FORMULATION, IMPLEMENTATION, AND CONTROL OF COMPETITIVE STRATEGY

JOHN A. PEARCE II

College of Commerce and Finance
Villanova University

RICHARD B. ROBINSON, JR.

College of Business Administration
University of South Carolina

Sixth Edition

IRWIN

Chicago • Bogotá • Boston • Buenos Aires • Caracas
London • Madrid • Mexico City • Sydney • Toronto

Irwin Book Team

Publisher: *Rob Zwettler*
Executive editor: *Craig S. Beytien*
Developmental editor: *Jennifer R. Boxell*
Marketing manager: *Michael Campbell*
Project editor: *Gladys True*
Production supervisor: *Dina L. Genovese*
Graphics supervisor: *Bethany Stubbe*
Manager, Prepress Purchasing: *Kimberly Meriwether David*
Compositor: *Weimer Graphics, Inc., Division of Shepard Poorman Communications Corp.*
Typeface: *10/12 Times Roman*
Printer: *Times Mirror Higher Education Group, Inc., Print Group*

Times Mirror
Higher Education Group

Library of Congress Cataloging-in-Publication Data
Pearce, John A.
    Formulation, implementation, and control of competitive strategy /
John A. Pearce II, Richard B. Robinson, Jr. — 6th ed.
        p.   cm.
    Includes bibliographical references and index.
    ISBN 0-256-21660-6
    1. Strategic planning.   2. Strategic planning—Case studies.
    I. Robinson, Richard B. (Richard Braden), 1947-   . II. Title.
    HD30.28.P3385   1997
    658.4′012—dc20   96-28686

Printed in the United States of America
1 2 3 4 5 6 7 8 9 0 WCB 3 2 1 0 9 8 7 6

To
Mary Frances and Jack Pearce
Mattie and Frank Fletcher

PREFACE

This sixth edition of *Formulation, Implementation, and Control of Competitive Strategy* is both the culmination of almost 20 years of work by many people and a major revision designed to fit the 21st century needs of strategy students. We were pleased that the fifth edition was used by more teachers and students than any previous edition. This preface describes what we have done to make the sixth edition even more effective and relevant in preparing students for the exciting global economy they are about to enter. It also gives us the opportunity to recognize many outstanding contributors.

The sixth edition of *Formulation, Implementation, and Control of Competitive Strategy* provides a thoroughly revised, state-of-the art treatment of the critical business skills needed to plan and manage strategic activities. We have divided the text into 12 chapters filled with many real-world business examples. Sensitivity to the 21st century strategic ramifications of topics like the global economy, entrepreneurship, ethics, restructuring, continuous improvement, integrated operations and manufacturing, virtual organization, and cultural diversity are evident throughout this major revision of the text. A newly revised and exciting cohesion case on the world's most successful global business, The Coca-Cola Company, is included based on the popular reaction to the use of Coca-Cola in the 5th edition. Coca-Cola remains large but still entrepreneurial, innovative, growing, and cleverly managed—a collection of thousands of locally focused operations in every corner of the globe. It provides an extraordinarily useful example that students will find beneficial, recognizable, and motivational in their study of strategic management, entrepreneurship, and global business.

Contemporary research in strategic management, with an emphasis on conceptual tools and skills created by value-adding scholars and practitioners in the field, will be evident throughout the 12 chapters in this edition. While the text retains its solid academic connection, we have endeavored to create text material that is practical, skills oriented, and applicable on the job.

Components of our teaching package include a totally revised, comprehensive instructor's manual, a set of two-color transparencies, packaged with PowerPoint presentation slides, and a computerized test bank. These elements are coordinated and backed by Irwin's outstanding customer support capabilities.

Changes to Our Text Material

The literature and research comprising the strategic management field has been developing at a rapid pace in recent years both in the academic literature and the business press. We have endeavored to create an edition that incorporates major developments from both sources while keeping our focus centered on a straightforward and logical framework through which students can grasp the complexity and essence of strategic management. Some of the revisions that deserve particular note are:

- The text went from 11 chapters in the fifth edition to 12 chapters in this edition. The reason was to provide a treatment of strategic analysis and choice over two chapters instead of one chapter as in previous editions. A new Chapter 8 focuses on tools and techniques for strategic analysis at the business level—single- or dominant-product/service companies. A new Chapter 9 covers strategic analysis in multibusiness companies and covers behavioral considerations shaping strategic choice.

- Previous adopters will note a revised model of the strategic management process. Covered in Chapter 1, our revisions sought to reflect strategic analysis at different organizational levels while also portraying the role of action plans, continuous improvement, and employee empowerment within the strategic management process. While the model has been revised, we went to great efforts to keep the useful attributes mentioned by so many previous adopters as being a key distinctive competence present in our book: a logical flow, distinct elements, and easy-to-understand guide to strategic management.

- The role of the CEO and the board of directors has received prominent attention in Chapter 1. We have developed the exciting examples of Saturn and Nissan to explain company philosophy. Complementing this material, Chapter 2 has also increased its attention to customer influences on strategy, customer-driven organizations, and the essence of quality as a part of mission development.

- Our three-chapter set examining the environment has undergone considerable revision. Some key highlights include adding a major section on ecological issues; examining issues of regulation and innovation-friendly regulation as entry barriers; and highlighting techniques and concepts to create meaningful customer profiles and unique customer segmentation early on in strategic management.

- Globalization is certainly a defining theme in environmental analysis, and we have added important new examples and a discussion of factors that drive global companies. Forecasting competitive behavior and the creation of early warning systems when confronting competitive or environmental problems received new coverage in Chapter 5. Accompanying these new developments is a revised, three-chapter core replete with dynamic examples and contemporary discussion linking them to the field's most important concepts in a breadth of coverage (three chapters) that continues to be one of the most expansive available.

- Attention to value chain analysis as a framework for examining a firm's strengths and weaknesses was expanded along with a major new discussion of benchmarking as a means to leverage the use of value chain analysis and other techniques for understanding firm capabilities. New examples—an exciting global female entrepreneur at England's Laura Ashley, Avery Dennison's global benchmarking, and the dramatic changes in the global PC industry—illustrate these topics.

· Our discussion of strategic alternatives in Chapter 7 was expanded in two ways. First, we sought to help students understand the linkage between strategic intent and corporate purpose—the big picture. Second, we added significantly to our discussion of market development as a grand strategy while expanding the coverage of strategic alliances and outsourcing as strategy elements—all changes intended to emphasis the focus and partnering trends among the best businesses around the globe.

· Already mentioned above, our treatment of strategic analysis and choice has been expanded from one large chapter to two chapters of more modest length. Our major concern here was to create a more user-friendly coverage of strategic analysis in the somewhat distinct venues of single- or dominant-product businesses and multibusiness companies. Chapter 8 seeks to focus on the single-product business by discussing techniques and concepts managers use to examine business strategy alternatives—identifying and choosing the best way to build sustainable competitive advantage. The chapter emphasizes speed and market focus, as well as the traditional cost leadership and differentiation sources of competitive advantage. Strategic analysis focused on identifying sources of each type of competitive advantage along with organizational resources required to support and sustain them form the basis for strategic analysis and choice at the business level.

· Strategic analysis and choice facing managers of multibusiness companies as they seek to maximize long-term shareholder value is the focus of a new Chapter 9. Rationalizing diversification, and examining opportunities for sharing infrastructure and capabilities are developed as key conceptual "tools" to make corporate strategic decisions. This chapter also retains a revised, reduced coverage of portfolio techniques and a focused coverage of key behavioral considerations in strategic choice.

· The three chapters on implementation and strategic control underwent major revision. Creating value activities provides a current, integrating theme for Chapter 10's material on action plans and functional tactics. Major revisions include coverage of flexible manufacturing systems, JIT, SPC, and outsourcing as operating tactical options; marketing responses to diversity, the decreasing importance of size, and HRM in a downsized, outsourcing environment; and a major emphasis on the use of policies as a source of employee empowerment.

· New material in Chapter 11 examines (1) guidelines to match structure to strategy emphasizing restructuring to support strategically critical activities, (2) business process engineering as a means to do the restructuring, and (3) downsizing, outsourcing, and self-managing work teams as ways to truly redefine the way an organization's "work" or strategically critical activities get done with speed, quality, and cost effectiveness. The discussion of leadership and culture has been reworked to place embracing change through three fundamental means as a central theme. Examples from prominent companies that have visibly restructured themselves in the 1990s provide many useful strategy-in-action examples.

· Chapter 12's well-received coverage of strategic control was revised to include updated literature on strategic control and to add significant new material on continuous improvement. The emphasis was placed on strategic control; operational control and budgets were given reduced, yet focused coverage; and a new section was added on continuous improvement to build customer value, replete with how-to guidelines and current examples.

Overall, we found ourselves reenergized by the challenge to "continuously improve" on well-received text material. A lot has changed during the 1990s—changes that have revitalized and redefined the nature and focus of strategic management. The challenge and result for us has been a major revitalization and revision of our book while keeping a structured, student-friendly flow an overriding requirement.

We have updated, increased, and improved our *Strategy in Action* capsules. The fundamental idea behind them remains the same—provide interesting, separate examples that enrich text material and engage students as they read the text. The 12 chapters contain 42 of these illustration vignettes, 36 of which are completely new to the sixth edition. Each Strategy in Action provides a contemporary business example of a key chapter topic designed to enhance student interest and aid learning.

We also have 14 *Global Strategy in Action* capsules in this edition, with at least one in every chapter. These cases are introduced to help students appreciate how strategic managers worldwide meet global competition, and we are excited about the interesting, all-new set assembled for this edition. They are more diverse, personal, and educational, taking students into a variety of surprising businesses around the world. They also offer North American student users the chance in a sense to "benchmark" companies most familiar to them with several best-practice companies across a variety of industries throughout the global economy.

We have responded to adopters' positive response to the introduction of The Coca-Cola Company as our cohesion case in the last edition by retaining the company as the cohesion case for this edition. While the company is the same, users of the cohesion case will be pleased to see a virtually totally rewritten coverage of strategic management at Coca-Cola. This company has made incredible progress since 1995. It has refined and built sustainable competitive advantages based on speed, market focus, differentiation, and cost leadership. Its strategies are specific, varied, and very educational. Numerous visual as well as narrative illustrations of each aspect of strategic management at Coca-Cola around the globe have been provided to help students learn strategic management from one of, if not, the best global business system in the history of world commerce.

Three supplements accompany or are available to accompany our text to increase readers' ability to enhance their competence in the practice of strategic management: A guide to industry information sources follows Chapter 5. Students will find it helpful in rapidly orienting them to where and how to get company and industry data.

Also following Chapter 5 is a supplement on strategic planning tools and techniques for forecasting. It offers a practical assessment of each of 20 planning aids as well as source information on these detailed how-to materials.

A revised guide to financial analysis is provided following Chapter 6. It provides a thorough, easy-to-use guide to the quantitative analysis of financial and operating information, which will help refamiliarize students with previously learned techniques and introduce them to others.

Acknowledgments

We have benefited from the help of many people in the evolution of this book over six editions. Students, adopters, colleagues, reviewers, and business contacts have provided hundreds of insightful comments, suggestions, and contributions that have progressively enhanced this book. We are indebted to the researchers, writers, and practicing managers who have accelerated the development of the literature on strategic management.

The development of this book through six editions has been greatly enhanced by the generous time, energy and ideas from the following people (we apologize if the affiliation has changed):

A. J. Almaney
DePaul University

B. Alpert
San Francisco State University

Alan Amason
University of Georgia

Sonny Aries
University of Toledo

Amy Vernberg Beekman
University of South Carolina

Robert Earl Bolick
Metropolitan State University

Bill Boulton
Auburn University

Charles Boyd
Southwest Missouri State University

Jeff Bracker
University of Louisville

Dorothy Brawley
Kennesaw State College

James W. Bronson
Washington State University

William Burr
University of Oregon

Gene E. Burton
California State University–Fresno

Edgar T. Busch
Western Kentucky University

Charles M. Byles
Virginia Commonwealth University

Gerard A. Cahill

Jim Callahan
University of LaVerne

James W. Camerius
Northern Michigan University

Richard Castaldi
San Diego State University

Gary J. Castogiovanni
Louisiana State University

Jafor Chowdbury
University of Scranton

James J. Chrisman
University of South Carolina

J. Carl Clamp
University of South Carolina

Earl D. Cooper
Florida Institute of Technology

Louis Coraggio
Troy State University

Jeff Covin
Georgia Institute of Technology

John P. Cragin
Oklahoma Baptist University

Larry Cummings
Northwestern University

Peter Davis
Memphis State University

William Davis
Auburn University

Julio DeCastro
University of Colorado

D. Keith Denton
Southwest Missouri State University

F. Derakhshan
*California State University–
San Bernardino*

Brook Dobni
University of Saskatchewan

Mark Dollinger
Indiana University

Max E. Douglas
Indiana State University

Derrick Dsouza
University of North Texas

Thomas J. Dudley
Pepperdine University

John Dunkelberg
Wake Forest University

Norbert Esser
Central Wesleyan College

Forest D. Etheredge
Aurora University

Liam Fahey

Mark Fiegener
Oregon State University

Calvin D. Fowler
Embry–Riddle Aeronautical University

Debbie Francis
Auburn University–Montgomery

Elizabeth Freeman
Southern Methodist University

Mahmound A. Gaballa
Mansfield University

Donna M. Gallo
Boston College

Diane Garsombke
University of Maine

Betsy Gatewood
University of Houston

Michael Geringer
Southern Methodist University

Manton C. Gibbs
Indiana University of Pennsylvania

Nicholas A. Glaskowsky, Jr.
University of Miami

Tom Goho
Wake Forest University

Jon Goodman
University of Southern California

Pradeep Gopalakrishna
Hofstra University

R. H. Gordon
Hofstra University

Barbara Gottfried
Bentley College

Peter Goulet
University of Northern Iowa

Walter E. Greene
University of Texas–Pan American

Sue Greenfeld
*California State University–
San Bernardino*

David W. Grigsby
Clemson University

Daniel E. Hallock
St. Edward's University

Don Hambrick
Columbia University

Barry Hand
Indiana State University

Samuel Hazen
Tarleton State University

W. Harvey Hegarty
Indiana University

Edward A. Hegner
*California State University–
Sacramento*

Marilyn M. Helms
University of Tennessee–Chattanooga

Lanny Herron
University of Baltimore

D. Higginbothan
University of Missouri

Roger Higgs
Western Carolina University

William H. Hinkle
Johns Hopkins University

Charles T. Hofer
University of Georgia

Alan N. Hoffman
Bentley College

Richard Hoffman
College of William and Mary

Eileen Hogan
George Mason University

Gary L. Holman
St. Martin's College

Don Hopkins
Temple University

Cecil Horst
*Keller Graduate School of
Management*

Henry F. House
Auburn University–Montgomery

William C. House
University of Arkansas–Fayetteville

Frank Hoy
University of Texas–El Paso

Warren Huckabay

Eugene H. Hunt
Virginia Commonwealth University

Tammy G. Hunt
*University of North Carolina–
Wilmington*

John W. Huonker
University of Arizona

Stephen R. Jenner
California State University

Shailendra Jha
Wilfrid Laurier University–Ontario

C. Boyd Johnson
California State University–Fresno

Troy Jones
University of Central Florida

Jon Kalinowski
Mankato State University

Al Kayloe
Lake Erie College

Michael J. Keefe
Southwest Texas State University

Kay Keels
Louisiana State University

James A. Kidney
Southern Connecticut State University

John D. King
Embry-Riddle Aeronautical University

Raymond M. Kinnunen
Northeastern University

John B. Knauff
University of St. Thomas

Rose Knotts
University of North Texas

Dan Kopp
Southwest Missouri State University

Michael Koshuta
Valparaiso University

Myroslaw Kyj
Widener University of Pennsylvania

Dick LaBarre
Ferris State University

Ryan Lancaster
The University of Phoenix

Anne T. Lawrence
San Jose State University

Joseph Leonard
Miami University–Ohio

Robert Letovsky
Saint Michael's College

Benjamin Litt
Lehigh University

Frank S. Lockwood
University of South Carolina

John Logan
University of South Carolina

Sandra Logan
Newberry College

Jean M. Lundin
Lake Superior State University

Rodney H. Mabry
Clemson University

Donald C. Malm
University of Missouri–St. Louis

Charles C. Manz
Arizona State University

John Maurer
Wayne State University

Denise Mazur
Aquinas College

Edward McClelland
Roanoke College

Bob McDonald
Central Wesleyan College

Patricia P. McDougall
Georgia Institute of Technology

S. Mehta
San Jose State University

Ralph Melaragno
Pepperdine University

Richard Merner
University of Delaware

Timothy Mescon
Kennesaw State College

Philip C. Micka
Park College

Bill J. Middlebrook
Southwest Texas State University

James F. Molly, Jr.
Northeastern University

Cynthia Montgomery
Harvard University

Robert Mookler
St. John's University

Gary W. Muller
Hofstra University

Terry Muson
Northern Montana College

Stephanie Newell
Bowling Green State University

Michael E. Nix
Trinity College of Vermont

Kenneth Olm
University of Texas–Austin

Benjamin M. Oviatt
Georgia State University

Joseph Paolillo
University of Mississippi

Gerald Parker
St. Louis University

Paul J. Patinka
University of Colorado

James W. Pearce
Western Carolina University

Michael W. Pitts
Virginia Commonwealth University

Douglas Polley
St. Cloud State University

Valerie J. Porciello
Bentley College

Mark S. Poulous
St. Edward's University

John B. Pratt
Saint Joseph's College

Oliver Ray Price
West Coast University

John Primus
Golden Gate University

Norris Rath
Shepard College

Paula Rechner
University of Illinois

Richard Reed
Washington State University

J. Bruce Regan
University of St. Thomas

F. A. Ricci
Georgetown University

Keith Robbins
George Mason University

Gary Roberts
Kennesaw State College

Lloyd E. Roberts
Mississippi College

John K. Ross III
Southwest Texas State University

Les Rue
Georgia State University

J. A. Ruslyk
Memphis State University

Ronald J. Salazar
Idaho State University

Jack Scarborough
Barry University

Paul J. Schlachter
Florida International University

John Seeger
Bentley College

Martin Shapiro
Iona College

Arthur Sharplin
McNeese State University

Frank Shipper
Salisbury State University

Rodney C. Shrader
Georgia State University

Lois Shufeldt
Southwest Missouri State University

F. Bruce Simmons III
The University of Akron

Mark Simon
Georgia State University

Michael Skipton
Memorial University

Fred Smith
Western Illinois University

Scott Snell
Michigan State University

Coral R. Snodgrass
Canisius College

Rudolph P. Snowadzky
University of Maine

Neil Snyder
University of Virginia

Melvin J. Stanford
Mankato State University

Warren S. Stone
Virginia Commonwealth University

Ram Subramanian
Grand Valley State University

Paul M. Swiercz
Georgia State University

Robert L. Swinth
Montana State University

Russell Teasley
University of South Carolina

George H. Tompson
University of New Zealand

Jody Tompson
University of New Zealand

Melanie Trevino
University of Texas–El Paso

Howard Tu
Memphis State University

Craig Tunwall
Ithaca College

Elaine M. Tweedy
University of Scranton

Arieh A. Ullmann
SUNY–Binghamton

P. Veglahn
James Madison University

George Vozikis
The Citadel

William Waddell
*California State University–
Los Angeles*

Bill Warren
College of William and Mary

Kirby Warren
Columbia University

Steven J. Warren
Rutgers University

Michael White
University of Tulsa

Randy White
Auburn University

Sam E. White
Portland State University

Frank Winfrey
Kent State University

Joseph Wolfe
University of Tulsa

Robley Wood
Virginia Commonwealth University

Edward D. Writh, Jr.
Florida Institute of Technology

John Young
University of Colorado

Jan Zahrly
Old Dominion University

Alan Zeiber
Portland State University

As the Endowed Chair holder of the College of Commerce and Finance at Villanova University, Jack is able to combine his scholarly and teaching activities with his co-authorship of this text. He is grateful to Villanova University and his colleagues for the support and encouragement that they provide.

Richard deeply appreciates the support and assistance of USC strategy colleagues Alan Bauerschmidt, Carl Clamp, John Logan, Michael Leiblein, Harry Sapienza, Bill Sandberg, and David Schweiger, as well as doctoral candidates James Almeida, Amy Beeckman, and Jim Bloodgood. Susie VanHuss, Program Director, Dean David Shrock, and Associate Deans Bob Markland and Randy Martin provided much appreciated encouragement, recognition, and support. A special thanks goes to Cheryl Fowler, Susie Gorsage, and Sandy Bennett for their clerical and logistical support.

None of this would have been possible without the outstanding Irwin organization. We thank Gerald Saykes for getting us started over 20 years ago and continuing to support this project. Craig Beytein's editorial leadership is outstanding. His team including Jenny Boxell, Gladys True, Kim Kanakes, and Harriet Stockanes continue the Irwin legacy of professionalism and excellence. The Irwin field organization deserves special recognition for six successful editions. And John Black's leadership through much strategic change has been a calming force that kept us focused.

In using this text, we hope that you will share our enthusiasm both for the rich subject of strategic management and for the learning approach that we have taken. We value your

recommendations and thoughts about our material. Plea
following addresses:

Dr. John A. Pearce II
College of Commerce & Finance
Villanova University
Villanova, PA 19085-1678
610-519-4332
Jpearce@email.vill.edu

Dr. Richard Robinson
College of Business Administration
University of South Carolina
Columbia, SC 29205
803-777-5961
Robinson@darla.badm.sc.edu

We wish you the very best as you advance your knowledge in the exciting and
ing field of strategic management.

Jack Pearce
Richard Robinson

ABOUT THE AUTHORS

John A. Pearce, II, Ph.D., is the endowed chair holder of the College of Commerce and Finance at Villanova University. Previously, Dr. Pearce was holder of the Eakin Endowed Chair in Strategic Management at George Mason University and was a State of Virginia Eminent Scholar. In 1994, he received the Fulbright U.S. Professional Award for service in Malaysia. Professor Pearce has taught at Penn State, West Virginia University, the University of Malta where as a Fulbright Senior Professor in International Management he served as the Head of Business Faculties, and at the University of South Carolina where he was Director of Ph.D. Programs in Strategic Management. He received a Ph.D. degree in Business Administration from the Pennsylvania State University.

Professor Pearce is coauthor of 24 books that have been used to help educate more than 1,000,000 students and managers. He has also authored more than 165 articles and professional papers. These have been published in journals that include the *Academy of Management Journal*, *California Management Review*, *Journal of Applied Psychology*, *Journal of Business Venturing*, *Sloan Management Review*, and *Strategic Management Journal*. Several of these publications have resulted from Professor Pearce's work as a principal on research projects funded for more than $2 million. He is a recognized expert in the field of strategic management, with special accomplishments in the areas of strategy formulation, implementation, and control, management during recessions, mission statement development, competitive assessment, industry analysis, joint ventures, and tools for strategy evaluation and design.

A frequent leader of executive development programs and an active consultant to business and industry, Dr. Pearce's client list includes domestic and multinational firms engaged in manufacturing, service, and nonprofit industries.

Richard B. Robinson, Jr., Ph.D., is Professor of Strategy and Entrepreneurship and is a Business Partnership Foundation Fellow in the College of Business Administration at the University of South Carolina. Professor Robinson recently returned to USC after serving for three years as president and CEO of a rapidly growing hazardous waste management company.

Professor Robinson has published numerous articles and professional papers in preeminent journals and associations dedicated to improving the practice of strategic management and the art of entrepreneurship. He has coauthored 26 texts, proceedings, and supplements for book publishers that include Richard D. Irwin, McGraw-Hill, Random House, and the Academy of Management.

Professor Robinson is the recipient of several awards in recognition of his work in strategic management and entrepreneurship. He also has held offices in the Academy of Management, the Southern Management Association, and the International Council of Small Business.

Professor Robinson currently serves on the investment advisory committee of two venture capital funds.

CONTENTS

I OVERVIEW OF STRATEGIC MANAGEMENT

The first chapter of this book introduces strategic management, the set of decisions and actions that result in the design and activation of strategies to achieve the objectives of an organization. The chapter provides an overview of the nature, benefits, and terminology of and the need for strategic management. Subsequent chapters provide greater detail.

The first major section of Chapter 1, "The Nature and Value of Strategic Management," emphasizes the practical value and benefits of strategic management for a firm. It also distinguishes between a firm's strategic decisions and its other planning tasks.

The section stresses the key point that strategic management activities are undertaken at three levels: corporate, business, and functional. The distinctive characteristics of strategic decision making at each of these levels affect the impact of activities at these levels on company operations. Other topics dealt with in this section are the value of formality in strategic management and the alignment of strategy makers in strategy formulation and implementation. The section concludes with a review of the planning research on business, which demonstrates that the use of strategic management processes yields financial and behavioral benefits that justify their costs.

The second major section of Chapter 1 presents a model of the strategic management process. The model, which will serve as an outline for the remainder of the text, describes approaches currently used by strategic planners. Its individual components are carefully defined and explained, as is the process for integrating them into the strategic management process. The section ends with a discussion of the model's practical limitations and the advisability of tailoring the recommendations made to actual business situations.

STRATEGIC MANAGEMENT

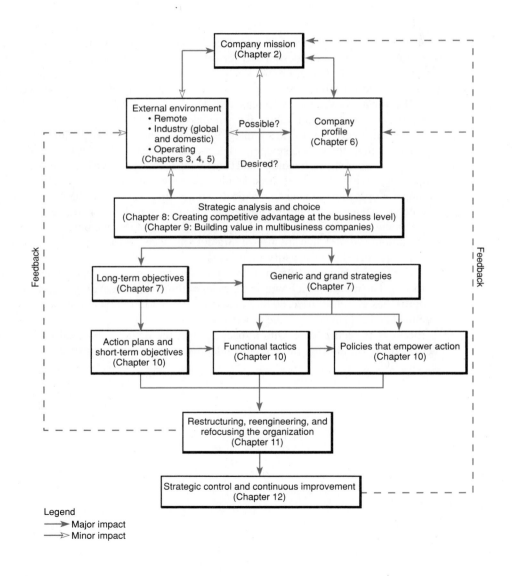

Company mission (Chapter 2)

External environment
• Remote
• Industry (global and domestic)
• Operating
(Chapters 3, 4, 5)

Possible?

Desired?

Company profile (Chapter 6)

Strategic analysis and choice
(Chapter 8: Creating competitive advantage at the business level)
(Chapter 9: Building value in multibusiness companies)

Long-term objectives (Chapter 7)

Generic and grand strategies (Chapter 7)

Action plans and short-term objectives (Chapter 10)

Functional tactics (Chapter 10)

Policies that empower action (Chapter 10)

Restructuring, reengineering, and refocusing the organization (Chapter 11)

Strategic control and continuous improvement (Chapter 12)

Feedback

Feedback

Legend
⟶ Major impact
⟶ Minor impact

THE NATURE AND VALUE OF STRATEGIC MANAGEMENT

Managing activities internal to the firm is only part of the modern executive's responsibilities. The modern executive also must respond to the challenges posed by the firm's immediate and remote external environments. The immediate external environment includes competitors, suppliers, increasingly scarce resources, government agencies and their ever more numerous regulations, and customers whose preferences often shift inexplicably. The remote external environment comprises economic and social conditions, political priorities, and technological developments, all of which must be anticipated, monitored, assessed, and incorporated into the executive's decision making. However, the executive often is compelled to subordinate the demands of the firm's internal activities and external environment to the multiple and often inconsistent requirements of its stakeholders: owners, top managers, employees, communities, customers, and country. To deal effectively with everything that affects the growth and profitability of a firm, executives employ management processes that they feel will position it optimally in its competitive environment by maximizing the anticipation of environmental changes and of unexpected internal and competitive demands.

Broad-scope, large-scale management processes became dramatically more sophisticated after World War II. These processes responded to increases in the size and number of competing firms; to the expanded role of government as a buyer, seller, regulator, and competitor in the free enterprise system; and to greater business involvement in international trade. Perhaps the most significant improvement in management processes came in the 1970s, when "long-range planning," "new venture management," "planning, programming, budgeting," and "business policy" were blended. At the same time, increased emphasis was placed on environmental forecasting and external considerations in formulating and implementing plans. This all-encompassing approach is known as strategic management or strategic planning.[1]

Strategic management is defined as the set of decisions and actions that result in the formulation and implementation of plans designed to achieve a company's objectives. It comprises nine critical tasks:

1. Formulate the company's mission, including broad statements about its purpose, philosophy, and goals.
2. Develop a company profile that reflects its internal conditions and capabilities.
3. Assess the company's external environment, including both the competitive and general contextual factors.
4. Analyze the company's options by matching its resources with the external environment.
5. Identify the most desirable options by evaluating each option in light of the company's mission.
6. Select a set of long-term objectives and grand strategies that will achieve the most desirable options.
7. Develop annual objectives and short-term strategies that are compatible with the selected set of long-term objectives and grand strategies.
8. Implement the strategic choices by means of budgeted resource allocations in which the matching of tasks, people, structures, technologies, and reward systems is emphasized.

---

[1] In this text, the term *strategic management* refers to the broad overall process. To some scholars and practitioners, the term connotes only the formulation phase of total management activities.

9. Evaluate the success of the strategic process as an input for future decision making.

As these nine tasks indicate, strategic management involves the planning, directing, organizing, and controlling of a company's strategy-related decisions and actions. By *strategy,* managers mean their large-scale, future-oriented plans for interacting with the competitive environment to achieve company objectives. A strategy is a company's "game plan." Although that plan does not precisely detail all future deployments (of people, finances, and material), it does provide a framework for managerial decisions. A strategy reflects a company's awareness of how, when, and where it should compete; against whom it should compete; and for what purposes it should compete.

DIMENSIONS OF STRATEGIC DECISIONS

What decisions facing a business are strategic and therefore deserve strategic management attention? Typically, strategic issues have the following dimensions.

Strategic Issues Require Top-Management Decisions   Since strategic decisions overarch several areas of a firm's operations, they require top-management involvement. Usually only top management has the perspective needed to understand the broad implications of such decisions and the power to authorize the necessary resource allocations. As top manager of Volvo GM Heavy Truck Corporation, Karl-Erling Trogen, president, wanted to push the company closer to the customer by overarching operations with service and customer relations empowering the work force closest to the customer with greater knowledge and authority. This strategy called for a major commitment to the parts and service end of the business where customer relations was first priority. Trogen's philosophy was to so empower the work force that more operating questions were handled on the line where workers worked directly with customers. He believed that the corporate headquarters should be more focused on strategic issues, such as engineering, production, quality, and marketing.

Strategic Issues Require Large Amounts of the Firm's Resources   Strategic decisions involve substantial allocations of people, physical assets, or moneys that either must be redirected from internal sources or secured from outside the firm. They also commit the firm to actions over an extended period. For these reasons, they require substantial resources. Whirlpool Corporation's "Quality Express" product delivery program exemplified a strategy that required a strong financial and personnel commitment from the company. The plan was to deliver products to customers when, where, and how they wanted them. This proprietary service uses contract logistics strategy to deliver Whirlpool, Kitchen Aid, Roper, and Estate brand appliances to 90 percent of the company's dealer and builder customers within 24 hours and to the other 10 percent within 48 hours. In highly competitive service-oriented businesses, achieving and maintaining customer satisfaction frequently involves a commitment from every facet of the organization.

Strategic Issues Often Affect the Firm's Long-Term Prosperity   Strategic decisions ostensibly commit the firm for a long time, typically five years; however, the impact of such decisions often lasts much longer. Once a firm has committed itself to a particular strategy, its image and competitive advantages usually are tied to that strategy. Firms become known in certain markets, for certain products, with certain technologies. They would jeopardize their previous gains if they shifted from these markets, products, or technologies by adopting a radically different strategy. Thus, strategic decisions have enduring effects on firms—for better or worse.

Strategic Issues Are Future Oriented Strategic decisions are based on what managers forecast, rather than on what they know. In such decisions, emphasis is placed on the development of projections that will enable the firm to select the most promising strategic options. In the turbulent and competitive free enterprise environment, a firm will succeed only if it takes a proactive (anticipatory) stance toward change.

Strategic Issues Usually Have Multifunctional or Multibusiness Consequences Strategic decisions have complex implications for most areas of the firm. Decisions about such matters as customer mix, competitive emphasis, or organizational structure necessarily involve a number of the firm's strategic business units (SBUs), divisions, or program units. All of these areas will be affected by allocations or reallocations of responsibilities and resources that result from these decisions.

Strategic Issues Require Considering the Firm's External Environment All business firms exist in an open system. They affect and are affected by external conditions that are largely beyond their control. Therefore, to successfully position a firm in competitive situations, its strategic managers must look beyond its operations. They must consider what relevant others (e.g., competitors, customers, suppliers, creditors, government, and labor) are likely to do.

Global Strategy in Action 1–1 tells the strategy of a small but rapidly growing restaurant chain. Notice that even such a brief overview of an entrepreneurial firm covers many of the issues that we described above as critical to the strategic management process.

Three Levels of Strategy

The decision-making hierarchy of a firm typically contains three levels. At the top of this hierarchy is the corporate level, composed principally of a board of directors and the chief executive and administrative officers. They are responsible for the firm's financial performance and for the achievement of nonfinancial goals, such as enhancing the firm's image and fulfilling its social responsibilities. To a large extent, attitudes at the corporate level reflect the concerns of stockholders and society at large. In a multibusiness firm, corporate-level executives determine the businesses in which the firm should be involved. They also set objectives and formulate strategies that span the activities and functional areas of these businesses. Corporate-level strategic managers attempt to exploit their firm's distinctive competencies by adopting a portfolio approach to the management of its businesses and by developing long-term plans, typically for a five-year period. A key corporate strategy of Airborne Express's operations involved direct sale to high-volume corporate accounts and developing an expansive network in the international arena. Instead of setting up operations overseas, Airborne's long-term strategy was to form direct associations with national companies within foreign countries to expand and diversify their operations.

Another example of the portfolio approach involved a plan by state-owned Saudi Arabian Oil to spend $1.4 billion to build and operate an oil refinery in Korea with its partner, Ssangyong. To implement their program, the Saudis embarked on a new "cut-out-the-middleman" strategy to reduce the role of international oil companies in the processing and selling of Saudi crude oil.

WHERE THE MAITRE D' OUTRANKS THE CHEF

Blocking the north side of 54th Street between Fifth and Madison avenues each day at lunchtime is a well-dressed but hungry mob. It's crowding the sidewalk outside Bice, the chic Italian eatery that has made itself the Lourdes of pasta.

The airy dining room seats 160 people and serves some 600 meals a day—average check, about $40 per person at lunch, $60 at dinner. Average daily take: $30,000. But even at these prices, the crowds keep coming. Gianfranco Sorrentino, Bice's unflappable maitre d', dispenses choice front tables to Henry Kissinger and Ronald Perelman, shuffling shoppers and Japanese tourists off behind the massive floral arrangement.

What makes Bice (pronounced beechay) different is owner Roberto Ruggeri's notion that it can be cloned worldwide—doing with a $22.00 black risotto with cuttlefish what McDonald's did with the $1.80 Big Mac.

So Bices are popping up everywhere, 14 so far. Branches in Chicago and Beverly Hills opened in 1989; Paris and Palm Beach in 1990; Washington, Atlanta, Miami, and Scottsdale, Arizona, last year. Bice has since sprouted in San Diego and Tokyo. Coming up are new outposts in Aspen, Montreal, Toronto, Mexico City, Caracas, London, and Sydney. The U.S. operations are all wholly owned. The foreign Bices are joint ventures or are licensed to local owners. "I don't know Caracas," Ruggeri says, explaining why he prefers not to entirely own his deals overseas. "You wake up, they shoot, a new government comes in, and I lose my restaurant."

Potential coups aside, Bice looks enviably solid in a notoriously treacherous industry. The New York flagship had revenues of around $10 million last year, a level that only a handful of New

Source: Excerpted from J. Levine, "Where the Maitre d' Outranks the Chef," *Forbes*, June 8, 1992, pp. 70–71. Reprinted by permission of FORBES Magazine © Forbes Inc., 1995.

In the middle of the decision-making hierarchy is the business level, composed principally of business and corporate managers. These managers must translate the statements of direction and intent generated at the corporate level into concrete objectives and strategies for individual business divisions, or SBUs. In essence, business-level strategic managers determine how the firm will compete in the selected product-market arena. They strive to identify and secure the most promising market segment within that arena. This segment is the piece of the total market that the firm can claim and defend because of its competitive advantages.

At the bottom of the decision-making hierarchy is the functional level, composed principally of managers of product, geographic, and functional areas. They develop annual objectives and short-term strategies in such areas as production, operations, research and development, finance and accounting, marketing, and human relations. However, their principal responsibility is to implement or execute the firm's strategic plans. Whereas corporate- and business-level managers center their attention on "doing the right things," managers at the functional level center their attention on "doing things right." Thus, they address such issues as the efficiency and effectiveness of production and marketing systems, the quality of customer service, and the success of particular products and services in increasing the firm's market shares.

Figure 1–1 depicts the three levels of strategic management as structured in practice. In alternative 1, the firm is engaged in only one business and the corporate- and business-level responsibilities are concentrated in a single group of directors, officers, and managers. This is the organizational format of most small businesses.

York restaurants—like Tavern on the Green and Windows on the World—can beat. Pasta ingredients are relatively cheap, so New York profit margins are high: 20 percent. Bice's satellite restaurants have revenues of around $3.0 million to $3.5 million, considered hearty performance by the trade. Only one so far is a dud: Scottsdale. Price cuts loom there.

"This is unique," says Clark Wolf, a New York food and restaurant consultant. "No one before has opened the same restaurant of this caliber all over the world."

To finance his growth, Ruggeri sold a half-interest in his company to a Japanese restaurant chain, WDI, for roughly $2 million in 1989—with the provision that he could buy back his stake. He did so last year for about $6 million. The Japanese got back their $2 million in cash and financed the rest in notes. Now Ruggeri is hoping that investors have noticed his success. He says he's contemplating a public offering to raise $15 million for around 30 percent to 40 percent of the company. With that new money he can expand still further.

Ruggeri, 49, an affable, somewhat rumpled Milanese with unruly brown and gray hair, has a simple marketing strategy: predictability and ambiance, rather than to-die-for food. Explains Ruggeri: "A customer would rather go to a happy place with exceptional food. I'm giving people comfort, not a peak experience." So at Bice the key job is maitre d', not chef. "Italian cuisine is very simple—any good chef can do it. Personality, you can't teach," says Ruggeri.

The trick in the restaurant trade is to survive when the fickle fashion crowd moves on, as they inevitably do. So Ruggeri makes sure he finds locations close to swank stores like Tiffany and Cartier and to commercial hubs to pull in a diverse clientele. "When the trendies stopped coming, the shopping ladies and business people took over," he says.

Alternative 2, the classical corporate structure, comprises three fully operative levels: the corporate level, the business level, and the functional level. The approach taken throughout this text assumes the use of alternative 2. Moreover, whenever appropriate, topics are covered from the perspective of each level of strategic management. In this way, the text presents a comprehensive discussion of the strategic management process.

Characteristics of Strategic Management Decisions

The characteristics of strategic management decisions vary with the level of strategic activity considered. As shown in Figure 1–2, decisions at the corporate level tend to be more value oriented, more conceptual, and less concrete than decisions at the business or functional level. For example, at Alcoa, the world's largest aluminum maker, chairman Paul O'Neill made Alcoa one of the nation's most centralized organizations by imposing a dramatic management reorganization that wiped out two layers of management. He found that this effort not only reduced costs but also enabled him to be closer to the front-line operations managers. Corporate-level decisions are often characterized by greater risk, cost, and profit potential; greater need for flexibility; and longer time horizons. Such decisions include the choice of businesses, dividend policies, sources of long-term financing, and priorities for growth.

Functional-level decisions implement the overall strategy formulated at the corporate and business levels. They involve action-oriented operational issues and are relatively short range and low risk. Functional-level decisions incur only modest costs, because they are

FIGURE 1–1
Alternative Strategic Management Structures

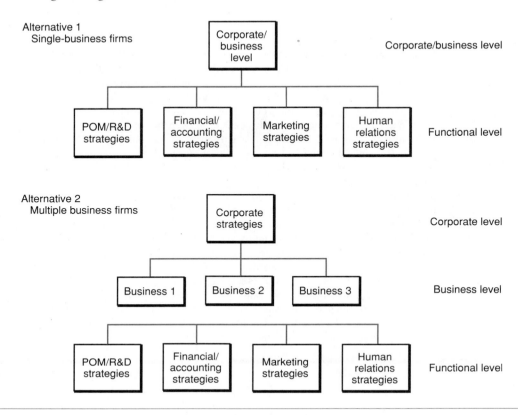

dependent on available resources. They usually are adaptable to ongoing activities and, therefore, can be implemented with minimal cooperation. For example, in 1991, Nordstrom and Dillard Department Stores reported first-quarter profits of $26 million, a 95 percent increase over the previous year. They attributed the increased earnings to tighter inventory and operating controls in the parent company. In a second example, the corporate headquarters of Sears, Roebuck & Company spent $60 million to automate 6,900 clerical jobs by installing 28,000 computerized cash registers at its 868 stores in the United States. Though this move eliminated many functional-level jobs, top management believed that reducing annual operating expenses by at least $50 million was crucial to competitive survival.

Because functional-level decisions are relatively concrete and quantifiable, they receive critical attention and analysis even though their comparative profit potential is low. Common functional-level decisions include decisions on generic versus brand-name labeling, basic versus applied research and development (R&D), high versus low inventory levels, general-purpose versus specific-purpose production equipment, and close versus loose supervision.

Business-level decisions help bridge decisions at the corporate and functional levels. Such decisions are less costly, risky, and potentially profitable than corporate-level decisions, but they are more costly, risky, and potentially profitable than functional-level decisions. Common business-level decisions include decisions on plant location, marketing segmentation and geographic coverage, and distribution channels.

FIGURE 1–2
Hierarchy of Objectives and Strategies

Ends (What is to be achieved?)	Means (How is it to be achieved?)	Strategic Decision Makers			
		Board of Directors	Corporate Managers	Business Managers	Functional Managers
Mission, including goals and philosophy		✓✓	✓✓	✓	
Long-term objectives	Grand strategy	✓	✓✓	✓✓	
Annual objectives	Short-term strategies and policies		✓	✓✓	✓✓

Note: ✓✓ indicates a principal responsibility; ✓ indicates a secondary responsibility.

FORMALITY IN STRATEGIC MANAGEMENT

The formality of strategic management systems varies widely among companies. *Formality* refers to the degree to which participants, responsibilities, authority, and discretion in decision making are specified. It is an important consideration in the study of strategic management, because greater formality is usually positively correlated with the cost, comprehensiveness, accuracy, and success of planning.

A number of forces determine how much formality is needed in strategic management. The size of the organization, its predominant management styles, the complexity of its environment, its production process, its problems, and the purpose of its planning system all play a part in determining the appropriate degree of formality.[2]

In particular, formality is associated with the size of the firm and with its stage of development. Methods of evaluating strategic success also are linked to formality. Some firms, especially smaller ones, follow an *entrepreneurial* mode. They are basically under the control of a single individual, and they produce a limited number of products or services. In such firms, strategic evaluation is informal, intuitive, and limited. Very large firms, on the other hand, make strategic evaluation part of a comprehensive, formal planning system, an approach that Henry Mintzberg called the *planning mode*. Mintzberg also identified a third mode (the *adaptive mode*), which he associated with medium-sized firms in relatively stable environments.[3] For firms that follow the adaptive mode, the identification and evaluation of alternative strategies are closely related to existing strategy. It is not unusual to find different modes within the same organization. For example, Exxon might follow an entrepreneurial mode in developing and evaluating the strategy of its solar subsidiary but follow a planning mode in the rest of the company.

The Strategy Makers

The ideal strategic management team includes decision makers from all three company levels (the corporate, business, and functional)—for example, the chief executive officer (CEO), the product managers, and the heads of functional areas. In addition, the team obtains input from company planning staffs, when they exist, and from lower-level managers and supervisors. The latter provide data for strategic decision making and then implement strategies.

---

[2] M. Goold and A. Campbell, "Managing the Diversified Corporation: The Tensions Facing the Chief Executive," *Long Range Planning*, August 1988, pp. 12–24.

[3] H. Mintzberg, "Strategy Making in Three Modes," *California Management Review* 16, no. 2 (1973), pp. 44–53.

Because strategic decisions have a tremendous impact on a company and require large commitments of company resources, top managers must give final approval for strategic action. Figure 1–2 aligns levels of strategic decision makers with the kinds of objectives and strategies for which they are typically responsible.

Planning departments, often headed by a corporate vice president for planning, are common in large corporations. Medium-sized firms often employ at least one full-time staff member to spearhead strategic data-collection efforts. Even in small firms or less progressive larger firms, strategic planning often is spearheaded by an officer or by a group of officers designated as a planning committee.

Precisely what are managers' responsibilities in the strategic planning process at the corporate and business levels? Top management shoulders broad responsibility for all the major elements of strategic planning and management. It develops the major portions of the strategic plan and reviews, and it evaluates and counsels on all other portions. General managers at the business level typically have principal responsibilities for developing environmental analysis and forecasting, establishing business objectives, and developing business plans prepared by staff groups.

A firm's president or CEO characteristically plays a dominant role in the strategic planning process. In many ways, this situation is desirable. The CEO's principal duty often is defined as giving long-term direction to the firm, and the CEO is ultimately responsible for the firm's success and, therefore, for the success of its strategy. In addition, CEOs are typically strong-willed, company-oriented individuals with high self-esteem. They often resist delegating authority to formulate or approve strategic decisions.

However, when the dominance of the CEO approaches autocracy, the effectiveness of the firm's strategic planning and management processes are likely to be diminished. For this reason, establishing a strategic management system implies that the CEO will allow managers at all levels to participate in the strategic posture of the company.

In implementing a company's strategy, the CEO must have an appreciation for the power and responsibility of the board, while retaining the power to lead the company with the guidance of informed directors. The interaction between the CEO and board is key to any corporation's strategy. Empowerment of the board has been a recent trend across major management teams. Strategy in Action 1–1 presents descriptions of the changes that companies have made in an attempt to monitor the relationships between the role of the board and the role of CEO.

Benefits of Strategic Management

Using the strategic management approach, managers at all levels of the firm interact in planning and implementing. As a result, the behavioral consequences of strategic management are similar to those of participative decision making. Therefore, an accurate assessment of the impact of strategy formulation on organizational performance requires not only financial evaluation criteria but also nonfinancial evaluation criteria—measures of behavior-based effects. In fact, promoting positive behavioral consequences also enables the firm to achieve its financial goals.[4] However, regardless of the profitability of strategic plans, several behavioral effects of strategic management improve the firm's welfare:

1. Strategy formulation activities enhance the firm's ability to prevent problems. Managers who encourage subordinates' attention to planning are aided in their monitoring and forecasting responsibilities by subordinates who are aware of the needs of strategic planning.

[4] A. Langely, "The Roles of Formal Strategic Planning," *Long Range Planning,* June 1988, pp. 400–50.

STRATEGY
IN ACTION
1–1

THE PROGRESS OF BOARD EMPOWERMENT

Company	Innovation
Dayton Hudson Corporation	Requires the inside directors to conduct an annual evaluation of the CEO.
Medtronic	Solicits opinions on board procedures by requiring all directors to complete a questionnaire; then the full board reviews the results at an annual meeting and tries to make improvements.
Stanhome	Developed a formal document that specifies the board's purpose, size, proportion of outside directors, annual calendar, and expectations of directors and management.
Mallinckrodt	Separated the roles of chair and CEO.
Lukens	Formed a committee of outside directors to study a major acquisition proposal, hold discussions with management, and recommend action to the full board.
Campbell Soup Company	Designated a lead director with the title of vice chairman.
Monsanto	Increased the proportion of the board's time that would be focused on strategic direction and considered specific capital proposals within that framework.
General Motors	Developed an explicit set of guidelines that outline how the board will function and be structured.

Source: Reprinted by permission of *Harvard Business Review.* An exhibit from "Empowering the Board," by Jay W. Lorsch, January–February 1995. Copyright © 1995 by the President and Fellows of Harvard University, all rights reserved.

2. Group-based strategic decisions are likely to be drawn from the best available alternatives. The strategic management process results in better decisions because group interaction generates a greater variety of strategies and because forecasts based on the specialized perspectives of group members improve the screening of options.

3. The involvement of employees in strategy formulation improves their understanding of the productivity-reward relationship in every strategic plan and, thus, heightens their motivation.

4. Gaps and overlaps in activities among individuals and groups are reduced as participation in strategy formulation clarifies differences in roles.

5. Resistance to change is reduced. Though the participants in strategy formulation may be no more pleased with their own decisions than they would be with authoritarian decisions, their greater awareness of the parameters that limit the available options makes them more likely to accept those decisions.

Risks of Strategic Management

Managers must be trained to guard against three types of unintended negative consequences of involvement in strategy formulation.

First, the time that managers spend on the strategic management process may have a negative impact on operational responsibilities. Managers must be trained to minimize that impact by scheduling their duties to allow the necessary time for strategic activities.

Second, if the formulators of strategy are not intimately involved in its implementation, they may shirk their individual responsibility for the decisions reached. Thus, strategic managers must be trained to limit their promises to performance that the decision makers and their subordinates can deliver.

Third, strategic managers must be trained to anticipate and respond to the disappointment of participating subordinates over unattained expectations. Subordinates may expect their involvement in even minor phases of total strategy formulation to result in both acceptance of their proposals and an increase in their rewards, or they may expect a solicitation of their input on selected issues to extend to other areas of decision making.

Sensitizing managers to these possible negative consequences and preparing them with effective means of minimizing such consequences will greatly enhance the potential of strategic planning.

Executives' Views of Strategic Management

How do managers and corporate executives view the contribution of strategic management to the success of their firms? To answer this question, a survey was conducted that included over 200 executives from the Fortune 500, Fortune 500 Service, and INC 500 companies.[5] Their responses are summarized in Strategy in Action 1–2.

Overall, these responses indicate that corporate America sees strategic management as instrumental to high performance, evolutionary and perhaps revolutionary in its ever-growing sophistication, action oriented, and cost effective. Clearly, the responding executives view strategic management as critical to their individual and organizational success.

THE STRATEGIC MANAGEMENT PROCESS

Businesses vary in the processes they use to formulate and direct their strategic management activities. Sophisticated planners, such as General Electric, Procter & Gamble, and IBM, have developed more detailed processes than less-formal planners of similar size. Small businesses that rely on the strategy formulation skills and limited time of an entrepreneur typically exhibit more basic planning concerns than those of larger firms in their industries. Understandably, firms with multiple products, markets, or technologies tend to use more complex strategic management systems. However, despite differences in detail and the degree of formalization, the basic components of the models used to analyze strategic management operations are very similar.

Because of the similarity among the general models of the strategic management process, it is possible to develop an eclectic model representative of the foremost thought in the strategic management area. This model is shown in Figure 1–3. It serves three major functions. First, it depicts the sequence and the relationships of the major components of the strategic management process. Second, it is the outline for this book. This chapter provides a general overview of the strategic management process, and the major components of the model will be the principal theme of subsequent chapters. Notice that the chapters of the text that discuss each of the strategic management process components are shown in each block. Finally, the model offers one approach

[5] V. Ramanujam, J. C. Camillus, and N. Venkatraman, "Trends in Strategic Planning," in *Strategic Planning and Management Handbook,* ed. W. R. King and D. I. Cleland (New York: Van Nostrand Reinhold, 1987), pp. 611–28.

EXECUTIVES' GENERAL OPINIONS AND ATTITUDES

Item	Percent of Respondents Indicating		
	Agreement	Neutral	Disagreement
1. Reducing emphasis on strategic planning will be detrimental to our long-term performance.	88.7%	4.9%	6.4%
2. Our plans today reflect implementation concerns.	73.6	16.9	9.5
3. We have improved the sophistication of our strategic planning systems.	70.6	18.6	10.8
4. Our previous approaches to strategic planning are not appropriate today.	64.2	16.2	19.6
5. Today's systems emphasize creativity among managers more than our previous systems did.	62.6	20.2	17.2
6. Our strategic planning systems today are more consistent with our organization's culture.	55.6	30.7	13.7
7. We are more concerned about the evaluation of our strategic planning systems today.	54.0	29.7	16.3
8. There is more participation from lower-level managers in our strategic planning.	56.6	18.0	25.4
9. Our tendency to rely on outside consultants for strategic planning has been on the decrease.	50.8	23.0	26.2
10. Our systems emphasize control more than before.	41.3	33.0	25.7
11. Planning in our company or unit is generally viewed as a luxury today.	15.0	13.0	72.0

Source: Adapted from V. Ramanujam, J. C. Camillus, and N. Venkatraman, "Trends in Strategic Planning," in *Strategic Planning and Management Handbook,* ed. W. R. King and D. I. Cleland (New York: Van Nostrand Reinhold, 1987), p. 619.

for analyzing the case studies in this text and thus helps the analyst develop strategy formulation skills.

COMPONENTS OF THE STRATEGIC MANAGEMENT MODEL

This section will define and briefly describe the key components of the strategic management model. Each of these components will receive much greater attention in a later chapter. The intention here is simply to introduce them.

Company Mission

The mission of a company is the unique purpose that sets it apart from other companies of its type and identifies the scope of its operations. In short, the mission describes the company's product, market, and technological areas of emphasis in a way that reflects the values and priorities of the strategic decision makers. For example, Lee Hun-Hee, the new chairman of the Samsung Group, revamped the company mission by stamping his own brand of management on Samsung. Immediately, Samsung separated Chonju

FIGURE 1–3
Strategic Management Model

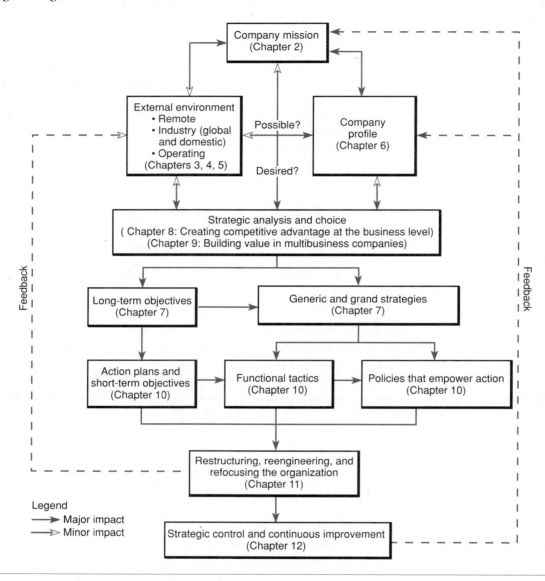

Paper Manufacturing and Shinsegae Department Store from other operations. This corporate act of downscaling reflected a revised management philosophy that favored specialization, thereby changing the direction and scope of the organization.

Company Profile

The company profile depicts the quantity and quality of the company's financial, human, and physical resources. It also assesses the strengths and weaknesses of the company's management and organizational structure. Finally, it contrasts the company's past successes and traditional concerns with the company's current capabilities in an attempt to identify the company's future capabilities.

External Environment

A firm's external environment consists of all the conditions and forces that affect its strategic options and define its competitive situation. The strategic management model shows the external environment as three interactive segments: the operating, industry, and remote environments.

Strategic Analysis and Choice

Simultaneous assessment of the external environment and the company profile enables a firm to identify a range of possibly attractive interactive opportunities. These opportunities are *possible* avenues for investment. However, they must be screened through the criterion of the company mission to generate a set of possible and *desired* opportunities. This screening process results in the selection of options from which a *strategic choice* is made. The process is meant to provide the combination of long-term objectives and generic and grand strategies that optimally position the firm in its external environment to achieve the company mission.

Strategic analysis and choice in single or dominant product/service businesses centers around identifying strategies that are most effective at building sustainable competitive advantage based on key value chain activities and capabilities—core competencies of the firm. Multibusiness companies find their managers focused on the question of which combination of businesses maximizes shareholder value as the guiding theme during their strategic analysis and choice.

Long-Term Objectives

The results that an organization seeks over a multiyear period are its *long-term objectives.* Such objectives typically involve some or all of the following areas: profitability, return on investment, competitive position, technological leadership, productivity, employee relations, public responsibility, and employee development.

Generic and Grand Strategies

Many businesses explicitly and all implicitly adopt one or more *generic strategies* characterizing their competitive orientation in the marketplace. Low cost, differentiation, or focus strategies define the three fundamental options. Enlightened managers seek to create ways their firm possesses both low cost and differentiation competitive advantages as part of their overall generic strategy. They usually combine these capabilities with a comprehensive, general plan of major actions through which their firm intends to achieve its long-term objectives in a dynamic environment. Called the *grand strategy,* this *statement of means* indicates how the objectives are to be achieved. Although every grand strategy is, in fact, a unique package of long-term strategies, 14 basic approaches can be identified: concentration, market development, product development, innovation, horizontal integration, vertical integration, joint venture, strategic alliances, consortia, concentric diversification, conglomerate diversification, turnaround, divestiture, and liquidation.

Each of these grand strategies will be covered in detail in Chapter 7.

Action Plans and Short-Term Objectives

Action plans translate generic and grand strategies into "action" by incorporating four elements. First, they identify *specific* functional *tactics and actions* to be undertaken in the next week, month or quarter as part of the business's effort to build competitive advantage. The second element is a clear *time frame for completion.* Third, action plans *create accountability* by identifying who is responsible for each "action" in the plan. Fourth, each "action" in an action plan has one or more specific, immediate objectives that are identified as *outcomes* that action should generate.

Functional Tactics

Within the general framework created by the business's generic and grand strategies, each business function needs to identify and undertake activities unique to the function that help build a sustainable competitive advantage. Managers in each business function develop tactics which delineate the functional activities undertaken in their part of the business and usually include them as a core part of their action plan. Functional tactics are detailed statements of the "means" or activities that will be used to achieve short-term objectives and establish competitive advantage.

Policies that Empower Action

Speed is a critical necessity for success in today's competitive, global marketplace. One way to enhance speed and responsiveness is to force/allow decisions to be made whenever possible at the lowest level in organizations. *Policies* are broad, precedent-setting decisions that guide or substitute for repetitive or time-sensitive managerial decision making. Creating policies that guide and "preauthorize" the thinking, decisions, and actions of operating managers and their subordinates in implementing the business's strategy is essential for establishing and controlling the ongoing operating process of the firm in a manner consistent with the firm's strategic objectives. Policies often increase managerial effectiveness by standardizing routine decisions and empowering or expanding the discretion of managers and subordinates in implementing business strategies.

The following are examples of the nature and diversity of company policies:

A requirement that managers have purchase requests for items costing more than $5,000 cosigned by the controller.

The minimum equity position required for all new McDonald's franchises.

The standard formula used to calculate return on investment for the 43 strategic business units of General Electric.

A decision that Sears service and repair employees have the right to waive repair charges to appliance customers they feel have been poorly served by their Sears appliance.

Restructuring, Reengineering, and Refocusing the Organization

Until this point in the strategic management process, managers have maintained a decidedly market-oriented focus as they formulate strategies and begin implementation through action plans functional tactics. Now the process takes and internal focus—getting the work of the business done efficiently and effectively so as to make the srategy work. What is the best way to organize ourselves to accomplish the mission? Where should leadership come from? What values should guide our daily activities—what should the organization and its people "be like?" How can we shape rewards to encourage appropriate action? The intense competition in the global marketplace has made this tradition "internally focused" set of questions—how the activities within their business are conducted—recast themselves with unprecedented attentiveness to the marketplace. Downsizing, restructuring, reengineering, outsourcing, and empowerment are all terms that reflect the critical stage in strategy implementation wherein managers attempt to rationalize and recast their organizational structure, leadership, culture, and reward systems to ensure a basic level of cost competitiveness, capacity for responsive quality, and the need to shape each one to accomodate unique requirements of their strategies.

Strategic Control and Continuous Improvement

Strategic control is concerned with tracking a strategy as it is being implemented, detecting problems or changes in its underlying premises, and making necessary adjustments. In contrast to postaction control, strategic control seeks to guide action on behalf of the generic and grand strategies as they are taking place and when the end results are still several years away. The rapid, accelerating change of the global marketplace of the last 10 years has made continuous improvement another aspect of strategic control in many organizations. Continuous improvement provides a way for managers to provide a form of strategic control that allows their organization to respond more proactively and timely to rapid developments in hundreds of areas that influence a business's success.

STRATEGIC MANAGEMENT AS A PROCESS

A *process* is the flow of information through interrelated stages of analysis toward the achievement of an aim. Thus, the strategic management model in Figure 1–3 depicts a process. In the strategic management process, the flow of information involves historical, current, and forecast data on the operations and environment of the business. Managers evaluate these data in light of the values and priorities of influential individuals and groups—often called *stakeholders*—that are vitally interested in the actions of the business. The interrelated stages of the process are the 12 components discussed in the last section. Finally, the aim of the process is the formulation and implementation of strategies that work, achieving the company's long-term mission and near-term objectives.

Viewing strategic management as a process has several important implications. First, a change in any component will affect several or all of the other components. Most of the arrows in the model point two ways, suggesting that the flow of information usually is reciprocal. For example, forces in the external environment may influence the nature of a company's mission, and the company may in turn affect the external environment and heighten competition in its realm of operation. A specific example is a power company that is persuaded, in part by governmental incentives, to include a commitment to the development of energy alternatives in its mission statement. The company then might promise to extend its R&D efforts in the area of coal liquefaction. The external environment has affected the company's mission, and the revised mission signals a competitive condition in the environment.

A second implication of viewing strategic management as a process is that strategy formulation and implementation are sequential. The process begins with development or reevaluation of the company mission. This step is associated with, but essentially followed by, development of a company profile and assessment of the external environment. Then follow, in order, strategic choice, definition of long-term objectives, design of the grand strategy, definition of short-term objectives, design of operating strategies, institutionalization of the strategy, and review and evaluation.

The apparent rigidity of the process, however, must be qualified.

First, a firm's strategic posture may have to be reevaluated in response to changes in any of the principal factors that determine or affect its performance. Entry by a major new competitor, the death of a prominent board member, replacement of the chief executive officer, and a downturn in market responsiveness are among the thousands of changes that can prompt reassessment of a firm's strategic plan. However, no matter where the need for a reassessment originates, the strategic management process begins with the mission statement.

Second, not every component of the strategic management process deserves equal attention each time planning activity takes place. Firms in an extremely stable environment may find that an in-depth assessment is not required every five years. Companies often are satisfied with their original mission statements even after a decade of operation and spend only a minimal amount of time addressing this subject. In addition, while formal strategic planning may be undertaken only every five years, objectives and strategies usually are updated each year, and rigorous reassessment of the initial stages of strategic planning rarely is undertaken at these times.

A third implication of viewing strategic management as a process is the necessity of feedback from institutionalization, review, and evaluation to the early stages of the process. *Feedback* can be defined as the collection of postimplementation results to enhance future decision making. Therefore, as indicated in Figure 1–3, strategic managers should assess the impact of implemented strategies on external environments. Thus, future planning can reflect any changes precipitated by strategic actions. Strategic managers also should analyze the impact of strategies on the possible need for modifications in the company mission.

A fourth implication of viewing strategic management as a process is the need to regard it as a dynamic system. The term *dynamic* characterizes the constantly changing conditions that affect interrelated and interdependent strategic activities. Managers should recognize that the components of the strategic process are constantly evolving but that formal planning artificially freezes those components, much as an action photograph freezes the movement of a swimmer. Since change is continuous, the dynamic strategic planning process must be monitored constantly for significant shifts in any of its components as a precaution against implementing an obsolete strategy.

Changes in the Process

The strategic management process undergoes continual assessment and subtle updating. Although the elements of the basic strategic management model rarely change, the relative emphasis that each element receives will vary with the decision makers who use the model and with the environments of their companies.

Strategy in Action 1–3 is an update on general trends in strategic management, summarizing the responses of over 200 corporate executives. This update shows there has been an increasing companywide emphasis on and appreciation for the value of strategic management activities. It also provides evidence that practicing managers have given increasing attention to the need for frequent and widespread involvement in the formulation and implementation phases of the strategic management process. Finally, it indicates that, as managers and their firms gain knowledge, experience, skill, and understanding in how to design and manage their planning activities, they become better able to avoid the potential negative consequences of instituting a vigorous strategic management process.

STRATEGY
IN ACTION
1–3

GENERAL TRENDS IN STRATEGIC MANAGEMENT

Item	Percent of Respondents Indicating		
	Increase	No Change	Decrease
1. Overall emphasis on strategic planning systems.	81.2%	7.7%	11.1%
2. Perceived usefulness of strategic planning.	82.0	10.2	7.8
3. Involvement of line managers in strategic planning activities.	75.2	21.4	3.4
4. Time spent by the chief executive in strategic planning.	78.7	17.8	3.5
5. Acceptance of the outputs of the strategic planning exercise by top management.	74.0	20.6	5.4
6. Perceived usefulness of annual planning.	53.9	38.7	7.4
7. Involvement of staff managers in the annual planning exercise.	52.9	39.3	7.8
8. Involvement of the board of directors in strategic planning.	51.4	47.0	1.6
9. Resources provided for strategic planning.	62.9	23.9	13.2
10. Consistency between strategic plans and budgets.	53.4	38.2	8.3
11. Use of annual plans in monthly performance review.	42.3	55.6	2.1
12. Overall satisfaction with the strategic planning system.	57.4	24.5	18.1
13. Number of planners (i.e., those management personnel whose primary task is planning).	52.9	24.8	22.3
14. Attention to stakeholders other than stockholders.	32.8	63.0	4.2
15. Use of planning committees.	40.9	46.1	13.1
16. Attention to societal issues in planning.	33.2	59.8	7.0
17. The planning horizon (i.e., the number of years considered in the strategic plan).	28.8	56.6	14.6
18. The distance between the CEO and the chief of planning.	13.3	45.1	41.5
19. Threats to the continuation of strategic planning.	12.0	47.0	41.0
20. Resistance to planning in general.	10.2	31.7	58.0

Source: Adapted from V. Ramanujam, J. C. Camillus, and N. Venkatraman, "Trends in Strategic Planning," in *Strategic Planning and Management Handbook,* ed. W. R. King and D. I. Cleland (New York: Van Nostrand Reinhold, 1987), p. 614.

SUMMARY

Strategic management is the set of decisions and actions that result in the formulation and implementation of plans designed to achieve a company's objectives. Because it involves long-term, future-oriented, complex decision making and requires considerable resources, top-management participation is essential.

Strategic management is a three-tier process involving corporate, business, and functional-level planners, and support personnel. At each progressively lower level, strategic activities were shown to be more specific, narrow, short term, and action oriented, with lower risks but fewer opportunities for dramatic impact.

The strategic management model presented in this chapter will serve as the structure for understanding and integrating all the major phases of strategy formulation and implementation. The chapter provided a summary account of these phases, each of which is given extensive individual attention in subsequent chapters.

The chapter stressed that the strategic management process centers on the belief that a firm's mission can be best achieved through a systematic and comprehensive assessment of both its internal capabilities and its external environment. Subsequent evaluation of the firm's opportunities leads, in turn, to the choice of long-term objectives and grand strategies and, ultimately, to annual objectives and operating strategies, which must be implemented, monitored, and controlled.

QUESTIONS FOR DISCUSSION

1. Find a recent copy of *Business Week* and read the "Corporate Strategies" section. Was the main decision discussed strategic? At what level in the organization was the key decision made?

2. In what ways do you think the subject matter in this strategic management-business policy course will differ from that of previous courses you have taken?

3. After graduation, you are not likely to move directly to a top-level management position. In fact, few members of your class will ever reach the top-management level. Why, then, is it important for all business majors to study the field of strategic management?

4. Do you expect outstanding performance in this course to require a great deal of memorization? Why or why not?

5. You undoubtedly have read about individuals who seemingly have given singled-handed direction to their corporations. Is a participative strategic management approach likely to stifle or suppress the contributions of such individuals?

6. Think about the courses you have taken in functional areas, such as marketing, finance, production, personnel, and accounting. What is the importance of each of these areas to the strategic planning process?

7. Discuss with practicing business managers the strategic management models used in their firms. What are the similarities and differences between these models and the one in the text?

8. In what ways do you believe the strategic planning approach of not-for-profit organizations would differ from that of profit-oriented organizations?

9. How do you explain the success of firms that do not use a formal strategic planning process?

10. Think about your postgraduation job search as a strategic decision. How would the strategic management model be helpful to you in identifying and securing the most promising position?

BIBLIOGRAPHY

Adler, P. S.; D. W. McDonald; and F. MacDonald. "Strategic Management of Technical Functions." *Sloan Management Review* (Winter 1992), pp. 19–38.

Allen, M. G. "Strategic Management Hits Its Stride." *Planning Review* (September 1985), pp. 6–9.

Arkam, J. D., and S. S. Cowen. "Strategic Planning for Increased Profit in the Small Business." *Long Range Planning* (December 1990), pp. 63–70.

Baron, David P. "Integrated Strategy: Market and Nonmarket Components." *California Management Review* 37, no. 2 (Winter 1995), p. 47.

Blair, J. D., and K. B. Boal. "Strategy Formation Processes in Health Care Organizations: A Context-Specific Examination of Context-Free Strategy Issues." *Journal of Management* (June 1991), pp. 305–44.

Borch, Odd Jarl, and Michael B. Arthur. "Strategy Networks among Small Firms: Implications for Strategy Research Methodology." *Journal of Management Studies* 32, no. 4 (July 1995), p. 419.

Brandenburger, Adam M., and Barry J. Nalebuff. "The Right Game: Use Game Theory to Shape Strategy." *Harvard Business Review* 73, no. 4 (July–August 1995), p. 57.

Brooker, R. E., Jr. "Orchestrating the Planning Process." *The Journal of Business Strategy* (July–August 1991), pp. 4–9.

Carlson, F. P. "The Long and Short of Strategic Planning." *The Journal of Business Strategy* (May–June 1990), pp. 15–21.

Collins, James C., and Jerry I. Porras. "Building a Visionary Company." *California Management Review* 37, no. 2 (Winter 1995).

Collis, David J., and Cynthia A. Montgomery. "Competing on Resources: Strategy in the 1990s." *Harvard Business Review* 73, no. 4 (July–August 1995), p. 118.

Goold, M., and A. Campbell. "Many Best Ways to Make Strategy." *Harvard Business Review* (November–December 1987), pp. 70–76.

Gopinath, C., and Richard C. Hoffman. "The Relevance of Strategy Research: Practitioner and Academic Viewpoints." *Journal of Management Studies* 32, no. 5 (September 1995), p. 575.

Hahn, D. "Strategic Management—Tasks and Challenges in the 1990s." *Long Range Planning* (February 1991), pp. 26–39.

Hax, A. C. "Redefining the Concept of Strategy and the Strategy Formation Process." *Planning Review* (May–June 1990), pp. 34–41.

Hinterhuber, H. H., and W. Popp. "Are You a Strategist or Just a Manager." *Harvard Business Review* (January–February 1992), pp. 105–14.

Hitt, M. A.; R. E. Hoskisson; and J. S. Harrison. "Strategic Competitiveness in the 1990s: Challenges and Opportunities for U.S. Executives." *Academy of Management Executive* (May 1991), pp. 7–22.

Larwood, Laurie; Cecilia M. Falbe; Mark P. Krieger; and Paul Miesing. "Structure and Meaning of Organizational Vision." *The Academy of Management Journal* 38, no. 3 (June 1995), p. 740.

Meyer, A. D. "What Is Strategy's Distinctive Competence?" *Journal of Management* (December 1991), pp. 821–34.

Miles, Raymond E.; Henry J. Coleman, Jr.; and W. E. Dougles Creed. "Keys to Success in Corporate Redesign." *California Management Review* 37, no. 3 (Spring 1995), p. 128.

Mintzberg, H. "Strategy Making in Three Modes." *California Management Review* (Spring 1973), pp. 44–53.

Pearce, J. A., II. "An Executive-Level Perspective on the Strategic Management Process." *California Management Review* (Spring 1982), pp. 39–48.

Peker, Peter, Jr., and Stan Abraham. "Is Strategic Management Living Up to Its Promise?" *Long Range Planning* 28, no. 5 (October 1995), p. 32.

Rappaport, A. "CFOs and Strategists: Forging a Common Framework." *Harvard Business Review* (May–June 1992), pp. 84–93.

Rouleau, Linda, and Francine Ségun. "Strategy and Organizational Theories: Common Forms of Discourse." *Journal of Management Studies* 32, no. 1 (January 1995), p. 101.

Schonberger, R. J. "Is Strategy Strategic? Impact of Total Quality Management on Strategy." *Academy of Management Executive* (August 1992), pp. 80–97.

Stalk, G.; P. Evans; and L. E. Shulman. "Competing on Capabilities: The New Rules of Corporate Strategy." *Harvard Business Review* (March–April 1992), pp. 57–69.

Stonich, P. J. "Time: The Next Strategic Frontier." *Planning Review* (November–December 1990), pp. 4–7.

Taylor, Bernard. "The New Strategic Leadership—Driving Charge, Getting Results." *Long Range Planning* 28, no. 5 (October 1995), p. 71.

Veliyath, R. "Strategic Planning: Balancing Short-Run Performance and Longer Term Prospects." *Long Range Planning* (June 1992), pp. 86–97.

Yon, E. T. "Corporate Strategy and the New Europe." *Academy of Management Executive* (August 1990), pp. 61–65.

CHAPTER 1 COHESION CASE ILLUSTRATION

THE COCA-COLA COMPANY

Celebrating its 110th birthday in 1996, The Coca-Cola Company has become perhaps the world's most well-known company. Behind the world's most ubiquitous trademark is an international corporation—or as Coke's management likes to say: "a truly global business system"—that has many lessons to share with strategic management students. As you prepare for a successful business career in the 21st century, you must be fine-tuning your understanding of how to help your company achieve and sustain global competitiveness while building stockholder value in a social and environmentally responsible manner. This book and this Cohesion Case about Coca-Cola will help you do that.

The Cohesion Case is a set of 12 comprehensive illustrations, one accompanying each chapter in the book, that uses The Coca-Cola Company to illustrate and apply key concepts presented in the chapter. Taken together, they provide a "cohesive" journey through experiences, strategies, and decisions at The Coca-Cola Company that will enhance your understanding of strategic management in today's global marketplace.

The remainder of this introductory section will give you a brief history and overview of The Coca-Cola Company. More complete information about The Coca-Cola Company will be provided in the Cohesion Case illustrations following each chapter. And there is a wealth of information about The Coca-Cola Company in various company and trade publications, as well as the popular business press, that we encourage you to seek out as a way to enhance your strategic management skills.

HISTORY OF THE COCA-COLA COMPANY

Coca-Cola's origin dates to 1886 when an Atlanta, Georgia, pharmacist, Dr. John S. Pemberton, cooked up the first medicinal syrup extract of "Coca" in a three-legged brass pot in his backyard. Derived as a potential patent medicine, the first glass of the new soda fountain drink went on sale for 5 cents a glass on May 8, 1886, in an Atlanta pharmacy where, by design or accident, carbonated water was blended with the new syrup to produce the drink. Dr. Pemberton sold 25 gallons of the syrup that year, generating approximately $50 in total sales.

Two years later, Atlanta businessman Asa G. Candler bought all rights to Coca-Cola for $2,300. Candler placed major emphasis on promotional activities and quickly expanded distribution of the syrup and registered the Coca-Cola trademark. The bottling of Coca-Cola started in 1894 in Vicksburg, Mississippi, and continued until 1899, when the company granted rights to bottle and sell Coca-Cola in practically the entire continental United States. By 1904, the annual sales for Coca-Cola syrup reached 1 million gallons, and there were 123 plants authorized or licensed to bottle the finished drink.

Ernest Woodruff, an Atlanta banker, led an investor group that bought The Coca-Cola Company from Candler for $25 million in 1919. Robert Woodruff was made president, and the company moved aggressively to expand sales, establishing a foreign sales office and developing a concentrate for the syrup to reduce transportation costs. Shortly after the Woodruff group purchased the company, Coca-Cola stock was sold to the public at $40 per share, helping to lay the capital foundation for its rapid domestic and international expansion. By 1995, consumers in almost 200 countries purchased over 845 million servings daily of soft drinks provided by The Coca-Cola Company.

COCA-COLA'S RECENT HISTORY

The 1960s saw The Coca-Cola Company expand its business focus beyond soft drinks. In rapid succession, Coca-Cola acquired more than 15 different businesses, ranging from food, wine, and soft drinks to film and water treatment. By 1977, The Coca-Cola Company looked something like this:

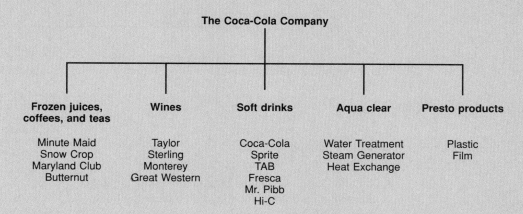

The company reported that, in 1977, 76 percent of total sales ($3.5 billion) and 89 percent of operating profit ($0.6 billion) came from soft drinks. It also reported that 60 percent of worldwide soft-drink volume came from non-U.S. markets. On a companywide basis, sales and profitability looked as follows during that year:

1977 (in millions)

	United States	Latin America	Europe and Africa	Canada and Pacific	Total
Net sales	$2,008	$270	$669	$613	$3,556
Operating profit	264	67	189	114	634
Identifiable assets	1,060	196	414	273	1,943

By 1983, The Coca-Cola Company had become a major player in movie entertainment, acquiring Columbia Pictures. Along the way it sold its wine, water treatment, and plastics businesses. It adopted an aggressive product development effort in soft drinks, with diet, caffeine-free, and citrus soft-drink additions. Introduced one year earlier, Diet Coke became the No. 1 low-calorie beverage in the United States and No. 4 soft drink overall. On a companywide basis, sales and profitability looked as follows during that year:

1983 (in millions)

	United States	Latin America	Europe and Africa	Canada and Pacific	Total
Net sales	$4,071	$401	$1,226	$1,131	$6,829
Operating profit	499	69	295	207	993
Identifiable assets	2,997	421	607	473	4,496

The 12 years that followed saw The Coca-Cola Company make several fundamental changes in its strategic posture, while also accelerating its globalization and achieving some extraordinary results. Having completed the divestiture of Columbia Pictures (to Sony), The Coca-Cola Company of 1994 returned to its roots, operating in only two lines of business:

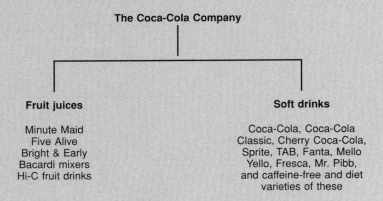

The Coca-Cola Company

Fruit juices

Minute Maid
Five Alive
Bright & Early
Bacardi mixers
Hi-C fruit drinks

Soft drinks

Coca-Cola, Coca-Cola
Classic, Cherry Coca-Cola,
Sprite, TAB, Fanta, Mello
Yello, Fresca, Mr. Pibb,
and caffeine-free and diet
varieties of these

In addition, the company has reversed its traditional approach and started aggressively making major equity investments in bottling facilities. These facilities are owned by bottling franchisees or joint ventures, or are company-owned. Another action was to create and sell 51 percent—the largest IPO in U.S. history—of a new publicly traded company (Coca-Cola Enterprises), which buys and invests in Coca-Cola bottling companies worldwide.

As Coca-Cola generously helped Atlanta host the 1996 Olympics, Coca-Cola's emphasis on globalization is unmistakable. Indeed, Coca-Cola's board chairman and chief executive officer, Robert C. Goizueta, had the following recent remarks about Coca-Cola's global perspective:

The global marketplace is something people have been writing about for years, and, while it may not be completely here yet, it is a fact that most U.S.–based companies of any size today think and act in international terms. At The Coca-Cola Company, we view ourselves today as an international corporation headquartered in the United States, as opposed to a U.S. company with a sizable international business. Coca-Cola's globalization is unquestioned and long a part of our company. Our attention, therefore, has moved beyond, to what we call "the Coca-Cola system," arguably the only truly global business system in existence today.

The trend toward globalization by U.S.–based companies will continue. Not only do 95 percent of the world's 5+ billion people live outside the United States, but the global climate today is generally favorable for companies disposed to expansion:

First, disposable income is rising around the world and, with it, people's ability to purchase more consumer products.

Second, outside the United States and Europe, the world is getting younger, and young people are the most enthusiastic purchasers of many consumer products.

Third, the world's markets are becoming easier to reach. Events in eastern Europe and the former Soviet Union are good examples.

Finally, in many important ways, the world's markets are also becoming more alike. Every corner of the free world is increasingly subjected to intense and similar communications: commercial, cultural, social, and hard news. Thus, people around the world are today connected to each other by brand name consumer products as much as by anything else. Tokyo, London, New York, and Los Angeles resemble each other today far more than they did 25 years ago, in large part because their residents' tastes in consumer products have converged.

Through our advertising and marketing we have encouraged consumers to associate Coca-Cola with their best feelings and memories . . . friends and family . . . joy and laughter . . . sports and music. Through our insistence on product integrity, we have made sure that wherever and whenever they drink a Coke, the product will live up to their expectations.

Through our worldwide business system we have made sure that Coca-Cola is there, so that wherever consumers travel they can always find a point of reference, a friendly reminder of home, regardless of where home may be. And through our efforts to serve our customers and consumers with a passion, they have come to feel passionate about Coca-Cola . . . It is this deep, heartfelt bond shared by Coca-Cola consumers and the members of the Coca-Cola system around the world that The Coca-Cola Company and its management cherish and value above all else. We cherish it because it is, more than anything else, the true measure of success in the global marketplace.

Goizueta, a Cuban refugee who as a young man worked for a Coke bottler in Cuba until fleeing the country with his family after Castro's rise to power, brings a unique perspective to his insistence on a global perspective. And The Coca-Cola Company has prospered under his leadership. Since becoming CEO in 1980, Goizueta has led Coca-Cola to a virtually unsurpassed level of performance. Compounded annual growth rates for several key indicators through 1995 are shown below:

Compound Annual Growth through 1995

	3 Year (%)	5 Year (%)	10 Year (%)
Operating revenues	11%	13%	12%
Operating income	16	17	16
Pretax income	17	16	15
Net income, continuing operations	24	16	17
EPS	23	17	18
EPS, continuing operations	15	17	21
Dividends	18	18	13
Average return on equity	50	47	38
Share appreciation	11	25	27

At January 1, 1982, Coca-Cola's market value stood at $4.3 billion. Fifteen years later, it exceeded $80 billion—an 18-fold growth. By any standard, these results were (and still are) truly extraordinary. It is certainly an indication of sound strategic decision making.

The remainder of this book will provide a Cohesion Case discussion at the end of each chapter. Each segment will examine aspects of strategic management at Coca-Cola that should help you understand Coca-Cola's success, while also serving to illustrate the ideas, concepts, and techniques we will present in each chapter of this book. We are excited about being able to "team up" with Coca-Cola to provide you with this unique perspective. And we strongly encourage you to supplement our coverage by obtaining and reviewing past Coca-Cola annual reports and recent business periodicals about the company to broaden your understanding of the company and its willingness to embrace sensible risk-taking and to welcome global change.

II STRATEGY FORMULATION

Strategy formulation guides executives in defining the business their firm is in, the ends it seeks, and the means it will use to accomplish those ends. The approach of strategy formulation is an improvement over that of traditional long-range planning. As discussed in the next seven chapters—about developing a firm's competitive plan of action—strategy formulation combines a future-oriented perspective with concern for the firm's internal and external environments.

The strategy formulation process begins with definition of the company mission, as discussed in Chapter 2. In that chapter, the purpose of business is defined to reflect the values of a wide variety of interested parties.

Chapter 3 deals with the principal factors in a firm's external environment that strategic managers must assess so they can anticipate and take advantage of future business conditions. It emphasizes the importance to a firm's planning activities of factors in the firm's remote, industry, and operating environments. A key theme of the chapter is the problem of deciding whether to accept environmental constraints or to maneuver around them.

Chapter 4 describes the key differences in strategic planning and implementation among domestic, multinational, and global firms. It gives special attention to the new vision that a firm must communicate in a revised company mission when it multinationalizes.

Chapter 5 focuses on the environmental forecasting approaches currently used by strategic managers in assessing and anticipating changes in the external environment.

Chapter 6 shows how firms evaluate their internal strengths and weaknesses to produce a company profile. Strategic managers use such profiles to target competitive advantages they can emphasize and competitive disadvantages they should correct or minimize.

Chapter 7 examines the types of long-range objectives strategic managers set and specifies the qualities these objectives must have to provide a basis for direction and evaluation. The chapter also examines the generic and grand strategies that firms use to achieve long-range objectives.

Comprehensive approaches to the evaluation of strategic opportunities and to the final strategic decision are the focus of Chapter 8. The chapter shows how a firm's strategic options can be compared in a way that allows selection of the best available option.

DEFINING THE COMPANY MISSION

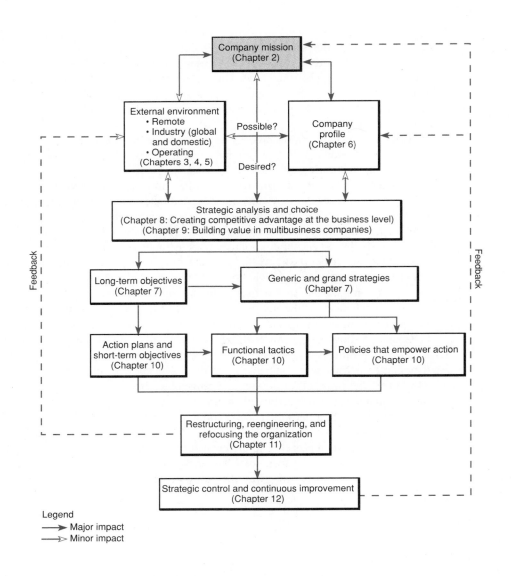

Legend
⟶ Major impact
⟶▷ Minor impact

What Is a Company Mission?

Whether a firm is developing a new business or reformulating direction for an ongoing business, it must determine the basic goals and philosophies that will shape its strategic posture. This fundamental purpose that sets a firm apart from other firms of its type and identifies the scope of its operations in product and market terms is defined as the company mission. As discussed in Chapter 1, the company mission is a broadly framed but enduring statement of a firm's intent. It embodies the business philosophy of the firm's strategic decision makers, implies the image the firm seeks to project, reflects the firm's self-concept, and indicates the firm's principal product or service areas and the primary customer needs the firm will attempt to satisfy. In short, it describes the firm's product, market, and technological areas of emphasis, and it does so in a way that reflects the values and priorities of the firm's strategic decision makers. An excellent example is the company mission statement of Nicor, Inc., shown in Strategy in Action 2–1.

The Need for an Explicit Mission

No external body requires that the company mission be defined, and the process of defining it is time-consuming and tedious. Moreover, it contains broadly outlined or implied objectives and strategies rather than specific directives. Characteristically, it is a statement, not of measurable targets but of attitude, outlook, and orientation.

A company mission is designed to accomplish seven outcomes:

1. To ensure unanimity of purpose within the organization.
2. To provide a basis for motivating the use of the organization's resources.
3. To develop a basis, or standard, for allocating organizational resources.
4. To establish a general tone or organizational climate; for example, to suggest a businesslike operation.
5. To serve as a focal point for those who can identify with the organization's purpose and direction and to deter those who cannot do so from participating further in its activities.
6. To facilitate the translation of objectives and goals into a work structure involving the assignment of tasks to responsible elements within the organization.
7. To specify organizational purposes and the translation of these purposes into goals in such a way that cost, time, and performance parameters can be assessed and controlled.[1]

Formulating a Mission

The process of defining the company mission for a specific business can perhaps be best understood by thinking about the business at its inception. The typical business begins with the beliefs, desires, and aspirations of a single entrepreneur. Such an owner-manager's sense of mission usually is based on the following fundamental beliefs:

1. The product or service of the business can provide benefits at least equal to its price.
2. The product or service can satisfy a customer need of specific market segments that is currently not being met adequately.

Note: Portions of this chapter are adopted from John A. Pearce II, "The Company Mission as a Strategic Tool," *Sloan Management Review,* Spring 1992, pp. 15–24.

[1] William R. King and David I. Cleland, *Strategic Planning and Policy* (New York: Van Nostrand Reinhold, 1978), p. 124.

MISSION STATEMENT OF NICOR, INC.

PREAMBLE

We, the management of Nicor, Inc., here set forth our belief as to the purpose for which the company is established and the principles under which it should operate. We pledge our effort to the accomplishment of these purposes within these principles.

BASIC PURPOSE

The basic purpose of Nicor, Inc., is to perpetuate an investor-owned company engaging in various phases of the energy business, striving for balance among those phases so as to render needed satisfactory products and services and earn optimum, long-range profits.

WHAT WE DO

The principal business of the company, through its utility subsidiary, is the provision of energy through a pipe system to meet the needs of ultimate consumers. To accomplish its basic purpose, and to ensure its strength, the company will engage in other energy-related activities, directly or through subsidiaries or in participation with other persons, corporations, firms, or entities.

All activities of the company shall be consistent with its responsibilities to investors, customers, employees, and the public and its concern for the optimum development and utilization of natural resources and for environmental needs.

WHERE WE DO IT

The company's operations shall be primarily in the United States, but no self-imposed or regulatory geographical limitations are placed upon the acquisition, development, processing, transportation, or storage of energy resources, or upon other energy-related ventures in which the company may engage. The company will engage in such activities in any location where, after careful review, it has determined that such activity is in the best interest of its stockholders.

Utility service will be offered in the territory of the company's utility subsidiary to the best of its ability, in accordance with the requirements of regulatory agencies and pursuant to the subsidiary's purposes and principles.

3. The technology that is to be used in production will provide a cost- and quality-competitive product or service.

4. With hard work and the support of others, the business can not only survive but also grow and be profitable.

5. The management philosophy of the business will result in a favorable public image and will provide financial and psychological rewards for those who are willing to invest their labor and money in helping the business to succeed.

6. The entrepreneur's self-concept of the business can be communicated to and adopted by employees and stockholders.

As the business grows or is forced by competitive pressures to alter its product–market–technology, redefining the company mission may be necessary. If so, the revised mission statement will contain the same components as the original. It will state the

STRATEGY IN ACTION 2–2	**IDENTIFYING MISSION STATEMENT COMPONENTS: A COMPILATION OF EXCERPTS FROM ACTUAL CORPORATE MISSION STATEMENTS**

1. Customer-market

We believe our first responsibility is to the doctors, nurses, and patients, to mothers and all others who use our products and services. (Johnson & Johnson)

To anticipate and meet market needs of farmers, ranchers, and rural communities within North America. (CENEX)

2. Product-service

AMAX's principal products are molybdenum, coal, iron ore, copper, lead, zinc, petroleum and natural gas, potash, phosphates, nickel, tungsten, silver, gold, and magnesium. (AMAX)

3. Geographic domain

We are dedicated to the total success of Corning Glass Works as a worldwide competitor. (Corning Glass)

4. Technology

Control Data is the business of applying microelectronics and computer technology in two general areas: computer-related hardware and computing-enhancing services, which include computation, information, education, and finance. (Control Data)

The common technology in these areas relates to discrete particle coatings. (NASHUA)

5. Concern for survival

In this respect, the company will conduct its operation prudently, and will provide the profits and growth which will assure Hoover's ultimate success. (Hoover Universal)

6. Philosophy

We are committed to improve health care throughout the world. (Baxter Travenol)

We believe human development to be the worthiest of the goals of civilization and independence to be the superior condition for nurturing growth in the capabilities of people. (Sun Company)

7. Self-concept

Hoover Universal is a diversified, multi-industry corporation with strong manufacturing capabilities, entrepreneurial policies, and individual business unit autonomy. (Hoover Universal)

8. Concern for public image

We are responsible to the communities in which we live and work and to the world community as well. (Johnson & Johnson)

Also, we must be responsive to the broader concerns of the public, including especially the general desire for improvement in the quality of life, equal opportunity for all, and the constructive use of natural resources. (Sun Company)

Source: John A Pearce II and F. R. David, "Corporate Mission Statements: The Bottom Line," *Academy of Management Executive,* May 1987, pp. 109–16.

basic type of product or service to be offered, the primary markets or customer groups to be served, and the technology to be used in production or delivery; the firm's fundamental concern for survival through growth and profitability; the firm's managerial philosophy; the public image the firm seeks; and the self-concept those affiliated with the firm should have of it. This chapter will discuss in detail these components. The examples shown in Strategy in Action 2–2 provide insights into how some major corporations handle them.

Basic Product or Service; Primary Market; Principal Technology

Three indispensable components of the mission statement are specification of the basic product or service, specification of the primary market, and specification of the principal technology for production or delivery. These components are discussed under one heading because only in combination do they describe the company's business activity. A good example of the three components is to be found in the business plan of ITT Barton, a division of ITT. Under the heading of business mission and area served, the following information is presented:

The unit's mission is to serve industry and government with quality instruments used for the primary measurement, analysis, and local control of fluid flow, level, pressure, temperature, and fluid properties. This instrumentation includes flow meters, electronic readouts, indicators, recorders, switches, liquid level system, analytical instruments such as titrators, integrators, controllers, transmitters, and various instruments for the measurement of fluid properties (density, viscosity, gravity) used for processing variable sensing, data collecting, control, and transmission. The unit's mission includes fundamental loop- closing control and display devices, when economically justified, but excludes broadline central control room instrumentation, systems design, and turnkey responsibility.

Markets served include instrumentation for oil and gas production, gas transportation, chemical and petrochemical processing, cryogenics, power generation, aerospace, government, and marine, as well as other instrument and equipment manufacturers.

In only 129 words, this segment of the mission statement clearly indicates to all readers—from company employees to casual observers—the basic products, primary markets, and principal technologies of ITT Barton.

Often the most referenced public statement of a company's selected products and markets appears in "silver bullet" form in the mission statement; for example, "Dayton-Hudson Corporation is a diversified retailing company whose business is to serve the American consumer through the retailing of fashion-oriented quality merchandise."[2] Such an abstract of company direction is particularly helpful to outsiders who value condensed overviews.

Company Goals: Survival, Growth, Profitability

Three economic goals guide the strategic direction of almost every business organization. Whether or not the mission statement explicitly states these goals, it reflects the firm's intention to secure *survival* through *growth* and *profitability.*

A firm that is unable to survive will be incapable of satisfying the aims of any of its stakeholders. Unfortunately, the goal of survival, like the goals of growth and profitability, often is taken for granted to such an extent that it is neglected as a principal criterion in strategic decision making. When this happens, the firm may focus on short-term aims at the expense of the long run. Concerns for expediency, a quick fix, or a bargain may displace the assessment of long-term impact. Too often, the result is near-term economic failure owing to a lack of resource synergy and sound business practice. For example, Consolidated Foods, maker of Shasta soft drinks and L ' eggs hosiery, sought growth through the acquisition of bargain businesses. However, the erratic sales patterns of its diverse holdings forced it to divest itself of more than four dozen companies. This process cost Consolidated Foods millions of dollars and hampered its growth.

Profitability is the mainstay goal of a business organization. No matter how profit is measured or defined, profit over the long term is the clearest indication of a firm's ability to satisfy the principal claims and desires of employees and stockholders. The key phrase here is "over the long term." Obviously, basing decisions on a short-term concern for profitability would lead to a strategic myopia. Overlooking the enduring concerns of customers, suppliers, creditors, ecologists, and regulatory agents may produce profit in the short term, but, over time, the financial consequences are likely to be detrimental.

---

[2] See W. Ouchi, *Theory Z* (Reading, Mass.: Addison-Wesley Publishing, 1981). Ouchi presents more complete mission statements of three of the companies discussed in this chapter: Dayton-Hudson, Hewlett-Packard, and Intel.

The following excerpt from the Hewlett-Packard statement of mission ably expresses the importance of an orientation toward long-term profit:

> To achieve sufficient profit to finance our company growth and to provide the resources we need to achieve our other corporate objectives.
>
> In our economic system, the profit we generate from our operation is the ultimate source of the funds we need to prosper and grow. It is the one absolutely essential measure of our corporate performance over the long term. Only if we continue to meet our profit objective can we achieve our other corporate objectives.

A firm's growth is tied inextricably to its survival and profitability. In this context, the meaning of growth must be broadly defined. Although the product impact market studies (PIMS) have shown that growth in market share is correlated with profitability, other important forms of growth do exist. Growth in the number of markets served, in the variety of products offered, and in the technologies that are used to provide goods or services frequently lead to improvements in a firm's competitive ability. Growth means change, and proactive change is essential in a dynamic business environment.

Hewlett-Packard's mission statement provides an excellent example of corporate regard for growth:

> Objective: To let our growth be limited only by our profits and our ability to develop and produce technical products that satisfy real customer needs.
>
> We do not believe that large size is important for its own sake; however, for at least two basic reasons, continuous growth is essential for us to achieve our other objectives.
>
> In the first place, we serve a rapidly growing and expanding segment of our technological society. To remain static would be to lose ground. We cannot maintain a position of strength and leadership in our field without growth.
>
> In the second place, growth is important in order to attract and hold high-caliber people. These individuals will align their future only with a company that offers them considerable opportunity for personal progress. Opportunities are greater and more challenging in a growing company.

The issue of growth raises a concern about the definition of the company mission. How can a firm's product, market, and technology be specified sufficiently to provide direction without precluding the exercise of unanticipated strategic options? How can a firm so define its mission that it can consider opportunistic diversification while maintaining the parameters that guide its growth decision? Perhaps such questions are best addressed when a firm's mission statement outlines the conditions under which the firm might depart from ongoing operations. General Electric Company's extensive global mission provided the foundation for its GE Appliances (GEA) in Louisville, Kentucky, to grow in spite of the 1990–91 recession. GEA did not see consumer preferences in the world market becoming Americanized. Instead, its expansion goals allowed for flexibility in examining the unique characteristics of individual foreign markets and tailoring strategies to fit them.

The growth philosophy of Dayton-Hudson also embodies this approach:

> The stability and quality of the corporation's financial performance will be developed through the profitable execution of our existing businesses, as well as through the acquisition or development of new businesses. Our growth priorities, in order, are as follows:
>
> 1. Development of the profitable market preeminence of existing companies in existing markets through new store development or new strategies within existing stores.

2. Expansion of our companies to feasible new markets.
3. Acquisition of other retailing companies that are strategically and financially compatible with Dayton-Hudson.
4. Internal development of new retailing strategies.

Capital allocations to fund the expansion of existing Dayton-Hudson operating companies will be based on each company's return on investment (ROI), in relationship to its ROI objective and its consistency in earnings growth and on the ability of its management to perform up to the forecasts contained in its capital requests. Expansion via acquisition or new venture will occur when the opportunity promises an acceptable rate of long-term growth and profitability, an acceptable degree of risk, and compatibility with Dayton-Hudson's long-term strategy.

Company Philosophy

The statement of a company's philosophy, often called the *company creed,* usually accompanies or appears within the mission statement. It reflects or specifies the basic beliefs, values, aspirations, and philosophical priorities to which strategic decision makers are committed in managing the company. Fortunately, the philosophies vary little from one firm to another. Owners and managers implicitly accept a general, unwritten, yet pervasive code of behavior that governs business actions and permits them to be largely self-regulated. Unfortunately, statements of company philosophy are often so similar and so platitudinous that they read more like public relations handouts than the commitment to values they are meant to be.

Saturn's statement of philosophy, presented in Strategy in Action 2–3, indicates the company's clearly defined initiatives for satisfying the needs of its customers, employees, suppliers, and dealers.

Despite the similarity of these statements, the intentions of the strategic managers in developing them do not warrant cynicism. Company executives attempt to provide a distinctive and accurate picture of the firm's managerial outlook. One such statement of company philosophy is that of Dayton-Hudson Corporation. As Strategy in Action 2–4 shows, Dayton-Hudson's board of directors and executives have established especially clear directions for company decision making and action.

Perhaps most noteworthy in the Dayton-Hudson statement is its delineation of responsibility at both the corporate and business levels. In many ways, the statement could serve as a prototype for the three-tier approach to strategic management. This approach implies that the mission statement must address strategic concerns at the corporate, business, and functional levels of the organization. Dayton-Hudson's management philosophy does this by balancing operating autonomy and flexibility on the one hand with corporate input and direction on the other.

As seen in Global Strategy in Action 2–1, the philosophy of Nissan Motor Manufacturing is expressed by the company's People Principles and Key Corporate Principles. These principles form the basis of the way the company operates on a daily basis. They address the principal concepts used in meeting the company's established goals. Nissan focuses on the distinction between the role of the individual and the corporation. In this way, employees can link their productivity and success to the productivity and success of the company. Given these principles, the company is able to concentrate on the issues most important to its survival, growth, and profitability.

Strategy in Action 2–5 provides an example of how General Motors uses a statement of company philosophy to clarify its environmental principles. Strategy in Action 2–6

STRATEGY
IN ACTION
2–3

SATURN'S STATEMENT OF PHILOSOPHY

We, the Saturn Team, in concert with the UAW and General Motors, believe that meeting the needs of customers, Saturn members, suppliers, dealers, and neighbors is fundamental to fulfilling our mission.

To meet our customers' needs . . .
· our products and services must be world leaders in value and satisfaction.

To meet our members' needs, we . . .
· will create a sense of belonging in an environment of mutual trust, respect, and dignity;
· believe that all people want to be involved in decisions that affect them, care about their jobs and each other, take pride in themselves and in their contributions, and want to share in the success of their efforts;
· will develop the tools, training, and education for each member, recognizing individual skills and knowledge;
· believe that creative, motivated, responsible team members who understand that change is critical to success are Saturn's most important asset.

To meet our suppliers' and dealers' needs, we . . .
· will strive to create real partnerships with them;
· will be open and fair in our dealings, reflecting trust, respect, and their importance to Saturn;
· want dealers and suppliers to feel ownership in Saturn's mission and philosophy as their own.

To meet the needs of our neighbors, the communities in which we live and operate, we . . .
· will be good citizens, protect the environment, and conserve natural resources;
· will seek to cooperate with government at all levels and strive to be sensitive, open, and candid in all our public statements.

Source: Excerpted from Robert R. Rehder, ''Is Saturn Competitive?'' p. 9. Reprinted from *Business Horizons*, March–April 1994. Copyright 1994 by the Foundation for the School of Business at Indiana University. Used with permission.

describes the changes in corporate philosophy that enabled a subsidiary of Johnson & Johnson to achieve an organizational turnaround.

Public Image

Both present and potential customers attribute certain qualities to particular businesses. Gerber and Johnson & Johnson make safe products; Cross Pen makes high-quality writing instruments; Étienne Aigner makes stylish but affordable leather products; Corvettes are power machines; and Izod Lacoste stands for the preppy look. Thus, mission statements should reflect the public's expectations, since this makes achievement of the firm's goals more likely. Gerber's mission statement should not open the possibility for diversification into pesticides, and Cross Pen's should not open the possibility for diversification into $0.59 brand-name disposables.

On the other hand, a negative public image often prompts firms to reemphasize the beneficial aspects of their mission. For example, in response to what it saw as a disturbing

MANAGEMENT PHILOSOPHY OF
DAYTON-HUDSON CORPORATION

The corporation will:

Set standards for return on investment (ROI) and earnings growth.

Approve strategic plans.

Allocate capital.

Approve goals.

Monitor, measure, and audit results.

Reward performance.

Allocate management resources.

The operating companies will be accorded the freedom and responsibility:

To manage their own business.

To develop strategic plans and goals that will optimize their growth.

To develop an organization that can ensure consistency of results and optimum growth.

To operate their businesses consistent with the corporation's statement of philosophy.

The corporate staff will provide only those services that are:

Essential to the protection of the corporation.

Needed for the growth of the corporation.

Wanted by operating companies and that provide a significant advantage in quality or cost.

The corporation will insist on:

Uniform accounting practices by type of business.

Prompt disclosure of operating results.

A systematic approach to training and developing people.

Adherence to appropriately high standards of business conduct and civic responsibility in accordance with the corporation's statement of philosophy.

trend in public opinion, Dow Chemical undertook an aggressive promotional campaign to fortify its credibility, particularly among "employees and those who live and work in [their] plant communities." Dow described its approach in its annual report:

All around the world today, Dow people are speaking up. People who care deeply about their company, what it stands for, and how it is viewed by others. People who are immensely proud of their company's performance, yet realistic enough to realize it is the public's perception of that performance that counts in the long run.

Firms seldom address the question of their public image in an intermittent fashion. Although public agitation often stimulates greater attention to this question, firms are concerned about their public image even in the absence of such agitation. The following excerpt from the mission statement of Intel Corporation is an example of this attitude:

We are sensitive to our *image with our customers and the business community*. Commitments to customers are considered sacred, and we are upset with ourselves when we do not meet our

GLOBAL
STRATEGY IN
ACTION 2–1

PRINCIPLES OF NISSAN MOTOR MANUFACTURING (UK) LTD.

People Principles
(All Other Objectives Can Only Be Achieved by People)

Selection	Hire the highest caliber people; look for technical capabilities and emphasize attitude.
Responsibility	Maximize the responsibility; staff by devolving decision making.
Teamwork	Recognize and encourage individual contributions, with everyone working toward the same objectives.
Flexibility	Expand the role of the individual: multiskilled, no job description, generic job titles.
Kaizen	Continuously seek 100.1 percent improvements; give "ownership of change."
Communications	"Every day, face to face."
Training	Establish individual "continuous development programs."
Supervisors	Regard as "the professionals at managing the production process"; give them much responsibility normally assumed by individual departments; make them the genuine leaders of their teams.
Single status	Treat everyone as a "first class" citizen; eliminate all illogical differences.
Trade unionism	Establish single union agreement with AEU emphasizing the common objective for a successful enterprise.

Key Corporate Principles

Quality	Building profitably the highest quality car sold in Europe.
Customers	Achieve target of no. 1 customer satisfaction in Europe.
Volume	Always achieve required volume.
New products	Deliver on time, at required quality, within cost.
Suppliers	Establish long-term relationships with single-source suppliers; aim for zero defects and just-in-time delivery; apply Nissan principles to suppliers.
Production	Use "most appropriate" technology; develop predictable "best method" of doing job; build in quality.
Engineering	Design "quality" and "ease of working" into the product and facilities; establish "simultaneous engineering" to reduce development time.

Source: Excerpted from Judith Kenner Thompson and Robert R. Rehder, "Nissan U.K.: A Worker's Paradox?" p. 51. Reprinted from *Business Horizons,* January–February 1995. Copyright 1995 by the Foundation for the School of Business at Indiana University. Used with permission.

commitments. We strive to demonstrate to the business world on a continuing basis that we are credible in describing the state of the corporation, and that we are well organized and in complete control of all things that determine the numbers.

Company Self-Concept

A major determinant of a firm's success is the extent to which the firm can relate functionally to its external environment. To achieve its proper place in a competitive situation, the firm realistically must evaluate its competitive strengths and weaknesses. This idea—that

GENERAL MOTORS ENVIRONMENTAL PRINCIPLES

As a responsible corporate citizen, General Motors is dedicated to protecting human health, natural resources, and the global environment. This dedication reaches further than compliance with the law to encompass the integration of sound environmental practices into our business decisions.

The following environmental principles provide guidance to General Motors personnel worldwide in the conduct of their daily business practices:

1. We are committed to actions to restore and preserve the environment.
2. We are committed to reducing waste and pollutants, conserving resources, and recycling materials at every stage of the product life cycle.
3. We will continue to participate actively in educating the public regarding environmental conservation.
4. We will continue to pursue vigorously the development and implementation of technologies for minimizing pollutant emissions.
5. We will continue to work with all governmental entities for the development of technically sound and financially responsible environmental laws and regulations.
6. We will continually assess the impact of our plants and products on the environment and the communities in which we live and operate with a goal of continuous improvement.

Source: 1991 General Motors Public Interest Report, p. 23.

the firm must know itself—is the essence of the company self-concept. The idea is not commonly integrated into theories of strategic management; its importance for individuals has been recognized since ancient times. As one scholar writes, "Man has struggled to understand himself, for how he thinks of himself will influence both what he chooses to do and what he expects from life. Knowing his identity connects him both with his past and with the potentiality of his future."[3]

Both individuals and firms have a crucial need to know themselves. The ability of either to survive in a dynamic and highly competitive environment would be severely limited if they did not understand their impact on others or of others on them.

In some senses, then, firms take on personalities of their own. Much behavior in firms is organizationally based; that is, a firm acts on its members in other ways than their individual interactions. Thus, firms are entities whose personality transcends the personalities of their members. As such, they can set decision-making parameters based on aims different and distinct from the aims of their members. These organizational considerations have pervasive effects.

Organizations do have policies, do and do not condone violence, and may or may not greet you with a smile. They also manufacture goods, administer policies, and protect the citizenry. These are organizational actions and involve properties of organizations, not individuals. They are carried out by individuals, even in the case of computer-produced letters, which are programmed by individuals—but the genesis of the actions remains in the organization.[4]

---

[3] J. Kelly, *Organizational Behavior* (Burr Ridge, IL: Irwin, 1974), p. 258.

[4] R. H. Hall, *Organizational Structure and Process* (Englewood Cliffs, NJ: Prentice-Hall, 1972), p. 13.

The characteristics of the corporate self-concept have been summarized as follows:

1. It is based on management's perception of the way in which others (society) will respond to the company.
2. It directs the behavior of people employed by the company.
3. It is determined in part by the responses of others to the company.
4. It is incorporated into mission statements that are communicated to individuals inside and outside the company.[5]

Ordinarily, descriptions of the company self-concept per se do not appear in mission statements. Yet such statements often provide strong impressions of the company self-concept. For example, ARCO's environment, health, and safety (EHS) managers were adamant about emphasizing the company's position on safety and environmental performance as a part of the mission statement. The challenges facing the ARCO EHS managers in the early 1990s included dealing with concerned environmental groups and a public that has become environmentally aware. They hoped to motivate employees toward safer behavior while reducing emissions and waste. They saw this as a reflection of the company's positive self-image.

The following excerpts from the Intel Corporation mission statement describe the corporate persona that its top management seeks to foster:

> Management is self-critical. The leaders must be capable of recognizing and accepting their mistakes and learning from them.
>
> Open (constructive) confrontation is encouraged at all levels of the corporation and is viewed as a method of problem solving and conflict resolution.
>
> Decision by consensus is the rule. Decisions once made are supported. Position in the organization is not the basis for quality of ideas.
>
> A highly communicative, open management is part of the style.
>
> Management must be ethical. Managing by telling the truth and treating all employees equitably has established credibility that is ethical.
>
> We strive to provide an opportunity for rapid development.
>
> Intel is a results-oriented company. The focus is on substance versus form, quality versus quantity.
>
> We believe in the principle that hard work, high productivity is something to be proud of.
>
> The concept of assumed responsibility is accepted. (If a task needs to be done, assume you have the responsibility to get it done.)
>
> Commitments are long term. If career problems occur at some point, reassignment is a better alternative than termination.
>
> We desire to have all employees involved and participative in their relationship with Intel.

Newest Trends in Mission Components

Recently, two new issues have become so prominent in the strategic planning for organizations that they are increasingly becoming integral parts in the development and revisions of mission statements: sensitivity to consumer wants and concern for quality.

Customers

"The customer is our top priority" is a slogan that would be claimed by the majority of businesses in the United States and abroad. For companies including Caterpillar Tractor, General Electric, and Johnson & Johnson, this means analyzing consumer needs before as

---

[5] E. J. Kelley, *Marketing Planning and Competitive Strategy* (Englewood Cliffs, NJ: Prentice Hall, 1972), p. 5.

ORGANIZATIONAL RENEWAL CENTERS ON
STRATEGIC COLLABORATION

When William Crouse took over as president of Ortho Diagnostic Systems, Inc. (ODSI), he knew this Johnson & Johnson subsidiary was in danger of becoming yet another victim of growth. In its effort to serve its customers and maintain market share, ODSI hit its markets with a dizzying array of products. Its customer base was deep but too wide. Its sales force devoted as much attention to small hospitals as it did to those with greater potential. All of this pointed to a lack of strategic focus, which usually translates into higher operating costs and profit margin deterioration. Clearly, the company needed to change in order to maintain its leadership position in the competitive diagnostic segment of the global healthcare marketplace.

So change it did. The strategy now is more focused, and there's a greater responsiveness to customers and less product-market clutter. Since the transformation began, turnover has been arrested, volume has more than doubled, profits have skyrocketed, and morale has improved.

The turnaround was achieved through a multistep approach to organizational transformation, which began with setting vision and strategy and included diagnosing an organization's structure, systems, culture, and capabilities for strategic fit. The process also included developing action plans and designing a tracking system for monitoring and updating.

When Crouse assumed the presidency, the first thing he did was nothing—except wander down the hallways of the organization, making stops at all levels and functions, soliciting ideas, asking questions, and listening. "I learned about the company and got to know the people by speaking with them about problems and opportunities," he recalls. "By the end of the first three months, I knew exactly what had to be done."

But Crouse felt that was not enough, so he spent another three months talking with virtually every employee. "I then reported back to them saying, 'This is what you've told me about the company, and here are my conclusions based on what you've told me. This is what I think we should do; now, what do you think?' "

Source: W. A. Schiemann, "Organizational Change: Lessons from a Turnaround," *Management Review,* April 1992, pp. 34–37.

well as after a sale. The bonus plan at Xerox allows for a 40 percent annual bonus, based on high customer reviews of the service that they receive, and a 20 percent penalty if the feedback is especially bad. For these firms and many others, the overriding concern for the company has become consumer satisfaction.

In addition many U.S. firms maintain extensive product safety programs to help assure consumer satisfaction. RCA, Sears, and 3M boast of such programs. Other firms including Calgon Corporation, Amoco, Mobil Oil, Whirlpool, and Zenith provide toll-free telephone lines to answer customer concerns and complaints.

The focus on customer satisfaction is demonstrated by retailer J. C. Penney in this excerpt from its statement of philosophy: "The Penney Idea is (1) To serve the public as nearly as we can to its complete satisfaction; (2) To expect for the service we render a fair remuneration, and not all the profit the traffic will bear; (3) To do all in our power to pack the customer's dollar full of value, quality, and satisfaction."

A focus on customer satisfaction causes managers to realize the importance of providing quality customer service. Strong customer service initiatives have led some firms to gain competitive advantages in the marketplace. Hence, many corporations have made the customer service initiative a key component of their corporate mission. Some key elements of customer service–driven organizations are listed in Figure 2–1.

Strategy then evolved from this broadly based, back-and-forth process of questioning and testing conclusions. "Strategy is not only about what you are going to do, it's also about getting people to buy in and commit to what's going to happen and having them understand their role in implementation."

The evolutionary approach paid off in terms of the quality of thinking that went into the strategy and the commitment to it down through the ranks. It worked because Crouse was personally involved, and he substituted the top-down textbook approach with a more collaboratively strategy-setting model.

At ODSI, an effort was made to channel people's anxiety over change by focusing their energies on a basic strategic mission. That mission had to meet three criteria: uniqueness (it had to set ODSI apart from competitors); altruism (it had to capture employees' spirit and get them to look beyond themselves); and simplicity (it had to be easily understood, remembered, and enacted). As the business mission states: "ODSI provides customers with fast, simple, accurate means of diagnosing patients and protects the safety of the world's blood supply."

This mission could be accomplished only if everyone remained focused. Crouse's six-month journey through the organization taught him that employees were caught in an activity trap. They were bouncing from one crisis to the next and doing too many things. There were too many customers, too many marginal products, and too many small orders. There was a sense that everyone was looking for silver bullets to solve problems, instead of striving to maintain ODSI's leadership position. To move forward, the company had to go back to the basics.

Although the mission provided a good framework, it needed greater specification. The top-management team developed a business protocol that spelled out how ODSI would conduct business; how it would manage and motivate the work force; new decision-making patterns that pushed responsibility downward; and new structures that promoted teamwork and focus. Developing a clear, specific sense of strategic direction and thinking throughout the organization was key to the ODSI turnaround.

Quality

"Quality is job one!" is a rallying point not only for Ford Motor Corporation but for many resurging U.S. businesses as well. Since the 1950s, two U.S. management experts have fostered a worldwide emphasis on quality in manufacturing. W. Edwards Deming and J. M. Juran's messages were first embraced by Japanese managers, whose quality consciousness led to global dominance in several industries including automobile, TV, audio equipment, and electronic components manufacturing. Deming summarizes his approach in 14 now well-known points:

1. Create constancy of purpose.
2. Adopt the new philosophy.
3. Cease dependence on mass inspection to achieve quality.
4. End the practice of awarding business on price tag alone. Instead, minimize total cost, often accomplished by working with a single supplier.
5. Improve constantly the system of production and service.
6. Institute training on the job.
7. Institute leadership.
8. Drive out fear.
9. Break down barriers between departments.

FIGURE 2–1
Key Elements of Customer Service–Driven Organizations

1. A mission statement or sense of mission makes customer service a priority.
2. Customer service goals are clearly defined.
3. Customer service standards are clearly defined.
4. Customer satisfaction with existing products and services is continuously measured.
5. Ongoing efforts are made to understand customers to determine where the organization should be headed.
6. Corrective action procedures are in place to remove barriers to servicing customers in a timely and effective fashion.
7. Customer service goals have an impact on organizational action.

Source: An excerpt from "Peters, 1987," p. 78. Reprinted from *Business Horizons,* July–August 1995. Copyright 1995 by the Foundation for the School of Business at Indiana University. Used with permission.

10. Eliminate slogans, exhortations, and numerical targets.
11. Eliminate work standards (quotas) and management by objective.
12. Remove barriers that rob workers, engineers, and managers of their right to pride of workmanship.
13. Institute a vigorous program of education and self-improvement.
14. Put everyone in the company to work to accomplish the transformation.

Beginning in the late 1980s, firms in the United States responded aggressively. The new philosophy is that quality should be the norm. For example, Motorola's 1993 production goal was 60 or fewer defects per every billion components that it manufactures. Managers who emphasize quality have even created their own jargon, as reviewed in Figure 2–2.

Strategy in Action 2–7 presents the integration of the quality initiative into the mission statements of three corporations. The emphasis on quality has received added emphasis in many corporate philosophies since the Congress created the Malcolm Baldrige Quality Award in 1987. Each year up to two Baldrige Awards can been given in three categories of a company's operations: manufacturing, services, and small businesses.

OVERSEEING THE STRATEGY MAKERS

Who is responsible for determining the firm's mission? Who is responsible for acquiring and allocating resources so the firm can thoughtfully develop and implement a strategic plan? Who is responsible for monitoring the firm's success in the competitive marketplace to determine whether that plan was well designed and activated? The answer to all of these questions is "strategic decision makers." As you saw in Figure 1–3, most organizations have multiple levels of strategic decision makers; typically, the larger the firm, the more levels it will have. The strategic managers at the highest level are responsible for decisions that affect the entire firm, commit the firm and its resources for the longest periods, and declare the firm's sense of values. In other words, this group of strategic managers is responsible for overseeing the creation and accomplishment of the company mission. The term that describes the group is *board of directors.*

In overseeing the management of a firm, the board of directors operates as the representatives of the firm's stockholders. Elected by the stockholders, the board has these major responsibilities:

FIGURE 2–2
A Glossary of Quality-Speak

Acceptable Quality Level (AQL)

Minimum number of parts that must comply with quality standards, usually stated as a percentage.

Competitive Benchmarking

Rating a company's practices, processes, and products against the world's best, including those in other industries.

Continuous-Improvement Process (CIP)

Searching unceasingly for ever-higher levels of quality by isolating sources of defects. The goal: zero defects. The Japanese call it Kaizen.

Control Charts

Statistical plots derived from measuring factory processes, they help detect "process drift," or deviation, before it generates defects. Charts also help spot inherent variations in manufacturing processes that designers must account for to achieve "robust design" (below).

Just-in-Time (JIT)

When suppliers deliver materials and parts at the moment a factory needs them, thus eliminating costly inventories. Quality is paramount: A faulty part delivered at the last minute won't be detected.

Pareto Chart

A bar graph that ranks causes of process variation by the degree of impact on quality.

Poka-Yoke

Making the workplace mistake-proof. A machine fitted with guide rails permits a part to be worked on in just one way.

Quality Function Deployment (QFD)

A system that pays special attention to customer wants. Activities that don't contribute are considered wasteful.

Robust Design

A discipline for making designs "production-proof" by building in tolerances for manufacturing variables that are known to be unavoidable.

Six-Sigma Quality

A statistical measure expressing how close a product comes to its quality goal. One-sigma means 68% of products are acceptable; three-sigma means 99.7%. Six-sigma is 99.999997% perfect: 3.4 defects per million parts.

Statistical Process Control (SPC)

A method of analyzing deviations in production processes during manufacturing.

Statistical Quality Control (SQC)

A method of analyzing measured deviations in manufactured materials, parts, and products.

Taguchi Methods

Statistical techniques developed by Genichi Taguchi, a Japanese consultant, for optimizing design and production. These are used often on "robust design" projects.

Total Quality Control (TQC)

The application of quality principles to all company endeavors, including satisfying internal "customers." Manufacturing engineers, for instance, are customers of the design staff. Also known as total quality management (TQM).

Source: Reprinted from October 25, 1991, issue of *Business Week,* by special permission, copyright © 1991 by McGraw-Hill, Inc.

1. To establish and update the company mission.
2. To elect the company's top officers, the foremost of whom is the CEO.
3. To establish the compensation levels of the top officers, including their salaries and bonuses.
4. To determine the amount and timing of the dividends paid to stockholders.

STRATEGY
IN ACTION
2–7

VISIONS OF QUALITY

CADILLAC

The Mission of the Cadillac Motor Company is to engineer, produce, and market the world's finest automobiles known for uncompromised levels of distinctiveness, comfort, convenience, and refined performance. Through its people, who are its strength, Cadillac will continuously improve the quality of its products and services to meet or exceed customer expectations and succeed as a profitable business.

MOTOROLA

Dedication to quality is a way of life at our company, so much so that it goes far beyond rhetorical slogans. Our ongoing program of continued improvement reaches out for change, refinement, and even revolution in our pursuit of quality excellence.

It is the objective of Motorola, Inc., to produce and provide products and services of the highest quality. In its activities, Motorola will pursue goals aimed at the achievement of quality excellence. These results will be derived from the dedicated efforts of each employee in conjunction with supportive participation from management at all levels of the corporation.

ZYTEC

Zytec is a company that competes on value; is market driven; provides superior quality and service; builds strong relationships with its customers; and provides technical excellence in its products.

Source: Excerpted from Richard M. Hodgets, "Quality Lessons from America's Baldrige Winners," p. 75. Reprinted from *Business Horizons,* July–August 1995. Copyright 1995 by the Foundation for the School of Business at Indiana University. Used with permission.

5. To set broad company policy on such matters as labor-management relations, product or service lines of business, and employee benefit packages.
6. To set company objectives and to authorize managers to implement the long-term strategies that the top officers and the board have found agreeable.
7. To mandate company compliance with legal and ethical dictates.

This chapter considers the board of directors because the board's greatest impact on the behavior of a firm results from its determination of the company mission. The philosophy espoused in the mission statement sets the tone by which the firm and all of its employees will be judged. As logical extensions of the mission statement, the firm's objectives and strategies embody the board's view of proper business demeanor. Through its appointment of top executives and its decisions about their compensation, the board reveals its priorities for organizational achievement.

Board Success Factors

A review of writings and research on the behavior of boards discloses that they are judged to be most successful when:[6]

---

[6] S. A. Zahra and J. A. Pearce II, "Boards of Directors and Corporate Financial Performance: A Review and Integrative Model," *Journal of Management* 15 (1989), pp. 291–334.

1. They represent the interests of stockholders and carefully monitor the actions of senior executives to promote and protect those interests.[7]

2. They link the firm to influential stakeholders in its external environment, thereby promoting the company mission while ensuring attention to important societal concerns.[8]

3. They are composed of 8 to 12 highly qualified members.

4. They exercise independent and objective thinking in appraising the actions of senior executives and in introducing strategic changes.[9]

5. They pay special attention to their own composition to ensure an appropriate mix of inside and outside directors and the inclusion of minority representatives.[10]

6. They have a well-developed structure; that is, they are organized into appropriate committees to perform specialized tasks (e.g., to review executive compensation and to audit the company's financial transactions).[11]

7. They meet frequently to discuss progress in achieving organizational goals and to provide counsel to executives.[12]

8. They evaluate the CEO's performance at least annually to provide guidance on issues of leadership style.[13]

9. They conduct strategy reviews to determine the fit between the firm's strategy and the requirements of its competitive environment.[14]

10. They formulate the ethical codes that are to govern the behavior of the firm's executives and employees.[15]

11. They promote a future-oriented outlook on the company mission by challenging executives to articulate their visions for the firm and for its interface with society.

These criteria can enable board members, CEOs, and stockholders to judge board behavior. The question "What should boards do?" can be answered largely by studying the criteria.

THE STAKEHOLDER APPROACH TO COMPANY RESPONSIBILITY

In defining or redefining the company mission, strategic managers must recognize the legitimate rights of the firm's claimant. These include not only stockholders and employees but also outsiders affected by the firm's actions. Such outsiders commonly include customers,

---

[7] P. L. Rechner and D. R. Dalton, "The Impact of CEO as Board Chairperson on Corporate Performance: Evidence vs. Rhetoric," *Academy of Management Executive* 3, no. 2 (1989), pp. 141–43.

[8] M. S. Mizruchi, "Who Controls Whom?: An Examination of the Relation between Management and Board of Directors in Large American Corporations," *Academy of Management Review,* August 1983, pp. 426–35.

[9] T. M. Jones and L. D. Goldberg, "Governing the Large Corporation: More Arguments for Public Directors," *Academy of Management Review* 7 (1982), pp. 603–11.

[10] I. F. Kesner, "Directors' Characteristics and Committee Membership: An Investigation of Type, Occupation, Tenure, and Gender," *Academy of Management Journal* 31 (1988), pp. 66–84; and J. A. Pearce II, "The Relationship of Internal versus External Orientations to Financial Measures of Strategic Performance," *Strategic Management Journal* 4 (1983), pp. 297–306.

[11] R. Molz, "Managerial Domination of Boards of Directors and Financial Performance," *Journal of Business Research* 16 (1988), pp. 235–50.

[12] A. Tashakori and W. Boulton, "A Look at the Board's Role Planning," *Journal of Business Strategy* 3, no. 3 (1985), pp. 64–70.

[13] R. Nader, "Reforming Corporate Governance," *California Management Review,* Winter 1984, pp. 126–32.

[14] J. R. Harrison, "The Strategic Use of Corporate Board Committees," *California Management Review* 30 (1987), pp. 109–25; and J. W. Henke, Jr., "Involving the Board of Directors in Strategic Planning," *Journal of Business Strategy* 7, no. 2 (1986), pp. 87–95.

[15] K. R. Andrews, *The Concept of Corporate Strategy* (Burr Ridge, IL: Irwin, 1987).

suppliers, governments, unions, competitors, local communities, and the general public. Each of these interest groups has justifiable reasons for expecting (and often for demanding) that the firm satisfy their claims in a responsible manner. In general, stockholders claim appropriate returns on their investment; employees seek broadly defined job satisfactions; customers want what they pay for; suppliers seek dependable buyers; governments want adherence to legislation; unions seek benefits for their members; competitors want fair competition; local communities want the firm to be a responsible citizen; and the general public expects the firm's existence to improve the quality of life.

According to a recent survey of 2,361 directors in 291 of the largest southeastern U.S. companies:

1. Directors perceived the existence of distinct stakeholder groups.
2. Directors have high stakeholder orientations.
3. Directors view some stakeholders differently, depending on their occupation (CEO directors versus non-CEO directors) and type (inside versus outside directors).

The study also found that the perceived stakeholders were, in the order of their importance, customers and government, stockholders, employees, and society. The results clearly indicated that boards of directors no longer believe that the stockholder is the only constituency to whom they are responsible.

However, when a firm attempts to incorporate the interests of these groups into its mission statement, broad generalizations are insufficient. These steps need to be taken:

1. Identification of the stakeholders.
2. Understanding the stakeholders' specific claims vis-à-vis the firm.
3. Reconciliation of these claims and assignment of priorities to them.
4. Coordination of the claims with other elements of the company mission.

Identification The left-hand column of Figure 2–3 lists the commonly encountered stakeholder groups, to which the executive officer group often is added. Obviously, though, every business faces a slightly different set of stakeholder groups, which vary in number, size, influence, and importance. In defining the company, strategic managers must identify all of the stakeholder groups and weigh their relative rights and their relative ability to affect the firm's success.

Understanding The concerns of the principal stakeholder groups tend to center on the general claims listed in the right-hand column of Figure 2–3. However, strategic decision makers should understand the specific demands of each group. They then will be better able to initiate actions that satisfy these demands.

Reconciliation and Priorities Unfortunately, the claims of various stakeholder groups often conflict. For example, the claims of governments and the general public tend to limit profitability, which is the central claim of most creditors and stockholders. Thus, claims must be reconciled in a mission statement that resolves the competing, conflicting, and contradicting claims of stakeholders. For objectives and strategies to be internally consistent and precisely focused, the statement must display a single-minded, though multidimensional, approach to the firm's aims.

There are hundreds, if not thousands, of claims on any firm–high wages, pure air, job security, product quality, community service, taxes, occupational health and safety regulations, equal employment opportunity regulations, product variety, wide markets, career

FIGURE 2–3
A Stakeholder View of Company Responsibility

Stakeholder	Nature of the Claim
Stockholders	Participation in distribution of profits, additional stock offerings, assets on liquidation; vote of stock; inspection of company books; transfer of stock; election of board of directors; and such additional rights as have been established in the contract with the corporation.
Creditors	Legal proportion of interest payments due and return of principal from the investment. Security of pledged assets; relative priority in event of liquidation. Management and owner prerogatives if certain conditions exist with the company (such as default of interest payments).
Employees	Economic, social, and psychological satisfaction in the place of employment. Freedom from arbitrary and capricious behavior on the part of company officials. Share in fringe benefits, freedom to join union and participate in collective bargaining, individual freedom in offering up their services through an employment contract. Adequate working conditions.
Customers	Service provided with the product; technical data to use the product; suitable warranties; spare parts to support the product during use; R&D leading to product improvement; facilitation of credit.
Suppliers	Continuing source of business; timely consummation of trade credit obligations; professional relationship in contracting for, purchasing, and receiving goods and services.
Governments	Taxes (income, property, and so on); adherence to the letter and intent of public policy dealing with the requirements of fair and free competition; discharge of legal obligations of businesspeople (and business organizations); adherence to antitrust laws.
Unions	Recognition as the negotiating agent for employees. Opportunity to perpetuate the union as a participant in the business organization.
Competitors	Observation of the norms for competitive conduct established by society and the industry. Business statesmanship on the part of peers.
Local communities	Place of productive and healthful employment in the community. Participation of company officials in community affairs, provision of regular employment, fair play, reasonable portion of purchases made in the local community, interest in and support of local government, support of cultural and charitable projects.
The general public	Participation in and contribution to society as a whole; creative communications between governmental and business units designed for reciprocal understanding; assumption of fair proportion of the burden of government and society. Fair price for products and advancement of the state-of-the-art technology that the product line involves.

Source : William R. King and David I. Cleland, *Strategic Planning and Policy.* ©1978 by Litton Educational Publishing, Inc., p. 153. Reprinted by permission of Van Nostrand Reinhold Company.

opportunities, company growth, investment security, high ROI, and many, many more. Although most, perhaps all, of these claims may be desirable ends, they cannot be pursued with equal emphasis. They must be assigned priorities in accordance with the relative emphasis that the firm will give them. That emphasis is reflected in the criteria that the firm uses in its strategic decision making; in the firm's allocation of its human, financial, and physical resources; and in the firm's long-term objectives and strategies.

Coordination with Other Elements   The demands of stakeholder groups constitute only one principal set of inputs to the company mission. The other principal sets are the managerial operating philosophy and the determinants of the product-market offering. Those determinants constitute a reality test that the accepted claims must pass. The key question is: How can the firm satisfy its claimants and at the same time optimize its economic success in the marketplace?

Social Responsibility

As indicated in Figure 2–4, the various stakeholders of a firm can be divided into inside stakeholders and outside stakeholders. The insiders are the individuals or groups that are stockholders or employees of the firm. The outsiders are all the other individuals or groups

FIGURE 2–4
Inputs to the Development of the Company Mission

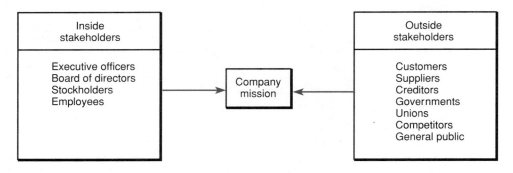

that the firm's actions affect. The extremely large and often amorphous set of outsiders makes the general claim that the firm be socially responsible.[16]

Perhaps the thorniest issues faced in defining a company mission are those that pertain to responsibility. The stakeholder approach offers the clearest perspective on such issues. Broadly stated, outsiders often demand that insiders' claims be subordinated to the greater good of the society; that is, to the greater good of outsiders. They believe that such issues as pollution, the disposal of solid and liquid wastes, and the conservation of natural resources should be principal considerations in strategic decision making. Also broadly stated, insiders tend to believe that the competing claims of outsiders should be balanced against one another in a way that protects the company mission. For example, they tend to believe that the need of consumers for a product should be balanced against the water pollution resulting from its production if the firm cannot eliminate that pollution entirely and still remain profitable. Some insiders also argue that the claims of society, as expressed in government regulation, provide tax money that can be used to eliminate water pollution and the like if the general public wants this to be done.

The issues are numerous, complex, and contingent on specific situations. Thus, rigid rules of business conduct cannot deal with them. Each firm *regardless of size* must decide how to meet its perceived social responsibility. While large, well-capitalized companies may have easy access to environmental consultants, this is not an affordable strategy for smaller companies. However, the experience of many small businesses demonstrates that it is feasible to accomplish significant pollution prevention and waste reduction without big expenditures and without hiring consultants. Once a problem area has been identified, a company's line employees frequently can develop a solution. Other important pollution prevention strategies include changing the materials used or redesigning how operations are bid out. Making pollution prevention a social responsibility can be beneficial to smaller companies. Publicly traded firms also can benefit directly from socially responsible strategies, as indicated in Global Strategy in Action 2–2.

Different approaches adopted by different firms reflect differences in competitive position, industry, country, environmental and ecological pressures, and a host of other factors. In other words, they will reflect both situational factors and differing priorities in the acknowledgment of claims. Obviously, winning the loyalty of the growing legions of

[16] J. S. Bracker and A. J. Kinicki, "Strategic Management, Plant Closings and Social Responsibility: An Integrative Process Model," *Employee Responsibilities and Rights Journal* 1, no. 3 (1988), pp. 201–13.

GLOBAL
STRATEGY IN
ACTION 2–2

SOCIAL INDEX LISTS RESPONSIBLE FIRMS

At one time, socially conscious investing was as simple as Just Say No—no investing in companies that produce alcohol, tobacco, or weapons, or are involved in gambling, nuclear energy, or South Africa.

But social investing has matured since arriving in the early 1970s, and it's no longer a cut-and-dried process. "In the past, it has primarily been a boycott movement with social change as a goal," says Amy Domini. "Newer criteria are more about corporate responsibility, and they're more difficult to apply."

Domini, with her husband, Peter Kinder, created the Domini Social Index of 400 socially responsible companies in May 1990. Their Cambridge, Massachusetts, firm screens more than 800 companies for product quality and consumer relations, environmental performance, corporate citizenship, and employee relations.

Companies on the Domini Social Index are not 1960s holdouts making tie-dye T-shirts or macramé plant hangers. The list includes Wal-Mart, Merck, Coca-Cola, PepsiCo, McDonald's, the Federal National Mortgage, and Sears.

The index should perform on a par with the Standard & Poor's 500 index over the long term, says Domini. But it can be more volatile short term, because it has more small companies than the S&P 500.

Source: Excerpted from Chris Wloszczyna, "Social Index Lists Responsible Firms," *USA Today*, March 30, 1992, Section 3B. Copyright 1992, USA TODAY. Reprinted with permission.

consumers will require new marketing strategies and new alliances in the year 2000. Many marketers already have discovered these new marketing facts of life by adopting strategies that can be called the "4 e's": (1) make it easy for the consumer to be green, (2) empower consumers with solutions, (3) enlist the support of the consumer, and (4) establish credibility with all publics and help to avoid a backlash.

Despite differences in their approaches, most American firms now try to assure outsiders that they attempt to conduct business in a socially responsible manner. Many firms, including Abt Associates, Dow Chemical, Eastern Gas and Fuel Associates, Exxon, and the Bank of America, conduct and publish annual social audits. The Equal Employment Opportunity element of an Exxon social audit and the philanthropy element of an audit published in General Motors Public Interest Report are shown in Strategy in Action 2–8 and Strategy in Action 2–9. Such audits attempt to evaluate a firm from the perspective of social responsibility. Private consultants often conduct them for the firm and offer minimally biased evaluations on what are inherently highly subjective issues.

Guidelines for a Socially Responsible Firm

After decades of public debate on the social responsibility of business, the individual firm must still struggle to determine its own orientation. However, public debate and business concern have led to a jelling of perspectives. Sawyer has provided an excellent summary of guidelines for a socially responsible firm that is consistent with the stakeholder approach:

1. The purpose of the business is to make a profit; its managers should strive for the optimal profit that can be achieved over the long run.

STRATEGY
IN ACTION
2–8

EQUAL EMPLOYMENT OPPORTUNITY/ CONTRIBUTION AT EXXON

STEADY PROGRESS FOR WOMEN AND MINORITIES

The percentage of women in Exxon's U.S. work force grew from 25.3 to 25.9 percent, while minority groups increased from 22.5 to 22.9 percent.

At year-end, minorities held 11.4 percent of managerial assignments, compared with 10.3 percent, while minority groups increased from 11.5 to 11.7 percent.

Women employees held 10 percent of managerial posts, compared with 8.9 percent last year, while the women's share of professional jobs rose from 18.9 to 19.5 percent.

The focus on recruitment of minorities and women was expanded through summer jobs, co-op assignments, and scholarships.

EXXON GRANTED $49 MILLION TO NONPROFIT ORGANIZATIONS, INCLUDING $35 MILLION IN THE UNITED STATES

Educational institutions and programs accounted for 59 percent of total U.S. grants. To encourage support for higher education for minority students, the Exxon Education Foundation amended its matching gift program. Employees and annuitants may now make gifts to three organizations with which the donors or their families may have had no prior affiliation. Those educational fits will be matched three-to-one by the Foundation. The three organizations are the United Negro College Fund, the American Indian College Fund, and the Hispanic Association of Colleges and Universities.

A solid grounding in mathematics is a critical asset in many careers in industry. The Exxon Education Foundation began a program in 1988 with these main goals: To foster use of college-level math teaching resources and to address major national math education policy issues.

In its elementary school program, the Foundation's initial 1988 K–3 (kindergarten through third grade) math specialist Planning Grants went to some 50 school districts across America, representing a cross-section of rural, suburban, and inner-city schools. Grantees are now seeking more effective approaches for improving math teaching and learning in these early, formative years.

Of the 24 percent of Exxon's U.S. contributions that were directed to health, welfare, and community service programs, a number addressed problems common to the nation's inner cities. A $50,000 grant was made to the Institute on Black Chemical Abuse in St. Paul, Minnesota, to help develop a national technical assistance, training, and information center.

A $200,000 grant was made to the Environmental and Occupational Health Sciences Institute, a joint program of Rutgers University and the University of Medicine and Dentistry of New Jersey. This grant will contribute to a better understanding of how the environment affects human health.

Source: Exxon 1988 annual report to stockholders.

2. No true profits can be claimed until business costs are paid. This includes all social costs, as determined by detailed analysis of the social balance between the firm and society.

3. If there are social costs in areas where no objective standards for correction yet exist, managers should generate corrective standards. These standards should be based on the managers' judgment of what ought to exist and should simultaneously encourage individual involvement of firm members in developing necessary social standards.

4. Where competitive pressure or economic necessity precludes socially responsible action, the business should recognize that its operation is depleting social capital and, therefore, represents a loss. It should attempt to restore profitable operation through either better management, if the problem is internal, or by advocating corrective legislation, if

STRATEGY
IN ACTION
2–9

PHILANTHROPIC ACTIVITIES

General Motors is committed to being a socially aware and responsible corporate citizen. It believes that it has an obligation to make reasonable and appropriate contributions to charitable and community organizations and educational institutions.

The Corporation has consistently ranked among the top companies in the United States in terms of dollars contributed. While GM seeks to contribute to worthy local activities in the cities and states in which GM facilities are located, it also works to benefit the nation as a whole.

An important tool in managing GM's contributions is the General Motors Foundation, established in 1976 and funded by the Corporation. As a means to offset fluctuations in charitable and educational contributions which result from economic downturns—times when nonprofit organizations most need support—the Foundation helps GM maintain a consistent response to the needs and challenges of these organizations.

In 1990, combined educational and other charitable contributions from the General Motors Corporation and the General Motors Foundation totaled over $65 million.

With a variety of philanthropic activities being supported at both the plant and corporate levels, it is not possible to list all of them.

Source: 1991 General Motors Public Interest Report, p. 55.

society is suffering as a result of the way that the rules for business competition have been made.[17]

Corporate philanthropy dates back to the 17th century when it was common for prominent business leaders to make significant donations. However, these contributions were made solely from wealthy individuals without ties to specific corporations. In the past, legal restrictions made it difficult for firms to become involved in social and philanthropic affairs. However, a Supreme Court ruling in the 1950s put an end to regulations and as a result, corporations began creating their own internal organizations. It became common for larger corporations to give up to 5 percent of their pretax income to charities as a means of improving public image.

Today, as philanthropic strategies become more and more of a key success factor, companies are assuming larger roles on social issues. Strategy in Action 2–10 outlines some of the more prominent national movements in corporate America.

SUMMARY

Defining the company mission is one of the most often slighted tasks in strategic management. Emphasizing the operational aspects of long-range management activities comes much more easily for most executives. But the critical role of the mission statement repeatedly is demonstrated by failing firms whose short-run actions have been at odds with their long-run purposes.

The principal value of the mission statement is its specification of the firm's ultimate aims. A firm gains a heightened sense of purpose when its board of directors and its top

[17] G. E. Sawyer, *Business and Society: Managing Corporate Social Impact* (Boston: Houghton Mifflin, 1979), p. 401.

HOW CORPORATE PHILANTHROPY PROMOTES CAUSES

N ow that U.S. companies are adopting strategic philanthropy, they are assuming an activist
stance on social issues. As a result, many fringe causes, including the following, have become
national movements.

HUNGER

Before the new approach to corporate philanthropy, the foundations of food companies gave cash
donations to antihunger organizations. But when the ranks of the hungry increased tenfold in the
1980s, contributions managers in companies such as General Mills, Grand Metropolitan, Kraft
General Foods, and Sara Lee decided to play a larger role *and* establish a rallying point around which
disparate units of their companies could come together. Marketers arranged for a portion of product
sales to be donated to antihunger programs, human resources staffs deployed volunteers, operating
units provided free food, and CEOs joined the board of Chicago-based Second Harvest, the food
industry's antihunger voice. As a result of those efforts, a complex infrastructure of food banks and
soup kitchens was developed.

Now the trend is toward deeper political involvement. In 1993, Kraft General Foods became the
first company to use its political capital to press for more funding for food stamps and other federal
initiatives.

COMMUNITY AND ECONOMIC DEVELOPMENT

In the late 1980s, major banks such as Bank of America, Chase Manhattan, Citicorp, Morgan
Guaranty, and Wells Fargo explored how philanthropy could be tied to marketing, human resources,
government affairs, investment, and even trust management. Those banks had given mostly to the
arts, but their business managers were concerned about the Community Reinvestment Act, which
requires lenders to be responsive to low-income communities. Philanthropy managers used the act to
gain internal support for positioning their companies as leaders in the antipoverty struggle. They
pointed out that by going beyond the CRA requirements, they could develop positive relationships
with regulators while scoring public relations points.

At least 60 banks in the United States have created community development corporations to assist
run-down neighborhoods. An executive at Wells Fargo organized a national network of bankers who
make low-interest loans to nonprofits working to bring enterprise to inner cities. About 20 percent of
those banks' donations now go to those developers.

LITERACY

The effort to increase literacy in the United States is the favorite cause of the communications
industry. Print media companies such as McGraw-Hill, Prentice Hall, the *Los Angeles Times,* the

Source: Reprinted by permission of *Harvard Business Review.* An excerpt from "The New Corporate Philanthropy," by
Jay W. Lorsch, May–June 1994. Copyright © 1994 by the President and Fellows of Harvard University, all rights reserved.

executives address these issues: "What business are we in?" "What customers do we
serve?" "Why does this organization exist?" However, the potential contribution of the
company mission can be undermined if platitudes or ambiguous generalizations are accepted in response to these questions. It is not enough to say that Lever Brothers is in the
business of "making anything that cleans anything" or that Polaroid is committed to

continued

Washington Post, and the *New York Times* are trying to halt the drop in readership, and broadcasters and cable companies are compensating for their role in the decline of literacy. Those companies have mobilized their marketing, human resources, and lobbying power to establish workplace literacy programs. While human resources budgets fund such programs, philanthropy dollars go mostly to volunteer organizations.

SCHOOL REFORM

Under the old corporate philanthropy paradigm, elementary and secondary education received no more than 5 percent of the typical corporate philanthropy budget, and most of the institutions that received aid were private. Now about 15 percent of the country's cash gifts go to school reform, and a recent study estimated that at least one-third of U.S. school districts have partnership programs with business.

Even so, as a recent Conference Board report argues, those programs have not halted the decline of the public school system. The next step toward reform, promoted by the Business Roundtable, is for companies to mobilize their lobbying power at the state level to press for the overhaul of state educational agencies.

AIDS

AIDS is a top cause for insurance companies, who want to reduce claims; pharmaceutical companies, who want public support for the commercialization of AIDS drugs; and design-related companies, who want to support the large number of gays in their work force. Those industries put the first big money into AIDS prevention measures, and they've helped turn the American Foundation for AIDS Research into an advocate for more and better research by the National Institutes of Health.

ENVIRONMENTALISM

Until recently, corporate America feared environmentalism. But the new corporate philanthropy professionals consult their companies' environmental officers to find ways to link donations and volunteer programs to internal efforts at environmental stewardship. Environmental support varies across industries. In high-tech companies, environmentalism is largely a human resources issue because it's the favorite cause of many employees. Contribution managers in such companies typically conduct activities that elicit employee support for conservation. Among the makers of outdoor apparel, environmentalism is largely a marketing issue, so companies donate a portion of the purchase price to environmental nonprofits. In industries that pollute or extract natural resources, environmentalism is often a government affairs matter. Companies in those industries forge alliances with nonprofit adversaries in the hope of circumventing regulations.

businesses that deal with "the interaction of light and matter." Only if a firm clearly articulates its long-term intentions can its goals serve as a basis for shared expectations, planning, and performance evaluation.

A mission statement that is developed from this perspective provides managers with a unity of direction transcending individual, parochial, and temporary needs. It promotes a sense of shared expectations among all levels and generations of employees. It consolidates values over time and across individuals and interest groups. It projects a sense of worth and intent that can be identified and assimilated by outside stakeholders; that is, customers, suppliers, competitors, local committees, and the general public. Finally, it asserts the firm's commitment to responsible action in symbiosis with the preservation and protection of the essential claims of insider stakeholders' survival, growth, and profitability.

QUESTIONS FOR DISCUSSION

1. Reread Nicor, Inc.'s mission statement in Strategy in Action 2–1. List five insights into Nicor that you feel you gained from knowing its mission.

2. Locate the mission statement of a company not mentioned in the chapter. Where did you find it? Was it presented as a consolidated statement, or were you forced to assemble it yourself from various publications of the firm? How many of the mission statement elements outlined in this chapter were discussed or revealed in the statement you found?

3. Prepare a two-page typewritten mission statement for your school of business or for a firm selected by your instructor.

4. List five potentially vulnerable areas of a firm without a stated company mission.

5. The partial social audits shown in Strategy in Action 2–8 and 2–9 included only a few of the possible indicators of a firm's social responsibility performance. Name five other potentially valuable indicators and describe how company performance in each could be measured.

6. Define the term *social responsibility.* Find an example of a company action that was legal but not socially responsible. Defend your example on the basis of your definition.

BIBLIOGRAPHY

Board of Directors

Bartlett, Christopher A., and Sumantha Ghoshal. "Changing the Role of Top Management: Beyond Systems to People." *Harvard Business Review* 73, no. 3 (May–June 1995), p. 132.

Donaldson, Gordon. "The New Task for Boards: The Strategic Audit." *Harvard Business Review* 73, no. 4 (July–August 1995), p. 99.

Hambrick, Donald C. "Fragmentation and the Other Problems CEOs Have with Their Top Management Teams." *California Management Review* 37, no. 3 (Spring 1995), p. 110.

Harrison, J. R. "The Strategic Use of Corporate Board Committees." *California Management Review* 30 (1987), pp. 109–25.

Henke, J. W., Jr. "Involving the Board of Directors in Strategic Planning." *Journal of Business Strategy* 7, no. 2 (1986), pp. 87–95.

Hout, Thomas M., and John C. Carter. "Getting It Done: New Roles for Senior Executives." *Harvard Business Review* 73, no. 6 (November–December 1995), p. 133.

Kerr, J., and R. A. Bettis. "Boards of Directors, Top Management Compensation, and Shareholder Returns." *Academy of Management Journal* 30 (1987), pp. 645–64.

Kesner, I. F. "Directors' Characteristics and Committee Membership: An Investigation of Type, Occupation Tenure, and Gender." *Academy of Management Journal* 31 (1988), pp. 66–84.

Lorsch, Jay W. "Empowering the Board." *Harvard Business Review* 73, no. 1 (January–February 1995), p. 107.

Molz, R. "Managerial Domination of Boards of Directors and Financial Performance." *Journal of Business Research* 16 (1988), pp. 235–50.

Park, Jae C. "Reengineering Boards of Directors." *Business Horizons* 38, no. 2 (March–April 1995), p. 63.

Pearce, J. A., II. "The Relationship of Internal versus External Orientations to Financial Measures of Strategic Performance." *Strategic Management Journal* 4 (1983), pp. 297–306.

Pound, John. "The Promise of the Governed Corporation." *Harvard Business Review* 73, no. 2 (March–April 1995), p. 89

Rosenstein, J. "Why Don't U.S. Boards Get More Involved in Strategy?" *Long Range Planning* (June 1987), pp. 20–34.

Savage, G. T.; T. W. Nix; C. J. Whitehead; and J. D. Blair. "Strategies for Assessing and Managing Organizational Stakeholders." *Academy of Management Executive* (May 1991), pp. 61–75.

Smale, John G.; Alan J. Patricot; Denys Henderson; Bernard Marcus; and David N. Johnson. "Redraw the Line Between the Board and the CEO." *Harvard Business Review* 73, no. 2 (March–April 1995), p. 153.

Tichy, Noel M., and Ram Charan. "The CEO as Coach: An Interview with Allied Signal's Lawrence A. Bussidy." *Harvard Business Review* 73, no. 2 (March–April 1995), p. 68.

Zahra, S. A., and J. A. Pearce II. "Boards of Directors and Corporate Financial Performance: A Review and Integrative Model." *Journal of Management* 15 (1989), pp. 291–334.

Mission Statements

Bertodo, R. "Implementing a Strategic Vision." *Long Range Planning* (October 1990), pp. 22–30.

Campbell, A.; M. Gorld; and M. Alexander. "Corporate Strategy—The Quest for Parenting Advantage." *Harvard Business Review* 73, no. 2 (March–April 1995), p. 120.

Ireland, R. D., and M. A. Hitt. "Mission Statements; Importance, Challenge, and Recommendation for Development." *Business Horizons* (May–June 1992), pp. 34–42.

Klemm, M.; S. Sanderson; and G. Luffman. "Mission Statements: Selling Corporate Values to Employees." *Long Range Planning* (June 1991), pp. 73–78.

Osborne, R. L. "Core Value Statements: The Corporate Compass." *Business Horizons* (September–October 1991), pp. 28–34.

Pearce, J. A. II. "The Company Mission as a Strategic Tool." *Sloan Management Review* (Spring 1982), pp. 15–24.

Pearce, J. A. II, and F. R. David. "Corporate Mission Statements: The Bottom Line." *Academy of Management Executive* (May 1987), pp. 109–16.

Pearce, J. A. II; R. B. Robinson, Jr.; and Kendall Roth. "The Company Mission as a Guide to Strategic Action." In *Strategic Planning and Management Handbook,* ed. William R. King and David I. Cleland. New York: Van Nostrand Reinhold, 1987.

Rogers, J. E., Jr. "Adopting and Implementing a Corporate Environmental Charter." *Business Horizons* (March–April 1992), pp. 29–33.

Rothstein, Lawrence R. "The Empowerment Effort that Came Undone." *Harvard Business Review* 73, no. 1 (January–February 1995), p. 20.

Schmitt, Bernd H.; Alex Simonson; and Joshua Marcus. "Managing Corporate Image and Identity." *Long Range Planning* 28, no. 5 (October 1995), p. 82.

Tregoe, B. B.; J. W. Zimmerman; R. A. Smith; and P. M. Tobia. "The Driving Force." *Planning Review* (March–April 1990), pp. 4–17.

Social Responsibility and Business Ethics

Aupperle, K.; A. Carroll; and J. Hatfield. "An Empirical Examination of the Relationship between Corporate Social Responsibility and Profitability." *Academy of Management Journal* 28 (1985), pp. 446–63.

Badaracco, J. L., Jr. "Business Ethics: Four Spheres of Executive Responsibility." *California Management Review* (Spring 1992), pp. 64–79.

Bavaria, S. "Corporate Ethics Should Start in the Boardroom." *Business Horizons* (January–February 1991), pp. 9–12.

Bowie, N. "New Directions in Corporate Social Responsibility." *Business Horizons* (July–August 1991), pp. 56–65.

Cadbury, A. "Ethical Managers Make Their Own Rules." *Harvard Business Review* (September–October 1987), pp. 69–73.

Carroll, A. B. "The Pyramid of Corporate Social Responsibility: Toward the Moral Management of Organizational Stakeholders." *Business Horizons* (July–August 1991), pp. 39–48.

Dalton, D. R., and C. M. Daily. "The Constituents of Corporate Responsibility: Separate, But Not Separable, Interests?" *Business Horizons* (July–August 1991), pp. 74–78.

Day, G. S., and L. Fahey. "Putting Strategy into Shareholder Value Analysis." *Harvard Business Review* (March–April 1990), pp. 156–62.

Freeman, R. E., and J. Liedtka. "Corporate Social Responsibility: A Critical Approach." *Business Horizons* (July–August 1991), pp. 92–98.

Harrington, S. J. "What Corporate America Is Teaching about Ethics." *Academy of Management Executive* (February 1991), pp. 21–30.

Litzinger, W. D., and T. E. Schaefer. "Business Ethics Bogeyman: The Perpetual Paradox." *Business Horizons* (March–April 1987), pp. 16–21.

Waddock, Sandra A., and Mary-Ellen Boyle. "The Dynamics of Change in Corporate Community Relations." *Management Review* 37, no. 4 (Summer 1995), p. 125.

Wood, D. J. "Social Issues in Management: Theory and Research in Corporate Social Performance." *Journal of Management* (June 1991), pp. 383–406.

———. "Toward Improving Corporate Social Performance." *Business Horizons* (July–August 1991), pp. 66–73.

CHAPTER 2 COHESION CASE ILLUSTRATION

COMPANY MISSION AT THE COCA-COLA COMPANY

At the heart of Coca-Cola, especially in its first 100 years, there has been a commitment to intense marketing and to the preservation of its patented formulas and processes to make its special syrup. The intense secrecy that always has surrounded Coke's formula has long fostered an organizational obsession with secrecy pertaining to other information about Coke and its operations. While reaching almost 40,000 employees working in 135 countries and almost 80,000 stockholders by 1978, Coke's statements of mission and long-term goals or values remained very abbreviated and direct. Excerpts from 1978 company documents show its mission to be a brief description of the business and, later in the document, a reference to very general and typical goals or priorities:

> The Coca-Cola Company is the largest manufacturer and distributor of soft-drink concentrates and syrups in the world. Its product, "Coca-Cola," has been sold in the United States since 1886, is now sold in over 135 countries as well, and is the leading soft-drink product in most of these countries . . . Through the Foods Division, the Company manufactures and markets Minute Maid and Snow Crop frozen concentrated citrus juices . . . The Company manufactures and markets still and sparkling wines under the "Taylor" trademark . . . a subsidiary designs and manufactures water treatment systems . . . and a subsidiary is engaged in the manufacture and distribution of plastic film products . . . Our goal is to continue the strong financial growth trends into the future.

By the mid-1980s, Coke had diversified into movie entertainment, yet its commitment to brevity and secrecy remained, as can be seen in these excerpts from its 1986 mission statements:

> The Coca-Cola Company is the worldwide soft-drink leader, as well as one of the world's leading producers and distributors of filmed entertainment and the leading U.S. marketer of orange juice and juice products . . . Management's primary objective is to increase shareholder value. To accomplish this objective, The Coca-Cola Company and subsidiaries have developed a comprehensive business strategy that emphasizes improving volume and margins, maximizing long-term cash flow by increasing investments in areas offering attractive returns, divesting low-return assets, and maintaining appropriate financial policies. The Company operates in three markets: soft drinks, entertainment, and food, each of which is consumer oriented and offers attractive rates of returns. In each market, the Company focuses on maximizing unit volume growth, exercising effective asset management, and increasing utilization of its distribution systems . . . A principal goal for the Soft Drink Business Sector is to increase unit volume at rates in excess of the respective industry rates . . . Key goals of the Entertainment Business Sector are to leverage its motion picture and television distribution systems and to increase its library of filmed entertainment products . . . Following a strategy of product and package segmentation, the Foods Business Sector increases unit volume by adding new products into its existing distribution systems.

By the end of the 1980s, Roberto Goizueta had weathered a few storms and enjoyed several successes in Coca-Cola's last 10 years. "New Coke" had caused an unprecedented consumer revolt. The entertainment business was sold to Sony for an impressive gain. An increasing hallmark of Goizueta's leadership was greater openness about the mission and intention of Coca-Cola. In the early 1990s, Goizueta shared the following mission statement in a booklet entitled *Coca-Cola, a Business System toward 2000: Our Mission in the 1990s:*

OUR OPPORTUNITY

Bringing refreshment to a thirsty world is a unique opportunity for our Company . . . and for all of our Coca-Cola associates . . . to create shareholder value. Ours is the only production and distribution business system capable of realizing that opportunity on a global scale. And we are committed to realizing it.

OUR GOAL

With Coca-Cola as the centerpiece, ours is a worldwide system of superior brands and services through which we, our franchisees, and other business partners deliver satisfaction and value to customers and consumers. By doing so, we enhance brand equity on a global basis. As a result, we increase shareholder wealth over time.

Our goal for the 1990s sounds deceptively simple. *It is to expand our global business system, reaching increasing numbers of consumers who will enjoy our brands and products more and more often.*

OUR CHALLENGE

The 1990s promise to be a paradoxical time for our business. Distribution channels will continue to consolidate, while new ones will emerge . . . yet, *customers* will demand more choices, as well as customized service and marketing programs at the lowest possible cost. *Consumers* in developed countries will grow in age and affluence but not in numbers . . . while strong population growth in lesser developed countries means the vitality of these young consumer markets will depend on job creation and expanding economies.

To succeed in this environment we will make *effective use* of our fundamental resources:

· Brands,
· Systems,
· Capital, and, most important,
· People.

Because these resources are already available, one might assume we need only to draw on them for achieving our goal. Nothing could be more wrong. *The challenge of the 1990s will be not only to use these resources but to expand them . . . to adapt them . . . to reconfigure them in constantly changing ways in order to bring about an ever renewed relationship between the Coca-Cola system and the consumers of the world . . . to make the best even better.*

OUR RESOURCES

Brands   Increasing globalization of the communications industry means we can more effectively expose our advertising and other image-building programs through a worldwide brand framework. This places a premium on maintaining our traditional excellence as a premier brand advertiser. Yet, we must remember that it is our franchisee network around the world which will distribute and locally market our brands. To appropriately leverage these brands, we must recognize that we and our franchisees are fundamentally in the business of servicing our customers and meeting the needs, real or perceived, of our consumers.

Tactical decisions regarding the marketing of our products must stay as close to the customer and consumer as possible, within a clear, but flexible, global brand strategy. This is another way of saying that we must think globally but act locally. Thus, intimate knowledge of an account, a channel, or a consumer segment will be required to design specific programs which generate satisfaction and value to that customer or consumer. The Coca-Cola Company does not sell commodities—we will not sell commodities—and we will not cheapen our relationships with customers and consumers.

Coca-Cola, in every form . . . classic, diet, caffeine free, cherry, light . . . is the most widely recognized and esteemed brand in the world. Coca-Cola was, is, and always will be . . . it! It is the centerpiece of our entire refreshment system.

Sprite and Fanta are worldwide brands. They must play a role in our brand strategy. We will continually strive to develop new brands where the opportunity presents itself.

Systems   Moving closer to the consumer both in our own organizational structure and in timely decision-making will be mandated by the global, yet diverse, marketplace of the 1990s.

Structurally, a flatter organization of our Company will be required. Functional groups must be reorganized around business units which focus on market opportunities. And as a company, we must be players, not just cheerleaders or critics.

It will be essential that our franchisees understand this new role we see for ourselves. Our increased equity participation in the Coca-Cola production and distribution network, which may include complete franchise consolidations in some areas of the world, will be carried out only whenever it becomes necessary for achieving our goal. A greater involvement in our franchise system will likely necessitate our making investments to help bring about production and distribution capabilities which meet the service demands of customers at the lowest possible cost. This is to ensure a competitive advantage for the entire system.

Entirely new distribution systems may be needed to realize new opportunities in vending and in new and emerging post-mix markets, particularly outside the United States. Joint ventures, in many forms, with our franchisees and suppliers will put our capital directly into building new avenues to reach consumers.

Success in managing these flatter, market-driven structures will depend largely on our information systems. To reach our goal, our information systems—the processes, reports, procedures, and communication linkages that hold the organization together—must lead, rather than trail, developments in the marketplace. Effective and timely information is vital to effective and timely allocation of resources.

Ours is a multilocal business. Its relative state of development varies dramatically from the soft drink frontiers of Asia to the sophisticated markets of North America. Throughout our 103-year history there has been an evolutionary process or cycle of development continuously at work. That cycle, which often evolved over decades in the past, will quicken in astonishing dimensions in the future. By the year 2000, our business system in developing countries must function at levels nearly equal to those seen in today's sophisticated markets. Where lack of hard currency or difficult political realities are constraints to reaching consumers, we must build new strategic alliances and enhance our trading capabilities to overcome constraints.

Capital   Shaping business systems which are close to consumers will require not only the investment of our capital for new assets but more sophisticated management of existing ones. Existing assets will be evaluated as potential resources for meeting our goal. Those assets include not only physical assets but also equity ownership positions, financial capacity, and information systems, as well as creative management of key business relationships.

Capital management is no longer just the process of earning a rate of return above our cost of capital. It is the innovative endeavor of finding more productive uses and new purposes for assets, of trading or leveraging existing assets to meet our goal and to create new strategic alliances.

Our organization has a rich history of effectively allocating resources and of utilizing our financial strength to build value. That will continue. And given our growing experience at managing greater financial leverage, we will periodically evaluate higher leverage ceilings, primarily for investments in our business system or in strategic alliances and, secondarily, in our own shares.

People   Through the years, The Coca-Cola Company has always had an international cadre of individuals. To capture the global soft-drink opportunity in the 1990s, we need more than the right brands, systems, and infrastructure. We need the right people for the 21st century.

We must have people who use facts and knowledge to add something . . . to add value to our customers' businesses. In an age where everyone has basically the same information at the same time, the advantage goes to people who can take information and quickly put it to effective and profitable use. It means having people with what can be called the "mind of the strategist" . . . people who can create a competitive advantage . . . out of common knowledge.

Few are born with such skill. This skill can be developed, however, and should be rewarded. We must recruit and nurture the growth of associates to match the needs of the business. In the 1990s, "internationalists" with multilingual, multicultural capabilities will be the norm. And we must continue to refine our compensation systems to reflect our operating culture and reward value-adding performance.

The responsibility for developing people cannot be delegated to training courses, academic exercises, or professionals in the area of human resources. Those have a role to play but do not constitute an adequate process. *The development of our best people is the personal responsibility of Management*. It requires each manager to see his or her most important responsibility as teaching and developing people. Our charge is that simple—recruiting and training the best talent by the best managers. As that talent grows and develops, they become the next managers capable of and responsible for developing new talent, thus perpetuating a strength.

This process is the link to maintaining the sense of dissatisfaction that has resulted in much of the success we enjoy today. We must continue to cultivate intelligent risk taking and flexible decision making, realizing that, while not every risk taken or decision made brings success, the alternative is complacency and stagnation . . . a stance totally unacceptable to our Company.

OUR REWARDS

The rewards of meeting these challenges and flourishing in a state of rapid change are enormous:

· Satisfied consumers who return again and again to our brands for refreshment.
· Profitable customers who rely on our worldwide brands and services.
· Communities around the world where we are an economic contributor and welcomed guest.
· Successful business partners.
· Shareholders who are building value through the power of the Coca-Cola system.

OUR SHARED VISION

The Coca-Cola system is indeed a special business. One hundred and three years of dedicated effort by literally millions of individuals have combined to create in Coca-Cola a remarkable trademark presence and economic value unchallenged since the dawn of commercial history.

However, any edge we have is fragile. Our journey to the year 2000 requires that our brands, systems, capital, and people grow and change to meet our goal and thus realize our opportunity. To borrow a recent popular phrase, we see 6 billion points of light in a thirsty world—6 billion consumers in the world of the year 2000—all being refreshed as never before by the Coca-Cola system.

That is a wonderful goal we all can share and strive for as we move together—toward 2000.

The evolution of Coca-Cola's use of mission statements from the 1970s to the 1990s displays a consistent commitment to specific, direct statements defining the business of Coca-Cola, while evidencing a move from brevity and secrecy toward greater clarification of values, priorities, and the "Coca-Cola system." Goizueta's elaborate statement of Coke's mission for the 1990s is rather lengthy by comparison to several mission statements excerpted in Chapter 2. But while sensitive to the virtues of brevity, Mr. Goizueta felt a detailed, complete elaboration upon Coke's mission and related components was essential to focusing a diverse, worldwide group of employees and "partners" on the key ingredients for global success in the next century. He felt that providing order and clarity to a detailed "vision" of what the Coca-Cola system is and what it intends to become would provide a framework for future decisions and actions throughout the Coke system to enhance its opportunity for success.

THE EXTERNAL ENVIRONMENT

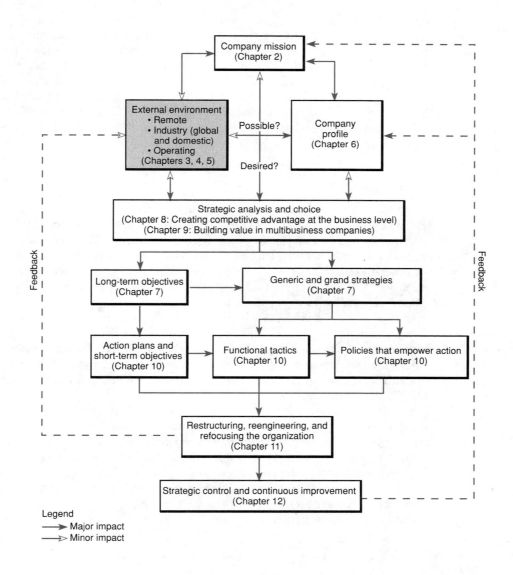

Legend
⟶ Major impact
⟶▷ Minor impact

A host of external factors influence a firm's choice of direction and action and, ultimately, its organizational structure and internal processes. These factors, which constitute the *external environment,* can be divided into three interrelated subcategories: factors in the *remote* environment, factors in the *industry* environment, and factors in the *operating* environment.[1] This chapter describes the complex necessities involved in formulating strategies that optimize a firm's market opportunities. Figure 3–1 suggests the interrelationship between the firm and its remote, its industry, and its operating environments. In combination, these factors form the basis of the opportunities and threats that a firm faces in its competitive environment.

REMOTE ENVIRONMENT

The remote environment comprises factors that originate beyond, and usually irrespective of, any single firm's operating situation: (1) economic, (2) social, (3) political, (4) technological, and (5) ecological factors. That environment presents firms with opportunities, threats, and constraints, but rarely does a single firm exert any meaningful reciprocal influence. For example, when the economy slows and construction starts to decrease, an individual contractor is likely to suffer a decline in business, but that contractor's success in stimulating local construction activities would be unable to reverse the overall decrease in construction starts. The trade agreements that resulted from improved relations between the United States and China and the United States and Russia are examples of the effects of political factors on individual firms. The agreements provided individual U.S. manufacturers with opportunities to broaden their international operations.

1. Economic Factors

Economic factors concern the nature and direction of the economy in which a firm operates. Because consumption patterns are affected by the relative affluence of various market segments, in its strategic planning each firm must consider economic trends in the segments that affect its industry. On both the national and international level, it must consider the general availability of credit, the level of disposable income, and the propensity of people to spend. Prime interest rates, inflation rates, and trends in the growth of the gross national product are other economic factors it must consider.

Until recently, the potential impact of international economic forces appeared to be severely restricted and was largely discounted. However, the emergence of new international power brokers has changed the focus of economic environmental forecasting. Among the most prominent of these power brokers are the European Economic Community (EEC, or Common Market), the Organization of Petroleum Exporting Countries (OPEC), and coalitions of developing countries.

The EEC, whose members include most of the West European countries, was established by the Treaty of Rome in 1957. It has eliminated quotas and established a tariff-free trade area for industrial products among its members. By fostering intra-European economic cooperation, it has helped its member countries compete more effectively in non-European international markets.

Vying with the opening of Eastern European borders to commerce as the most significant marketplace occurrence of the 1990s has been the opening of protected markets by the European Community. Commonly referred to as *EC 92,* the stated goal of this cooperative

---

[1] Many authors refer to the operating environment as the *task* or *competitive* environment.

FIGURE 3–1
The Firm's External Environment

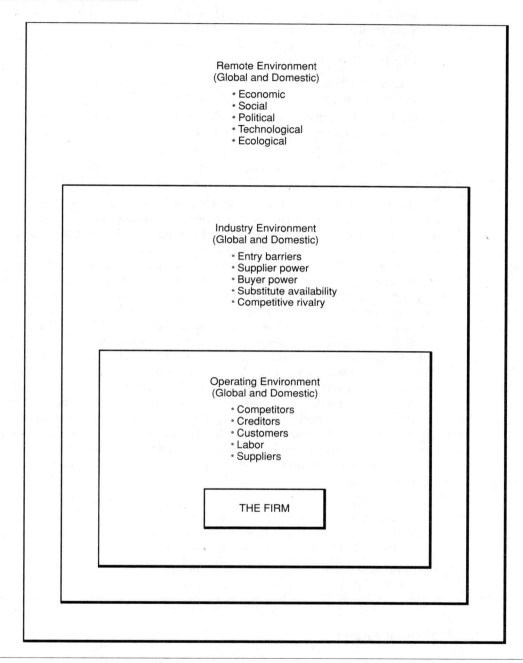

effort is the elimination of all technical, physical, and fiscal barriers to the conduct of international trade in Europe by 1992. While pragmatists see the EC 92 as a concept and not a deadline, significant progress is being made each year toward the attainment of aims of the collaboration. As of early 1990, 125 of the 265 directives related to 1992 had become EC law.

Much of the excitement over EC 92 stems from the size of the market in Europe, which exceeds 320 million consumers. As Europeans' incomes rise and their tastes become less geocentric, a booming market is expected for consumer goods, from appliances to soft drinks. As evidence of their enthusiasm for the EC 92 marketplace, U.S. companies spent $20.9 billion in 1987 alone to build plants and buy companies in Europe, an amount 28 times greater than their expenditures in 1982.

Among the U.S. firms that invested heavily and early in Europe in the hope of profiting from the EC 92 developments were:

American Express, which projected a 20 percent annual growth rate in Europe in the 1990s owing to weak competition from "mom-and-pop" travel agencies.

AT&T, which completed a five-year, $27 billion deal with Italy's state-owned telephone equipment maker to overhaul the country's aging telephone system.

Federal Express, which was among the early organizers of warehousing and distribution services for European companies. Its $200 million-a-year business in Europe is forecasted to grow 80 percent annually during this decade.

Following the original EEC initiative of economic cooperation, the United States, Canada, Japan, the EEC, and other countries conducted multilateral trade negotiations in 1979 to establish rules for international trade and conduct. Those negotiations had a profound effect on almost every aspect of U.S. business activity.

In terms of impact on the United States, OPEC is at present among the most powerful international economic forces. This cartel includes most of the world's major oil and gas suppliers. Its drastic price increases impeded U.S. recovery from the recession of the early 1970s and fueled inflationary fires throughout the world. Those price increases in particular affected the U.S. automobile industry by raising the fuel costs of automobile users and by giving rise to legislation on engine design and performance standards.

Historically underdeveloped countries recently have assumed a greater role in international commerce as a source of both threats and opportunities. Following OPEC's success, these countries found it economically beneficial to directly confront the established powers. Since 1974, producers of primary commodities in the developing countries have formed or greatly strengthened trade organizations to enforce higher prices and achieve larger real incomes for their members. Even developing countries not desiring or unable to form cartels now exhibit an aggressive attitude in their international economic relations. On the other hand, developing countries offer U.S. firms huge new markets for foodstuffs and capital equipment.

The intense nationalism of the developing countries, with nearly three fourths of the world's population, represents perhaps the greatest challenge our industrialized society and multinational corporations will face. As one Third World expert puts it, "the vastly unequal relationship between the rich and poor nations is fast becoming the central issue of our time."[2]

All of these international forces can affect—for better or worse—the economic well being of the U.S. business community. Consequently, firms must try to forecast the repercussions of major actions taken in both the domestic and international economic arenas.

2. Social Factors

The social factors that affect a firm involve the beliefs, values, attitudes, opinions, and lifestyles of persons in the firm's external environment, as developed from cultural, ecological, demographic, religious, educational, and ethnic conditioning. As social attitudes

---

[2] R. Steade, "Multinational Corporations and the Changing World Economic Order," *California Management Review*, Winter 1978, p. 5.

change, so too does the demand for various types of clothing, books, leisure activities, and so on. Like other forces in the remote external environment, social forces are dynamic, with constant change resulting from the efforts of individuals to satisfy their desires and needs by controlling and adapting to environmental factors. Teresa Iglesias-Soloman hoped to benefit from social changes with *Ninos,* a children's catalog written in both English and Spanish. The catalog featured books, videos, and Spanish cultural offerings for English-speaking children who wanted to learn Spanish and for Spanish-speaking children who wanted to learn English. *Ninos'* target market included middle-to-upper income Hispanic parents and a greater number of consumers, educators, bilingual schools, libraries, and purchasing agents. Iglesias-Solomon had reason to be optimistic about the future of *Ninos,* because the Hispanic population was growing five times faster than the general U.S. population.

One of the most profound social changes in recent years has been the entry of large numbers of women into the labor market. This has not only affected the hiring and compensation policies and the resource capabilities of their employers; it also has created or greatly expanded the demand for a wide range of products and services necessitated by their absence from the home. Firms that anticipated or reacted quickly to this social change offered such products and services as convenience foods, microwave ovens, and day-care centers.

A second profound social change has been the accelerating interest of consumers and employees in quality-of-life issues. Evidence of this change is seen in recent contract negotiations. In addition to the traditional demand for increased salaries have been worker demands for such benefits as sabbaticals, flexible hours or four-day workweeks, lump-sum vacation plans, and opportunities for advanced training.

A third profound social change has been the shift in the age distribution of the population. Changing social values and a growing acceptance of improved birth control methods are expected to raise the mean age of the U.S. population, which was 27.9 in 1970, to 34.9 by the year 2000. This trend will have an increasingly unfavorable impact on most producers of predominantly youth-oriented goods and will necessitate a shift in their long-range marketing strategies. Producers of hair- and skin-care preparations already have begun to adjust their research and development to reflect anticipated changes in demand.

A consequence of the changing age distribution of the population has been a sharp increase in the demands made by a growing number of senior citizens. Constrained by fixed incomes, these citizens have demanded that arbitrary and rigid policies on retirement age be modified and have successfully lobbied for tax exemptions and increases in Social Security benefits. Such changes have significantly altered the opportunity-risk equations of many firms—often to the benefit of firms that anticipated the changes.

Translating social change into forecasts of business effects is a difficult process, at best. Nevertheless, informed estimates of the impact of such alterations as geographic shifts in populations and changing work values, ethical standards, and religious orientation can only help a strategizing firm in its attempts to prosper.

3. Political Factors

The direction and stability of political factors is a major consideration for managers on formulating company strategy. Political factors define the legal and regulatory parameters within which firms must operate. Political constraints are placed on firms through fair-trade decisions, antitrust laws, tax programs, minimum wage legislation, pollution and pricing policies, administrative jawboning, and many other actions aimed at protecting employees, consumers, the general public, and the environment. Since such laws and regulations are most commonly restrictive, they tend to reduce the potential profits of firms. However, some political actions are designed to benefit and protect firms. Such actions include patent laws, government subsidies, and product research grants. Thus, political factors either may limit or benefit the firms they influence. For example, when Ethiopian Airlines organized in 1945, it received assistance from TWA and various Ethiopian governments. This support made Ethiopian Airlines one of the most successful members of the African air transport industry. The airline pioneered the hub concept in Africa and arranged its schedules to provide easy connections between many of the continent's countries, as well as between Africa and points in Europe and the Middle East and Asia. Without the political support of the Ethiopian governments, it would have been impossible for the airline to operate.[3]

Political activity also has a significant impact on two governmental functions that influence the remote environment of firms:

Supplier Function

Government decisions regarding the accessibility of private businesses to government-owned natural resources and national stockpiles of agricultural products will affect profoundly the viability of the strategies of some firms.

Customer Function

Government demand for products and services can create, sustain, enhance, or eliminate many market opportunities. For example, in the same way that the Kennedy administration's emphasis on landing a man on the moon spawned a demand for thousands of new products, the Carter administration's emphasis on developing synthetic fuels created a demand for new skills, technologies, and products; and the Reagan administration's strategic defense initiative (the "Star Wars" defense) sharply accelerated the development of laser technologies.

Entrepreneurial firms often feel such influences especially strongly. For example, in the six months following the August invasion of Kuwait, D. M. Offray & Son, a Chester, New Jersey, bow and ribbon manufacturer, sold about 28,409 miles of yellow ribbon in support of the armed forces. In order to keep up with the demand, the plant manager had to go to a triple-shift, six-day work week.[4]

4. Technological Factors

The fourth set of factors in the remote environment involves technological change. To avoid obsolescence and promote innovation, a firm must be aware of technological changes that might influence its industry. Creative technological adaptations can suggest possibilities for new products, for improvements in existing products, or in manufacturing and marketing techniques.

A technological breakthrough can have a sudden and dramatic effect on a firm's environment. It may spawn sophisticated new markets and products or significantly shorten the anticipated life of a manufacturing facility. Thus, all firms, and most particularly those in turbulent growth industries, must strive for an understanding both of the existing technological advances and the probable future advances that can affect their products and services. This quasi-science of attempting to foresee advancements and estimate their impact on an organization's operations is known as technological forecasting.

---

[3] *Air Transport World,* February 1992, pp. 110–12.

[4] *Fortune,* March 11, 1991, p. 14.

Technological forecasting can help protect and improve the profitability of firms in growing industries. It alerts strategic managers to both impending challenges and promising opportunities. As examples: (1) advances in xerography were a key to Xerox's success but caused major difficulties for carbon paper manufacturers, and (2) the perfection of transistors changed the nature of competition in the radio and television industry, helping such giants as RCA while seriously weakening smaller firms whose resource commitments required that they continue to base their products on vacuum tubes.

The key to beneficial forecasting of technological advancement lies in accurately predicting future technological capabilities and their probable impacts. A comprehensive analysis of the effect of technological change involves study of the expected impact of new technologies on the remote environment, on the competitive business situation, and on the business-society interface. In recent years, forecasting in the last area has warranted particular attention. For example, as a consequence of increased concern over the environment, firms must carefully investigate the probable effect of technological advances on quality-of-life factors, such as ecology and public safety.

5. Ecological Factors

As strategic managers forecast past the year 2000, the most prominent factor in the remote environment is often the reciprocal relationship between business and the ecology. The term ecology refers to the relationships among human beings and other living things and the air, soil, and water that support them. Threats to our life-supporting ecology caused principally by human activities in an industrial society are commonly referred to as *pollution*. Specific concerns include global warming, loss of habitat and biodiversity, as well as air, water, and land pollution.

The global climate has been changing for ages; however, it is now evident that humanity's activities are accelerating this tremendously. A change in atmospheric radiation, due in part to ozone depletion, causes global warming. Solar radiation that is normally absorbed into the atmosphere reaches the earth's surface, heating the soil, water, and air.

Another area of great importance is the loss of habitat and biodiversity. Ecologists agree that the extinction of important flora and fauna is occurring at a rapid rate, and if this pace is continued, could constitute a global extinction on the scale of those found in fossil records. The earth's life forms are dependent on a well-functioning ecosystem. In addition, immeasurable advances in disease treatment can be attributed to research involving substances found in plants. As species become extinct, the life-support system is irreparably harmed. The primary cause of extinction on this scale is a disturbance of natural habitat. For example, current data suggest that the earth's primary tropical forests, a prime source of oxygen and potential plant "cure," could be destroyed in only five decades.

Air pollution is created by dust particles and gaseous discharges that contaminate the air. Acid rain, or rain contaminated by sulfur dioxide, which can destroy aquatic and plant life, is believed to result from coal-burning factories in 70 percent of all cases. A health-threatening "thermal blanket" is created when the atmosphere traps carbon dioxide emitted from smokestacks in factories burning fossil fuels. This "greenhouse effect" can have disastrous consequences, making the climate unpredictable and raising temperatures. An interesting example of a way in which the free market system can help to reduce air pollution problems is discussed in Strategy in Action 3–1.

Water pollution occurs principally when industrial toxic wastes are dumped or leak into the nation's waterways. Since fewer than 50 percent of all municipal sewer systems are in compliance with Environmental Protection Agency requirements for water safety, contaminated waters represent a substantial present threat to public welfare.

COLD CASH FOR OLD CLUNKERS

Waddya bid me for this 1971 Ford? Forget the Blue Book. The value of this beauty depends on how much choking black smoke blasts out of its rusted tailpipe—and the more the better. Thanks to the Bush Administration, there is a thriving free market in dirty old cars: companies that pollute the air buy them, junk them, and earn a "pollution credit" for saving however much smog- and ozone-forming exhaust the cars would have belched out before they died. The company— anything from a utility to a paint factory—subtracts the amount of the credit from the quantity of air pollution they're required to cut under the 1990 Clean Air Act. The idea of this and other market- based approaches to environmental cleanup is to get the most clean for the least green. "Lots of little smokestacks on the highway are equivalent to one big smokestack," says energy-policy analyst Will Schroeer of the U.S. Environmental Protection Agency. "But it will be cheaper to scrap cars than to put emission controls on smokestacks."

Adam Smith would love it. Say a factory must reduce its nitrogen oxide (NO_x) emissions by 130,000 pounds a year. And say it will cost $1 million to do that by installing scrubbers on its smokestacks. If the factory buys 1,000 old cars for an average $700 each, and if each car spews out 130 pounds of NO_x a year, the company will have met its clean-air mandate and saved $300,000 in the bargain. People who sold their old clunkers could buy a cleaner, later-model car. That's how it worked in 1990 in California, when Unocal bought 8,376 pre-1971 cars for $700 apiece. The junked cars accounted for nearly 13 million pounds of emissions per year—as much as the hydrocarbons from 250,000 new cars, one large oil refinery, or all the barbecue lighter fluid used in the Los Angeles basin.

Such "green economics" has become as trendy as recycling newspaper. In 1993, southern Cali- fornia allowed factories to meet clean-air standards by buying pollution credits from companies that had exceeded their mandated emissions cuts. Still, although using market forces to clean up the planet has found support in Congress, the administration, and even among environmental groups, cash-for-clunkers has its detractors. Dan Becker of the Sierra Club calls it "the Cheshire Cat ap- proach. Pollution from the car will continue after the [car] has disappeared"—because the car's "quota" is now coming from the smokestack of the buyer, who can avoid cleaning up his own act. But there is no debate that old cars make a tempting target. The 37.6 million cars that predate 1980 are responsible for 86 percent of the smog-making gases from autos but represent only 38 percent of the fleet; the 5.9 million dirtiest cars cause a whopping 50 percent of all hydrocarbons. Next up for the green marketers: giving companies pollution credits if they switch to alternative-fuel fleets. Capitalism may turn out to be an environmentalist's friend after all.

Land pollution is caused by the need to dispose of ever-increasing amounts of waste. Routine, everyday packaging is a major contributor to this problem, as described in Global Strategy in Action 3–1. Land pollution is more dauntingly caused by the disposal of industrial toxic wastes in underground sites. With approximately 90 percent of the annual U.S. output of 500 million metric tons of hazardous industrial wastes being placed in underground dumps, it is evident that land pollution and its resulting endangerment of the ecology have become a major item on the political agenda.

As a major contributor to ecological pollution, business now is being held responsible for eliminating the toxic by-products of its current manufacturing processes and for clean- ing up the environmental damage that it did previously. Increasingly, managers are being

GLOBAL
STRATEGY IN   **PACKAGING FOR THE ENVIRONMENT**
ACTION 3–1

Packaging is the ultimate symbol of the 20th century's consumer culture. It protects what we buy and raises our standard of living. In developing countries, 30 percent to 50 percent of food shipments are spoiled because of inadequate packaging and distribution systems. In developed countries with more sophisticated packaging, storage, and distribution, only 2 percent to 3 percent is wasted.

Packaging not only protects goods but also conveys information about their contents and preparation or administration, and—in some cases—foils would-be tamperers. It plays a vital and growing role in the global economy.

At the same time, packaging is on the environmental frontline. It is the largest and fastest growing contributor to one of the most troubling environmental problems: garbage.

In the United States, packaging accounted for more than 30 percent of the municipal solid waste stream in 1990. Where is all this packaging going? In this country, most packaging and other waste is buried in landfills. But even with its abundance of open land, America is running out of room for its garbage.

One quarter of the country's municipalities are expected to exhaust their landfill capacity before 1995, and more than half the population lives in regions with less than 10 years of landfill capacity.

Meanwhile, the environmentally sound alternatives to burying garbage—recycling, reuse, and energy recovery—are only just beginning. For the throwaway society, the 1990s are the decade of reckoning.

While packaging is not the only culprit in the solid waste crisis, it is a highly visible component, and one that directly involves consumers. And its short lifetime exacerbates the problem. Although the useful lives of some packages—such as paint cans and reusable canisters—may be as long as several years, the useful lives of others—such as fast-food hamburger wrappers—can be as fleeting as a few minutes.

Fortunately, because of the sheer volume of packaging in the solid waste stream, even relatively small improvements in packaging can make a real difference in the magnitude of the garbage crisis. Packaging, thus, offers a unique opportunity for companies to assume a leadership role in environmental responsibility.

In terms of packaging choices, industry's response to the environmental challenge has so far focused on recycling and source reduction. But the complexity of the issues involved demands a more systemic, integrated approach based on comprehensive analysis and long-term vision as well as innovative solutions.

Among the analytical tools now being deployed is life-cycle analysis. This is a fairly new technique for exploring the environmental implications of a given product decision—in this case, a packaging choice from raw material acquisition through manufacturing, energy consumption, design, and transportation to final use and disposal of the package. Life-cycle thinking is an important step toward understanding the full environmental implications of packaging choices.

required by the government or are being expected by the public to incorporate ecological concerns into their decision making. For example, between 1975 and 1992, 3M cut its pollution in half by reformulating products, modifying processes, redesigning production equipment, and recycling by-products. Similarly, steel companies and public utilities have invested billions of dollars in costlier but cleaner-burning fuels and pollution control equipment. The automobile industry has been required to install expensive emission controls in

FIGURE 3–2
Environmental Costs and Competitiveness

Several recent efforts to quantify environmental spending have suggested that enormous costs are being incurred. A 1990 study by the U.S. EPA concluded that environmental spending was approaching 2 percent of GNP. Manufacturers then used this information to support their claim that regulation was harming industrial growth and putting the nation at a competitive disadvantage vis-á-vis foreign suppliers. The claims, however, simply did not hold up to closer inspection. First, only a small share of pollution abatement and control spending was incurred by industrial facilities. By one estimate (one used as a source for the EPA study), manufacturers incurred a total of $31.1 billion in environmental costs in 1990. This amounted to only 1.1 percent of product shipments. The costs identified by the EPA resulted from such areas as the requirement for catalytic converters on all automobiles ($14 billion in 1990), the construction and operation of public sewer systems ($20 billion), and the disposal of household wastes ($10 billion).

Even if environmental spending made up only 1 percent of costs, it would not be unreasonable for manufacturers to claim that these costs had a significant influence on competitiveness if international competitors were not required to meet similar requirements. Comparisons of international spending suggest, however, that manufacturers in important production areas around the world are experiencing costs similar to those faced by U.S. producers. Pollution control's share of capital expenditures in Germany was 12 percent in 1990, matching the costs incurred by American manufacturers. Similarly, recent environmental spending by U.S. pulp and paper manufacturers is closely matched by key competitors in Canada and Sweden.

These comparisons suggest that although pollution abatement expenditures are clearly a material part of total costs, the impact of these costs on competitiveness is mild. In fact, no clear link can be made between environmental regulation and measurably adverse effects on net exports, overall trade flows, or plant location decisions. It appear that little advantage has been gained by foreign firms based on the environmental requirements in the areas of their production.

Source: Excerpted from Benjamin C. Bonifant, Matthew R. Arnold, and Frederick J. Long, "Gaining Competitive Advantage through Environmental Investments," p. 39. Reprinted from *Business Horizons,* July–August 1995. Copyright 1995 by the Foundation for the School of Business at Indiana University. Used with permission.

cars. The gasoline industry has been forced to formulate new low-lead and no-lead products. And thousands of companies have found it necessary to direct their R&D resources into the search for ecologically superior products, such as Sears's phosphate-free laundry detergent and Pepsi-Cola's biodegradable plastic soft-drink bottle.

Environmental legislation impacts corporate strategies worldwide. Many companies fear the consequences of highly restrictive and costly environmental regulations. However, some manufacturers view these new controls as an opportunity, capturing markets with products that help customers satisfy their own regulatory standards. Other manufacturers contend that the costs of environmental spending inhibit the growth and productivity of their operations. Figure 3–2 takes a deeper look into the costs of environmental regulations.

The increasing attention by companies to protect the environment is evidenced in the attempts by firms to establish proecology policies. One such approach to environmental activism is described in Global Strategy in Action 3–2.

Despite cleanup efforts to date, the job of protecting the ecology will continue to be a top strategic priority—usually because corporate stockholders and executives choose it, increasingly because the public and the government require it. As evidenced by Figure 3–3, the government has made numerous interventions into the conduct of business for the purpose of bettering the ecology.

Benefits of Eco-Efficiency

Many of the world's largest corporations are realizing that business activities must no longer ignore environmental concerns. Every activity is linked to thousands of other transactions and their environmental impact; therefore, corporate environmental responsibility must be taken seriously and environmental policy must be implemented to ensure a

GLOBAL
STRATEGY IN
ACTION 3–2

TAKING A STEP IN THE RIGHT DIRECTION

"The ongoing occurrence of environmental incidents has become unacceptable in the public's mind," says George Pilko, president of Houston-based Pilko & Associates, an environmental consulting firm. That's why companies today are taking a proactive stance when it comes to managing environmental issues. The public just won't tolerate any more Love Canals, Bhopals, or major oil spills. "You've got strong public sentiment, increasingly stringent environmental regulations at the local, state, and federal level, stricter enforcement of existing regulations, and an exponential rise in environmentally oriented lawsuits. It clearly doesn't make sense for companies to continue to operate as they had been up until the late 1980s where they focused in on just remaining in compliance with existing regulations," Pilko adds.

Instead, according to Pilko, companies need to make sure they've got an environmental policy that clearly explains their commitment to being proactive and is communicated clearly to all employees. Companies also should be aware of the effectiveness of their current programs and where they stand relative to their competitors, because "there is a tremendous discrepancy between executives' perception of how they are doing and what is reality." In fact, a recent Pilko & Associates survey of 200 senior executives representing large industrial firms found that 40 percent of the respondents believed their company was doing an excellent job of managing their environmental problems, while only 8 percent thought their competitors were doing an excellent job.

Regardless of perception, however, management of environmental issues must be supported from the top. "Corporate environmental policy is most effectively communicated by the president or CEO," Pilko says. For those CEOs or senior executives interested in getting out the message that they are serious about dealing with the environment, Pilko advises them to ask themselves the following 10 questions:

1. Do you have a clearly articulated environmental policy that has been communicated throughout the company?
2. Have you had an objective, third-party assessment of the effectiveness of your environmental programs?
3. Have you analyzed how your company's environmental performance compares with that of the leading firms in your industry?
4. Does your company view environmental performance not just as a staff function but as the responsibility of all employees?
5. Have you analyzed the potential impact of environmental issues on the future demand for your products and the competitive economics in your industry?
6. Are environmental issues and activities discussed frequently at your board meetings?
7. Do you have a formal system for monitoring proposed regulatory changes and for handling compliance with changing regulations?
8. Do you routinely conduct environmental due-diligence studies on potential acquisitions?
9. Have you successfully budgeted for environmental expenditures, without incurring surprise expenses that materially affected your profitability?
10. Have you identified and quantified environmental liabilities from past operations, and do you have a plan for minimizing those liabilities?

Source: Excerpted from Julie Cohen Mason, "Taking a Step in the Right Direction," p. 23. Reprinted by permission of the publisher from *Management Review,* December 1991, © 1991 American Management Association, New York. All rights reserved.

FIGURE 3–3
Federal Ecological Legislation

Centerpiece Legislation

National Environmental Policy Act, 1969 Established Environmental Protection Agency; consolidated federal environmental activities under it. Established Council on Environmental Quality to advise president on environmental policy and to review environmental impact statements.

Air Pollution

Clean Air Act, 1963 Authorized assistance to state and local governments in formulating control programs. Authorized limited federal action in correcting specific pollution problems.
Clean Air Act, Amendments (Motor Vehicle Air Pollution Control Act), 1965 Authorized federal standards for auto exhaust emission. Standards first set for 1968 models.
Air Quality Act, 1967 Authorized federal government to establish air quality control regions and to set maximum permissible pollution levels. Required states and localities to carry out approved control programs or else give way to federal controls.
Clean Air Act Amendments, 1970 Authorized EPA to establish nationwide air pollution standards and to limit the discharge of six principal pollutants into the lower atmosphere. Authorized citizens to take legal action to require EPA to implement its standards against undiscovered offenders.
Clean Air Act Amendments, 1977 Postponed auto emission requirements. Required use of scrubbers in new coal-fired power plants. Directed EPA to establish a system to prevent deterioration of air quality in clean areas.

Solid Waste Pollution

Solid Waste Disposal Act, 1965 Authorized research and assistance to state and local control programs.
Resource Recovery Act, 1970 Subsidized construction of pilot recycling plants; authorized development of nationwide control programs.
Resource Conservation and Recovery Act, 1976 Directed EPA to regulate hazardous waste management, from generation through disposal.
Surface Mining and Reclamation Act, 1976 Controlled strip mining and restoration of reclaimed land.

Water Pollution

Refuse Act, 1899 Prohibited dumping of debris into navigable waters without a permit. Extended by court decision to industrial discharges.

comprehensive organizational strategy. Because of increases in government regulations and consumer environmental concerns, the implementation of environmental policy has become a point of competitive advantage. Therefore, the rational goal of business should be to limit its impact on the environment, thus ensuring long-run benefits to both the firm and society. To neglect this responsibility is to ensure the demise of both the firm and our ecosystem.

Stephen Schmidheiny, chairman of the Business Council for Sustainable Development, has coined the term *eco-efficiency* to describe corporations that produce more-useful goods and services while continuously reducing resource consumption and pollution. He cites a number of reasons for corporations to implement environmental policy: customers demand cleaner products, environmental regulations are increasingly more stringent, employees prefer to work for environmentally conscious firms, and financing is more readily available for eco-efficient firms. In addition, the government provides incentives for environmentally responsible companies.

Setting priorities, developing corporate standards, controlling property acquisition and use to preserve habitats, implementing energy-conserving activities, and redesigning products (e.g., minimizing packaging) are a number of measures the firm can implement to enhance an eco-efficient strategy. One of the most important steps a firm can take in achieving a competitive position with regard to the eco-efficient strategy is to fully capitalize on technological developments as a method of gaining efficiency.

FIGURE 3–3
(concluded)

Federal Water Pollution Control Act, 1956   Authorized grants to states for water pollution control. Gave federal government limited authority to correct specific pollution problems.

Water Quality Act, 1965   Provided for adoption of water quality standards by states, subject to federal approval.

Water Quality Improvement Act, 1970   Provided for federal cleanup of oil spills. Strengthened federal authority over water pollution control.

Federal Water Pollution Control Act Amendments, 1972   Authorized EPA to set water quality and effluent standards; provided for enforcement and research.

Safe Drinking Water Act, 1974   Set standards for drinking water quality.

Clean Water Act, 1977   Ordered control of toxic pollutants by 1984 with best available technology economically feasible.

Other Points

Federal Insecticide, Fungicide and Rodenticide Act, 1947   To protect farmers, prohibited fraudulent claims by salespersons. Required registration of poisonous products.

Federal Insecticide, Fungicide, and Rodenticide Amendments, 1967, 1972   Provided new authority to license users of pesticides.

Pesticide Control Act, 1972   Required all pesticides shipped in interstate commerce to be certified as effective for their stated purposes and harmless to crops, animal feed, animal life, and humans.

Noise Control Act, 1972   Required EPA to set noise standards for major sources of noise and to advise Federal Aviation Administration on standards for airplane noise.

Federal Environmental Pesticide Control Act Amendments, 1975   Set 1977 deadline (not met) for registration, classification, and licensing of many pesticides.

Toxic Substances Control Act, 1976   Required testing of chemicals; authorized EPA to restrict the use of harmful substances.

Comprehensive Environmental Response, Compensation, and Liability Act, 1980   Commonly called "Superfund Act"; created a trust fund (paid for in part by toxic-chemical manufacturers) to clean up hazardous waste sites.

Four key characteristics of eco-efficient corporations are:

· Eco-efficient firms are proactive, not reactive. Policy is initiated and promoted by business because it is in their own interests and the interest of their customers, not because it is imposed by one or more external forces.

· Eco-efficiency is designed in, not added on. This characteristic implies that the optimization of eco-efficiency requires that every business effort regarding the product and process must internalize the strategy.

· Flexibility is imperative for eco-efficient strategy implementation. Continuous attention must be paid to technological innovation and market evolution.

· Eco-efficiency is encompassing, not insular. In the modern global business environment, efforts must not only cross industrial sectors but national and cultural boundaries as well.

INDUSTRY ENVIRONMENT

Harvard professor Michael E. Porter's book *Competitive Strategy* propelled the concept of industry environment into the foreground of strategic thought and business planning. The cornerstone of the book is an article from the *Harvard Business Review,* in which Porter explains the five forces that shape competition in an industry. His well-defined analytic framework helps strategic managers to link remote factors to their effects on a firm's operating environment.

With the special permission of Professor Porter and the *Harvard Business Review,* we present in this section of the chapter the major portion of his seminal article on the industry environment and its impact on strategic management.[5]

OVERVIEW

The nature and degree of competition in an industry hinge on five forces: the threat of new entrants, the bargaining power of customers, the bargaining power of suppliers, the threat of substitute products or services (where applicable), and the jockeying among current contestants. To establish a strategic agenda for dealing with these contending currents and to grow despite them, a company must understand how they work in its industry and how they affect the company in its particular situation. This chapter will detail how these forces operate and suggest ways of adjusting to them, and, where possible, of taking advantage of them.

HOW COMPETITIVE FORCES SHAPE STRATEGY

The essence of strategy formulation is coping with competition. Yet it is easy to view competition too narrowly and too pessimistically. While one sometimes hears executives complaining to the contrary, intense competition in an industry is neither coincidence nor bad luck.

Moreover, in the fight for market share, competition is not manifested only in the other players. Rather, competition in an industry is rooted in its underlying economics, and competitive forces exist that go well beyond the established combatants in a particular industry. Customers, suppliers, potential entrants, and substitute products are all competitors that may be more or less prominent or active depending on the industry.

The state of competition in an industry depends on five basic forces, which are diagrammed in Figure 3–4. The collective strength of these forces determines the ultimate profit potential of an industry. It ranges from intense in industries like tires, metal cans, and steel, where no company earns spectacular returns on investment, to mild in industries like oil-field services and equipment, soft drinks, and toiletries, where there is room for quite high returns.

In the economists' "perfectly competitive" industry, jockeying for position is unbridled and entry to the industry very easy. This kind of industry structure, of course, offers the worst prospect for long-run profitability. The weaker the forces collectively, however, the greater the opportunity for superior performance.

Whatever their collective strength, the corporate strategist's goal is to find a position in the industry where his or her company can best defend itself against these forces or can influence them in its favor. The collective strength of the forces may be painfully apparent to all the antagonists; but to cope with them, the strategist must delve below the surface and analyze the sources of competition. For example, what makes the industry vulnerable to entry? What determines the bargaining power of suppliers?

Knowledge of these underlying sources of competitive pressure provides the groundwork for a strategic agenda of action. They highlight the critical strengths and weaknesses

---

[5] M. E. Porter, "How Competitive Forces Shape Strategy," *Harvard Business Review,* March–April 1979, pp. 137–45.

FIGURE 3–4
Forces Driving Industry Competition

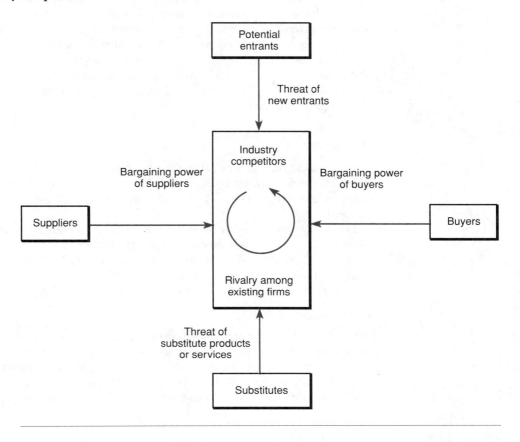

of the company, animate the positioning of the company in its industry, clarify the areas where strategic changes may yield the greatest payoff, and highlight the places where industry trends promise to hold the greatest significance as either opportunities or threats.

Understanding these sources also proves to be of help in considering areas for diversification.

CONTENDING FORCES

The strongest competitive force or forces determine the profitability of an industry and so are of greatest importance in strategy formulation. For example, even a company with a strong position in an industry unthreatened by potential entrants will earn low returns if it faces a superior or a lower-cost substitute product—as the leading manufacturers of vacuum tubes and coffee percolators have learned to their sorrow. In such a situation, coping with the substitute product becomes the number one strategic priority.

Different forces take on prominence, of course, in shaping competition in each industry. In the oceangoing tanker industry, the key force is probably the buyers (the major oil companies), while in tires it is powerful OEM buyers coupled with tough competitors. In the steel industry the key forces are foreign competitors and substitute materials.

Every industry has an underlying structure, or a set of fundamental economic and technical characteristics, that gives rise to these competitive forces. The strategist, wanting to position his or her company to cope best with its industry environment or to influence that environment in the company's favor, must learn what makes the environment tick.

This view of competition pertains equally to industries dealing in services and to those selling products. To avoid monotony, I refer to both products and services as *products*. The same general principles apply to all types of business.

A few characteristics are critical to the strength of each competitive force. They will be discussed in this section.

A. Threat of Entry

New entrants to an industry bring new capacity, the desire to gain market share, and often substantial resources. Companies diversifying through acquisition into the industry from other markets often leverage their resources to cause a shake-up, as Philip Morris did with Miller beer.

The seriousness of the threat of entry depends on the barriers present and on the reaction from existing competitors that the entrant can expect. If barriers to entry are high and a newcomer can expect sharp retaliation from the entrenched competitors, he or she obviously will not pose a serious threat of entering.

There are six major sources of barriers to entry:

1. Economies of Scale

These economies deter entry by forcing the aspirant either to come in on a large scale or to accept a cost disadvantage. Scale economies in production, research, marketing, and service are probably the key barriers to entry in the mainframe computer industry, as Xerox and GE sadly discovered. Economies of scale also can act as hurdles in distribution, utilization of the sales force, financing, and nearly any other part of a business.

2. Product Differentiation

Brand identification creates a barrier by forcing entrants to spend heavily to overcome customer loyalty. Advertising, customer service, being first in the industry, and product differences are among the factors fostering brand identification. It is perhaps the most important entry barrier in soft drinks, over-the-counter drugs, cosmetics, investment banking, and public accounting. To create high fences around their business, brewers couple brand identification with economies of scale in production, distribution, and marketing.

3. Capital Requirements

The need to invest large financial resources in order to compete creates a barrier to entry, particularly if the capital is required for unrecoverable expenditures in up-front advertising or R&D. Capital is necessary not only for fixed facilities but also for customer credit, inventories, and absorbing start-up losses. While major corporations have the financial resources to invade almost any industry, the huge capital requirements in certain fields, such as computer manufacturing and mineral extraction, limit the pool of likely entrants.

4. Cost Disadvantages Independent of Size

Entrenched companies may have cost advantages not available to potential rivals, no matter what their size and attainable economies of scale. These advantages can stem from the effects of the learning curve (and of its first cousin, the experience curve), proprietary technology, access to the best raw materials sources, assets purchased at preinflation prices, government subsidies, or favorable locations. Sometimes cost advantages are enforceable legally, as they are through patents. (For analysis of the much-discussed experience curve as a barrier to entry, see Strategy in Action 3–2.)

5. Access to Distribution Channels

The new boy or girl on the block must, of course, secure distribution of his or her product or service. A new food product, for example, must displace others from the supermarket shelf via price breaks, promotions, intense selling efforts, or some other means. The more limited the wholesale or retail channels are and the more that existing competitors have these tied up, obviously the tougher that entry into the industry will be. Sometimes this barrier is so high that, to surmount it, a new contestant must create its own distribution channels, as Timex did in the watch industry in the 1950s.

6. Government Policy

The government can limit or even foreclose entry to industries, with such controls as license requirements and limits on access to raw materials. Regulated industries like trucking, liquor retailing, and freight forwarding are noticeable examples; more subtle government restrictions operate in fields like ski-area development and coal mining. The government also can play a major indirect role by affecting entry barriers through such controls as air and water pollution standards and safety regulations.

The potential rival's expectations about the reaction of existing competitors also will influence its decision on whether to enter. The company is likely to have second thoughts if incumbents have previously lashed out at new entrants, or if:

> The incumbents possess substantial resources to fight back, including excess cash and unused borrowing power, productive capacity, or clout with distribution channels and customers.

> The incumbents seem likely to cut prices because of a desire to keep market shares or because of industrywide excess capacity.

> Industry growth is slow, affecting its ability to absorb the new arrival and probably causing the financial performance of all the parties involved to decline.

B. Powerful Suppliers

Suppliers can exert bargaining power on participants in an industry by raising prices or reducing the quality of purchased goods and services. Powerful suppliers, thereby, can squeeze profitability out of an industry unable to recover cost increases in its own prices. By raising their prices, soft-drink concentrate producers have contributed to the erosion of profitability of bottling companies because the bottlers—facing intense competition from powdered mixes, fruit drinks, and other beverages—have limited freedom to raise their prices accordingly.

The power of each important supplier (or buyer) group depends on a number of characteristics of its market situation and on the relative importance of its sales or purchases to the industry compared with its overall business.

A *supplier* group is powerful if:

1. It is dominated by a few companies and is more concentrated than the industry it sells.

2. Its product is unique or at least differentiated, or if it has built-up switching costs. Switching costs are fixed costs that buyers face in changing suppliers. These arise because, among other things, a buyer's product specifications tie it to particular suppliers, it has

THE EXPERIENCE CURVE AS AN ENTRY BARRIER

In recent years, the experience curve has become widely discussed as a key element of industry structure. According to this concept, unit costs in many manufacturing industries (some dogmatic adherents say in all manufacturing industries) as well as in some service industries decline with "experience," or a particular company's cumulative volume of production. (The experience curve, which encompasses many factors, is a broader concept than the better-known learning curve, which refers to the efficiency achieved over time by workers through much repetition.)

The causes of the decline in unit costs are a combination of elements, including economies of scale, the learning curve for labor, and capital-labor substitution. The cost decline creates a barrier to entry because new competitors with no "experience" face higher costs than established ones, particularly the producer with the largest market share, and have difficulty catching up with the entrenched competitors.

Adherents of the experience curve concept stress the importance of achieving market leadership to maximize this barrier to entry, and they recommend aggressive action to achieve it, such as price cutting in anticipation of falling costs in order to build volume. For the combatant that cannot achieve a healthy market share, the prescription is usually, "Get out."

Is the experience curve an entry barrier on which strategies should be built? The answer is: not in every industry. In fact, in some industries, building a strategy on the experience curve can be potentially disastrous. That costs decline with experience in some industries is not news to corporate executives. The significance of the experience curve for strategy depends on what factors are causing the decline.

A new entrant may well be more efficient than the more experienced competitors; if it has built the newest plant, it will face no disadvantage in having to catch up. The strategic prescription, "You must have the largest, most efficient plant," is a lot different from "You must produce the greatest cumulative output of the item to get your costs down."

Whether a drop in costs with cumulative (not absolute) volume erects an entry barrier also depends on the sources of the decline. If costs go down because of technical advances known generally in the industry or because of the development of improved equipment that can be copied or purchased from equipment suppliers, the experience curve is not an entry barrier at all—in fact, new or less- experienced competitors may actually enjoy a cost advantage over the leaders. Free of the legacy of heavy past investments, the newcomer or less-experienced competitor can purchase or copy the newest and lowest-cost equipment and technology.

If, however, experience can be kept proprietary, the leaders will maintain a cost advantage. But new entrants may require less experience to reduce their costs than the leaders needed. All this suggests that the experience curve can be a shaky entry barrier on which to build a strategy.

While space does not permit a complete treatment here, I want to mention a few other crucial elements in determining the appropriateness of a strategy built on the entry barrier provided by the experience curve:

> The height of the barrier depends on how important costs are to competition compared with other areas like marketing, selling, and innovation.
>
> The barrier can be nullified by product or process innovations leading to a substantially new technology and, thereby, creating an entirely new experience curve. New entrants can leapfrog the industry leaders and alight on the new experience curve, to which those leaders may be poorly positioned to jump.
>
> If more than one strong company is building its strategy on the experience curve, the consequences can be nearly fatal. By the time only one rival is left pursuing such a strategy, industry growth may have stopped and the prospects of reaping the spoils of victory may long since have evaporated.

invested heavily in specialized ancillary equipment or in learning how to operate a supplier's equipment (as in computer software), or its production lines are connected to the supplier's manufacturing facilities (as in some manufacturing of beverage containers).

3. It is not obliged to contend with other products for sale to the industry. For instance, the competition between the steel companies and the aluminum companies to sell to the can industry checks the power of each supplier.

4. It poses a credible threat of integrating forward into the industry's business. This provides a check against the industry's ability to improve the terms on which it purchases.

5. The industry is not an important customer of the supplier group. If the industry is an important customer, suppliers' fortunes will be tied closely to the industry, and they will want to protect the industry through reasonable pricing and assistance in activities like R&D and lobbying.

C. Powerful Buyers

Customers likewise can force down prices, demand higher quality or more service, and play competitors off against each other—all at the expense of industry profits.

A *buyer* group is powerful if:

1. It is concentrated or purchases in large volumes. Large-volume buyers are particularly potent forces if heavy fixed costs characterize the industry—as they do in metal containers, corn refining, and bulk chemicals, for example—which raise the stakes to keep capacity filled.

2. The products it purchases from the industry are standard or undifferentiated. The buyers, sure that they always can find alternative suppliers, may play one company against another, as they do in aluminum extrusion.

3. The products it purchases from the industry form a component of its product and represent a significant fraction of its cost. The buyers are likely to shop for a favorable price and purchase selectively. Where the product sold by the industry in question is a small fraction of buyers' costs, buyers are usually much less price sensitive.

4. It earns low profits, which create great incentive to lower its purchasing costs. Highly profitable buyers, however, are generally less price sensitive (i.e., of course, if the item does not represent a large fraction of their costs).

5. The industry's product is unimportant to the quality of the buyers' products or services. Where the quality of the buyers' products is very much affected by the industry's product, buyers are generally less price sensitive. Industries in which this situation exists include oil-field equipment, where a malfunction can lead to large losses and enclosures for electronic medical and test instruments, where the quality of the enclosure can influence the user's impression about the quality of the equipment inside.

6. The industry's product does not save the buyer money. Where the industry's product or service can pay for itself many times over, the buyer is rarely price sensitive; rather, he or she is interested in quality. This is true in services like investment banking and public accounting, where errors in judgment can be costly and embarrassing, and in businesses like the mapping of oil wells, where an accurate survey can save thousands of dollars in drilling costs.

7. The buyers pose a credible threat of integrating backward to make the industry's product. The Big Three auto producers and major buyers of cars often have used the threat of self-manufacture as a bargaining lever. But sometimes an industry so engenders a threat to buyers that its members may integrate forward.

Most of these sources of buyer power can be attributed to consumers as a group as well as to industrial and commercial buyers; only a modification of the frame of reference is necessary. Consumers tend to be more price sensitive if they are purchasing products that are undifferentiated, expensive relative to their incomes, and of a sort where quality is not particularly important.

The buying power of retailers is determined by the same rules, with one important addition. Retailers can gain significant bargaining power over manufacturers when they can influence consumers' purchasing decisions, as they do in audio components, jewelry, appliances, sporting goods, and other goods.

D. Substitute Products

By placing a ceiling on the prices it can charge, substitute products or services limit the potential of an industry. Unless it can upgrade the quality of the product or differentiate it somehow (as via marketing), the industry will suffer in earnings and possibly in growth.

Manifestly, the more attractive the price-performance trade-off offered by substitute products, the firmer the lid placed on the industry's profit potential. Sugar producers confronted with the large-scale commercialization of high-fructose corn syrup, a sugar substitute, are learning this lesson today.

Substitutes not only limit profits in normal times but also reduce the bonanza an industry can reap in boom times. In 1978, the producers of fiberglass insulation enjoyed unprecedented demand as a result of high energy costs and severe winter weather. But the industry's ability to raise prices was tempered by the plethora of insulation substitutes, including cellulose, rock wool, and Styrofoam. These substitutes are bound to become an even stronger force once the current round of plant additions by fiberglass insulation producers has boosted capacity enough to meet demand (and then some).

Substitute products that deserve the most attention strategically are those that *(a)* are subject to trends improving their price-performance trade-off with the industry's product or *(b)* are produced by industries earning high profits. Substitutes often come rapidly into play if some development increases competition in their industries and causes price reduction or performance improvement.

E. Jockeying for Position

Rivalry among existing competitors takes the familiar form of jockeying for position—using tactics like price competition, product introduction, and advertising slugfests. This type of intense rivalry is related to the presence of a number of factors:

1. Competitors are numerous or are roughly equal in size and power. In many U.S. industries in recent years, foreign contenders, of course, have become part of the competitive picture.

2. Industry growth is slow, precipitating fights for market share that involve expansion-minded members.

3. The product or service lacks differentiation or switching costs, which lock in buyers and protect one combatant from raids on its customers by another.

4. Fixed costs are high or the product is perishable, creating strong temptation to cut prices. Many basic materials businesses, like paper and aluminum, suffer from this problem when demand slackens.

5. Capacity normally is augmented in large increments. Such additions, as in the chlorine and vinyl chloride businesses, disrupt the industry's supply-demand balance and often lead to periods of overcapacity and price cutting.

6. Exit barriers are high. Exit barriers, like very specialized assets or management's loyalty to a particular business, keep companies competing even though they may be

earning low or even negative returns on investment. Excess capacity remains functioning, and the profitability of the healthy competitors suffers as the sick ones hang on. If the entire industry suffers from overcapacity, it may seek government help—particularly if foreign competition is present.

7. The rivals are diverse in strategies, origins, and "personalities." They have different ideas about how to compete and continually run head-on into each other in the process.

As an industry matures, its growth rate changes, resulting in declining profits and (often) a shakeout. In the booming recreational vehicle industry of the early 1970s, nearly every producer did well; but slow growth since then has eliminated the high returns, except for the strongest members, not to mention many of the weaker companies. The same profit story has been played out in industry after industry—snowmobiles, aerosol packaging, and sports equipment are just a few examples.

An acquisition can introduce a very different personality to an industry, as has been the case with Black & Decker's takeover of McCullough, the producer of chain saws. Technological innovation can boost the level of fixed costs in the production process, as it did in the shift from batch to continuous-line photo finishing in the 1960s.

While a company must live with many of these factors—because they are built into the industry economics—it may have some latitude for improving matters through strategic shifts. For example, it may try to raise buyers' switching costs or increase product differentiation. A focus on selling efforts in the fastest-growing segments of the industry or on market areas with the lowest fixed costs can reduce the impact of industry rivalry. If it is feasible, a company can try to avoid confrontation with competitors having high exit barriers and, thus, can sidestep involvement in bitter price cutting.

INDUSTRY ANALYSIS AND COMPETITIVE ANALYSIS

Designing viable strategies for a firm requires a thorough understanding of the firm's industry and competition. The firm's executives need to address four questions: (1) What are the boundaries of the industry? (2) What is the structure of the industry? (3) Which firms are our competitors? (4) What are the major determinants of competition? The answers to these questions provide a basis for thinking about the appropriate strategies that are open to the firm.

INDUSTRY BOUNDARIES

An industry is a collection of firms that offer similar products or services. By "similar products," we mean products that customers perceive to be substitutable for one another. Consider, for example, the brands of personal computers (PCs) that are now being marketed. The firms that produce these PCs, such as AT&T, IBM, Apple, and Compaq, form the nucleus of the microcomputer industry.

Suppose a firm competes in the microcomputer industry. Where do the boundaries of this industry begin and end? Does the industry include desktops? Laptops? These are the kinds of questions that executives face in defining industry boundaries.

Why is a definition of industry boundaries important? First, it helps executives determine the arena in which their firm is competing. A firm competing in the microcomputer industry participates in an environment very different from that of the broader electronics business. The microcomputer industry comprises several related product families, including personal computers, inexpensive computers for home use, and workstations. The unifying characteristic of these product families is the use of a central processing unit (CPU) in a microchip. On the other hand, the electronics industry is far more extensive; it includes computers, radios, supercomputers, superconductors, and many other products.

The microcomputer and electronics industries differ in their volume of sales, their scope (some would consider microcomputers a segment of the electronics industry), their rate of growth, and their competitive makeup. The dominant issues faced by the two industries also are different. Witness, for example, the raging public debate being waged on the future of the "high-definition TV." U.S. policymakers are attempting to ensure domestic control of that segment of the electronics industry. They also are considering ways to stimulate "cutting-edge" research in superconductivity. These efforts are likely to spur innovation and stimulate progress in the electronics industry. In contrast, the same policymakers are attempting to ensure that microcomputer technology does not reach Eastern Bloc countries. These efforts will restrict the scope of international markets for microcomputer producers.

Second, a definition of industry boundaries focuses attention on the firm's competitors. Defining industry boundaries enables the firm to identify its competitors and producers of substitute products. This is critically important to the firm's design of its competitive strategy.

Third, a definition of industry boundaries helps executives determine key factors for success. Survival in the premier segment of the microcomputer industry requires skills that are considerably different from those required in the lower end of the industry. Firms that compete in the premier segment need to be on the cutting edge of technological development and to provide extensive customer support and education. On the other hand, firms that compete in the lower end need to excel in imitating the products introduced by the premier segment, to focus on customer convenience, and to maintain operational efficiency that permits them to charge the lowest market price. Defining industry boundaries enables executives to ask these questions: Do we have the skills it takes to succeed here? If not, what must we do to develop these skills?

Finally, a definition of industry boundaries gives executives another basis on which to evaluate their firm's goals. Executives use that definition to forecast demand for their firm's products and services. Armed with that forecast, they can determine whether those goals are realistic.

Problems in Defining Industry Boundaries

Defining industry boundaries requires both caution and imagination. Caution is necessary because there are no precise rules for this task and because a poor definition will lead to poor planning. Imagination is necessary because industries are dynamic—in every industry, important changes are under way in such key factors as competition, technology, and consumer demand.

Defining industry boundaries is a very difficult task. The difficulty stems from three sources:

1. The evolution of industries over time creates new opportunities and threats. Compare the financial services industry as we know it today with that of the 1970s and 1980s, and then try to imagine how different the industry will be in the year 2000.

2. Industrial evolution creates industries within industries. The electronics industry of the 1960s has been transformed into many "industries"—TV sets, transistor radios, micro- and macrocomputers, supercomputers, superconductors, and so on. Such transformation allows some firms to specialize and others to compete in different, related industries.

3. Industries are becoming global in scope. Consider the civilian aircraft manufacturing industry. For nearly three decades, U.S. firms dominated world production in that

FIGURE 3–5
Computer Industry Product Segments

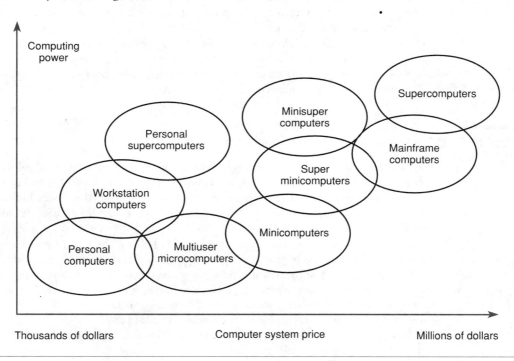

Source: Egil Juliussen and Karen Juliussen, *The Computer Industry Almanac* (New York: Simon & Schuster, 1988), p. 1.11.

industry. But small and large competitors were challenging their dominance by 1990. At that time, Airbus Industries (a consortium of European firms) and Brazilian, Korean, and Japanese firms were actively competing in the industry.

Developing a Realistic Industry Definition

Given the difficulties outlined above, how do executives draw accurate boundaries for an industry? The starting point is a definition of the industry in global terms; that is, in terms that consider the industry's international components as well as its domestic components.

Having developed a preliminary concept of the industry (e.g., computers), executives flesh out its current components. This can be done by defining its product segments, as illustrated in Figure 3–5. Executives need to select the scope of their firm's potential market from among these related but distinct areas.

To understand the makeup of the industry, executives adopt a longitudinal perspective. They examine the emergence and evolution of product families. Why did these product families arise? How and why did they change? The answers to such questions provide executives with clues about the factors that drive competition in the industry.

Executives also examine the companies that offer different product families, the overlapping or distinctiveness of customer segments, and the rate of substitutability among product families.

To realistically define their industry, executives need to examine five issues:

1. Which part of the industry corresponds to our firm's goals?
2. What are the key ingredients of success in that part of the industry?
3. Does our firm have the skills needed to compete in that part of the industry? If not, can we build those skills?
4. Will the skills enable us to seize emerging opportunities and deal with future threats?
5. Is our definition of the industry flexible enough to allow necessary adjustments to our business concept as the industry grows?

INDUSTRY STRUCTURE

Defining an industry's boundaries is incomplete without an understanding of its structural attributes. *Structural attributes* are the enduring characteristics that give an industry its distinctive character. Consider the cable television and financial services industries. Both industries are competitive, and both are important for our quality of life. But these industries have very different requirements for success. To succeed in the cable television industry, firms require vertical integration, which helps them lower their operating costs and ensures their access to quality programs; technological innovation, to enlarge the scope of their services and deliver them in new ways; and extensive marketing, using appropriate segmentation techniques to locate potentially viable niches. To succeed in the financial services industry, firms need to meet very different requirements, among which are extensive orientation of customers and an extensive capital base.

How can we explain such variations among industries? The answer lies in examining the four variables that industry comprises: (1) concentration, (2) economies of scale, (3) product differentiation, and (4) barriers to entry.

Concentration

This variable refers to the extent to which industry sales are dominated by only a few firms. In a highly concentrated industry (i.e., an industry whose sales are dominated by a handful of companies), the intensity of competition declines over time. High concentration serves as a barrier to entry into an industry, because it enables the firms that hold large market shares to achieve significant economies of scale (e.g., savings in production costs due to increased production quantities) and, thus, to lower their prices to stymie attempts of new firms to enter the market.

The U.S. aircraft manufacturing industry is highly concentrated. In 1988, its concentration ratio—the percent of market share held by the top four firms in the industry—was 67 percent. Competition in the industry has not been vigorous. Firms in the industry have been able to deter entry through proprietary technologies and the formation of strategic alliances (e.g., joint ventures).

Economies of Scale

This variable refers to the savings that companies within an industry achieve due to increased volume. Simply put, when the volume of production increases, the long-range average cost of a unit produced will decline.

Economies of scale result from technological and nontechnological sources. The technological sources are a higher level of mechanization or automation and a greater up-to-dateness of plant and facilities. The nontechnological sources include better managerial coordination of production functions and processes, long-term contractual agreements with suppliers, and enhanced employee performance arising from specialization.

Economies of scale are an important determinant of the intensity of competition in an industry. Firms that enjoy such economies can charge lower prices than their competitors. They also can create barriers to entry by reducing their prices temporarily or permanently to deter new firms from entering the industry.

Product Differentiation

This variable refers to the extent to which customers perceive products or services offered by firms in the industry as different.

The differentiation of products can be real or perceived. The differentiation between Apple's Macintosh and IBM's PS/2 Personal Computer is a prime example of real differentiation. These products differ significantly in their technology and performance. Similarly, the civilian aircraft models produced by Boeing differ markedly from those produced by Airbus. The differences result from the use of different design principles and different construction technologies. For example, the newer Airbus planes follow the principle of "fly by wire," whereas Boeing planes utilize the laws of hydraulics. Thus, in Boeing planes, wings are activated by mechanical handling of different parts of the plane, whereas in the Airbus planes, this is done almost automatically.

Perceived differentiation results from the way in which firms position their products and from their success in persuading customers that their products differ significantly from competing products. Marketing strategies provide the vehicles through which this is done. Witness, for example, the extensive advertising campaigns of the automakers, each of which attempts to convey an image of distinctiveness. BMW ads highlight the excellent engineering of the BMW and its symbolic value as a sign of achievement. Some automakers focus on roominess and durability, which are desirable attributes for the family segment of the automobile market.

Real and perceived differentiations often intensify competition among existing firms. On the other hand, successful differentiation poses a competitive disadvantage for firms that attempt to enter an industry.

Barriers to Entry

As Porter noted earlier in this chapter, barriers to entry are the obstacles that a firm must overcome to enter an industry. The barriers can be tangible or intangible. The tangible barriers include capital requirements, technological know-how, resources, and the laws regulating entry into an industry. The intangible barriers include the reputation of existing firms, the loyalty of consumers to existing brands, and access to the managerial skills required for successful operation in an industry.

Entry barriers both increase and reflect the level of concentration, economies of scale, and product differentiation in an industry, and such increases make it more difficult for new firms to enter the industry. Therefore, when high barriers exist in an industry, competition in that industry declines over time.

In summary, analysis of concentration, economies of scale, product differentiation, and barriers to entry in an industry enables a firm's executives to understand the forces that determine competition in an industry and sets the stage for identifying the firm's competitors and how they position themselves in the marketplace.

Industry regulations are a key element of industry structure and can constitute a significant barrier to entry for corporations. Escalating regulatory standards costs have been a

FIGURE 3–6
Innovation-Friendly Regulation

Regulation, properly conceived, need not drive up costs. The following principles of regulatory design will promote innovation, resource productivity, and competitiveness.

Focus on Outcomes, Not Technologies.

Past regulations have often prescribed particular remediation technologies, such as catalysts or scrubbers for air pollution. The phrases "best available technology" (BAT) and "best available control technology" (BACT) are deeply rooted in U.S. practice and imply that one technology is best, thus discouraging innovation.

Enact Strict Rather Than Lax Regulation.

Companies can handle lax regulation incrementally, often with end-of-pipe or secondary treatment solutions. Regulation, therefore, needs to be stringent enough to promote real innovation.

Regulate as Close to the End User as Practical, While Encouraging Upstream Solutions.

This will normally allow more flexibility for innovation in the end product and in all the production and distribution stages. Avoiding pollution entirely or, second best, mitigating it early in the value chain is almost always less costly than late-stage remediation or cleanup.

Employ Phase-In Periods.

Ample but well-defined phase-in periods tied to industry-capital-investment cycles will allow companies to develop innovative resource-saving technologies rather than force them to implement expensive solutions hastily, merely patching over problems.

Use Market Incentives.

Market incentives such as pollution charges and deposit-refund schemes draw attention to resource inefficiencies. In addition, tradable permits provide continuing incentives for innovation and encourage creative use of technologies that exceed current standards.

Harmonize or Converge Regulations in Associated Fields.

Liability exposure in the United States leads companies to stick to safe, BAT approaches, and inconsistent regulation on alternative technologies deters beneficial innovation. For example, one way to eliminate refrigerator cooling agents suspected of damaging the ozone layer involves replacing them with small amounts of propane and butane. But narrowly conceived safety regulations covering these gases seem to have impeded development of the new technology in the United States, while several leading European companies are already marketing the new products.

serious concern for corporations for years. As legislative bodies continue their stronghold on corporate activities, businesses feel the impact on their bottom line. In-house counsel departments have been perhaps the most significant additions to corporate structure in the past decade. Legal fees have skyrocketed and managers have learned the hard way about the importance of adhering to regulatory standards. Figure 3–6 presents some key principles that enable corporations to abide by the ever-increasing regulations while keeping costs down, maintaining competitiveness, and enhancing creativity.

COMPETITIVE ANALYSIS

Competitive analysis usually has these objectives: (1) to identify current and potential competitors, (2) to identify potential moves by competitors, and (3) to help the firm devise effective competitive strategies.

How to Identify Competitors

In identifying their firm's current and potential competitors, executives consider several important variables:

FIGURE 3–6
(concluded)

Develop Regulations in Sync with Other Countries or Slightly Ahead of Them.

It is important to minimize possible competitive disadvantages relative to foreign companies that are not yet subject to the same standard. Developing regulations slightly ahead of other countries will also maximize export potential in the pollution-control sector by raising incentives for innovation.

Make the Regulatory Process More Stable and Predictable.

The regulatory process is as important as the standards. If standards and phase-in periods are set and accepted early enough and if regulators commit to keeping standards in place for, say, five years, industry can lock in and tackle root-cause solutions instead of government philosophy.

Require Industry Participation in Setting Standards from the Beginning.

U.S. regulation differs sharply from European regulation in its adversarial approach. Industry should help in designing phase-in periods, the content of regulations, and the most effective regulatory process.

Develop Strong Technical Capabilities among Regulators.

Regulators must understand an industry's economics and what drives its competitiveness. Better information exchange will help avoid costly gaming in which ill-informed companies use an array of lawyers and consultants to try to stall the poorly designed regulations of ill-informed regulators.

Minimize the Time and Resources Consumed in the Regulatory Process Itself.

Time delays in granting permits are usually costly for companies. Self-regulation with periodic inspections would be more efficient than requiring formal approvals. Potential and actual litigation creates uncertainty and consumes resources. Mandatory arbitration procedures or rigid arbitration steps before litigation would lower costs and encourage innovation.

Source: Reprinted by permission of *Harvard Business Review*. An excerpt from "Green and Competitive," by Michael E. Porter and Claas van der Linde, September–October 1995. Copyright © 1995 by the President and Fellows of Harvard University, all rights reserved.

1. How do other firms define the scope of their market? The more similar the definitions of firms, the more likely the firms will view each other as competitors.

2. How similar are the benefits the customers derive from the products and services that other firms offer? The more similar the benefits of products or services, the higher the level of substitutability between them. High substitutability levels force firms to compete fiercely for customers.

3. How committed are other firms to the industry? Although this question may appear to be far removed from the identification of competitors, it is in fact one of the most important questions that competitive analysis must address, because it sheds light on the long-term intentions and goals. To size up the commitment of potential competitors to the industry, reliable intelligence data are needed. Such data may relate to potential resource commitments (e.g., planned facility expansions).

Common Mistakes in Identifying Competitors

Identifying competitors is a milestone in the development of strategy. But it is a process laden with uncertainty and risk, a process in which executives sometimes make costly mistakes. Examples of these mistakes are:

1. Overemphasizing current and known competitors while giving inadequate attention to potential entrants.

2. Overemphasizing large competitors while ignoring small competitors.

3. Overlooking potential international competitors.

4. Assuming that competitors will continue to behave in the same way they have behaved in the past.

5. Misreading signals that may indicate a shift in the focus of competitors or a refinement of their present strategies or tactics.

6. Overemphasizing competitors' financial resources, market position, and strategies while ignoring their intangible assets, such as a top-management team.

7. Assuming that all of the firms in the industry are subject to the same constraints or are open to the same opportunities.

8. Believing that the purpose of strategy is to outsmart the competition, rather than to satisfy customer needs and expectations.

OPERATING ENVIRONMENT

The operating environment, also called the *competitive* or *task environment,* comprises factors in the competitive situation that affect a firm's success in acquiring needed resources or in profitably marketing its goods and services. Among the most important of these factors are the firm's competitive position, the composition of its customers, its reputation among suppliers and creditors, and its ability to attract capable employees. The operating environment is typically much more subject to the firm's influence or control than the remote environment. Thus, firms can be much more proactive (as opposed to reactive) in dealing with the operating environment than in dealing with the remote environment.

1. Competitive Position

Assessing its competitive position improves a firm's chances of designing strategies that optimize its environmental opportunities. Development of competitor profiles enables a firm to more accurately forecast both its short- and long-term growth and its profit potentials. Although the exact criteria used in constructing a competitor's profile are largely determined by situational factors, the following criteria are often included:

1. Market share
2. Breadth of product line.
3. Effectiveness of sales distribution.
4. Proprietary and key-account advantages.
5. Price competitiveness.
6. Advertising and promotion effectiveness.
7. Location and age of facility.
8. Capacity and productivity.
9. Experience.
10. Raw materials costs.
11. Financial position.
12. Relative product quality.
13. R&D advantages position.
14. Caliber of personnel.
15. General images.[6]

Once appropriate criteria have been selected, they are weighted to reflect their importance to a firm's success. Then the competitor being evaluated is rated on the criteria, the ratings are multiplied by the weight, and the weighted scores are summed to yield a numerical profile of the competitor, as shown in Figure 3–7.

---

[6] These items were selected from a matrix for assessing competitive position proposed by C. W. Hofer and D. Schendel, *Strategy Formulation: Analytical Concepts* (St. Paul, MN: West Publishing, 1978), p. 76.

FIGURE 3–7
Competitor Profile

Key Success Factors	Weight	Rating†	Weighted Score
Market share	0.30	4	1.20
Price competitiveness	0.20	3	0.60
Facilities location	0.20	5	1.00
Raw materials costs	0.10	3	0.30
Caliber of personnel	0.20	1	0.20
	1.00*		3.30

* The total of the weights must always equal 1.00.
† The rating scale suggested is as follows: very strong competitive position (5 points), strong (4), average (3), weak (2), very weak (1).

This type of competitor profile is limited by the subjectivity of its criteria selection, weighting, and evaluation approaches. Nevertheless, the process of developing such profiles is of considerable help to a firm in defining its perception of its competitive position. Moreover, comparing the firm's profile with those of its competitors can aid its managers in identifying factors that might make the competitors vulnerable to the strategies the firm might choose to implement.

2. Customer Profiles

Perhaps the most vulnerable result of analyzing the operating environment is the understanding of a firm's customers that this provides. Developing a profile of a firm's present and prospective customers improves the ability of its managers to plan strategic operations, to anticipate changes in the size of markets, and to reallocate resources so as to support forecast shifts in demand patterns. The traditional approach to segmenting customers is based on customer profiles constructed from geographic, demographic, psychographic, and buyer behavior information, as illustrated in Figure 3–8.

Enterprising companies have quickly learned the importance of identifying target segments. In recent years, market research has increased tremendously as companies realize the benefits of demographic and psychographic segmentation. Research by American Express showed that competitors were stealing a prime segment of the company's business, affluent business travelers. AMEX's competing companies, including Visa and Mastercard, began offering high-spending business travelers frequent flier programs and other rewards including discounts on new cars. In turn, AMEX began to invest heavily in rewards programs, while also focusing on its strongest capabilities, assets, and competitive advantage. Unlike most credit card companies, AMEX cannot rely on charging interest to make money because its customers pay in full each month. Therefore, the company charges higher transaction fees to its merchants. In this way, increases in spending by AMEX customers who pay off their balances each month are more profitable to AMEX than to competing credit card companies. As Strategy in Action 3–3 shows, successful segmentation has paid off.

Assessing consumer behavior is a key element in the process of satisfying your target market needs. Many firms lose market share as a result of assumptions made about target segments. Market research and industry surveys can help to reduce a firm's chances of relying on illusive assumptions. Firms most vulnerable are those that have had success with one or more products in the marketplace and as a result try to base consumer behavior on past data and trends. Some dangerous implicit assumptions are listed in Figure 3–9.

FIGURE 3–8
Major Segmentation Variables for Consumer Markets

Variable	Typical Breakdowns
Geographic	
Region	Pacific, Mountain, West North Central, West South Central, East North Central, East South Central, South Atlantic, Middle Atlantic, New England.
County size	A, B, C, D.
City or SMSA size	Under 5,000; 5,000–20,000; 20,000–50,000; 50,000–100,000; 100,000–250,000; 250,000–500,000; 500,000–1,000,000; 1,000,000–4,000,000; 4,000,000 or over.
Density	Urban, suburban, rural.
Climate	Northern, southern.
Demographic	
Age	Under 6, 6–11, 12–19, 20–34, 35–49, 50–64, 65+.
Sex	Male, female.
Family size	1–2, 3–4, 5+.
Family life cycle	Young, single; young, married, no children; young, married, youngest child under 6; young, married, youngest child 6 or over; older, married, with children; older, married, no children under 18; older, single; other.
Income	Under $10,000; $10,000–$15,000; $15,000–$20,000; $20,000–$25,000; $25,000–$30,000; $30,000–$50,000; $50,000 and over.
Occupation	Professional and technical; managers, officials, and proprietors; clerical, sales; craftspeople, foremen; operatives; farmers; retired; students; housewives; unemployed.
Education	Grade school or less; some high school; high school graduate; some college; college graduate.
Religion	Catholic, Protestant, Jewish, other.
Race	White, Black, Oriental.
Nationality	American, British, French, German, Scandinavian, Italian, Latin American, Middle Eastern, Japanese.
Psychographic	
Social class	Lower lowers, upper lowers, working class, middle class, upper middles, lower uppers, upper uppers.
Lifestyle	Straights, swingers, longhairs.
Personality	Compulsive, gregarious, authoritarian, ambitious.
Behavioral	
Occasions	Regular occasion, special occasion.
Benefits	Quality, service, economy.
User status	Nonuser, ex-user, potential user, first-time user, regular user.
Usage rate	Light user, medium user, heavy user.
Loyalty status	None, medium, strong, absolute.
Readiness stage	Unaware, aware, informed, interested, desirous, intending to buy.
Attitude toward product	Enthusiastic, positive, indifferent, negative, hostile.

SMSA stands for standard metropolitan statistical area.
Source: *Marketing Management,* 7/e by Kotler, © 1991. Adapted by permission of Prentice Hall, Inc., Upper Saddle River, NJ.

Geographic

It is important to define the geographic area from which customers do or could come. Almost every product or service has some quality that makes it variably attractive to buyers from different locations. Obviously, a Wisconsin manufacturer of snow skis should think twice about investing in a wholesale distribution center in South Carolina. On the other

CUSTOMER SEGMENTATION AT AMEX

Self-selecting, individually correcting offers are new in customer segmentation. American Express is using the approach to reduce cost and shorten time-to-market when it tests new value propositions. One example is its recent *zero spender stimulation test*.

Zero spenders are customers who hold the American Express Card and pay the annual fee but rarely or never use the card. Since those customers not only generate lower profits but also are more likely to defect than an average AMEX customer, they are an obvious target for a loyalty program. However, not all customers in this segment are of equal potential value to American Express. Some are not using the card simply because they can't afford much discretionary spending, but others are using cash or a competitor's card instead. It is the zero spender in the second category that American Express wants to target. Easier said than done.

Although zero spenders consist of two different groups, the behavior of one is indistinguishable from that of the other. To identify the subsegments, AMEX has begun testing a series of self-selecting offers designed to attract the customers who have the highest potential value.

One such offer, high in value and likely to appeal only to those with significant discretionary spending ability, is two airline tickets for heavy card use during a six-month period. The cost of the offer is high, but the cost of losing potentially valuable customers and acquiring new ones would be higher. And trying to identify valuable customers through market research could be expensive and time consuming, given the size of the company's worldwide base of customers.

Customer rewards at AMEX are, in effect, a means of delivering mass-customized value. Most companies think of mass customization as it applies to packaging and delivery, but American Express is using reward to mass-customize the value proposition itself. The approach allows the company to test an unprecedented variety of offers and products while lowering costs and speeding time-to-market. All products and offers are designed not only to appeal to desired target segments but also to allow the customers to select the relevant propositions, thereby identifying themselves and making targeted marketing easier in the future. As a global company, AMEX can correlate lessons learned from one market with other markets—lessons showing which products and offers customers prefer and which behavior and profits each proposition generates.

hand, advertising in the *Milwaukee Sun-Times* could significantly expand the geographically defined customer market of a major Myrtle Beach hotel in South Carolina.

Demographic

Demographic variables most commonly are used to differentiate groups of present or potential customers. Demographic information (e.g., information on sex, age, marital status, income, and occupation) is comparatively easy to collect, quantify, and use in strategic forecasting, and such information is the minimum basis for a customer profile.

Psychographic

Personality and lifestyle variables often are better predictors of customer purchasing behavior than geographic or demographic variables. In such situations, a psychographic study is an important component of the customer profile. Recent advertising campaigns by soft-drink producers—Pepsi-Cola ("the Pepsi generation"), Coca-Cola ("catch the

FIGURE 3–9
Some Dangerous Implicit Assumptions

1. Customers will buy our product because we think it's a good product.
2. Customers will buy our product because it's technically superior.
3. Customers will agree with our perception that the product is "great."
4. Customers run no risk in buying from us instead of continuing to buy from their past suppliers.
5. The product will sell itself.
6. Distributors are desperate to stock and service the product.
7. We can develop the product on time and on budget.
8. We will have no trouble attracting the right staff.
9. Competitors will respond rationally.
10. We can insulate our product from competition.
11. We will be able to hold down prices while gaining share rapidly.
12. The rest of our company will gladly support our strategy and provide help as needed.

Source: Reprinted by permission of *Harvard Business Review*. An excerpt from "Discovery-Driven Planning," by Rita Gunther McGrath and Ian C. MacMillan, July–August 1995. Copyright © by the President and Fellows of Harvard University, all rights reserved.

wave"), and 7UP ("America's turning 7UP")—reflect strategic management's attention to the psychographic characteristics of their largest customer segment—physically active, group-oriented nonprofessionals.

Buyer Behavior

Buyer behavior data also can be a component of the customer profile. Such data are used to explain or predict some aspect of customer behavior with regard to a product or service. As Figure 3–8 indicates, information on buyer behavior (e.g., usage rate, benefits sought, and brand loyalty) can provide significant aid in the design of more accurate and profitable strategies.

A second approach to identifying customer groups is by segmenting industrial markets. As shown in Figure 3–10, there is considerable overlap between the variables used to segment individual and industrial consumers, but the definition of the customer differs.

3. Suppliers

Dependable relationships between a firm and its suppliers are essential to the firm's long-term survival and growth. A firm regularly relies on its suppliers for financial support, services, materials, and equipment. In addition, it occasionally is forced to make special requests for such favors as quick delivery, liberal credit terms, or broken-lot orders. Particularly at such times, it is essential for a firm to have had an ongoing relationship with its suppliers.

In assessing a firm's relationships with its suppliers, several factors, other than the strength of that relationship, should be considered. With regard to its competitive position with its suppliers, the firm should address the following questions:

Are the suppliers' prices competitive? Do the suppliers offer attractive quantity discounts?

How costly are their shipping charges? Are the suppliers competitive in terms of production standards?

In terms of deficiency rates, are the suppliers' abilities, reputations, and services competitive?

Are the suppliers reciprocally dependent on the firm?

FIGURE 3–10
Major Segmentation Variables for Industrial Markets

Demographic

Industry: Which industries that buy this product should we focus on?
Company size: What size companies should we focus on?
Location: What geographical areas should we focus on?

Operating Variables

Technology: What customer technologies should we focus on?
User-nonuser status: Should we focus on heavy, medium, light users or nonusers?
Customer capabilities: Should we focus on customers needing many services or few services?

Purchasing Approaches

Purchasing-function organization: Should we focus on companies with highly centralized or decentralized purchasing organizations?
Power structure: Should we focus on companies that are engineering dominated? financially dominated? other ways dominated?
Nature of existing relationships: Should we focus on companies with which we have strong existing relationships or simply go after the most desirable companies?
General purchase policies: Should we focus on companies that prefer leasing? service contracts? systems purchases? sealed bidding?
Purchasing criteria: Should we focus on companies that are seeking quality? service? price?

Situational Factors

Urgency: Should we focus on companies that need quick and sudden delivery or service?
Specific application: Should we focus on certain applications of our product, rather than all applications?
Size of order: Should we focus on large or small orders?

Perfect Characteristics

Buyer-seller similarity: Should we focus on companies whose people and values are similar to ours?
Attitudes toward risk: Should we focus on risk-taking or risk-avoiding customers?
Loyalty: Should we focus on companies that show high loyalty to their suppliers?

Source: Adapted from Thomas V. Bonoma and Benson P. Shapiro, *Segmenting the Industrial Market* (Lexington, MA: Lexington Books, 1983).

4. Creditors

Because the quantity, quality, price, and accessibility of financial, human, and material resources are rarely ideal, assessment of suppliers and creditors is critical to an accurate evaluation of a firm's operating environment. With regard to its competitive position with its creditors, among the most important questions that the firm should address are the following:

Do the creditors fairly value and willingly accept the firm's stock as collateral?

Do the creditors perceive the firm as having an acceptable record of past payment? A strong working capital position? Little or no leverage?

Are the creditors' loan terms compatible with the firm's profitability objectives?

Are the creditors able to extend the necessary lines of credit?

The answers to these and related questions help a firm forecast the availability of the resources it will need to implement and sustain its competitive strategies.

5. Human Resources: Nature of the Labor Market

A firm's ability to attract and hold capable employees is essential to its success. However, a firm's personnel recruitment and selection alternatives often are influenced by the nature of its operating environment. A firm's access to needed personnel is affected primarily by three factors: the firm's reputation as an employer, local employment rates, and the ready availability of people with the needed skills.

Reputation

A firm's reputation within its operating environment is a major element of its ability to satisfy its personnel needs. A firm is more likely to attract and retain valuable employees if it is seen as permanent in the community, competitive in its compensation package, and concerned with the welfare of its employees, and if it is respected for its product or service and appreciated for its overall contribution to the general welfare.

Employment Rates

The readily available supply of skilled and experienced personnel may vary considerably with the stage of a community's growth. A new manufacturing firm would find it far more difficult to obtain skilled employees in a vigorous industrialized community than in an economically depressed community in which similar firms had recently cut back operations.

Availability

The skills of some people are so specialized that relocation may be necessary to secure the jobs and the compensation that those skills commonly command. People with such skills include oil drillers, chefs, technical specialists, and industry executives. A firm that seeks to hire such a person is said to have broad labor market boundaries; that is, the geographic area within which the firm might reasonably expect to attract qualified candidates is quite large. On the other hand, people with more common skills are less likely to relocate from a considerable distance to achieve modest economic or career advancements. Thus, the labor market boundaries are fairly limited for such occupational groups as unskilled laborers, clerical personnel, and retail clerks.

EMPHASIS ON ENVIRONMENTAL FACTORS

This chapter has described the remote, industry, and operating environments as encompassing five components each. While that description is generally accurate, it may give the false impression that the components are easily identified, mutually exclusive, and equally applicable in all situations. In fact, the forces in the external environment are so dynamic and interactive that the impact of any single element cannot be wholly disassociated from the impact of other elements. For example, are increases in OPEC oil prices the result of economic, political, social, or technological changes? Or are a manufacturer's surprisingly good relations with suppliers a result of competitors', customers', or creditors' activities or of the supplier's own activities? The answer to both questions is probably that a number of forces in the external environment have combined to create the situation. Such is the case in most studies of the environment.

In a recent study involving more than 200 company executives, the respondents were asked to identify key planning issues in terms of their increasing importance to strategic success. As shown in Figure 3–11, domestic competitive trends, customer or end-user preferences, and technological trends were the issues they selected most often.

Strategic managers are frequently frustrated in their attempts to anticipate the environment's changing influences. Different external elements affect different strategies at different times and with varying strengths. The only certainty is that the impact of the remote and operating environments will be uncertain until a strategy is implemented. This leads many

FIGURE 3–11
Key Planning Issues

Issue	Percent of Respondents Indicating		
	Increase	No Change	Decrease
1. Competitive (domestic) trends	83.6%	13.5%	2.9%
2. Customer or end-user preferences	69.0	29.1	2.0
3. Technological trends	71.4	25.6	3.0
4. Diversification opportunities	61.7	30.3	8.0
5. Worldwide or global competition	59.4	34.4	6.3
6. Internal capabilities	55.4	40.2	4.4
7. Joint venture opportunities	56.6	36.7	6.6
8. Qualitative data	55.9	38.1	5.9
9. General economic and business conditions	46.4	47.3	6.3
10. Regulatory issues	42.8	51.2	6.0
11. Supplier trends	26.0	69.1	5.0
12. Reasons for past failures	27.6	62.3	10.1
13. Quantitative data	36.8	40.7	22.5
14. Past performance	27.3	51.2	21.5

Source: Adapted from V. Ramanujam, J. C. Camillus, and N. Venkatraman, "Trends in Strategic Planning," in *Strategic Planning and Management Handbook,* ed. W. R. King and D. I. Cleland (New York: Van Nostrand Reinhold, 1987), p. 615.

managers, particularly in less-powerful or smaller firms to minimize long-term planning, which requires a commitment of resources. Instead, they favor allowing managers to adapt to new pressures from the environment. While such a decision has considerable merit for many firms, there is an associated trade-off, namely that absence of a strong resource and psychological commitment to a proactive strategy effectively bars a firm from assuming a leadership role in its competitive environment.

There is yet another difficulty in assessing the probable impact of remote, industry, and operating environments on the effectiveness of alternative strategies. Assessment of this kind involves collecting information that can be analyzed to disclose predictable effects. Except in rare instances, however, it is virtually impossible for any single firm to anticipate the consequences of a change in the environment; for example, the precise effect on alternative strategies of a 2 percent increase in the national inflation rate, a 1 percent decrease in statewide unemployment, or the entry of a new competitor in a regional market.

Still, assessing the potential impact of changes in the external environment offers a real advantage. It enables decision makers to narrow the range of the available options and to eliminate options that are clearly inconsistent with the forecast opportunities. Environmental assessment seldom identifies the best strategy, but it generally leads to the elimination of all but the most promising options.

SUMMARY

A firm's external environment consists of three interrelated sets of factors that play a principal role in determining the opportunities, threats, and constraints that the firm faces. The remote environment comprises factors originating beyond, and usually irrespective of, any single firm's operating situation—economic, social, political, technological, and ecological factors. Factors that more directly influence a firm's prospects originate in the environment of its industry, including entry barriers, competitor rivalry, the availability of substitutes, and the bargaining power of buyers and suppliers. The operating environment comprises factors that influence a firm's immediate competitive situation—competitive position, customer profiles, suppliers, creditors, and the labor market. These three sets of factors provide many of the challenges that a particular firm faces in its attempts to attract or acquire needed resources and to profitably market its goods and services. Environmental assessment is more complicated for multinational corporations (MNCs) than for domestic firms because multinationals must evaluate several environments simultaneously.

Thus, the design of business strategies is based on the conviction that a firm able to anticipate future business conditions will improve its performance and profitability. Despite the uncertainty and dynamic nature of the business environment, an assessment process that narrows, even if it does not precisely define, future expectations is of substantial value to strategic managers.

QUESTIONS FOR DISCUSSION

1. Briefly describe two important recent changes in the remote environment of U.S. business in each of the following areas:
   a. Economic.
   b. Social.
   c. Political.
   d. Technological.
   e. Ecological.

2. Describe two major environmental changes that you expect to have a major impact on the wholesale food industry in the next 10 years.

3. Develop a competitor profile for your college and of the one geographically closest to it. Next, prepare a brief strategic plan to improve the competitive position of the weaker of the two colleges.

4. Assume the invention of a competitively priced synthetic fuel that could supply 25 percent of U.S. energy needs within 20 years. In what major ways might this change the external environment of U.S. business?

5. With your instructor's help, identify a local firm that has enjoyed great growth in recent years. To what degree and in what ways do you think this firm's success resulted from taking advantage of favorable conditions in its remote, industry, and operating environments?

6. Choose a specific industry and, relying solely on your impressions, evaluate the impact of the five forces that drive competition in that industry.

7. Choose an industry in which you would like to compete. Use the five-forces method of analysis to explain why you find that industry attractive.

8. Many firms neglect industry analysis. When does this hurt them? When does it not?

9. The model below depicts industry analysis as a funnel that focuses on remote-factor analysis to better understand the impact of factors in the operating environment. Do you find this model satisfactory? If not, how would you improve it?

10. Who in a firm should be responsible for industry analysis? Assume that the firm does not have a strategic planning department.

BIBLIOGRAPHY

Aaker, D. A. "Managing Assets and Skills: The Key to a Sustainable Competitive Advantage." *California Management Review* (Winter 1989), pp. 91–106.

Allen, M. G. "Competitive Confrontation in Consumer Services." *Planning Review* (January–February 1989), pp. 4–9.

Bleeke, J. A. "Strategic Choices for Newly Opened Markets." *Harvard Business Review* (September–October 1990), pp. 158–66.

Bonifant, Benjamin C., Matthew B. Arnold, and Frederick J. Long. "Gaining Competitive Advantage through Environmental Investments." *Business Horizons* 38, no. 1 (July–August 1995), p. 37.

Bylinsky, G. "Manufacturing for Reuse." *Fortune* (February 6, 1995), p. 102.

Covin, J. G., and D. P. Slevin. "Strategic Management of Small Firms in Hostile and Benign Environments." *Strategic Management Journal* (January–February 1989), pp. 75–87.

Cowley, R. R. "Market Structure and Business Performance: An Evaluation of Buyer/Seller Power in the PIMS Database." *Strategic Management Journal* (May–June 1988), pp. 271–78.

Fiesinger, E. G. "Dealing with Environmental Regulations and Agencies: An Industry Perspective." *Business Horizons* (March–April 1992), pp. 41–45.

Filho, P. V. "Environmental Analysis for Strategic Planning." *Managerial Planning* (January–February 1985), pp. 23–30.

Ginter, P. M., and W. J. Duncan. "Macroenvironmental Analysis for Strategic Management." *Long Range Planning* (December 1990), pp. 63–70.

Hooper, T. L., and B. T. Rocca. "Environmental Affairs: Now on the Strategic Agenda." *The Journal of Business Strategy* (May–June 1991), pp. 26–31.

Ilinitch, Anne Y., and Stefan C. Schaltegger. "Developing a Green Business Portfolio." *Long Range Planning* 28, no. 2 (April 1995), p. 79.

Ketelhöhn, Werner. "Re-engineering Strategic Management." *Long Range Planning* 28, no. 3 (June 1995), p. 68.

Lieberman, M. B. "The Learning Curve, Technology Barriers to Entry, and Competitive Survival in the Chemical Processing Industries." (Strategic Management Journal) (September–October 1989), pp. 431–47.

MacMillan, I. C. "Controlling Competitive Dynamics by Taking Strategic Initiative." *Academy of Management Executive* (May 1988), pp. 111–18.

Mascarenhas, B., and D. A. Aaker. "Mobility Barriers and Strategic Groups." *Strategic Management Journal* (September–October 1989), pp. 475–85.

May, Douglas R., and Brenda L. Flannery. "Cutting Waste with Employee Involvement Teams." *Business Horizons* 38, no. 5 (September–October 1995), p. 28.

Mayer, R. "Winning Strategies for Manufacturers in Mature Industries." *Journal of Business Strategy* (Fall 1987), pp. 23–31.

Miles, R. E. "Adapting to Technology and Competition: A New Industrial Relations System for the 21st Century." *California Management Review* (Winter 1989), pp. 9–28.

Miller, D. "Relating Porter's Business Strategies to Environment and Structure: Analysis and Performance Implications." *Academy of Management Journal* (June 1988), pp. 280–308.

Ottman, J. A. "Industry's Response to Green Consumerism." *Journal of Business Strategy* (July–August 1992), pp. 3–7.

Porter, Michael E., and Claas van der Linde. "Toward a New Conception of the Environment-Competitiveness Relationship." *Journal of Economic Perspectives* (Fall 1995).

———. "Green and Competitive: Ending the Stalemate." *Harvard Business Review* 73, no. 5 (September–October 1995), p. 120.

Prescott, J. E., and J. H. Grant. "A Manager's Guide for Evaluating Competitive Analysis Techniques." *Interfaces* (May–June 1988), pp. 10–22.

Rafferty, J. "Exit Barriers and Strategic Position in Declining Markets." *Long Range Planning* (April 1987), pp. 86–91.

Reilly, W. K. "Environment, Inc." *Business Horizons* (March–April 1992), pp. 9–11.

Reimann, B. C. "Sustaining the Competitive Advantage." *Planning Review* (March–April 1989), pp. 30–39.

Robertson, T. S., and H. Gatignon. "How Innovators Thwart New Entrants into Their Market." *Planning Review* (September–October 1991), pp. 4–11.

Sarkis, Joseph, and Abdul Rasheed. "Greening the Manufacturing Function." *Business Horizons* 38, no. 5 (September–October 1995), p. 17.

Schoemaker, Paul J. H., and Joyce A. Shoemaker. "Estimating Environmental Liability." *California Management Review* 37, no. 3 (Spring 1995), p. 29.

———. "Ecocentric Management in Industrial Ecosystems: Management Paradigm for a Risk Society." *Academy of Management Review* 20, no. 1 (1995), p. 118.

Thomas, L. M. "The Business Community and the Environment: An Important Partnership." *Business Horizons* (March–April 1992), pp. 21–24.

Ulrich, D., and F. Wiersema. "Gaining Strategic and Organizational Capability in a Turbulent Business Environment." *Academy of Management Executive* (May 1988), pp. 115–22.

Vesey, J. T. "The New Competitors: They Think in Terms of 'Speed to Market.' " *Academy of Management Executive* (May 1991), pp. 23–33.

Winsemius, P., and U. Guntram. "Responding to the Environmental Challenge." *Business Horizons* (March–April 1992), pp. 12–20.

Yoffie, D. B. "How an Industry Builds Political Advantage." *Harvard Business Review* (May–June 1988), pp. 82–89.

CHAPTER 3 COHESION CASE ILLUSTRATION

ASSESSING THE EXTERNAL ENVIRONMENT AT THE COCA-COLA COMPANY

Coca-Cola managers place a great deal of emphasis on constant renewal and preparedness of their "worldwide business system." Part of their reasoning emanates from the reality of trying to predict future circumstances of different environmental factors across the thousands of essentially local markets in which they compete throughout the world. Roberto Goizueta addressed this when he said:

> Although we cannot foretell the future, we approach it with the premise that in the coming years organizations will be successful to the extent of their effectiveness in managing and coping with change . . . It is our belief that, in the future, fast change, even chaotic change at times, will pose an equal, if not a greater, challenge. If our premise is correct, then organizations must be sharply focused, flexible, and capable of fast reaction to external forces to succeed in this environment that we foresee.

And a year later, he offered:

> We don't view the future as preordained, but as an infinite series of openings, of possibilities. What is required to succeed in the middle of this uncertainty is what the Greeks called "practical intelligence." Above all else, this "practical intelligence" forces adaptability and teaches constant preparedness. It acknowledges that nothing succeeds quite as planned, and that the model is not the reality. But it also teaches that choice and preparedness can influence the future.

While *preparedness* appears the watchword of Coke management, attention to key environmental factors is evident in Coca-Cola's strategic management perspective. Let's look at a few ways this seems evident.

ECONOMIC

Coca-Cola's products are consumer products, and as such are somewhat sensitive to consumers' disposable income. Coca-Cola's management reports two trends that serve to shape its planning related to this factor. First, Coca-Cola consumers view soft drinks as inexpensive pleasure. As such, even in a temporary environment of steady or slightly declining disposable income, Coca-Cola's research suggests that consumers are unlikely to forgo soft drinks. Second, Coca-Cola monitors disposable income in over 200 countries where it sells soft drinks. In 1993, this information suggests that disposable income is generally rising around the world. Coca-Cola interprets this to mean more purchases of consumer products, particularly in countries where consumer product purchasing has been minimal.

Inflation is another economic factor that influences Coca-Cola's success. Asked about this recently, Coca-Cola's CFO offered this comment:

> Inflation is a factor in many markets around the world and consequently impacts the way the company operates. In general, our management believes that we are able to adjust prices to counteract the effects of increasing costs and generate sufficient cash flow to maintain our productive capacity. In highly inflationary countries, Coca-Cola has benefited from its net monetary liability position in recent years. This position is viewed as a hedge against the effects of country-specific inflation, since net liabilities would ultimately be paid with devalued currency.

DEMOGRAPHIC/SOCIAL

Consumption of soft drinks has long been inversely correlated with a person's age. In other words, as you age you drink fewer soft drinks, while younger people drink most soft drinks. Coca-Cola subscribes to this basic phenomenon.

The average age of the populations in the United States and most European countries is increasing. Outside the United States and Europe, Coke management observes, *"The world is getting younger and young people are the most enthusiastic purchasers of consumer products."*

TECHNOLOGICAL

Many of us have heard the phrase, "The world is getting smaller and smaller." Ease of travel and increasingly sophisticated, instantaneous worldwide communication capabilities drive this phenomenon. Coca-Cola's management views this phenomenon as favorable:

> As the world has gotten smaller, a "global teenager" has emerged. In Germany and around the world, these teenagers share similar tastes in music, clothing, and consumer brands. With its global scope and the power of the world's most ubiquitous trademark, the Coca-Cola system is uniquely equipped to market to this group.

These are a few of the remote environmental factors that influence Coca-Cola's future and how Coke management views them. Let's now look at some factors within their more immediate "industry environment" and see how Coca-Cola's management views these, too.

RIVALRY

The Coca-Cola Company is rather vague on how it assesses rivals. Recent comments are both brief and generic, such as:

> The commercial beverages industry, of which the soft-drink business is a part, is competitive. The soft-drink business itself is highly competitive. In any parts of the world in which Coca-Cola does business, demand for soft drinks is growing at the expense of other commercial beverages. Advertising and sales promotional programs, product innovation, increased efficiency in production techniques, the introduction of new packaging, new vending and dispensing equipment, and brand and trademark developments and protection are important competitive factors.

Translated, this statement acknowledges that Coke's intense rivalry with Pepsi results in a "rivalry ante" that virtually eliminates other, lesser rivals. That intense rivalry (known as the "cola wars"), unceasing for 20 years, has resulted in an ever-increasing share of a growing market for both Pepsi and Coke at the expense of other players.

A "third front," *private labels,* has opened up to challenge Coke and Pepsi. Pioneered by Toronto-based Cott Corp., private labels like Wal-Mart's Sam's Choice have begun to impact on cola sales. Cott bottles most of these beverages, and has seen a five-year growth rate exceeding 200 percent, bringing it $1 billion in revenue. Wal-Mart sold over 1 billion 12-ounce servings of Cott-produced cola beverages last year. Cott has over a 23 percent market share of all soda sold in Canadian supermarkets. Douglas Ivester, Roberto Goizueta's heir apparent, said of Cott and other private labelers: "Parasites! On our turf, the parasite is nothing but a tiny bug, waiting to be crushed." Private label beverages typically sell for half Coke or Pepsi's retail price. Cott's profit has slid as its sales increased, leading Goizueta to comment: "Those who continue to rely on pricing as their only point of distinctiveness are meeting with difficult times, on Main Street and Wall Street. In a highly competitive market for every consumer dollar and investment dollar, we believe the failure to differentiate brands in every aspect of marketing eventually erodes the value of the brand and the investment."

The "front line troops" in the cola wars are Coke and Pepsi bottlers, half of whom are independent bottling franchises. Both companies work incessantly to keep these troops at a fever pitch, because of the critical role these local distributors play—soda moves fast in stores and machines; and, if supplies aren't restocked daily, that firm loses sales. At one recent bottlers' convention, Coke bottlers watched a giant screen where a "Coke" battle tank clanked over a valley, swung its turret while zeroing in on a target, and blew a Pepsi vending machine into a million pieces. The attendees went wild! Similarly, a recent Pepsi bottlers' convention featured, along with its regular speakers, a muscle-bound Pepsi bottler who took a sledgehammer and dismantled a Coke machine on stage.

And now, while Coke and Pepsi pummel each other, they must consider retailer comments about Cott-provided products such as "having a store brand improved the way Coke and Pepsi deal with us" and "we can give consumers value and still earn better margins than on national brands." Analysts project Cott to hold 8 percent of U.S. supermarket soda sales by 2000. Cott's beverages already make up over half of the canned soda sold by its first Japanese customer, the 5,000-store Ito Yokado chain, where retail soda prices are sky high.

SUPPLIERS

The principal raw material used by the soft-drink industry in the United States is high fructose corn syrup, a form of sugar, which is available from numerous domestic sources. The principal raw material used by the soft-drink industry outside the United States is sucrose. It likewise is available from numerous sources.

Another raw material increasingly used by the soft-drink industry is aspartame, a sweetening agent used in low-calorie soft-drink products. Until January 1993, in the United States aspartame was available from just one source—the NutraSweet Company, a subsidiary of the Monsanto Company—due to its patent, which expired at the end of 1992.

Coke managers have long held "power" over sugar suppliers. They view the recently expired aspartame patent as only enhancing their power relative to suppliers.

BUYERS

Individual consumers are the ultimate buyers of soft drinks. However, Coke and Pepsi's real "buyers" have been local bottlers who are franchised to bottle the companies' products and to whom each company sells its patented syrups or concentrates. While Coke and Pepsi issue their franchises, these bottlers are in effect the "conduit" through which these international cola brands get to local consumers.

Through the early 1980s, Coke's domestic bottlers were typically independent family businesses deriving from franchises issued early in the century. Pepsi had a collection of similar franchises, plus a few large franchisees that owned many locations. Until 1980, Coke and Pepsi were somewhat restricted in owning bottling facilities, which was viewed as a restraint of free trade. Then President Jimmy Carter, a Coke fan, changed that by signing legislation to allow soft-drink companies to own bottling companies or territories, plus upholding the territorial integrity of soft-drink franchises, shortly before he left office.

Prior to this development, Coke "power" relative to its key buyers was weak when compared with Pepsi, which had fewer, larger, better capitalized franchisees. This advantage helped Pepsi grow aggressively until Coca-Cola was legally allowed to "integrate forward," creating similarly large, modern Coke bottlers.

The other critical buyer is the retailer, particularly grocery chains, which provide the shelf space to products from Coke and other beverage companies. There are numerous chains and stores large and small in virtually every town worldwide. Chain stores have shown increasing interest in private labels or store brands for many national branded products including soft drinks. For example, Wal-Mart now sells over 1 billion 12-ounce bottles or cans of their brand, Sam's Choice, annually. While Coke's power relative to its bottlers' retail outlets has traditionally been imposing, the continued acceptance of private-label brands may begin to change this.

THREAT OF SUBSTITUTES AND POTENTIAL ENTRANTS

Numerous beverages are available as substitutes for soft drinks. Citrus beverages and fruit juices are the more popular substitutes, along with plain ol' water. Availability of shelf space in retail stores, as well as advertising and promotion, has a significant effect on beverage purchasing behavior. Total liquid consumption in the United States has been approximately the following in the 1990s:

Drink	Percent of Liquid Consumed in the United States
Coca-Cola beverages	10%
Other carbonated soft drinks	15
Fruit juices	6
Milk	15
Coffee	11
Beer	12
Tap water	19
Other	12
	100%

For the first half of the 1990s, Coca-Cola USA sales grew at an annualized rate of 4 percent, twice the industry average. Coca-Cola sold almost half of all soft drinks sold in the United States in 1995, finishing off a five-year annualized growth in market share of 18 percent per annum.

"New Age" beverages, the 1,000 to 2,000 new brands or varieties of fruit-flavored drinks, teas, and bottled waters, have been catching some attention in the early 1990s. With rising demand for alternative drinks, small beverage companies have begun to make inroads into places that have long been the strongholds of major cola brands. Snapple, Clearly Canadian, and Tropicana Twisters are among the more well known vanguards in this substitute beverage class. Kroger is one large grocery chain that has allotted considerable space to New Age beverages. Says a key Kroger buyer, "From a retailer's standpoint, it would not bother us at all to see consumers move from the major brands to the New Age beverages."

The New Age beverage category is estimated at 6 percent of 1995 soft-drink sales. But the category seems to be steadily growing at between 10 and 20 percent annually. Observed one Pepsi executive, "The whole New Age, better-for-you phenomenon is out there and it's affecting the soft drink business, especially on the diet side."

4 THE GLOBAL ENVIRONMENT: STRATEGIC CONSIDERATIONS FOR MULTINATIONAL FIRMS

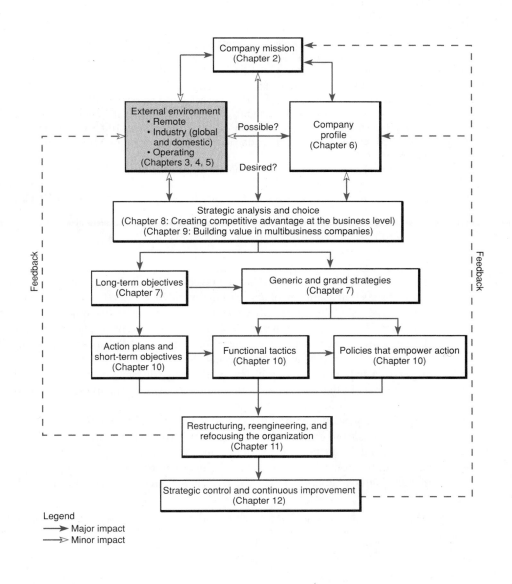

Legend
→ Major impact
⇢ Minor impact

YAMANOUCHI PHARMACEUTICAL READIES ITSELF FOR GLOBALIZATION

The basic policy of the top management of Yamanouchi Pharmaceutical Co., Ltd., represented by Chairman Shigeo Morioka and President Masayoshi Onoda, is summarized by the concepts of big dual enterprise, three-pole tactics, and GBS (global big seven) 005. Big dual enterprise means the dual management diversification into pharmaceuticals and health foods. Three-pole tactics means concentrating activities in Asia (including Japan), America, and Europe, starting from Japan. The GSB 005 envisages the development of seven original new drugs acceptable to the world market until the year 2005, according to Managing Director Junichiro Matsumoto.

The company is actively engaged in project evolution aimed at the establishment of an integrated system covering research and development, and production and sales, as well as a strategy serving local communities. These steps are aimed at converting Yamanouchi into a global enterprise during the first decade of the 21st century.

Yamanouchi achieved excellent business results during fiscal 1994 (March 1995 term). Sales totaled ¥273,048 million, of which exports accounted for ¥12,770 million. Ordinary profit totaled ¥57,990 million. Sales and profit grew by 5.1 percent and 6.6 percent, respectively, from the previous year. The combined group including 54 subsidiaries (for example, Shaklee Corp. of the United States) showed sales of ¥384,323 million and ¥77,390 million, up 4.2 percent and 10.5 percent, respectively. The ordinary profit of the Yamanouchi Group thus achieved even higher growth than the parent company, reflecting the good performance of overseas subsidiaries.

In particular, Yamanouchi Ireland is playing a vital role as the production base of bulk famotidine (Gaster), an anti-ulcer drug agent, which is sold in over 100 countries and recorded annual sales surpassing $1,200 million worldwide. The globalization of Yamanouchi has thus entered a new stage.

Intensified activities related to Yamanouchi's globalization have been seen in the past decade. The firm established Yamanouchi Ireland and started the construction of a manufacturing plant in 1986. The construction was completed in 1988 and the plant moved into full-scale bulk production of

Source: Excerpted from *Japan*, August 21, 1995, p. 30.

Special complications confront a firm involved in the globalization of its operations. *Globalization* refers to the strategy of approaching worldwide markets with standardized products. Such markets are most commonly created by end consumers that prefer lower-priced, standardized products over higher-priced, customized products and by global corporations that use their worldwide operations to compete in local markets.[1] Global corporations headquartered in one country with subsidiaries in other countries experience difficulties that are understandably associated with operating in several distinctly different competitive arenas.

Awareness of the strategic opportunities faced by global corporations and of the threats posed to them is important to planners in almost every domestic U.S. industry. Among corporations headquartered in the United States that receive more than 50 percent of their annual profits from foreign operations are Citicorp, Coca-Cola, Exxon, Gillette, IBM, Otis Elevator, and Texas Instruments. In fact, the 100 largest U.S. globals earn an average of 37 percent of their operating profits abroad. Equally impressive is the impact of foreign-based globals that operate in the United States. Their "direct foreign investment" in the United

[1] T. Levitt, "The Globalization of Markets," *Harvard Business Review*, September-October 1982, p. 91; and T. Hout, M. E. Porter, and E. Rudden, "How Global Companies Win Out," *Harvard Business Review*, September-October 1982, pp. 98–108.

| GLOBAL STRATEGY IN ACTION 4–1 | **continued** |

Gaster. Yamanouchi Research Institute (United Kingdom) was inaugurated at Oxford in 1990 as the firm's British research center mainly engaged in basic research centered on cell biology.

In 1991 Yamanouchi bought the pharmaceutical division of Royal Gist–Brocades (the Netherlands) and reorganized it as Brocades Pharma, a base for research and development, and production and sales of pharmaceuticals in Europe. The firm's name was again changed, to Yamanouchi Europe and Yamanouchi Pharma, in 1994 with the establishment of the head office in the Netherlands and sales branches in 12 countries including France, Germany, and Russia. A research center and two plants have been established to bolster development and production.

In the United States, Yamanouchi USA is engaged in clinical development and study. In addition, the firm carried out capital participation (29%) in Roberts, Inc., a middle-level pharmaceutical maker in the United States in 1992.

In the health food sector, in 1989 Yamanouchi bought San Francisco–based Shaklee Corp., a major producer of preparation-enriched foods, with a significant market share and Shaklee Japan, its Japanese subsidiary.

To consolidate its presence in Asia, Yamanouchi established Korea Yamanouchi Pharmaceutical in Seoul, ROK, and Shenyang Yamanouchi Pharmaceutical in Shenyang, China, in 1994. A new plant is slated to start operation in Shenyang in March 1997. The consolidation of the company's foundation in fast-growing Asia is thus making steady progress.

Matsumoto explains: "Our present state is compared to the Step in the Hop, Step, Jump. Jump, the last stage, is crucial." In fact, the next coming few years would be critically important. The structuring of the company's own sales network must be expedited." Overseas production is assisted by the plants of Shacklee and Yamanouchi Europe, but the sales network cannot be established so speedily. "The preparation of a more powerful sales system is essential in order to survive competition with European and American pharmaceutical firms," Matsumoto said. The company's strategy on this point is highly significant.

States now exceeds $90 billion, with Japanese, German, and French firms leading the way. As Global Strategy in Action 4–1 describes, Yamanouchi Pharmaceutical is a fast growth company in the process of globalizing.

Understanding the myriad and sometimes subtle nuances of competing in global markets or against global corporations is rapidly becoming a required competence of strategic managers. For example, experts in the advertising community contend that Korean companies only recently recognized the importance of making their names known abroad. In the 1980s, there was very little advertising of Korean brands, and the country had very few recognizable brands abroad. Korean companies tended to emphasize sales and production more than marketing. The opening of the Korean advertising market in 1991 indicated that Korean firms had acquired a new appreciation for the strategic competencies that are needed to compete globally and created an influx of global firms like Saatchi and Saatchi, J. W. Thompson, Ogilvy and Mather, and Bozell. Many of them established joint ventures or partnerships with Korean agencies. An excellent example of such a strategic approach to globalization by Philip Morris's KGFI is described in Global Strategy in Action 4–2.

Because the growth in the number of global firms continues to overshadow other changes in the competitive environment, this section will focus on the nature, outlook, and operations of global corporations.

GLOBAL
STRATEGY IN
ACTION 4–2

THE GLOBALIZATION OF PHILIP MORRIS'S KGFI

Outside of its core Western markets, Kraft General Foods International's (KGFI) food products have a growing presence in one of the most dynamic business environments in the world—the Asia-Pacific region. Its operations there are expanding rapidly, often aided by links with local manufacturers and distributors.

Japan and Korea, two of the world's fastest-growing economies in the last decade, are important examples. In both countries, local alliances can be crucial to market entry and success. Realizing this fact in the early 1970s, General Foods established joint ventures in both Japan and Korea. In 1993, these joint ventures, combined with Kraft General Foods International's (KGFI) stand-alone operations, generated more than $1 billion in revenues. In the aggregate, their combined food operations in Japan and Korea are larger than many Fortune 500 companies.

Whereas soluble coffee accounts for just over 25 percent of the coffee consumed in U.S. homes, it fills over 70 percent of the cups consumed in the homes of convenience-minded Japan. Additionally, Japan is the origin of a unique form of packaged coffee—liquid—and a unique channel of distribution—vending machines. Japanese consumers have purchased packaged liquid coffee for years, and in 1993 it amounted to a $5 billion category. Some 2 million vending machines dispense 9 billion cans of liquid coffee annually—an average of 75 cans per person.

Japan offers a culturally unique distribution channel for coffee products—the gift-set market. Many Japanese exchange specially packaged food or beverage assortments at least twice a year to commemorate holidays as well as special personal or business occasions. The gift-set business has helped Maxim products reinforce their quality image; it also will be a launching pad and support vehicle for Carte Noire coffees.

Outside the Ajinomoto General Foods joint venture, KGFI is developing a freestanding food business under the name Kraft Japan. It is building a cheese business with imported Philadelphia

DEVELOPMENT OF A GLOBAL CORPORATION

The evolution of a global corporation often entails progressively involved strategy levels. The first level, which often entails export-import activity, has minimal effect on the existing management orientation or on existing product lines. The second level, which can involve foreign licensing and technology transfer, requires little change in management or operation. The third level typically is characterized by direct investment in overseas operations, including manufacturing plants. This level requires large capital outlays and the development of global management skills. Although the domestic operations of a firm at this level continue to dominate its policy, such a firm is commonly categorized as a true multinational corporation (MNC). The most involved strategy level is characterized by a substantial increase in foreign investment, with foreign assets comprising a significant portion of total assets. At this level, the firm begins to emerge as a global enterprise with global approaches to production, sales, finance, and control.

Some firms downplay their global nature (to never appear distracted from their domestic operations), whereas others highlight it. For example, General Electric's formal statement of mission and business philosophy includes the following commitment:

> To carry out a diversified, growing, and profitable worldwide manufacturing business in electrical apparatus, appliances, and supplies, and in related materials, products, systems, and services for industry, commerce, agriculture, government, the community, and the home.

Brand cream cheese, the leading cream cheese in the Tokyo metropolitan market, as well as locally manufactured and licensed Kraft Milk Farm cheese slices. The cheese market is expected to grow approximately 5 percent per year. This is a rapid growth rate for a large food category. In addition to cheese, KGFI also imports Oscar Mayer prepared meats and Jacobs Suchard chocolates.

KGFI's joint venture in Korea, Doug Suh Foods Corporation, is one of the top 10 food companies in the country. Doug Suh manufactures coffees and cereals and has its own distribution network. One of Doug Suh's other businesses in Korea, Post Cereals, is also a strong number two, with a 42 percent category share.

Korea's $400 million coffee market is the fastest-growing major coffee market in the world, expanding at an average annual rate of 14 percent in 1990–91. Growing with the market, Maxim and Maxwell soluble coffees, in both traditional "agglomerate" and freeze-dried forms, account for more than 70 percent of the country's soluble coffee sales. The strength of these brands also brings the company a strong number one position in coffee mix, a mixture of soluble coffee, creamer, and sugar. In addition, its Frima brand leads the market in the nondairy creamer segment.

Beyond Australia, where it has a long-established, wholly owned business, and operations in Japan and Korea, KGFI is targeting many other countries for geographic expansion. In Indonesia, for instance, KGFI has established a rapidly growing cheese business through a licensee and introduced other KGFI products in 1993. In Taiwan, the joint venture company, PremierFoods Corporation, holds a 34 percent share of the soluble coffee market and is aggressively developing a Kraft cheese and Jacobs Suchard import business. KGF Philippines, a wholly owned subsidiary, has a leading position in the cheese and powdered soft-drink markets in its country. In the People's Republic of China, the company produces and markets Maxwell House coffees and Tang powdered soft drinks through two successful and rapidly growing joint ventures.

A similar global orientation is evident at IBM, which operates in 125 countries, conducts business in 30 languages and more than 100 currencies, and has 23 major manufacturing facilities in 14 countries.

The question for many firms is not *whether* to globalize, but rather how, how fast, and how to measure progress over time. Six factors that drive global companies are listed in Figure 4–1. They address key aspects of globalizing a business's operations and provide a framework within which companies can effectively pursue the global marketplace.

WHY FIRMS GLOBALIZE

The technological advantage once enjoyed by the United States has declined dramatically during the past 30 years. In the late 1950s, over 80 percent of the world's major technological innovations were first introduced in the United States. By 1990, the figure had declined to less than 50 percent. In contrast, France is making impressive advances in electric traction, nuclear power, and aviation. Germany leads in chemicals and pharmaceuticals, precision and heavy machinery, heavy electrical goods, metallurgy, and surface transport equipment. Japan leads in optics, solid-state physics, engineering, chemistry, and process metallurgy. Eastern Europe and the former Soviet Union, the so-called COMECON (Council for Mutual Economic Assistance) countries, generate 30

FIGURE 4–1
Factors That Drive Global Companies

1. **Global Management Team**
   Possesses global vision and culture.
   Includes foreign nationals.
   Leaves management of subsidiaries to foreign nationals.
   Frequently travels internationally.
   Has cross-cultural training.

2. **Global Strategy**
   Implement strategy as opposed to independent country strategies.
   Develop significant cross-country alliances.
   Select country targets strategically rather than opportunistically.
   Perform business functions where most efficient—no home-country bias.
   Emphasize participation in the triad—North America, Europe, and Japan.

3. **Global Operations and Products**
   Use common core operating processes worldwide to ensure quantity and uniformity.
   Product globally to obtain best cost and market advantage.

4. **Global Technology and R&D**
   Design global products but take regional differences into account.
   Manage development work centrally but carry out globally.
   Do not duplicate R&D and product development; gain economies of scale.

5. **Global Financing**
   Finance globally to obtain lowest cost.
   Hedge when necessary to protect currency risk.
   Price in local currencies.
   List shares on foreign exchanges.

6. **Global Marketing**
   Market global products but provide regional discretion if economies of scale are not affected.
   Develop global brands.
   Use core global marketing practices and themes.
   Simultaneously introduce new global products worldwide.

Source: Robert N. Lussier, Robert W. Baeder, and Joel Corman, "Measuring Global Practices: Global Strategic Planning through Company Situational Analysis," p. 57. Reprinted from *Business Horizons*, September–October 1994. Copyright 1994 by the Foundation for the School of Business at Indiana University. Used with permission.

percent of annual worldwide patent applications. However, the United States can regain some of its lost technological advantage. Through globalization, U.S. firms often can reap benefits from industries and technologies developed abroad. Even a relatively small service firm that possesses a distinct competitive advantage can capitalize on large overseas operations. One such firm that has done this is Domino's Pizza, described in Global Strategy in Action 4–3.

In many situations, global development makes sense as a competitive weapon. Direct penetration of foreign markets can drain vital cash flows from a foreign competitor's domestic operations. The resulting lost opportunities, reduced income, and limited production can impair the competitor's ability to invade U.S. markets. This fact is well understood by the Japanese. As evidence, in 1993 there were 1,500 Japanese-owned or -operated factories in the United States (up 40 percent since 1989) that employed about 300,000 American workers. More than 75 percent of these plants were in six industries, including electronics, food, and cars. Another case in point is IBM's move to establish a position of strength in the Japanese mainframe computer industry before two key competitors, Fiyitsue and Hitachi, could dominate it. Once IBM had achieved a substantial share of the Japanese market, it worked to deny its Japanese competitors the vital cash and production experience they needed to invade the U.S. market.

GLOBAL
STRATEGY IN
ACTION 4–3

THE MULTINATIONALIZATION OF DOMINO'S

Domino's Pizza International, adding stores in Japan at an astounding rate of 1 every four weeks, had 10 in operation by mid-October 1987. By the end of 1988, another 16 stores were to be added. A good reason exists for this expansion. Sales in Japan average $25,000 per store each week, compared with an average of $8,000–$8,500 in the United States.

Domino's works through the Y. Higa Corporation under a licensing agreement to set up pizza franchises. Donald K. Cooper, controller of Domino's Pizza International, said:

> The key to success is spending a lot of time training the workers. It takes a year and a half for a driver to move up to manager-in-training and eventually become a store manager. Early on, managers-in-training learn how to complete a profit and loss statement every four weeks, and, after six months, they know their inventories and how to run a business.

Another reason for Domino's success is the attention it gives to standards. The International stores of Domino's Pizza are kept as close to the U.S. version as possible. Employee uniforms, outdoor signs, and logos are the same as those in the United States. Delivery in 30 minutes or $3 off the price is guaranteed no matter where in the world a Domino's is located, and the menu is always kept simple. Each store must limit the number of toppings it offers, and only two pizza sizes are available.

Domino's operates 200 stores worldwide. It hopes to double that number of stores each year. Cooper said, "Everyone realizes that International is going to be the force in the future."

Source: Adapted from Andrea Chancellor, "Domino's Finds Japanese Sales as Easy as Pie," *Journal of Commerce*, October 13, 1987, p. 1A; and M. R. Czinkota, P. Rivoli, and I. A. Ronkainen, *International Business* (Hinsdale, IL: Dryden Press, 1989).

CONSIDERATIONS PRIOR TO GLOBALIZATION

To begin globalization, firms are advised to take four steps.[2]

Scan the Global Situation   Scanning includes reading journals and patent reports and checking other printed sources—as well as meeting people at scientific-technical conferences and in-house seminars.

Make Connections with Academia and Research Organizations   Firms active in overseas R&D often pursue work-related projects with foreign academics and sometimes enter into consulting agreements with them.

Increase the Firm's Global Visibility   Common methods that firms use to attract global attention include participating in trade fairs, circulating brochures on their products and inventions, and hiring technology acquisition consultants.

Undertake Cooperative Research Projects   Some firms engage in joint research projects with foreign firms to broaden their contacts, reduce expenses, diminish the risk for each partner, or forestall the entry of competitors into their markets.

In a similar vein, external and internal assessments may be conducted before a firm enters global markets. For example, Japanese investors conduct extensive assessments and

[2] R. Rondstadt and R. Kramer, "Getting the Most out of Innovation Abroad," *Harvard Business Review*, March–April 1982, pp. 94–99.

GLOBAL
STRATEGY IN
ACTION 4–4

CHECKLIST OF FACTORS TO CONSIDER IN CHOOSING A FOREIGN MANUFACTURING SITE

The following considerations were drawn from an 88-point checklist developed by Business International Corporation.

Economic factors:

1. Size of GNP and projected rate of growth.
2. Foreign exchange position.
3. Size of market for the firm's products; rate of growth.
4. Current or prospective membership in a customs union.

Political factors:

5. Form and stability of government.
6. Attitude toward private and foreign investment by government, customers, and competition.
7. Practice of favored versus neutral treatment for state industries.
8. Degree of antiforeign discrimination.

Geographic factors:

9. Efficiency of transport (railways, waterways, highways).
10. Proximity of site to export markets.
11. Availability of local raw materials.
12. Availability of power, water, gas.

Labor factors:

13. Availability of managerial, technical, and office personnel able to speak the language of the parent company.

---

analyses before selecting a U.S. site for a Japanese-owned firm. They prefer states with strong markets, low unionization rates, and low taxes. In addition, Japanese manufacturing plants prefer counties characterized by manufacturing conglomeration; low unemployment and poverty rates; and concentrations of educated, productive workers.[3]

External assessment involves careful examination of critical features of the global environment, particular attention being paid to the status of the host nations in such areas as economic progress, political control, and nationalism. Expansion of industrial facilities, favorable balances of payments, and improvements in technological capabilities over the past decade are gauges of the host nation's economic progress. Political status can be gauged by the host nation's power in and impact on global affairs.

Internal assessment involves identification of the basic strengths of a firm's operations. These strengths are particularly important in global operations, because they are often the characteristics of a firm that the host nation values most and, thus, offer significant bargaining leverage. The firm's resource strengths and global capabilities must be analyzed. The resources that should be analyzed include, in particular, technical and managerial skills, capital, labor, and raw materials. The global capabilities that should be analyzed include the firm's product delivery and financial management systems.

---

[3] D. Woodward, "Locational Determinants of Japanese Manufacturing Start-Ups in the United States," *Southern Economic Journal*, January 1992, pp. 690–708.

14. Degree of skill and discipline at all levels.
15. Presence or absence of militant or Communist-dominated unions.
16. Degree and nature of labor voice in management.

Tax factors:

17. Tax-rate trends (corporate and personal income, capital, withholding, turnover, excise, payroll, capital gains, customs, and other indirect and local taxes).
18. Joint tax treaties with home country and others.
19. Duty and tax drawbacks when imported goods are exported.
20. Availability of tariff protection.

Capital source factors:

21. Cost of local borrowing.
22. Local availability of convertible currencies.
23. Modern banking systems.
24. Government credit aids to new businesses.

Business factors:

25. State of marketing and distribution system.
26. Normal profit margins in the firm's industry.
27. Competitive situation in the firm's industry: do cartels exist?
28. Availability of amenities for expatriate executives and their families.

A firm that gives serious consideration to internal and external assessment is Business International Corporation, which recommends that seven broad categories of factors be considered. As shown in Global Strategy in Action 4–4, these categories include economic, political, geographic, labor, tax, capital source, and business factors.

COMPEXITY OF THE GLOBAL ENVIRONMENT

Global strategic planning is more complex than purely domestic planning. There are at least five factors that contribute to this increase in complexity:

1. Globals face multiple political, economic, legal, social, and cultural environments as well as various rates of changes within each of them.

2. Interactions between the national and foreign environments are complex, because of national sovereignty issues and widely differing economic and social conditions.

3. Geographic separation, cultural and national differences, and variations in business practices all tend to make communication and control efforts between headquarters and the overseas affiliates difficult.

4. Globals face extreme competition, because of differences in industry structures.

5. Globals are restricted in their selection of competitive strategies by various regional blocs and economic integrations, such as the European Economic Community, the European Free Trade Area, and the Latin American Free Trade Area. Indications of how these

FIGURE 4–2

Differences between Factors That Affect Strategic Management in the United States and Internationally

Factor	U.S. Operations	International Operations
Language	English used almost universally.	Use of local language required in many situations.
Culture	Relatively homogenous.	Quite diverse, both between countries and within countries.
Politics	Stable and relatively unimportant.	Often volatile and of decisive importance.
Economy	Relatively uniform.	Wide variations among countries and among regions within countries.
Government interference	Minimal and reasonably predictable.	Extensive and subject to rapid change.
Labor	Skilled labor available.	Skilled labor often scarce, requiring training or redesign of production methods.
Financing	Well-developed financial markets.	Poorly developed financial markets; capital flows subject to government control.
Media research	Data easy to collect.	Data difficult and expensive to collect.
Advertising	Many media available; few restrictions.	Media limited; many restrictions; low literacy rates rule out print media in some countries.
Money	U.S. dollar used universally.	Must change from one currency to another; problems created by changing exchange rates and government restrictions.
Transportation/ communication	Among the best in the world.	Often inadequate.
Control	Always a problem, but centralized control will work.	A worse problem—centralized control won't work; must walk a tightrope between overcentralizing and losing control through too much decentralizing.
Contracts	Once signed, are binding on both parties even if one party makes a bad deal.	Can be avoided and renegotiated if one party becomes dissatisfied.
Labor relations	Collective bargaining; layoff of workers easy.	Layoff of workers often not possible; may have mandatory worker participation in management; workers may seek change through political process rather than collective bargaining.

Source: Adapted from R. G. Murdick, R. C. Moor, R. H. Eckhouse, and T. W. Zimmerer, *Business Policy: A Framework for Analysis*, 4th ed. (Columbus, OH: Grid, 1984), p. 275.

factors contribute to the increased complexity of global strategic management are provided in Figure 4–2.

CONTROL PROBLEMS OF THE GLOBAL FIRM

An inherent complicating factor for many global firms is that their financial policies typically are designed to further the goals of the parent company and pay minimal attention to the goals of the host countries. This built-in bias creates conflict between the different parts of the global firm, between the whole firm and its home and host countries, and between the home and host countries themselves. The conflict is accentuated by the use of various schemes to shift earnings from one country to another in order to avoid taxes, minimize risk, or achieve other objectives.

Moreover, different financial environments make normal standards of company behavior concerning the disposition of earnings, sources of finance, and the structure of capital more problematic. Thus, it becomes increasingly difficult to measure the performance of international divisions.

In addition, important differences in measurement and control systems often exist. Fundamental to the concept of planning is a well-conceived, future-oriented approach to decision making that is based on accepted procedures and methods of analysis. Consistent approaches to planning throughout a firm are needed for effective review and evaluation by corporate headquarters. In the global firm, planning is complicated by differences in national attitudes toward work measurement, and by differences in government requirements about disclosure of information.

Although such problems are an aspect of the global environment, rather than a consequence of poor management, they are often most effectively reduced through increased attention to strategic planning. Such planning will aid in coordinating and integrating the firm's direction, objectives, and policies around the world. It enables the firm to anticipate and prepare for change. It facilitates the creation of programs to deal with worldwide development. Finally, it helps the management of overseas affiliates become more actively involved in setting goals and in developing means to more effectively utilize the firm's total resources.

As an example of the need for coordination in global ventures and as evidence that firms can successfully plan for global collaboration (e.g., through rationalized production), consider Figure 4–3. Ford Escort (Europe), the best-selling automobile in the world, has a component manufacturing network that consists of plants in 15 countries.

GLOBAL STRATEGIC PLANNING

It should be evident from the previous sections that the strategic decisions of a firm competing in the global marketplace become increasingly complex. In such a firm, managers cannot view global operations as a set of independent decisions. These managers are faced with trade-off decisions in which multiple products, country environments, resource sourcing options, corporate and subsidiary capabilities, and strategic options must be considered.

A recent trend toward increased activism of stakeholders has added to the complexity of strategic planning for the global firm. *Stakeholder activism* refers to demands placed on the global firm by the foreign environments in which it operates, principally by foreign governments. This section provides a basic framework for the analysis of strategic decisions in this complex setting.

Multidomestic Industries and Global Industries

Michael E. Porter has developed a framework for analyzing the basic strategic alternatives of a firm that competes globally.[4] The starting point of the analysis is an understanding of the industry or industries in which the firm competes. International industries can be ranked along a continuum that ranges from multidomestic to global.

Multidomestic Industries

A multidomestic industry is one in which competition is essentially segmented from country to country. Thus, even if global corporations are in the industry, competition in one country is independent of competition in other countries. Examples of such industries include retailing, insurance, and consumer finance.

---

[4] Michael E. Porter, "Changing Patterns of International Competition," *California Management Review*, Winter 1986, pp. 9–40.

FIGURE 4–3
The Global Manufacturing Network for the Ford Escort (Europe)

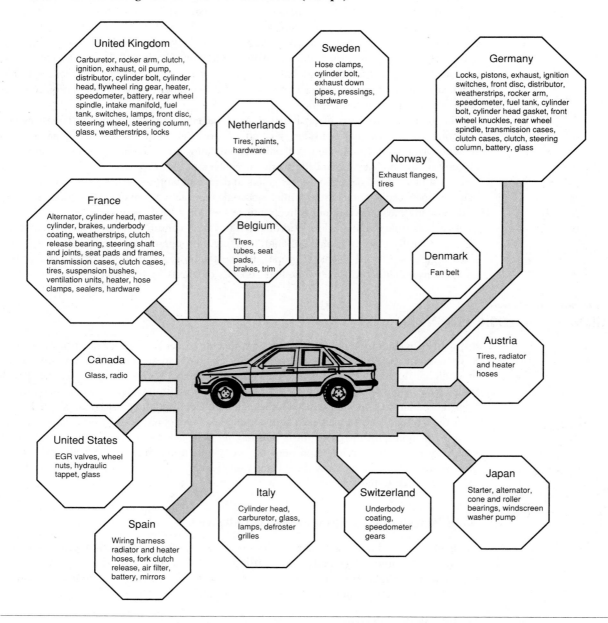

Note: Final assembly takes place in Halewood (United Kingdom) and Saarlouis (Germany).

Source: Peter Dicken, *Global Shift: Industrial Change in a Turbulent World* (London: Harper & Row, 1986), p. 304.

In a multidomestic industry, a global corporation's subsidiaries should be managed as distinct entities; that is, each subsidiary should be rather autonomous, having the authority to make independent decisions in response to local market conditions. Thus, the global strategy of such an industry is the sum of the strategies developed by subsidiaries operating in different countries. The primary difference between a domestic firm and a global firm competing in a multidomestic industry is that the latter makes decisions related to the countries in which it competes and to how it conducts business abroad.

Factors that increase the degree to which an industry is multidomestic include:[5]

The need for customized products to meet the tastes or preferences of local customers.

Fragmentation of the industry, with many competitors in each national market.

A lack of economies of scale in the functional activities of firms in the industry.

Distribution channels unique to each country.

A low technological dependence of subsidiaries on R&D provided by the global firm.

Global Industries

A global industry is one in which competition crosses national borders. In fact, it occurs on a worldwide basis. In such an industry, a firm's strategic moves in one country can be significantly affected by its competitive position in another country. The very rapidly expanding list of global industries includes commercial aircraft, automobiles, mainframe computers, and electronic consumer equipment. Many authorities are convinced that almost all product-oriented industries soon will be global. As a result, strategic management planning must be global for at least six reasons:

1. *The increased scope of the global management task.* Growth in the size and complexity of global firms made management virtually impossible without a coordinated plan of action detailing what is expected of whom during a given period. The common practice of management by exception is impossible without such a plan.

2. *The increased globalization of firms.* Three aspects of global business make global planning necessary: (1) differences among the environmental forces in different countries, (2) greater distances, and (3) the interrelationships of global operations.

3. *The information explosion.* It has been estimated that the world's stock of knowledge is doubling every 10 years. Without the aid of a formal plan, executives can no longer know all that they must know to solve the complex problems they face. A global planning process provides an ordered means for assembling, analyzing, and distilling the information required for sound decisions.

4. *The increase in global competition.* Because of the rapid increase in global competition, firms must constantly adjust to changing conditions or lose markets to competitors. The increase in global competition also spurs managements to search for methods of increasing efficiency and economy.

5. *The rapid development of technology.* Rapid technological development has shortened product life cycles. Strategic management planning is necessary to ensure the replacement of products that are moving into the maturity stage, with fewer sales and declining profits. Planning gives management greater control of all aspects of new product introduction.

6. *Strategic management planning breeds managerial confidence.* Like the motorist with a road map, managers with a plan for reaching their objectives know where they are going. Such a plan breeds confidence, because it spells out every step along the way and assigns responsibility for every task. The plan simplifies the managerial job.

A firm in a global industry must maximize its capabilities through a worldwide strategy. Such a strategy necessitates a high degree of centralized decision making in corporate headquarters so as to permit trade-off decisions across subsidiaries.

---

[5] Y. Doz and C. K. Prahalad, "Patterns of Strategic Control within Multinational Corporations," *Journal of International Business Studies*, Fall 1984, pp. 55–72.

Among the factors that make for the creation of a global industry are:

Economies of scale in the functional activities of firms in the industry.

A high level of R&D expenditures on products that require more than one market to recover development costs.

The presence in the industry of predominantly global firms that expect consistency of products and services across markets.

The presence of homogeneous product needs across markets, which reduces the requirement of customizing the product for each market. The presence of a small group of global competitors.

A low level of trade regulation and of regulation regarding foreign direction investment.[6]

The Multinational Challenge

Although industries can be characterized as global or multidomestic, few "pure" cases of either type exist. A global firm competing in a global industry must be responsive, to some degree, to local market conditions. Similarly, a global firm competing in a multidomestic industry cannot totally ignore opportunities to utilize intracorporate resources in competitive positioning. Thus, each global firm must decide which of its corporate functional activities should be performed where and what degree of coordination should exist among them.

Location and Coordination of Functional Activities

Typical functional activities of a firm include purchases of input resources, operations, research and development, marketing and sales, and after-sales service. A multinational corporation has a wide range of possible location options for each of these activities and must decide which sets of activities will be performed in how many and which locations. A multinational corporation may have each location perform each activity, or it may center an activity in one location to serve the organization worldwide. For example, research and development centered in one facility may serve the entire organization.

A multinational corporation also must determine the degree to which functional activities are to be coordinated across locations. Such coordination can be extremely low, allowing each location to perform each activity autonomously, or extremely high, tightly linking the functional activities of different locations. Coca-Cola tightly links its R&D and marketing functions worldwide to offer a standardized brand name, concentrate formula, market positioning, and advertising theme. However, its operations function is more autonomous, with the artificial sweetener and packaging differing across locations.

Location and Coordination Issues

Figure 4–4 presents some of the issues related to the critical dimensions of location and coordination in multinational strategic planning. It also shows the functional activities that the firm performs with regard to each of these dimensions. For example, in connection with the service function, a firm must decide where to perform after-sale service and whether to standardize such service.

How a particular firm should address location and coordination issues depends on the nature of its industry and on the type of international strategy that the firm is pursuing. As

---

[6] G. Harvel and C. K. Prahalad, "Managing Strategic Responsibility in the MNC," *Strategic Management Journal*, October–December 1983, pp. 341–51.

FIGURE 4-4
Location and Coordination Issues of Functional Activities

Functional Activity	Location Issues	Coordination Issues
Operations	Location of production facilities for components.	Networking of international plants.
Marketing	Product line selection. Country (market) selection.	Commonality of brand name worldwide. Coordination of sales to multinational accounts. Similarity of channels and product positioning worldwide. Coordination of pricing in different countries.
Service	Location of service organization.	Similarity of service standards and procedures worldwide.
Research and development	Number and location of R&D centers.	Interchange among dispersed R&D centers. Developing products responsive to market needs in many countries. Sequence of product introductions around the world.
Purchasing	Location of the purchasing function.	Managing suppliers located in different countries. Transferring market knowledge. Coordinating purchases of common items.

Source: Adapted from Michael E. Porter, "Changing Patterns of International Competition," *California Management Review*, Winter 1986, p. 18.

discussed earlier, an industry can be ranked along a continuum that ranges between multidomestic at one extreme and global at the other. Little coordination of functional activities across countries may be necessary in a multidomestic industry, since competition occurs within each country in such an industry. However, as its industry becomes increasingly global, a firm must begin to coordinate an increasing number of functional activities to effectively compete across countries.

Going global impacts every aspect of a company's operations and structure. As firms redefine themselves as global competitors, work forces are becoming increasingly diversified. The most significant challenge for firms, therefore, is the ability to adjust to a work force of varied cultures and lifestyles and the capacity to incorporate cultural differences to the benefit of the company's mission. Global Strategy in Action 4–5 illustrates Colgate-Palmolive's effort to become a truly global consumer products company, a vision that has impacted virtually every company function, including human resources.

International Strategy Options

Figure 4–5 presents the basic multinational strategy options that have been derived from a consideration of the location and coordination dimensions. Low coordination and geographic dispersion of functional activities are implied if a firm is operating in a multidomestic industry and has chosen a country-centered strategy. This allows each subsidiary to closely monitor the local market conditions it faces and to respond freely to these conditions.

High coordination and geographic concentration of functional activities result from the choice of a pure global strategy. Although some functional activities, such as after-sale

GLOBAL
STRATEGY IN   **COLGATE ALIGNS HR WITH ITS GLOBAL VISION**
ACTION 4–5

New York City–based Colgate-Palmolive Co. has a clear vision for its future: To become the best truly global consumer products company. This statement is telling. The few carefully chosen words demonstrate the commitment of this $7 billion firm to being more than a U.S.–based company that does business overseas. In the words of CEO Reuben Mark, taken from the company's 1992 annual report: "virtually every aspect of Colgate's business—from how we organize our operations to how we view new product development to how and where we manufacture—reflects our global orientation."

This global mindedness isn't a reaction to recent trends either. The company, which manages such internationally recognized brand-name products as Ajax, Fab, and Soft Soap, has been in 20 countries for more than 50 years, and in more than 50 countries for at least a decade. As far back as 30 years ago, Colgate created a global marketing training program to generate an international cadre of management.

Today, with operations in 75 countries and product distribution in at least 100 more, the company generates 64 percent of sales and 59 percent of operating profits overseas (Canada is included with the United States). As a consequence, two-thirds of the firm's employees now work outside of North America, providing strategic challenges for Colgate's human resources (HR) staff. More than ever before, they must ensure that the company attracts and retains *globalites*—those with the skills and interest to pursue international careers. And they must create systems for the fluid movement of workers across borders.

service, may need to be located in each market, tight control of those activities is necessary to ensure standardized performance worldwide. For example, IBM expects the same high level of marketing support and service for all of its customers, regardless of their location.

Two other strategy options are shown in Figure 4–5. High foreign investment with extensive coordination among subsidiaries would describe the choice of remaining at a particular growth stage, such as that of an exporter. Export-based strategy with decentralized marketing would describe the choice of moving toward globalization, which a multinational firm might make.

GLOBALIZATION OF THE COMPANY MISSION

Few strategic decisions bring about a more radical departure from the existing direction and operations of a firm than the decision to expand globally. Globalization subjects a firm to a radically different set of environmentally determined opportunities, constraints, and risks. To prevent these external factors from dictating the firm's direction, top management must reassess the firm's fundamental purpose, philosophy, and strategic intentions before globalization to ensure their continuation as decision criteria in proactive planning.

Expanding across national borders to secure new market or production opportunities initially may be viewed as consistent with the growth objectives outlined in a firm's existing mission statement. However, a firm's direction inherently is altered as globalization occurs.

GLOBAL
STRATEGY IN   **continued**
ACTION 4–5

In 1991, HR met these challenges head on. Following an initiative by Mark to refocus the company's energies into five key business areas, the company formed a global human resources strategy team to better align HR with the business needs. The team was composed of senior line managers and senior HR leaders. "The objective of our global human resources strategy team was to work in partnership with management to build organizational excellence," says Brian Smith, director of global staffing and strategy. "We define organizational excellence here as the continuous alignment of Colgate people and business processes with vision, values, and strategies to become the best."

The year-long development process yielded: a set of international values that emphasize care for Colgate people, consumers, shareholders, and business partners; an order for all employees to work as part of a global team; and a commitment to continuous improvement. The team also developed strategic initiatives for generating, reinforcing, and sustaining organizational excellence. These initiatives' central feature was the development of recruitment, training, compensation, and recognition systems that reinforce the technical, managerial, and leadership competencies needed to support the global business.

The global human resources strategic team's work was unveiled at a week-long global HR conference in 1992. The conference was attended by the chairman, the president, the chief operating officer, each division's president, and more than 200 of Colgate's HR leaders representing 35 countries. Smith says that the senior leadership's commitment to this project was extraordinary, demonstrating HR's role as a key player in the company's global outlook.

For example, as a firm expands overseas, its operations are physically relocated in foreign operating environments. Since strategic decisions are made in the context of some understanding of the environment, management will absorb information from new sources into its planning processes as the environment becomes pluralistic, with a revised corporate direction as a probable and desirable result. Thus, before reconsidering the firm's strategic choices, management must reassess its mission and institute the required changes as the appropriate environmental information is defined, collected, analyzed, and integrated into existing databases.

Management also must provide a mission that continues to serve as a basis for evaluating strategic alternatives as this information is incorporated into the firm's decision-making processes. Consider the financial component of Zale Corporation's mission statement from this standpoint:

> Our ultimate responsibility is to our shareholders. Our goal is to earn an optimum return on invested capital through steady profit growth and prudent, aggressive asset management. The attainment of this financial goal, coupled with a record of sound management, represents our approach toward influencing the value placed on our common stock in the market.

From a U.S. perspective, this component seems quite reasonable. In a global context, however, it could be unacceptable. Corporate financial goals vary in different countries. The clear preference of French, Japanese, and Dutch executives has been to maximize growth in after-tax earnings, and that of Norwegian executives has been to maximize earnings before interest and taxes. In contrast, these executives have assigned a low priority to the maximization of stockholder wealth. Thus, from a global perspective, a mission

FIGURE 4–5
International Strategy Options

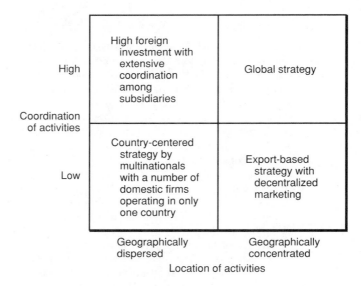

Source: Adapted from Michael E. Porter, "Changing Patterns of International Competition," *California Management Review*, Winter 1986, p. 19.

statement specifying that a firm's ultimate responsibility is to its stockholders may be an inappropriate basis for its financial operating philosophy. This example illustrates the critical need to review and revise the mission statement prior to global expansion so it will maintain its relevance in the new situations confronting the firm.

Components of the Company Mission Revisited

The mission statement must be revised to accommodate the changes in strategic decision making, corporate direction, and strategic alternatives mandated by globalization and must encompass the additional strategic capabilities that will result from globalizing operations. Therefore, each of its basic components needs to be analyzed in light of specific considerations that accompany globalization.

Product or Service, Market, and Technology

The mission statement defines the basic market need that the firm aims to satisfy. This definition is likely to remain essentially intact in the global corporation context, since competencies acquired in the firm's home country can be exploited as competitive advantages when they are transferred to other countries. However, confronted with a multiplicity of contexts, the firm must redefine its primary market to some extent.

The firm could define its market as global, which would necessitate standardization in product and company responses, or it could pursue a "market concept" orientation by focusing on the particular demands of each national market. The mission statement must provide a basis for strategic decision making in this trade-off situation. For example, the directive in Hewlett-Packard's mission statement, "HP customers must feel that they are dealing with one company with common policies and services," implies a standardized approach designed to provide comparable service to all customers. In contrast, Holiday Inn's mission statement reflects the marketing concept: "Basic to almost everything Holiday Inn, Inc., does is its interaction with its market, the consumer, and its consistent capacity to provide what the consumer wants, when, and where it is needed."

Company Goals: Survival, Growth, and Profitability

The mission statement specifies the firm's intention of securing its future through growth and profitability. In the United States, growth and profitability are considered essential to corporate survival. These goals also are acceptable in other countries supportive of the free enterprise system. Following global expansion, however, the firm may operate in countries that are not unequivocally committed to the profit motive. Many countries are committed to state ownership of industries that they view as critical to domestic prosperity. Austria, France, India, Italy, and Mexico are all good examples. A host country may view social welfare and development goals as taking precedence over the goals of free market capitalism. In developing countries, for example, employment and income distribution goals often take precedence over rapid economic growth.

Moreover, even countries that accept the profit motive may oppose the profit goals of global corporations. In such countries, the flow of global corporation profits often is viewed as unidirectional. At the extreme, the global is seen as a tool for exploiting the host country for the exclusive benefit of the parent company's home country, and its profits are regarded as evidence of corporate atrocities. This means that in a global context, a corporate commitment to profits may increase the risk of failure, rather than help secure survival.

Therefore, the mission statement of a global corporation must reflect the firm's intention of securing its survival through dimensions that extend beyond growth and profitability. A global corporation must develop a corporate philosophy that embodies its belief in a bidirectional flow of benefits among the firm and its multiple environments. The mission statement of Gulf & Western Americas Corporation expresses this view deftly: "We believe that in a developing country, revenue is inseparable from mandatory social responsibility and that a company is an integral part of the local and national community in which its activities are based." This statement maintains a commitment to profitability yet acknowledges the firm's responsibility to the host country.

The growth dimension of the mission statement remains closely tied to survival and profitability even in the global corporation context. Globalization disperses corporate resources and operations. This implies that strategic decision makers are no longer located exclusively at corporate headquarters, and that they are less accessible for participation in collective decision-making processes. To maintain the firm's cohesiveness in these circumstances, some mechanism is required to record its commitment to a unifying purpose. The mission statement can provide such a mechanism. It can provide the global corporation's decision makers with a common guiding thread of understanding and purpose.

Company Philosophy

Within the domestic setting, implicit understandings result in a general uniformity of corporate values and behavior even if a firm's philosophy goes unstated. Few domestic events challenge a firm to properly formulate and implement its implied or expressed philosophy. Globalization, however, is clearly such an event. A corporate philosophy developed from a singular perspective is inadequate for a firm that functions in variant cultures. A firm's values and beliefs are primarily culturally defined, reflecting the general philosophical perspective of the society in which the firm operates. Thus, when a firm extends its operations into another society, it encounters a new set of accepted corporate values and beliefs, which it must assimilate and incorporate into its own.

For example, numerous U.S. global corporations have been subjected to considerable criticism about the policies of their South African, Namibian, and Dominican Republic subsidiaries. In general, violations of corporate social responsibility pertaining to working standards have been alleged, not by coalitions within host countries but by coalitions within the United States, such as the Interfaith Center on Corporate Responsibility. Thus, if a global corporation tailors its values and beliefs to those of interest groups in various host countries, it will generate domestic opposition to which it must respond. Consequently, in adopting a company philosophy, a global corporation must recognize its accountability to such opposition.

Self-Concept

The globalized self-concept of a firm is dependent on management's understanding of the firm's strengths and weaknesses as a competitor in each of its operating arenas. The firm's ability to survive in multiple dynamic and highly competitive environments is severely limited if its management does not understand the impact it has or can have on those environments, and vice versa.

Public Image

Domestically, a firm's public image often is shaped from a marketing viewpoint. That image is managed as a marketing tool whose objective is customer acceptance of the firm's product. Although this consideration remains critical in the global environment, in that environment it must be balanced with consideration of other organizational claimants than the customer. In many countries, the global corporation is a major user of national resources and a major force in socialization processes. Thus, it must broaden its image so as to clearly convey its recognition of the additional internal and external claimants resulting from globalization. The following excerpt from Hewlett-Packard's mission statement exemplifies such an image: "As a corporation operating in many different communities throughout the world, we must assure ourselves that each of these communities is better for our presence . . . Each community has its particular set of social problems. Our company must help to solve these problems." These words convey an image of Hewlett-Packard's responsiveness to claimants throughout the world.

COMPETITIVE STRATEGIES FOR U.S. FIRMS IN FOREIGN MARKETS

Strategies for firms that are attempting to move toward globalization can be categorized by the degree of complexity of each foreign market being considered and by the diversity in a company's product line (see Figure 4–6).[7] Complexity refers to the number of critical success factors that are required to prosper in a given competitive arena. When a firm must consider many such factors, the requirements of success increase in complexity. Diversity, the second variable, refers to the breadth of a firm's business lines. When a company offers many product lines, diversity is high.

---

[7] Material in this section was developed in collaboration with Professors J. Kim DeDee, University of Wisconsin–Oskosh, and Shaker A. Zahra, Georgia State University.

FIGURE 4–6
International Strategy Options

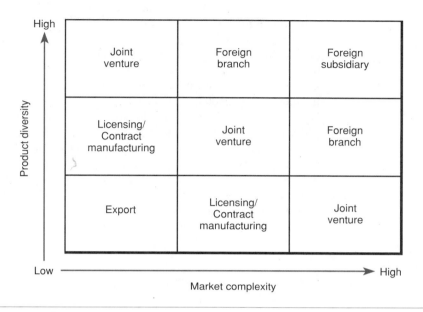

Together, the complexity and diversity dimensions form a continuum of possible strategic choices. Combining these two dimensions highlights many possible actions.

Niche Market Exporting

The primary niche market approach for the company that wants to export is to modify select product performance or measurement characteristics to meet special foreign demands. Combining product criteria from both the U.S. and the foreign markets can be slow and tedious. There are, however, a number of expansion techniques that provide the U.S. firm with the know-how to exploit opportunities in the new environment. For example, copying product innovations in countries where patent protection is not emphasized and utilizing nonequity contractual arrangements with a foreign partner can assist in rapid product innovation. N. V. Philips and various Japanese competitors, such as Sony and Matsushita, now are working together for common global product standards within their markets. Siemens, with a centralized R&D in electronics, also has been very successful with this approach.

Exporting usually requires minimal capital investment. The organization maintains its quality control standards over production processes and finished goods inventory, and risk to the survival of the firm is typically minimal. Additionally, the U.S. Commerce Department through its Export Now Program and related government agencies lowers the risks to smaller companies by providing export information and marketing advice.

Licensing/Contract Manufacturing

Establishing a contractual arrangement is the next step for U.S. companies that want to venture beyond exporting but are not ready for an equity position on foreign soil. Licensing involves the transfer of some industrial property right from the U.S. licensor to a motivated licensee. Most tend to be patents, trademarks, or technical know-how that are granted to the licensee for a specified time in return for a royalty and for avoiding tariffs or import quotas. Bell South and U.S. West, with various marketing and service competitive advantages valuable to Europe, have extended a number of licenses to create personal computer networks in the United Kingdom.

Another licensing strategy open to U.S. firms is to contract the manufacturing of its product line to a foreign company to exploit local comparative advantages in technology, materials, or labor.

U.S. firms that use either licensing option will benefit from lowering the risk of entry into the foreign markets. Clearly, alliances of this type are not for everyone. They are used best in companies large enough to have a combination of international strategic activities and for firms with standardized products in narrow margin industries.

Two major problems exist with licensing. One is the possibility that the foreign partner will gain the experience and evolve into a major competitor after the contract expires. The experience of some U.S. electronics firms with Japanese companies shows that licensees gain the potential to become powerful rivals. The other potential problem stems from the control that the licensor forfeits on production, marketing, and general distribution of its products. This loss of control minimizes a company's degrees of freedom as it reevaluates its future options.

Joint Ventures

As the multinational strategies of U.S. firms mature, most will include some form of joint venture (JV) with a target nation firm. AT&T followed this option in its strategy to produce its own personal computer by entering into several joint ventures with European producers to acquire the required technology and position itself for European expansion. Because JVs begin with a mutually agreeable pooling of capital, production or marketing equipment, patents, trademarks, or management expertise, they offer more permanent cooperative relationships than export or contract manufacturing.

Compared to full ownership of the foreign entity, JVs provide a variety of benefits to each partner. U.S. firms without the managerial or financial assets to make a profitable independent impact on the integrated foreign markets can share management tasks and cash requirements often at exchange rates that favor the dollar. The coordination of manufacturing and marketing allows ready access to new markets, intelligence data, and reciprocal flows of technical information.

For example, Siemens, the German electronics firm, has a wide range of strategic alliances throughout Europe to share technology and research developments. For years, Siemens grew by acquisitions, but now, to support its horizontal expansion objectives, it is engaged in joint ventures with companies like Groupe Bull of France, International Computers of Britain, General Electric Company of Britain, IBM, Intel, Philips, and Rolm. Another example is Airbus Industries, which produces wide-body passenger planes for the world market as a direct result of JVs among many companies in Britain, France, Spain, and Germany.

JVs speed up the efforts of U.S. firms to integrate into the political, corporate, and cultural infrastructure of the foreign environment, often with a lower financial commitment than acquiring a foreign subsidiary. General Electric's (GE) 3 percent share in the European lighting market was very weak and below expectations. Significant increases in competition throughout many of their American markets by the European giant, Philips Lighting, forced GE to retaliate by expanding in Europe. GE's first strategy was an attempted joint venture with the Siemens lighting subsidiary, Osram, and with the British electronics firm, Thorn EMI. Negotiations failed over control issues. When recent events in

Eastern Europe opened the opportunity for a JV with the Hungarian lighting manufacturer, Tungsram, which was receiving 70 percent of revenues from the West, GE capitalized on it.

Although joint ventures can address many of the requirements of complex markets and diverse product lines, U.S. firms considering either equity- or nonequity-based JVs face many challenges. For example, making full use of the native firm's comparative advantage may involve managerial relationships where no single authority exists to make strategic decisions or solve conflicts. Additionally, dealing with host-company management requires the disclosure of proprietary information and the potential loss of control over production and marketing quality standards. Addressing such challenges with well-defined covenants agreeable to all parties is difficult. Equally important is the compatibility of partners and their enduring commitments to mutually supportive goals. Without this compatibility and commitment, a joint venture is critically endangered.

Foreign Branching

A foreign branch is an extension of the company in its foreign market—a separately located strategic business unit directly responsible for fulfilling the operational duties assigned to it by corporate management, including sales, customer service, and physical distribution. Host countries may require that the branch be "domesticated"; that is, have some local managers in middle and upper-level positions. The branch most likely will be outside any U.S. legal jurisdiction, liabilities may not be restricted to the assets of the given branch, and business licenses for operations may be of short duration, requiring the company to renew them during changing business regulations.

Foreign Subsidiaries

Foreign subsidiaries are considered by companies that are willing and able to make the highest investment commitment to the foreign market. These companies insist on full ownership for reasons of control and managerial efficiency. Policy decisions about local product lines, expansion, profits, and dividends typically remain with the U.S. senior managers.

Fully owned subsidiaries can be started either from scratch or by acquiring established firms in the host country. U.S. firms can benefit significantly if the acquired company has complementary product lines or an established distribution or service network.

U.S. firms seeking to improve their competitive postures through a foreign subsidiary face a number of risks to their normal mode of operations. First, if the high capital investment is to be rewarded, managers must attain extensive knowledge of the market, the host nation's language, and its business culture. Second, the host country expects both a long-term commitment from the U.S. enterprise and a portion of their nationals to be employed in positions of management or operations. Fortunately, hiring or training foreign managers for leadership positions is commonly a good policy, since they are close to both the market and contacts. This is especially important for smaller firms when markets are regional. Third, changing standards mandated by foreign regulations may eliminate a company's protected market niche. Product design and worker protection liabilities also may extend back to the home office.

The strategies shown in Figure 4–6 are not mutually exclusive. For example, a firm may engage in any number of joint ventures while maintaining an export business. Additionally, there are a number of other strategies that a firm should consider before deciding on its long-term approach to foreign markets. These will be discussed in detail in Chapter 7 under the topic of grand strategies. However, the strategies discussed in this chapter provide the most popular starting points for planning the globalization of a firm.

SUMMARY

To understand the strategic planning options available to a corporation, its managers need to recognize that different types of industry-based competition exist. Specifically, they must identify the position of their industry along the global versus multidomestic continuum and then consider the implications of that position for their firm.

The differences between global and multidomestic industries about the location and coordination of functional corporate activities necessitate differences in strategic emphasis. As an industry becomes global, managers of firms within that industry must increase the coordination and concentration of functional activities.

The appendix at the end of this chapter lists many components of the environment with which global corporations must contend. This list is useful in understanding the issues that confront global corporations and in evaluating the thoroughness of global corporation strategies.

As a starting point for global expansion, the firm's mission statement needs to be reviewed and revised. As global operations fundamentally alter the direction and strategic capabilities of a firm, its mission statement, if originally developed from a domestic perspective, must be globalized.

The globalized mission statement provides the firm with a unity of direction that transcends the divergent perspectives of geographically dispersed managers. It provides a basis for strategic decisions in situations where strategic alternatives may appear to conflict. It promotes corporate values and commitments that extend beyond single cultures and satisfies the demands of the firm's internal and external claimants in different countries. Finally, it ensures the survival of the global corporation by asserting the global corporation's legitimacy with respect to support coalitions in a variety of operating environments.

Movement of a firm toward globalization often follows a systematic pattern of development. Commonly, businesses begin their foreign nation involvements progressively through niche market exporting, license-contract manufacturing, joint ventures, foreign branching, and foreign subsidiaries.

QUESTIONS FOR DISCUSSION

1. How does environmental analysis at the domestic level differ from global analysis?
2. Which factors complicate environmental analysis at the global level? Which factors are making such analysis easier?
3. Do you agree with the suggestion that soon all industries will need to evaluate global environments?
4. Which industries operate almost devoid of global competition? Which inherent immunities do they enjoy?

BIBLIOGRAPHY

Adler, N. J., and S. Bartholomew. "Managing Globally Competent People." *Academy of Management Executive* (August 1992), pp. 52–65.

Allio, R. J. "Formulating Global Strategy." *Planning Review* (March–April 1989), pp. 22–29.

Banks, Philip, and Ganesh Natarajan. "India: The New Asian Tiger." *Business Horizons* 38, no. 3 (May–June 1995), p. 47.

Beaver, William. "Levi's Is Leaving China." *Business Horizons* 38, no. 2 (March–April 1995), p. 35.

Bolt, J. F. "Global Competitors: Some Criteria for Success." *Business Horizons* (May–June 1988), pp. 62–72.

Calantone, R. J., and C. A. di Benedetto. "Defensive Marketing in Globally Competitive Industrial Markets." *Columbia Journal of World Business* (Fall 1988), pp. 3–14.

Chankin, W., and R. A. Mauborgne. "Becoming an Effective Global Competitor." *Journal of Business Strategy* (January–February 1988), pp. 33–37.

Chaponniere, J. R., and M. Lautier. "Breaking into the Korean Market—Invest or License?" *Long-Range Planning* 28, no. 1 (February 1995), p. 104.

Chilton, Kenneth. "How American Manufacturers Are Facing the Global Marketplace." *Business Horizons* 38, no. 4 (July–August 1995), p. 10.

Copeland, T.; T. Koller; and J. Murrin. "How to Value a Multinational Business." *Planning Review* (May–June 1990), pp. 16–25.

Cox, T., Jr. "The Multicultural Organization." *Academy of Management Executive* (May 1991), pp. 34–47.

Edmunds, John C. "The Multinational as an Engine of Value." *Business Horizons* 38, no. 4 (July–August 1995), p. 5.

Fagan, M. L. "A Guide to Global Sourcing." *The Journal of Business Strategy* (March–April 1991), pp. 21–25.

Franko, L. G. "Global Corporate Competition: Who's Winning, Who's Losing, and the R&D Factor as One Reason Why." *Strategic Management Journal* (September–October 1989), pp. 449–74.

Friedmann, R., and J. Kim. "Political Risk and International Marketing." *Columbia Journal of World Business* (Fall 1988), pp. 63–74.

Gomes-Casseres, B. "Joint Ventures in the Face of Global Competition." *Sloan Management Review* (Spring 1989), pp. 17–26.

Heenan, D. A. "Global Strategy: Why the U.S. Government Should Go to Bat for Business." *The Journal of Business Strategy* (March–April 1990), pp. 46–49.

————. "Global Strategy: The End of Centralized Power." *The Journal of Business Strategy* (March–April 1991), pp. 46–49.

Hitt, Michael A.; Beverly B. Tyler; Camilla Hardel; and Daewoo Park. "Understanding Strategic Intent in the Global Marketplace." *The Academy of Management Executive* 9, no. 2 (May 1995), p. 12.

Hordes, Mark W.; J. Anthony Clancy; and Julie Baddaley. "A Primer for Global Start-Ups." *The Academy of Management Executive* 9, no. 2 (May 1995), p. 7.

Hu, Y. S. "Global or Stateless Corporations Are National Firms with International Operations." *California Management Review* (Winter 1992), pp. 107–26.

Hu, Yao-Su. "The International Transferability of Competitive Advantage." *California Management Review* 37, no. 4 (Summer 1995), p. 73.

James, B. "Reducing the Risks of Globalization." *Long-Range Planning* (February 1990), pp. 80–88.

Johnston, W. B. "Global Work Force 2000: The New World Labor Market." *Harvard Business Review* (March–April 1991), pp. 115–29.

Kanter, Rosabeth Moss. "Thriving Locally in the Global Economy." *Harvard Business Review* 73, no. 5 (September–October 1995), p. 151.

Kester, W. C. "Global Players, Western Tactics, Japanese Outcomes: The New Japanese Market for Corporate Control." *California Management Review* (Winter 1991), pp. 58–70.

Koepfler, E. R. "Strategic Options for Global Market Players." *Journal of Business Strategy* (July–August 1989), pp. 46–50.

Kuhn, R. L. "Japanese-American Strategic Alliances." *Journal of Business Strategy* (March–April 1989), pp. 51–53.

Lasserre, Philippe. "Corporate Strategies for the Asia Pacific." *Long-Range Planning* 28, no. 1 (February 1995), p. 13.

Levy, B. "Korean and Taiwanese Firms as International Competitors." *Columbia Journal of World Business* (Spring 1988), pp. 43–51.

Luthans, Fred; Richard R. Patrick; and Brett C. Luthans. "Doing Business in Central and Eastern Europe: Political, Economic, and Cultural Diversity." *Business Horizons* 38, no. 5 (September–October 1995), p. 9.

Maruyama, M. "Changing Dimensions in International Business." *Academy of Management Executive* (August 1992), pp. 88–96.

Metzger, R. O., and A. Ginsburg. "Lessons from Japanese Global Acquisitions." *Journal of Business Strategy* (May–June 1989), pp. 32–36.

Ohmal, Kenschi. "Putting Global Logic First." *Harvard Business Review* 73, no. 1 (January–February 1995), p. 119.

O'Reilly, A. J. F. "Leading a Global Strategic Charge." *The Journal of Business Strategy* (July–August 1991), pp. 10–13.

Reich, R. B. "Who Is Them?" *Harvard Business Review*, (March–April 1991), pp. 77–89.

Reilly, Tom. "The Harmonization of Standards in the European Union and the Impact on U.S. Business." *Business Horizons* 38, no. 2 (March–April 1995), p. 28.

Reynolds, A. "Competitiveness and the 'Global Capital Shortage.' " Business Horizons (November–December 1991), pp. 23–26.

Sera, K. "Corporate Globalization: A New Trend." *Academy of Management Executive* (February 1992), pp. 89–96.

Shama, Avraham. "Entry Strategies of U.S. Firms to the Former Soviet Bloc and Eastern Europe." *California Management Review* 37, no. 3 (Spring 1995), p. 90.

Shetty, Y. K. "Strategies for U.S. Competitiveness: A Survey of Business Leaders." *Business Horizons* (November–December 1991), pp. 43–48.

Sugiura, H. "How Honda Localizes Its Global Strategy." *Sloan Management Review* (Fall 1990), pp. 77–82.

Von Glinow, Mary Ann, and Linda Clarke. "Vietnam: Tiger or Kitten?" *Academy of Management Executive* 9, no. 4 (November 1995), p. 35.

Williamson, P. "Successful Strategies for Export." *Long Range Planning* (February 1991), pp. 57–63.

Yip, G. S., and G. A. Coundouriotis. "Diagnosing Global Strategy Potential: The World Chocolate Confectionery Industry." *Planning Review* (January–February 1991), pp. 4–15.

APPENDIX

COMPONENTS OF THE MULTINATIONAL ENVIRONMENT

Multinational firms must operate within an environment that has numerous components. These components include:

I. Government, laws, regulations, and policies of home country (United States, for example).
   A. Monetary and fiscal policies and their effect on price trends, interest rates, economic growth, and stability.
   B. Balance-of-payments policies.
      1. Mandatory controls on direct investment.
      2. Interest equalization tax and other policies.
   C. Commercial policies, especially tariffs, quantitative import restrictions, and voluntary import controls.
   D. Export controls and other restrictions on trade.
   E. Tax policies and their impact on overseas business.
   F. Antitrust regulations, their administration, and their impact on international business.
   G. Investment guarantees, investment surveys, and other programs to encourage private investments in less-developed countries.
   H. Export-import and government export expansion programs.
   I. Other changes in government policy that affect international business.
II. Key political and legal parameters in foreign countries and their projection.
   A. Type of political and economic system, political philosophy, national ideology.
   B. Major political parties, their philosophies, and their policies.
   C. Stability of the government.
      1. Changes in political parties.
      2. Changes in governments.
   D. Assessment of nationalism and its possible impact on political environment and legislation.
   E. Assessment of political vulnerability.
      1. Possibilities of expropriation.
      2. Unfavorable and discriminatory national legislation and tax laws.
      3. Labor laws and problems.
   F. Favorable political aspects.
      1. Tax and other concessions to encourage foreign investments.
      2. Credit and other guarantees.
   G. Differences in legal system and commercial law.
   H. Jurisdiction in legal disputes.
   I. Antitrust laws and rules of competition.
   J. Arbitration clauses and their enforcement.
   K. Protection of patents, trademarks, brand names, and other industrial property rights.
III. Key economic parameters and their projection.
   A. Population and its distribution by age groups, density, annual percentage increase, percentage of working age, percentage of total in agriculture, and percentage in urban centers.

    B. Level of economic development and industrialization.

    C. Gross national product, gross domestic product, or national income in real terms and also on a per capita basis in recent years and projections over future planning period.

    D. Distribution of personal income.

    E. Measures of price stability and inflation, wholesale price index, consumer price index, other price indexes.

    F. Supply of labor, wage rates.

    G. Balance-of-payments equilibrium or disequilibrium, level of international monetary reserves, and balance-of-payments policies.

    H. Trends in exchange rates, currency stability, evaluation of possibility of depreciation of currency.

    I. Tariffs, quantitative restrictions, export controls, border taxes, exchange controls, state trading, and other entry barriers to foreign trade.

    J. Monetary, fiscal, and tax policies.

    K. Exchange controls and other restrictions on capital movements, repatriation of capital, and remission of earnings.

IV. Business system and structure.

    A. Prevailing business philosophy: mixed capitalism, planned economy, state socialism.

    B. Major types of industry and economic activities.

    C. Numbers, size, and types of firms, including legal forms of business.

    D. Organization: proprietorship, partnerships, limited companies, corporations, cooperatives, state enterprises.

    E. Local ownership patterns: public and privately held corporations, family-owned enterprises.

    F. Domestic and foreign patterns of ownership in major industries.

    G. Business managers available: their education, training, experience, career patterns, attitudes, and reputations.

    H. Business associations and chambers of commerce and their influence.

    I. Business codes, both formal and informal.

    J. Marketing institutions: distributors, agents, wholesalers, retailers, advertising agencies, advertising media, marketing research, and other consultants.

    K. Financial and other business institutions: commercial and investment banks, other financial institutions, capital markets, money markets, foreign exchange dealers, insurance firms, engineering companies.

    L. Managerial processes and practices with respect to planning, administration, operations, accounting, budgeting, and control.

V. Social and cultural parameters and their projections.

    A. Literacy and educational levels.

    B. Business, economic, technical, and other specialized education available.

    C. Language and cultural characteristics.

    D. Class structure and mobility.

    E. Religious, racial, and national characteristics.

    F. Degree of urbanization and rural-urban shifts.

    G. Strength of nationalistic sentiment.

    H. Rate of social change.

    I. Impact of nationalism on social and institutional change.

CHAPTER 4 COHESION CASE ILLUSTRATION

THE GLOBAL ENVIRONMENT AND THE COCA-COLA COMPANY

Roberto Goizueta has made it clear that, while Coca-Cola may have its corporate head-quarters in the United States, Coca-Cola is an international corporation, rather than a U.S. company with a sizable international business. Table 1 provides per capita consumption of Coca-Cola's soft-drink products in selected countries in 1994. Domestic per capita consumption is way ahead, while also suggesting the future opportunities in other countries where Coke is already strong. By 1995, over 80 percent of Coca-Cola's net revenues from soft drinks were generated outside the United States, as was a whopping 85 percent of its operating profits from soft drinks. Yes, Coca-Cola is certainly a global company. And as Mr. Goizueta claims, it may well be "the only truly global business system" in the 1990s. Recent comments by Mr. Goizueta further explain how Coca-Cola views the global environment:

> Geographic diversity not only helps insulate us from the sputters every economy inevitably endures, it also makes it impossible for us to miss out on the growth spurts—wherever those growth spurts may be.
>
> When an isolated downturn occurs in one of our markets, literally dozens more help take up the slack. When opportunities arise, we stand poised to seize them.
>
> Mexico serves as a timely example. When the sharp devaluation of the peso occurred, most companies ran for cover. Not us, because we view adversity as an opportunity for disciplined companies to shine. And through our long-term investment program in Mexico, we're doing just that. Even now, as the impact of the peso's devaluation continues, our volume and share of industry case sales in Mexico continue to climb.
>
> Our muscle, of course, comes from leading-edge markets such as the United States, Germany, and Japan, all of which generate substantial cash to help fuel our growth.
>
> Our growth potential comes not only from new and rapidly emerging markets such as China, India, East Central Europe, and Russia, but also from our established markets, which offer abundant opportunities for growth.

Fundamental to global growth of the sales of Coca-Cola's products is the need for local and regional bottlers within each country (almost 200 countries by 1996) that will bottle and distribute soft-drink products. Consistent with Figure 4–6 in this chapter, Coca-Cola (low product diversity and high market diversity) has used joint venturing with bottling partners as its major strategy for entering and dominating global markets. The percentage of Coca-Cola's investment in any country's bottler(s) depends on regulations in that country regarding foreign ownership, as well as the capital requirements of prospective bottling partners and the extent to which peculiarities exist within the country's retail distribution practices. Their resulting ownership of key, worldwide bottling operations are shown in the figure, "Worldwide Bottling Investments," on page 133. In just 10 years, Coca-Cola had invested over $2.5 billion in about 41 bottling and canning operations around the world. They ranged from joint ventures to minority positions in public companies to company-owned bottlers. Perhaps more important, this reversed a historical "hands off" approach, allowing Coca-Cola to help capitalize the direct efforts to build retail sales. We will examine this posture more in the Chapter 10 Cohesion Case.

Strategic bottling investments and aggressive marketing have made the Coca-Cola Company's global presence change drastically, as conveyed in Table 2. Since 1984, Coke has solidified a presence in all but 20 countries around the globe.

TABLE 1

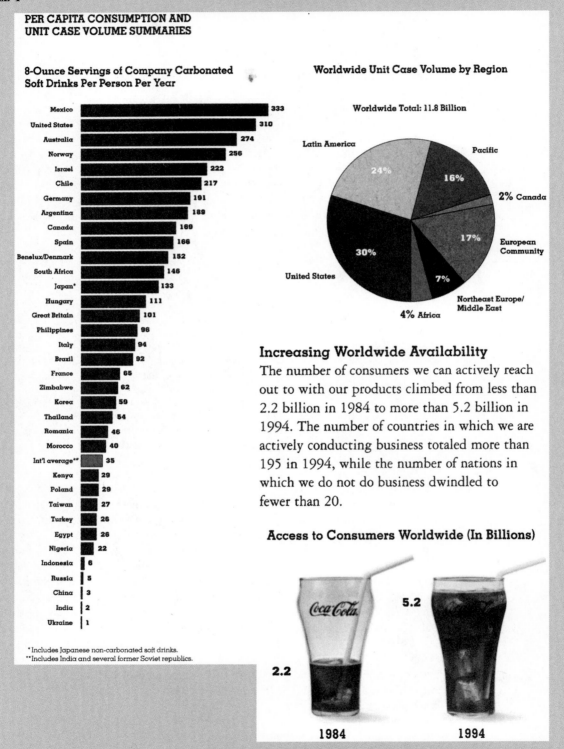

PER CAPITA CONSUMPTION AND UNIT CASE VOLUME SUMMARIES

8-Ounce Servings of Company Carbonated Soft Drinks Per Person Per Year

Mexico	333
United States	310
Australia	274
Norway	256
Israel	222
Chile	217
Germany	191
Argentina	189
Canada	169
Spain	166
Benelux/Denmark	152
South Africa	146
Japan*	133
Hungary	111
Great Britain	101
Philippines	96
Italy	94
Brazil	92
France	65
Zimbabwe	62
Korea	59
Thailand	54
Romania	46
Morocco	40
Int'l average**	35
Kenya	29
Poland	29
Taiwan	27
Turkey	26
Egypt	26
Nigeria	22
Indonesia	6
Russia	5
China	3
India	2
Ukraine	1

*Includes Japanese non-carbonated soft drinks.
**Includes India and several former Soviet republics.

Worldwide Unit Case Volume by Region

Worldwide Total: 11.8 Billion

- Latin America 24%
- Pacific 16%
- Canada 2%
- European Community 17%
- Northeast Europe/Middle East 7%
- Africa 4%
- United States 30%

Increasing Worldwide Availability

The number of consumers we can actively reach out to with our products climbed from less than 2.2 billion in 1984 to more than 5.2 billion in 1994. The number of countries in which we are actively conducting business totaled more than 195 in 1994, while the number of nations in which we do not do business dwindled to fewer than 20.

Access to Consumers Worldwide (In Billions)

Coca-Cola

2.2 5.2

1984 1994

Worldwide

Bottling Investments

NCCB 30%
(Netherlands)

Essen CBO 100%
Göttingen CBO 100%
Frankfurt Bottler 44%
Eastern Germany CBO 100%
Cologne CBO 80%
West Berlin CBO 100%
Düsseldorf Bottler 30%

Brussels Bottler 28%
Belgium CBO 100%
(Brugge/Hasselt/Aalst)

Coca-Cola
New York 53%

France CBO 100%

Brucephil 29%

Refresca AG 33%
(Switzerland)

Hainan 25%
Tianjin Bottler 50%
(China)

Coca-Cola Beverages 49%
(Canada)

Coca-Cola &
Schweppes
Beverages 49%

Taiwan Bottling
Company 34%

Coca-Cola
Consolidated
30%

Coca-Cola
Enterprises 44%

Swire Bottlers
(Hong Kong)
14%

Coca-Cola
Philippines 30%

Grupo Continental 11%
(Mexico)

Industria de Cafe 37%
(Guatemala)

BONAGUI
(Guinea)
44%

ANSAN 88%
MAKSAN 100%
(Turkey)

Industrias Roman 20%
(Colombia)

IAWC
(Egypt) 100%

Jakarta
Bottler 29%

Refrescos
do Brasil 13%
(Brazil)

Nairobi CBO 77%

Coca-Cola
Amatil 51%

Coca-Cola S.A. 100%
Inti S.A. 57%
(Argentina)

Montevideo
Refrescos 55%
(Uruguay)

Zambia Bottlers Ltd.
100%

Thai Pure
Drinks Ltd.
44%

Bucharest
CBO 51%

Milan CBO 100%
Rome CBO 100%
Turin CBO 100%
Piacenza CBO 100%

TABLE 2
The Coca-Cola Company's Expanding Global Presence

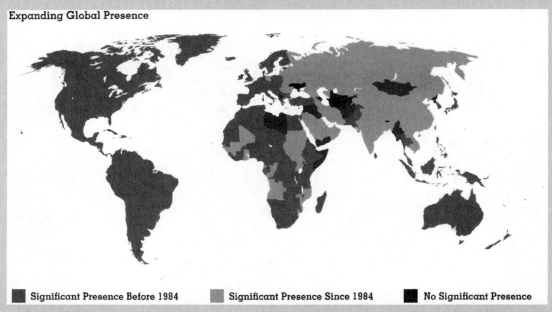

Expanding Global Presence

■ **Significant Presence Before 1984**   ■ **Significant Presence Since 1984**   ■ **No Significant Presence**

Trends in global markets, while impressive, are beginning to present Coca-Cola with some challenges. Consider the following two examples, one from Eastern Europe and another from Japan:

TOKYO—Tomiichi Murayama, Japan's Socialist prime minister, has been saying all the right things about deregulation. But of course everybody in Japan now favors deregulation—some just want it slower than others. That's why foreign marketers are better off putting their faith in Isao Nakauchi.

Mr. Nakauchi's Daiei department-store chain is groaning under a heavy load of debt, and that has helped motivate the maverick retailer to take on his country's brand-name cartels. In the process, he's offering Japan's consumers a better deal.

Specifically, Mr. Nakauchi has been driving pins into the Coca-Cola folks, who've had their markets locked up for decades and have gouged the Japanese mercilessly. Coke shows that Japan isn't closed to Western companies, just as long as they're willing to front the money to play by the same rules as Japanese firms. That means investing heavily in the capacity and troops to make and distribute your product locally—and to freeze out potential competitors.

Coke runs 17 bottling plants in Japan, including the world's biggest in Tokyo. Like any good Japanese giant—Coke controls 90% of Japan's cola market—it uses its clout to punish mom-and-pop retailers who dare to place a rival on the shelves.

It dawned on Mr. Nakauchi that Japanese consumers probably weren't thrilled to pay the equivalent of $1.10, even for "the real thing." He's begun importing a no-name Canadian cola, pasting on the Daiei label and selling pop for the equivalent of 39 cents a pop. That he has a big success on his hands is clear from Coke's response last week. The company announced plans to import Coca-Cola Classic from North America to compete with its own high-cost Japanese bottlers. The imported brew will sell for about 40% less.

Coke isn't happy about this, as indeed other entrenched U.S. companies in Japan aren't happy about the coming of a freer market. You won't notice Procter & Gamble, NCR and other such companies cheering deregulation from the rooftops. They've invested millions in doing things the Japanese way, and now the Japanese way is becoming obsolete.

BUDAPEST—Sitting at an outdoor cafe overlooking the Danube in the Hungarian capital, Istvan Fischer breaks into a smile as he picks up a glass of Coca-Cola.

"I drank my first Coke in 1963, in Vienna, and my hands trembled," says Mr. Fischer, a 69-year-old pensioner. "I was afraid because the Communists told us that Coca-Cola was an intoxicating potion that left people in a stupor."

Today, Eastern Europeans are guzzling soda after decades of a Western soft-drink drought. That's because a battle raging between those icons of American consumer culture, Coca-Cola and Pepsi, has filled shop shelves to overflowing. Since the collapse of communism in 1989, the two companies have been bent on capturing the markets of Eastern Europe, pouring a total of $2 billion into the region to modernize production and distribution facilities.

After just a few years, Coke, Pepsi and a slew of other cola brands can be found not only in Budapest and Warsaw, but also along the back roads to remote Transylvanian towns and secluded villages from Bohemia to central Bulgaria.

Yet the skirmish for this largely untapped market is just now reaching a fever pitch. After years of clashes in which Coca-Cola Co. emerged as the clear winner, PepsiCo Inc. is striking back.

The payoff could be huge, officials from both companies predict. Like China and India, Eastern Europe is a premier emerging market, they note, with more than 300 million consumers. Analysts forecast as many as two decades of dramatic growth in Eastern Europe before it levels off.

5 ENVIRONMENTAL FORECASTING

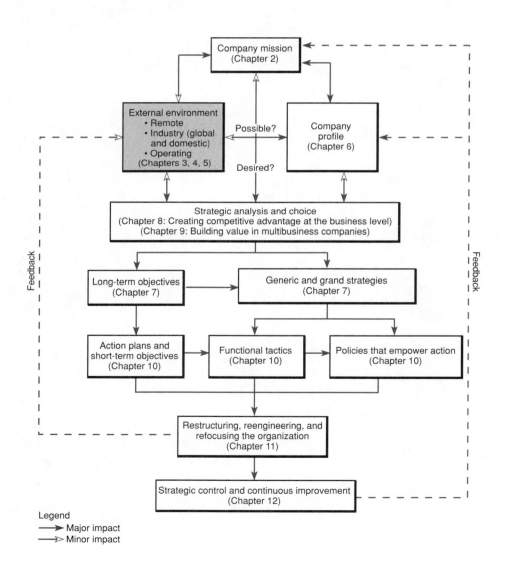

Legend
⟶ Major impact
⟶▷ Minor impact

IMPORTANCE OF FORECASTING

Change is occurring rapidly, and even greater changes and challenges are forecast for the year 2000. The crucial responsibility for managers will be ensuring their firm's capacity for survival. This will be done by anticipating and adapting to environmental changes in ways that provide new opportunities for growth and profitability. The impact of changes in the remote industry and task environments must be understood and predicted.

Even large firms in established industries will be actively involved in transitions. The $5.5 billion loss in the U.S. auto industry in the early 1980s is a classic example of what can happen when firms fail to place a priority on environmental forecasting. The preceding decade saw a 20 percent penetration of the U.S. new car market by foreign competition, a nation-crippling oil embargo, rapidly climbing fuel prices, and uncertain future supplies of crude oil. Yet the long-range implications of these predictable factors on future auto sales were largely ignored by U.S. automakers. Because it was not open to changes in technology, Detroit was left without viable, fuel-efficient, quality alternatives for the American market. On the other hand, Japanese automakers anticipated the future need for fuel efficiency, quality, and service through careful market research and environmental forecasting. As a result, they gained additional market share at Detroit's expense.

In retaliation, American automakers spent $80 billion over a three-year period on product and capital-investment strategies that were meant to recapture their lost market share. They realized that success in strategic decisions rests not solely on dollar amounts but also on anticipation of and preparation for the future.

Accurate forecasting of changing elements in the environment is an essential part of strategic management. Forecasting the business environment for the 1990s led many firms to diversify. For example, USX Corporation (formerly U.S. Steel) purchased Marathon Oil so as to have a profit generator whose proceeds could be used to turn USX into a low-cost steel producer. Similarly, predicting future demand for new products is an arduous process. As Strategy in Action 5–1 suggests, the accuracy of new product forecasts can be critically important.

Other firms have forecast a need for massive retrenchment. One such firm is IBM, which laid off 40,000 employees in 1991–92 and another 25,000 employees in 1993 to streamline its cost of doing business. Still other firms have cut back in one area of operations to underwrite growth in another. For example, CBS sold its records division to Sony for $2 billion to raise the capital it needed for its planned expansion in television stations in the 1990s.

These and many other examples indicate that strategic managers need to develop skills in predicting significant environmental changes. To aid in the search for future opportunities and constraints, they should take the following steps:

1. Select the environmental variables that are critical to the firm.
2. Select the sources of significant environmental information.
3. Evaluate forecasting techniques.
4. Integrate forecast results into the strategic management process.
5. Monitor the critical aspects of managing forecasts.

SELECT CRITICAL ENVIRONMENTAL VARIABLES

Management experts have argued that an important cause of the turbulent business environment is the change in population structure and dynamics. This change, in turn, produced other major changes in the economic, social, and political environments.

FORECASTING DEMAND FOR NEW PRODUCTS ALWAYS DIFFICULT

The major new project of the 90s, the so-called information superhighway, is developing rapidly. One sure sign is the increasing frequency of reported misuse for stock swindles, assorted sexual solicitations, slanderous communications, and other undesirable traffic.

When the Haloid company developed the dry-process copier in the later 1950s, it retained Stewart, Dougall & Associates, a now-defunct research and consulting firm, to estimate market potential and assist in developing market strategy. A common initial reaction to the product concept was that it seemed like a good idea that could replace some then-current methods like thermography because of the better appearance and durability of its plain-paper copies. The forecast seemed unbelievably high and turned out to be a serious underestimate.

It is difficult to project uses that go beyond replacements of current use and beyond the needs currently anticipated by potential users, even assuming that all potential users have been correctly identified. A little earlier, the same firm had forecast demand for another new product, polyethylene film; this forecast also turned out to be far short of reality.

The main obstacle to the prediction of demand is our limited vision. It is hard for us to realize how severely we are hemmed in by assumptions of the persistence of current patterns. Because early xerography equipment turned out relatively expensive copies compared to the mimeograph and multigraph, few analysts foresaw that it would virtually eliminate their use, and even affect traditional printing.

We tend to resist the notion of great supply-driven demand growth. It smacks of hucksterism that runs counter to the traditionally desirable posture of conservatism in forecasting and in research generally. This conservative posture has a severe downside, a risk of underestimation resulting in opportunity loss.

A closely related risk is failure to recognize problems that may arise, such as undesirable uses. In the last century, the great advantages offered by dynamite in mining and construction obscured realization of its destructive potential. Similarly, the information superhighway's potential for misuse, while realized by some, could not compete with the enthusiastic media hype of its benefits.

Anyone trying to forecast new-product demand should be well aware of the trade-off between the optimistic and the conservative views. That trade-off should be carefully modulated in accordance with the relative risks involved, an assessment that requires close cooperation of top management. After all, the company's future may depend on it.

There is no such thing as objectivity when we try to look into the future, except in data collection. The decision as to what data to collect, how to collect them, and how to interpret them cannot be objective, no matter how hard we try and it shouldn't be.

Source: "Forecasting Demand for New Products Always Difficult," by Thomas T. Semon, *Marketing News*, March 27, 1995, p. 10. Reprinted by permission of the American Marketing Association.

Historically, population shifts tended to occur over 40–50 year periods and, therefore, had little relevance to business decisions. During the second half of the 20th century, however, population changes have become radical, erratic, contradictory, and, therefore, of great importance.

For example, the U.S. baby boom between 1945 and the mid-1960s has had and will have a dramatic impact on all parts of society—from maternity wards and schools to the labor force and the marketplace. This population bulge is facing heavy competition for jobs, promotions, and housing, despite a highest-ever educational level. Compounding the problem are the heightened expectations of women and of racial minorities. The lack of high-status jobs to fit these expectations poses a potential impetus for major social and

FIGURE 5–1
The New Work Force

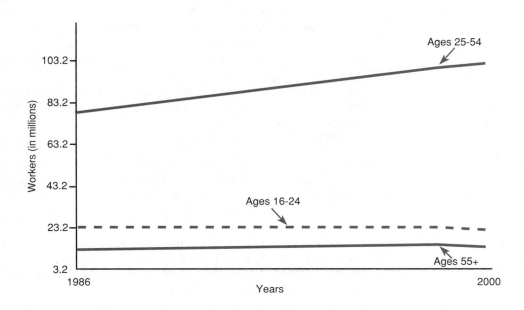

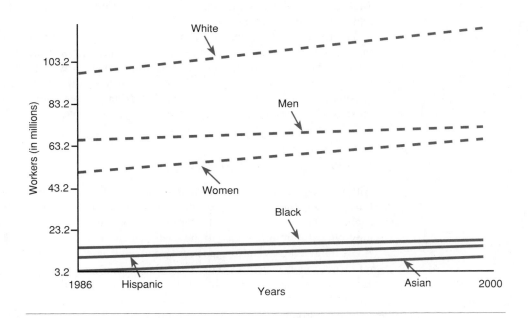

Source: *American Demographics*

economic changes. In addition, an increasingly aging labor force finds it difficult to give up status, power, and employment when retirement programs are either not financially attractive or not available at the traditional age of 65. (See Figure 5–1 for work force projections through the year 2000.)

Obviously, the demands of these groups will have important effects on social and political changes in terms of lifestyle, consumption patterns, and political decisions. In economic terms, the size and potential affluence of these groups suggest increasing markets for housing, consumer products, and leisure goods and services.

Interestingly, the same shifts in population, life expectancy, and education have occurred in many developed nations. However, developing nations face the opposite population configurations. Although birthrates have declined, high survival rates resulting from medical improvements have created a large population of people who are reaching adulthood in the 1990s. Jobs and food are expected to be in short supply. Therefore, many developing countries will face severe social and political instability unless they can find appropriate work for their surplus labor.

The rates of population increase obviously can be of great importance, as indicated by the contrasting effects forecast above. If a growing population has sufficient purchasing power, new markets will be developed to satisfy its needs. However, too much growth in a country with a limited amount of resources or a drastic inequity in their distribution may result in major social and political upheavals that pose substantial risks for businesses.

If forecasting were as simple as predicting population trends, strategic managers would only need to examine census data to predict future markets. But economic interpretations are more complex. Population statistics are complicated by migration rates; mobility trends; birth, marriage, and death rates; and racial, ethnic, and religious structures. In addition, resource development and its political use in this interdependent world further confuse the problem—as evidenced by the actions of some of the oil states (e.g., Saudi Arabia, Iraq, Libya, and Kuwait). Changes in political situations, technology, or culture add further complications.

Domestically, the turbulence is no less severe. Continually changing products and services, changing competitors, uncertain government priorities, rapid social change, and major technological innovations all add to the complexity of planning for the future. To grow, to be profitable, and at times even to survive in this turbulent world, a firm needs sensitivity, commitment, and skill in recognizing and predicting these variables that will most profoundly affect its future.

Who Selects the Key Variables?

Although executives or committees in charge of planning may assist in obtaining the forecast data, the responsibility for environmental forecasting usually lies with top management. This is the case at the Sun (Oil) Company, where responsibility for the firm's long-range future is assigned to the chairman and vice chairman of the board of directors. A key duty of the vice chairman is environmental assessment. In this context, environment refers not to air, water, and land but rather to the general business setting created by the economic, technological, political, social, and ecological forces in which Sun plans to operate.

The environmental assessment group consists of Sun's chief economist, a specialist in technological assessment, and a public issues consultant—who all report to the vice president of environmental assessment. The chief economist evaluates and forecasts the state of the economy; the technological assessment specialist covers technology and science; and the public issues consultant concentrates on politics and society.

However, headquarters may lack the capability and proficiency needed to analyze political, economic, and social variables around the world. Therefore, on-the-spot personnel, outside consultants, or company task forces may be assigned to assist in forecasting.

What Variables Should Be Selected?

A list of the key variables that will have make-or-break consequences for the firm must be developed. Some of these variables may have been crucial in the past, and others may be expected to have future importance. This list can be kept manageable by limiting it in the following ways:[1]

1. Include all variables that would have a significant impact although their probability of occurrence is low (e.g., trucking deregulation). Also include highly probable variables regardless of their impact (e.g., a minimal price increase by a major supplier). Delete others with little impact and low probabilities.

2. Disregard major disasters, such as nuclear war.

3. When possible, aggregate variables into gross variables (e.g., a bank loan is based more on the dependability of a firm's cash flow than on the flow's component sources).

4. If the value of one variable is based on the value of another, separate the dependent variable for future planning.

Limits of money, time, and forecasting skill prevent a firm from predicting many variables. The task of predicting even a dozen is substantial. Firms often try to select a set of key variables by analyzing the environmental factors in the industry that are most likely to foster sharp growth or decline in the marketplace. For the furniture, appliance, and textiles industries, housing starts are a key variable. Housing starts, in turn, are greatly affected by interest rates. Figure 5–2 identifies some issues that may have critical impacts on a firm's future success.

Another key consideration in attempting to forecast future performance is the amount of data needed. Data requirements are situation specific, but, as Figure 5–3 shows, depend on how quickly the data patterns change, the type of industry, the type of product, the analytical model selected, the forecast horizon, and ex-post forecast results.

SELECT SOURCES OF SIGNIFICANT ENVIRONMENTAL INFORMATION

Before formal forecasting can begin, appropriate sources of environmental information should be identified. Casual gathering of strategic information—through reading, interactions, and meetings—is part of the normal course of executive behavior but is subject to bias and must be balanced with alternative viewpoints. Although *The Wall Street Journal, Business Week, Fortune, Harvard Business Review, Forbes,* and other popular trade and scholarly journals are important sources of forecasting information, formal, deliberate, and structured searches are desirable. Appendix 5–A lists published sources that strategic managers can use to meet their specific forecasting needs. If the firm can afford the time and expense, it should also gather primary data in such areas as market factors, technological changes, and competitive and supplier strategies.

EVALUATE FORECASTING TECHNIQUES

Debate exists over the accuracy of quantitative versus qualitative approaches to forecasting (see Figure 5–4), with most research supporting quantitative models. However, the differences in the predictions derived from these approaches are often minimal. Moreover, subjective or judgmental approaches are often the only practical method of forecasting political, legal, social, and technological trends in the remote external environment. The same is true of several factors in the task environment, especially customer and competitive considerations.

---

[1] R. E. Linneman and J. D. Kennell, "Shirt-Sleeve Approach to Long-Range Plans," *Harvard Business Review*, March–April 1977, p. 145.

FIGURE 5–2
Strategic Forecasting Issues

Key Issues in the Remote Environment

Economy

What are the probable future directions of the economies in the firm's regional, national, and international markets? What changes in economic growth, inflation, interest rates, capital availability, credit availability, and consumer purchasing power can be expected? What income differences can be expected between the wealthy upper-middle class, the working class, and the underclass in various regions? What shifts in relative demand for different categories of goods and services can be expected?

Society and demographics

What effects will changes in social values and attitudes regarding childbearing, marriage, lifestyle, work, ethics, sex roles, racial equality, education, retirement, pollution, and energy have on the firm's development? What effects will population changes have on major social and political expectations—at home and abroad? What constraints or opportunities will develop? What pressure groups will increase in power?

Ecology

What natural or pollution-caused disasters threaten the firm's employees, customers, or facilities? How rigorously will existing environmental legislature be enforced? What new federal, state, and local laws will affect the firm, and in what ways?

Politics

What changes in government policy can be expected with regard to industry cooperation, antitrust activities, foreign trade, taxation, depreciation, environmental protection, deregulation, defense, foreign trade barriers, and other important parameters? What success will a new administration have in achieving its stated goals? What effect will that success have on the firm? Will specific international climates be hostile or favorable? Is there a tendency toward instability, corruption, or violence? What is the level of political risk in each foreign market? What other political or legal constraints or supports can be expected in international business (e.g., trade barriers, equity requirements, nationalism, patent protection)?

Technology

What is the current state of the art? How will it change? What pertinent new products or services are likely to become technically feasible in the foreseeable future? What future impact can be expected from technological breakthroughs in related product areas? How will those breakthroughs interface with the other remote considerations, such as economic issues, social values, public safety, regulations, and court interpretations?

Key Issues in the Industry Environment

New entrants

Will new technologies or market demands enable competitors to minimize the impact of traditional economies of scale in the industry? Will consumers accept our claims of product or service differentiation? Will potential new entrants be able to match the capital requirements that currently exist? How permanent are the cost disadvantages (independent of size) in our industry? Will conditions change so that all competitors have equal access to marketing channels? Is government policy toward competition in our industry likely to change?

Bargaining power of suppliers

How stable are the size and composition of our supplier group? Are any suppliers likely to attempt forward integration into our business level? How dependent will our suppliers be in the future? Are substitute suppliers likely to become available? Could we become our own supplier?

Ultimately, the choice of technique depends not on the environmental factor under review but on such considerations as the nature of the forecast decision, the amount and accuracy of available information, the accuracy required, the time available, the importance of the forecast, the cost, and the competence and interpersonal relationships of the managers and forecasters involved. Frequently, assessment of such considerations leads to the selection of a combination of quantitative and qualitative techniques, thereby strengthening the accuracy of the ultimate forecast.

FIGURE 5–2
concluded

Substitute products or services

Are new substitutes likely? Will they be price competitive? Could we fight off substitutes by price competition? By advertising to sharpen product differentiation? What actions could we take to reduce the potential for having alternative products seen as legitimate substitutes?

Bargaining power of buyers

Can we break free of overcommitment to a few large buyers? How would our buyers react to attempts by us to differentiate our products? What possibilities exist that our buyers might vertically integrate backward? Should we consider forward integration? How can we make the value of our components greater in the products of our buyers?

Rivalry among existing firms

Are major competitors likely to undo the established balance of power in our industry? Is growth in our industry slowing such that competition will become fiercer? What excess capacity exists in our industry? How capable are our major competitors of withstanding intensified price competition? How unique are the objectives and strategies of our major competitors?

Key Issues in the Operating Environment

Competitive position

What strategic moves are expected by existing rivals—inside and outside the United States? What competitive advantage is necessary in selected foreign markets? What will be our competitors' priorities and ability to change? Is the behavior of our competitors predictable?

Customer profiles and market changes

What will our customer regard as needed value? Is marketing research done, or do managers talk to each other to discover what the customer wants? Which customer needs are not being met by existing products? Why? Are R&D activities under way to develop means for fulfilling these needs? What is the status of these activities? What marketing and distribution channels should we use? What do demographic and population changes portend for the size and sales potential of our market? What new market segments or products might develop as a result of these changes? What will be the buying power of our customer groups?

Supplier relationships

What is the likelihood of major cost increases because of dwindling supplies of a needed natural resource? Will sources of supply, especially of energy, be reliable? Are there reasons to expect major changes in the cost or availability of inputs as a result of money, people, or subassembly problems? Which suppliers can be expected to respond to emergency requests?

Creditors

What lines of credit are available to help finance our growth? What changes may occur in our creditworthiness? Are creditors likely to feel comfortable with our strategic plan and performance? What is the stock market likely to feel about our firm? What flexibility would our creditors show toward us during a downturn? Do we have sufficient cash reserves to protect our creditors and our credit rating?

Labor market

Are potential employees with desired skills and abilities available in the geographic areas in which our facilities are located? Are colleges and vocational-technical schools that can aid in meeting our training needs located near our plant or store sites? Are labor relations in our industry conducive to meeting our expanding needs for employees? Are workers whose skills we need shifting toward or away from the geographic location of our facilities?

Techniques Available

Economic Forecasts

At one time, only forecasts of economic variables were used in strategic management. The forecasts were primarily concerned with remote factors, such as general economic conditions, disposable personal income, the consumer price index, wage rates, and productivity. Derived from government and private sources, these economic forecasts served as the framework for industry and company forecasts, which dealt with task-environment concerns, such as sales, market share, and other pertinent economic trends.

FIGURE 5–3
How Much Data Should You Use to Prepare Forecasts?

Sooner or later a decision has to be made as to how much data should be used to prepare the next period's forecast. Should you use all the data you have or a part of it? If you use part of the data, which part should be used? There is no simple answer to these questions; it depends on: (1) how quickly the data pattern changes, (2) the type of industry, (3) the type of product, (4) the model selected, (5) the forecast horizon, and (6) ex-post forecast results.

Data Pattern

As we know: Actual value = Pattern + Error. The best forecasting model is the one that most accurately captures the underlying pattern in a data set. The more a given model captures the pattern, the less will be the error. In a given company, the data pattern can change from one time to another because of a change in legislation, product mix, socio-demographic makeup, and the competitive environment. Technological developments and acquisitions and mergers can also change the data pattern. In that case, you need data from where the most recent data pattern starts. For example, if the most recent pattern starts in 1991, you should be using data starting 1991.

Type of Industry

The change in the data pattern is not the same in each and every industry. Some industries experience changes more rapidly than others. This may be because some industries are more prone to technological developments and/or mergers and acquisitions than others. In industries where the data pattern changes rapidly, forecasters often use data of a shorter period. In consumer product industries, for example, forecasters use data of the previous three years in preparing operations forecasts—forecasts of less than one year.

Type of Product

The type of product also makes a difference. Some products have a longer life than others. The life of essential products is generally much longer than that of fashion products. Other things being constant, the longer the life of a product the more data will be required and vice versa.

Forecast Horizon

How much data is needed also depends on whether we wish to prepare a short- or long-term forecast. Generally speaking, less data are needed for short-term forecasts and more data for long-term forecasts. If you wish to make a forecast for the next week or month, by and large, projecting the current trend adjusted for seasonal elements will be sufficient. This means a couple of years of data will be enough. However, if you wish to make a forecast for four or five years into the future, you will need much more data.

Model Selected

The data required also depends on the selected model because each model has its own requirement. For example, the "three-period moving average change model" needs at least four periods of data, and at the same time the "three-period double moving average change model" requires at least six periods of data. For a Box Jenkins model, some feel at least six years of data are needed if weekly or monthly forecasts are to be prepared and the data contain seasonality. In a regression-based model, the minimum observations required depend, among other things, on the number of independent variables. The more independent variables you incorporate in a model, the more observations will be needed.

Ex-Post Forecasts

Above all, the data required depend on how many observations, on the average, give the best forecasts. Using the best model, one can prepare ex-post forecasts on the basis of, say, one year of data, two years of data, and three years of data. (Ex-post forecasts are forecasts of those periods for which actuals are known.) If, on the average, three years of data give the lowest error, you need three years of data; if two years of data give the lowest error, you need two years of data; and so on.

Source: Chaman L. Jain, "How Much Data Should You Use to Prepare Forecasts?" *The Journal of Business Forecasting*, Winter 1994–1995, p. 2.

Econometric Models

With the advent of sophisticated computers, the government and some wealthy firms contracted with private consulting firms to develop "casual models," especially models involving econometrics. These econometric models utilize complex simultaneous regression equations to relate economic occurrences to areas of corporate activity. They are especially useful when

FIGURE 5–4
Popular Approaches to Forecasting

Technique	Short Description	Cost	Popularity	Complexity	Association with Life-Cycle Stage
Quantitative–Causal Models					
Econometric models	Simultaneous systems of multiple regression equations.	High	High	High	Steady state
Single and multiple regression	Variations in dependent variables are explained by variations in one or more independent variables.	High/ medium	High	Medium	Steady state
Time series models	Linear, exponential, S-curve, or other types of projections.	Medium	High	Medium	Steady state
Trend extrapolation	Forecasts obtained by linear or exponential smoothing or averaging of past actual values.	Medium	High	Medium	Steady state
Qualitative or Judgmental Models					
Sales force estimate	A bottom-up approach aggregating salespersons' forecasts.	Low	High	Low	All stages
Juries of executive opinion	Forecasts jointly prepared by marketing, production, finance, and purchasing executives.	Low	High	Low	Product development
Customer surveys; market research	Learning about intentions of potential customers or plans of businesses.	Medium	Medium	Medium	Market testing and early introduction
Scenario development	Impacts of anticipated conditions imagined by forecasters.	Low	Medium	Low	All stages
Delphi method	Experts guided toward a consensus.	Low	Medium	Medium	Product development
Brainstorming	Idea generation in a noncritical group situation.	Low	Medium	Medium	Product development

information on casual relationships is available and large changes are anticipated. During the relatively stable decade of the 1970s, econometrics was one of the nation's fastest-growing industries. In the 1980s, however, the three biggest econometric firms—Data Resources (Mc-Graw-Hill), Chase Econometric (Chase Manhattan Bank), and Wharton Econometric Forecasting Associates (Ziff-Davis Publishing)—fell on hard times. The explosion of oil prices, inflation, and the growing interdependence in the world economy created problems that fell beyond the inherent limits of econometric models. And despite enormous technological resources, such models still depend on the often undependable judgment of the model builders.

Two more widely used and less expensive forecasting techniques are *time series models* and *judgmental models*. Time series models attempt to identify patterns based on combinations of historical trends and seasonal and cyclical factors. This technique assumes that the past is a prologue to the future. Time series techniques, such as exponential smoothing and linear projections, are relatively simple, well known, inexpensive, and accurate.

Of the time series models, *trend analysis* models are the most frequently used. Such models assume that the future will be a continuation of the past, following some long-range trend. If sufficient historical data are available, such as annual sales, a trend analysis can be done quickly at a modest cost.

In the trend analysis depicted in Figure 5–5, concern should focus on long-term trends, such as Trend C, which is based on 11 years of fluctuating sales. Trend A, which is based

FIGURE 5–5
Interpretations in Trend Analysis

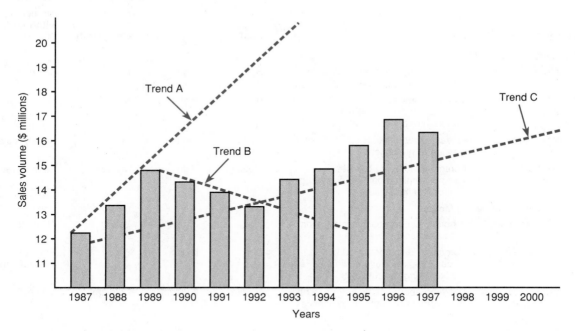

on three excellent years, is much too optimistic. Similarly, Trend B, which is based on four bad years, is much too pessimistic.

The major limitation of trend analysis is the assumption that all of the relevant conditions will remain relatively constant. Sudden changes in these conditions falsify trend predictions.

Judgmental models are useful when historical data are unavailable or hard to use. *Sales force estimates* and *juries of executive opinion* are examples of such models. Sales force estimates consolidate salespeople's opinions of customer intentions regarding specific products. These estimates can be relevant if customers respond honestly and their intentions remain consistent. Juries of executive opinion average the estimates made by executives from marketing, production, finance, and purchasing. No elaborate math or statistics are required.

Customer surveys are conducted by means of personal interviews or telephone questionnaires. The questions must be well stated and easily understood. The respondents are a random sample of the relevant population. Customer surveys can provide valuable in-depth information. Although they are often difficult to construct and time-consuming to administer, many marketing research firms use them.

Social Forecasts

If strategic forecasting relies only on economic indicators, social trends that can have a profound impact may be neglected. Some firms have recognized this and identify social trends and underlying attitudes as part of their environmental scanning. Recent social forecasting efforts have involved analysis of such areas as population, housing, Social Security and welfare, health and nutrition, education and training, income, and wealth and expenditures.

A variety of approaches are used in social forecasting, including time series analysis and the judgmental techniques described earlier. However, *scenario development* is probably the most popular approach. Scenarios, the imagined stories that integrate objective and subjective parts of other forecasts, are designed to help prepare strategic managers for alternative possibilities, thus enabling them to develop contingency plans. Because scenarios can be presented in easily understood forms, they often are used in social forecasting. They can be developed by the following process:

1. Prepare the background by assessing the overall social environment under investigation (such as social legislation).
2. Select critical indicators, and search for future events that may affect them (e.g., growing distrust of business).
3. Analyze the reasons for the past behavior of each indicator (e.g., perceived disregard for air and water quality).
4. Forecast each indicator in three scenarios—showing the least favorable environment, the likely environment, and the most favorable environment.
5. Write the scenarios from the viewpoint of someone at a given future time.
6. Condense each scenario to a few paragraphs.

Strategy in Action 5–2 presents the "most likely" scenario of the ecology in the 21st century as judged by a panel of experts. It shows how social, political, and technological concerns can be blended to produce a useful forecast.

Strategy in Action 5–3 presents a scenario that was developed in 1987 for Georgia Power Company. Its purpose was to determine how the future environment might influence the firm's load and energy growth to the year 1995. With the help of Battelle Columbus Division, a consulting firm, Georgia Power identified five broad areas of influence—the same areas you studied in Chapter 3 as the constituents of the remote external environment. From these areas, 15 key factors were isolated for investigation, of which 5 were judged to be critical to Georgia Power's planning. The scenario in Strategy in Action 5–3 was built on forecasts regarding these five factors. Several scenarios were developed, of which the one presented in Strategy in Action 5–3 showed the greatest economic growth.

Political Forecasts

Some strategic planners want to give political forecasts the same serious consideration that is given to economic forecasts. They believe that business success can be profoundly affected by shifts in a broad range of political factors, such as the size of government budgets, tariffs, tax rates, defense spending, the growth of regulatory bodies, and the extent of business leaders' participation in government planning.

Political forecasts for foreign countries also are important. Political risks in those countries affect firms that are in any way dependent on international subsidiaries, on suppliers for customers, or on critical resources. Increasing worldwide interdependence makes it imperative for firms of all sizes to consider the international political implications of their strategies.

Because of the billions of U.S. dollars lost in the last two decades as a result of revolutions, nationalization, and other manifestations of political instability, multinational firms and consultants have developed a variety of approaches to international forecasting. Some of the better known are:

Haner's Business Environmental Risk Index, which monitors 15 economic and political variables in 42 countries.

SCENARIO ON THE ECOLOGY IN THE 21ST CENTURY

Imagine how the world will look from a technological standpoint in the year 2050. It seems likely that the combination of environmental constraints and consumer desires for functionality rather than ownership will have had profound impacts on the global economy, government policies, private corporations, and individuals. As a result of environmental constraints, for example, energy and resource conservation will have become increasingly critical. Energy- and resource-efficient corporations will have gained substantial competitive advantages. This trend in particular may favor Japanese companies, because as an island nation, the Japanese have already internalized a parsimonious attitude toward energy and resources. This attitude, which at least initially was quite independent of the environment, will serve them well in an environmentally constrained world. Americans, on the other hand, with their "cowboy economy" and propensity for resource depletion, may have a considerably rougher time.

Price structures, a serious impediment to industrial ecology during the 1990s, will undergo considerable evolution in the next few decades, as more and more externalities become captured either through market mechanisms or fees and taxes. The adjustment of the pricing structure will be sporadic and will make business planning quite difficult. Those corporations that fail to internalize environmental considerations into their product and process planning in the late twentieth or early twenty-first centuries will find their costs escalating wildly and unpredictably, and will have few options when changes have to be made rapidly.

A concomitant development will be the ascendancy of materials science in many corporations. The ability to predict environmental impacts of materials across their life cycles and to implement alternatives in response to regulatory bans and rapidly changing costs will prove to be an important competency for any extractive or manufacturing corporation. Much of the progress in achieving sustainable manufacturing practices will rely on new materials—superconductors, buckyball derivatives, and enzymes used in bioprocessing factories, for example—and those corporations that stay abreast of the "learning curve" on new materials will do well.

The crucial role of new materials will be reinforced by an explicit policy on the part of many governments to allocate the transfer of functionality to the consumer marketplace and to place the responsibility for the underlying product on manufacturing corporations. The trend, initiated by postconsumer product take-back legislation in Germany and Japan in the 1990s, will be extended to most product categories. Governments will increasingly realize that environmental impacts arise predominantly from the nature of the material stocks and flows underlying the economy rather than

Source: *Industrial Ecology* by Graedel/Allenby, © 1995. Adapted by permission of Prentice Hall, Inc., Upper Saddle River, NJ.

Frost and Sullivan's World Political Risks Forecasts, which predict the likelihood of various catastrophes befalling an individual firm.

Probe International's custom reports for specific firms, which examine broad social trends.

The developmental forecasts of Arthur D. Little (ADL), which examine a country's progress.

Of all the approaches in use, those of ADL may be the most ambitious and sophisticated. With computer assistance, ADL follows the progress of each country by looking at five criteria: social development, technological advancement, abundance of natural resources, level of domestic tranquility, and type of political system. When a country's

from the quality of life the economy provides to consumers. They will react more and more by imposing on business the responsibility for materials, from extraction to rebirth to safe disposal.

On a broader front, as more and more operations of corporations become subject to public approval processes, either formally through regulatory mechanisms or informally through public activism, manufacturing will become a true partnership among the corporation, the community in which it exists, and the society in which it is embedded. The idea of a corporation as responsible to only its shareholders and perhaps to its employees or management is rapidly becoming obsolescent, although the details of balancing desirable competitive incentives against a broader social role are difficult and still evolving. Nonetheless, in the future corporations will not quickly put profit ahead of social responsibility; so deeply will environmental concerns redefine our society.

What of various industrial sectors? Electronics manufacturing and software development will boom as the creation of intelligent resource- and energy-conserving systems permeates the economy. Some power utilities will suffer, but many will prosper by increasing their energy networking capabilities and becoming turnkey energy-efficiency consultants, an extension of the demand management efforts that began in the early 1990s. The transportation sector will see enormous change, best characterized by saying that customers will be offered "transparent transportation" for goods and services, where conditions and timing are specified but modes and interconnections are chosen by the service vendor. "Transparent commuting" will operate much the same way, except that many people will remain where they are and commute electronically. An economy based on intellectual capital requires an infrastructure emphasizing electronic networks, not civil engineering.

A SUMMARY OF THE VISION

The future for purposes of the practitioner of industrial ecology is essentially captured in two propositions: that it is an increasingly environmentally constrained world, and that customers will soon be buying functionality, not material. Thus, the long-term vision of industrial ecology centers both on a technological development and on changes in the structure of societal demand. Industrial ecology recognizes that technology is the source of our environmental problems and that it may be the only feasible way to solve them. Technology alone cannot achieve the transformation we envision; it must work within the societal system to move closer to that goal.

development in any one of these areas gets too far ahead of its development in the other areas, tension builds and violence often follows. Using this system, ADL forecast political turbulence in Iran eight years before the U.S. hostage crisis. ADL foresees that uneven development probably will produce similar turmoil in 20 other countries, such as Peru, Chile, Malaysia, and the Philippines. It believes the world is highly predictable if the right questions are asked. Unfortunately, too many executives fail to use the same logic in analyzing political affairs that they use in other strategic areas. Political analysis should be routinely incorporated into economic analyses. Ford, General Motors, PepsiCo, Singer, Du Pont, and United Technologies are among the many firms that follow ADL's advice.

Global Strategy in Action 5–1 provides a guide to political evaluation that is popular among executives who are responsible for international operations. Global Strategy in Action 5–2 presents an actual scenario that was developed to assess political and economic conditions in the Americas.

GEORGIA POWER PLANNING SCENARIOS FOR 1995

HIGH ECONOMIC GROWTH SCENARIO

The average annual growth rate of the real U.S. gross national product (GNP) will exceed 3.2 percent between now and the year 2010. This growth rate is about the same as the growth rate of 3.4 percent experienced during the post–World War II era but is greater than the average growth rate for the 1980s. Economic growth in Georgia will exceed that of the nation as a whole by as much as one percentage point. This growth pattern is expected to result from a continuation of the Sunbelt phenomenon that drove Georgia's strong growth over the past two decades. With higher economic growth elsewhere, net migration to Georgia will slow down.

Higher productivity growth and lower real interest rates will be associated with higher U.S. economic growth. Higher productivity growth will occur as the baby boom generation matures and the work experience of its members increases. Interest rates will remain lower as long as inflationary pressures do not reemerge.

The average price of oil in 1985 dollars will remain under $18 per barrel as a result of the transformation of the OPEC-dominated world oil market into a commodity-based market. The surplus of natural gas will diminish, but not until the middle 1990s. Industrial demand for natural gas will dampen, as lower oil prices encourage substitution to oil. Coal prices will increase more slowly. Real electricity prices will decline if the free market energy policy pursued by the Reagan Administration continues. Emissions will remain essentially stable through 1995.

Real U.S. GNP will grow at an annual rate of less than 2.7 percent, a rate lower than the average growth rate experienced so far in the 1980s. This decline will result from a worsening trade imbalance and from large deficit spending that exerts an upward pressure on interest rates. Georgia's personal income growth will exceed that of the United States as a whole by over one percentage point. Higher levels of net migration into Georgia will occur as economic circumstances worsen elsewhere. This will accelerate growth in the state.

The annual increase in U.S. productivity will be less than 1.5 percent, an increase consistent with the slow growth of the 1970s. The low growth rate will result from a decline in demand for most goods and services as the population ages. Taxes will increase to support the aged population. Both higher taxes and higher interest rates will accelerate the shift from a manufacturing to a service economy.

By 1995, oil prices will average over $30 per barrel in 1985 dollars. The current world surplus will erode quickly in the early years as the current strong economic growth increases oil demand. This will cause a return to OPEC price controls. Deregulation will free natural gas prices to adjust rapidly to supply and demand imbalances. Exploration and development will be dampened by the initial lower prices and by inconsistent and unpredictable government energy policy. Real electricity prices will decline. Some acid rain legislation will be passed, but not enough to significantly discourage growth in the utility industry.

Source: D. L. Goldfarb and W. R. Huss, "Building Scenarios for an Electric Utility," *Long Range Planning*, June 1988, pp. 78–85.

Technological Forecasts

Such rapidly developed and revolutionary technological innovations as lasers, nuclear energy, satellites and other communication devices, desalination of water, electric cars, and miracle drugs have prompted many firms to invest in technological forecasts. Knowledge of probable technological development helps strategic managers prepare their firms to benefit from change. Except for econometrics, all of the previously described techniques can be used to make technological forecasts. However, uncertainty of information favors the use of scenarios and two additional forecasting approaches: brainstorming and the Delphi technique.

Brainstorming helps a group generate new ideas and forecasts. With this technique, analysis or criticisms of participants' contributions are postponed so creative thinking is not stifled or restricted. Because there are no interruptions, group members are encouraged to offer original ideas and to build on one another's innovative thoughts. The most promising ideas generated in this way are thoroughly evaluated at a later time.

The *Delphi method* is a systematic procedure for obtaining consensus among a group of experts. This method includes:

1. A detailed survey of opinions of experts, usually obtained through a mail questionnaire.
2. Anonymous evaluation of the responses by the experts involved.
3. One or more revisions of the experts' answers until convergence has been achieved.

Relatively inexpensive, the Delphi method can be successful in social and political forecasting.

A firm's use of a particular forecasting technique is often highly dependent on the industry in which it is involved. For product necessities such as electric power, food, and pharmaceuticals, corporations are often able to perform forecasts several months in advance. However, for newly introduced products or products with volatile demand, forecasting efforts become daily challenges in satisfying fluctuating demand patterns. A means to alleviate the pressures of dealing with such patterns can be the recognition of early warning signals. Proactive steps such as customer surveys or early tests of response can help to promote early warning signs. Figure 5–6 provides a comparison of where early warning systems have greater or less value in predicting demand.

At the end of this chapter, Appendix 5–B briefly describes the 20 most frequently used forecasting approaches.

INTEGRATE FORECAST RESULTS INTO THE STRATEGIC MANAGEMENT PROCESS

Once the forecasting techniques have been selected and the forecasts made, the results must be integrated into the strategic management process. For example, the economic forecast must be related to analyses of the industry, suppliers, competition, and key resources. Figure 5–7 presents a format for displaying interrelationships between forecast remote environment variables and the influential task environment variables. The resulting predictions become a part of the assumed environment in formulating strategy.

It is critical that strategic decision makers understand the assumptions on which environmental forecasts are based. The experience of Itel, a computer-leasing firm, illustrates the consequences of a failure to understand these assumptions. Itel had been able to lease 200 plug-in computers made by Advance Systems and by Hitachi largely because IBM could not deliver its newest AT systems. Consequently, Itel bullishly forecast that it would place 430 of its systems in the following year—despite the rumor that IBM would announce a new line of aggressively priced systems in the first quarter of that year. Even Itel's competitors felt that customers would hold off their purchasing decisions until IBM made the announcement. However, Itel signed long-term purchase contracts with its suppliers and increased its marketing staff by 80 percent. Itel's forecasting mistake and its failure to examine its sales forecasts in relationship to the actions of competitors and suppliers were nearly disastrous. It slipped close to bankruptcy within less than a year.

A GUIDE TO POLITICAL EVALUATION

The following is an abridged version of the popular Political Agenda Worksheet developed by Probe, a consulting firm that specializes in political analysis, which may serve as a guide for corporate executives initiating their own political evaluations.

EXTERNAL FACTORS AFFECTING SUBJECT COUNTRY

Prospects for foreign conflict.

Relations with border countries.

Regional instabilities.

Alliances with major and regional powers.

Sources of key raw materials.

Major foreign markets.

Policy toward United States.

U.S. policy toward country.

INTERNAL GROUPINGS (POINTS OF POWER)

Government in Power

Key agencies and officials.

Legislative entrenched bureaucracies.

Policies—economic, financial, social, labor, and so on.

Pending legislation.

Attitude toward private sector.

Power networks.

Political Parties (in and out of power)

Policies.

Leading and emerging personalities.

Source: Benjamin Weiner, "What Executives Should Know about Political Risk," *Management Review,* January 1992, p. 21.

Forecasting external events enables a firm to identify its probable requirements for future success, to formulate or reformulate its basic mission, and to design strategies for achieving its goals and objectives. If the forecast identifies any gaps or inconsistencies between the firm's desired position and its present position, strategic managers can respond with plans and actions. When Apple successfully introduced its new low-priced personal computers, sales climbed 85 percent for the quarter. However, because the firm failed to forecast that sales of the low-price computers would cannibalize the sales of its more expensive models, profits slipped, forcing Apple to lay off 10 percent of its work force, or 1,500 employees.

Dealing with the uncertainty of the future is a major function of strategic managers. The forecasting task requires systematic information gathering coupled with the utilization of a

continued

Internal power struggles.

Sector and area strengths.

Future prospects for retaining or gaining power.

Other Important Groups

Unions and labor movements.

Military, special groups within military.

Families.

Business and financial communities.

Intelligentsia.

Students.

Religious groups.

Media.

Regional and local governments.

Social and environmental activists.

Cultural, linguistic, and ethnic groups.

Separatist movements.

Foreign communities.

Potential competitors and customers.

INTERNAL FACTORS

Power struggles among elites.

Ethnic confrontations.

Regional struggles.

Economic factors affecting stability (consumer inflation, price and wage controls, unemployment, supply shortages, taxation, and so on).

Anti-establishment movements.

variety of forecasting approaches. A high level of insight also is needed to integrate risks and opportunities in formulating strategy. However, intentional or unintentional delays or the inability to understand certain issues may prevent a firm from using the insights gained in assessing the impact of broad environmental trends. Sensitivity and openness to new and better approaches and opportunities, therefore, are essential.

MONITOR THE CRITICAL ASPECTS OF MANAGING FORECASTS

Although almost all aspects of forecast management may be critical in specific situations, three aspects are critical over the lifetime of a firm.

GLOBAL
STRATEGY IN   THE AMERICAS
ACTION 5–2

In general, political and economic conditions are likely to be more stable in Central and South America in 1992 than they have been for several years. The debt crisis has receded as a prime concern; and while political violence may increase, most regimes are not likely to change during 1992. The biggest headlines will be devoted to the free-trade movements in the region, especially the North American Free Trade Area (NAFTA).

Some type of free-trade agreement between Mexico and the United States is likely in 1992, but its economic impact will not be nearly as important as its symbolic significance. Rather than stimulating new trade in Mexico, it will open up new opportunities for joint venture investments. The most important consequence of such an agreement may well be to sustain political support for President Salinas of Mexico. Other free-trade agreements among South American countries will also evolve during 1992, but they will have only limited impact on the local economies.

Since Brazil and Argentina together account for 50 percent of all economic activity in South America, these are the countries to watch closely. Brazil continues to make little headway against inflation or toward meaningful economic reform. Prospects for improvement are not good while President Collor battles a recalcitrant congress and the stubbornly independent state governments.

Argentina, on the other hand, has shown significant signs of economic improvement under a new minister of the economy and President Menem, who has regained much of his earlier popularity. As more privatization has occurred, the international financial community appears to have talked itself back into believing in Argentina. Nevertheless, prospects for comprehensive privatization remain limited, and labor is becoming increasingly opposed to Menem's policies. A new acceleration of inflation could destroy Menem's chances of implementing the nascent program of far-reaching economic reform now in process.

Source: *Planning Review* 20, no. 2 (March–April 1992), p. 27. Published with permission of The Planning Forum, P.O. Box 70, Oxford, OH 45056.

The first is the identification of the environmental factors that deserve forecasting. Hundreds of factors may affect a firm, but often the most important of these factors are a few of immediate concern, such as sales forecasts and competitive trends. The time and resources needed to completely understand all the environmental factors that might be critical to the success of a strategy are seldom available. Therefore, executives must depend on their collective experience and perception to determine which factors are worth the expense of forecasting.

The second aspect is the selection of reputable, cost-efficient forecasting sources outside the firm that can expand its forecasting database. Strategic managers should identify federal and state government agencies, trade and industry associations, and individuals or other groups that can provide data forecasts at reasonable costs.

The third aspect is the selection of forecasting tasks that are to be done in-house. Given the great credence that often is accorded to formally developed forecasts—despite the inherent uncertainty of the database—the selection of forecasting techniques is indeed critical. A firm beginning its forecasting efforts is well advised to start with less technical methods, such as sales force estimates and the jury of executive opinion, rather than highly sophisticated forecasting techniques, such as econometrics, and to add approaches requiring greater analytic sophistication as its experience and understanding increase. In this way, its managers can learn how to deal with the varied weaknesses and strengths of forecasting techniques.

FIGURE 5–6
Where an Early Warning System Has Greater or Less Value in Business

Greater Value	Less Value
Long or lengthening supply lead times.	Easy resupply "off the shelf."
Lean inventories.	Ample inventories.
High fraction of new products; apparel, book publishing.	Well-established products such as aspirin and corn flakes.
Customers can easily go elsewhere if item is unavailable: department stores, airlines.	Unique items with limited competition: high-performance car accessories.
Perishable or rapid-obsolescence items: theater seats, cut flowers.	Products can be easily carried over for future sale: blue jeans, office supplies.
Short, intense selling season: Christmas decorations, skiwear.	Selling seasons that permit enough time to expand or contract supplies.
Suppliers to JIT or Quick Response customers, for example, to auto companies, Wal-Mart.	Suppliers of capital equipment and systems that are made to order: mainframe computers, aircraft.

Source: Paul V. Teplitz, "Do You Need an Early Warning System?" *The Journal of Forecasting*, 1995, p. 9.

SUMMARY

Environmental forecasting starts with the identification of critical factors external to the firm that might provide opportunities or pose threats in the future. Both quantitative and qualitative strategic forecasting techniques are used to project the long-range direction and impact of these factors in the remote and task environments. To select the forecasting techniques that are most appropriate for the firm, the strengths and weaknesses of the various techniques must be understood. To offset the potential biases or errors individual techniques involve, employment of more than one technique usually is advisable.

Critical aspects in forecast management include the identification of the environmental factors that deserve forecasting, the selection of forecasting sources outside the firm, and the selection of forecasting tasks that are to be done in-house.

QUESTIONS FOR DISCUSSION

1. Identify five changes in the remote environment that you believe will affect major U.S. industries over the next decade. What forecasting techniques could be used to assess the probable impact of these changes?

2. Construct a matrix with forecasting techniques on the horizontal axis and at least five qualities of forecasting techniques across the vertical axis. Indicate the relative strengths and weaknesses of each technique.

3. Develop three rules of thumb for guiding strategic managers in their use of forecasting.

4. Develop a typewritten two-page forecast of a variable that you believe will affect the prosperity of your business school over the next 10 years.

5. Using prominent business journals, find two examples of firms that either benefited or suffered from environmental forecasts.

6. Describe the background, skills, and abilities of the individual you would hire as the environmental forecaster for a firm with $500 million in annual sales. How would the qualifications of such an individual differ for a much smaller firm? For a much larger firm?

FIGURE 5–7
Task and Remote Environment Impact Matrix

Remote Environments	Task Environments			
	Key Customer Trends	**Key Competitor Trends**	**Key Supplier Trends**	**Key Labor Market Trends**
Economic	*Example:* Trends in inflation and unemployment rates.		*Example:* Annual domestic oil demand and worldwide sulfur demand through the year 2020.	
Social	*Example:* Increasing numbers of single-parent homes.			*Example:* Rising education level of U.S. population.
Political	*Example:* Increasing numbers of punitive damage awards in product liability cases.		*Example:* Possibility of oil boycotts	
Technological		*Example:* Increasing use of superchips and computer-based instrumentation for synthesizing genes.	*Example:* Use of cobalt 60 gamma irradiation to extend shelf life of perishables.	
Ecological		*Example:* Increased use of biodegradable fast-food packaging.		*Example:* Increasing availability of mature workers with experience in "smokestack" industries.

BIBLIOGRAPHY

Alerthal, Lester M., Jr. "Keeping the Lead in an Ever-Changing Global Landscape." *Planning Review* 23, no. 8 (September–October 1995), p. 13.

Alexander, Marcus; Andrew Campbell; and Michael Gorld. "A New Model for Reforming the Planning Review Process." *Planning-Review* 23, no. 1 (January–February 1995), p. 12.

Allaire, Y., and M. E. Firsirotu. "Coping with Strategic Uncertainty." *Sloan Management Review*, Spring 1989, pp. 7–16.

Barndt, W. D., Jr. "Profiling Rival Decision Makers." *The Journal of Business Strategy*, January–February 1991, pp. 8–11.

Barrett, F. D. "Strategies for the Use of Artificial and Human Intelligence." *Business Quarterly*, Summer 1986, pp. 18–27.

Coplin, W. D., and M. K. O'Leary. "1991 World Political Risk Forecast." *Planning Review*, January–February 1991, pp. 16–23.

Czinkota, M. R. "International Information Needs for U.S. Competitiveness." *Business Horizons*, November–December 1991, pp. 86–91.

Fuld, L. "A Recipe for Business Intelligence Success." *The Journal of Business Strategy*, January–February 1991, pp. 12–17.

———. "Achieving Total Quality through Intelligence." *Long Range Planning*, February 1992, pp. 109–15.

Fulmer, W., and R. Fulmer. "Strategic Group Technique: Involving Managers in Strategic Planning." *Long Range Planning*, April 1990, pp. 79–84.

Gelb, B. D.; M. J. Saxton; G. M. Zinkhan; and N. D. Albers. "Competitive Intelligence: Insights from Executives." *Business Horizons*, January–February 1991, pp. 43–47.

Gilad, B. "U.S. Intelligence System: Model for Corporate Chiefs?" *The Journal of Business Strategy*, May–June 1991, pp. 20–25.

Herring, J. P. "The Role of Intelligence in Formulating Strategy." *The Journal of Business Strategy*, September–October 1992, pp. 54–60.

Kahane, A. "Scenarios for Energy: Sustainable World vs. Global Mercantilism." *Long Range Planning*, August 1992, pp. 38–46.

Keiser, B. "Practical Competitor Intelligence." *Planning Review*, September 1987, pp. 14–19.

Lederer, A. L., and V. Sethi. "Guidelines for Strategic Information Planning." *The Journal of Business Strategy*, November–December 1991, pp. 38–43.

Pant, P. N., and W. H. Starbuck. "Innocents in the Forest: Forecasting and Research Methods." *Yearly Review of Management*, June 1990, pp. 433–60.

Pine, B. Joseph, II. "Peter Schwartz Offers Two Scenarios for the Future." *Planning Review* 23, no. 5 (September–October 1995), p. 30.

Premkumar, G., and W. R. King. "Assessing Strategic Information Systems Planning." *Long Range Planning*, October 1991, pp. 41–58.

Rousch, G. B. "A Program for Sharing Corporate Intelligence." *The Journal of Business Strategy*, January–February 1991, pp. 4–7.

Schoemaker, Paul J. H. "Scenario Planning: A Tool for Strategic Thinking." *Sloan Management Review* 36, no. 2 (Winter 1995), p. 25.

———. "Getting the Most Out of Scenarios: Some Questions and Answers." *Planning Review* 23, no. 6 (November–December 1995), p. 37.

Schriefer, Audrey E. "Getting the Most Out of Scenarios: Advice from the Experts." *Planning Review* 23, no. 5 (September–October 1995), p. 33.

Simpson, Daniel. "The Planning Process and the Role of the Planner." *Planning Review* 23, no. 1 (January–February 1995), p. 20.

———. "Planning in a Global Business." *Planning Review* 23, no. 2 (March–April 1995), p. 25.

Stokke, P. R.; W. K. Ralston; T. A. Boyce; and I. H. Wilson. "Scenario Planning for Norwegian Oil and Gas." *Long Range Planning*, April 1990, pp. 17–26.

Thurow, Lester C. "Surviving in a Turbulent Environment." *Planning Review* 23, no. 5 (September–October 1995), p. 24.

Wilson, Ian; Oliver W. Markley; Joseph F. Coates; and Clement Bezold. "A Forum of Futurists." *Planning Review* 23, no. 6 (November–December 1995), p. 10.

APPENDIX 5–A

SOURCES FOR ENVIRONMENTAL FORECASTS

REMOTE AND INDUSTRY ENVIRONMENTS

A. Economic considerations:
   1. *Predicasts* (most complete and up-to-date review of forecasts).
   2. National Bureau of Economic Research.
   3. *Handbook of Basic Economic Statistics.*
   4. *Statistical Abstract of the United States* (also includes industrial, social, and political statistics).
   5. Publications by Department of Commerce agencies:
      a. Office of Business Economics (e.g., *Survey of Business*).
      b. Bureau of Economic Analysis (e.g., *Business Conditions Digest*).
      c. Bureau of the Census (e.g., *Survey of Manufacturers* and various reports on population, housing, and industries).
      d. Business and Defense Services Administration (e.g., *United States Industrial Outlook*).
   6. Securities and Exchange Commission (various quarterly reports on plant and equipment, financial reports, working capital of corporations).
   7. The Conference Board.
   8. *Survey of Buying Power.*
   9. *Marketing Economic Guide.*
   10. *Industrial Arts Index.*
   11. U.S. and national chambers of commerce.
   12. American Manufacturers Association.
   13. *Federal Reserve Bulletin.*
   14. *Economic Indicators*, annual report.
   15. *Kiplinger Newsletter.*
   16. International economic sources:
      a. *Worldcasts.*
      b. Master key index for business international publications.
      c. Department of Commerce.
         (1) Overseas business reports.
         (2) Industry and Trade Administration.
         (3) Bureau of the Census—*Guide to Foreign Trade Statistics.*
   17. *Business Periodicals Index.*
B. Social considerations:
   1. Public opinion polls.

Sources: Adapted with numerous additions from C. R. Goeldner and L. M. Kirks, "Business Facts: Where to Find Them," *MSU Business Topics*, Summer 1976, pp. 23–76, reprinted by permission of the publisher, Division of Research, Graduate School of Business Administration, MSU; F. E. deCarbonnel and R. G. Donance, "Information Source for Planning Decisions," *California Management Review*, Summer 1973, pp. 42–53; and A. B. Nun, R. C. Lenz, Jr., H. W. Landford, and M. J. Cleary, "Data Source for Trend Extrapolation in Technological Forecasting," *Long Range Planning*, February 1972, pp. 72–76.

    2. Surveys such as *Social Indicators and Social Reporting,* the annals of the American Academy of Political and Social Sciences.

    3. Current controls: Social and behavioral sciences.

    4. Abstract services and indexes for articles in sociological, psychological, and political journals.

    5. Indexes for *The Wall Street Journal, New York Times*, and other newspapers.

    6. Bureau of the Census reports on population, housing, manufacturers, selected services, construction, retail trade, wholesale trade, and enterprise statistics.

    7. Various reports from such groups as the Brookings Institution and the Ford Foundation.

    8. World Bank Atlas (population growth and GNP data).

    9. World Bank–World Development Report.

C. Political considerations:

    1. *Public Affairs Information Services Bulletin.*

    2. CIS Index (Congressional Information Index).

    3. Business periodicals.

    4. Funk & Scott (regulations by product breakdown).

    5. Weekly compilation of presidential documents.

    6. *Monthly Catalog of Government Publications.*

    7. *Federal Register* (daily announcements of pending regulations).

    8. *Code of Federal Regulations* (final listing of regulations).

    9. Business International Master Key Index (regulations, tariffs).

    10. Various state publications.

    11. Various information services (Bureau of National Affairs, Commerce Clearing House, Prentice Hall).

D. Technological considerations:

    1. *Applied Science and Technology Index.*

    2. *Statistical Abstract of the United States.*

    3. Scientific and Technical Information Service.

    4. University reports, congressional reports.

    5. Department of Defense and military purchasing publishers.

    6. Trade journals and industrial reports.

    7. Industry contacts, professional meetings.

    8. Computer-assisted information searches.

    9. National Science Foundation annual report.

    10. *Research and Development Directory* patent records.

E. Industry considerations:

    1. *Concentration Ratios in Manufacturing* (Bureau of the Census).

    2. *Input-Output Survey* (productivity ratios).

    3. *Monthly Labor Review* (productivity ratios).

    4. *Quarterly Failure Report* (Dun & Bradstreet).

    5. *Federal Reserve Bulletin* (capacity utilization).

    6. *Report on Industrial Concentration and Product Diversification in the 1,000 Largest Manufacturing Companies* (Federal Trade Commission).

    7. Industry trade publications.

    8. Bureau of Economic Analysis, Department of Commerce (specialization ratios).

INDUSTRY AND OPERATING ENVIRONMENTS

A. Competition and supplier considerations:
   1. Target Group Index.
   2. U.S. Industrial Outlook.
   3. Robert Morris annual statement studies.
   4. Troy, Leo Almanac of Business & Industrial Financial Ratios.
   5. Census of Enterprise Statistics.
   6. Securities and Exchange Commission (10-K reports).
   7. Annual reports of specific companies.
   8. *Fortune 500 Directory, The Wall Street Journal, Barron's, Forbes, Dun's Review.*
   9. Investment services and directories: Moody's, Dun & Bradstreet, Standard & Poor's, Starch Marketing, Funk & Scott Index.
   10. Trade association surveys.
   11. Industry surveys.
   12. Market research surveys.
   13. *Country Business Patterns.*
   14. *Country and City Data Book.*
   15. Industry contacts, professional meetings, salespeople.
   16. *NFIB Quarterly Economic Report for Small Business.*

B. Customer profile:
   1. *Statistical Abstract of the United States*, first source of statistics.
   2. *Statistical Sources* by Paul Wasserman (a subject guide to data—both domestic and international).
   3. *American Statistics Index* (Congressional Information Service Guide to statistical publications of U.S. government—monthly).
   4. Office to the Department of Commerce:
      a. Bureau of the Census reports on population, housing, and industries.
      b. *U.S. Census of Manufacturers* (statistics by industry, area, and products).
      c. *Survey of Current Business* (analysis of business trends, especially February and July issues).
   5. Market research studies (*A Basic Bibliography on Market Review*, compiled by Robert Ferber et al., American Marketing Association).
   6. *Current Sources of Marketing Information: A Bibliography of Primary Marketing Data* by Gunther & Goldstein, AMA.
   7. *Guide to Consumer Markets*, The Conference Board (provides statistical information with demographic, social, and economic data—annual).
   8. *Survey of Buying Power.*
   9. *Predicasts* (abstracts of publishing forecasts of all industries, detailed products, and end-use data).
   10. *Predicasts Basebook* (historical data from 1960 to present, covering subjects ranging from population and GNP to specific products and services; series are coded by Standard Industrial Classifications).
   11. *Market Guide* (individual market surveys of over 1,500 U.S. and Canadian cities; includes population, location, trade areas, banks, principal industries, colleges and universities, department and chain stores, newspapers, retail outlets, and sales).
   12. *Country and City Data Book* (includes bank deposits, birth and death rates, business firms, education, employment, income of families, manufacturers, population, savings, and wholesale and retail trade).

13. *Yearbook of International Trade Statistics* (UN).
14. *Yearbook of National Accounts Statistics* (UN).
15. *Statistical Yearbook* (UN—covers population, national income, agricultural and industrial production, energy, external trade, and transport).
16. *Statistics of (Continents): Sources for Market Research* (includes separate books on Africa, America, Europe).

C. Key natural resources:

1. *Minerals Yearbook, Geological Survey* (Bureau of Mines, Department of the Interior).
2. *Agricultural Abstract* (Department of Agriculture).
3. Statistics of electric utilities and gas pipeline companies (Federal Power Commission).
4. Publications of various institutions: American Petroleum Institute, Atomic Energy Commission, Coal Mining Institute of America, American Steel Institute, and Brookings Institution.

APPENDIX 5–B

STRATEGIC PLANNING FORECASTING TOOLS AND TECHNIQUES

1. **Dialectical Inquiry.**
   Development, evaluation, and synthesis of conflicting points of view by (1) having separate assigned groups use debate format to formulate and refine each point of view and (2) then bringing two groups together for presentation of debate between and synthesis of their points of view.

2. **Nominal Group Technique.**
   Development, evaluation, and synthesis of individual points of view through an interactive process in a group setting.

3. **Delphi Method.**
   Development, evaluation, and synthesis of individual points of view by systematically soliciting and collating judgments on a particular topic through a set of carefully designed sequential questionnaires interspersed with summarized information and feedback of opinions derived from earlier responses.

4. **Focus Groups.**
   Bringing together recognized experts and qualified individuals in an organized setting to develop, evaluate, and synthesize their individual points of view on a particular topic.

5. **Simulation Technique.**
   Computer-based technique for simulating future situations and then predicting the outcome of various courses of action against each of these situations.

6. **PIMS Analysis.**
   Application of the experiences of a diverse sample of successful and unsuccessful firms.

7. **Market Opportunity Analysis.**
   Identification of markets and market factors in the economy and the industry that will affect the demand for and marketing of a product or service.

8. **Benchmarking.**
   Comparative analysis of competitor programs and strategic positions for use as reference points in the formulation of organization objectives.

9. **Situational Analysis** (SWOT or TOWS).
   Systematic development and evaluation of past, present, and future data to identify internal strengths and weaknesses and external threats and opportunities.

10. **Critical Success Factors/Strategic Issues Analysis.**
    Identification and analysis of a limited number of areas in which high performance will ensure a successful competitive position.

11. **Product Life Cycle Analysis.**
    Analysis of market dynamics in which a product is viewed according to its position within distinct stages of its sales history.

12. **Future Studies.**
    Development of future situations and factors based on agreement of a group of "experts," often from a variety of functional areas within a firm.

Source: Excerpted with updates from J. Webster, W. Reif, and J. Bracker, "The Manager's Guide to Strategic Planning Tools and Techniques," *Planning Review*, November–December 1989, pp. 4–13, 48.

13. **Multiple Scenarios.**
   Smoothly unfolding narratives that describe an assumed future expressed through a sequence of time frames and snapshots.
14. **SPIRE** (Systematic Procedure for Identification of Relevant Environments).
   A computer-assisted, matrix-generating tool for forecasting environmental changes that can have a dramatic impact on operations.
15. **Environmental Scanning, Forecasting, and Trend Analysis.**
   Continuous process, usually computer based, of monitoring external factors, events, situations, and projections of forecasts of trends.
16. **Experience Curves.**
   An organizing framework for dynamic analyses of cost and price for a product, a company, or an industry over an extended period.
17. **Portfolio Classification Analysis.**
   Classification and visual display of the present and prospective positions of firms and products according to the attractiveness of the market and the ability of the firms and products to compete within that market.
18. **Metagame Analysis.**
   Arriving at a strategic direction by thinking through a series of viewpoints on a contemplated strategy in terms of every competitor and every combination of competitive responses.
19. **Strategic Gap Analysis.**
   Examination of the difference between the extrapolation of current performance levels (e.g., current sales) and the projection of desired performance objectives (e.g., a desired sales level).
20. **Sustainable Growth Model.**
   Financial analysis of the sales growth rate that is required to meet market share objectives and the degree to which capacity must be expanded to achieve that growth rate.

CHAPTER 5 COHESION CASE ILLUSTRATION

FORECASTING AND THE COCA-COLA COMPANY

Coca-Cola's chief executive officer, Roberto Goizueta, communicating with Coke share-holders, appeared to suggest that Coke's strategic management process avoids significant emphasis on forecasting when he said:

> As an organization we are not wasting our energy forecasting what the soft-drink industry will be like in the many countries around the world in which we operate. And neither are we spending our time forecasting what the future holds for this company. We will use our resources to construct today the foundation on which OUR future . . . THE FUTURE WE ARE CREATING FOR OURSELVES . . . will be built.

* * * * *

> We do not want to leave our shareowners with the false impression that this wonderful soft-drink business of The Coca-Cola Company is totally impervious to any and all setbacks. How-ever, we are running this business today at a high efficiency, and we have the attitude and the financial resources, as well as the management team, needed to take care of any negative eventu-ality which may come our way. So . . . when it does, if we don't completely neutralize it, at the very least, we will minimize its impact.
>
> On the other hand, and as with everything in life, there will also surely be unexpected positive events in the future of this Company. When they happen, we will quickly put them to work to our advantage. In the past we have demonstrated our system has such capabilities, and we will continue to take advantage of every opportunity in the future.

On the surface, it would appear that Mr. Goizueta places little faith in efforts to forecast future events. A closer reading and review of Coke's management actions suggest other-wise. In other words, Mr. Goizueta is at least in part saying that Coca-Cola is a very focused company. While it serves a myriad of markets worldwide, it has learned some very simple and powerful lessons about the fundamentals of success in the soft-drink business. And it is his belief that Coke's ability to do those things and to adjust those things to changing conditions will perhaps more profoundly influence its success in an unknown future than will reactions generated by any single forecast. According to Mr. Goizueta, successful global marketing of soft-drink products requires certain conditions be in place that require a long time to develop: (1) a company must have, build, or buy a powerful trademark to be a globally successful soft-drink company, and (2) that company must have a global business system through which to reach consumers. (3) Such a business system must be able to appeal to cultures as diverse as Switzerland and Swaziland—to tailor products and messages to local markets. And finally, (4) there must be an intangible yet powerful ingredient—a central theme, idea, or symbol—that binds together the business system, the brands, and the consumers into an association with their best feelings and memories each time they drink a Coke. And it is sensitivity to ways that these key condi-tions can be applied, refined, and expanded that shapes future success at Coke.

While Goizueta eschews forecasts, he recently told *Financial World*:

> In the United States, we will be growing 6 percent in volume with double-digit earnings growth. But outside the United States, where we have 9–10 percent volume growth, we will have higher double-digit earnings increases.

Apparently there is keen management interest in charting and projecting soft-drink consumption patterns. An internal company trend analysis of soft-drink consumption during 1991 and the preceding 10 years is shown in the table, "Selected Country Results," from The Coca-Cola Company 1994 Annual Report.

Another area where Coca-Cola management appears sensitive to monitoring are changes in key countries, which have large populations, that support introduction or re-introduction of the "Coca-Cola Business System." Coke management calls this "seeding for the future," as is illustrated regarding India, China, and Indonesia in the excerpt on page 167.

Finally, several soft-drink-related facts or trends have appeared in various industry forums that provide Coke management with confirmation of its inclinations or possible "forecasts." Some of these include:

1. While annual per capita soft-drink consumption in the United States is about 770 servings, in markets abroad per capita rates average only 62 servings. In less developed markets, such as India, consumers drink less than three servings a year.

2. In international markets, most soft drinks are sold in single-serve bottles, one at a time. Getting consumers to take home bigger packages means they'll drink more.

3. In the United States, vending machines account for 12 percent of soft-drink sales; but they're still a rarity in many countries.

4. Soft drinks represent about one quarter of all beverages consumed in the United States. That means replacing other beverages or expanding into them represents growth for soft-drink companies.

5. Eastern Europe is developing rapidly as a soft-drink market from a negligible base in 1992. The breakup of the Soviet Union has opened new markets that represent sustained volume growth opportunities.

SELECTED COUNTRY RESULTS

Estimated Unit Case[1] Volume

| | Average Annual Growth | | | | 1994 Results | | | |
| | 10 Years | | 5 Years | | Unit Case Growth | | Company | |
	Company[3]	Industry[4]	Company[3]	Industry[4]	Company[3]	Industry[4]	Share[4]	Per Capita[4] Consumption
Worldwide[6]	7%	5%	6%	3%	10%	6%	46%	49
North America Business Sector[2]	4	3	4	3	7	4	41	296
United States	4	3	4	3	7	4	41	310
International Business Sector[6]	8	5	7	3	11	7	49	35
European Community	9	5	6	3	7	5	49	130
Benelux/Denmark	8	4	8	4	9	4	46	152
France	13	7	11	5	9	(1)	47	65
Germany	7	5	8	1	4	3	55	191
Great Britain	12	6	2	3	7	10	31	101
Italy	8	6	4	3	5	2	55	94
Spain	8	4	5	2	9	8	54	166
Pacific[5]	8	8	7	6	12	12	39	20
Australia	9	7	8	3	10	9	65	274
Japan[5]	6	1	6	2	8	8	30	133
Korea	5	5	4	1	11	5	52	59
Philippines	6	3	3	3	14	14	75	96
Thailand	12	14	9	9	14	11	48	54
Northeast Europe/Middle East (NEME)[6]	14	4	17	1	35	17	32	11
Egypt	5	2	4	0	47	4	55	26
Hungary	20	2	37	6	4	12	42	111
Norway	11	7	8	5	9	15	59	256
Poland	33	2	69	8	44	47	24	29
Africa	5	2	5	(1)	1	(7)	84	23
Nigeria	2	0	6	0	(14)	(25)	82	22
South Africa	5	3	5	1	4	0	88	146
Zimbabwe	8	6	5	(1)	9	4	87	62
Latin America	8	6	6	4	10	4	55	148
Argentina	7	6	14	11	12	12	57	189
Brazil	8	7	0	1	10	14	56	92
Chile	15	14	12	8	8	6	64	217
Mexico	8	6	6	4	11	7	57	333

[1] Unit case equals 24 8-ounce drinks.
[2] Consists of United States and Canada.
[3] Includes non-carbonated soft drinks.
[4] Includes only flavored, carbonated soft drinks.
[5] Company share and per capita include Japanese non-carbonated soft drinks; revised to conform with Japanese industry standards (equivalent Company share for Japan in 1993 was 31).
[6] The calculation of per capita consumption includes India and several former Soviet republics.

Seeding for the Future

Over the past five years, the Company's international unit case sales have increased at an average annual rate of 8 percent. No countries better exemplify the Company's long-term opportunity to maintain or exceed that sort of growth than the three profiled on this page. **Nearly 45 percent of the more than 5 billion people on earth live in China, India or Indonesia, but the per capita soft drink consumption rates for the countries are only 8, 3 and 6, respectively.** *While explosive short-term growth is unlikely, the potential for tremendous, sustained growth over time is extraordinary, and the Company is taking aggressive actions now to prepare the ground. Set forth below are some of the ways in which we are seeding for the future.*

INDIA

With 860 million people, India is, by far, the largest market in which Company products are not currently produced. That should change in 1993, thanks to the Indian government's approval of a joint venture formed in late 1991.

The Company will not, however, be starting from scratch. During the 1970s, the Coca-Cola system in India comprised 21 bottlers selling more than 32 million unit cases annually and accounting for 60 percent of the country's carbonated soft drink sales. The Company left India in 1977, but the Coca-Cola trademark continues to enjoy strong, positive recognition and recall among consumers.

The immediate task is to re-establish bottling and distribution networks in and around large metropolitan areas. Once up and running, we will be addressing several marketing opportunities, including packaging, where we see tremendous potential for large, multiserve containers.

Last year, the entire Indian carbonated soft drink industry sold only 113 million unit cases, less than the Company sold in Korea, a country with only 5 percent as many people. To say that the opportunity is enormous is an understatement. No market in the world shows greater promise for rapid, sustained growth for years to come.

CHINA

The Company resumed operations in China in 1981 after an absence of 41 years. Since our re-entry, we have invested $75 million in 13 bottling plants and a concentrate plant in Shanghai, which makes it possible for bottlers to purchase concentrate with local currency, a distinct advantage.

Company products have long been acceptable in China — in 1933 the country became the first market outside the United States to post annual sales of more than a million unit cases — and we are continuing to invest as necessary to make them available and affordable to every one of China's 1.2 billion people.

INDONESIA

If there is such a thing as an ideal soft drink market, it probably looks like Indonesia. Fifty-five percent of its 180 million people are under age 25; the average year-round temperature is a humid 80°F; gross national product is growing 6 to 7 percent a year; and the government welcomes foreign investment.

Last year, the Coca-Cola system sold 34 million unit cases of Company products, accounting for 71 percent of all carbonated soft drinks sold in the country. Because we see the potential for a vastly larger market, we have, over the past few years, rationalized our bottling system and entered, directly and indirectly, into three joint ventures that last year posted 87 percent of our system's unit case sales. Since we began making these investments in 1987, unit case sales have grown at a compound annual rate of 15 percent, and the business is well positioned for continued rapid growth in the years to come.

35

6

INTERNAL ANALYSIS

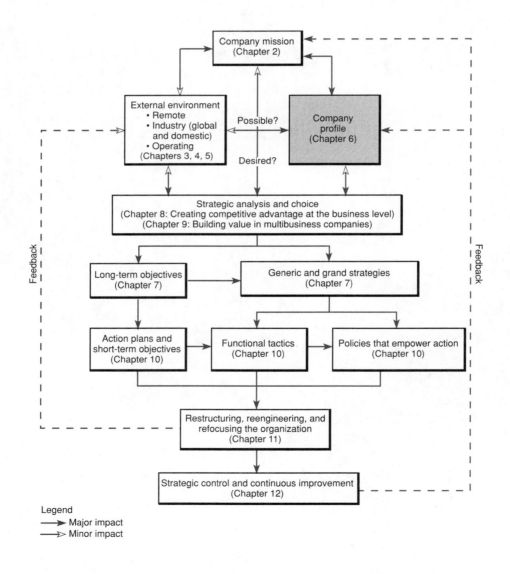

Company mission
(Chapter 2)

External environment
• Remote
• Industry (global and domestic)
• Operating
(Chapters 3, 4, 5)

Possible?

Desired?

Company profile
(Chapter 6)

Strategic analysis and choice
(Chapter 8: Creating competitive advantage at the business level)
(Chapter 9: Building value in multibusiness companies)

Long-term objectives
(Chapter 7)

Generic and grand strategies
(Chapter 7)

Action plans and short-term objectives
(Chapter 10)

Functional tactics
(Chapter 10)

Policies that empower action
(Chapter 10)

Restructuring, reengineering, and refocusing the organization
(Chapter 11)

Strategic control and continuous improvement
(Chapter 12)

Feedback

Feedback

Legend
⟶ Major impact
⟶▹ Minor impact

Three ingredients are critical to the success of a strategy. First, the strategy must be *consistent* with conditions in the competitive environment. Specifically, it must take advantage of existing or projected opportunities and minimize the impact of major threats. Second, the strategy must place *realistic* requirements on the firm's internal capabilities. In other words, the firm's pursuit of market opportunities must be based not only on the existence of such opportunities but also on the firm's key internal strengths. Finally, the strategy must be *carefully executed*. The focus of this chapter is on the second ingredient: *realistic analysis of the firm's internal capabilities.*

Managers often do this subjectively, based on intuition and "gut feel." Years of seasoned industry experience positions managers to make sound subjective judgments. But just as often, or more often, this may not be the case. In fast-changing environments, reliance on past experiences can cause management myopia or a tendency to accept the status quo and disregard signals that change is needed. And with managers new to strategic decision making, subjective decisions are particularly suspect. A lack of experience is easily replaced by emotion, narrow functional expertise, and the opinions of others creating the foundation on which newer managers build strategic recommendations. So it is that new managers' subjective assessments often come back to haunt them.

This chapter looks at several ways managers achieve greater objectivity and rigor as they analyze their company's internal capabilities. Managers often start their internal analysis with questions like: "How well is the current strategy working? What is our current situation? Or what are our strengths and weaknesses?" *SWOT analysis* and *functional analysis* are two approaches discussed in this chapter that managers frequently use to introduce realism and greater objectivity into their attempts to answer these questions. More recently, insightful managers have begun to look at their business as a chain of activities that add value by creating the products or services they sell. Associated with this perspective is a powerful concept for introducing rigor and objectivity into internal analysis, the *value chain*, which this chapter will examine in great detail. Finally, objectivity and realism are enhanced when managers use meaningful standards for comparison regardless of the particular analytical framework they employ in internal analysis. We conclude this chapter examining how managers do this using *past performance*, stages of industry evolution, *comparison with competitors* or other *"benchmarks," industry norms*, and traditional *financial analysis*.

Laura Ashley Holdings PLC, the famous United Kingdom-based retail chain, recently convinced American Ann Iverson to leave her position as President and CEO of Kay Bee Toys to move to London and become Laura Ashley's new President and CEO. She is the first female CEO since the late Laura Ashley founded the company 42 years ago. Iverson spent the first four months traveling to stores in the United Kingdom, Europe, and the United States conducting a realistic analysis of Laura Ashley's internal capabilities and situation. You should read Global Strategy in Action 6–1 to see what she found and you should use this example to help you understand the focus of this chapter.

TRADITIONAL APPROACHES TO INTERNAL ANALYSIS

Managers have historically relied on two approaches to structure their analysis of internal capabilities so that they introduce greater objectivity into their firm's strategic decision-making process: SWOT analysis and functional analysis.

ENGLAND'S FAMOUS RETAILER LAURA ASHLEY HOLDINGS PLC NEEDED A WOMAN AT THE HELM TO CONDUCT A REALISTIC INTERNAL ANALYSIS

When Ann Iverson became CEO of Laura Ashley, she found the Laura Ashley name meant different things to different people. Unfortunately, most of those people worked at Laura Ashley stores. Stores in the United States and Europe offered vastly different items. Buyers and designers around the globe created hundreds of styles, and many clashed with Laura Ashley's English country fashions.

The chain's mail-order catalog showed the problem. Fall 1995 found three different versions for the United States, United Kingdom, and European markets. Iverson traveled throughout the various stores and quickly concluded that Laura Ashley had lost its focus. "We didn't have a single point of view or great conviction . . . people didn't understand what we stood for or even who they reported to." Iverson went to work.

First, she was the fourth CEO in five years. She was the first woman since the founder 40 years earlier, and she was the first with retail experience among the last five. Heading into 1996 she offered the following assessment of Laura Ashley's current internal capabilities.

"One of our main problems is a vast range of product lines, many filled with weak sellers and duplicate styles." When she joined the firm, 83 percent of its sales came from 22 percent of the merchandise. She quickly eliminated 30 percent of the clothing styles and 20 percent of the home furnishings.

"Our U.S. stores are too small and cramped for our large range. Most U.S. stores are only 600 square feet while newer shops in the United Kingdom average 4,700 square feet. And many U.S. stores are second rate. Of the 500 best U.S. shopping malls, Laura Ashley has stores in only 150."

Although the famous Laura Ashley "green box" store front is likely to remain intact, Iverson says she hopes to create a common store front design and format. "Of the famous brands in more than one market—Estee Lauder, Ralph Lauren, the Gap—they all have a common theme. They have a common way they talk to the customer. We don't."

"Many of our costs are too high. Distribution costs rose 1.6 million pounds in six months due to a contract with a shipper that costs the company far too much money. And shipping is chaotic at times—products shipped from the Far East go to a facility in Wales where they were then packaged and reshipped to the United States—and then repackaged and sent to Japan."

Iverson is also reviewing the company's heavy vertical integration with significant manufacturing capacity. She says retailers should not be manufacturers and distributors as well as retailers.

British analysts are encouraged for 1997 based on her initial efforts. They are optimistic about her predictions that Laura Ashley can move from operating margins around 2 percent to double-digit levels in 1998. Her concluding comment after completing her internal analysis and charting her direction: "There's no question that it's a brilliant brand, but we're finally behaving like a retailer."

It appears Iverson conducted a realistic internal analysis.

Source: Tara Parker-Pope, "Laura Ashley's Chief Tries to Spruce Up Company That Isn't Dressed for Success," *The Wall Street Journal*, September 22, 1995. Reprinted by permission of *The Wall Street Journal*, © 1995 Dow Jones & Company, Inc. All rights reserved worldwide.

SWOT Analysis

SWOT is an acronym for the internal Strengths and Weaknesses of a firm and the environmental Opportunities and Threats facing that firm. SWOT analysis is an easy technique through which managers create a quick overview of a company's strategic situation. It is based on the assumption that an effective strategy derives from a sound "fit" between a firm's internal capabilities (strengths and weaknesses) and its external situation (opportunities and threats). A good fit maximizes a firm's strengths and opportunities and minimizes its weaknesses and threats. Accurately applied, this simple assumption has powerful implications for the design of a successful strategy.

Environmental industry analysis (Chapters 3 through 5) provides the information needed to identify opportunities and threats in a firm's environment, the first fundamental focus in SWOT analysis. We define opportunities and threats first.

Opportunities

An *opportunity* is a major favorable situation in a firm's environment. Key trends are one source of opportunities. Identification of a previously overlooked market segment, changes in competitive or regulatory circumstances, technological changes, and improved buyer or supplier relationships could represent opportunities for the firm.

Threats

A *threat* is a major unfavorable situation in a firm's environment. Threats are key impediments to the firm's current or desired position. The entrance of new competitors, slow market growth, increased bargaining power of key buyers or suppliers, technological changes, and new or revised regulations could represent threats to a firm's success.

Japanese acceptance of superior U.S. technology in personal computers is proving a major opportunity for Apple and IBM. Deregulation of the airline industry was a major opportunity for regional carriers (such as Southwest Airlines) to serve routes previously closed to them. Some traditional carriers (such as United) saw deregulation as a threat to the profitability of their high-traffic routes. So an opportunity for one firm can be a threat to another. Moreover, the same factor can be seen as both an opportunity and a threat. For example, the baby boom generation moving into its prime earning years presents a major opportunity for financial service firms like Merrill Lynch. However, this generation wants convenient inexpensive financial services, which is a major threat to Merrill Lynch's established broker network—historically a Merrill Lynch strength.

Understanding the key opportunities and threats facing a firm helps its managers identify realistic options from which to choose an appropriate strategy and clarifies the most effective niche for the firm.

The second fundamental focus in SWOT analysis is the identification of internal strengths and weaknesses.

Strengths

A *strength* is a resource, skill, or other advantage relative to competitors and the needs of the markets a firm serves or expects to serve. It is a *distinctive competence* when it gives the firm a comparative advantage in the marketplace. Strengths may exist with regard to financial resources, image, market leadership, buyer-supplier relations, and other factors.

Weaknesses

A *weakness* is a limitation or deficiency in resource, skills, or capabilities that seriously impedes a firm's effective performance. Facilities, financial resources, management capabilities, marketing skills, and brand image can be sources of weaknesses.

The sheer size and level of Microsoft's user base have proven to be a key strength on which it built its initially successful strategy in applications software like word processing, financial services, and operating systems. Limited financial capacity was a weakness recognized by Southwest Airlines, which charted a selective route expansion strategy to build the best profit record in a deregulated airline industry.

FIGURE 6–1
SWOT Analysis Diagram

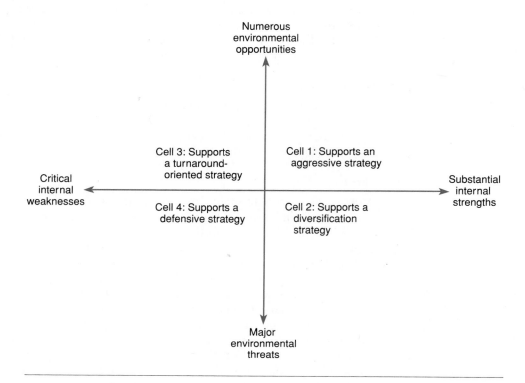

SWOT analysis can be used in many ways to aid strategy analysis. The most common way is to use it as a logical framework guiding systematic discussion of a firm's situation and the basic alternatives that the firm might consider. What one manager sees as an opportunity, another may see as a potential threat. Likewise, a strength to one manager may be a weakness to another. Different assessments may reflect underlying power considerations within the firm or differing factual perspectives. Systematic analysis of these issues facilitates objective internal analysis.

A second way in which SWOT analysis can be used to aid strategic analysis is illustrated in Figure 6–1. Key external opportunities and threats are systematically compared with internal strengths and weaknesses in a structured approach. The objective is identification of one of four distinct patterns in the match between a firm's internal and external situations. These patterns are represented by the four cells in Figure 6–1. Cell 1 is the most favorable situation; the firm faces several environmental opportunities and has numerous strengths that encourage pursuit of those opportunities. This situation suggests growth-oriented strategies to exploit the favorable match. America OnLine's intensive market development strategy in the online services market is the result of a favorable match of its strengths of technical expertise, early entry, and reputation with an opportunity for impressive market growth as millions of people joined the "information highway" in the latter 1990s. Cell 4 is the least favorable situation, with the firm facing major environmental threats from a position of relative weakness. This situation clearly calls for strategies that reduce or redirect involvement in the products or markets examined by means of SWOT analysis. Citicorp's successful turnaround from the verge of insolvency due to massive defaults on many international loans is an example of such a strategy in the early 1990s.

In cell 2, a firm with key strengths faces an unfavorable environment. In this situation, strategies would use current strengths to build long-term opportunities in more opportunistic product markets. Greyhound, possessing many strengths in intercity bus transportation, still faced an environment dominated by fundamental, long-term threats, such as airline competition and high costs. The result was product development into nonpassenger (freight) services, followed by diversification into other businesses (e.g., financial services).

A firm in cell 3 faces impressive market opportunity but is constrained by internal weaknesses. The focus of strategy for such a firm is eliminating the internal weaknesses so as to more effectively pursue the market opportunity. Disney's late 1995 acquisition of ABC/Capital Cities was in part an attempt to overcome key weaknesses in Disney's control of distribution outlets for its varied, excellent programming so that it could more easily pursue global opportunities in the entertainment industry of the 21st century.

Overall, SWOT analysis highlights the central role that the identification of internal strengths and weaknesses plays in a manager's search for effective strategies. The careful matching of a firm's opportunities and threats with its strengths and weaknesses is the essence of sound strategy formulation. Global Strategy in Action 6–2 shows three key players in the global PC industry attempting to do just this in 1996.

Although SWOT analysis provides an excellent framework through which managers can view their firm's strategic situation, it does not explain how managers identify internal strengths and weaknesses. The functional approach is one way managers have traditionally sought to isolate and evaluate internal strengths and weaknesses.

The Functional Approach

Key internal factors are a firm's basic capabilities, limitations, and characteristics. Figure 6–2 lists typical internal factors, some of which would be the focus of internal analysis in most firms. The list is broken along functional lines for one logical reason. Most firms organize their operations at some level along functional lines to get their products or services sold, produced, delivered, financed, and accounted. It stands to reason that close scrutiny of each of these functions serves as a compelling, strategically relevant focus for internal analysis.

Firms are not likely to evaluate all of the factors listed in Figure 6–2 (pp. 176–77) as potential strengths or weaknesses. To develop or revise a strategy, managers would prefer to identify the few factors on which its success is most likely to depend. Equally important, a firm's reliance on particular internal factors will vary by industry, market segment, product life cycle, and the firm's current position. Managers are looking for what Chester Barnard calls the "strategic factors," those internal capabilities that are most critical for success in a particular competitive area. The strategic factors of firms in the oil industry, for example, will be quite different from those of firms in the construction industry or the hospitality industry. Strategic factors also can vary among firms within the same industry. In the mechanical writing industry, for example, the strategies of BIC and Cross, both successful firms, are based on different internal strengths: BIC's on its strength in mass production, extensive advertising, and mass distribution channels; Cross's on high quality, image, and selective distribution channels.

Strategists examine a firm's past performance to isolate key internal contributors to favorable (or unfavorable) results. What did we do well, or poorly, in marketing, operations, and financial management that had a major influence on our past results? Was our sales force effectively organized? Were we in the right channels of distribution? Did we have the financial resources needed to support our past strategy? The same examination can be applied to a firm's current situation, with particular emphasis on changes in the

GLOBAL
STRATEGY IN
ACTION 6–2

THREE GLOBAL PC MAKERS TAKE A "SWOT" AT THE U.S. HOME PC MARKET

The PC industry is becoming very competitive. Forrester Research, which predicted a "golden age" for home PCs in the late 1990s, now says the market will slow significantly by 1998. They say that "PC makers will need new strategies to endure, such as really cheap, specialized models. Dell Computer's wizard founder Mr. Dell says: "There's no way all these companies are going to survive." Here's what other "experts" are saying:

Profit margins are very thin, the products are obsolete in six months, and buyers are fickle with endless options. More and more companies are jumping into the home PC market. But 1996 sees too many players and cut-throat competition.

Packard Bell leads the home PC market with a 32 percent share, but doesn't make much money and recently sold 20 percent of itself to NEC–Japan. Hewlett Packard operates at a loss; IBM lost $1 billion in 1995. "We don't know if anyone is making money,"says an IBM spokesman, "yet you need a lot of inventory on which prices come down all the time!"

New players keep coming. NEC and ACER–Taiwan re-entered the home PC market. And solid players like Dell, Gateway, Apple, AST, and Compaq already have serious positions. AT&T and Radio Shack have cut their losses and exited.

PC makers argue that the business segment is 90 percent penetrated; the home market is growing and only 30 percent of U.S. homes (smaller overseas) have PCs, leaving 68 million homes without them. "We have the opportunity to become a market leader in the major growth opportunities—home PCs—over the next 20 years" say HP's home PC general manager.

But recent surveys suggest only 5 percent of homes without PCs are likely to purchase within one year. Replacement sales are less likely with easily upgraded Pentium models. The price tag of $2,000 + is way above mass merchandising standards. Some outsiders like Oracle's Larry Ellison are pushing a $500 stripped-down model that will "surf" the Internet. It's hotly rejected by major PC makers, maybe because it could redefine the whole industry.

Gross profit margins for PC makers range from 8 percent to 14 percent—well below the 20 percent to 30 percent in traditional consumer electronics. Microsoft generates an 80 percent margin on its Windows operating system; Intel gets a 50 percent gross margin on its Pentium chips.

Source: Bart Ziegler, "PC Makers' Big Push into the Home Market Comes at Risky Time," *The Wall Street Journal* 226, no. 86; Jeff Trachtenberg and Bart Ziegler, "Sony Expected in U.S. Market for Home PCs,"*The Wall Street Journal*, November 13, 1995; "Making Over the IBM PC Co.," *Information Week*, November 13, 1995, p. 97; Peter Burrows, "Is Spindler A Survivor?" *Business Week*, October 2, 1995, p. 62.

importance of key dimensions over time. For example, heavy advertising, mass production, and mass distribution were strategic internal factors in BIC's initial strategy for ballpoint pens and disposable lighters. With the product life cycle fast reaching maturity, BIC later determined that cost-conscious mass production was a strategic factor, whereas heavy advertising was not.

Analysis of past trends in a firm's sales, costs, and profitability is of major importance in identifying its strategic internal factors. And that identification should be based on a clear picture of the nature of the firm's sales. An anatomy of past sales trends broken down by product lines, channels of distribution, key customers or types of customers, geographic region, and sales approach should be developed in detail. A similar anatomy should be developed on costs and profitability. Detailed investigation of the firm's performance history helps isolate the internal factors that influence its sales, costs, and profitability or their interrelationships. For example, one firm may find that 83 percent of its sales result from 25 percent of its products, and another firm may find that 30 percent of its products (or

continued

Let's look at three industry players.

SONY—Japanese electronic giant Sony chose 1996 to enter the U.S. home PC market. It has concluded that it can use its powerful brand name and reservoir of electronics expertise to elbow its way into this "growth market." It also believes synergies with its semiconductor and computer peripheral businesses, which are its fastest growing U.S. businesses, represent key strengths. Unknown to many is the fact that Sony has long manufactured portable computers and workstations for Dell and Apple. It also sells monitors to virtually all U.S. computer manufacturers.

IBM—The new head of the IBM PC Co., Robert Stephenson, taking over a group that lost $1 billion in 1995, said this: "I'm spending my time reengineering the whole process of becoming a reliable supplier. We have good strategies. We just are not executing well. If we can get the reengineering of our manufacturing, procurement, and distribution right, marketing and sales will follow. To put it bluntly, if we can't correct our reliability as a supplier, we won't be in business. . . . In home PCs, we have a good product but its $2,000–$3,000 price is too high . . . And we have got to change the way we develop products and make brand managers and marketing people think in tune."

Apple—Demand for Macintosh has been booming with a $1 billion backlog in 1996. But Apple's stock price has plunged. Apple can't cash in on the surge because it lacks critical parts, especially modems and custom chips. That's because many of its components are custom-designed and sourced to only one supplier. That makes accurate forecasts critical . . . and that's where Apple screwed up. 1995 sales surged 25 percent, Apple predicted 15 percent growth based on "sandbagged" estimates Apple salespeople gave Apple executives that they knew they could easily surpass in order to enhance their bonuses. And analysts predict consumers unable to buy Macintosh will opt for computers running Windows 95 and will not return to the Apple fold. Michael Spindler, Apple's CEO, says "I resent the idea that we have systemic problems" as he argues their problems are fixable.

When you apply a SWOT analysis to the home PC market and these three players, what do you see and what do you think will happen?

services) contribute 78 percent of its profitability. On the basis of such results, a firm may determine that certain key internal factors (e.g., experience in particular distribution channels, pricing policies, warehouse location, technology) deserve major attention in the formulation of future strategy.

The identification of strategic internal factors requires an external focus. A strategist's efforts to isolate key internal factors are assisted by analysis of industry conditions and trends and by comparisons with competitors. BIC's identification of mass production and advertising as key internal factors was based as much on analysis of industry and competitive characteristics as on analysis of its own past performance. Changing conditions in an industry can lead to the need to reexamine a firm's internal strengths and weaknesses in light of newly emerging determinants of success in that industry.

It is important for you to see that a functional approach, regardless of situational differences, focuses managers on basic business functions leading to a more objective, relevant internal analysis that enhances strategic decision making. Whether looking at attributes of marketing, production, financing, information systems, or human resource management, the functional approach structures managers' thinking in a focused, potentially objective manner.

FIGURE 6–2
Key Internal Factors: Potential Strengths or Weaknesses

Marketing

Firm's products-services: breadth of product line.
Concentration of sales in a few products or to a few customers.
Ability to gather needed information about markets.
Market share or submarket shares.
Product-service mix and expansion potential: life cycle of key products; profit-sales balance in product-service.
Channels of distribution: number, coverage, and control.
Effective sales organization; knowledge of customer needs.
Product-service image, reputation, and quality.
Imaginativeness, efficiency, and effectiveness of sales promotion and advertising.
Pricing strategy and pricing flexibility.
Procedures for digesting market feedback and developing new products, services, or markets.
After-sale service and follow-up.
Goodwill—brand loyalty.

Financial and Accounting

Ability to raise short-term capital.
Ability to raise long-term capital; debt-equity.
Corporate-level resources (multibusiness firm).
Cost of capital relative to that of industry and competitors.
Tax considerations.
Relations with owners, investors, and stockholders.
Leverage position; capacity to utilize alternative financial strategies, such as lease or sale and leaseback.
Cost of entry and barriers to entry.
Price-earnings ratio.
Working capital; flexibility of capital structure.
Effective cost control; ability to reduce cost.
Financial size.
Efficiency and effectiveness of accounting system for cost, budget, and profit planning.

Production, Operations, Technical

Raw materials cost and availability, supplier relationships.
Inventory control systems; inventory turnover.
Location of facilities; layout and utilization of facilities.
Economies of scale.
Technical efficiency of facilities and utilization of capacity.
Effectiveness of subcontracting use.
Degree of vertical integration; value added and profit margin.
Efficiency and cost-benefit of equipment.

While the functional approach offers logical advantages focusing internal analysis, managers that endured the downsizing and reengineering 1990s found the need for an approach that focused them even more narrowly on how work actually took place within their companies as they sought to meet customer needs. What these managers were responding to was the reality that producing goods or services and handling customers often necessitated the simultaneous involvement of multiple functions to be effective. They needed a way to look at their business as a series of activities that took place to create value for a customer—and to use this view as the framework to guide internal analysis. The value chain concept became their framework.

Value Chain Analysis

Value chain analysis is based on the assumption that a business's basic purpose is to create value for users of its products or services. In value chain analysis, managers divide the activities of their firm into sets of separate activities that add value. Their firm is viewed as

FIGURE 6–2
(concluded)

Production, Operations, Technical (cont.)

Effectiveness of operation control procedures: design, scheduling, purchasing, quality control, and
    efficiency.
Costs and technological competencies relative to those of industry and competitors.
Research and development–technology–innovation.
Patents, trademarks, and similar legal protection.

Personnel

Management personnel.
Employees' skill and morale.
Labor relations costs compared to those of industry and competitors.
Efficiency and effectiveness of personnel policies.
Effectiveness of incentives used to motivate performance.
Ability to level peaks and valleys of employment.
Employee turnover and absenteeism.
Specialized skills.
Experience.

Quality Management

Relationship with suppliers, customers.
Internal practices to enhance quality of products and services.
Procedures for monitoring quality.

Information Systems

Timeliness and accuracy of information about sales, operations, cash, and suppliers.
Relevance of information for tactical decisions.
Information to manage quality issues; customer service.
Ability of people to use the information that is provided.

Organization and General Management

Organizational structure.
Firm's image and prestige.
Firm's record in achieving objectives.
Organization of communication system.
Overall organizational control system (effectiveness and utilization).
Organizational climate; organizational culture.
Use of systematic procedures and techniques in decision making.
Top-management skill, capabilities, and interest.
Strategic planning system.
Intraorganizational synergy (multibusiness firms).

a chain of value-creating activities starting with procuring raw materials or inputs and
continuing through design, component production, manufacturing and assembly, distribution, sales, delivery, and support of the ultimate user of its products or services. Each of
these activities can add value and each can be a source of competitive advantage. By
identifying and examining these activities, managers often acquire an in-depth understanding of their firm's capabilities, its cost structure, and how these create competitive advantage or disadvantage.

Value chain analysis divides a firm's activities into two major categories, primary activities and support activities, as shown in Figure 6–3. *Primary activities* are those involved in
the physical creation of the product, marketing and transfer to the buyer, and after-sale
support. *Support activities* assist the primary activities by providing infrastructure or inputs
that allow them to take place on an ongoing basis. The value chain includes a *profit margin*
since a markup above the cost of providing a firm's value-adding activities is normally part
of the price paid by the buyer—creating value that exceeds cost so as to generate a return
for the effort.

FIGURE 6–3
The Value Chain

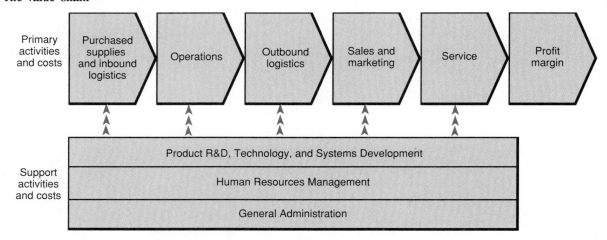

Primary Activities

- **Purchased Supplies and Inbound Logistics**—Activities, costs, and assets associated with purchasing fuel, energy, raw materials, parts components, merchandise, and consumable items from vendors; receiving, storing, and disseminating inputs from suppliers; inspection; and inventory management.

- **Operations**—Activities, costs, and assets associated with converting inputs into final product form (production, assembly, packaging, equipment maintenance, facilities, operations, quality assurance, environmental protection).

- **Outbound Logistics**—Activities, costs, and assets dealing with physically distributing the product to buyers (finished goods warehousing, order processing, order picking and packing, shipping, delivery vehicle operations).

- **Sales and Marketing**—Activities, costs, and assets related to sales force efforts, advertising and promotion, market research and planning, and dealer/distributor support.

- **Service**—Activities, costs, and assets associated with providing assistance to buyers, such as installation, spare parts delivery, maintenance and repair, technical assistance, buyer inquiries, and complaints.

Support Activities

- **Research, Technology, and Systems Development**—Activities, costs, and assets relating to product R&D, process R&D, process design improvement, equipment design, computer software development, telecommunications systems, computer-assisted design and engineering, new database capabilities, and development of computerized support systems.

- **Human Resources Management**—Activities, costs, and assets associated with the recruitment, hiring, training, development, and compensation of all types of personnel; labor relations activities; development of knowledge-based skills.

- **General Administration**—Activities, costs, and assets relating to general management, accounting and finance, legal and regulatory affairs, safety and security, management information systems, and other "overhead" functions.

Note: Purchasing, also called *procurement*, was listed as a support activity in the original value chain model. We have chosen to list it as part of the inbound primary activities because of the prominent role it plays at this stage for most value-sensitive companies today. At the same time, keep in mind that many companies retain a procurement function that provides purchasing support to all the organization's primary activities. For example, office supplies or other routine supplies, from safety gear in operations to recurring ads in newspapers sought by marketing, may all be handled through one suport activity or procurement department.

Source: Adapted from Michael E. Porter, *Competitive Advantage* (New York: The Free Press, 1985), pp 37–43; and A. A. Thompson and A. Strickland, *Strategic Management* (Burr Ridge, IL: Richard D. Irwin, 1995), p. 98.

FIGURE 6–4

The Difference between Traditional Cost Accounting and Activity-Based Cost Accounting

Traditional Cost Accounting in a Purchasing Department		Activity-Based Cost Accounting in the Same Purchasing Department	
Wages and Salaries	$350,000	Evaluate supplier capabilities	$135,750
Employee benefits	115,000	Process purchase orders	82,100
Supplies	6,500	Expedite supplier deliveries	23,500
Travel	2,400	Expedite internal processing	15,840
Depreciation	17,000	Check quality of items purchased	94,300
Other fixed charges	124,000	Check incoming deliveries against purchase orders	48,450
Miscellaneous operating expenses	25,250	Resolve problems	110,000
		Internal administration	130,210
	$640,150		$640,150

Source: Terence P. Pare, "A New Tool for Managing Costs," *Fortune*, June 14, 1993, pp. 124–29. © 1993, Time, Inc. All rights reserved.

Conducting a Value Chain Analysis

The initial step in value chain analysis is to divide a company's operations into specific activities or business processes, usually grouping them similarly to the primary and support activity categories provided in Figure 6–3. Within each category, a firm typically performs a number of discrete activities that may represent key strengths or weaknesses. Service activities, for example, may include such discrete activities as installation, repair, parts distribution, and upgrading—any of which could be a major source of competitive advantage or disadvantage. The manager's challenge at this point is to be very detailed attempting to "disaggregate" what actually goes on into numerous distinct, analyzable activities rather than settling for a broad, general categorization.

The next step is to attempt to attach costs to each discrete activity. Each activity in the value chain incurs costs and ties up time and assets. Value chain analysis requires managers to assign costs and assets to each activity, thereby providing the basis to estimate costs of each activity. The result provides managers with a very different way of viewing costs than traditional cost accounting procedures would produce, as seen in Figure 6–4. Many managers find the value activity costs more useful in drawing conclusions about and managing internal strengths and weaknesses.

The data necessary to support value chain analysis can be formidable, particularly given its nontraditional format. Traditional accounting identifies costs in broad expense categories—wages, benefits, travel, supplies, depreciation, and so on. Activity-based costing requires managers to "disaggregate" these broad numbers across specific tasks and activities. Figure 6–5 gives a good illustration of the challenge, and the benefit, in doing this in a purchasing department.

Once the company's value chain has been documented and costs determined, managers need to identify the activities that are critical to buyer satisfaction and market success. It is those that are deserving major scrutiny in an internal analysis. Three considerations are essential at this stage in the value chain analysis. First, the company's basic mission needs to influence managers' choice of activities they examine in detail. If the company is focused on being a low-cost provider, then management attention to lower costs should be very visible; and missions built around commitment to differentiation should find managers spending more on activities that are differentiation cornerstones. Retailer Wal-Mart focuses intensely on costs related to inbound logistics and purchasing to build its competitive advantage while

FIGURE 6–5
The Value Chain System

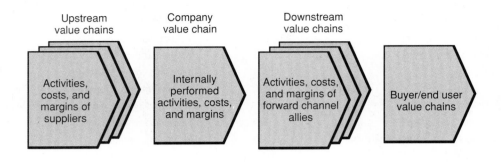

Source: Adapted from Michael E. Porter, *Competitive Advantage* (New York: The Free Press, 1985), p. 35.

Nordstrom builds its distinct position in retailing emphasizing sales and support activities on which they spend twice the retail industry average. The Gap's use of value chain analysis to guide its spectacular retail success is described in Strategy in Action 6–1.

Second, the nature of value chains and the relative importance of the activities within them vary by industry. Lodging firms like Holiday Inn's major costs and concerns involve operational activities—it provides its service instantaneously at each location—and marketing activities, while having minimal concern for outbound logistics. Yet for a distributor, such as the food distributor PYA, inbound and outbound logistics are the most critical area. Major retailers like Wal-Mart have built value advantages focusing on purchasing and inbound logistics while the most successful personal computer companies have built via sales, outbound logistics, and service through the mail order process.

Third, the relative importance of value activities can vary by a company's position in a broader value system that includes the value chains of its upstream suppliers and downstream customers or partners involved in providing products or services to end users (see Figure 6–5). A producer of roofing shingles depends heavily on the activities of wholesale distributors and building supply retailers to reach roofing contractors and do-it-yourselfers. Paint manufacturers typically have a similar situation, although some strong regional independent paint producers (Kelly-Moore in California; Rose Talbert in the Carolinas) have built their own wholesale/retail outlets creating a whole different position in the value system that exists to provide paint products to home and business paint users. They created value-building activities that meet customer needs more cost effectively than the downstream retail partners of typical paint producers. Kelly-Moore has also worked closely with pigment suppliers and equipment suppliers to ensure coordinated shipment of paint supplies and state-of-the-art mixing capabilities—thereby building a value-creating inbound logistics and operation advantage via upstream suppliers'/partners' service activities in the California paint industry.

As these examples suggest, it is important that managers take into account their level of vertical integration when comparing their cost structure for activities on their value chain to the value chain of key competitors. Comparing a fully integrated rival with a partially integrated one requires adjusting for the scope of activities performed to achieve meaningful comparison. It also suggests the need for examining costs associated with activities provided by upstream or downstream companies the activities of which ultimately determine comparable, final costs to end users. Said another way, one company's comparative cost disadvantage (or advantage) may emanate more from activities undertaken by upstream or downstream "partners" than from activities under the direct control of that company—therefore suggesting less of a relative advantage or disadvantage within the company's direct value chain.

The final basic consideration when applying value chain analysis is the need to have a meaningful comparison to use when evaluating a value activity as a strength or weakness. Whether using the value chain approach or an examination of functional areas, or both approaches, the strategist's next step in a systematic internal analysis is to compare the firm's status with meaningful standards to determine which of its value activities are strengths or weaknesses. Four sources of meaningful standards for evaluating internal factors and value activities are discussed in the next section.

INTERNAL ANALYSIS: MAKING MEANINGFUL COMPARISONS

Managers need an objective standard to use when examining internal capabilities or value-building activities. Whether using SWOT analysis, the functional approach, or the value chain, strategists rely on four basic perspectives to evaluate where their firm stacks up on its internal capabilities. These four perspectives are discussed in this section.

Comparison with Past Performance

Strategists use the firm's historical experience as a basis for evaluating internal factors. Managers are most familiar with the internal capabilities and problems of their firm because they have been immersed in its financial, marketing, production, and R&D activities. Not surprisingly, a manager's assessment of whether a certain internal factor—such as production facilities, sales organization, financial capacity, control systems, or key personnel—is a strength or a weakness will be strongly influenced by his or her experience in connection with that factor. In the capital-intensive airline industry, for example, debt capacity is a strategic internal factor. Delta Airlines managers view Delta's debt-equity ratio of less than 1.5 brought on by its acquisition of PanAm's international operations as a real weakness limiting its flexibility to invest in facilities because it maintained a ratio less than 0.6 for over 20 years. American Airlines managers, on the other hand, view American's much higher 1.8 debt-equity ratio as a growing strength, because it is down 50 percent from its 3.5 level five years earlier.

Although historical experience can provide a relevant evaluation framework, strategists must avoid tunnel vision in making use of it. NEC, Japan's IBM, has dominated Japan's PC market with a 70 percent market share using a proprietary hardware system, much higher screen resolution, powerful distribution channels, and a large software library from third-party vendors. Far from worried, Hajime Ikeda, manager of NEC's planning division, said recently: "We don't hear complaints from our users." But the 1990s has seen IBM and Macintosh filling shelves in Japan's famous consumer electronics district, Akihabara. Hiroki Kamata, president of a Japanese computer research firm, reports that Japan's PC market is worth over $15 billion in 1996, with Apple and IBM compatibles each having more market share than NEC because of better technology, software, and the restrictions created by NEC's proprietary technology. Clearly, using only historical experience as a basis for identifying strengths and weaknesses can prove dangerously inaccurate.

Stage of Industry Evolution

The requirements for success in industry segments change over time. Strategists can use these changing requirements, which are associated with different stages of industry evolution, as a framework for identifying and evaluating the firm's strengths and weaknesses.

THE GAP'S SPECTACULAR RETAILING SUCCESS
WAS BASED ON VALUE CHAIN ANALYSIS

Melvin Jacobs, chairman of the New York–based Saks Fifth Avenue, observed: "The Gap is a huge success, while retailers around the world are struggling like crazy." Dean Witter analyst Donald Trott says The Gap hit 2,000 stores and $5 billion in sales in 1995—an impressive accomplishment for its 25th birthday after a one-store start in San Francisco. While The Gap has been a Wall Street darling for some time, president Mickey Drexler says, "We've been doing the same thing for seven or eight years. This company is no overnight success."

What Drexler and founder Donald Fisher did was apply a type of value chain look at specialty retail clothing to identify key value activities around which they could build a long-term competitive advantage. They identified four components of the value chain within which they saw the opportunity to create new, value-added approaches that could become sustained competitive advantages.

1. PROCUREMENT

Drexler's concept for The Gap was and is: simple, quality, and comfort. Gap's designers are told to design clothes they themselves would wear, to guide their search for merchandise. At an early 1992 meeting in San Francisco, about 30 merchandisers were showing their proposed fall collection for GapKids to Drexler and his staff. The woman in charge of jackets held up a hooded coat. After viewing it, Drexler's reaction: "I hate it." A loud cheer among the staff goes up—the New York designers were pushing the item, but The Gap staff found it ugly.

The Gap staff members feel their strong involvement in clothing design choices, rather than the usual reliance on New York or Dallas merchandisers, is a distinct advantage. The Gap designs its own clothes, chooses its own material, and monitors manufacturing so closely that it can keep quality high and costs low.

2. INBOUND LOGISTICS

The Gap has over 200 quality-control inspectors working inside factories in 40 countries to make sure specifications are met right from the start. Like Wal-Mart, The Gap has computerized, highly automated, carefully located distribution centers serving as hubs directly linked to store groupings. For example, a $75 million automated distribution center recently opened outside Baltimore,

Source: The Gap annual reports, 1991–1995; The Gap, *Business Week*, March 9, 1992, p. 58.

Figure 6–6 depicts four stages of industry evolution and the typical changes in functional capabilities that are often associated with business success at each of these stages. The early development of a product market, for example, entails minimal growth in sales, major R&D emphasis, rapid technological change in the product, operating losses, and a need for sufficient resources or slack to support a temporarily unprofitable operation. Success at this introduction stage may be associated with technical skill, with being first in new markets, or with having a marketing advantage that creates widespread awareness. Radio Shack's initial success with its TRS–80 home computer was based in part on its ability to gain widespread exposure and acceptance in the ill-defined home computer market via the large number of existing Radio Shack outlets throughout the country.

The strengths necessary for success change in the growth stage. Rapid growth brings new competitors into the product market. At this stage, such factors as brand recognition, product differentiation, and the financial resources to support both heavy marketing expenses and the

allowing The Gap to supply New York City stores daily instead of three times a week. Few in specialty retailing can match this logistical capability.

3. OPERATIONS

Every Gap store is the same—a clean, well-lit place where harried consumers can shop easily and quickly. Every detail is fussed over, from cleaning the store's floors to rounding the counter corners at GapKids for safety's sake to the detailed instructions on where to display clothes and touching up white walls weekly and polishing wood floors every three days. Already in 800 of the U.S.'s 1,500 largest malls, it lowered operating costs long term by taking advantage of the 1992 recession's impact, locking up sweet lease deals, moving into downtowns and urban neighborhoods, and opening new stores on the declining main streets of midsized cities. Each of these operational activities ensured higher quality and ease of management, and sustained lower costs.

4. HUMAN RESOURCE MANAGEMENT

In an industry that is low base pay and commission based, The Gap salespeople receive no commission. But compensation exceeds the industry average. The Gap's COO motivates salespeople with constant contests. The most multiple purchases to the register in one day wins a Gap-logo watch. The Thanksgiving weekend rush saw COO O'Donnell have Pizza Hut and Domino's deliver 15,000 pizzas and 72,000 Pepsis to store personnel on the job. And The Gap's training program is detailed and rigorous before you are free to "work the floor." Again, The Gap pursues policies that differentiate it from current industry practices in a way that adds incremental value—well trained, fairly compensated, highly motivated store personnel, resulting in lower turnover costs and a favorable image for service-leery retail shoppers.

Drexler and Fisher have driven The Gap's success in these and many other ways. But disaggregating specialty clothing retailing into distinct activities in order to better understand their costs and sources of differentiation has led them to design unique approaches (described above) in four strategically important activities that created sustained competitive advantages through lower costs, higher quality, and clear differentiation from all other clothing retailers.

---

effect of price competition on cash flow can be key strengths. IBM entered the personal computer market in the growth stage and was able to rapidly become the market leader with a strategy based on its key strengths in brand awareness and possession of the financial resources needed to support consumer advertising. But IBM lost that lead in the next stage as speed in distribution and cost structures became the key success factors—strengths for Compaq and several mail order–oriented computer assemblers.

As the industry moves through a shakeout phase and into the maturity stage, industry growth continues, but at a decreasing rate. The number of industry segments expands, but technological change in product design slows considerably. As a result, competition usually becomes more intense, and promotional or pricing advantages and differentiation become key internal strengths. Technological change in process design becomes intense as the many competitors seek to provide the product in the most efficient manner. Where R&D was critical in the introduction stage, efficient production is now crucial to continued success in the broader industry segments. Ford's emphasis on quality control and modern,

FIGURE 6–6
Sources of Distinctive Competence at Different Stages of Industry Evolution

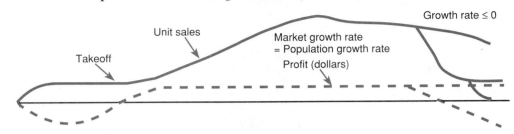

Functional Area	Introduction	Growth	Maturity	Decline
Marketing	Resources/skills to create widespread awareness and find acceptance from customers; advantageous access to distribution	Ability to establish brand recognition, find niche, reduce price, solidify, strong distribution relations, and develop new channels	Skills in aggressively promoting products to new markets and holding existing markets; pricing flexibility; skills in differentiating products and holding customer loyalty	Cost-effective means of efficient access to selected channels and markets; strong customer loyalty or dependence; strong company image
Production operations	Ability to expand capacity effectively, limit number of designs, develop standards	Ability to add product variants, centralize production, or otherwise lower costs; ability to improve product quality; seasonal subcontracting capacity	Ability to improve product and reduce costs; ability to share or reduce capacity; advantageous supplier relationships; subcontracting	Ability to prune product line; cost advantage in production, location or distribution; simplified inventory control; subcontracting or long production runs
Finance	Resources to support high net cash overflow and initial losses; ability to use leverage effectively	Ability to finance rapid expansion, to have net cash outflows but increasing profits; resources to support product improvements	Ability to generate and redistribute increasing net cash inflows; effective cost control systems	Ability to reuse or liquidate unneeded equipment; advantage in cost of facilities; control system accuracy; streamlined management control
Personnel	Flexibility in staffing and training new management; existence of employees with key skills in new products or markets	Existence of an ability to add skilled personnel; motivated and loyal work force	Ability to cost effectively, reduce work force, increase efficiency	Capacity to reduce and reallocate personnel; cost advantage
Engineering and research and development	Ability to make engineering changes, have technical bugs in product and process resolved	Skill in quality and new feature development; ability to start developing successor product	Ability to reduce costs, develop variants, differentiate products	Ability to support other grown areas or to apply product to unique customer needs
Key functional area and strategy focus	Engineering: market penetration	Sales: consumer loyalty; market share	Production efficiency; successor products	Finance; maximum investment recovery

Source: Adapted from Peter Doyle, "The Realities of the Product Life Cycle," *Quarterly Review of Marketing*, Summer 1976, pp. 1–6; Harold Fox, "A Framework for Functional Coordination," *Atlantic Economic Review* November–December 1973; Charles W. Hofer, *Conceptual Conflicts for Formulating Corporate and Business Strategy* (Boston: Intercollegiate Case Clearing House 1977), p. 7; Philip Kotler, *Marketing Management* (Englewood Cliffs, NJ: Prentice Hall, 1988); and Charles Wasson, *Dynamic Competitive Strategy and Product Cycles* (Austin, TX: Austin Press, 1978).

GLOBAL
STRATEGY IN
ACTION 6–3

AVERY DENNISON USES BENCHMARKING AND STAGE OF INDUSTRY EVALUATION TO TURN WEAKNESS INTO STRENGTH

Avery Dennison has long made adhesives and what it calls "sticky papers" for business customers. Ten years ago, AD decided to take on 3M with its own version of 3M's highly successful Post-It notes and Scotch transparent tape.

How frequently did you buy Avery Notes and Avery Tape? You probably have never heard of them, right? That is because Avery was beat up in that market by 3M and AD exited the business after just a few years. Key strengths, distribution and brand name, that 3M used to build those products were major weaknesses at AD. Plus, in President Charles Miller's way of viewing it, 3M remained aggressive and true to an innovative culture to back its products while AD had grown rusty and "me too" rather than being the innovator it had traditionally been with pressure-sensitive papers. So faced with considerable weakness competing against a major threat (see Figure 6–2), Miller refocused AD on getting innovative in areas of traditional technical strength.

Today, AD has 30 percent of its sales from products introduced in the past five years. It has half the market for adhesive paper stock and 40 percent of the market for coated paper films for package labels. Says Miller, "We believe in market evolution. The best way to control a market is to invent it. With innovative products, superstores aren't able to squeeze margins, as they can in commodity products." New products now pour out of AD labs to position AD strengths against early life cycle stage opportunities.

Source: Damon Darlin, "Thank You, 3M," *Forbes*, September 25, 1995, p. 86. Reprinted by permission of *Forbes* Magazine © Forbes, Inc., 1995.

efficient production has helped it prosper in the maturing U.S. auto industry, while General Motors, which pays almost 50 percent more than Ford to produce a comparable car, continues to decline.

When the industry moves into the decline stage, strengths and weaknesses center on cost advantages, superior supplier or customer relationships, and financial control. Competitive advantage can exist at this stage, at least temporarily, if a firm serves gradually shrinking markets that competitors are choosing to leave.

Figure 6–6 is a rather simple model of the stages of industry evolution. These stages can and do vary from the model. What should be borne in mind is that the relative importance of various determinants of success differs across the stages of industry evolution. Thus, the state of that evolution must be considered in internal analysis. Figure 6–6 suggests dimensions that are particularly deserving of in-depth consideration when a company profile is being developed.

Benchmarking—Comparison with Competitors

A major focus in determining a firm's strengths and weaknesses is comparison with existing (and potential) competitors. Firms in the same industry often have different marketing skills, financial resources, operating facilities and locations, technical know-how, brand images, levels of integration, managerial talent, and so on. These different internal capabilities can become relative strengths (or weaknesses) depending on the strategy a firm chooses. In choosing a strategy, managers should compare the firm's key internal capabilities with those of its rivals, thereby isolating its key strengths and weaknesses.

SAS Airlines Benchmarks Using Delta Airlines

For many years, Scandinavian Airline System (SAS) was a premier European airline. Benefiting from International Airline Transportation Association (IATA), a protective European airline industry trade organization, SAS was profitable for 17 straight years. But changes in the global

We've got some tough competition. Like the "street fighters" from the rough-and-tumble American domestic

market. Efficient. In shape. Like Delta. . .

Or European companies which have pursued more consistent and purposeful policies than we have.

And who keep making money, hard times or not.

In the home appliance industry, for example, Sears and General Electric are major rivals. Sears's principal strength is its retail network. For GE, distribution—through independent franchised dealers—has traditionally been a relative weakness. GE's possession of the financial resources needed to support modernized mass production has enabled it to maintain both cost and technological advantages over its rivals, particularly Sears. This major strength for GE is a relative weakness for Sears, which depends solely on subcontracting to produce its Kenmore appliances. On the other hand, maintenance and repair service are important in the appliance industry. Historically, Sears has had strength in this area because it maintains fully staffed service components and spreads the costs of components over numerous departments at each retail location. GE, on the other hand, has had to depend on regional service centers and on local contracting with independent service firms by its independent local dealers. Among the internal factors that Sears and GE must

continued

airline industry caused its earnings to plummet in the last few years. When SAS was on the verge of folding, its new CEO undertook an extensive competitor comparison as a basis for finding a strategy to turn it around. The CEO shared the following assessment in an employee pamphlet communicating the firm's new strategy and rationale behind it.

Look at the Differences:

	Swissair International	SAS International
Cabin Factor	63.60	59.30
Load Factor	59.20	47.60
Passenger revenue USD/RPK*	0.09	0.08
Cargo revenue USD/RFTK	0.37	0.31
Total revenue USD/RTK	0.79	0.73
Operating cost USD/ATK	0.45	0.42
Revenue-cost relationship (Over 100% profit)	103.50	99.70
Average flight leg/km	1051.00	967.00

Delta Has:

40% more revenue tonne kms per employee

120% more passengers per employee

14% more available tonne kms per pilot

40% more passenger kms per cabin attendant

35% more passenger kms per passenger sales employee

It is difficult to make similar comparisons in the technical and maintenance fields, but even in these areas Delta has a substantially higher productivity than SAS.

* USD = U.S. Dollars; RPK = Revenue passenger-kilometers; RFTK = Revenue freight tonne-kilometers; RTK = Revenue tonne-kilometers; ATK = Available tonne-kilometers. Exchange rate: one USD = 4.65 Swedish kronor.

consider in developing a strategy are distribution networks, technological capabilities, operating costs, and service facilities. Managers in both organizations have built successful strategies yet those strategies are quite different. Benchmarking each other, they have identified ways to build on relative strengths while avoiding dependence on capabilities at which the other firm excels.

Benchmarking, comparing the way "our" company performs a specific activity with a competitor or other company doing the same thing, has become a central concern of managers in quality commitment companies worldwide. Particularly as the value chain framework has taken hold in structuring internal analysis, managers seek to systematically benchmark the costs and results of the smallest value activities against relevant competitors or other useful standards because it has proven to be an effective way to continuously improve that activity. The ultimate objective in benchmarking is to identify the "best

KMART GETS SOME BAD NEWS BY BENCHMARKING INDUSTRY SUCCESS FACTORS AGAINST A KEY RIVAL

Kmart's new management team has a problem. Kmart is in serious trouble, perhaps more so than they originally thought when they took over the firm in 1995.

Key success factors in discount retailing include the obvious—good locations, solid supplier relations, selection, and efficient inbound logistics. But recent focus among investment analysts charting the industry has centered around four key indicators: Core customers, sales/square foot, shopper visits/year, and loyalty to the chain. ᐧ

Their 1996 benchmarking of Kmart compared to Wal-Mart revealed the following on these key success factors:

Key Success Factor to Benchmark	Kmart	Wal-Mart
Core customer	Over 55; more than $20k income and no kids at home	Under 44, $40k income and kids at home
Sales/square foot	$185	$379
Shopper visits/year	15 times per year	32 times per year
Loyal to the chain	19 percent of Kmart customers	46 percent of Wal-Mart customers
Location	36 percent of Americans find their newest Kmart inconvenient compared to other stores	49 percent of Wal-Mart customers drive past a Kmart to go to Wal-Mart

Sources: Wal-Mart 1995 Annual Report; Kmart 1995 Annual Report; "Can This Chain Be Saved?" *Chain Store Age Executive,* May 1995, pp. 31–44; "Kmart Is Down for the Count," *Fortune,* January 15, 1996, pp. 102–3; "As Kmart Teeters, an Industry Holds Its Breath," *Chain Store Age Executive,* January 1996, p. 70.

practices'' in performing an activity, to learn how lower costs, fewer defects, or other outcomes linked to excellence are achieved. Companies committed to benchmarking attempt to isolate and identify where their costs or outcomes are out of line with what the best practicers of a particular activity experience (competitors and noncompetitors) and then attempt to change their activities to achieve the new best practices standard.

Comparison with key competitors can prove useful in ascertaining whether their internal capabilities on these and other factors are strengths or weaknesses. Significant favorable differences (existing or expected) from competitors are potential cornerstones of a firm's strategy. Moreover, through comparison with major competitors, a firm may avoid strategic commitments that it cannot competitively support. Global Strategy in Action 6–4 shows how the Scandinavian Airline System (SAS) used competitor comparison to assess its strengths and weaknesses in the global airline industry.

Comparison with Success Factors in the Industry

Industry analysis (see Chapter 3) involves identifying the factors associated with successful participation in a given industry. As was true for the evaluation methods discussed above, the key determinants of success in an industry may be used to identify a firm's internal strengths and weaknesses. By scrutinizing industry competitors, as well as customer needs, vertical industry structure, channels of distribution, costs, barriers to entry, availability of substitutes, and suppliers, a strategist seeks to determine whether a firm's current internal capabilities represent strengths or weaknesses in new competitive arenas. The discussion in Chapter 3 provides a useful framework—five industry forces—against which to examine a firm's potential strengths and weaknesses. General Cinema Corporation, the largest U.S. movie theater operator, determined that its internal skills in marketing, site analysis, creative financing, and management of geographically dispersed operations were key strengths relative to major success factors in the soft-drink bottling industry. This assessment proved accurate. Within 10 years after it entered the soft-drink bottling industry, General Cinema became the largest franchised bottler of soft drinks in the United States, handling Pepsi, 7UP, Dr Pepper, and Sunkist. Strategy in Action 6–2 provides a very current example where Kmart has used industry factors to benchmark itself against industry leader Wal-Mart to find out just how weak Kmart is on some key factors. Global Strategy in Action 6–3 describes how Avery Dennison used similar industry evolution benchmarking versus 3M to create a new, successful strategy.

SUMMARY

This chapter looked at several ways managers achieve greater objectivity and rigor as they analyze their company's internal capabilities. Managers often start their internal analysis with questions like: "How well is the current strategy working? What is our current situation? Or what are our strengths and weaknesses?" *SWOT analysis* and *functional analysis* are two traditional approaches discussed in this chapter. Managers frequently use them to introduce realism and greater objectivity into their attempts to answer these questions. This chapter then described how insightful managers have begun to look at their business as a chain of activities that add value creating the products or services they sell. Associated with this perspective is a powerful concept for introducing rigor and objectivity into internal analysis, *value chain analysis*, which this chapter examined in great detail. Managers who use value chain to understand the value structure within their firm's activities and look at the value system, which also includes upstream suppliers and downstream partners and buyers, often gain very meaningful insights into their company's strategic capabilities and options. Finally, this chapter covered four ways objectivity and realism are enhanced when managers use meaningful standards for comparison regardless of the particular analytical framework they employ in internal analysis. This chapter is followed by an appendix covering traditional financial analysis to serve as a refresher and reminder about this basic internal analysis tool.

When matched with management's environmental analyses and mission priorities, the process of internal analysis provides the critical foundation for strategy formulation. Armed with an accurate, thorough, and timely internal analysis, managers are in a better position to formulate effective strategies. The next chapter describes basic strategy alternatives that any firm may consider.

QUESTIONS FOR DISCUSSION

1. Describe SWOT analysis as a way to guide internal analysis. How does this approach reflect the basic strategic management process?

2. Why would the functional approach be considered a "traditional" approach to internal analysis? Would you expect managers to prefer this approach or shy away from it? Why? What do you think are the strengths and weaknesses of this approach?

3. Apply SWOT analysis to yourself and your career aspirations. What are your major strengths and weaknesses? How might you use your knowledge of these strengths and weaknesses to develop your future career plans?

4. Why do you think value chain analysis has become a preferred approach to guide internal analysis? What are its strengths? Weaknesses?

5. In what ways do the approaches to internal analysis at The Gap (see Strategy in Action 6–1) and Scandinavian Airline Systems (see Global Strategy in Action 6–4) appear to be similar and different?

BIBLIOGRAPHY

Aaker, David A. "Managing Assets and Skills: The Key to a Sustainable Competitive Advantage." *California Management Review*, Winter 1989, pp. 91–106.

Barney, J. B. "Firm Resources and Sustained Competitive Advantage." *Journal of Management* 17 (1991), pp. 99–120.

Berman, S. J., and R. F. Kautz. "A Sophisticated Tool That Facilitates Strategic Analysis." *Planning Review* 18, no. 4 (1990), pp. 35–39.

Bukszar, Ed, and Terry Connolly. "Hindsight Bias and Strategy Choice." *Academy of Management Journal*, September 1988, p. 828.

Cvitkovic, Emillo. "Profiling Your Competitors." *Planning Review*, May–June 1989, pp. 28–31.

De Geus, A. P. "Planning as Learning." *Harvard Business Review*, March 1988. pp. 70–74.

Fann, G. L., and L. R. Smittzer. "The Use of Information from and about Competitors in Small Business Management." *Entrepreneurship: Theory and Practice*, Summer 1989, pp. 35–46.

Feinman, B. C. "Sustaining the Competitive Market Advantage." *Planning Review*, May 1989, pp. 30–39.

Fifer, R. M. "Cost Bench Marketing Approach: Functions in Value Chain." *Planning Review*, May 1989, pp. 18–27.

Gale, B. T., and R. D. Buzzel. "Market Perceived Quality: Key Strategic Concept." *Planning Review*, March 1989, pp. 6–15.

Hergert, M., and D. Morris. "Accounting Data for Value Chain Analysis." *Strategic Management Journal*, March 1989, pp. 175–88.

Hinterhuber, H. H., and W. Popp. "Are You a Strategist or Just a Manager?" *Harvard Business Review* 70, no. 1 (1992), pp. 105–13.

Kazanjian, Robert K. "Relation of Dominant Problems to Stages of Growth in Technology-Based New Ventures." *Academy of Management Journal*, September 1988, p. 628.

Lado, A.; N. Boyd; and P. Wright. "A Competency-Based Model of Sustainable Competitive Advantage: Toward a Conceptual Integration." *Journal of Management* 18 (1992), pp. 77–91.

Langley, A. "The Roles of Formal Strategic Planning." *Long Range Planning*, June 1988, pp. 40–50.

Leigh, T. W. "Competitive Assessment in Service Industries." *Planning Review*, January 1989, pp. 10–19.

Morrisey, George L. "Executive Guide to Strategic Thinking." *Executive Excellence* 7, no. 6 (1990), pp. 5–6.

Porter, Michel E. "From Competitive Advantage to Corporate Strategy." *Harvard Business Review*, May–June 1987, p. 43.

Potts, G. W. "Exploit Your Product's Service Life Cycle." *Harvard Business Review*, September 1988, pp. 32–39.

Prahalad, C. K., and G. Hamel. "The Core Competence of the Corporation." *Harvard Business Review* 68, no. 3 (1990), pp. 79–91.

Quinn, J. B. "Strategic Change: Logical Incrementalism." *Sloan Management Review*, Summer 1989, pp. 45–60.

Schmidt, J. A. "The Strategic Review," *Planning Review*, July 1988, pp. 14–19.

Stalk, G.; P. Evans; and L. E. Shulman. "Competing on Capabilities: The New Rules for Corporate Strategy." *Harvard Business Review* 70 (1992), pp. 57–69.

Steiner, M. P., and O. Solem. "Factors for Success in Small Manufacturing Firms." *Journal of Small Business Management*, January 1988, pp. 51–56.

Stoner, Charles R. "Distinctive Competence and Competitive Advantage." *Journal of Small Business Management*, April 1987, p. 33.

USING FINANCIAL ANALYSIS

One of the most important tools for assessing the strength of an organization within its industry is financial analysis. Managers, investors, and creditors all employ some form of this analysis as the beginning point for their financial decision making. Investors use financial analyses in making decisions about whether to buy or sell stock, and creditors use them in deciding whether or not to lend. They provide managers with a measurement of how the company is doing in comparison with its performance in past years and with the performance of competitors in the industry.

Although financial analysis is useful for decision making, some weaknesses should be noted. Any picture that it provides of the company is based on past data. Although trends may be noteworthy, this picture should not automatically be assumed to be applicable to the future. In addition, the analysis is only as good as the accounting procedures that have provided the information. When making comparisons between companies, one should keep in mind the variability of accounting procedures from firm to firm.

There are four basic groups of financial ratios: liquidity, leverage, activity, and profitability.

Depicted in Exhibit 6–1 are the specific ratios calculated for each of the basic groups. Liquidity and leverage ratios represent an assessment of the risk of the firm. Activity and profitability ratios are measures of the return generated by the assets of the firm. The interaction between certain groups of ratios is indicated by arrows.

Typically, two common financial statements are used in financial analyses: the balance sheet and the income statement. Exhibit 6–2 is a balance sheet and Exhibit 6–3 an income statement for the ABC Company. These statements will be used to illustrate the financial analyses.

LIQUIDITY RATIOS

Liquidity ratios are used as indicators of a firm's ability to meet its short-term obligations. These obligations include any current liabilities, including currently maturing long-term debt. Current assets move through a normal cash cycle of inventories–sales—accounts receivable—cash. The firm then uses cash to pay off or reduce its current liabilities. The best-known liquidity ratio is the current ratio: current assets divided by current liabilities. For the ABC Company, the current ratio is calculated as follows:

$$\frac{\text{Current assets}}{\text{Current liabilities}} = \frac{\$4,125,000}{\$2,512,500} = 1.64 \ (1999)$$
$$= \frac{\$3,618,000}{\$2,242.250} = 1.161 \ (1998)$$

Most analysts suggest a current ratio of 2 to 3. A large current ratio is not necessarily a good sign; it may mean that an organization is not making the most efficient use of its assets. The optimum current ratio will vary from industry to industry, with the more volatile industries requiring higher ratios.

Prepared by Elizabeth Gatewood, University of Houston. ©Elizabeth Gatewood, 1997. Reprinted by permission of Elizabeth Gatewood.

EXHIBIT 6–1
Financial Ratios

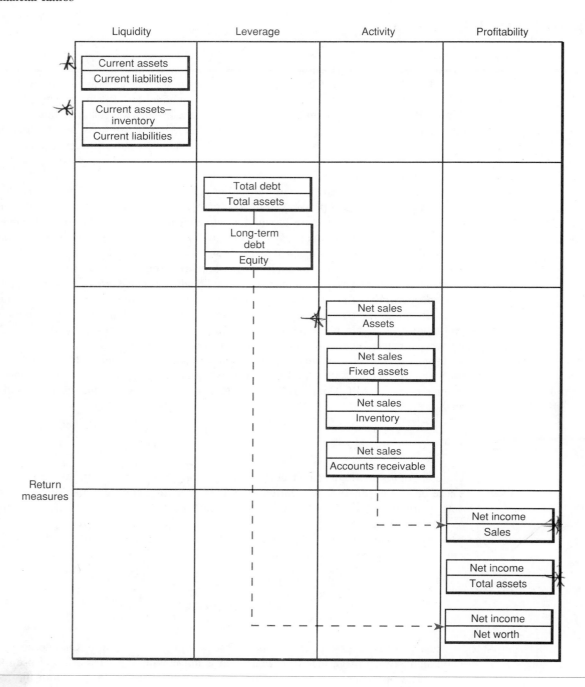

EXHIBIT 6–2

ABC COMPANY
Balance Sheet
As of December 31, 1998, and 1999

		1999		1998
Assets				
Current assets:				
Cash		$ 140,000		$ 115,000
Accounts receivable		1,760,000		1,440,000
Inventory		2,175,000		2,000,000
Prepaid expenses		50,000		63,000
Total current assets		4,125,000		3,618,000
Fixed assets:				
Long-term receivable		1,255,000		1,090,000
Property and plant	$2,037,000		$2,015,000	
Less: Accumulated depreciation	862,000		860,000	
Net property and plant		1,175,000		1,155,000
Other fixed assets		550,000		530,000
Total fixed assets		2,980,000		2,775,000
Total assets		$7,105,000		$6,393,000
Liabilities and Stockholders' Equity				
Current liabilities:				
Accounts payable		$1,325,000		$1,225,000
Bank loans payable		475,000		550,000
Accrued federal taxes		675,000		425,000
Current maturities (long-term debt)		17,500		26,000
Dividends payable		20,000		16,250
Total current liabilities		2,512,500		2,242,250
Long-term liabilities		1,350,000		1,425,000
Total liabilities		3,862,000		3,667,250
Stockholders' equity:				
Common stock (104,046 shares outstanding in 1995; 101,204 shares outstanding in 1994)		44,500		43,300
Additional paid-in capital		568,000		372,450
Retained earnings		2,630,000		2,310,000
Total stockholders' equity		3,242,500		2,725,750
Total liabilities and stockholders' equity		$7,105,000		$6,393,000

Since slow-moving or obsolescent inventories could overstate a firm's ability to meet short-term demands, the quick ratio is sometimes preferred to assess a firm's liquidity. The quick ratio is current assets minus inventories, divided by current liabilities. The quick ratio for the ABC Company is calculated as follows:

$$\frac{\text{Current assets} - \text{Inventories}}{\text{Current liabilities}} = \frac{\$1,950,000}{\$2,512,500} = 0.78 \ (1999)$$

$$= \frac{\$1,618,000}{\$2,242,250} = 0.72 \ (1998)$$

EXHIBIT 6–3

ABC COMPANY
Income Statement
For the Years Ending December 31, 1998, and 1999

	1999		1998
Net sales		$8,250,000	$8,000,000
Cost of goods sold	$5,100,000		$5,000,000
Administrative expenses	1,750,000		1,680,000
Other expenses	420,000		390,000
Total		7,270,000	7,070,000
Earnings before interest and taxes		980,000	930,000
Less: Interest expense		210,000	210,000
Earnings before taxes		770,000	720,000
Less: Federal income taxes		360,000	325,000
Earnings after taxes (net income)		$ 410,000	$ 395,000
Common stock cash dividends		$ 90,000	$ 84,000
Addition to retained earnings		$ 320,000	$ 311,000
Earnings per common share		$ 3.940	$ 3.90
Dividends per common share		$ 0.865	$ 0.83

A quick ratio of approximately 1 would be typical for American industries. Although there is less variability in the quick ratio than in the current ratio, stable industries would be able to operate safely with a lower ratio.

LEVERAGE RATIOS

Leverage ratios identify the source of a firm's capital—owners or outside creditors. The term *leverage* refers to the fact that using capital with a fixed interest charge will "amplify" either profits or losses in relation to the equity of holders of common stock. The most commonly used ratio is total debt divided by total assets. Total debt includes current liabilities and long-term liabilities. This ratio is a measure of the percentage of total funds provided by debt. A total debt–total assets ratio higher than 0.5 is usually considered safe only for firms in stable industries.

$$\frac{\text{Total debt}}{\text{Total assets}} = \frac{\$3,862,500}{\$7,105,000} = 0.54 \ (1999)$$

$$= \frac{\$3,667,250}{\$6,393,000} = 0.57 \ (1998)$$

The ratio of long-term debt to equity is a measure of the extent to which sources of long-term financing are provided by creditors. It is computed by dividing long-term debt by the stockholders' equity.

$$\frac{\text{Long-term debt}}{\text{Equity}} = \frac{\$1,350,000}{\$3,242,500} = 0.42 \ (1999)$$

$$= \frac{\$1,425,000}{\$2,725,750} = 0.52 \ (1998)$$

ACTIVITY RATIOS

Activity ratios indicate how effectively a firm is using its resources. By comparing revenues with the resources used to generate them, it is possible to establish an efficiency of operation. The asset turnover ratio indicates how efficiently management is employing total assets. Asset turnover is calculated by dividing sales by total assets. For the ABC Company, asset turnover is calculated as follows:

$$\text{Asset turnover} = \frac{\text{Sales}}{\text{Total assets}} = \frac{\$8,250,000}{\$7,105,000} = 1.16 \ (1999)$$

$$= \frac{\$8,000,000}{\$6,393,000} = 1.25 \ (1998)$$

The ratio of sales to fixed assets is a measure of the turnover on plant and equipment. It is calculated by dividing sales by net fixed assets.

$$\text{Fixed asset turnover} = \frac{\text{Sales}}{\text{Net fixed assets}} = \frac{\$8,250,000}{\$2,980,000} = 2.77 \ (1999)$$

$$= \frac{\$8,000,000}{\$2,775,000} = 2.88 \ (1998)$$

Industry figures for asset turnover will vary with capital-intensive industries, and those requiring large inventories will have much smaller ratios.

Another activity ratio is inventory turnover, estimated by dividing sales by average inventory. The norm for American industries is 9, but whether the ratio for a particular firm is higher or lower normally depends on the product sold. Small, inexpensive items usually turn over at a much higher rate than larger, expensive ones. Since inventories normally are carried at cost, it would be more accurate to use the cost of goods sold in place of sales in the numerator of this ratio. Established compilers of industry ratios, such as Dun & Bradstreet, however, use the ratio of sales to inventory.

$$\text{Inventory turnover} = \frac{\text{Sales}}{\text{Inventory}} = \frac{\$8,250,000}{\$2,175,000} = 3.79 \ (1999)$$

$$= \frac{\$8,000,000}{\$2,000,000} = 4 \ (1998)$$

The accounts receivable turnover is a measure of the average collection period on sales. If the average number of days varies widely from the industry norm, it may be an indication of poor management. A too-low ratio could indicate the loss of sales because of a too restrictive credit policy. If the ratio is too high, too much capital is being tied up in accounts receivable, and management may be increasing the chance of bad debts. Because of varying industry credit policies, a comparison for the firm over time or within an industry is the only useful analysis. Because information on credit sales for other firms generally is unavailable, total sales must be used. Since not all firms have the same percentage of credit sales, there is only approximate comparability among firms.

$$\frac{\text{Accounts}}{\text{receivable turnover}} = \frac{\text{Sales}}{\text{Accounts receivable}} = \frac{\$8,250,000}{\$1,760,000} = 4.69 \ (1999)$$

$$= \frac{\$8,000,000}{\$1,440,000} = 5.56 \ (1998)$$

$$\text{Average collection period} = \frac{360}{\text{Accounts receivable turnover}}$$

$$= \frac{360}{4.69} = 77 \text{ days (1999)}$$

$$= \frac{360}{5.56} = 65 \text{ days (1998)}$$

PROFITABILITY RATIOS

Profitability is the net result of a large number of policies and decisions chosen by an organization's management. Profitability ratios indicate how effectively the total firm is being managed. The profit margin for a firm is calculated by dividing net earnings by sales. This ratio is often called *return on sales* (ROS). There is wide variation among industries, but the average for American firms is approximately 5 percent.

$$\frac{\text{Net earnings}}{\text{Sales}} = \frac{\$410,000}{\$8,250,000} = 0.0497 \text{ (1999)}$$

$$= \frac{\$395,000}{\$8,000,000} = 0.0494 \text{ (1998)}$$

A second useful ratio for evaluating profitability is the return on investment—or *ROI*, as it is frequently called—found by dividing net earnings by total assets. The ABC Company's ROI is calculated as follows:

$$\frac{\text{Net earnings}}{\text{Total assets}} = \frac{\$410,000}{\$7,105,000} = 0.0577 \text{ (1999)}$$

$$= \frac{\$395,000}{\$6,393,000} = 0.0618 \text{ (1998)}$$

The ratio of net earnings to net worth is a measure of the rate of return or profitability of the stockholders' investment. It is calculated by dividing net earnings by net worth, the common stock equity and retained earnings account. ABC Company's return on net worth, also called ROE, is calculated as follows:

$$\frac{\text{Net earnings}}{\text{Net worth}} = \frac{\$410,000}{\$3,242,500} = 0.1264 \text{ (1999)}$$

$$= \frac{\$395,000}{\$2,725,750} = 0.1449 \text{ (1998)}$$

It is often difficult to determine causes for lack of profitability. The Du Pont system of financial analysis provides management with clues to the lack of success of a firm. This financial tool brings together activity, profitability, and leverage measures and shows how these ratios interact to determine the overall profitability of the firm. A depiction of the system is set forth in Exhibit 6–4.

The right side of the exhibit develops the turnover ratio. This section breaks down total assets into current assets (cash, marketable securities, accounts receivable, and inventories) and fixed assets. Sales divided by these total assets gives the turnover on assets.

The left side of the exhibit develops the profit margin on sales. The individual expense items plus income taxes are subtracted from sales to produce net profits after taxes. Net profits divided by sales gives the profit margin on sales. When the asset turnover ratio on the right side of Exhibit 6–4 is multiplied by the profit margin on sales developed on the left side of the exhibit, the product is the return on assets (ROI) for the firm. This can be shown by the following formula:

EXHIBIT 6–4
Du Pont's Financial Analysis

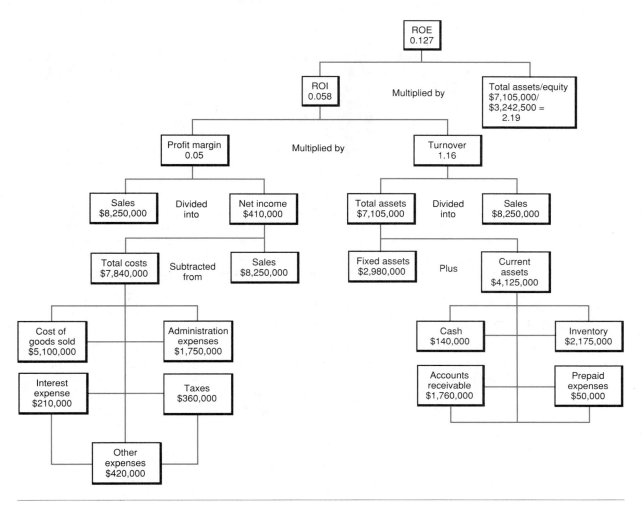

$$\frac{\text{Sales}}{\text{Total assets}} \times \frac{\text{Net earnings}}{\text{Sales}} = \frac{\text{Net earnings}}{\text{Total assets}} = \text{ROI}$$

The last step in the Du Pont analysis is to multiply the rate of return on assets (ROI) by the equity multiplier, which is the ratio of assets to common equity, to obtain the rate of return on equity (ROE). This percentage rate of return, of course, could be calculated directly by dividing net income by common equity. However, the Du Pont analysis demonstrates how the return on assets and the use of debt interact to determine the return on equity.

The Du Pont system can be used to analyze and improve the performance of a firm. On the left, or profit, side of the exhibit, attempts to increase profits and sales could be investigated. The possibilities of raising prices to improve profits (or lowering prices to improve volume) or seeking new products or markets, for example, could be studied. Cost accountants and production engineers could investigate ways to reduce costs. On the right, or turnover, side, financial officers could analyze the effect of reducing investment in various assets as well as the effect of using alternative financial structures.

There are two basic approaches to using financial ratios. One approach is to evaluate the corporation's performance over several years. Financial ratios are computed for different years, and then an assessment is made about whether there has been an improvement or deterioration over time. Financial ratios also can be computed for projected, pro forma, statements and compared with present and past ratios.

The other approach is to evaluate a firm's financial condition and compare it with the financial conditions of similar firms or with industry averages in the same period. Such a comparison gives insight into the firm's relative financial condition and performance. Financial ratios for industries are provided by Robert Morris Associates, Dun & Bradstreet, and various trade association publications. (Associations and their addresses are listed in the *Encyclopedia of Associations* and in the *Directory of National Trade Associations*.) Information about individual firms is available through *Moody's Manual*, Standard & Poor's manuals and surveys, annual reports to stockholders, and the major brokerage houses.

To the extent possible, accounting data from different companies must be so standardized that companies can be compared or so a specific company can be compared with an industry average. It is important to read any footnotes of financial statements, since various accounting or management practices can have an effect on the financial picture of the company. For example, firms using sale-leaseback methods may have leverage pictures quite different from what is shown as debts or assets on the balance sheet.

ANALYSIS OF THE SOURCES AND USES OF FUNDS

The purpose of this analysis is to determine how the company is using its financial resources from year to year. By comparing balance sheets from one year to the next, one may determine how funds were obtained and how these funds were employed during the year.

To prepare a statement of the sources and uses of funds, it is necessary to (1) classify balance sheet changes that increase and decrease cash, (2) classify from the income statement those factors that increase or decrease cash, and (3) consolidate this information on a sources and uses of funds statement form.

Sources of funds that increase cash are:

1. A net decrease in any other asset than a depreciable fixed asset.
2. A gross decrease in a depreciable fixed asset.
3. A net increase in any liability.
4. Proceeds from the sale of stock.
5. The operation of the company (net income, and depreciation if the company is profitable).

Uses of funds include:

1. A net increase in any other asset than a depreciable fixed asset.
2. A gross increase in depreciable fixed assets.
3. A net decrease in any liability.
4. A retirement or purchase of stock.
5. Payment of cash dividends.

We compute gross changes to depreciable fixed assets by adding depreciation from the income statement for the period to net fixed assets at the end of the period and then subtracting from the total net fixed assets at the beginning of the period. The residual represents the change in depreciable fixed assets for the period.

For the ABC Company, the following change would be calculated:

Net property and plant (1999)	$1,175,000
Depreciation for 1999	+ 80,000
	$1,255,000
Net property and plant (1998)	−1,155,000
	$ 100,000

To avoid double counting, the change in retained earnings is not shown directly in the funds statement. When the funds statement is prepared, this account is replaced by the earnings after taxes, or net income, as a source of funds, and dividends paid during the year as a use of funds. The difference between net income and the change in the retained earnings account will equal the amount of dividends paid during the year. The accompanying sources and uses of funds statement was prepared for the ABC Company.

A funds analysis is useful for determining trends in working-capital positions and for demonstrating how the firm has acquired and employed its funds during some period.

ABC COMPANY
Sources and Uses of Funds Statement
For 1999

Sources:

Prepaid expenses	$ 13,000
Accounts payable	100,000
Accrued federal taxes	250,000
Dividends payable	3,750
Common stock	1,200
Additional paid-in capital	195,000
Earnings after taxes (net income)	410,000
Depreciation	80,000
Total sources	$1,053,500

ABC COMPANY
Sources and Uses of Fund Statement
For 1999

Uses:

Cash	$ 25,000
Accounts receivable	320,000
Inventory	175,000
Long-term receivables	165,000
Property and plant	100,000
Other fixed assets	20,000
Bank loans payable	75,000
Current maturities of long-term debt	8,500
Long-term liabilities	75,000
Dividends paid	90,000
Total uses	1,053,500

CONCLUSION

It is recommended that you prepare a chart, such as that shown in Exhibit 6–5, so you can develop a useful portrayal of these financial analyses. The chart allows a display of the ratios over time. The "Trend" column could be used to indicate your evaluation of the ratios over time (e.g., "favorable," "neutral," or "unfavorable"). The "Industry Average" column could include recent industry averages on these ratios or those of key competitors. These would provide information to aid interpretation of the analyses. The "Interpretation" column could be used to describe your interpretation of the ratios for this firm. Overall, this chart gives a basic display of the ratios that provides a convenient format for examining the firm's financial condition.

Finally, Exhibit 6–6 is included to provide the quick reference summarizing the calculation and meaning of the ratios discussed earlier.

EXHIBIT 6–5
A Summary of the Financial Position of a Firm

Ratios and Working Capital	1995	1996	1997	1998	1999	Trend	Industry Average	Interpre-tation
Liquidity: Current								
Quick								
Leverage: Debt-assets								
Debt-equity								
Activity: Asset turnover								
Fixed asset ratio								
Inventory turnover								
Accounts receivable turnover								
Average collection period								
Profitability: ROS								
ROI								
ROE								
Working-capital position								

EXHIBIT 6–6
A Summary of Key Financial Ratios

Ratio	Calculation	Meaning
Liquidity Ratios:		
Current ratio	$\dfrac{\text{Current assets}}{\text{Current liabilities}}$	The extent to which a firm can meet its short-term obligations.
Quick ratio	$\dfrac{\text{Current assets} - \text{Inventory}}{\text{Current liabilities}}$	The extent to which a firm can meet its short-term obligations without relying on the sale of inventories.
Leverage Ratios:		
Debt-to-total-assets ratio	$\dfrac{\text{Total debt}}{\text{Total assets}}$	The percentage of total funds that are provided by creditors.
Debt-to-equity ratio	$\dfrac{\text{Total debt}}{\text{Total stockholders' equity}}$	The percentage of total funds provided by creditors versus the percentage provided by owners.
Long-term-debt-to-equity ratio	$\dfrac{\text{Long-term debt}}{\text{Total stockholders' equity}}$	The balance between debt and equity in a firm's long-term capital structure.
Times-interest-earned ratio	$\dfrac{\text{Profits before interest and taxes}}{\text{Total interest charges}}$	The extent to which earnings can decline without the firm becoming unable to meet its annual interest costs.
Activity Ratios:		
Inventory turnover	$\dfrac{\text{Sales}}{\text{Inventory of finished goods}}$	Whether a firm holds excessive stocks of inventories and whether a firm is selling its inventories slowly compared to the industry average.
Fixed assets turnover	$\dfrac{\text{Sales}}{\text{Fixed assets}}$	Sales productivity and plant equipment utilization.
Total assets turnover	$\dfrac{\text{Sales}}{\text{Total assets}}$	Whether a firm is generating a sufficient volume of business for the size of its assets investment.
Accounts receivable turnover	$\dfrac{\text{Annual credit sales}}{\text{Accounts receivable}}$	In percentage terms, the average length of time it takes a firm to collect on credit sales.
Average collection period	$\dfrac{\text{Accounts receivable}}{\text{Total sales/365 days}}$	In days, the average length of time it takes a firm to collect on credit sales.
Profitability Ratios:		
Gross profit margin	$\dfrac{\text{Sales} - \text{Cost of goods sold}}{\text{Sales}}$	The total margin available to cover operating expenses and yield a profit.
Operating profit margin	$\dfrac{\text{Earnings before interest and taxes (EBIT)}}{\text{Sales}}$	Profitability without concern for taxes and interest.
Net profit margin	$\dfrac{\text{Net income}}{\text{Sales}}$	After-tax profits per dollar of sales.
Return on total assets (ROA)	$\dfrac{\text{Net income}}{\text{Total assets}}$	After-tax profits per dollar of assets; this ratio is also called *return on investment* (ROI).
Return on stockholders' equity (ROE)	$\dfrac{\text{Net income}}{\text{Total stockholders' equity}}$	After-tax profits per dollar of stockholders' investment in the firm.

EXHIBIT 6–6
(concluded)

Ratio	Calculation	Meaning
Earnings per share (EPS)	$$\frac{\text{Net income}}{\text{Number of shares of common stock outstanding}}$$	Earnings available to the owners of common stock.
Growth Ratio:		
Sales	Annual percentage growth in total sales	Firm's growth rate in sales.
Income	Annual percentage growth in profits	Firm's growth rate in profits.
Earnings per share	Annual percentage growth in EPS Firm's growth rate in EPS.	
Dividends per share	Annual percentage growth in dividends per share	Firm's growth rate in dividends per share.
Price-earnings ratio	$$\frac{\text{Market price per share}}{\text{Earnings per share}}$$	Faster-growing and less risky firms tend to have higher price-earnings ratios.

CHAPTER 6 COHESION CASE ILLUSTRATION

INTERNAL ANALYSIS AT THE COCA-COLA COMPANY

One way to gauge the strengths and weaknesses at Coca-Cola is to compare it to competitors on key indicators. Perhaps the best starting point for comparison is to look at recent data on sales and market share. Listed below are the sales results in the U.S. market for the first half of the 1990s.

CORPORATE COLA LEADERS
Top 10 Parent Companies in 1995

Rank	Brand	Gallonage (millions)	Market Share	1994 Growth	Industry Growth Index Factor*	Five-Year Growth
1	Coca-Cola	*5,580.8*	*42.0%*	+5.1%	*+49.0%*	+18.1%
2	Pepsi-Cola	4,070.6	30.7	+4.4	+31.1	+12.1
3	Dr Pepper/Seven-Up*	1,520.8	11.5	+6.3	+16.4	+33.9
4	Cadbury Beverages†	632.3	4.8	+1.1	+1.2	+10.3
5	Cott‡	300.7	2.3	*+37.7*	+14.9	NA
6	Royal Crown	267.3	2.0	–3.2	–1.6	–12.8
7	National Beverage	227.8	1.7	+5.5	+2.2	+13.6
8	Monarch	208.0	1.6	–0.4	–0.1	+8.4
9	Barq's	82.5	0.6	+6.5	+0.9	*+66.7*
10	Double-Cola	53.2	0.4	+2.9	+0.3	–2.7
	Top 10 Soft-Drink Companies	12,944.0	97.6	+5.1	+114.3	+21.4
	All Others	331.0	2.4	–19.2	–14.3	–68.8
	Total Soft-Drink Industry	13,275.0	100.0	+4.3	+100.0	+13.5

Bold italics indicate best among top 10.
*GIF = Brand gallonage growth ÷ Industry gallonage growth.
†Acquired by Cadbury Schweppes in 1995.
‡Includes A&W Brands, acquired in 1993.
§Cott tracked since 1992.
Source: Beverage Marketing Corporation.

Coca-Cola has sustained a dominant domestic market share lead over Pepsi throughout the decade. Internationally, Coca-Cola is even more dominant as the following exhibit indicates:

THE WORLD'S FAVORITE SOFT DRINK?

	Market Leader	Leadership Margin	Second Place
Australia	Coca-Cola	3.9–1	Diet Coke
Belgium	Coca-Cola	9.0–1	Fanta
Brazil	Coca-Cola	3.7–1	Brazilian brand
Chile	Coca-Cola	4.5–1	Fanta
France	Coca-Cola	4.2–1	French brand
Germany	Coca-Cola	3.5–1	Fanta
Great Britain	Coca-Cola	1.8–1	Diet Coke
Greece	Coca-Cola	3.7–1	Fanta
Italy	Coca-Cola	2.8–1	Fanta
Japan	Coca-Cola	2.2–1	Fanta
Korea	Coca-Cola	1.6–1	Korean brand
Norway	Coca-Cola	2.7–1	Coca-Cola light
South Africa	Coca-Cola	3.8–1	Sparletta
Spain	Coca-Cola	2.4–1	Spanish brand
Sweden	Coca-Cola	3.6–1	Fanta

Share of flavored, carbonated soft drink sales.
Source: Company data/store audit data.

Further comparison of Coca-Cola, Pepsi-Cola, and upstart Cott Corporation gives a sense that Coke has major strength in traditional brands and is experiencing the best growth in the diet and "new age" categories among these major players. Cott's success with retailers is impressive, representing a potential challenge to Coke's traditional dominance.

Soft Drink	Gallonage (millions)	Market Share	Corporate Share	1994 Growth	Industry Growth Index Factor*	Five-Year Growth
Coca-Cola	**5,580.8**	**42.0%**	**100.0%**	**+5.1%**	**+49.0%***	**+18.1%**
Coca-Cola Classic	2,621.1	19.7	47.0	+5.7	+25.6	+16.4
Diet Coke	1,267.5	9.5	22.7	+3.6	+8.0	+16.8
Sprite	580.6	4.4	10.4	+10.8	+10.2	+37.6
Caffeine-Free Diet Coke	264.8	2.0	4.7	−1.7	−0.8	+10.0
Diet Sprite	97.1	0.7	1.7	−3.2	−0.6	+3.1
Cherry Coke	94.6	0.7	1.7	+4.9	+0.8	−20.8
Mello Yello	89.0	0.7	1.7	+1.0	+0.2	+65.7
Fanta	73.9	0.6	1.4	−0.1	(−)0.0	−11.4
Minute Maid	69.4	0.5	1.2	+16.1	+1.7	+37.4
Caffeine-Free Coca-Cola Classic	69.3	0.5	1.1	+11.1	−1.2	+179.4
Mr. PIBB	54.2	0.4	1.0	+10.4	+0.9	+160.6
Diet Minute Maid	49.6	0.4	0.9	+11.5	+0.9	+49.8
Coke II	37.6	0.3	0.8	−29.5	−2.8	−77.2
Fresca	17.9	0.1	0.3	+13.3	+0.4	+588.5
Tab	15.8	0.1	0.3	−5.4	−0.2	−54.2
Diet Cherry Coke	10.8	0.1	0.2	−15.6	−0.4	−55.6
All other Coke products	167.6	1.3	2.9	+14.6	+3.9	+805.9

Soft Drink	Gallonage (millions)	Market Share	Corporate Share	1994 Growth	Industry Growth Index Factor*	Five-Year Growth
Pepsi-Cola	**4,070.6**	**30.7**	**100.0**	**+4.4**	**+31.1**	**+12.1**
Pepsi-Cola	2,066.3	15.6	50.7	+5.4	+19.2	+1.3
Diet Pepsi	760.3	5.7	18.7	+4.0	+5.3	+15.8
Mountain Dew	682.6	5.1	16.8	+17.4	+18.3	+61.5
Caffeine-Free Diet Pepsi	152.7	1.2	3.8	+1.7	+0.5	+10.2
Slice	126.8	1.0	3.1	+6.8	+1.5	+23.6
Caffeine-Free Pepsi	105.8	0.8	2.6	−6.4	+0.6	+3.1
Diet Mountain Dew	85.0	0.6	2.1	+3.4	+1.3	+66.0
Mug	38.2	0.3	0.9	+9.5	+0.2	+32.6
Diet Slice	22.5	0.2	0.6	+1.1	−0.7	−63.2
Caffeine-Free Mountain Dew	12.1	0.1	0.3	NA	+2.2[†]	NA
Caffeine-Free Diet Mountain Dew	7.8	0.1	0.2	NA	+1.4[†]	NA
Crystal Pepsi	5.6	0.0	0.1	−90.4	−9.5	NA
Diet Crystal Pepsi	1.9	0.0	0.0	−94.0	−5.4	NA
All other Pepsi products	3.0	0.0	0.0	−91.1	−3.7	−87.3
Cott Total[‡]	**300.7**	**2.3**	**100.0**	**+37.7**	**+14.9**	**218.5**
Sam's Choice	104.0	0.8	34.6	+31.5	+4.5	+54.3
Safeway Select	50.8	0.4	16.9	+11.6	+1.0	NA
President's Choice	38.0	0.3	12.6	+33.3	+1.7	+544.1
World Classics	13.2	0.1	4.4	+37.5	+0.7	NA
Marquee	9.6	0.1	3.2	NA	NA	NA
Q&V	7.5	0.1	2.5	NA	NA	NA
Bi-Lo	6.6	NS	2.2	NA	NA	NA
Smith's	5.4	NS	1.8	NA	NA	NA
Wegman's	4.5	NS	1.5	NA	NA	NA
Ralph's	4.5	NS	1.5	NA	NA	NA
Top's	4.2	NS	1.4	NA	NA	NA
Master Choice	3.0	NS	1.0	NA	NA	NA
Randall's	2.5	NS	0.8	NA	NA	NA
Schnuck's	2.4	NS	0.8	NA	NA	NA
All other Cott products	44.5	0.3	14.8	−20.0	−1.8	+110.9

[‡]Cott tracked since 1992.

NA = Not available. NS = not significant.

*IGIF = Brand gallonage growth ÷ Industry gallonage growth.

[†]Represents first-year gallonage.

Source: Beverage Marketing Corporation.

Pepsi's main strength is in the supermarket area, but Coca-Cola maintains a virtually equal portion of this market. Pepsi has strong sales through the restaurant chains it owns (Pizza Hut, Kentucky Fried Chicken, Taco Bell), although a recent decision by Burger King to leave Pepsi for Coke, plus McDonald's continued relationship with Coca-Cola, seem to confirm Goizueta's long-held policy that Coca-Cola will not compete with its customers, such as restaurant chains, by entering their industry.

Coca-Cola was a weak relative to Pepsi in the early 1980s in terms of the strength of franchisee bottlers. Coke's bottlers, as mentioned in an earlier case, were second- and third-generation family businesses that had been with Coke from its very early days. Pepsi's franchises, led by what was then the world's largest soft-drink bottler, General Cinema Corporation, had better capitalized and more sophisticated bottlers in many key urban areas in the United States. But Coca-Cola recognized this and, over the 1980s, became more aggressively involved with its bottlers, including over $2 billion in investment, which makes its bottling network, particularly abroad, a relative advantage in the 1990s.

Cott Corporation's efforts to reach Japanese consumers through large Japanese retailers by selling cola beverages for less than half Coke's price has begun to cause Coca-Cola management to question its relative weakness in this geographic region and channel. Coca-Cola's conclusion appears to be that a relative weakness could potentially develop unless Coca-Cola responds to minimize the threat and reestablish its competitive advantage.

Coca-Cola likes to assess its strengths and weaknesses against an internal sense of what is required for success in the global soft-drink industry. Based on quotes of Roberto Goizueta, Coca-Cola's chief executive officer, provided in the Chapter 5 Cohesion Case, it appears Coke is exceptionally strong on dimensions it deems key determinants of success. An outside evaluation of Coke's strengths vis-à-vis international markets appears to confirm Coke's perception:

> International volume growth [at Coke] has outpaced domestic growth for several years, reflecting the relative immaturity of those markets in terms of soft-drink consumption and, more importantly, The Coca-Cola Company's aggressive efforts to expand distribution and emphasize marketing. While The Coca-Cola Company participates in U.S. bottling activities primarily as an equity investor (albeit a highly involved investor), the international involvement has been varied. In most countries, the preferred avenue has been to establish a joint venture with a strong local business entity, with Coke contributing equity and management expertise. In some markets, notably France and the former East Germany, Coca-Cola has stepped in with direct ownership and investment.

Overall the company's increasing emphasis on bottling investment and support represent a major strength for the company in virtually every market.

Brand loyalty is another major strength for Coca-Cola. In the United States, Coke's mid-1980s debacle—withdrawing regular Coke in favor of New Coke only to have consumers react so negatively that regular Coke, "Coke Classic," was brought back to head off consumer lawsuits and other demands—showed Coke the depth of brand loyalty it had engendered. The net result was greater market share and profitability for Coke as it realized the depth of its brand loyalty. The selected financial data provided on the following two pages portray the strong position of the Coke brand abroad, and suggest a similar brand loyalty in those markets.

1995 saw Coca-Cola using the billboard below to communicate the strength of its brand identity. A recent global analysis ranked Coca-Cola as the world's most valuable brand, assigning it a value of $39 billion.

THE COCA-COLA COMPANY AND SUBSIDIARIES

SELECTED FINANCIAL DATA

(In millions except per share data, ratios and growth rates)	Compound Growth Rates 5 Years	10 Years	Year Ended December 31, 1994[2]	1993[3]
Summary of Operations				
Net operating revenues	13.4%	11.5%	$ 16,172	$ 13,957
Cost of goods sold	11.7%	8.5%	6,167	5,160
Gross profit	14.5%	14.0%	10,005	8,797
Selling, administrative and general expenses	13.5%	13.0%	6,297	5,695
Operating income	16.5%	15.9%	3,708	3,102
Interest income			181	144
Interest expense			199	168
Equity income			134	91
Other income (deductions)-net			(96)	4
Gain on issuance of stock by equity investees			—	12
Income from continuing operations before income taxes and changes in accounting principles	16.1%	15.2%	3,728	3,185
Income taxes	16.2%	12.5%	1,174	997
Income from continuing operations before changes in accounting principles	16.1%	16.6%	$ 2,554	$ 2,188
Net income	10.7%[6]	15.0%	$ 2,554	$ 2,176
Preferred stock dividends			—	—
Net income available to common share owners	11.0%[6]	15.0%	$ 2,554	$ 2,176
Average common shares outstanding			1,290	1,302
Per Common Share Data				
Income from continuing operations before changes in accounting principles	18.1%	18.9%	$ 1.98	$ 1.68
Net income	12.5%	17.3%	1.98	1.67
Cash dividends	18.1%	13.0%	.78	.68
Market price at December 31	21.7%	25.8%	51.50	44.63
Balance Sheet Data				
Cash, cash equivalents and current marketable securities			$ 1,531	$ 1,078
Property, plant and equipment–net			4,080	3,729
Depreciation			382	333
Capital expenditures			878	800
Total assets			13,873	12,021
Long-term debt			1,426	1,428
Total debt			3,509	3,100
Share-owners' equity			5,235	4,584
Total capital[1]			8,744	7,684
Other Key Financial Measures[1]				
Total-debt-to-total-capital			40.1%	40.3%
Net-debt-to-net-capital			22.6%	26.2%
Return on common equity			52.0%	51.7%
Return on capital			32.7%	31.2%
Dividend payout ratio			39.4%	40.6%
Economic profit			$ 2,012	$ 1,495

[1]See Glossary on page 70.
[2]In 1994, the Company adopted SFAS No. 115, "Accounting for Certain Investments in Debt and Equity Securities."
[3]In 1993, the Company adopted SFAS No. 112, "Employers' Accounting for Postemployment Benefits."
[4]In 1992, the Company adopted SFAS No. 106, "Employers' Accounting for Postretirement Benefits Other Than Pensions."
[5]The Company adopted SFAS No. 109, "Accounting for Income Taxes," in 1992 by restating financial statements beginning in 1989.

THE COCA-COLA COMPANY AND SUBSIDIARIES

1992[4,5]	1991[5]	1990[5]	1989[5]	1988	1987	1986	1985	1984
$ 13,074	$ 11,572	$ 10,236	$ 8,622	$ 8,065	$ 7,658	$ 6,977	$ 5,879	$ 5,442
5,055	4,649	4,208	3,548	3,429	3,633	3,454	2,909	2,738
8,019	6,923	6,028	5,074	4,636	4,025	3,523	2,970	2,704
5,249	4,604	4,076	3,348	3,038	2,701	2,626	2,163	1,855
2,770	2,319	1,952	1,726	1,598	1,324	897	807	849
164	175	170	205	199	232	154	151	133
171	192	231	308	230	297	208	196	128
65	40	110	75	92	64	45	52	42
(82)	41	13	66	(33)	—	35	69	13
—	—	—	—	—	40	375	—	—
2,746	2,383	2,014	1,764	1,626	1,363	1,298	883	909
863	765	632	553	537	496	471	314	360
$ 1,883	$ 1,618	$ 1,382	$ 1,211	$ 1,089	$ 867	$ 827	$ 569	$ 549
$ 1,664	$ 1,618	$ 1,382	$ 1,537	$ 1,045	$ 916	$ 934	$ 722	$ 629
—	1	18	21	7	—	—	—	—
$ 1,664	$ 1,617	$ 1,364	$ 1,516[6]	$ 1,038	$ 916	$ 934	$ 722	$ 629
1,317	1,333	1,337	1,384	1,458	1,509	1,547	1,573	1,587
$ 1.43	$ 1.21	$ 1.02	$ .86	$ .74	$ .57	$ .53	$ .36	$ .35
1.26	1.21	1.02	1.10[6]	.71	.61	.60	.46	.40
.56	.48	.40	.34	.30	.28	.26	.25	.23
41.88	40.13	23.25	19.31	11.16	9.53	9.44	7.04	5.20
$ 1,063	$ 1,117	$ 1,492	$ 1,182	$ 1,231	$ 1,489	$ 895	$ 843	$ 768
3,526	2,890	2,386	2,021	1,759	1,602	1,538	1,483	1,284
310	254	236	181	167	152	151	130	119
1,083	792	593	462	387	304	346	412	300
11,052	10,189	9,245	8,249	7,451	8,606	7,675	6,341	5,241
1,120	985	536	549	761	909	996	801	631
3,207	2,288	2,537	1,980	2,124	2,995	1,848	1,280	1,310
3,888	4,239	3,662	3,299	3,345	3,187	3,479	2,948	2,751
7,095	6,527	6,199	5,279	5,469	6,182	5,327	4,228	4,061
45.2%	35.1%	40.9%	37.5%	38.8%	48.4%	34.7%	30.3%	32.3%
31.9%	19.2%	23.7%	14.7%	18.9%	15.4%	10.9%	15.6%	19.7%
46.4%	41.3%	41.4%	39.4%	34.7%	26.0%	25.7%	20.0%	19.4%
29.4%	27.5%	26.8%	26.5%	21.3%	18.3%	20.1%	16.8%	16.7%
44.3%	39.5%	39.2%	31.0%[6]	42.1%	46.0%	43.1%	53.8%	57.9%
$ 1,293	$ 1,029	$ 878	$ 821	$ 748	$ 417	$ 311	$ 269	$ 268

[6]Net income available to common share owners in 1989 includes after-tax gains of $604 million ($.44 per common share) from the sales of the Company's equity interest in Columbia Pictures Entertainment, Inc. and the Company's bottled water business and the transition effect of $265 million related to the change in accounting for income taxes. Excluding these nonrecurring items, the dividend payout ratio in 1989 was 39.9 percent.

FORMULATING LONG-TERM OBJECTIVES AND GRAND STRATEGIES

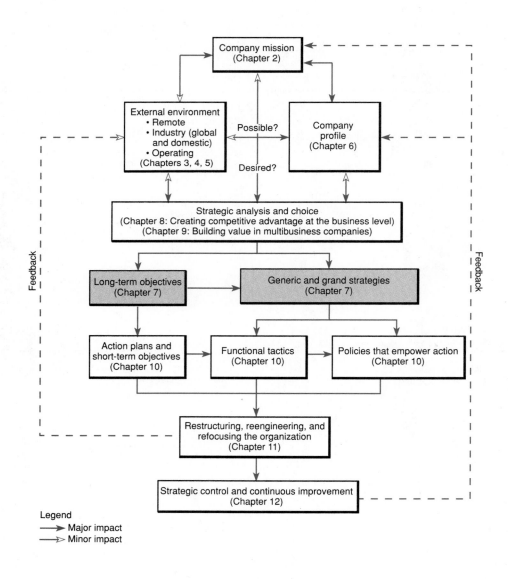

Company mission
(Chapter 2)

External environment
• Remote
• Industry (global
and domestic)
• Operating
(Chapters 3, 4, 5)

Possible?

Company
profile
(Chapter 6)

Desired?

Strategic analysis and choice
(Chapter 8: Creating competitive advantage at the business level)
(Chapter 9: Building value in multibusiness companies)

Long-term objectives
(Chapter 7)

Generic and grand strategies
(Chapter 7)

Action plans and
short-term objectives
(Chapter 10)

Functional tactics
(Chapter 10)

Policies that empower action
(Chapter 10)

Restructuring, reengineering, and
refocusing the organization
(Chapter 11)

Strategic control and continuous improvement
(Chapter 12)

Feedback

Feedback

Legend
⟶ Major impact
⟶ Minor impact

The company mission was described in Chapter 2 as encompassing the broad aims of the firm. The most specific statement of aims presented in that chapter appeared as the goals of the firm. However, these goals, which commonly dealt with profitability, growth, and survival, were stated without specific targets or time frames. They were always to be pursued but could never be fully attained. They gave a general sense of direction but were not intended to provide specific benchmarks for evaluating the firm's progress in achieving its aims. Providing such benchmarks is the function of objectives.[1]

The first part of this chapter will focus on long-term objectives. These are statements of the results a firm seeks to achieve over a specified period, typically five years. The second part will focus on the formulation of grand strategies. These provide a comprehensive general approach in guiding major actions designed to accomplish the firm's long-term objectives.

The chapter has two major aims: (1) to discuss in detail the concept of long-term objectives, the topics they cover, and the qualities they should exhibit; and (2) to discuss the concept of grand strategies and to describe the 14 principal grand strategy options that are available to firms singly or in combination, including three newly popularized options that are being used to provide the basis for global competitiveness.

LONG-TERM OBJECTIVES

Strategic managers recognize that short-run profit maximization is rarely the best approach to achieving sustained corporate growth and profitability. An often repeated adage states that if impoverished people are given food, they will eat it and remain impoverished; however, if they are given seeds and tools and shown how to grow crops, they will be able to improve their condition permanently. A parallel choice confronts strategic decision makers:

1. Should they eat the seeds to improve the near-term profit picture and make large dividend payments through cost saving measures such as laying off workers during periods of slack demand, selling off inventories, or cutting back on research and development?
2. Or should they sow the seeds in the effort to reap long-term rewards by reinvesting profits in growth opportunities, committing resources to employee training, or increasing advertising expenditures?

For most strategic managers, the solution is clear—distribute a small amount of profit now but sow most of it to increase the likelihood of a long-term supply. This is the most frequently used rationale in selecting objectives.

To achieve long-term prosperity, strategic planners commonly establish long-term objectives in seven areas:

Profitability   The ability of any firm to operate in the long run depends on attaining an acceptable level of profits. Strategically managed firms characteristically have a profit objective, usually expressed in earnings per share or return on equity.

---

[1] Throughout this text, the terms *goals* and *objectives* are each used to convey a special meaning, with goals being the less specific and more encompassing concept. Most authors follow this usage; however, some use the two words interchangeably, while others reverse the usage.

GLOBAL
STRATEGY IN
ACTION 7–1

**FROM STRATEGIC INTENT TO CORPORATE
PURPOSE: THE REMAKING OF KOMATSU**

When he succeeded his father as Komatsu's president in 1964, Ryoichi Kawai articulated an objective that the company would pursue for more than 20 years. Komatsu's strategic intent, Kawai announced, was to "catch up with and surpass Caterpillar."

The management approach Kawai adopted to pursue this goal became a well-studied and widely emulated model in the West. Each year, Kawai would define a clear and specific operating priority—for example, improving quality, reducing costs, or expanding exports—that used Catepillar's performance as a standard and sited Caterpillar itself as the competitive target. Then each year's priority would be translated into detailed action plans through PDCA (plan, do, check, act), Komatsu's tightly controlled management system.

Kawai's strategy worked well, and by 1982, when he was choosing his successor, Komatsu had grown from a tiny local competitor with poor product quality to Caterpillar's most serious global challenger in the construction equipment market. But the market was about to change. By 1989, when Tetsuya Katada became the third president to follow Kawai, worldwide demand for construction equipment was down, competition was up, and Komatsu's profits were in steady decline.

As Katada saw the situation, Komatsu's management had become so obsessed with catching Caterpillar that it had stopped thinking about strategic choices. For instance, its product development efforts were biased toward Caterpillar's high-end bulldozers rather than toward smaller, lower-priced products like hydraulic excavators, for which market demand was growing. Katada worried that Komatsu's top management had stopped questioning the business the company was in. Further, he was concerned that the inflexible, top-down style that had become embedded at Komatsu had crushed "the spirit of enterprise" among middle and frontline managers.

Productivity   Strategic managers constantly try to improve the productivity of their systems. Firms that can improve the input-output relationship normally increase profitability. Thus, firms almost always state an objective for productivity. Commonly used productivity objectives are the number of items produced or the number of services rendered per unit of input. However, productivity objectives sometimes are stated in terms of desired cost decreases. For example, objectives may be set for reducing defective items, for customer complaints leading to litigation, or for overtime. Achieving such objectives increases profitability if unit output is maintained.

Competitive Position   One measure of corporate success is relative dominance in the marketplace. Larger firms commonly establish an objective in terms of competitive position, often using total sales or market share as measures of their competitive position. An objective with regard to competitive position may indicate a firm's long-term priorities. For example, Gulf Oil set a five-year objective of moving from third to second place as a producer of high-density polypropylene. Total sales were the measure.

Competitive positioning, however, may sometimes result in a firm subordinating its main objective. As was the case with Komatsu, management became so concerned with the company's performance relative to its competitor, Caterpillar, that the company found itself forgoing opportunities for growth, which led to the company's decline in profits. As Global Strategy in Action 7–1 demonstrates, the company's strategy was successfully restructured before any further damage was caused.

Managers, Katada decided, "can no longer operate within the confines of a defined objective. They need to go out and see the needs and opportunities and operate in a creative and innovative way, always encouraging initiative from below." In other words, he told the company, "I want everyone to stop concentrating simply on catching up with Caterpillar."

At meetings and discussions, Katada challenged managers at several levels to find ways for the company to double its sales by the mid-1990s. What emerged from these and subsequent discussions was a new definition of the company. Rather than thinking of Komatsu as a construction equipment company trying to catch Caterpillar, management began to describe it as a "total technology enterprise" with an opportunity to leverage its existing resources and expertise in electronics, robotics, and plastics.

Under a new banner of "Growth, Global, Groupwide" (the Three Gs), Katada encouraged management at all levels to find new growth opportunities through expanding geographically and leveraging competences. He appointed a Committee for the 1990s to determine how Komatsu could enrich its corporate philosophy, broaden its social contributions, and revitalize its human resources. His objective was to create an organization that could attract and stimulate the best people. "Compared with our old objective," Katada acknowledged, "the Three Gs slogan may seem abstract, but it was this abstract nature that stimulated people to ask what they could do and respond creatively."

More than a strategy, Komatsu now had a corporate purpose, to which its managers could commit and in which they had a voice. In the first three years after Katada articulated the Three Gs, Komatsu's sales, which had been declining since 1982, perked up. That surge was driven almost entirely by a 40 percent growth in Komatsu's nonconstruction equipment business.

Employee Development   Employees value growth and career opportunities. Providing such opportunities often increases productivity and decreases turnover. Therefore, strategic decision makers frequently include an employee development objective in their long-range plans. For example, PPG has declared an objective of developing highly skilled and flexible employees and, thus, providing steady employment for a reduced number of workers.

Employee Relations   Whether or not they are bound by union contracts, firms actively seek good employee relations. In fact, proactive steps in anticipation of employee needs and expectations are a characteristic concern of strategic managers. Strategic managers believe that productivity is linked to employee loyalty and to perceived management interest in workers' welfare. They, therefore, set objectives to improve employee relations. Among the outgrowths of such objectives are safety programs, worker representation on management committees, and employee stock option plans.

Technological Leadership   Firms must decide whether to lead or follow in the marketplace. Either approach can be successful, but each requires a different strategic posture. Therefore, many firms state an objective with regard to technological leadership. For example, Caterpillar Tractor Company established its early reputation and dominant position in its industry by being in the forefront of technological innovation in the manufacture of large earthmovers. Because of an advanced technological design, Daihatsu Mira became the most popular car in Japan in 1991. The four-seat minicar held a 660cc engine that provided the customer with 30 percent more miles per gallon than any competitor, and it had a 25 percent smaller sales tax.

Public Responsibility   Firms recognize their responsibilities to their customers and to society at large. In fact, many firms seek to exceed the demands made by government. They work not only to develop reputations for fairly priced products and services but also to establish themselves as responsible corporate citizens. For example, they may establish objectives for charitable and educational contributions, minority training, public or political activity, community welfare, or urban revitalization. In an attempt to exhibit their sense of public responsibility in the United States, Japanese companies, such as Toyota, Hitachi, and Matsushita, contributed more than $500 million to American educational projects, charities, and nonprofit organizations, a 67 percent increase over the previous year.

Qualities of Long-Term Objectives

What distinguishes a good objective from a bad one? What qualities of an objective improve its chances of being attained? Perhaps these questions are best answered in relation to seven criteria that should be used in preparing long-term objectives: acceptable, flexible, measurable over time, motivating, suitable, understandable, and achievable.

Acceptable   Managers are most likely to pursue objectives that are consistent with their preferences. They may ignore or even obstruct the achievement of objectives that offend them (e.g., promoting a non-nutritional food product) or that they believe to be inappropriate or unfair (e.g., reducing spoilage to offset a disproportionate allocation of fixed overhead). In addition, long-term corporate objectives frequently are designed to be acceptable to groups external to the firm. An example is efforts to abate air pollution that are undertaken at the insistence of the Environmental Protection Agency.

Flexible   Objectives should be adaptable to unforeseen or extraordinary changes in the firm's competitive or environmental forecasts. However, such flexibility usually is increased at the expense of specificity. Moreover, employee confidence may be tempered because adjustment of flexible objectives may affect their jobs. One way of providing flexibility while minimizing its negative effects is to allow for adjustments in the level, rather than in the nature, of objectives. For example, the personnel department objective of providing managerial development training for 15 supervisors per year over the next five-year period might be adjusted by changing the number of people to be trained. In contrast, changing the personnel department's objective of "assisting production supervisors in reducing job-related injuries by 10 percent per year" after three months had gone by would understandably create dissatisfaction.

Measurable   Objectives must clearly and concretely state what will be achieved and when it will be achieved. Thus, objectives should be measurable over time. For example, the objective of "substantially improving our return on investment" would be better stated as "increasing the return on investment on our line of paper products by a minimum of 1 percent a year and a total of 5 percent over the next three years."

Motivating   Studies have shown that people are most productive when objectives are set at a motivating level—one high enough to challenge but not so high as to frustrate or so low as to be easily attained. The problem is that individuals and groups differ in their perceptions of what is high enough. A broad objective that challenges one group frustrates another and minimally interests a third. One valuable recommendation is that objectives be tailored to specific groups. Developing such objectives requires time and effort, but objectives of this kind are more likely to motivate.

| STRATEGY IN ACTION 7–1 | CACI'S LONG-TERM OBJECTIVES, 1990–1997 |

REVENUE

Increase revenue range to $167–$176M or better in FY 90 (FY 90 bookings at $170M).

FY 91: Revenue in the $193–$202M range; bookings at $195–$205M range.

Increase company revenue 15–20 percent per year steadily over next decade.

Consistently increase revenues to $500 M per annum by 1997 or earlier. Steady manageable and consistent profitable growth.

PROFITABILITY

Achieve 4 percent NAT or better as an annual corporate target for return on revenues, moving to 5 percent CAT by mid-90s.

Individual departments and divisions must target NAT percentage profits at 50–100 percent above company levels (i.e., 6–8 percent moving to 7.5–10 percent).

SHAREHOLDERS' VALUE

Increase stock price (market value) to $20 per share or better by 1997 (current share basis).

Suitable   Objectives must be suited to the broad aims of the firm, which are expressed in its mission statement. Each objective should be a step toward the attainment of overall goals. In fact, objectives that do not coincide with the company mission can subvert the firm's aims. For example, if the mission is growth oriented, the objective of reducing the debt-to-equity ratio to 1.00 would probably be unsuitable and counterproductive.

Understandable   Strategic managers at all levels must understand what is to be achieved. They also must understand the major criteria by which their performance will be evaluated. Thus, objectives must be so stated that they are as understandable to the recipient as they are to the giver. Consider the misunderstandings that might arise over the objective of "increasing the productivity of the credit card department by 20 percent within five years." What does this objective mean? Increase the number of outstanding cards? Increase the use of outstanding cards? Increase the employee workload? Make productivity gains each year? Or hope that the new computer-assisted system, which should improve productivity, is approved by year 5? As this simple example illustrates, objectives must be clear, meaningful, and unambiguous.

Achievable   Finally, objectives must be possible to achieve. This is easier said than done. Turbulence in the remote and operating environments affects a firm's internal operations, creating uncertainty, and limiting the accuracy of the objectives set by strategic management. To illustrate, the wildly fluctuating prime interest rates in 1980 made objective setting extremely difficult for the years 1981 to 1985, particularly in such areas as sales projections for producers of consumer durable goods like General Motors and General Electric.

An especially fine example of long-term objectives is provided in CACI, Inc.'s strategic plan. Shown in Strategy in Action 7–1 are CACI's major financial objectives for the period. The firm's approach is wholly consistent with the list of desired qualities for long-term objectives. In particular, CACI's objectives are flexible, measurable over time, understand-able, and suitable for a high-technology and professional services organization.

GENERIC STRATEGIES

Many planning experts believe that the general philosophy of doing business declared by the firm in the mission statement must be translated into a holistic statement of the firm's strategic orientation before it can be further defined in terms of a specific long-term strategy. In other words, a long-term or grand strategy must be based on a core idea about how the firm can best compete in the marketplace.

The popular term for this core idea is *generic strategy*. From a scheme developed by Michael Porter, many planners believe that any long-term strategy should derive from a firm's attempt to seek a competitive advantage based on one of three generic strategies:

1. Striving for overall low-cost leadership in the industry.
2. Striving to create and market unique products for varied customer groups through *differentiation*.
3. Striving to have special appeal to one or more groups of consumer or industrial buyers, *focusing* on their cost or differentiation concerns.

Advocates of generic strategies believe that each of these options can produce above-average returns for a firm in an industry. However, they are successful for very different reasons.

Low-cost leaders depend on some fairly unique capabilities to achieve and sustain their low-cost position. Examples of such capabilities are: having secured suppliers of scarce raw materials, being in a dominant market share position, or having a high degree of capitalization. Low-cost producers usually excel at cost reductions and efficiencies. They maximize economies of scale, implement cost-cutting technologies, stress reductions in overhead and in administrative expenses, and use volume sales techniques to propel themselves up the earning curve. The commonly accepted requirements for successful implementation of the low-cost and other two generic strategies are overviewed in Figure 7–1.

A low-cost leader is able to use its cost advantage to charge lower prices or to enjoy higher profit margins. By so doing, the firm effectively can defend itself in price wars, attack competitors on price to gain market share, or, if already dominant in the industry, simply benefit from exceptional returns. As an extreme case, it has been argued that National Can Company, a corporation in an essentially stagnant industry, is able to generate attractive and improving profits by being the low-cost producer.

Strategies dependent on differentiation are designed to appeal to customers with a special sensitivity for a particular product attribute. By stressing the attribute above other product qualities, the firm attempts to build customer loyalty. Often such loyalty translates into a firm's ability to charge a premium price for its product. Cross-brand pens, Brooks Brothers suits, Porsche automobiles, and Chivas Regal Scotch whiskey are all examples.

The product attribute also can be the marketing channels through which it is delivered, its image for excellence, the features it includes, and the service network that supports it. As a result of the importance of these attributes, competitors often face "perceptual" barriers to entry when customers of a successfully differentiated firm fail to see largely identical products as being interchangeable. For example, General Motors hopes that customers will accept "only genuine GM replacement parts."

A focus strategy, whether anchored in a low-cost base or a differentiation base, attempts to attend to the needs of a particular market segment. Likely segments are those that are ignored by marketing appeals to easily accessible markets, to the "typical" customer, or to

FIGURE 7–1
Requirements for Generic Competitive Strategies

Generic Strategy	Commonly Required Skills and Resources	Common Organizational Requirements
Overall cost leadership	Sustained capital investment and access to capital.	Tight cost control.
	Process engineering skills.	Frequent, detailed control reports.
	Intense supervision of labor.	Structured organization and responsibilities.
	Products designed for ease in manufacture.	Incentives based on meeting strict quantitative targets.
	Low-cost distribution system.	
Differentiation	Strong marketing abilities.	Strong coordination among functions in R&D, product development, and marketing.
	Product engineering.	
	Creative flare.	Subjective measurement and incentives instead of quantitative measures.
	Strong capability in basic research.	
	Corporate reputation for quality or technological leadership.	Amenities to attract highly skilled labor, scientists, or creative people.
	Long tradition in the industry or unique combination of skills drawn from other businesses.	
	Strong cooperation from channels.	
Focus	Combination of the above policies directed at the particular strategic target.	Combination of the above policies directed at the regular strategic target.

Source: Free Press COMPETITIVE STRATEGY: Techniques for Analyzing Industries and Competitors, pp. 40–41. Reprinted with permission of the Free Press, a division of Simon & Schuster, from Competitive Strategy: Techniques for Analyzing Industries and Competitors, by Michael E. Porter. Copyright © 1980 by Michael E. Porter.

customers with common applications for the product. A firm pursuing a focus strategy is willing to service isolated geographic areas; to satisfy the needs of customers with special financing, inventory, or servicing problems; or to tailor the product to the somewhat unique demands of the small-to-medium-sized customer. The focusing firms profit from their willingness to serve otherwise ignored or under-appreciated customer segments. The classic example is cable television. An entire industry was born because of a willingness of cable firms to serve isolated rural locations that were ignored by traditional television services. Brick producers that typically service a radius of less than 100 miles and commuter airlines that serve regional geographic areas are other examples of industries where a focus strategy frequently yields above-average industry profits.

While each of the generic strategies enables a firm to maximize certain competitive advantages, each one also exposes the firm to a number of competitive risks. For example, a low-cost leader fears a new low-cost technology that is being developed by a competitor; a differentiating firm fears imitators; and a focused firm fears invasion by a firm that largely targets customers. As Figure 7–2 suggests, each generic strategy presents the firm with a number of risks.

GRAND STRATEGIES

While the need for firms to develop generic strategies remains an unresolved debate, designers of planning systems agree about the critical role of grand strategies. Grand strategies, often called *master* or *business strategies*, provide basic direction for strategic

FIGURE 7–2
Risks of the Generic Strategies

Risks of Cost Leadership	Risks of Differentiation	Risk of Focus
Cost of leadership is not sustained: • Competitors imitate. • Technology changes. • Other bases for cost leadership erode.	Differentiation is not sustained: • Competitors imitate. • Bases for differentiation becomes less important to buyers.	The focus strategy is imitated. The target segment becomes structurally unattractive: • Structure erodes. • Demand disappears.
Proximity in differentiation is lost.	Cost proximity is lost.	Broadly targeted competitors overwhelm the segment: • The segment's differences from other segments narrow • The advantages of a broad line increase.
Cost focusers achieve even lower cost in segments.	Differentiation focusers achieve even greater differentiation in segments.	New focusers subsegment the industry.

Source: Free Press *Competitive Advantage: Creating and Sustaining Superior Performance*, p. 21. Adapted with the permission of the Free Press, a division of Simon & Schuster, from *Competitive Strategy: Creating and Sustaining Superior Performance*, by Michael E. Porter. Copyright © 1985 by Michael E. Porter.

actions. They are the basis of coordinated and sustained efforts directed toward achieving long-term business objectives.

The purpose of this section is twofold: (1) to list, describe, and discuss 14 grand strategies that strategic managers should consider and (2) to present approaches to the selection of an optimal grand strategy from the available alternatives.

Grand strategies indicate the time period over which long-range objectives are to be achieved. Thus, a grand strategy can be defined as a comprehensive general approach that guides a firm's major actions.

The 14 principal grand strategies are: concentrated growth, market development, product development, innovation, horizontal integration, vertical integration, concentric diversification, conglomerate diversification, turnaround, divestiture, liquidation, joint ventures, strategic alliances, and consortia. Any one of these strategies could serve as the basis for achieving the major long-term objectives of a single firm. But a firm involved with multiple industries, businesses, product lines, or customer groups—as many firms are—usually combines several grand strategies. For clarity, however, each of the principal grand strategies is described independently in this section, with examples to indicate some of its relative strengths and weaknesses.

Concentrated Growth

Many of the firms that fell victim to merger mania were once mistakenly convinced that the best way to achieve their objectives was to pursue unrelated diversification in the search for financial opportunity and synergy.[2] By rejecting that "conventional wisdom," such firms as Martin-Marietta, Kentucky Fried Chicken, Compaq, Avon, Hyatt Legal Services, and Tenant have demonstrated the advantages of what is increasingly proving to be sound business strategy. A firm that has enjoyed special success through a strategic emphasis

---

[2] Portions of this section were adapted from John A. Pearce II and J. Harvey, "Risks and Rewards of a Concentrated Growth Strategy," *Academy of Management Executive*, February 1990, pp. 62–69.

on increasing market share through concentration is Chemlawn. With headquarters in Columbus, Ohio, Chemlawn is the North American leader in professional lawn care. Like others in the lawn-care industry, Chemlawn is experiencing a steadily declining customer base. Market analysis shows that the decline is fueled by negative environmental publicity, perceptions of poor customer service, and concern about the price versus the value of the company's services, given the wide array of do-it-yourself alternatives. Chemlawn's approach to increasing market share hinges on addressing quality, price, and value issues; discontinuing products that the public or environmental authorities perceive as unsafe; and improving the quality of its work force.

These firms are just a few of the majority of American firms that pursue a concentrated growth strategy by focusing on a specific product and market combination. Concentrated growth is the strategy of the firm that directs its resources to the profitable growth of a single product, in a single market, with a single dominant technology. The main rationale for this approach, sometimes called a *market penetration* or *concentration strategy*, is that the firm thoroughly develops and exploits its expertise in a delimited competitive arena.

Rationale for Superior Performance

Concentrated growth strategies lead to enhanced performance. The ability to assess market needs, knowledge of buyer behavior, customer price sensitivity, and effectiveness of promotion are characteristics of a concentrated growth strategy. Such core capabilities are a more important determinant of competitive market success than are the environmental forces faced by the firm. The high success rates of new products also are tied to avoiding situations that require undeveloped skills, such as serving new customers and markets, acquiring new technology, building new channels, developing new promotional abilities, and facing new competition.

A major misconception about the concentrated growth strategy is that the firm practicing it will settle for little or no growth. This is certainly not true for a firm that correctly utilizes the strategy. A firm employing concentrated growth grows by building on its competences, and it achieves a competitive edge by concentrating in the product-market segment it knows best. A firm employing this strategy is aiming for the growth that results from increased productivity, better coverage of its actual product-market segment, and more efficient use of its technology. Strategy in Action 7–2 provides an excellent example of how Hechinger, the home supply chain, is attempting to improve its competitiveness by refocusing its concentration strategy.

Conditions That Favor Concentrated Growth

Specific conditions in the firm's environment are favorable to the concentrated growth strategy. The first is a condition in which the firm's industry is resistant to major technological advancements. This is usually the case in the late growth and maturity stages of the product life cycle and in product markets where product demand is stable and industry barriers, such as capitalization, are high. Machinery for the paper manufacturing industry, in which the basic technology has not changed for more than a century, is a good example.

An especially favorable condition is one in which the firm's targeted markets are not product saturated. Markets with competitive gaps leave the firm with alternatives for growth, other than taking market share away from competitors. The successful introduction of traveler services by Allstate and Amoco demonstrates that even an organization as entrenched and powerful as the AAA could not build a defensible presence in all segments of the automobile club market. Similarly, General Motors attempted to increase its share of the Japanese car market in 1992 with the introduction of its Pontiac Grand AM and Buick

HECHINGER REBUILDS STORE CONCEPT

Hechinger—the company that's helped thousands of weekend do-it-yourselfers with everything from fixing a leaky faucet to building a deck—is kicking up a little dust of its own with the remodeling of its Washington area stores to a new "Home Project Center" format.

In addition to new warehouse-style shelving, the stores cluster products around "project areas" and displays and have more workers on hand to answer questions.

"The most important thing we must do as a retailer . . . is to focus on what the customer wants and give it to them better than anyone else," said John W. Hechinger, Jr., the company's president since 1986. "That's really what's driving us."

"The wave of the present, if not the future, is the warehouse concept," said Neal Kaplan, an analyst at Scott & Stringfellow, a Richmond-based brokerage. "It seems some Hechinger stores aren't really as competitive as they'd like them to be."

Analysts also see Hechinger's rapid move as a "preemptive strike" against expansion by Atlanta-based The Home Depot, Inc., and other specialty hardware retailers, such as Lowes, a North Carolina-based chain that is opening larger "superstores."

The Home Depot, rapidly becoming the dominant company in the nation's $25 billion home improvement products industry, has 200 stores in 18 states and is looking to open its first Washington store in Alexandria next year.

Hechinger expects to convert its two dozen Washington area stores to Home Project Centers by the middle of the decade. In early 1992, the Landover, Maryland-based, company set aside $83 million for the work, which also involves closing or consolidating some stores.

It costs about $6 million to open a new store and about $2 million to convert an older Hechinger to the Home Project Center format. Most of the Washington area stores—in prime locations—will be remodeled.

Hechinger's new centers sell more goods, but operating costs are higher, meaning lower gross margins, according to the company's financial records. In response to competition, the company also cut prices in several markets and started a lowest-price guarantee, which has pared profits.

Analysts say it's important for Hechinger to pick its battles in key markets, in part because of the evolution of the home improvement supplies business. For example, they point to the fact that it's possible to buy a tub of spackle or a hacksaw at a drug store or mulch at the neighborhood grocery.

"We need to be the most flexible, leanest operator in the business," Hechinger said.

Source: Excerpted from "Hechinger Rebuilds Store Concept," by Lloyd Batzler, *The Fairfax Journal Weekly*, December 2, 1992, p. A3.

Park Avenue. The move was based on GM's knowledge that import auto sales in Japan rose 5.2 percent in 1990, with large cars accounting for most of those sales.

A third condition that favors concentrated growth exists when the firm's product markets are sufficiently distinctive to dissuade competitors in adjacent product markets from trying to invade the firm's segment. John Deere scrapped its plans for growth in the construction machinery business when mighty Caterpillar threatened to enter Deere's mainstay, the farm machinery business, in retaliation. Rather than risk a costly price war on its own turf, Deere scrapped these plans.

A fourth favorable condition exists when the firm's inputs are stable in price and quantity and are available in the amounts and at the times needed. Maryland-based Giant Foods is able to concentrate in the grocery business largely due to its stable long-term arrangements with suppliers of its private-label products. Most of these suppliers are makers of the national brands that compete against the Giant labels. With a high market share and aggressive retail distribution, Giant controls the access of these brands to the consumer. Consequently, its suppliers have considerable incentive to honor verbal agreements, called *bookings*, in which they commit themselves for a one-year period with regard to the price, quality, and timing of their shipments to Giant.

The pursuit of concentrated growth also is favored by a stable market—a market without the seasonal or cyclical swings that would encourage a firm to diversify. Night Owl Security, the District of Columbia market leader in home security services, commits its customers to initial four-year contracts. In a city where affluent consumers tend to be quite transient, the length of this relationship is remarkable. Night Owl's concentrated growth strategy has been reinforced by its success in getting subsequent owners of its customers' homes to extend and renew the security service contracts. In a similar way, Lands' End reinforced its growth strategy by asking customers for names and addresses of friends and relatives living overseas who would like to receive Lands' End catalogs.

A firm also can grow while concentrating, if it enjoys competitive advantages based on efficient production or distribution channels. These advantages enable the firm to formulate advantageous pricing policies. More efficient production methods and better handling of distribution also enable the firm to achieve greater economies of scale or, in conjunction with marketing, result in a product that is differentiated in the mind of the consumer. Graniteville Company, a large South Carolina textile manufacturer, enjoyed decades of growth and profitability by adopting a "follower" tactic as part of its concentrated growth strategy. By producing fabrics only after market demand had been well established, and by featuring products that reflected its expertise in adopting manufacturing innovations and in maintaining highly efficient long production runs, Graniteville prospered through concentrated growth.

Finally, the success of market generalists creates conditions favorable to concentrated growth. When generalists succeed by using universal appeals, they avoid making special appeals to particular groups of customers. The net result is that many small pockets are left open in the markets dominated by generalists, and that specialists emerge and thrive in these pockets. For example, hardware store chains, such as Stanbaugh-Thompsons and Hechinger, focus primarily on routine household repair problems and offer solutions that can be easily sold on a self-service, do-it-yourself basis. This approach leaves gaps at both the "semiprofessional" and "neophyte" ends of the market—in terms of the purchaser's skill at household repairs and the extent to which available merchandise matches the requirements of individual homeowners.

Risk and Rewards of Concentrated Growth

Under stable conditions, concentrated growth poses lower risk than any other grand strategy; but, in a changing environment, a firm committed to concentrated growth faces high risks. The greatest risk is that concentrating in a single product market makes a firm particularly vulnerable to changes in that segment. Slowed growth in the segment would jeopardize the firm because its investment, competitive edge, and technology are deeply entrenched in a specific offering. It is difficult for the firm to attempt sudden changes if its product is threatened by near-term obsolescence, a faltering market, new substitutes, or changes in technology or customer needs. For example, the manufacturers of IBM clones faced such a problem when IBM adopted the OS/2 operating system for its personal computer line. That change made existing clones out of date.

The concentrating firm's entrenchment in a specific industry makes it particularly susceptible to changes in the economic environment of that industry. For example, Mack Truck, the second-largest truck maker in America, lost $20 million as a result of an 18-month slump in the truck industry.

Entrenchment in a specific product market tends to make a concentrating firm more adept than competitors at detecting new trends. However, any failure of such a firm to properly forecast major changes in its industry can result in extraordinary losses. Numerous makers of inexpensive digital watches were forced to declare bankruptcy because they failed to anticipate the competition posed by Swatch, Guess, and other trendy watches that emerged from the fashion industry.

A firm pursuing a concentrated growth strategy is vulnerable also to the high opportunity costs that result from remaining in a specific product market and ignoring other options that could employ the firm's resources more profitably. Overcommitment to a specific technology and product market can hinder a firm's ability to enter a new or growing product market that offers more attractive cost-benefit trade-offs. Had Apple Computers maintained its policy of making equipment that did not interface with IBM equipment, it would have missed out on what have proved to be its most profitable strategic opinions.

Concentrated Growth Is Often the Most Viable Option

Examples abound of firms that have enjoyed exceptional returns on the concentrated growth strategy. Such firms as McDonald's, Goodyear, and Apple Computers have used firsthand knowledge and deep involvement with specific product segments to become powerful competitors in their markets. The strategy is associated even more often with successful smaller firms that have steadily and doggedly improved their market position.

The limited additional resources necessary to implement concentrated growth, coupled with the limited risk involved, also make this strategy desirable for a firm with limited funds. For example, through a carefully devised concentrated growth strategy, medium-sized John Deere & Company was able to become a major force in the agricultural machinery business even when competing with such firms as Ford Motor Company. While other firms were trying to exit or diversify from the farm machinery business, Deere spent $2 billion in upgrading its machinery, boosting its efficiency, and engaging in a program to strengthen its dealership system. This concentrated growth strategy enabled it to become the leader in the farm machinery business despite the fact that Ford was more than 10 times its size.

The firm that chooses a concentrated growth strategy directs its resources to the profitable growth of a narrowly defined product and market, focusing on a dominant technology. Firms that remain within their chosen product market are able to extract the most from their technology and market knowledge and, thus, are able to minimize the risk associated with unrelated diversification. The success of a concentration strategy is founded on the firm's use of superior insights into its technology, product, and customer to obtain a sustainable competitive advantage. Superior performance on these aspects of corporate strategy has been shown to have a substantial positive effect on market success.

A grand strategy of concentrated growth allows for a considerable range of action. Broadly speaking, the firm can attempt to capture a larger market share by increasing the usage rates of present customers, by attracting competitors' customers, or by selling to nonusers. In turn, each of these options suggests more specific options, some of which are listed in the top section of Figure 7–3.

When strategic managers forecast that their current products and their markets will not provide the basis for achieving the company mission, they have two options that involve moderate costs and risk: market development and product development.

Market Development

Market development commonly ranks second only to concentration as the least costly and least risky of the 14 grand strategies. It consists of marketing present products, often with only cosmetic modifications, to customers in related market areas by adding

FIGURE 7–3
Specific Options under the Grand Strategies of Concentration, Market Development, and Product Development

Concentration (increasing use of present products in present markets):

1. Increasing present customers' rate of use:
   a. Increasing the size of purchase.
   b. Increasing the rate of product obsolescence.
   c. Advertising other uses.
   d. Giving price incentives for increased use.
2. Attracting competitors' customers:
   a. Establishing sharper brand differentiation.
   b. Increasing promotional effort.
   c. Initiating price cuts.
3. Attracting nonusers to buy the product:
   a. Inducing trial use through sampling, price incentives, and so on.
   b. Pricing up or down.
   c. Advertising new uses.

Market development (selling present products in new markets):

1. Opening additional geographic markets:
   a. Regional expansion.
   b. National expansion.
   c. International expansion.
2. Attracting other market segments:
   a. Developing product versions to appeal to other segments.
   b. Entering other channels of distribution.
   c. Advertising in other media.

Product development (developing new products for present markets):

1. Developing new product features:
   a. Adapt (to other ideas, developments).
   b. Modify (change color, motion, sound, odor, form, shape).
   c. Magnify (stronger, longer, thicker, extra value).
   d. Minify (smaller, shorter, lighter).
   e. Substitute (other ingredients, process, power).
   f. Rearrange (other patterns, layout, sequence, components).
   g. Reverse (inside out).
   h. Combine (blend, alloy, assortment, ensemble; combine units, purposes, appeals, ideas).
2. Developing quality variations.
3. Developing additional models and sizes (product proliferation).

Source: Adapted from Philip Kotler, *Marketing Management Analysis, Planning, and Control*, 6th ed., 1987. Reprinted by permission of Prentice Hall, Inc., Englewood Cliffs, NJ.

channels of distribution or by changing the content of advertising or promotion. Several specific approaches are listed under this heading in Figure 7–3. Thus, as suggested by the figure, firms that open branch offices in new cities, states, or countries are practicing market development. Likewise, firms are practicing market development if they switch from advertising in trade publications to advertising in newspapers or if they add jobbers to supplement their mail-order sales efforts. One company that has mastered the strategy of market development is Tandy Corporation, as explained in Strategy in Action 7–3.

Market development allows firms to practice a form of concentrated growth by identifying new uses for existing products and new demographically, psychographically, or geographically defined markets. Frequently, changes in media selection, promotional appeals, and distribution are used to initiate this approach. Du Pont used market development when it found a new application for Kevlar, an organic material that police, security, and military personnel had used primarily for bulletproofing. Kevlar now is being used to refit and maintain wooden-hulled boats, since it is lighter and stronger than glass fibers and has 11 times the strength of steel.

TANDY REMAKES ITSELF AGAIN AND AGAIN AND AGAIN

Only months after heralding its Incredible Universe megastore as the shop of the future, the venerable merchant Tandy Corp. announced that it would open mini electronics and computer stores in several big cities. In another surprising flip-flop, the $3.8 billion retailer scrapped plans to spin off its computer-manufacturing subsidiary, TE Electronics. Instead, it agreed to sell its money-losing plants to computer maker AST Research for an estimated $175 million.

If the reshuffling seems to defy logic, there may be some method in the madness. Central to Tandy's hope for redemption is Incredible Universe, which some analysts have called the most exciting retailing concept in years. The 160,000-square-foot stores, which are about 70 times larger than a Radio Shack, seem to offer 70 times more products than anyone else. They peddle, for instance, 315 kinds of televisions, 181 varieties of refrigerators, and 45,000 music and movie titles. As Tandy CEO John Roach puts it, "If it's not in the Universe, it doesn't exist."

If the stores' guaranteed low prices don't draw the crowds, the Disney-like atmosphere may. Customers are greeted by karaoke singers and salespeople dubbed "cast members" who offer product information and door-prize entry blanks. The stores have their own child-care center stocked with—what else?—electronic toys sold elsewhere in the store. The hope, of course, is that the kid will beg Mom and Dad to take some home. Said one father in Dallas: "One hour of babysitting cost me $400."

If Incredible Universe wants to be everything to everybody, Tandy's latest concepts promise specialized merchandise to a few. A sampling: Energy Express Plus stores will be free-standing kiosks in high-traffic malls that sell mostly impulse purchases like batteries and electronic date books. And Computer City Express will stock the top-selling products carried by the chain's larger computer superstores. Tandy is also out to capitalize on the outlet mall craze. Its new Famous Brand Electronics will carry factory overstocks and clearance merchandise.

Tandy executives report that the first of 16 planned Incredible Universe stores is expected to ring up sales of $60 million in its first year.

The medical industry provides other examples of new markets for existing products. The National Institutes of Health's report of a study showing that the use of aspirin may lower the incidence of heart attacks was expected to boost sales in the $2.2 billion analgesic market. It was predicted that the expansion of this market would lower the market share of nonaspirin brands, such as industry leaders Tylenol and Advil. Product extensions currently planned include Bayer Calendar Pack, 28-day packaging to fit the once-a-day prescription for the prevention of a second heart attack.

Another example is Chesebrough-Ponds, a major producer of health and beauty aids, which decided several years ago to expand its market by repacking its Vaseline Petroleum Jelly in pocket-size squeeze tubes as Vaseline "Lip Therapy." The corporation decided to place a strategic emphasis on market development, because it knew from market studies that its petroleum-jelly customers already were using the product to prevent chapped lips. Company leaders reasoned that their market could be expanded significantly if the product were repackaged to fit conveniently in consumers' pockets and purses.

As shown in Global Strategy in Action 7–2, a British joint venture called "Mercury One 2 One" was able to successfully market its cellular service to a new target segment. The company changed the promotion of its existing product to appeal to more than the

GLOBAL
STRATEGY IN
ACTION 7–2

IN ENGLAND THEY GIVE IT AWAY

A s U.S. companies try to figure out how to sell consumers on national cellular service, they should ponder the Pythonesque misadventures of a British operator called Mercury One 2 One that dared to cut prices too much.

A joint venture of US West and Britain's Cable 7 Wireless, Mercury was determined to make cellular more than a plaything for rich businessmen. So it launched a marketing campaign in which it offered customers across England free calling services 7 PM to 7 AM when call volume had been low.

The two-year campaign, which ended in September, was successful beyond hope. Mercury signed up over 300,000 new customers, two-thirds of whom had never used a cellular phone. In Britain, even local calls are metered, costing you more the longer you speak. Besides adapting their behavior in obvious ways, like never using the regular phone to make a call in the evening, the happy multitude showed typical British pluck in making the best of a good thing. Some customers took to keeping a line open all night and using their cell phones as crib monitors. The night hours became the time of peak traffic, and circuits soon overloaded. To avoid a PR disaster, Mercury had to install additional transmitters—for calls that brought in zero revenue.

Mercury points out that each customer pays a monthly fee, and that the volume of calls during the daylight hours has also soared. Still, the company now has 300,000 customers who will get free nighttime phone service for as long as they keep their contracts up, which can mean the rest of their lives. Says Mercury spokesman Andrew Donovan: "They can't, however, pass these rights on to their heirs."

Source: "The Trouble with Cellular," November 13, 1995, p. 186. By Andrew Jupfer, FORTUNE, © 1995, Time, Inc. All rights reserved.

traditional wealthy businessman, offering free calling services during downtime hours. The company's strategy proved disastrously successful as the company has gained over 300,000 new customers.

Product Development

Product development involves the substantial modification of existing products or the creation of new but related products that can be marketed to current customers through established channels. The product development strategy often is adopted either to prolong the life cycle of current products or to take advantage of a favorite reputation or brand name. The idea is to attract satisfied customers to new products as a result of their positive experience with the firm's initial offering. The bottom section in Figure 7–3 lists some of the options available to firms undertaking product development. A revised edition of a college textbook, a new car style, and a second formula of shampoo for oily hair are examples of the product development strategy.

The product development strategy is based on the penetration of existing markets by incorporating product modifications into existing items or by developing new products with a clear connection to the existing product line. The telecommunications industry provides an example of product extension based on product modification. To increase its estimated 8–10 percent share of the $5–$6 billion corporate user market, MCI Communication Corporation extended its direct-dial service to 146 countries, the same as those serviced by AT&T, at lower average rates than those of AT&T. MCI's recent addition of 79 countries to its network underscores its belief in this market, which it expects to grow 15–20 percent annually. Another example of expansions linked to existing lines is Gerber's decision to engage in general merchandise marketing. Gerber's recent introduction included 52 items that ranged from feeding accessories to toys and children's wear. Likewise, Nabisco Brands seeks competitive advantage by placing its strategic emphasis on product development. With headquarters in Parsippany, New Jersey, the company is one of three operating units of RJR Nabisco. It is the leading producer of biscuits, confections, snacks, shredded cereals, and processed fruits and vegetables. To maintain its position as leader, Nabisco pursues a strategy of developing and introducing new products and expanding its existing product line. Spoon Size Shredded Wheat and Ritz Bits crackers are two examples of new products that are variations on existing products.

Innovation

In many industries, it has become increasingly risky not to innovate. Both consumer and industrial markets have come to expect periodic changes and improvements in the products offered. As a result, some firms find it profitable to make innovation their grand strategy. They seek to reap the initially high profits associated with customer acceptance of a new or greatly improved product. Then, rather than face stiffening competition as the basis of profitability shifts from innovation to production or marketing competence, they search for other original or novel ideas. The underlying rationale of the grand strategy of innovation is to create a new product life cycle and thereby make similar existing products obsolete. Thus, this strategy differs from the product development strategy of extending an existing product's life cycle. For example, Intel, a leader in the semiconductor industry, pursues expansion through a strategic emphasis on innovation. With headquarters in California, the company is a designer and manufacturer of semiconductor components and related computers, of microcomputer systems, and of software. Its Pentium microprocessor gives a desktop computer the capability of a mainframe. The innovation strategy pursued at Nippondenso has led to a creative research approach of micronization as described in Global Strategy in Action 7–3.

While most growth-oriented firms appreciate the need to be innovative occasionally, a few firms use it as their fundamental way of relating to their markets. An outstanding example is Polaroid, which heavily promotes each of its new cameras until competitors are able to match its technological innovation; by this time, Polaroid normally is prepared to introduce a dramatically new or improved product. For example, it introduced consumers in quick succession to the Swinger, the SX-70, the One Step, and the Sun Camera 660.

Few innovative ideas prove profitable because the research, development, and premarketing costs of converting a promising idea into a profitable product are extremely high. A study by the Booz Allen & Hamilton management research department provides some understanding of the risks. As shown in Figure 7–4, Booz Allen & Hamilton found that less than 2 percent of the innovative projects initially considered by 51 companies eventually reached the marketplace. Specifically, out of every 58 new product ideas, only 12 pass an initial screening test that finds them compatible with the firm's mission and long-term objectives, only 7 remain after an evaluation of their potential, and only 3 survive development attempts. Of the three survivors, two appear to have profit potential after test marketing and only one is commercially successful.

GLOBAL
STRATEGY IN
ACTION 7–3

THE TINIEST TOYOTA

The technological edge in the car industry is shifting away from vehicle assemblers to the components makers. They are the ones responsible for such wonders as engine-management chips and antilock braking systems. Now, one of the world's biggest car-components companies, Japan's Nippondenso, has taken the process even further, and built its own car. Although it has yet to make some bits work—such as the engine—the car is still pretty impressive. That is because it is just 4.8mm long.

Nippondenso's microcar is a classic: a replica of the Toyota Model AA, which was developed in 1936 when the Toyota Automatic Loom Works decided to open an automobile division. That division became the third-biggest carmaker in the world. Toyota is Nippondenso's largest shareholder.

It took staff at Nippondenso's basic-research laboratory (one of the first to be opened by a carparts firm) 2½ months to build the little car. It was assembled from components produced by a number of processes.

Nippondenso now is trying to make the microcar go under its own steam, so to speak. An internal combustion engine is out of the question: too complex to make small enough to fit under the bonnet. Instead, the laboratory has decided to use an environmentally friendly miniaturized electric engine. There is still a problem, though, in supplying the energy. Shrinking the batteries and the necessary electrical connections to fit inside such a small vehicle appear impossible with current technology. So the company plans to supply the engine's energy externally.

The plan is to make what Nippondenso calls an *electromagnetic wave engine*—a tiny device capable of converting the energy contained in microwaves (which would be beamed at the car) into some kind of driving force. The laboratory is coy about the details, but it hopes to put together the components of such an engine within the next two years.

The purpose of all this, of course, is not to build cars for amoebae but to develop micromachining techniques that may be useful in making future products—and not just cars. Nippondenso talks of a self-propelled microcamera that can be driven through human blood vessels, or a microrobot that can repair, from the inside, the small cooling tubes surrounding the core of a nuclear reactor. Toyotas soon could be everywhere.

Horizontal Integration

When a firm's long-term strategy is based on growth through the acquisition of one or more similar firms operating at the same stage of the production-marketing chain, its grand strategy is called *horizontal integration*. Such acquisitions eliminate competitors and provide the acquiring firm with access to new markets. One example is Warner-Lambert's acquisition of Parke Davis, which reduced competition in the ethical drugs field for Chilcott Laboratories, a firm that Warner-Lambert previously had acquired. Another example is the long-range acquisition pattern of White Consolidated Industries, which expanded in the refrigerator and freezer market through a grand strategy of horizontal integration, by acquiring Kelvinator Appliance, the Refrigerator Products Division of Bendix Westinghouse Automotive Air Brake, and Frigidaire Appliance from General Motors. Nike's acquisition in the dress shoes business and N. V. Homes's purchase of Ryan Homes have vividly exemplified the success that horizontal integration strategies can bring.

FIGURE 7–4
Decay of New Product Ideas (51 Companies)

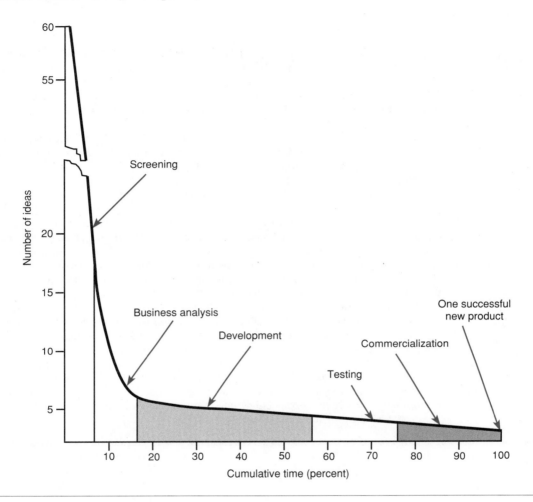

Vertical Integration

When a firm's grand strategy is to acquire firms that supply it with inputs (such as raw materials) or are customers for its outputs (such as warehousers for finished products), *vertical integration* is involved. To illustrate, if a shirt manufacturer acquires a textile producer—by purchasing its common stock, buying its assets, or exchanging ownership interests—the strategy is vertical integration. In this case, it is *backward* vertical integration, since the firm acquired operates at an earlier stage of the production-marketing process. If the shirt manufacturer had merged with a clothing store, it would have been *forward* vertical integration—the acquisition of a firm nearer to the ultimate consumer.

Amoco emerged as North America's leader in natural gas reserves and products in 1988 as a result of its acquisition of Dome Petroleum. This backward integration by Amoco was made in support of its downstream businesses in refining and in gas stations, whose profits made the acquisition possible.

FIGURE 7–5
Vertical and Horizontal Integrations

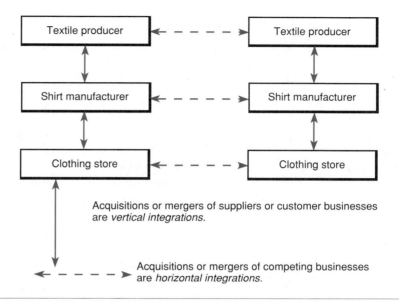

Acquisitions or mergers of suppliers or customer businesses are *vertical integrations*.

Acquisitions or mergers of competing businesses are *horizontal integrations*.

Figure 7–5 depicts both horizontal and vertical integration. The principal attractions of a horizontal integration grand strategy are readily apparent. The acquiring firm is able to greatly expand its operations, thereby achieving greater market share, improving economies of scale, and increasing the efficiency of capital use. In addition, these benefits are achieved with only moderately increased risk, since the success of the expansion is principally dependent on proven abilities.

The reasons for choosing a vertical integration grand strategy are more varied and sometimes less obvious. The main reason for backward integration is the desire to increase the dependability of the supply or quality of the raw materials used as production inputs. That desire is particularly great when the number of suppliers is small and the number of competitors is large. In this situation, the vertically integrating firm can better control its costs and, thereby, improve the profit margin of the expanded production-marketing system. Forward integration is a preferred grand strategy if great advantages accrue to stable production. A firm can increase the predictability of demand for its output through forward integration; that is, through ownership of the next stage of its production-marketing chain.

Some increased risks are associated with both types of integration. For horizontally integrated firms, the risks stem from increased commitment to one type of business. For vertically integrated firms, the risks result from the firm's expansion into areas requiring strategic managers to broaden the base of their competences and to assume additional responsibilities.

Concentric Diversification

Grand strategies involving diversification represent distinctive departures from a firm's existing base of operations, typically the acquisition or internal generation (spin-off) of a separate business with synergistic possibilities counterbalancing the strengths and weaknesses of the two businesses. For example, Head Ski initially sought to diversify into summer sporting goods and clothing to offset the seasonality of its "snow" business. However, diversifications occasionally are undertaken as unrelated investments, because of their high profit potential and their otherwise minimal resource demands.

Regardless of the approach taken, the motivations of the acquiring firms are the same:

Increase the firm's stock value. In the past, mergers often have led to increases in the stock price or the price-earnings ratio.

Increase the growth rate of the firm.

Make an investment that represents better use of funds than plowing them into internal growth.

Improve the stability of earnings and sales by acquiring firms whose earnings and sales complement the firm's peaks and valleys.

Balance or fill out the product line.

Diversify the product line when the life cycle of current products has peaked.

Acquire a needed resource quickly (e.g., high-quality technology or highly innovative management).

Achieve tax savings by purchasing a firm whose tax losses will offset current or future earnings.

Increase efficiency and profitability, especially if there is synergy between the acquiring firm and the acquired firm.[3]

Concentric diversification involves the acquisition of businesses that are related to the acquiring firm in terms of technology, markets, or products. With this grand strategy, the selected new businesses possess a high degree of compatibility with the firm's current businesses. The ideal concentric diversification occurs when the combined company profits increase the strengths and opportunities and decrease the weaknesses and exposure to risk. Thus, the acquiring firm searches for new businesses whose products, markets, distribution channels, technologies, and resource requirements are similar to but not identical with its own, whose acquisition results in synergies but not complete interdependence.

Conglomerate Diversification

Occasionally a firm, particularly a very large one, plans to acquire a business because it represents the most promising investment opportunity available. This grand strategy is commonly known as conglomerate diversification. The principal concern, and often the sole concern, of the acquiring firm is the profit pattern of the venture. Unlike concentric diversification, *conglomerate diversification* gives little concern to creating product-market synergy with existing businesses. What such conglomerate diversifiers as ITT, Textron, American Brands, Litton, U.S. Industries, Fuqua, and I.C. Industries seek is financial synergy. For example, they may seek a balance in their portfolios between current businesses with cyclical sales and acquired businesses with countercyclical sales, between high-cash/low-opportunity and low-cash/high-opportunity businesses, or between debt-free and highly leveraged businesses.

The principal difference between the two types of diversification is that concentric diversification emphasizes some commonality in markets, products, or technology, whereas conglomerate diversification is based principally on profit considerations.

---

[3] Godfrey Devlin and Mark Bleackley, "Strategic Alliances—Guidelines for Success," *Long Range Planning*, October 1988, pp. 18–23.

Several of the grand strategies discussed above, including concentric and conglomerate diversification and horizontal and vertical integration, often involve the purchase or acquisition of one firm by another. It is important to know that the majority of such acquisitions fail to produce the desired results for the companies involved. Strategy in Action 7–4 provides seven guidelines that can improve a company's chances of a successful acquisition.

Turnaround

For any one of a large number of reasons, a firm can find itself with declining profits. Among these reasons are economic recessions, production inefficiencies, and innovative break-throughs by competitors. In many cases, strategic managers believe that such a firm can survive and eventually recover if a concerted effort is made over a period of a few years to fortify its distinctive competences. This grand strategy is known as *turnaround*. It typically is begun through one of two forms of retrenchment, employed singly or in combination:

1. *Cost reduction.* Examples include decreasing the work force through employee attrition, leasing rather than purchasing equipment, extending the life of machinery, eliminating elaborate promotional activities, laying off employees, dropping items from a production line, and discontinuing low-margin customers.

2. *Asset reduction.* Examples include the sale of land, buildings, and equipment not essential to the basic activity of the firm and the elimination of "perks," such as the company airplane and executives' cars.

Interestingly, the turnaround most commonly associated with this approach is in management positions. In a study of 58 large firms, researchers Shendel, Patton, and Riggs found that turnaround almost always was associated with changes in top management.[4] Bringing in new managers was believed to introduce needed new perspectives on the firm's situation, to raise employee morale, and to facilitate drastic actions, such as deep budgetary cuts in established programs.

Strategic management research provides evidence the firms that have used a *turnaround strategy* have successfully confronted decline. The research findings have been assimilated and used as the building blocks for a model of the turnaround process shown in Figure 7–6 on page 234.[5]

The model begins with a depiction of external and internal factors as causes of a firm's performance downturn. When these factors continue to detrimentally impact the firm, its financial health is threatened. Unchecked decline places the firm in a turnaround situation.

A *turnaround situation* represents absolute and relative-to-industry declining performance of a sufficient magnitude to warrant explicit turnaround actions. Turnaround situations may be the result of years of gradual slowdown or months of sharp decline. In either case, the recovery phase of the turnaround process is likely to be more successful in accomplishing turnaround when it is preceded by planned retrenchment that results in the achievement of near-term financial stabilization. For a declining firm, stabilizing operations and restoring profitability almost always entail strict cost reduction followed by a shrinking back to those segments of the business that have the best prospects of attractive profit margins. The need for retrenchment was shown during the 1990–92 recession when

---

[4] Other forms of joint ventures (such as leasing, contract manufacturing, and management contracting) offer valuable support strategies. They are not included in the categorization, however, because they seldom are employed as grand strategies.

[5] J. A. Pearce II and D. K. Robbins, "Toward Improved Theory and Research on Business Turnaround," *Journal of Management*, 1993; D. K. Robbins and J. A. Pearce II, "Turnaround: Recovery and Retrench-ment," *Strategic Management Journal* 13, no. 4 (1992), pp. 287–309.

SEVEN DEADLY SINS OF STRATEGY ACQUISITION

1. *The wrong target.* This error becomes increasingly visible as time passes after the acquisition, when the acquiror may realize that anticipated synergies just don't exist, that the expanded market just isn't there, or that the acquiror's and target's technologies simply were not complementary.

The first step to avoid such a mistake is for the acquiror and its financial advisors to determine the strategic goals and identify the mission. The product of this strategic review will be specifically identified criteria for the target.

The second step required to identify the right target is to design and carry out an effective due diligence process to ascertain whether the target indeed has the identified set of qualities selected in the strategic review.

2. *The wrong price.* Even in a strategic acquisition, paying too much will lead to failure. For a patient strategic acquiror with long-term objectives, overpaying may be less of a problem than for a financial acquiror looking for a quick profit. Nevertheless, overpaying may divert needed acquiror resources and adversely affect the firm's borrowing capacity. In the extreme case, it can lead to continued operating losses and business failure.

The key to avoiding this problem lies in the acquiror's valuation model. The model will incorporate assumptions concerning industry trends and growth patterns developed in the strategic review.

3. *The wrong structure.* Both financial and strategic acquisitions benefit by the structure chosen. This may include the legal structure chosen for the entities, the geographic jurisdiction chosen for newly created entities, and the capitalization structure selected for the business after the acquisition. The wrong structure may lead to an inability to repatriate earnings (or an ability to do so only at a prohibitive tax cost), regulatory problems that delay or prevent realization of the anticipated benefits, and inefficient pricing of debt and equity securities or a bar to chosen exit strategies due to inflexibility in the chosen legal structure.

The two principal aspects of the acquisition process that can prevent this problem are a comprehensive regulatory compliance review and tax and legal analysis.

Source: Excerpted from D. A. Tanner, "Seven Deadly Sins of Strategic Acquisition," *Management Review,* June 1991, pp. 50–53. Reprinted by permission of publisher, from MANAGEMENT REVIEW, June 1991, © 1991. American Management Association, New York, All rights reserved.

half of all U.S. companies reduced their work forces by an average of 11 percent (especially hard hit were real estate, transportation, and electronic company middle managers).

The immediacy of the resulting threat to company survival posed by the turnaround situation is known as *situation severity.* Severity is the governing factor in estimating the speed with which the retrenchment response will be formulated and activated. When severity is low, a firm has some financial cushion. Stability may be achieved through cost retrenchment alone. When turnaround situation severity is high, a firm must immediately stabilize the decline or bankruptcy is imminent. Cost reductions must be supplemented

4. *The lost deal*. Lost deals often can be traced to poor communication. A successful strategic acquisition requires agreement upon the strategic vision, both with the acquiring company and between the acquiror and the continuing elements of the target. This should be established in the preliminary negotiations that lead to the letter of intent.

The letter must spell out not only the price to be paid but also many of the relational aspects that will make the strategic acquisition successful. Although an acquiror may justifiably focus on expenses, indemnification, and other logical concerns in the letter of intent, relationship and operational concerns are also important.

5. *Management difficulties*. Lack of attention to management issues may lead to a lost deal. These problems can range from a failure to provide management continuity or clear lines of authority after a merger to incentives that cause management to steer the company in the wrong direction.

The remedy for this problem must be extracted from the initial strategic review. The management compensation structure must be designed with legal and business advisors to help achieve those goals. The financial rewards to management must depend upon the financial and strategic success of the combined entity.

6. *The closing crisis*. Closing crises may stem from unavoidable changed conditions, but most often they result from poor communication. Negotiators sometimes believe that problems swept under the table maintain a deal's momentum and ultimately allow for its consummation. They are sometimes right—and often wrong. Charting a course through an acquisition requires carefully developed skills for every kind of professional—business, accounting, and legal.

7. *The operating transition crisis*. Even the best conceived and executed acquisition will prevent significant transition and postclosing operation issues. Strategic goals cannot be achieved by quick asset sales or other accelerated exit strategies. Management time and energy must be spent to assure that the benefits identified in the strategic review are achieved.

The principal constraints on smooth implementation are usually human: poor interaction of personnel between the two preexisting management structures and resistance to new systems. Problems also may arise from too much attention to the by now well-communicated strategic vision and too little attention to the nuts and bolts of continuing business operations.

with more drastic asset reduction measures. Assets targeted for divestiture are those determined to be underproductive. In contrast, more productive resources are protected from cuts and represent critical elements of the future core business plan of the company (i.e., the intended recovery response).

Turnaround responses among successful firms typically include two stages of strategic activities: retrenchment and the recovery response. *Retrenchment* consists of cost-cutting and asset-reducing activities. The primary objective of the retrenchment phase is to stabilize the firm's financial condition. Situation severity has been associated with retrenchment responses among successful turnaround firms. Firms in danger of bankruptcy or failure (i.e., severe situations) attempt to halt decline through cost and asset reductions. Firms in

FIGURE 7–6
A Model of the Turnaround Process

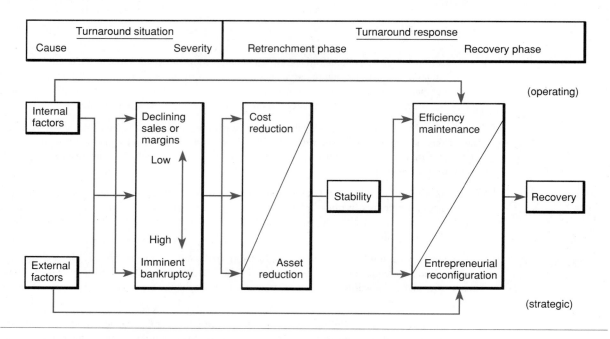

Source: J. A. Pearce II and D. K. Robbins, "Toward Improved Theory and Research on Business Turnaround," *Journal of Management*, 1993.

less severe situations have achieved stability merely through cost retrenchment. However, in either case, for firms facing declining financial performance, the key to successful turnaround rests in the effective and efficient management of the retrenchment process.

The primary causes of the turnaround situation have been associated with the second phase of the turnaround process, the *recovery response*. For firms that declined primarily as a result of external problems, turnaround most often has been achieved through creative new entrepreneurial strategies. For firms that declined primarily as a result of internal problems, turnaround has been most frequently achieved through efficiency strategies. *Recovery* is achieved when economic measures indicate that the firm has regained its pre-downturn levels of performance.

Divestiture

A *divestiture strategy* involves the sale of a firm or a major component of a firm. For example, in March 1992, Goodyear Tire and Rubber announced its decision to sell its polyester business to Shell Chemical to cut its $2.6 billion debt. The sale was part of Goodyear's strategy to bring its debt below $2 billion within 18 months.

When retrenchment fails to accomplish the desired turnaround, as was the Goodyear situation, or when a nonintegrated business activity achieves an unusually high market value, strategic managers often decide to sell the firm. However, because the intent is to find a buyer willing to pay a premium above the value of a going concern's fixed assets, the term *marketing for sale* is often more appropriate. Prospective buyers must be convinced that, because of their skills and resources or because of the firm's synergy with their existing businesses, they will be able to profit from the acquisition.

The reasons for divestiture vary. They often arise because of partial mismatches between the acquired firm and the parent corporation. Some of the mismatched parts cannot be integrated into the corporation's mainstream activities and, thus, must be spun off. A second reason is corporate financial needs. Sometimes the cash flow or financial stability of the corporation as a whole can be greatly improved if businesses with high market value can be sacrificed. The result can be a balancing of equity with long-term risks or of long-term debt payments to optimize the cost of capital. A third, less frequent reason for divestiture is government antitrust action when a firm is believed to monopolize or unfairly dominate a particular market.

Although examples of the divestiture grand strategy are numerous, CBS, Inc., recently provided an outstanding example. In a two-year period, the once diverse entertainment and publishing giant sold its Records Division to Sony, its magazine publishing business to Diamandis Communications, its book publishing operations to Harcourt Brace Jovanovich, and its music publishing operations to SBK Entertainment World. Other firms that recently have pursued this type of grand strategy include Esmark, which divested Swift & Company, and White Motors, which divested White Farm.

The unfortunate but frequent consequence of a firm's failure to achieve turnaround—through a combination of retrenchment, divestiture, and new strategies—is financial bankruptcy. Firms filing for Chapter 11 bankruptcy protection are allowed by federal law to undertake a comprehensive reorganization while being protected from creditor actions. Believed to be in trouble because of serious mismanagement, such firms are allowed to reorganize with "proper management" in the hope they may be able to repay their debts over time and to become profitable operations. One of the hundreds of thousands of troubled businesses that have sought protection under Chapter 11 is Wang, as described in Strategy in Action 7–5.

Liquidation

When liquidation is the grand strategy, the firm typically is sold in parts, only occasionally as a whole—but for its tangible asset value and not as a going concern. In selecting liquidation, the owners and strategic managers of a firm are admitting failure and recognize that this action is likely to result in great hardships to themselves and their employees. For these reasons, liquidation usually is seen as the least attractive of the grand strategies. As a long-term strategy, however, it minimizes the losses of all the firm's stockholders. Faced with bankruptcy, the liquidating firm usually tries to develop a planned and orderly system that will result in the greatest possible return and cash conversion as the firm slowly relinquishes its market share.

Planned liquidation can be worthwhile. For example, Columbia Corporation, a $130 million diversified firm, liquidated its assets for more cash per share than the market value of its stock.

CORPORATE COMBINATIONS

The 11 grand strategies discussed above, used singly and much more often in combinations, represent the traditional alternatives used by firms in the United States. Recently, three new grand types have gained in popularity; all fit under the broad category of corporate combinations. Although they do not fit the criterion by which executives retain a high degree of control over their operations, these grand strategies deserve special attention and consideration especially by companies that operate in global, dynamic, and technologically

BLINDSIDED BY THE FUTURE

On the streets of Boston, they're calling it Black Tuesday. The same day that basketball legend Larry Bird said he would end his career with the Boston Celtics, computer giant Wang Laboratories announced it would file for Chapter 11 bankruptcy protection and lay off 5,000 of its 13,000 workers. In many ways, it seemed fitting that Wang, based in Lowell, Massachusetts, and once a heroic player in the computer industry, bowed out during the same 24-hour period as did Boston's beloved hoopster. Like Bird, the 41-year-old industry icon was an old-timer crippled by past injuries that had failed to heal; a pain-racked veteran, it could no longer compete in a world filled with fastmoving rookies. Calling the bankruptcy "a drastic step that I deeply regret," chairman Richard W. Miller said the company, which will continue to operate, had simply "run out of resources."

The announcement was the end of a long, slow slide for the computer maker. Founded by Dr. An Wang, a Harvard-educated Chinese immigrant, Wang Laboratories revolutionized offices around the world with its minicomputers. But as the industry began to shift to personal computers in the mid-1980s, Wang was left behind. Its meteoric growth rates slowed, and earnings fell dramatically. Before the elder Wang's death from esophageal cancer in 1990, he already was preparing bankruptcy papers—but just in case the company rose from the ashes, he named Miller, an experienced turn-around artist, to succeed him.

Since then, Miller has been fighting to stave off the inevitable: The company has talked with more than 40 investors and has bargained with lenders for 56 amendments to its borrowing plan over the last three years. But analysts say Miller wasn't listening to customers—and last week Wang reported an operating loss of $45.4 million for the last fiscal year. "[The company] fell prey to the enormous success of the PC," says Thomas Willmont, a Boston-based computer consultant. "They simply did not react fast enough to compete in the workplace."

Wang could undergo transformation. In any case, the company will emerge from Chapter 11 much changed—if it emerges at all. Miller says, "We're in business today just as we were yesterday." Some analysts are doubtful. Like a wornout basketball player, they say, Wang may finally have benched itself for good.

driven industries. These three newly popularized grand strategies are joint ventures, strategic alliances, and consortia.

Joint Ventures

Occasionally two or more capable firms lack a necessary component for success in a particular competitive environment. For example, no single petroleum firm controlled sufficient resources to construct the Alaskan pipeline. Nor was any single firm capable of processing and marketing all of the oil that would flow through the pipeline. The solution was a set of *joint ventures*, which are third commercial companies (children) created and operated for the benefit of the co-owners (parents). These cooperative arrangements provided both the funds needed to build the pipeline and the processing and marketing capacities needed to profitably handle the oil flow.

The particular form of joint ventures discussed above is *joint ownership*. In recent years, it has become increasingly appealing for domestic firms to join foreign firms by means of this form. For example, Diamond-Star Motors is the result of a joint venture between a U.S. company, Chrysler Corporation, and Japan's Mitsubishi Motors corporation. Located in Normal, Illinois, Diamond-Star was launched because it offered Chrysler and Mitsubishi a chance to expand on their long-standing relationship in which subcompact cars (as well as Mitsubishi engines and other automotive parts) are imported to the United States and sold under the Dodge and Plymouth names.

The joint venture extends the supplier-consumer relationship and has strategic advantages for both partners. For Chrysler, it presents an opportunity to produce a high-quality car using expertise brought to the venture by Mitsubishi. It also gives Chrysler the chance to try new production techniques and to realize efficiencies by using the work force that was not included under Chrysler's collective bargaining agreement with the United Auto Workers. The agreement offers Mitsubishi the opportunity to produce cars for sale in the United States, without being subjected to the tariffs and restrictions placed on Japanese imports.

As a second example, Bethlehem Steel acquired an interest in a Brazilian mining venture to secure a raw material source. The stimulus for this joint ownership venture was grand strategy, but such is not always the case. Certain countries virtually mandate that foreign firms entering their markets do so on a joint ownership basis. India and Mexico are good examples. The rationale of these countries is that joint ventures minimize the threat of foreign domination and enhance the skills, employment, growth, and profits of local firms.

It should be noted that strategic managers understandably are wary of joint ventures. Admittedly, joint ventures present new opportunities with risks that can be shared. On the other hand, joint ventures often limit the discretion, control, and profit potential of partners, while demanding managerial attention and other resources that might be directed toward the firm's mainstream activities. Nevertheless, increasing globalization in many industries may require greater consideration of the joint venture approach, if historically national firms are to remain viable. Advantages and disadvantages of an international joint venture are highlighted in Global Strategy in Action 7–4.

Strategic Alliances

Strategic alliances are distinguished from joint ventures because the companies involved do not take an equity position in one another. In many instances, strategic alliances are synonymous with licensing agreements. Licensing involves the transfer of some industrial property right from the U.S. licensor to a motivated licensee in a foreign country. Most tend to be patents, trademarks, or technical know-how that are granted to the licensee for a specified time in return for a royalty and for avoiding tariffs or import quotas. Bell South and U.S. West, with various marketing and service competitive advantages valuable to Europe, have extended a number of licenses to create personal computer networks in the United Kingdom (U.K.).

Another licensing strategy open to U.S. firms is to contract the manufacturing of its product line to a foreign company to exploit local comparative advantages in technology, materials, or labor. For example, MIPS Computer Systems has licensed Digital Equipment Corporation, Texas Instruments, Cypress Semiconductor, and Bipolar Integrated Technology in the United States, and Fujitsu, NEC, and Kubota in Japan to market computers based on its designs in the partner's country.

Service and franchise-based firms—including Anheuser-Busch, Avis, Coca-Cola, Hilton, Hyatt, Holiday Inns, Kentucky Fried Chicken, McDonald's, and Pepsi—have long engaged in licensing arrangements with foreign distributors as a way to enter new markets with standardized products that can benefit from marketing economies.

JOINT VENTURE BOOSTS SIBERIAN OIL FLOW

The name White Nights Joint Enterprise plays off the Siberian summer and off the reason U.S. oil companies are here. And while the mission of the first working Russian–U.S. oil venture is simple, the details aren't.

"This is the first arrangement of its kind in all of the oil industry," says Gerald Walston, the Denver oil man who is White Nights' director.

The arrangement he refers to is incremental sharing, which entitles White Nights to all the oil recovered from three fields, above what the Russians had expected to get out, for 25 years.

Varyegan Oil and Gas, the state-owned company that controls the oil, is the Russian partner in White Nights. In exchange for turning its oil fields over to the joint venture, Varyegan gets all the oil up to its production estimates, plus half the oil that comes in addition to that. It also gets 10 percent in royalties.

The U.S. partners, Anglo-Suisse and Philbro Energy Production, split what's left, which is 40 percent of the extra production. They can make their money by shipping their oil out of the country to sell for hard currency.

The venture is pumping ahead of the Russians' estimated production. "Production in all of Russia was down 9.5 percent in 1991. Our fields were up about 40 percent," says Walston.

Anatoly Sivak, director general of Varyegan Oil and Gas, says, "This joint venture will serve as an example. It is the wave of the future."

The reason Sivak turned to the West for help was simple: "The question was how to stop the production decline. For that, we needed money and equipment and technology not available here." Completed wells were sitting idle for lack of parts.

Although the venture has succeeded in boosting production, "We've had some problems," Sivak says.

Anglo-Suisse was designated operator of the venture, and Russian oil people, who have been drilling here since the 1960s, couldn't understand why a U.S. company is running the show.

On top of that resentment were more obvious obstacles: different languages, clashing cultures, huge gaps in economic circumstances among the workers, different drilling techniques, and radically different organizational mindsets.

The Russians, with their five-year plans and strict instructions, "tended to organize and plan down to the last jot and tiddle," says Walston, a graying, unflappable gentleman who appears to keep the joint venture on an even keel via strings of Post-It notes splayed over the top of his desk. "The watchword for us is flexibility," he says.

Source: Excerpted from J. T. Buckley, "Joint Venture Boosts Siberian Oil Flows," *USA Today*, March 12, 1992, section 5B. Copyright 1992, USA TODAY. Reprinted with permission.

Outsourcing is another approach to strategic alliances that enables firms to gain a competitive advantage. Corporate use of outsourcing has increased dramatically in recent years as corporations realize its tremendous benefits. Significant changes within many segments of American business have encouraged the use of outsourcing practices. Within the healthcare arena, an industry survey recorded 67 percent of hospitals using provider outsourcing for at least one department within their organization. Services such as information systems, reimbursement, and risk and physician practice management are outsourced by 51 percent of the hospitals that use outsourcing.

Another successful application of outsourcing is found in human resources. A survey of human resource executives revealed 85 percent having personal experience with leading an

FIGURE 7–7
The Top Five Strategic Reasons for Outsourcing

1. **Improve Business Focus.**
   For many companies, the single most compelling reason for outsourcing is that several "how" issues are siphoning off huge amounts of management's resources and attention.

2. **Access to World-Class Capabilities.**
   By the very nature of their specialization, outsourcing providers bring extensive worldwide, world-class resources to meeting the needs of their customers. According to Norris Overton, vice president of reengineering, AMTRAK, partnering with an organization with world-class capabilities, can offer access to new technology, tools, and techniques that the organization may not currently possess; better career opportunities for personnel who transition to the outsourcing provider; more structured methodologies, procedures, and documentation; and competitive advantage through expanded skills.

3. **Accelerated Reengineering Benefits.**
   Outsourcing is often a byproduct of another powerful management tool—business process reengineering. It allows an organization to immediately realize the anticipated benefits of reengineering by having an outside organization—one that is already reengineered to world-class standards—take over the process.

4. **Shared Risks.**
   There are tremendous risks associated with the investments an organization makes. When companies outsource they become more flexible, more dynamic, and better able to adapt to changing opportunities.

5. **Free Resources for Other Purposes.**
   Every organization has limits on the resources available to it. Outsourcing permits an organization to redirect its resources from noncore activities toward activities that have the greater return in serving the customer.

Source: Material prepared for a paid advertising section which appeared in the October 16, 1995, issue of *Fortune* © 1995, Time, Inc. All rights reserved.

outsourcing effort within their organization. In addition, it was found that two-thirds of pension departments have outsourced at least one human resource function.

Within customer service and sales departments, outsourcing increased productivity in such areas as product information, sales and order taking, sample fulfillment, and complaint handling. Figure 7–7 presents the top five strategic and five tactical reasons for exploiting the benefits of outsourcing.

Consortia, Keiretsus, and Chaebols

Consortia are defined as large interlocking relationships between businesses of an industry. In Japan such consortia are known as *keiretsus*, in South Korea as *chaebols*.

In Europe, consortia projects are increasing in number and in success rates. Examples include the Junior Engineers' and Scientists' Summer Institute, which underwrites cooperative learning and research; the European Strategic Program for Research and Development in Information Technologies, which seeks to enhance European competitiveness in fields related to computer electronics and component manufacturing; and EUREKA, which is a joint program involving scientists and engineers from several European countries to coordinate joint research projects.

A Japanese *keiretsu* is an undertaking involving up to 50 different firms that are joined around a large trading company or bank and are coordinated through interlocking directories and stock exchanges. It is designed to use industry coordination to minimize risks of competition, in part through cost sharing and increased economies of scale. Examples include Sumitomo, Mitsubishi, Mitsui, and Sanwa.

FIGURE 7–8
A Profile of Strategic Choice Options

	Six Strategic Choice Options					
	1	2	3	4	5	6
Interactive opportunities	West Coast markets present little competition		Current markets sensitive to price competition		Current industry product lines offer too narrow a range of markets	
Appropriate long-range objectives (limited sample): Average 5-year ROI. Company sales by year 5. Risk of negative profits.	15% +50% .30	19% +40% .25	13% +20% .10	17% +0% .15	23% +35% .20	15% +25% .05
Grand strategies	Horizontal integration	Market development	Concentration	Selective retrenchment	Product development	Concentration

A South Korean chaebol resembles a consortium or keiretsu except that they are typically financed through government banking groups and largely are run by professional managers trained by participating firms expressly for the job.

SELECTION OF LONG-TERM OBJECTIVES AND GRAND STRATEGY SETS

At first glance, the Strategic Management Model, which provides the framework for study throughout this book, seems to suggest that strategic choice decision making leads to the sequential selection of long-term objectives and grand strategies. In fact, however, strategic choice is the simultaneous selection of long-range objectives and grand strategies. When strategic planners study their opportunities, they try to determine which are most likely to result in achieving various long-range objectives. Almost simultaneously, they try to forecast whether an available grand strategy can take advantage of preferred opportunities so the tentative objectives can be met. In essence, then, three distinct but highly interdependent choices are being made at one time. Several triads, or sets, of possible decisions are usually considered.

A simplified example of this process is shown in Figure 7–8. In this example, the firm has determined that six strategic choice options are available. These options stem from three interactive opportunities (e.g., West Coast markets) that present little competition. Because each of these interactive opportunities can be approached through different grand strategies—for options 1 and 2, the grand strategies are horizontal integration and market development—each offers the potential for achieving long-range objectives to varying degrees. Thus, a firm rarely can make a strategic choice only on the basis of its preferred opportunities, long-range objectives, or grand strategy. Instead, these three elements must be considered simultaneously, because only in combination do they constitute a strategic choice.

In an actual decision situation, the strategic choice would be complicated by a wider variety of interactive opportunities, feasible company objectives, promising grand strategy options, and evaluative criteria. Nevertheless, Figure 7–8 does partially reflect the nature and complexity of the process by which long-term objectives and grand strategies are selected.

In the next chapter, the strategic choice process will be fully explained. However, knowledge of long-term objectives and grand strategies is essential to understanding that process.

SEQUENCE OF OBJECTIVES AND STRATEGY SELECTION

The selection of long-range objectives and grand strategies involves simultaneous, rather than sequential, decisions. While it is true that objectives are needed to prevent the firm's direction and progress from being determined by random forces, it is equally true that objectives can be achieved only if strategies are implemented. In fact, long-term objectives and grand strategies are so interdependent that some business consultants do not distinguish between them. Long-term objectives and grand strategies are still combined under the heading of company strategy in most of the popular business literature and in the thinking of most practicing executives.

However, the distinction has merit. Objectives indicate what strategic managers want but provide few insights about how they will be achieved. Conversely, strategies indicate what types of actions will be taken but do not define what ends will be pursued or what criteria will serve as constraints in refining the strategic plan.

Does it matter whether strategic decisions are made to achieve objectives or to satisfy constraints? No, because constraints are themselves objectives. The constraint of increased inventory capacity is a desire (an objective), not a certainty. Likewise, the constraint of an increase in the sales force does not assure that the increase will be achieved, given such factors as other company priorities, labor market conditions, and the firm's profit performance.

SUMMARY

Before learning how strategic decisions are made, it is important to understand the two principal components of any strategic choice; namely, long-term objectives and the grand strategy. The purpose of this chapter was to convey that understanding.

Long-term objectives were defined as the results a firm seeks to achieve over a specified period, typically five years. Seven common long-term objectives were discussed: profitability, productivity, competitive position, employee development, employee relations, technological leadership, and public responsibility. These, or any other long-term objectives, should be acceptable, flexible, measurable over time, motivating, suitable, understandable, and achievable.

Grand strategies were defined as comprehensive approaches guiding the major actions designed to achieve long-term objectives. Fourteen grand strategy options were discussed: concentrated growth, market development, product development, innovation, horizontal integration, vertical integration, concentric diversification, conglomerate diversification, turnaround, divestiture, liquidation, joint ventures, strategic alliances, and consortia.

QUESTIONS FOR DISCUSSION

1. Identify firms in the business community nearest to your college or university that you believe are using each of the 14 grand strategies discussed in this chapter.
2. Identify firms in your business community that appear to rely principally on 1 of the 14 grand strategies. What kind of information did you use to classify the firms?
3. Write a long-term objective for your school of business that exhibits the seven qualities of long-term objectives described in this chapter.
4. Distinguish between the following pairs of grand strategies:
   a. Horizontal and vertical integration.
   b. Conglomerate and concentric diversification.

    c. Product development and innovation.

    d. Joint venture and strategic alliance.

5. Rank each of the 14 grand strategy options discussed in this chapter on the following three scales:

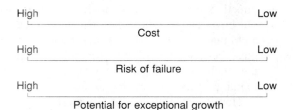

6. Identify firms that use one of the eight specific options shown in Figure 7–1 under the grand strategies of concentration, market development, and product development.

BIBLIOGRAPHY

Anderson, E. "Two Firms, One Frontier: On Assessing Joint Venture Performance." *Sloan Management Review*, Winter 1990, pp. 19–30.

Badaracco, J. L. "Alliances Speed Knowledge Transfer." *Planning Review*, March–April 1991, pp. 10–17.

Beamish, Paul W., and Andrew C. Inkpen. "Keeping International Joint Ventures Stable and Profitable." *Long Range Planning* 28, no. 3 (June 1995), p. 26.

Bleeke, J., and D. Ernst. "The Way to Win in Cross-Border Alliances." *Harvard Business Review*, November–December 1991, pp. 127–35.

Brannen, M. Y. "Culture as the Critical Factor in Implementing Innovation." *Business Horizons*, November–December 1991, pp. 59–67.

Bronthers, Keith D.; Lane Eliot Bronthers; and Timothy J. Wilkinson. "Strategic Alliances: Choose Your Partners." *Long Range Planning* 28, no. 3 (June 1995), p. 68.

Clarke, C. J., and K. Brennan. "Defensive Strategies against Takeovers: Creating Shareholder Value." *Long Range Planning*, February 1990, pp. 95–101.

Erickson, T. J.; J. F. Magee; P. A. Roussel; and K. N. Saad. "Managing Technology as a Business Strategy." *Sloan Management Review*, Spring 1990, pp. 73–78.

Ettlie, J. E. "What Makes a Manufacturing Firm Innovative?" *Academy of Management Executive*, November 1990, pp. 7–20.

Evan, W. M., and P. Olk. "R&D Consortia: A New U.S. Organizational Form." *Sloan Management Review*, Spring 1990, pp. 37–46.

Gopinath, C. "Turnaround: Recognizing Decline and Initiating Intervention." *Long Range Planning*, December 1991, pp. 96–101.

Grossi, G. "Promoting Innovation in a Big Business." *Long Range Planning*, February 1990, pp. 41–52.

Haspeslagh, P. C., and D. B. Jemison. "The Challenge of Renewal through Acquisitions." *Planning Review*, March–April 1991, pp. 27–33.

Houlden, Brian T. "How Corporate Planning Adopts and Survives." *Long Range Planning* 28, no. 4 (August 1995), p. 99.

Hughes, G. D. "Managing High-Tech Product Cycles." *Academy of Management Executive*, May 1990, pp. 44–55.

Kanter, R. M. "When Giants Learn Cooperative Strategies." *Planning Review*, January–February 1990, pp. 15–25.

Keller, R., and R. Chinta. "International Technology Transfer: Strategies for Success." *Academy of Management Executive*, May 1990, pp. 33–43.

Kukolis, Sal, and Mark Jungemann. "Strategic Planning for a Joint Venture." *Long Range Planning* 28, no. 3 (June 1995), p. 46.

Lengnick-Hall, C. A. "Innovation and Competitive Advantage: What We Know and What We Need to Learn." *Journal of Management*, June 1992, p. 399.

Leontiades, M. "The Case for Nonspecialized Diversification." *Planning Review*, January–February 1990, pp. 26–33.

Lewis, J. "Using Alliances to Build Market Power." *Planning Review*, September–October 1990, pp. 4–9.

Littler, Dole, and Fiona Leverick. "Joint Ventures for Product Development: Learning from Experience." *Long Range Planning* 28, no. 3 (June 1995), p. 58.

Lowry, James R. "A Partnering Approach to Mass Merchandising in Russia." *Business Horizons* 38, no. 4 (July–August 1995), p. 28.

McLeod, Raymond, Jr.; Jack William Jones; and Carol Saunders. "The Difficulty in Solving Strategic Problems: The Experiences of Three CIO's." *Business Horizons* 38, no. 1 (January–February 1995), p. 28.

Miller, D. "The Generic Strategy Trap." *The Journal of Business Strategy*, January–February 1992, pp. 37–41.

Newman, W. H. "Focused Joint Ventures in Transforming Economies." *Academy of Management Executive*, February 1992, pp. 67–75.

Paap, J. E. "A Venture Capitalist's Advice for Successful Strategic Alliances." *Planning Review*, September–October 1990, pp. 20–26.

Pearce, J. A., II, and J. W. Harvey. "Concentrated Growth Strategies." *Academy of Management Executive*, February 1990, pp. 61–68.

Pearce, J. A., II, and D. K. Robbins. "Toward Improved Theory and Research on Business Turnaround." *Journal of Management*, 1993.

———. "Entrepreneurial Recovery Strategies among Small Market Share Manufacturers." *Journal of Business Venturing*, 1994.

Peters, T. "Get Innovative or Get Dead." *California Management Review*, Winter 1991, pp. 9–23.

Randall, R. M. "The Coyote and the Bear Form a Strategic Alliance." *Planning Review*, September–October 1990, p. 27.

Reimann, B. C. "Corporate Strategies That Work." *Planning Review*, January–February 1992, pp. 41–46.

Robbins, D. K., and Pearce, J. A., II. "Entrepreneurial Retrenchment among Small Manufacturing Firms." *Journal of Business Venturing*, July 1993, pp. 301–18.

Sankar, Chetan S.; William R. Boulton; Nancy W. Davidson; Charles A. Snyder; and Richard W. Ussery. "Building a World-Class Alliance: The Universal Card—TSYS Case." *The Academy of Management Executive* 9, no. 2 (May 1995), p. 20.

Shanklin, William L. "Offensive Strategies for Defense Companies." *Business Horizons* 38, no. 4 (July–August 1995), p. 53.

Stiles, Jan. "Collaboration for Competitive Advantage: The Changing World of Alliances and Partnerships." *Long Range Planning* 28, no. 5 (October 1995), p. 109.

CHAPTER 7 COHESION CASE ILLUSTRATION

FORMULATING LONG-TERM OBJECTIVES AND GRAND STRATEGIES AT THE COCA-COLA COMPANY

Coca-Cola management sets forth several long-term objectives toward which the company is focused for the year 2000. First, they offer a statement about what they call "rewards." In the booklet entitled *Coca-Cola, a Business System toward 2000: Our Mission in the 1990s*, Coke management sets forth the four key "rewards" it seeks:

· Satisfied consumers who return again and again to our brands for refreshment.
· Profitable customers who rely on our worldwide brands and services.
· Communities around the world where we are an economic contributor and welcomed guest.
· Successful business partners.
· Shareholders who are building value through the power of the Coca-Cola system.

LONG-TERM OBJECTIVES

The company identifies several long-term objectives that support these reward intentions. The first objective most often mentioned is:

Management's primary objective is to maximize shareowner value over time.

The company then indicates that the following objectives help accomplish this over-arching objective:

Maximize long-term cash flow by increasing gallon sales, optimizing profit margins, expanding global business systems through investment in areas offering attractive returns.
   The principal objective of bottling investments is to ensure the strongest and most efficient production, distribution, and marketing systems possible, in order to maximize long-term growth in volume, cash flow, and shareowner value of the bottler and the Company.

The Coca-Cola Company pursues several inherent objectives as follows:

Profitability. Double-digit levels annually equal to or exceeding historical levels.
Productivity. Each Coca-Cola facility has as its objective maintenance or improvement of its operating profit margin.
Competitive Position. Coca-Cola seeks to be the market leader in markets in which it competes.
Technological Leadership. Coca-Cola seeks to be the leader in the production and marketing technologies used in the markets in which it competes.

What are the qualities of Coca-Cola's long-term objectives? It would appear Coca-Cola's objectives meet several criteria that this chapter has suggested characterize effective objectives. Specifically, each of these publicly stated Coke objectives appears to be acceptable, flexible, motivating, suitable, reasonable, and achievable.

These objectives all appear deficient in terms of being measurable. None of these publicly stated objectives identifies a quantifiable result to be achieved or a specific time period within which to accomplish those results. Coke officials indicate a preference for stating objectives publicly in broad terms. They prefer to retain key results and timetables for internal consumption only. While this may be quite appropriate, you should nonetheless be able to recognize that objectives without measurable results or measurable timetables within which to accomplish them lose a lot of their value in focusing and directing strategic activities. A recent interview with Coca Cola USA president Jack Stahl and vice president Charlie Frenette about their Year 2000 goals for the U.S. market shows that Coca Cola's use of measurable objectives is very much a way they work internally. It also suggests a willingness to be more open publicly. Finally, some people question whether the market share objectives are too ambitious. What do you think?

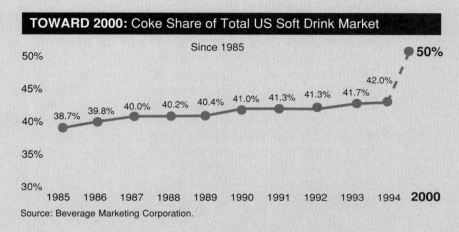

TOWARD 2000: Coke Share of Total US Soft Drink Market

Since 1985

Source: Beverage Marketing Corporation.

Frenette: Right now we estimate that the average person consumes 64 ounces of liquid daily. We have about 11 percent of that intake in the U.S., which translates into per capita consumption of 333 eight-ounce servings of our beverage products annually. We want to position our product portfolio to satisfy this physiological need for refreshment. As we set an aspiration for 400 per capita consumption and a 50 percent share—which is what our international business enjoys today—we're going to source everything, including tap water.

Beverage World **[BW]:** What makes 50 percent the right share target? Why not more?

Stahl: We had 42 percent entering 1995. We have to look at the power of our system today, look at the capabilities that we believe we can put in place over the next several years, and then say, "How much better can we do all of that vis-à-vis our competitors." We believe we can really distance ourselves in terms of our ability to service customers and meet the needs of consumers. We believe we can grow at a dramatically higher rate than the 3 percent industry average.

BW: Your recent history of share growth makes 50 a pretty ambitious number, doesn't it?

Stahl: That's right. It's somewhat ambitious. Although, if you look at where we've been and look at our capturing most of the growth [90 percent of the U.S. cola growth in 1995], that kind of performance over time can get you there.

BW: But 50 by 2000? Having procured 4 corporate share points since 1985, Coke entered 1995 with 42 percent of the whole U.S. soft drink market. That means it must snare 8 percentage points in six years.

Salmon Brothers [analyst Andrew Conway]: It's extremely aggressive. Coke will have to grow two to three times faster than the total industry to pull it off.

COCA-COLA STRATEGIES

Coca-Cola is in the enviable position of being able to pursue numerous strategies. Among generic strategies, Coke is able to pursue low-cost strategies and still enjoy higher profit margins. Its unparalleled trademarks and syrup patent protection offer strong support for differentiation strategies. And the global reality that its success is determined in one local market at a time puts it in the unique posture of needing focus strategies by local geographic markets.

Among grand strategies, Coke has several options available to it. Concentrated growth appears a viable strategy, at least in key major markets like the U.S. market. But given its sizable financial resources, concentrated growth alone may not achieve long-term objectives. Rather, its extraordinary global "system" makes market development a related and potentially advantageous strategy. The many underdeveloped global markets available to Coca-Cola represent attractive targets for Coke's excess resources.

Coke long has been committed to a product development strategy, which creates new but related products that can be marketed to current customers through established channels. Not only does this allow Coke to penetrate existing markets and channels but it preempts new product efforts of weaker competitors.

The diversification strategies, concentric and conglomerate, are available to Coca-Cola given its financial resources and market clout. Since 1975, Coke has included both diversification strategies in the options it has chosen. Coke's move into movie entertainment, water treatment, plastic films, and certain foods were clear diversifications.

Finally, the latter part of the 1980s has seen Coca-Cola seriously consider a forward vertical integration strategy, allowing greater involvement in and control over bottling activity, given the removal of regulatory restrictions on doing so, and combined with the critical role local bottlers play in distributing national brands and the relative strength in this regard of PepsiCo's bottling network.

The global commitments and aspirations of Coca-Cola are another reason forward vertical integration in some form must be considered by the company. Whether this takes the form of joint ventures, strategic alliances, or consortia appears dependent on market and regulatory conditions within each country that Coke targets.

Coke has little need for retrenchment, turnaround, and liquidation strategies. It has a strong position in most of its businesses. Divestiture has been used by Coke when it has chosen to exit a variety of related and unrelated businesses. This strategy was continually considered by Coke's management as it increasingly emphasized the need to focus on soft-drink and clearly related business sectors.

8

STRATEGIC ANALYSIS AND CHOICE IN SINGLE- OR DOMINANT-PRODUCT BUSINESSES: BUILDING SUSTAINABLE COMPETITIVE ADVANTAGES

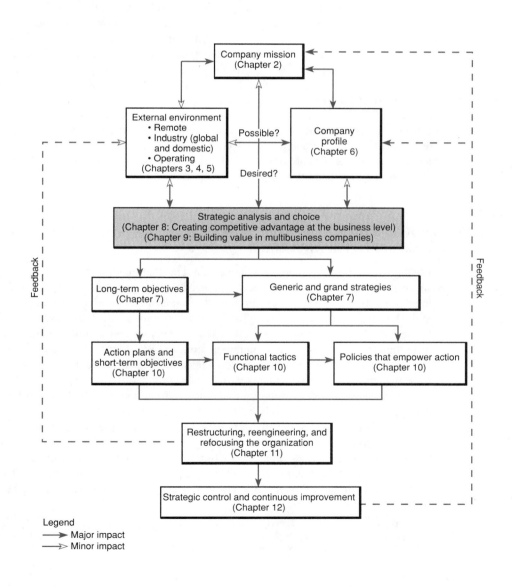

Company mission
(Chapter 2)

External environment
• Remote
• Industry (global and domestic)
• Operating
(Chapters 3, 4, 5)

Possible?

Desired?

Company profile
(Chapter 6)

Strategic analysis and choice
(Chapter 8: Creating competitive advantage at the business level)
(Chapter 9: Building value in multibusiness companies)

Long-term objectives
(Chapter 7)

Generic and grand strategies
(Chapter 7)

Action plans and short-term objectives
(Chapter 10)

Functional tactics
(Chapter 10)

Policies that empower action
(Chapter 10)

Restructuring, reengineering, and refocusing the organization
(Chapter 11)

Strategic control and continuous improvement
(Chapter 12)

Feedback

Feedback

Legend
⟶ Major impact
⟶ Minor impact

Strategic analysis and choice is the phase of the strategic management process when business managers examine and choose a business strategy that allows their business to sustain or create a sustainable competitive advantage. Their starting point is to evaluate and determine which value chain activities provide the basis for distinguishing itself in the customer's mind from other reasonable alternatives. Businesses with a dominant product or service line must also choose among alternate grand strategies to guide the firm's activities, particularly when they are trying to decide about broadening the scope of the firm's activities beyond its core business.

This chapter examines strategic analysis and choice in single- or dominant-product/ service businesses by addressing two basic issues:

1. **What strategies are most effective at building sustainable competitive advantages for single business units?** What competitive strategy positions a business most effectively in its industry? For example, Scania, the most productive truck manufacturer in the world, joins its major rival Volvo as two anchors of Sweden's economy. Scania's return on sales of 9.9 percent far exceeds Mercedes (2.6 percent) and Volvo (2.5 percent), which it has done most of the last 60 years. Scania has built a sustainable competitive advantage with a strategy of focusing solely on heavy trucks, in a limited geographic area—Europe—and by providing customized trucks with standardized components (20,000 components per truck versus 25,000 for Volvo and 40,000 for Mercedes). Scania is a low-cost producer of a differentiated truck that can be custom manufactured quickly and sold to a regionally focused market.

2. **Should dominant-product/service businesses diversify** to build value and competitive advantage? What grand strategies are most appropriate? For example, Compaq Computers and Coca-Cola managers have examined the question of diversification and apparently concluded that continued concentration on their core products and services and development of new markets for those same core products and services are best. IBM and Pepsi examined the same question and concluded that related diversification and vertical integration were best. Why?

EVALUATING AND CHOOSING BUSINESS STRATEGIES: SEEKING SUSTAINED COMPETITIVE ADVANTAGE

Business managers evaluate and choose strategies that they think will make their business successful. Businesses become successful because they possess some advantage relative to their competitors. The two most prominent sources of competitive advantage can be found in the business's cost structure and its ability to differentiate the business from competitors. Disney World in Orlando offers theme park patrons several unique, distinct features that differentiate it from other entertainment options. Wal-Mart offers retail customers the lowest prices on popular consumer items because they have created a low-cost structure resulting in a competitive advantage over most competitors.

Businesses that create competitive advantages from one or both of these sources usually experience above-average profitability within their industry. Businesses that lack a cost or differentiation advantage usually experience average or below-average profitability. Two recent studies found that businesses that do not have either form of competitive advantage perform the poorest among their peers while businesses that possess both forms of competitive advantage enjoy the highest levels of profitability within their industry.[1] The average return on investment for over 2,500 businesses across seven industries looked as follows:

[1] R. B. Robinson and J. A. Pearce, "Planned Patterns of Strategic Behavior and Their Relationship to Business Unit Performance," *Strategic Management Journal* 9, no. 1 (1988), pp. 43–60; G. G. Dess and A. Miller, *Strategic Management* (New York: McGraw Hill, 1993), pp. 110–11.

Differentiation Advantage	Cost Advantage	Overall Average ROI across Seven Industries
High	High	35.0%
Low	High	26.0
High	Low	22.0
Low	Low	9.5

Initially, managers were advised to evaluate and choose strategies that emphasized one type of competitive advantage. Often referred to as *generic strategies*, firms were encouraged to become either a differentiation-oriented or low-cost-oriented company. In so doing, it was logical that organizational members would develop a clear understanding of company priorities and, as these studies suggest, likely experience profitability superior to competitors without either a differentiation or low-cost orientation.

The studies mentioned above, and the experience of many other businesses, indicate that the highest profitability levels are found in businesses that possess both types of competitive advantage at the same time. In other words, businesses that have one or more value chain activities that truly differentiate them from key competitors and also have value chain activities that let them operate at a lower cost will consistently outperform their rivals that don't. So the challenge for today's business managers is to evaluate and choose business strategies based on core competencies and value chain activities that sustain both types of competitive advantage simultaneously.

Evaluating Cost Leadership Opportunities

Business success built on cost leadership requires the business to be able to provide its product or service at a cost below what its competitors can achieve. And it must be a sustainable cost advantage. Through the skills and resources identified in Figure 8–1, a business must be able to accomplish one or more activities in its value chain activities— procuring materials, processing them into products, marketing the products, and distributing the products or support activities—in a more cost-effective manner than that of its competitors or it must be able to reconfigure its value chain so as to achieve a cost advantage. Figure 8–1 provides examples of ways this might be done.

Strategists examining their business's value chain for low-cost leadership advantages evaluate the sustainability of those advantages by *benchmarking* (refer to Chapter 6 for a discussion of this comparison technique) their business against key competitors and by considering the impact of any cost advantage on the five forces in their business's competitive environment. Low-cost activities that are sustainable and that provide one or more of these advantages relative to key industry forces should become the basis for the business's competitive strategy.[2]

Low-Cost Advantages That Reduce the Likelihood of Pricing Pressure from Buyers When key competitors cannot match prices from the low-cost leader, customers pressuring the leader risk establishing a price level that drives alternate sources out of business.

Truly Sustained Low-Cost Advantages May Push Rivals into Other Areas, Lessening Price Competition Intense, continued price competition may be ruinous for all rivals, as seen occasionally in the airline industry.

---

[2] G. G. Dess and A. Miller, *Strategic Management* (New York: McGraw Hill, 1993), pp. 116.

FIGURE 8–1
Evaluating a Business's Cost Leadership Opportunities

A. Skills and Resources That Foster Cost Leadership

Sustained capital investment and access to capital.
Process engineering skills.
Intense supervision of labor or core technical operations.
Products or services designed for ease of manufacturer or delivery.
Low-cost distribution system.

B. Organizational Requirements to Support and Sustain Cost Leadership Activities

Tight cost control.
Frequent, detailed control reports.
Continuous improvement and benchmarking orientation.
Structured organization and responsibilities.
Incentives based on meeting strict, usually quantitative targets.

C. Examples of Ways Businesses Achieve Competitive Advantage via Cost Leadership

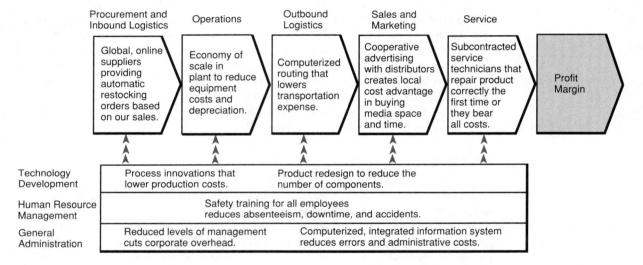

Source: Adapted with permission of The Free Press, a Division of Simon and Schuster, from *Competitive Advantage: Creating and Sustaining Superior Performance*, by Michael E. Porter. Copyright © 1985 by Michael E. Porter.

New Entrants Competing on Price Must Face an Entrenched Cost Leader without the Experience to Replicate Every Cost Advantage   Delite entered the fast food market with great fanfare in the 1980s as the first low-fat fast food chain emphasizing salads and lean hamburgers. Wendy's simply expanded its inexpensive salad bar and, already serving fresh lean meat, quickly saw Delite disappear from NASDAQ. Delite could not begin to match Wendy's cost structure, built on inbound logistics and lower location costs, and still charge a price close to what Wendy's charged for lean, fresh fast food.

Low-Cost Advantages Should Lessen the Attractiveness of Substitute Products   A serious concern of any business is the threat of a substitute product in which buyers can meet their original need. Low-cost advantages allow the holder to resist this happening because it allows them to remain competitive even against desirable substitutes and it allows them to lessen concerns about price facing an inferior, lower priced substitute.

Higher Margins Allow Low-Cost Producers to Withstand Supplier Cost Increases and Often Gain Supplier Loyalty over Time   Sudden, particularly uncontrollable increases in the costs suppliers face can be more easily absorbed by low-cost, higher margin producers. Severe droughts in California quadrupled the price of lettuce—a key restaurant demand. Some chains absorbed the cost; others had to confuse customers with a "lettuce tax." Furthermore, chains that worked well with produce suppliers gained a loyal, cooperative "partner" for possible assistance in a future, competitive situation.

Once managers identify opportunities to create cost advantage–based strategies, they must consider whether key risks inherent in cost leadership are present in a way that may mediate sustained success. The key risks with which they must be concerned are discussed next.

Many Cost-Saving Activities Are Easily Duplicated   Computerizing certain order entry functions among hazardous waste companies gave early adopters lower sales costs and better customer service for a brief time. Rivals quickly adapted, adding similar capabilities with similar impacts on their costs.

Exclusive Cost Leadership Can Become a Trap   Firms that emphasize lowest price and can offer it via cost advantages where product differentiation is increasingly not considered must truly be convinced of the sustainability of those advantages. Particularly with commodity-type products, the low-cost leader seeking to sustain a margin superior to lesser rivals may encounter increasing customer pressure for lower prices with great damage to both leader and lesser players.

Obsessive Cost Cutting Can Shrink Other Competitive Advantages Involving Key Product Attributes   Intense cost scrutiny can build margin, but it can reduce opportunities for or investment in innovation—processes and products. Similarly, such scrutiny can lead to the use of inferior raw materials, processes, or activities that were previously viewed by customers as a key attribute of the original products. Some mail order computer companies that sought to maintain or enhance cost advantages found reductions in telephone service personnel and automation of that function backfiring with a drop in demand for their products even though their low prices were maintained.

Cost Differences Often Decline over Time   As products age, competitors learn how to match cost advantages. Absolute volumes sold often decline. Market channels and suppliers mature. Buyers become more knowledgeable. All of these factors present opportunities to lessen the value or presence of earlier cost advantages. Said another way, cost advantages that are not sustainable over a period of time are risky.

Once business managers have evaluated the cost structure of their value chain, determined activities that provide competitive cost advantages, and considered their inherent risks, they start choosing the business's strategy. Those managers concerned with differentiation-based strategies, or those seeking optimum performance incorporating both sources of competitive advantage, move to evaluating their business's sources of differentiation.

Evaluating Differentiation Opportunities

Differentiation requires that the business have sustainable advantages that allow it to provide buyers with something uniquely valuable to them. A successful differentiation strategy allows the business to provide a product or service of perceived higher value to buyers at a "differentiation cost" below the "value premium" to the buyers. In other words, the buyer feels the additional cost to buy the product or service is well below what the product or service is worth compared to other available alternatives.

Differentiation usually arises from one or more activities in the value chain that create a unique value important to buyers. Perrier's control of a carbonated water spring in France,

FIGURE 8–2
Evaluating a Business's Differentiation Opportunities

A. Skills and Resources That Foster Differentiation

Strong marketing abilities.
Product engineering.
Creative talent and flair.
Strong capabilities in basic research.
Corporate reputation for quality or technical leadership.
Long tradition in an industry or unique combination of skills drawn from other businesses.
Strong cooperation from channels.
Strong cooperation from suppliers of major components of the product or service.

B. Organizational Requirements to Support and Sustain Differentiation Activities

Strong coordination among functions in R&D, product development, and marketing.
Subjective measurement and incentives instead of quantitative measures.
Amenities to attract highly skilled labor, scientists, and creative people.
Tradition of closeness to key customers.
Some personnel skilled in sales and operations—technical and marketing.

C. Examples of Ways Businesses Achieve Competitive Advantage via Differentiation

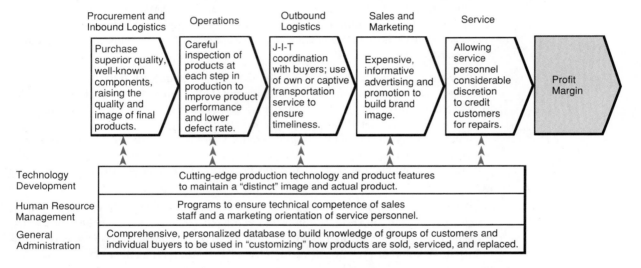

Source: Adapted with permission of The Free Press, a division of Simon and Schuster, from *Competitive Advantage: Creating and Sustaining Superior Performance*, by Michael E. Porter. Copyright © 1985 by Michael E. Porter.

Stouffer's frozen food packaging and sauce technology, Apple's highly integrated chip designs in its Macintosh computers, American Greeting Card's automated inventory system for retailers, and Federal Express's customer service capabilities are all examples of sustainable advantages around which successful differentiation strategies have been built. A business can achieve differentiation by performing its existing value activities or reconfiguring in some unique way. And the sustainability of that differentiation will depend on two things—a continuation of its high perceived value to buyers and a lack of imitation by competitors.

Figure 8–2 suggests key skills that managers should ensure are present to support an emphasis on differentiation. Examples of value chain activities that provide a differentiation advantage are also provided.

Strategists examining their business's value chain for differentiation advantages evaluate the sustainability of those advantages by *benchmarking* (refer to Chapter 6 for a discussion of this comparison technique) their business against key competitors and by considering the impact of any differentiation advantage on the five forces in their business's competitive environment. Sustainable activities that provide one or more of the following opportunities relative to key industry forces should become the basis for differentiation aspects of the business's competitive strategy:

Rivalry Is Reduced When a Business Successfully Differentiates Itself   BMW's new Z23 made up the road in Greer, South Carolina, does not compete with Saturns made in central Tennessee. A Harvard education does not compete with a local technical school. Both situations involve the same basic needs, transportation or education. However, one rival has clearly differentiated itself from others in the minds of certain buyers. In so doing, they do not have to respond competitively to that competitor.

Buyers Are Less Sensitive to Prices for Effectively Differentiated Products   The Highlands Inn in Carmel, California, and the Ventana Inn along the Big Sur charge a minimum of $400 per night for a room with a kitchen, fireplace, hot tub, and view. Other places are available along this beautiful stretch of California's spectacular coastline, but occupancy rates at these two locations remain over 90 percent. Why? You can't get a better view and a more relaxed, spectacular setting to spend a few days on the Pacific Coast. Similarly, buyers of differentiated products tolerate price increases low-cost–oriented buyers would not accept. The former become very loyal to certain brands.

Brand Loyalty Is Hard for New Entrants to Overcome   Many new beers are brought to market in the United States, but Budweiser continues to gain market share. Why? Brand loyalty is hard to overcome! And Anheuser Busch has been clever to extend its brand loyalty from its core brand into newer niches, like nonalcohol brews, that other potential entrants have pioneered.

Managers examining differentiation-based advantages must take potential risks into account as they commit their business to these advantages. Some of the more common ways risks arise are discussed next.

Imitation Narrows Perceived Differentiation, Rendering Differentiation Meaningless   AMC pioneered the Jeep passenger version of a truck 40 years ago. Ford created the Explorer, or luxury utility vehicle, in 1990. It took luxury car features and put them inside a jeep. Ford's payoff was substantial. The Explorer has become Ford's most popular domestic vehicle. However, virtually every vehicle manufacturer offered a luxury utility in 1997, with customers beginning to be hard pressed to identify clear distinctions between lead models. Ford's Explorer managers were looking for a new business strategy for the next decade that relied on new sources of differentiation and placed greater emphasis on low-cost components in their value chain.

Technological Changes That Nullify Past Investments or Learning   The Swiss controlled over 95 percent of the world's watch market into the 1970s. The bulk of the craftspeople, technology, and infrastructure resided in Switzerland. U.S.-based Texas Instruments decided to experiment with the use of its digital technology in watches. Swiss producers were not interested. Strategy in Action 8–1 shows how the Internet may be doing this to *Penthouse* magazine.

The Cost Difference between Low-Cost Competitors and the Differentiated Business Becomes Too Great for Differentiation to Hold Brand Loyalty   Buyers may begin to choose to sacrifice some of the features, services, or image possessed by the differentiated business for large cost savings. The rising cost of a college education, particularly at several "premier" institutions, has caused many students to opt for lower-cost destinations that offer very similar courses without image, frills, and professors that seldom teach undergraduate students anyway.

THE INTERNET ERASES *PENTHOUSE* MAGAZINE'S FUNDAMENTAL DIFFERENTIATION COMPETITIVE ADVANTAGE

WHY *PENTHOUSE* IS IN THE DOG HOUSE

The Pet of the Year may bear a come-hither look on the cover of the latest *Penthouse*, but there's much to be modest about at the skin mag these days.

Circulation continues to sag—off 61% over the past ten years—and for the nine months ended in September, the magazine's parent, General Media, lost $7.6 million, vs. a $2.2 million profit last year. Cash is tighter than a corset, and at least one analyst wonders whether the company can cover interest on $85 million of newly downgraded junk bonds.

Penthouse's woes are similar to those bedeviling such staid publishers as Times Mirror and Knight-Ridder. Competing electronic media—in *Penthouse*'s case, vavavoom videos and XXX Internet Web-sites—have readers browsing elsewhere. (Guess they weren't buying it for the articles after all.) Rising paper prices, up 50% last year, sent costs spiraling, as have postal rate hikes.

Skinzines also have distribution problems, stemming from the lingering effects of a 1990 boycott by religious groups against stores that displayed adult publications. *Penthouse* often gets bad exposure in the aisles, a fact that General Media President Richard Cohen admits cuts into sales. Says he: "For many people, we're an impulse buy." No kidding.

All of this has prompted retrenchment. The magazine, says Cohen, has cut costs by laying off employees, rejiggering production, and switching to cheaper paper stock. There are fewer pages too. General Media is also moving briskly into electronic distribution overseas: It recently rolled out a joint venture pay-per-view outlet in the U.K.

That may be too little too late, says analyst Brian Oak of Moody's Investors Service. He recently downgraded General Media debt from B2, just below investment grade, all the way to Caa, a scant two steps up from rock bottom. In particular, Oak is worried the company won't be able to make an interest payment of $4.2 million that's due on its junk bonds next June. Cohen insists the company has more than enough dough to meet current interest charges, but a closer look between General Media's balance sheets is revealing. Analyst Oak asserts the company's cash balance of some $9 million consists mostly of unearned revenue—upfront money paid by distributors that is supposed to pay for operating costs.

Penthouse founder and General Media CEO Bob Guccione need not fear for his tasteful art collection—Renoir to Van Gogh to Holbein. That isn't collateral. His two other publications, a health magazine called *Longevity* and science-fiction monthly *Omni*, operate separately.

Evaluating Speed as a Competitive Advantage

While most telecommunication companies used 1995 to leap aboard the information superhighway, GTE continued its impressive turnaround (income up 7% to $5 billion; revenues up 4%) focusing on its core business—providing local telephone services. Long lagging behind the Baby Bells in profitability and efficiency, GTE has emphasized improving its poor customer service that dates back to the 1980s. The service was so bad in Santa Monica, California, that officials once tried to remove GTE as the local phone company. Candidly saying "we were the pits," new CEO Chuck Lee largely did away with its old system of taking customer service requests by writing them down and passing them along for resolution. Now, using personal communication services and specially designed software, service reps can solve 70 percent of all problems on the initial call—triple the

FIGURE 8–3
Evaluating a Business's Rapid Response (Speed) Opportunities

A. Skills and Resources That Foster Speed

Process engineering skills.
Excellent inbound and outbound logistics.
Technical people in sales and customer service.
High levels of automation.
Corporate reputation for quality or technical leadership.
Flexible manufacturing capabilities.
Strong downstream partners.
Strong cooperation from suppliers of major components of the product or service.

B. Organizational Requirements to Support and Sustain Rapid Response Activities

Strong coordination among functions in R&D, product development, and marketing.
Major emphasis on customer satisfaction in incentive programs.
Strong delegation to operating personnel.
Tradition of closeness to key customers.
Some personnel skilled in sales and operations—technical and marketing.
Empowered customer service personnel.

C. Examples of Ways Businesses Achieve Competitive Advantage via Speed

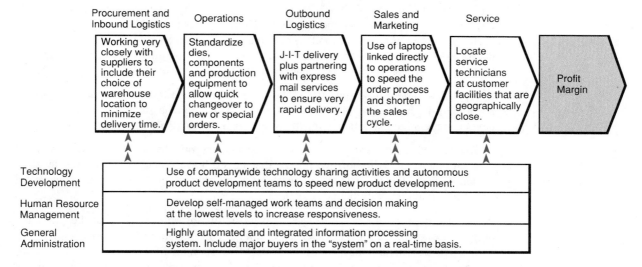

Source: Adapted with permission of The Free Press, a Division of Simon and Schuster, from *Competitive Advantage: Creating and Sustaining Superior Performance*, by Michael E. Porter. Copyright © 1985 by Michael E. Porter.

success rate at the beginning of the last decade. Repair workers meanwhile plan their schedules on laptops, cutting down time and speeding responses. CEO Lee has spent $1.5 billion on reengineering that slashed 17,000 jobs, replaced people with technology, and prioritized *speed* as the defining feature of GTE's business practices.

Speed, or rapid response to customer requests or market and technological changes, has become a major source of competitive advantage for numerous firms in today's intensely competitive global economy. Speed is certainly a form of differentiation, but it is more than that. Speed involves the *availability of a rapid response* to a customer by providing current products quicker, accelerating new product development or improvement, quickly adjusting production processes, and making decisions quickly. While low cost and differentiation may provide important competitive advantages, managers in tomorrow's successful companies will base their strategies on creating speed-based competitive advantages. Figure 8–3 describes and illustrates key skills and organizational requirements that are associated with speed-based competitive advantage. Jack Welch, the CEO who transformed General Electric from a fading company into one of Wall Street's best performers over the last 10 years, had this to say about speed:

> Speed is really the driving force that everyone is after. Faster products, faster product cycles to market. Better response time to customers. . . . Satisfying customers, getting faster communications, moving with more agility, all these things are easier when one is small. And these are all characteristics one needs in a fast-moving global environment.[3]

Speed-based competitive advantages can be created around several activities.

Customer Responsiveness   All consumers have encountered hassles, delays, and frustration dealing with various businesses from time to time. The same holds true when dealing business to business. Quick response with answers, information, and solutions to mistakes can become the basis for competitive advantage . . . one that builds customer loyalty quickly.

Product Development Cycles   Japanese car makers have focused intensely on the time it takes to create a new model because several experienced disappointing sales growth in the mid-1990s in Europe and North America competing against new vehicles like Ford's Explorer and Renault's Megane. By 1997, Honda, Toyota, and Nissan had lowered the cycle from 24 months to 11 months from conception to production. This capability is old hat to 3M Corporation, which is so successful at speedy product development that one-fourth of its sales and profits each year are from products that didn't exist five years earlier.

Product or Service Improvements   Like development time, companies that can rapidly adapt their products or services and do so in a way that benefits their customers or creates new customers have a major competitive advantage over rivals that cannot do this.

Speed in Delivery or Distribution   Firms that can get you what you need when you need it, even when that is tomorrow, realize that buyers have come to expect that level of responsiveness. Federal Express's success reflects the importance customers place on speed in inbound and outbound logistics.

Information Sharing and Technology   Speed in sharing information that becomes the basis for decisions, actions, or other important activities taken by a customer, supplier, or partner has become a major source of competitive advantage for many businesses. Telecommunications, the Internet, and networks are but a part of a vast infrastructure that is being used by knowledgeable managers to rebuild or create value in their businesses via information sharing.

These rapid response capabilities create competitive advantages in several ways. They create a way to lessen rivalry because they have *availability* of something that a rival may not have. It can allow the business to charge buyers more, engender loyalty, or otherwise enhance the business's position relative to its buyers. Particularly where impressive customer response is involved, businesses can generate supplier cooperation and concessions since their business ultimately benefits from increased revenue. Finally, substitute products and new entrants find themselves trying to keep up with the rapid changes rather than introducing them.

While the notion of speed-based competitive advantage is exciting, it has risks managers must consider. First, speeding up activities that haven't been conducted in a fashion that prioritizes rapid response should only be done after considerable attention to training,

---

[3] "Jack Welch on the Art of Thinking Small," *Business Week*, Enterprise 1993 issue, p. 212.

reorganization, and/or reengineering. Second, some industries—stable, mature ones that have very minimal levels of change—may not offer much advantage to the firm that introduces some forms of rapid response. Customers in such settings may prefer the slower pace or the lower costs currently available or they may have long time frames in purchasing such that speed is not that important to them.

Evaluating Market Focus as a Way to Competitive Advantage

Small companies, at least the better ones, usually thrive because they serve narrow market niches. This is usually called *focus*, the extent to which a business concentrates on a narrowly defined market. Take the example of Soho Beverages, a business former Pepsi manager Tom Cox bought from Seagram after Seagram had acquired it and was unable to make it thrive. The tiny brand, once a healthy niche product in New York and a few other east coast locations, muddled within Seagrams because its sales force was unused to selling in delis. Cox was able to double sales in one year. He did this on a lean marketing budget that didn't include advertising or database marketing. He hired Korean- and Arabic-speaking college students and had his people walk into practically every deli in Manhattan in order to reacquaint owners with the brand, spot consumption trends, and take orders. He provided rapid stocking services to all Manhattan-area delis, regardless of size. The business has continued sales growth at over 50 percent per year. Why? Cox says "It is attributable to focusing on a niche market, delis; differentiating the product and its sales force; achieving low costs in promotion and delivery; and making rapid, immediate response to any deli owner request its normal practice."

Two things are important in this example. First, this business focused on a narrow niche market in which to build a strong competitive advantage. But focus alone was not enough to build competitive advantage. Rather, Cox created several value chain activities that achieved differentiation, low cost, and rapid response competitive advantages within this niche market that would be hard for other firms, particularly mass market–oriented firms, to replicate.

Focus allows some businesses to compete on the basis of low cost, differentiation, and rapid response against much larger businesses with greater resources. Focus lets a business "learn" its target customers—their needs, special considerations they want accommodated—and establish personal relationships in ways that "differentiate" the smaller firm or make it more valuable to the target customer. Low costs can also be achieved filling niche needs in a buyer's operations that larger rivals either do not want to bother with or cannot do as cost effectively. Cost advantage often centers around the high level of customized service the focused, smaller business can provide. And perhaps the greatest competitive weapon that can arise is rapid response. With enhanced knowledge of its customers and intricacies of their operations, the small, focused company builds up organizational knowledge about timing sensitive ways to work with a customer. Often the needs of that narrow set of customers represent a large part of the small, focused business's revenues. Global Strategy In Action 8–1 illustrates how Sweden's Scania has become the global leader in heavy trucks via the focused application of low cost, differentiation, and speed.

The risk of focus is that you attract major competitors that have waited for your business to "prove" the market. Dominoes proved that a huge market for pizza delivery existed and now faces serious challenges. Likewise, publicly traded focused companies become takeover targets for large firms seeking to fill out a product portfolio. And perhaps the greatest risk of all is slipping into the illusion that it is focus itself, and not some special form of low cost, differentiation, or rapid response, that is creating the business's success.

GLOBAL
STRATEGY IN
ACTION 8–1

SCANIA LEAVES VOLVO AND OTHER GLOBAL TRUCK MANUFACTURERS IN ITS DUST

The preeminent consulting firm McKinsey and Company recently studied the global truck industry to understand which producers had the strongest competitive advantages and why they did. It quickly became a study of the Swedish firm, Scania, and its long time rival, Volvo. On an index that measured value added per hour worked, Scania scored 100 with Volvo close behind. The best Japanese, U.S., and German truck makers trailed by more than 25 points.

Leif Ostling, Scania's burly CEO, attributes the business's success to a determination to stick to its strategy of concentrating on heavy trucks, and rely on its own resources to deliver quality products commanding market leading prices. McKinsey's analysis broadens the explanation as it sought an answer to how Scania had arrived at its enviable position and what its prospects were for remaining a world leader. McKinsey concluded:

1. Intense competition between Scania and Volvo in tiny Sweden prepared them both to compete better than other rivals in the global market because the truck industry is much less international than the car industry, leaving newer rivals less competitive even on their home turf. Scania and Volvo have been benchmarking each other for years.

2. Scania uses a building principle of maximization of standardization of parts across many brands while also leading the industry in responding to the demand for customization of each vehicle that is sold. How? While every truck is a unique order, Scania uses less than 20,000 components to build their truck compared to 25,000 for Volvo and 40,000 for Mercedes. Fewer parts mean lower development costs, lower manufacturing costs, and lower distribution costs.

3. Scania produces all main components in house, which allows them to maximize integration of design, development, and production, thus saving time, allowing for greater customization, and fewer parts.

4. There is strong emphasis on customization of each vehicle: "We have to supply a specific truck to a customer's specific needs," said Kaj Holmelius, head of chassis development, pointing to a production line, "Each of these is for a specific order and almost every one will be different in some way when they come off the end of the line. At the same time we want to get as large volumes as possible for individual components."

5. Scania will not expand into lighter trucks because it would dilute the efficiencies it has wrung out of its modular system. It has no plans to enter the North American market because of very different truck specifications and lower margins. The intention is to grow chiefly in Central and Eastern Europe and in the Pacific region. "We will stick to what we know how to do in limited, margin favorable markets," said Ostling.

The bottom line is, Scania has built a variety of sustainable competitive advantages that promise to keep it on top the world heavy truck market for a long time.

Source: "Scania Pulls Ahead of the Crowd," *Financial Times*, October 16, 1995, p. 10.

Managers evaluating opportunities to build competitive advantage should link strategies to value chain activities that exploit low cost, differentiation, and rapid response competitive advantages. When advantageous, they should consider ways to use focus to leverage these advantages. One way business managers can enhance their likelihood of identifying these opportunities is to consider several different "generic" industry environments from the perspective of the typical value chain activities most often linked to sustained competitive advantages in those unique industry situations. The next section discusses five key generic industry environments and the value chain activities most associated with success.

SELECTED INDUSTRY ENVIRONMENTS AND BUSINESS STRATEGY CHOICES

The analysis and choice of the ways a business will seek to build competitive advantage can be enhanced when managers take industry conditions into account. Chapters 3 and 5 discussed ways to examine industry conditions, so we do not seek to repeat that here. Likewise, Chapter 6 shows how the market life cycle concept can be used to examine business strengths. What is important to recognize as managers evaluate opportunities to emphasize a narrow set of core competencies and potential competitive advantages is that different sets appear to be more useful in different, unique industry environments. We examine five "typical" industry settings and opportunities for generating competitive advantages that strategists should look for in their deliberations. Three of these five settings relate to industry life cycle. Managers use these as ways to evaluate their value chain activities and then select the ones around which it is most critical to build competitive advantage.[4]

Competitive Advantage in Emerging Industries

Emerging industries are newly formed or re-formed industries that typically are created by technological innovation, newly emerging customer needs, or other economic or sociological changes. Emerging industries of the last decade have been the Internet browser, fiber optic, solar heating, cellular telephone, and on-line services industries.

From the standpoint of strategy formulation, the essential characteristic of an emerging industry is that there are no "rules of the game." The absence of rules presents both a risk and an opportunity—a wise strategy positions the firm to favorably shape the emerging industry's rules.

Business strategies must be shaped to accommodate the following characteristics of markets in emerging industries.

Technologies that are mostly proprietary to the pioneering firms and technological uncertainty about how product standardization will unfold.

Competitor uncertainty because of inadequate information about competitors, buyers, and the timing of demand.

High initial costs but steep cost declines as the experience curve takes effect.

Few entry barriers, which often spurs the formation of many new firms.

First-time buyers requiring initial inducement to purchase and customers confused by the availability of a number of nonstandard products.

Inability to obtain raw materials and components until suppliers gear up to meet the industry's needs.

Need for high-risk capital because of the industry's uncertainty prospects.

For success in this industry setting, business strategies require one or more of these features:

1. The ability to *shape the industry's structure* based on the timing of entry, reputation, success in related industries or technologies, and role in industry associations.
2. The ability to *rapidly improve product quality* and performance features.
3. *Advantageous relationships* with key suppliers and promising distribution channels.

---

[4]These industry characterizations draw heavily on the work of Michael E. Porter, *Competitive Advantage: Creating and Sustaining Superior Performance.* (New York: Free Press, 1985).

STRATEGY
IN ACTION
8–2

DOES NETSCAPE HAVE A REAL, SUSTAINABLE COMPETITIVE ADVANTAGE IN THE EMERGING "INTERNET INDUSTRY?"

AS THE BIG GUYS AWAKE, CAN NETSCAPE PREVAIL?

Netscape, the tiny software company that the stock market values at nearly $6 billion, has come to symbolize the Internet the way Microsoft does PC computing. Investors treat this pup as a bellwether for the Internet phenomenon, the presumed Next Big Thing. Now, rapid-fire changes in the market are posing a threat to Netscape's ability to dominate Internet computing. Absent that, Netscape's hypervaluation is impossible to justify.

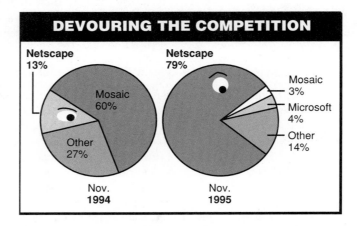

Source: "As the Big Guys Awake, Can Netscape Prevail?" January 15, 1996, p. 16. By David Kirkpatrick, *Fortune*, © 1996, Time, Inc. All rights reserved.

4. The ability to *establish the firm's technology as the dominant one* before technological uncertainty decreases.
5. The early acquisition of *a core group of loyal customers* and then the expansion of that customer base through model changes, alternative pricing, and advertising.
6. The ability to *forecast future competitors* and the strategies they are likely to employ.

A firm that has had repeated successes with business in emerging industries is 3M Corporation. In each of the last 20 years, over 25 percent of 3M's annual sales have come from products that did not exist 5 years earlier. Start-up companies enhance their success by having experienced entrepreneurs at the helm, a knowledgeable management team and board of directors, and patient sources of venture capital. Netscape's dramatic debut on Wall Street symbolically ushering in the emerging "Internet Industry" era for investors will certainly lead to questions about the lasting competitive advantage at Netscape. Strategy in Action 8–2 examines whether Netscape has the capacity to prevail in this emerging industry.

Competitive Advantage in the Transition to Industry Maturity

As an industry evolves, its rate of growth eventually declines. This "transition to maturity" is accompanied by several changes in its competitive environment:

Netscape's business consists primarily of two sectors—Internet "browsers" and software for the servers to which the browsers go for data. But new products announced by Microsoft and IBM's Lotus Development will be "Internet-enabled." That means such software as Microsoft Word or Excel, or Lotus Notes, can transport the user to the Internet directly, without help from Netscape's browser.

The company's biggest business right now—70% of this year's $60 million in revenues—is providing browsers and server software for so-called intranets. In these setups, businesses use Internet tools to build internal information-sharing systems. But if Microsoft inserts a browser in its operating systems, as it intends to in Windows 95, why should a customer buy another one? And Lotus Notes' primary function is for creating intranet-like systems but with vastly greater information control and security. In mid-December, Lotus raised the stakes by slashing Notes prices.

To fend off competitors like Lotus, Netscape has to add features to its software without raising prices. It also has to provide the kind of expensive support corporate customers demand. Given that its rivals are expert at just that, says David Marshak, a communications software expert at Boston's Patricia Seybold Group, "Netscape is vulnerable."

Jonathan Cohen, an analyst at Smith Barney, thinks naive investors assume Netscape can eventually rule the Internet and vanquish the challengers. "But it really will be difficult," he explains, "for any company to gain a proprietary competitive advantage by controlling the operating system of the Internet." At Netscape's recent price of $140, Cohen says sell.

Netscape co-founder Marc Andreessen takes a feisty view toward the more established competition. "Microsoft should have been all over this three years ago," he says. "It's premature to say a bunch of moribund companies are going to catch up and kill us."

Competition for market share becomes more intense as firms in the industry are forced to achieve sales growth at one another's expense.

Firms in the industry sell increasingly to experienced, repeat buyers that are now making choices among known alternatives.

Competition becomes more oriented to cost and service as knowledgeable buyers expect similar price and product features.

Industry capacity "tops out" as sales growth ceases to cover up poorly planned expansions.

New products and new applications are harder to come by.

International competition increases as cost pressures lead to overseas production advantages.

Profitability falls, often permanently, as a result of pressure to lower prices and the increased costs of holding or building market share.

These changes necessitate a fundamental strategic reassessment. Strategy elements of successful firms in maturing industries often include:

1. *Pruning the product line* by dropping unprofitable product models, sizes, and options from the firm's product mix.
2. *Emphasis on process innovation* that permits low-cost product design, manufacturing methods, and distribution synergy.

3. *Emphasis on cost reduction* through exerting pressure on suppliers for lower prices, switching to cheaper components, introducing operational efficiencies, and lowering administrative and sales overhead.
4. *Careful buyer selection* to focus on buyers that are less aggressive, more closely tied to the firm, and able to buy more from the firm.
5. *Horizontal integration* to acquire rival firms whose weaknesses can be used to gain a bargain price and are correctable by the acquiring firms.
6. *International expansion* to markets where attractive growth and limited competition still exist and the opportunity for lower-cost manufacturing can influence both domestic and international costs.

Business strategists in maturing industries must avoid several pitfalls. First, they must make a clear choice among the three generic strategies and avoid a middle-ground approach, which would confuse both knowledgeable buyers and the firm's personnel. Second, they must avoid sacrificing market share too quickly for short-term profit. Finally, they must avoid waiting too long to respond to price reductions, retaining unneeded excess capacity, engaging in sporadic or irrational efforts to boost sales, and placing their hopes on "new" products, rather than aggressively selling existing products.

Competitive Advantage in Mature and Declining Industries

Declining industries are those that make products or services for which demand is growing slower than demand in the economy as a whole or is actually declining. This slow growth or decline in demand is caused by technological substitution (such as the substitution of electronic calculators for slide rules), demographic shifts (such as the increase in the number of older people and the decrease in the number of children), and shifts in needs (such as the decreased need for red meat).

Firms in a declining industry should choose strategies that emphasize one or more of the following themes:

1. *Focus* on segments within the industry that offer a chance for higher growth or a higher return.
2. *Emphasize product innovation and quality improvement,* where this can be done cost effectively, to differentiate the firm from rivals and to spur growth.
3. *Emphasize production and distribution efficiency* by streamlining production, closing marginal productions facilities and costly distribution outlets, and adding effective new facilities and outlets.
4. *Gradually harvest the business*—generate cash by cutting down on maintenance, reducing models, and shrinking channels and make no new investment.

Strategists who incorporate one or more of these themes into the strategy of their business can anticipate relative success, particularly where the industry's decline is slow and smooth and some profitable niches remain. At the same time, three pitfalls must be avoided: (1) being overly optimistic about the prospects for a revival of the industry, (2) getting trapped in a profitless war of attrition, and (3) harvesting from a weak position.

Competitive Advantage in Fragmented Industries

A fragmented industry is one in which no firm has a significant market share and can strongly influence industry outcomes. Fragmented industries are found in many areas of the economy and are common in such areas as professional services, retailing, distribution, wood and metal fabrication, and agricultural products. Business strategists in fragmented industries pursue low-cost, differentiation, or focus competitive advantages in one of five ways.

Tightly Managed Decentralization

Fragmented industries are characterized by a need for intense local coordination, a local management orientation, high personal service, and local autonomy. Recently, however, successful firms in such industries have introduced a high degree of professionalism into the operations of local managers.

"Formula" Facilities

This alternative, related to the previous one, introduces standardized, efficient, low-cost facilities at multiple locations. Thus, the firm gradually builds a low-cost advantage over localized competitors. Fast food and motel chains have applied this approach with considerable success.

Increased Value Added

The products or services of some fragmented industries are difficult to differentiate. In this case, an effective strategy may be to add value by providing more service with the sale or by engaging in some product assembly that is of additional value to the customer.

Specialization

Focus strategies that creatively segment the market can enable firms to cope with fragmentation. Specialization can be pursued by:

1. *Product type.* The firm builds expertise focusing on a narrow range of products or services.
2. *Customer type.* The firm becomes intimately familiar with and serves the needs of a narrow customer segment.
3. *Type of order.* The firm handles only certain kinds of orders, such as small orders, custom orders, or quick turnaround orders.
4. *Geographic area.* The firm blankets or concentrates on a single area.

Although specialization in one or more of these ways can be the basis for a sound focus strategy in a fragmented industry, each of these types of specialization risks limiting the firm's potential sales volume.

Bare Bones/No Frills

Given the intense competition and low margins in fragmented industries, a "bare bones" posture—low overhead, minimum wage employees, tight cost control—may build a sustainable cost advantage in such industries.

Competitive Advantage in Global Industries

A global industry is one that comprises firms whose competitive positions in major geographic or national markets are fundamentally affected by their overall global competitive positions. To avoid strategic disadvantages, firms in global industries are virtually required to compete on a worldwide basis. Oil, steel, automobiles, apparel, motorcycles, televisions, and computers are examples of global industries.

Global industries have four unique strategy-shaping features:

Differences in prices and costs from country to country due to currency exchange fluctuations, differences in wage and inflation rates, and other economic factors.

Differences in buyer needs across different countries.

Differences in competitors and ways of competing from country to country.

Differences in trade rules and governmental regulations across different countries.

These unique features and the global competition of global industries require that two fundamental components be addressed in the business strategy: (1) the approach used to gain global market coverage and (2) the generic competitive strategy.

Three basic options can be used to pursue global market coverage:

1. *License* foreign firms to produce and distribute the firm's products.
2. *Maintain a domestic production base* and export products to foreign countries.
3. *Establish foreign-based plants and distribution* to compete directly in the markets of one or more foreign countries.

Along with the market coverage decision, strategists must scrutinize the condition of the global industry features identified earlier to choose among four generic global competitive strategies:

1. *Broad-line global competition*—directed at competing worldwide in the full product line of the industry, often with plants in many countries, to achieve differentiation or an overall low-cost position.
2. *Global focus* strategy—targeting a particular segment of the industry for competition on a worldwide basis.
3. *National focus* strategy—taking advantage of differences in national markets that give the firm an edge over global competitors on a nation-by-nation basis.
4. *Protected niche* strategy—seeking out countries in which governmental restraints exclude or inhibit global competitors or allow concessions, or both, that are advantageous to localized firms.

Competing in global industries is an increasing reality for many U.S. firms. Strategists must carefully match their skills and resources with global industry structure and conditions in selecting the most appropriate strategy option.

In conclusion, the analysis and choice of business strategy involves three basic considerations. First, strategists must recognize that their overall choice revolves around three sources of competitive advantage that require total, consistent commitment. Second, strategists must carefully weigh the skills, resources, organizational requirements, and risks associated with each source of competitive advantage. Finally, strategists must consider the unique influence that the generic industry environment most similar to the firm's situation will have on the set of value chain activities they choose to build competitive advantage.

DOMINANT-PRODUCT/SERVICE BUSINESSES: EVALUATING AND CHOOSING TO DIVERSIFY TO BUILD VALUE

McDonald's has frequently looked at numerous opportunities to diversify into related businesses or to acquire key suppliers. Its decision has consistently been to focus on its core business using the grand strategies of concentration, market development, and product development. Rival Pepsi, on the other hand, has chosen to diversify into related businesses and vertical integration as the best grand strategies for it to build long-term value. Both firms experienced unprecedented success during the last 20 years.

FIGURE 8–4
Grand Strategy Selection Matrix

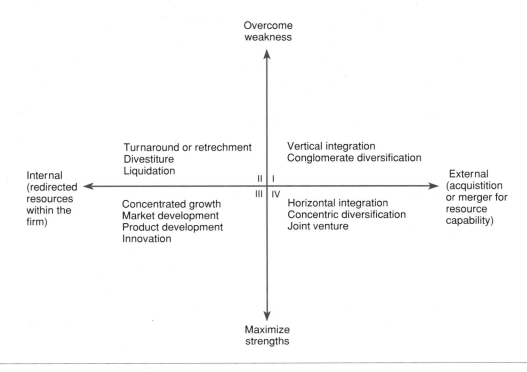

Many dominant product businesses face this question as their core business proves successful: What grand strategies are best suited to continue to build value? Under what circumstances should they choose an expanded focus (diversification, vertical integration); steady continued focus (concentration, market or product development); or a narrowed focus (turnaround or divestiture)? This section examines two ways you can analyze a dominant product company's situation and choose among the 12 grand strategies identified in Chapter 7.

Grand Strategy Selection Matrix

One valuable guide to the selection of a promising grand strategy is the matrix shown in Figure 8–4. The basic idea underlying the matrix is that two variables are of central concern in the selection process: (1) the principal purpose of the grand strategy and (2) the choice of an internal or external emphasis for growth or profitability, or both.

In the past, planners were advised to follow certain rules or prescriptions in their choice of strategies. Now, most experts agree that strategy selection is better guided by the conditions of the planning period and by the company strengths and weaknesses. It should be noted, however, that even the early approaches to strategy selection sought to match a concern over internal versus external growth with a desire to overcome weaknesses or maximize strengths.

The same considerations led to the development of the grand strategy selection matrix. A firm in quadrant I, with "all its eggs in one basket," often views itself as overcommitted to a particular business with limited growth opportunities or high risks. One reasonable solution is *vertical integration*, which enables the firm to reduce risk by reducing uncertainty about inputs or access to customers. Another is *conglomerate diversification*, which provides a profitable investment alternative with diverting management attention from the original business. However, the external approaches to overcoming weaknesses usually result in the most costly grand strategies. Acquiring a second business demands large investments of time and sizable financial resources. Thus, strategic managers considering these approaches must guard against exchanging one set of weaknesses for another.

More-conservative approaches to overcoming weaknesses are found in quadrant II. Firms often choose to redirect resources from one internal business activity to another. This approach maintains the firm's commitment to its basic mission, rewards success, and enables further development of proven competitive advantages. The least disruptive of the quadrant II strategies is *retrenchment*, pruning the current activities of a business. If the weaknesses of the business arose from inefficiencies, retrenchment can actually serve as a *turnaround* strategy—that is, the business gains new strength from the streamlining of its operations and the elimination of waste. However, if those weaknesses are a major obstruction to success in the industry and the costs of overcoming them are unaffordable or are not justified by a cost-benefit analysis, then eliminating the business must be considered. *Divestiture* offers the best possibility for recouping the firm's investment, but even *liquidation* can be an attractive option if the alternatives are bankruptcy or an unwarranted drain on the firm's resources.

A common business adage states that a firm should build from strength. The premise of this adage is that growth and survival depend on an ability to capture a market share that is large enough for essential economies of scale. If a firm believes that this approach will be profitable and prefers an internal emphasis for maximizing strengths, four grand strategies hold considerable promise. As shown in quadrant III, the most common approach is *concentrated growth*, that is, market penetration. The firm that selects this strategy is strongly committed to its current products and markets. It strives to solidify its position by reinvesting resources to fortify its strengths.

Two alternative approaches are *market development* and *product development*. With these strategies, the firm attempts to broaden its operations. Market development is chosen if the firm's strategic managers feel that its existing products would be well received by new customer groups. Product development is chosen if they feel that the firm's existing customers would be interested in products related to its current lines. Product development also may be based on technological or other competitive advantages. The final alternative for quadrant III firms is *innovation*. When the firm's strengths are in creative product design or unique production technologies, sales can be stimulated by accelerating perceived obsolescence. This is the principle underlying the innovative grand strategy.

Maximizing a firm's strengths by aggressively expanding its base of operations usually requires an external emphasis. The preferred options in such cases are shown in quadrant IV. *Horizontal integration* is attractive because it makes possible a quick increase in output capability. Moreover, in horizontal integration, the skills of the managers of the original business often are critical in converting newly acquired facilities into profitable contributors to the parent firm; this expands a fundamental competitive advantage of the firm—its management.

Concentric diversification is a good second choice for similar reasons. Because the original and newly acquired businesses are related, the distinctive competencies of the diversifying firm are likely to facilitate a smooth, synergistic, and profitable expansion.

The final alternative for increasing resource capability through external emphasis is a *joint venture* or *strategic alliance*. This alternative allows a firm to extend its strengths into competitive arenas that it would be hesitant to enter alone. A partner's production, technological, financial, or marketing capabilities can reduce the firm's financial investment significantly and increase its probability of success.

FIGURE 8–5
Model of Grand Strategy Clusters

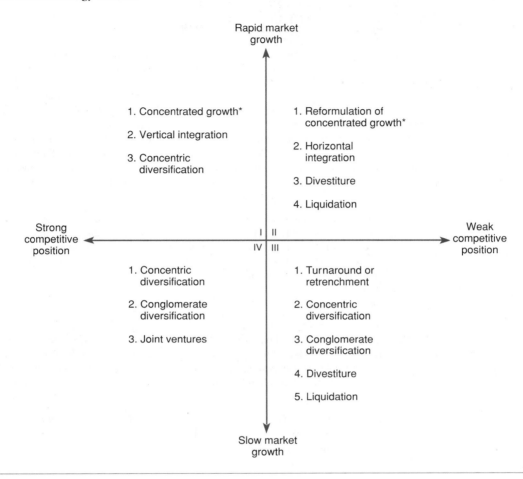

*This is usually via market development, product development, or a combination of both.

Model of Grand Strategy Clusters

A second guide to selecting a promising grand strategy is shown in Figure 8–5. The figure is based on the idea that the situation of a business is defined in terms of the growth rate of the general market and the firm's competitive position in that market. When these factors are considered simultaneously, a business can be broadly categorized in one of four quadrants: (I) strong competitive position in a rapidly growing market, (II) weak position in a rapidly growing market, (III) weak position in a slow-growth market, or (IV) strong position in a slow-growth market. Each of these quadrants suggests a set of promising possibilities for the selection of a grand strategy.

Firms in quadrant I are in an excellent strategic position. One obvious grand strategy for such firms is continued concentration on their current business as it is currently defined. Because consumers seem satisfied with the firm's current strategy, shifting notably from it would endanger the firm's established competitive advantages. McDonald's Corporation has followed this approach for 25 years. However, if the firm has resources that exceed the

CHOOSING AMONG GRAND STRATEGY ALTERNATIVES AT PEPSICO

Twenty-five years ago, PepsiCo was a sleepy and distant second to Coca-Cola in the U.S. soft-drink industry. Soda consumption by the baby boom generation made it easy for PepsiCo to double its sales to almost $1 billion while maintaining a steady ROE in the high teens and a 5 percent return on sales. This profitability allowed the company to generate an additional $40 million in working capital over that needed to operate the company's existing business.

PepsiCo's management team led by Donald Kendall and Andrall Pearson sought to heat up the company's growth, given the predictability of its soft-drink income stream. As they examined alternative grand strategies, they viewed PepsiCo as possessing proven strengths in selling an inexpensive consumable product (Pepsi) to a young, energetic consumer. Their first choice of strategy was one that sought to redirect internal resources (excess cash generated) toward maximizing these strengths. Their conclusion in this regard was a four-part program:

1. Continue to build sales of their Pepsi product in existing outlets. (Concentrated growth)
2. Expand distribution (and sales) of Pepsi by aggressively pursuing new and different outlets, especially grocery stores and international. (Market development)
3. Create related but new products like diet drinks to appeal to baby boomers reaching adulthood. (Product development)
4. Design revolutionary new packaging to reinforce the sales efforts emanating from above. (Innovation—plastics and 32 oz.)

Wisely anticipating that these strategies would continue to generate a growing stream of excess cash, these managers also realized that PepsiCo did not possess other resources (people, experience, and products) necessary to take advantage of related growth opportunities. So PepsiCo had to look externally for the management, experience, and product opportunities that could blend well with and maximize its proven strengths in cola marketing and sales. Their add-on grand strategies to pursue these conclusions were:

5. Acquire 7UP, Mountain Dew, and Mug Rootbeer to expand their product offerings. (Horizontal integration)
6. Diversify via acquisition into related products including Frito Lay. (Concentric diversification)

PepsiCo also rationalized the acquisition of Wilson Sporting Goods and United Van Lines as a part of this strategy. Wilson was seen as selling products to the same market—active young people. United complemented PepsiCo's growing transportation network by bringing the expertise to run it efficiently.

Source: PepsiCo, Inc., 1971 and 1994 annual reports.

demands of a concentrated growth strategy, it should consider vertical integration. Either forward or backward integration helps a firm protect its profit margins and market share by ensuring better access to consumers or material inputs. Finally, to diminish the risks associated with a narrow product or service line, a quadrant I firm might be wise to consider concentric diversification; with this strategy, the firm continues to invest heavily in its basic area of proven ability. Strategy in Action 8–3 describes how PepsiCo, a clear quadrant I firm, has followed these guidelines.

Firms in quadrant II must seriously evaluate their present approach to the marketplace. If a firm has competed long enough to accurately assess the merits of its current grand

STRATEGY
IN ACTION   **continued**
8–3

PepsiCo's choice of grand strategies generally proved successful. In 10 years net sales had increased sixfold to over $6 billion. Profitability and cash generation ratios remained consistent, meaning even greater excess financial resources to work with. Along the way, Wilson and United were divested, because management saw both businesses to contain several weaknesses not worth (from PepsiCo's perspective) investment to correct. With this overall growth in financial resources, PepsiCo managers concluded the same grand strategies applied that led to the acquisition of Pizza Hut, Kentucky Fried Chicken, and Taco Bell as a logical concentric diversification.

PepsiCo, now in soft drinks, snack foods, and restaurants, saw its net sales, net income, and cash flow grow at compounded annual rates of 17 percent, 19 percent, and 15 percent, respectively, into the first half of the 1990s. Over this period, operations generated over $15 billion for reinvestment, dividends, or acquisition.

Contributing to and reaping the bounty of this legacy, PepsiCo's colorful chairman and CEO, Wayne Calloway, observed:

> At PepsiCo, we've increased sales and net income at an exhilarating rate of nearly 15 percent for 26 years. That means we've doubled our business about every five years. But now that we're about $30 billion big, you might well ask, How long can this keep going on? Forever, as far as we're concerned. At least that's our intention.

Mr. Calloway views PepsiCo as being in the fortunate position of maximizing strengths via redirection of internally generated resources in each of its three business sections. Some of the specific strategies he outlines to back up his above assertion are:

1. In many international markets, consumers drink fewer soft drinks in a year than most Americans consume in a week. We're going to change that. (Concentrated growth)
2. Our (snack food) products are still unavailable to about 60 percent of the world's population. We're changing that. (Market development)
3. Soft drinks represent about one quarter of all beverages consumed in the United States. That means that three quarters of the beverage market provides opportunity. (Product development)
4. More than 40 percent of all adults in the United States have a meal delivered from a restaurant at least once a month. We're becoming a front runner in this market segment. (Concentrated growth)
5. International consumers eat about one sixth the amount of snack chips consumed by their U.S. counterparts, but snacking is becoming more popular every day. (Market and product development)

strategy, it must determine (1) why that strategy is ineffectual and (2) whether it is capable of competing effectively. Depending on the answers to these questions, the firm should choose one of four grand strategy options: formulation or reformulation of a concentrated growth strategy, horizontal integration, divestiture, or liquidation.

In a rapidly growing market, even a small or relatively weak business often is able to find a profitable niche. Thus, formulation or reformulation of a concentrated growth strategy is usually the first option that should be considered. However, if the firm lacks either a critical competitive element or sufficient economies of scale to achieve competitive cost efficiencies, then a grand strategy that directs its efforts toward horizontal integration is often a desirable alternative. A final pair of options involve deciding to stop competing in the market or product area of the business. A multiproduct firm may conclude that it is most likely to achieve the goals of its mission if the business is dropped through divestiture. This grand strategy not only eliminates a drain on resources but also may provide funds to promote other business activities. As an option of last resort, a firm may decide to liquidate the business. This means that the business cannot be sold as a going concern and is at best worth only the value of its tangible assets. The decision to liquidate is an undeniable admission of failure by a firm's strategic management and, thus, often is delayed—to the further detriment of the firm.

Strategic managers tend to resist divestiture because it is likely to jeopardize their control of the firm and perhaps even their jobs. Thus, by the time the desirability of divestiture is acknowledged, businesses often deteriorate to the point of failing to attract potential buyers. The consequences of such delays are financially disastrous for firm owners because the value of a going concern is many times greater than the value of its assets.

Strategic managers who have a business in quadrant III and expect a continuation of slow market growth and a relatively weak competitive position will usually attempt to decrease their resource commitment to that business. Minimal withdrawal is accomplished through retrenchment; this strategy has the side benefits of making resources available for other investments and of motivating employees to increase their operating efficiency. An alternative approach is to divert resources for expansion through investment in other businesses. This approach typically involves either concentric or conglomerate diversification because the firm usually wants to enter more promising arenas of competition than integration or concentrated growth strategies would allow. The final options for quadrant III businesses are divestiture, if an optimistic buyer can be found, and liquidation.

Quadrant IV businesses (strong competitive position in a slow-growth market) have a basis of strength from which to diversify into more promising growth areas. These businesses have characteristically high cash flow levels and limited internal growth needs. Thus, they are in an excellent position for concentric diversification into ventures that utilize their proven acumen. A second option is conglomerate diversification, which spreads investment risk and does not divert managerial attention from the present business. The final option is joint ventures, which are especially attractive to multinational firms. Through joint ventures, a domestic business can gain competitive advantages in promising new fields while exposing itself to limited risks.

Opportunities for Building Value as a Basis for Choosing Diversification or Integration

The grand strategy selection matrix or the model of grand strategy clusters are useful tools to help dominant product company managers evaluate and narrow their choices among alternative grand strategies. When considering grand strategies that would broaden the scope of their company's business activities through integration, diversification, or joint venture strategies, managers must examine whether opportunities to build value are present. Opportunities to build value via diversification, integration, or joint venture strategies are usually found in market-related, operating-related, and management activities. Such opportunities center around reducing costs, improving margins, or providing access to new revenue sources more cost effectively than traditional internal growth options via concentration, market development, or product development. Major opportunities for sharing and value building as well as ways to capitalize on core competencies are outlined in the next section about strategic analysis and choice in diversified companies.

Dominant product company managers who choose diversification or integration eventually create another management challenge. That challenge is charting the future of a company that becomes a collection of several distinct businesses. These distinct businesses often encounter different competitive environments, challenges, and opportunities. The next chapter examines ways managers of such diversified companies attempt to evaluate and choose corporate strategy. Central to their challenge is the continued desire to build value, particularly shareholder value.

SUMMARY

This chapter examined how managers in businesses that have a single or dominant product or service evaluate and choose their company's strategy. Two critical areas deserve their attention: first, their business's value chain; second, the appropriateness of 12 different grand strategies based on matching environmental factors with internal capabilities.

Managers in single-product-line business units examine their business's value chain to identify existing or potential activities around which they can create sustainable competitive advantages. As managers scrutinize their value chain activities, they are looking for three sources of competitive advantage: low cost, differentiation, and rapid response capabilities. They also examine whether focusing on a narrow market niche provides a more effective, sustainable way to build or leverage these three sources of competitive advantage.

Managers in single or dominant product/service businesses face two interrelated issues. First, they must choose which grand strategies make best use of their competitive advantages. Second, they must ultimately decide whether to diversify their business activity. Twelve grand strategies were identified in this chapter along with three frameworks that aid managers to choose which grand strategies should work best and when diversification or integration should be the best strategy for the business. The next chapter expands the coverage of diversification to look at how multibusiness companies evaluate continued diversification and how they construct corporate strategy.

QUESTIONS FOR DISCUSSION

1. Explain/illustrate how a business can build low-cost competitive advantages? Differentiation? Speed?
2. Is it better to concentrate on one type of competitive advantage or to nurture all three?
3. How does market focus help a business create any competitive advantage?
4. Select three grand strategies. Under what circumstances would you recommend one and not the other two for a business to pursue?

BIBLIOGRAPHY

Allaire, Yvon, and Michaela E. Firsirotu. "Coping with Strategic Uncertainty." *Sloan Management Review*, Spring 1987, p. 7.

Barwise, Patrick; Paul R. Marsh; and Robin Wensley. "Must Finance and Strategy Clash?" *Harvard Business Review*, September–October 1989, p. 85.

Berman, S. J., and R. F. Kautz. "Complete! A Sophisticated Tool That Facilitates Strategic Analysis." *Planning Review* 18 no. 4 (1990) pp. 35–39.

Bitner, Larry N., and Judith D. Powell. "Expansion Planning for Small Retail Firms." *Journal of Small Business Management*, April 1987, p. 47.

Chaganti, Rajeswararao, and Vijay Mahajan. "Portfolio Small Business Strategies under Different Types of Competition." *Entrepreneurship: Theory and Practice*, Spring 1989, p. 21.

Cravens, David W. "Gaining Strategic Marketing Advantage." *Business Horizons*, September–October 1988, p. 44.

Dess, Gregory G., and Nancy K. Orizer. "Environment, Structure, and Consensus in Strategy Formulation." *Academy of Management Review*, April 1987, p. 313.

Dodge, H. R.; S. Fullerton; and J. E. Robbins. "Stage of the Organizational Life Cycle and Competition as Mediators of Problem Perceptions for Small Businesses." *Strategic Management Journal* 15 (1994), pp. 121–34.

Eisenhardt, K. M. "Speed and Strategic Choice: How Managers Accelerate Decision Making." *California Management Review* 32, no. 3 (1990), pp. 39-54.

Eynn, P. J. "Avoid the Seven Deadly Sins of Strategic Risk Analysis." *Journal of Business Strategy*, September 1988, pp. 18–23.

Farnham, A. "America's Most Admired Companies." *Fortune*, February 7, 1994, pp. 50–62.

Fulmer, William E., and Jack Goodwin. "Differentiation: Begin with the Consumer." *Business Horizons*, September–October 1988, p. 55.

Govindarajan, Vijay. "A Contingency Approach to Strategy Selection at the Business Unit Level." *Academy of Management Journal*, December 1988, p. 828.

Hamilton, W. F.; J. Vila; and M. D. Dibner. "Patterns of Strategic Choice in Emerging Firms." *California Management Review* 32, no. 3 (1990), pp. 73–86.

Jones, T., and G. Seiler. "The Rapidly Growing Pump Company: Marketing for Competitive Advantage." *Planning Review*, May–June 1988, pp. 30–35.

Kelly, K. "Suddenly, Big Airlines Are Saying: 'Small Is Beautiful.' " *Business Week*, January 1994, p. 37.

Kennedy, C. "Planning Global Strategies for 3M." *Long Range Planning*, February 1988, pp. 9–17.

Krubasik, E. G. "Customize Your Product Development." *Harvard Business Review*, September–October 1988, pp. 46–53.

Lado, A. A.; N. G. Boyd; and P. Wright. "A Competency-Based Model of Sustainable Competitive Advantage: Toward a Conceptual Integration." *Journal of Management* 18, no. 1 (1992), pp. 77–91.

Mason, David H., and Robert G. Wilson. "Future-Mapping: A New Approach to Managing Strategic Uncertainty." *Planning Review*, May–June 1987, p. 20.

McConkey, Dale D. "Planning in a Changing Environment." *Business Horizons*, September–October 1988, p. 64.

Pelham, A. M., and D. E. Clayson. "Receptivity to Strategic Planning Tools." *Journal of Small Business Management*, January 1988, pp. 43–50.

Rudnitsky, H. "The King of Off-Price." *Forbes*, January 31, 1994, pp. 54–55.

Schofield, M., and D. Arnold. "Strategies for Mature Businesses." *Long Range Planning*, October 1988, p. 69–76.

Schrage, Michael. "A Japanese Firm Rethinks Globalization: Interview with Yoshihisa Tabuchi." *Harvard Business Review*, July–August 1989, p. 70.

Sfiligh, E. "Ice Beers Give Stroh Another Excuse to Keep Coming Out With New Brews." *Beverage World*, January 31, 1994, p. 3.

Stalk, G. "Time—The Next Source of Competitive Advantage." *Harvard Business Review*, July–August 1988, pp. 41–53.

————.; P. Evans; and L. E. Shulman. "Competing on Capabilities: The New Rules of Corporate Strategy." *Harvard Business Review* 70, no. 2 (1992), pp. 57–69.

Ulrich David. "Tie the Corporate Knot: Gaining Complete Customer Commitment." *Sloan Management Review*, Summer 1987, p. 139.

Varadarajan, P. R. "Product Portfolio Analysis and Market Share Objectives: An Exposition of Certain Underlying Relationships." *Journal of the Academy of Marketing Science* 18, no. 1 (1990), pp. 17–29.

————.; T. Clark; and W. M. Pride. "Controlling the Uncontrollable: Managing Your Market Environment." *Sloan Management Review* 33, no. 2 (1992), pp. 39–47.

Watts, L. R. "Degrees of Entrepreneurship and Small Firm Planning." *Journal of Business and Entrepreneurship* 2, no. 2 (1992), pp. 59–67.

CHAPTER 8 COHESION CASE ILLUSTRATION

BUILDING SUSTAINABLE COMPETITIVE ADVANTAGES AT COCA-COLA

Strategic analysis and choice at Coca-Cola in the 1990s has centered around how to build sustainable competitive advantages that create long-term shareholder value. Coca-Cola managers have emphasized differentiation, rapid response, and market focus competitive advantages during this time. Chief Executive Officer Roberto Goizueta likes to talk about these three sources of competitive advantage in terms of four key themes that define Coca-Cola's business strategy for the 1990s:

Since 1984, we have changed ourselves dramatically, a fact made obvious as our market value has climbed from $8 billion to nearly $66 billion. With a clear eye on the long run, we have deliberately assembled and fine-tuned a global machine capable of sustaining strong, profitable growth well into the next century. That assembly process continues today, but thus far, it can be characterized by these major initiatives: 1. Geographic expansion, 2. Financial reformation, 3. Infrastructure fortification, and 4. Consumer marketing.

Geographic Expansion

Refusing to neglect any territory anywhere in the world, we have long pursued geographic expansion as a fundamental means of growth. Through our own persistence, the end of the Cold War and the fundamental transformations of many important local economies, we have more than doubled since 1980 the number of potential consumers truly within our reach.

This has not been rocket science, just good, common business sense. After all, we market a brand with a uniquely universal appeal, and we have not entered a single new market where we did not benefit from a substantial existing demand for Coca-Cola.

Financial Reformation

We also began to capitalize on another significant resource: the naturally strong cash flow of our business. By the early 1980s, the financial prudence that protected our Company so well earlier in the century had ossified, effectively trapping a live organism within the hard constrictions of its own fossil shell.

One by one, we began taking important steps to reform our financial policies. We also shifted our focus to new, clearly superior measurements of our performance. We now evaluate our business units and opportunities based primarily on their ability to generate attractive economic profit, not just growth in revenues or earnings. We define economic profit as net operating profit after taxes, less a charge for the average cost of the capital employed to produce that profit.

Infrastructure Fortification

As we were moving ahead with geographic expansion and financial reformation, we began a third, complementary thrust. We began using our financial resources to fortify our global bottling network, taking a global distribution system that was already the world's most widespread and making it also the world's strongest and most efficient.

The methods we used varied. Some were as simple as encouraging the sale of bottling companies to owners who shared our prejudice for action and heavy reinvestment. Others involved injecting equity capital and management expertise in bottlers eager to have our participation. And still others were as complex as helping create the largest soft drink bottling company in the world, Coca-Cola Enterprises Inc.

Consumer Marketing

To drive that demand, we are taking the decisive actions that will effectively make us the world's premier consumer marketing company.

Some people tell us we're already there. After all, they would argue, wouldn't the company that has built the world's best-known and most admired brand also have to be the world's premier marketing organization?

Others would debate it, because there are a number of truly great marketing companies around the world.

To be perfectly honest, we don't care one way or the other what people say today. We simply intend to keep taking all the actions that will make our consumer marketing leadership undeniable tomorrow.

That's a bold proposition, and we know it. But we also know our success in generating value for you is largely tied to our ability to turn that proposition into reality.

When you think about it, any company can grow by expanding geographically and entering new markets. Only the best companies—the companies most worthy of your investment—can grow by building their businesses in their most developed markets.

For us, that means being able to generate solid growth in markets such as the United States, Japan, Western Europe, Mexico and Brazil. In 1994, we clearly showed that we can do just that.

We were able to do it because, while we continued to expand our brands *horizontally* across new geography in the Chinas and Indias of the world, we were also building our brands *vertically* in our established markets.

Building brands vertically means continually building new value into those brands, giving the people who buy your products more reasons to buy them than ever before. That task is particularly daunting when the brand you are building is already the world's most powerful.

How do we find new ways to make the world's most powerful brand even more powerful? How do we make that brand generate increased sales volume in a market like the United States, where, on average, every person is coming increasingly closer to consuming one of our products *every day*?

Through differentiation.

Differentiation

If the three keys to selling real estate are location, location, location, then the three keys to selling consumer products are differentiation, differentiation, differentiation. In recent years, whether it's product quality, packaging, advertising or any other element of the brand, our aim is to enhance the uniqueness of Coca-Cola by continuously making it different, better and special, relative to every possible competitor.

By further differentiating ourselves with consumers, we also further differentiated ourselves with our highly valued customers, adding value to their businesses with reliable sales growth, effective service and superior profitability.

And ultimately, by differentiating ourselves in the consumer marketplace, we were also able to differentiate ourselves in the investment marketplace, outperforming most other comparable investments while significantly enhancing the value of our Company.

In contrast, those who continued to rely on pricing as their *only* point of distinctiveness met with difficult times, on both Main Street and Wall Street. In a highly competitive environment for the consumer dollar and the investment dollar, we believe the failure to differentiate brands in *every* aspect of marketing eventually erodes the value of both the brand and the investment.

We will not allow ourselves to fall into that trap.

Market Focus

In sports, coaches can only be as good as their players. In business, the same holds true, as managers can only be as good as their businesses. Eager to be worthy managers of your investment, we purposefully narrowed our lines of business to those that would inherently make us shine. Today, we operate as an enterprise focused almost entirely on a soft drink concentrate business that consistently generates returns nearly three times greater than our average cost of capital. That core business is augmented by our selective holdings in key bottling operations around the world, and nicely complemented by Coca-Cola Foods, a solid long-term performer.

If you refer back to Figures 8–2, 8–3, and 8–4, the skills and resources required to support differentiation, rapid response, and market focus appear to be consistent with the resources available to Coke. Its decision to employ differentiation is easily apparent to any consumer. Its choice of market focus—beverages worldwide—leverages its increasing global presence and power. Rapid response through unmatched inbound and outbound logistics is supported and reinforced through its continued investment in infrastructure.

Another way to visualize strategic analysis and choice at Coke centers around the basic notion that strategists seek strategy alternatives offering a strong "fit" with a firm's overall situation. Two approaches—the grand strategy selection matrix and the model of grand strategy clusters—suggest sets of strategic alternatives associated with different strategic situations. Applying the first approach, Coca-Cola has long been in the situation of maximizing several strengths, while also preferring to emphasize "internally" generated growth. The grand strategy selection matrix would suggest concentrated growth, market development, product development, and innovation. These strategies are just what Coca-Cola has emphasized in its core soft-drink business, which it has returned to even more in the 1990s. Coke seeks first to hold and expand current market positions; then expand into new, particularly international as well as previously underemphasized outlets (e.g., restaurants, airlines); and also gradually add new product versions or those preferred in key local markets.

At the same time, Coca-Cola's management watched with some apprehension during the late 1970s as Pepsi's increasingly concentrated bottling network was out-distributing and out-marketing Coke's independent (franchised) bottlers in many local domestic markets. Pepsi's fewer, newer, and larger franchise bottlers were able to bring extra resources and professional management of marketing activities to bear in markets where they competed with smaller and usually older family-business franchises of Coca-Cola in the United States and in selected European countries. Applying the grand strategy selection matrix to overcome this relative "weakness," Coca-Cola had to look outside the company (externally) toward its existing bottling franchise network and seek to overcome a critical weakness—a situation wherein the matrix suggests a vertical integration strategy. Coca-Cola's analysis and choice reached the same conclusion—integrate forward into soft-drink bottling. To pursue this capital-intensive strategy, Coke decided to sell Columbia Pictures (net $1.3 billion) as well as create and take Coca-Cola Enterprises (CCE—a bottling franchise company) public to raise another source of funds. Coke remained a 49 percent owner and used CCE to buy old Coke bottling franchises in the United States and abroad so it could create bigger, more modern, and aggressive distributors-marketers of Coca-Cola's soft drinks in each local market. This allowed Coke to neutralize Pepsi's previous advantage in key markets.

The model of grand strategy clusters would focus on the market growth and strength of Coke's competitive position. The conclusion suggested by that model as portrayed in Figure 8–5 would have Coca-Cola's management following concentrated growth (includes market and product development), vertical integration, and, perhaps, concentric diversification when the success of the other strategies starts to fade. Indeed, this set of grand strategies is very similar to those suggested by the model of grand strategy clusters and appears to be the basic grand strategies Coca-Cola's management has charted toward the 21st century.

9

STRATEGIC ANALYSIS AND CHOICE IN THE MULTIBUSINESS COMPANY: RATIONALIZING DIVERSIFICATION AND BUILDING SHAREHOLDER VALUE

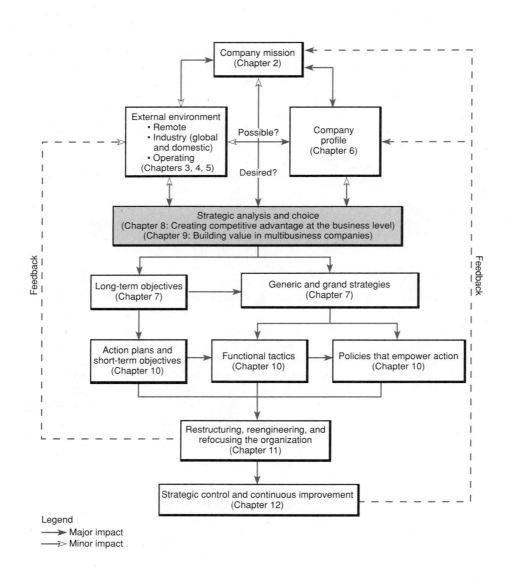

Legend
→ Major impact
⇢ Minor impact

Strategic analysis and choice is more complicated for corporate-level managers because they must create a strategy to guide a company that contains numerous businesses. They must examine and choose which businesses to own and which ones to forgo or divest. They must consider business managers' plans to capture competitive advantage, and then decide how to allocate resources among businesses as part of this phase. This chapter will first examine diversified, multibusiness companies. Specifically, how should the diversified business build shareholder value? For example, MCI has decided to pursue an aggressive diversification program to expand its presence in a variety of different industries; AT&T has recently decided to split into three separate companies while divesting itself of other businesses. Why?

A final topic that is important to an understanding of strategic analysis and choice in business organization is the "nonbusiness," behavioral factors that often exert a major influence on strategic decisions. This is true in the single-product business as well as the multibusiness company. What behavioral considerations often influence how managers analyze strategic options and make strategic choices? For example, J. E. Schrempp became CEO of Germany's Daimler Benz in mid-1995 as planned, having taken over from his mentor, Edzard Reuter, with whom he had charted a steady 10-year diversification to build a $74 billion company. Three months later, Schrempp reversed the strategy to break up the company, focus on core businesses, and reconstruct a new management team. How could such a dramatic, sudden shift take place? Answering that question requires you to consider behavioral factors as well as strategic issues at Daimler Benz.

RATIONALIZING DIVERSIFICATION AND INTEGRATION

When a single- or dominant-business company is transformed into a collection of numerous businesses across several industries, strategic analysis becomes more complex. Managers must deal not only with each business's strategic situation, they must set forth a corporate strategy that rationalizes the collection of businesses they have amassed. Two key audiences are listening. First, managers within the organization want to understand their role and access to resources relative to other businesses within the company. Second, and of greatest importance, stockholders deserve to understand how this collection of businesses is expected to build shareholder value over the long term more effectively than simply investing in separate businesses. In a sense the question is: "Are there compelling reasons why corporate management is better able to invest shareholder value in a variety of other businesses versus allowing shareholders to make that decision themselves?"

Stockholder value in a diversified company is ultimately determined by how well its various businesses perform and/or how compelling potential synergies and opportunities appear to be. Business-level performance is enhanced by sustained competitive advantages. Wise diversification has at its core the search for ways to build value and sustained competitive advantage across multiple business units. We saw several ways opportunities for sharing and building value may be present across different businesses. The bottom line is that diversification that shares skills and core competencies across multiple businesses to strengthen value chains and build competitive advantage enhances shareholder value. And so it is that strategic analysis and choice for corporate managers overseeing multibusiness companies involves determining whether their portfolio of business units is capturing the synergies they intended, how to respond accordingly, and choosing among future diversification or divestiture options. Managers address the following four basic questions to do this.

FIGURE 9–1
Value Building in Multibusiness Companies

Opportunities to Build Value or Sharing	Potential Competitive Advantage	Impediments to Achieving Enhanced Value
Market-Related Opportunities:		
Shared sales force activities or shared sales office, or both.	Lower selling costs. Better market coverage. Stronger technical advice to buyers. Enhanced convenience for buyers (can buy from single source). Improved access to buyers (have more products to sell).	• Buyers have different purchasing habits toward the products. • Different salespersons are more effective in representing the product. • Some products get more attention than others. • Buyers prefer to multiple-source rather than single-source their purchases.
Shared after-sale service and repair work.	Lower servicing costs. Better utilization of service personnel (less idle time). Faster servicing of customer calls.	• Different equipment or different labor skills, or both, are needed to handle repairs. • Buyers may do some in-house repairs.
Shared brand name.	Stronger brand image and company reputation. Increased buyer confidence in the brand.	• Company reputation is hurt if quality of one product is lower.
Shared advertising and promotional activities.	Lower costs. Greater clout in purchasing ads.	• Appropriate forms of messages are different. • Appropriate timing of promotions is different.
Common distribution channels.	Lower distribution costs. Enhanced bargaining power with distributors and retailers to gain shelf space, shelf positioning, stronger push and more dealer attention, and better profit margins.	• Dealers resist being dominated by a single supplier and turn to multiple sources and lines. • Heavy use of the shared channel erodes willingness of other channels to carry or push the firm's products.
Shared order processing.	Lower order processing costs. One-stop shopping for buyer enhances service and, thus, differentiation.	• Differences in ordering cycles disrupt order processing economies.

Are Opportunities for Sharing Infrastructure and Capabilities Forthcoming?

Opportunities to build value via diversification, integration, or joint venture strategies are usually found in market-related, operating-related, and management activities. Each business's basic value chain activities or infrastructure become a source of potential synergy and competitive advantage for another business in the corporate portfolio. Morrison's Cafeteria, long a mainstay in U.S. food services markets, rapidly accelerated its diversification into other restaurant concepts like Ruby Tuesdays. Numerous opportunities for shared operating capabilities and management capabilities drove this decision and, upon repeated strategic analysis, has accelerated corporate managers to move Morrison's totally out of the cafeteria segment by 1999. Some of the more common opportunities to share value chain activities and build value are identified in Figure 9–1.

Strategic analysis is concerned with whether or not the potential competitive advantages expected to arise from each value opportunity have materialized. Where advantage has not materialized, corporate strategists must take care to scrutinize possible impediments to achieving the synergy or competitive advantage. We have identified in Figure 9–1 several impediments associated with each opportunity, which strategists are well advised to examine. Good strategists assure themselves that their organization has ways to avoid or

FIGURE 9–1
concluded

Opportunities to Build Value or Sharing	Potential Competitive Advantage	Impediments to Achieving Enhanced Value
Operating Opportunities:		
Joint procurement of purchased inputs.	Lower input costs. Improved input quality. Improved service from suppliers.	• Input needs are different in terms of quality or other specifications. • Inputs are needed at different plant locations, and centralized purchasing is not responsive to separate needs of each plant.
Shared manufacturing and assembly facilities.	Lower manufacturing/assembly costs. Better capacity utilization, because peak demand for one product correlates with valley demand for other. Bigger scale of operation improves access to better technology and results in better quality.	• Higher changeover costs in shifting from one product to another. • High-cost special tooling or equipment is required to accommodate quality differences or design differences.
Shared inbound or outbound shipping and materials handling.	Lower freight and handling costs. Better delivery reliability. More frequent deliveries, such that inventory costs are reduced.	• Input sources or plant locations, or both, are in different geographic areas. • Needs for frequency and reliability of inbound/outbound delivery differ among the business units.
Shared product and process technologies or technology development or both.	Lower product or process design costs, or both, because of shorter design times and transfers of knowledge from area to area. More innovative ability, owing to scale of effort and attraction of better R&D personnel.	• Technologies are the same, but the applications in different business units are different enough to prevent much sharing of real value.
Shared administrative support activities.	Lower administrative and operating overhead costs.	• Support activities are not a large proportion of cost, and sharing has little cost impact (and virtually no differentiation impact).
Management Opportunities:		
Shared management know-how, operating skills, and proprietary information.	Efficient transfer of a distinctive competence—can create cost savings or enhance differentiation. More effective management as concerns strategy formulation, strategy implementation, and understanding of key success factors.	• Actual transfer of know-how is costly or stretches the key skill personnel too thinly, or both. • Increased risks that proprietary information will leak out.

Source: Adapted with the permission of The Free Press, a Division of Simon and Schuster, from *Competitive Advantage: Creating and Sustaining Superior Performance,* by Michael E. Porter. Copyright © 1985 by Michael E. Porter.

minimize the impact of any impediments or they recommend against further integration or diversification and consider divestiture options.

Two elements are critical in meaningful shared opportunities. First, the shared opportunities must be a significant portion of the value chain of the businesses involved. Returning to Morrison's Cafeteria, its purchasing and inbound logistics infrastructure give Ruby Tuesday's operators an immediate cost-effective purchasing and inventory management capability that lowered its cost in a significant cost activity. Second, the businesses involved must truly have shared needs—need for the same activity—or there is no basis for synergy in the first place. Novell, the U.S.-based networking software giant, paid $900 million for WordPerfect in late 1994, envisioning numerous synergies serving offices

DAIMLER'S DIVERSIFICATION DILEMMA

Inspired by the success of General Electric in the United States, where a dull electrical firm was turned into a successful diversified group by the drive and deal-making of Jack Welch, Edzard Reuter at Daimler Benz thought he could do the same by accelerating from luxury cars into aerospace and transport equipment. The early 1990s saw Germany's biggest company handing out a glossy document called *The New Age* in which Reuter boasted that he had transformed the firm from a luxury car maker into an "integrated technology group" involved in aerospace, microelectronics, and many kinds of transportation.

With a sense of conquest and closure, Reuter boasted of returning the company to profitability in 1994 ($DM 750 million on $DM 74 billion in diversified sales) as he predicted higher profits for 1995 and turned over the reins of the company to his heir-apparent of 10 years, Jurgen Schrempp. Three months into 1995, Daimler Benz was in disarray.

The soaring German mark, management disputes, and losses from Reuter's diversification strategy were causing analysts to turn negative on the company as Schrempp reversed Reuter's parting forecast and warned of severe 1995 losses by year-end ($DM 1.6 billion by mid-year).

By late 1995 analysts were saying that Schrempp had to act quickly and dismantle and reverse the diversification strategy his mentor, with Schrempp's help, had spent the previous 10 years implementing. Here were some of the recommendations analysts were making:

1. Make a decisive break with the failed diversification strategy.
2. Focus on the core automotive and truck business, which provides most of the profit anyway.
3. Close the money-losing Daimler Benz Industrie unit; sell off or transfer profitable operations.
4. Downsize Daimler Benz Aerospace by cutting its work force of 40,000 to 20,000 and accelerate outsourcing of parts from weak-currency areas. Consider divesting.
5. Accelerate globalization of manufacturing by locating big-ticket plants outside Germany.

Bottom line, analysts do not think the synergies originally expected in Reuter's diversification have occurred. Daimler's stock price, down 30 percent during Reuter's reign, doesn't compare with BMW's 50 percent increase.

Schrempp's remarks to the financial press during this uncertain time in late 1995 continued to publicly defend Reuter's strategy; however, he has begun to distance himself a bit by talking about strengthening Daimler as an "integrated transportation company" rather than the "integrated high-tech concern" as Reuter did.

Now it is your turn. What do you think he should have done? What do you suspect he has done since late 1995? Did diversification make sense or were the analysts right? Look up Daimler's stock price on the German DAX or the NYSE and read an article about Daimler Benz to see what Schrempp has done.

Sources: "A Tale of Two Conglomerates," *The Economist*, November 18, 1995, p. 20; "Dismantling Daimler Benz," *The Economist*, November 18, 1995, pp. 67–68, 77–78; "Failed Diversification," *German Brief*, April 8, 1994, pp. 4–5; and "There's Virtue in Diversification," *Euromoney*, November 1994, pp. 70–71.

globally not to mention 15 million WordPerfect users. By late 1995 Novell would sell WordPerfect for less than $300 million, because, as new CEO Bob Frankenberg said, "It is not because WordPerfect is not a business without a future, but for Novell it represented a distraction from our strategy." Corporate strategies have repeatedly rushed into diversification only to find perceived opportunities for sharing were nonexistent because the businesses did not really have shared needs. Global Strategy in Action 9–1 examines just this dilemma at Germany's Daimler Benz.

Are We Capitalizing on Our Core Competencies?

Perhaps the most compelling reason companies should diversify can be found in situations where core competencies—key value-building skills—can be leveraged with other products or into markets that are not a part of where they were created. Where this works well, extraordinary value can be built. Managers undertaking diversification strategies should dedicate a significant portion of their strategic analysis to this question.

General Cinema was a company that grew from drive-in theaters to eventually dominate the multicinema, movie exhibition industry. Next, they entered soft-drink bottling and became the largest bottler of soft drinks (Pepsi) in North America. Their stock value rose 2,000 percent in 10 years. They found that core competencies in movie exhibition— managing many small, localized businesses; dealing with a few large suppliers; applying central marketing skills locally; and acquiring or crafting a "franchise"—were virtually the same in soft-drink bottling. Disney and ABC see shared core competencies as central in the entertainment industry of the 21st century (see Strategy in Action 9–1). AT&T and McCall Cellular see shared core competencies as central to telecommunications success. These and many more companies look to three basic considerations to evaluate whether they are capitalizing on core competencies.[1]

Is Each Core Competency Providing a Relevant Competitive Advantage to the Intended Businesses?

The core competency must assist the intended business in creating strength relative to key competition. This could occur at any step in the business's value chain. But it must represent a major source of value to be a basis for competitive advantage—and the core competence must be transferrable. Honda of Japan viewed itself as having a core competence in manufacturing small, internal combustion engines. It diversified into small garden tools, perceiving that traditional electric tools would be much more attractive if powered by a lightweight, mobile, gas combustion motor. Their core competency created a major competitive advantage in a market void of gas-driven hand tools. When Coca-Cola added bottled water to its portfolio of products, it expected its extraordinary core competencies in marketing and distribution to rapidly build value in this business. Ten years later, Coke sold its water assets concluding that the product did not have enough margin to interest its franchised bottlers and that marketing was not a significant value-building activity among many small suppliers competing primarily on the cost of "producing" and shipping water.

Are Businesses in the Portfolio Related in Ways That Make the Company's Core Competence(s) Beneficial?

Earlier, we described General Cinema's spectacular success in both movie exhibition and soft-drink bottling. Seemingly unrelated, their management found that core competencies in various aspects of managing diverse business locations were key value chain components in both industries. So the products of various businesses do not necessarily have to be similar to leverage core competencies. While their products may not be related, it is essential that some activities in their value chains require similar skills to create competitive advantage if the company is going to leverage its core competence(s) in a value-creating way.

---

[1] C. K. Prahalad and G. Hamel, "The Core Competence of the Corporation," *Harvard Business Review*, May–June 1990, pp. 79–91; and M. Porter, "From Competitive Advantage to Corporate Strategy," *Harvard Business Review*, May–June 1987, pp. 43–59.

DISNEY DEMONSTRATES THE ABC'S
OF DIVERSIFICATION

The recent acquisition of ABC/Capital Cities by Disney was the most visible merger among the many that took place in 1995 as the rapidly changing media industry continued its dramatic upheavals. It was the second largest corporate takeover ever done. Walt Disney and ABC/Capital Cities have joined their businesses, including the following.

	Walt Disney	**ABC/Capital Cities**
Production	Walt Disney Pictures Touchstone Pictures	ABC Productions
Distribution		11 company-owned TV stations 228 TV affiliates 21 radio stations
Cable	Disney Channel	ESPN, Lifetime, A&E
Publishing		Newspapers in 13 states Fairchild Publications Chilton Publications

Most analysts viewed the Disney-ABC merger favorably. Here is what they said shortly after the deal was done:

1. The combination of the two companies creates a sizable player that transforms the balance of power in the entertainment industry by becoming the industry's most influential player.
2. Recent rule changes will permit networks (like ABC) to own more of their own programming, enhancing their value and challenging outside suppliers (like Disney), leaving the suppliers fearful of less "shelf space" for their products.

Are Our Combination of Competencies Unique or Difficult to Recreate?

Skills that corporate strategists expect to transfer from one business to another, or from corporate to various businesses, may be transferrable. They may also be easily replicated by competitors. When this is the case, no sustainable competitive advantage is created. Sometimes strategists look for a combination of competencies, a package of various inter-related skills, as another way to create a situation where seemingly easily replicated competencies become unique, sustainable competitive advantages. 3M Corporation has the enviable record of having 25 percent of its earnings always coming from products introduced within the last five years. 3M has been able to "bundle" the skills necessary to accelerate the introduction of new products so that it consistently extracts early life cycle value from adhesive-related products that hundreds of competitors with similar technical or marketing competencies cannot touch.

Does the Company's Business Portfolio Balance Financial Resources?

Multibusiness companies usually find that their various businesses generate and consume very different levels of cash. Some generate more cash than they can use to maintain or expand their business while others consume more than they generate. Corporate managers

3. The more forms of information delivery a company owns, the greater their power. Brands such as ABC and ESPN get people's attention.

4. "Content is king" was the traditional view attributing power to a studio like Disney; More recently distribution outlets have become key as demonstrated by Rupert Murdoch's Fox Network—many stations and satellite and cable channels to deliver product to viewers.

5. Eisner previously thought distribution was distasteful. Rupert Murdoch changed all of that. Cap Cities thrusts Disney into the distribution business in a big way. Eisner says it does more, since ABC produces and delivers programming over air and cable. And it provides a guaranteed platform for its first-run syndicated programs—shows that might otherwise die on the vine.

6. Financially, Disney takes on $10 billion in debt; however, it expects $5 billion annually in cash flow to quickly pay down the debt. Now Disney's growth can continue strongly like it has the last five years.

7. Disney has been weak internationally, but ABC has been strong. ESPN is well known. Disney can learn from ABC about developing foreign contacts and building distribution. In foreign markets, entertainment has become a leading U.S. export.

8. ABC is among the industry's best run. Disney reaps profits from all the shows the network airs, whether it produces them or not.

9. Disney has creative capabilities and a production track record second to none, which ABC can leverage.

face the very important challenge of determining the best way to generate and use financial resources among the businesses within their company. Faced with this challenge, managers historically looked to balance cash generators and cash users so that, along with outside capital sources, they can efficiently manage the cash flows across their business portfolio.

Responding to this challenge during the diversification explosion of the 1970s, the Boston Consulting Group pioneered an approach called *portfolio techniques* that attempted to help managers "balance" the flow of cash resources among their various businesses while also identifying their basic strategic purpose within the overall portfolio. Three of these techniques are reviewed here. Once reviewed, we will identify some of the problems with the portfolio approach that you should keep in mind when considering its use.

The BCG Growth-Share Matrix

Managers using the BCG matrix plotted each of the company's businesses according to market growth rate and relative competitive position. Market growth rate is the projected rate of sales growth for the market being served by a particular business. Usually measured as the percentage increase in a market's sales or unit volume over the two most recent years, this rate serves as an indicator of the relative attractiveness of the markets served by each business in the firm's portfolio of businesses. Relative competitive position usually is

FIGURE 9–2
The BCG Growth-Share Matrix

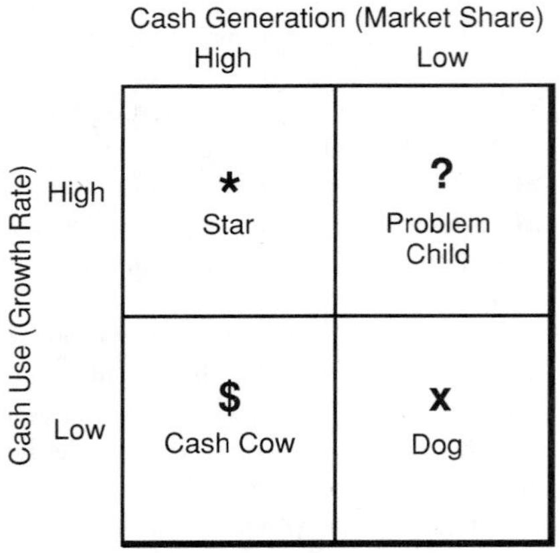

Cash Generation (Market Share)

Description of Dimensions

Market Share: Sales relative to those of other competitors in the market
(dividing point is usually selected to have only the two–three largest
competitors in any market fall into the high market share region)

Growth Rate: Industry growth rate in constant dollars
(dividing point is typically the GNP's growth rate)

Source: The growth-share matrix was originally developed by the Boston Consulting Group.

expressed as the market share of a business divided by the market share of its largest competitor. Thus, relative competitive position provides a basis for comparing the relative strengths of the businesses in the firm's portfolio in terms of their positions in their respective markets. Figure 9–2 illustrates the growth-share matrix.

The *stars* are businesses in rapidly growing markets with large market shares. These businesses represent the best long-run opportunities (growth and profitability) in the firm's portfolio. They require substantial investment to maintain (and expand) their dominant position in a growing market. This investment requirement is often in excess of the funds that they can generate internally. Therefore, these businesses are often short-term, priority consumers of corporate resources.

Cash cows are businesses with a high market share in low-growth markets or industries. Because of their strong positions and their minimal reinvestment requirements, these businesses often generate cash in excess of their needs. Therefore, they are selectively "milked" as a source of corporate resources for deployment elsewhere (to stars and question marks). Cash cows are yesterday's stars and the current foundation of corporate portfolios. They provide the cash needed to pay corporate overhead and dividends and provide debt capacity. They are managed to maintain their strong market share while generating excess resources for corporatewide use.

Low market share and low market growth businesses are the *dogs* in the firm's portfolio. Facing mature markets with intense competition and low profit margins, they are managed for short-term cash flow (through ruthless cost cutting, for example) to supplement corporate-level resource needs. According to the original BCG prescription, they are divested or liquidated once this short-term harvesting has been maximized.

Question marks are businesses whose high growth rate gives them considerable appeal but whose low market share makes their profit potential uncertain. Question marks are cash guzzlers because their rapid growth results in high cash needs, while their small market share results in low cash generation. At the corporate level, the concern is to identify the question marks that would increase their market share and move into the star group if extra corporate resources were devoted to them. Where this long-run shift from question mark to star is unlikely, the BCG matrix suggests divesting the question mark and repositioning its resources more effectively in the remainder of the corporate portfolio.

The Industry Attractiveness–Business Strength Matrix

Corporate strategists found the growth-share matrix's singular axes limiting in their ability to reflect the complexity of a business's situation. Therefore, some companies adopted a matrix with a much broader focus. This matrix, developed by McKinsey & Company at General Electric, is called the Industry Attractiveness–Business Strength Matrix. This matrix, shown in Figure 9–4, uses multiple factors to assess industry attractiveness and business strength rather than the single measures (market share and market growth, respectively) employed in the BCG matrix. It also has nine cells as opposed to four—replacing the high/low axes with high/medium/low axes to make finer distinctions among business portfolio positions.

The company's businesses are rated on multiple strategic factors within each axis, such as the factors described in Figure 9–3.[2] The position of a business is then calculated by "subjectively" quantifying its rating along the two dimensions of the matrix. Depending on the location of a business within the matrix, one of the following strategic approaches is suggested: (1) invest to grow, (2) invest selectively and manage for earnings, or (3) harvest or divest for resources. The resource allocation decisions remain quite similar to those of the BCG approach.

Although the strategic recommendations generated by the Industry Attractiveness–Business Strength Matrix are similar to those generated by the BCG matrix, the Industry Attractiveness–Business Strength Matrix improves on the BCG matrix in three fundamental ways. First, the terminology associated with the Industry Attractiveness–Business Strength Matrix is preferable because it is less offensive and more understandable. Second, the multiple measures associated with each dimension of the business strength matrix tap many factors relevant to business strength and market attractiveness besides market share and market growth. And this, in turn, makes for broader assessment during the planning process, bringing to light considerations of importance in both strategy formulation and strategy implementation. Strategy in Action 9–2 illustrates the matrix approach as applied at Holiday Inns over the last 20 years.

The Life Cycle–Competitive Strength Matrix

One criticism of the first two portfolio methods was their static quality—their portrayal of businesses as they exist at one point in time, rather than as they evolve over time. A third portfolio approach was introduced that attempted to overcome these deficiencies and better identify "developing winners" or potential "losers."[3] This approach used the multiple-factor approach to assess competitive strength as one dimension and stage of the market life cycle as the other dimension.

---

[2] G. G. Dess and A. Miller, *Strategic Management* (New York: McGraw-Hill, 1993), pp. 110–11.

[3] Attributed to Arthur D. Little, a consulting firm, and to Charles W. Hofer in "Conceptual Constructs for Formulating Corporate and Business Strategies" (Boston: Harvard Case Services, #9-378-754, 1977).

FIGURE 9-3
Factors Considered in Constructing an Industry Attractiveness–Business Strength Matrix

Industry Attractiveness	Business Strength
Nature of Competitive Rivalry	**Cost Position**
Number of competitors	Economies of scale
Size of competitors	Manufacturing costs
Strength of competitors' corporate parents	Overhead
Price wars	Scrap/waste/rework
Competition on multiple dimensions	Experience effects
	Labor rates
Bargaining Power of Suppliers/Customers	Proprietary processes
Relative size of typical players	**Level of Differentiation**
Numbers of each	Promotion effectiveness
Importance of purchases from or sales to	Product quality
Ability to vertically integrate	Company image
	Patented products
Threat of Substitute Products/New Entrants	Brand awareness
Technological maturity/stability	**Response Time**
Diversity of the market	Manufacturing flexibility
Barriers to entry	Time needed to introduce new products
Flexibility of distribution system	Delivery times
	Organizational flexibility
Economic Factors	
Sales volatility	**Financial Strength**
Cyclicality of demand	Solvency
Market growth	Liquidity
Capital intensity	Break-even point
	Cash flows
Financial Norms	Profitability
Average profitability	Growth in revenues
Typical leverage	**Human Assets**
Credit practices	Turnover
	Skill level
Sociopolitical Considerations	Relative wage/salary
Government regulation	Morale
Community support	Managerial commitment
Ethical standards	Unionization
	Public Approval
	Goodwill
	Reputation
	Image

The life cycle dimension allowed users to consider multiple strategic issues associated with each life cycle stage (refer to the discussion in Chapter 6), thereby enriching the discussion of strategic options. It also gave a "moving indication" of both issues—those strategy needs to address currently and those that could arise next. Figure 9–5 on page 291 provides an illustration of this matrix. It includes basic strategic investment parameters recommended for different positions in the matrix. While this approach seems valuable, its recommendations are virtually identical to the previous two portfolio matrices.

Limitations of Portfolio Approaches

Portfolio approaches made several contributions to strategic analysis by corporate managers convinced of their ability to transfer the competitive advantage of professional management across a broad array of businesses. They helped convey large amounts of information about diverse business units and corporate plans in a greatly simplified format. They

FIGURE 9–4
The Industry Attractiveness–Business Strength Matrix

Industry Attractiveness

	High	Medium	Low
High	Invest	Selective Growth	Grow or Let Go
Medium	Selective Growth	Grow or Let Go	Harvest
Low	Grow or Let Go	Harvest	Divest

(Business Strength on vertical axis)

Description of Dimensions

Industry Attractiveness: Subjective assessment based on broadest possible range of external opportunities and threats beyond the strict control of management

Business Strength: Subjective assessment of how strong a competitive advantage is created by a broad range of the firm's internal strengths and weaknesses.

Source: McKinsey & Company and General Electric.

illuminated similarities and differences between business units and helped convey the logic behind corporate strategies for each business with a common vocabulary. They simplified priorities for sharing corporate resources across diverse business units that generated and used those resources. They provided a simple prescription that gave corporate managers a sense of what they should accomplish—a balanced portfolio of businesses—and a way to control and allocate resources among them. While these approaches offered meaningful contributions, they had several critical limitations and shortcomings:

· A key problem with the portfolio matrix was that it did not address how value was being created across business units—the only relationship between them was cash. Because of this, its valued simplicity encouraged a tendency to trivialize strategic thinking among users that did not take proper time for thorough underlying analysis.

· Truly accurate measurement for matrix classification was not as easy as the matrices portrayed. Identifying individual businesses, or distinct markets, was not often as precise as underlying assumptions required.

· The underlying assumption about the relationship between market share and profitability—the experience curve effect—varied across different industries and

STRATEGY
IN ACTION
9–2

FROM HOLIDAY INNS TO HOLIDAY CORPORATION TO THE PROMUS COMPANIES: A STORY OF CORPORATE PORTFOLIO MANAGEMENT

In 1952, Kemmons Wilson started Holiday Inns to meet what he perceived to be a glaring need for affordable, consistent lodging throughout the United States and ultimately the world. Extraordinarily successful, Holiday Inns became and still is the largest lodging chain in the world, with three times the number of rooms as its nearest competitor. While this story generally is known to most of us, the fact Holiday Inns became a portfolio of businesses that has changed dramatically over the last 20 years is not. Following this latter story is an interesting journey in the application of corporate portfolio analysis.

By 1977, its 25th year, Holiday Inns Corporation was seen as a travel-related company, with several businesses Kemmons Wilson viewed as strategically related. The corporate portfolio looked as follows:

1977: Holiday Inn Corporation

	Revenue	Operating Income
A. Holiday Inns	$590 mm	$90 mm
B. Trailways Bus Lines	244 mm	16 mm
C. Delta Steamships	80 mm	17 mm
D. Products Group:	144 mm	6 mm
1. InnKeepers Supply		
2. Dohrmann		
3. Innkare		

Over the next five years, Kemmons Wilson would step down to be replaced by his long-time vice chairman and COO, Roy Winegardner. Holiday Inns' board, spurred by their young president, Mike Rose, began to view Holiday Inns as a portfolio of businesses needing significant change. Acting consistently with the strategic suggestions arising from the above portfolio analysis, Trailways, Delta, and the Products Group were divested, raising approximately $280 million. That money, along with new stock and debt, was used to reposition Holiday Inns as a "hospitality company" by acquiring Harrah's and Perkins Restaurants and by seeding two new hospitality ventures.

Source: Holiday Inns Corporation 1977 annual report; Holiday Corporation 1983 annual report; The Promus Companies 1995 annual report.

market segments. Some have no such link. Some find that firms with low market share can generate superior profitability with differentiation advantages.

· The limited strategic options, intended to describe the flow of resources in a company, came to be seen more as basic strategic missions. Doing this creates a false sense of what strategies were when none really existed. This becomes more acute when attempting to use the matrices to conceive strategies for average businesses in average growth markets.

· The portfolio approach portrayed the notion that firms needed to be self-sufficient in capital. This ignored capital raised in capital markets.

STRATEGY
IN ACTION
9–2   **continued**

1983: Holiday Corporation

	Revenue	Operating Income
A. Hotel Group: 1. Holiday Inns 2. Holiday Inn Crowne Plaza	$882 mm	$168 mm
B. Gaming Group: 1. Harrah's Nevada 2. Harrah's Atlantic City	592 mm	116 mm
C. Perkins Restaurants	106 mm	5 mm
D. New Ventures: 1. Hampton Inns 2. Embassy Suites	0	−8 mm

Mike Rose soon became chairman and CEO of what in 1983 was renamed Holiday Corporation. He offered these observations at the time:

> We have completed the divestiture of our nonhospitality businesses. The major story for 1983 and the remainder of the decade is execution of our segmentation strategy in the hotel industry and in the casino gaming markets.

What Mr. Rose had done was to restructure Holiday's business portfolio, diverting resources from weak or inconsistent businesses into those with greater future promise. The real question beginning to arise via portfolio analysis was the long-term status of the Holiday Inns chain with its segment, midpriced hotel accommodations, facing increased competition and less demand. By 1992, dramatic change had occurred again.

· The portfolio approach typically failed to compare the competitive advantage a business received from being owned by a particular company with the costs of owning it. The 1980s saw many companies build enormous corporate infrastructures that created only small gains at the business level. The deconstruction in the 1990s of some "model" portfolio companies reflects this important omission.

Constructing business portfolio matrices must be undertaken with these limitations in mind. Perhaps it is best to say that they provide one form of input to corporate managers seeking to balance financial resources. They should be used merely to provide a basis for further discussion of corporate strategy and the allocation of corporate resources, and to

STRATEGY
IN ACTION
9–2

continued

1994: The Promus Companies

	Revenue	Operating Income
A. Gaming Group:	$1.1 billion	$210 mm
1. Harrah's Atlantic City		
2. Harrah's Lake Tahoe		
3. Harrah's Las Vegas		
4. Harrah's Laughlin		
5. Harrah's Reno		
B. Hotel Group:	225 mm	75 mm
1. Hampton Inns		
2. Embassy Suites		
3. Homewood Suites		

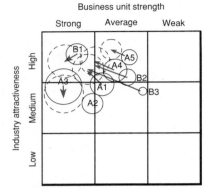

Consistent with the trend predicted and strategic recommendations emanating from the 1983 portfolio analysis, Holiday Corporation's board eventually would sell the Holiday Inns chain to the Bass group for approximately $2.5 billion. Also during this time, the Perkins Restaurant chain was sold at a net loss and Holiday Inn Crowne Suites was sold in a separate transaction. The newly created portfolio of businesses has what was originally the Holiday Inns, now Promus, positioned with two groups of businesses focused in the faster growing segments of gaming and lodging industries with what Mike Rose called "the leading brands" in each respective segment.

The evolution of Holiday Inns over the last 20 years to include getting out of the Holiday Inns business reflects a corporate portfolio management perspective very consistent with the suggestions of the BCG matrix or Industry Attractive–Business Strength matrix approaches. Indeed, so seriously were those suggestions taken to heart that Promus's largest business and the one from which it was founded was "harvested" to raise resources to support more promising business opportunities and building shareholder value.

A portfolio approach at Promus continued into 1995. On January 30, 1995, Promus announced plans to split the company into two separate, publicly traded companies. Said Mr. Rose:

> There are many good reasons for this decision. The most basic is we feel the two companies will achieve greater success as separate businesses than joined together. Like many other important decisions of the past two decades, this split narrows our focus. There are certainly similarities in our businesses and many lessons have been shared over the years. As the businesses have grown, however, the different attributes and needs of each have become more pronounced. Differences in such critical areas as sources of growth, regulatory and political issues, market visibility and capital needs all support the concept of a spin-off.

provide a picture of the "balance" of resource generators and users to test underlying assumptions about these issues in more involved corporate planning efforts to leverage core competencies to build sustained competitive advantages. For while the portfolio approaches have serious limitations, the challenge for corporate managers overseeing the allocation of resources among a variety of business units is still to maintain a balanced use of the company's financial resources.

FIGURE 9–5
The Market Life Cycle–Competitive Strength Matrix

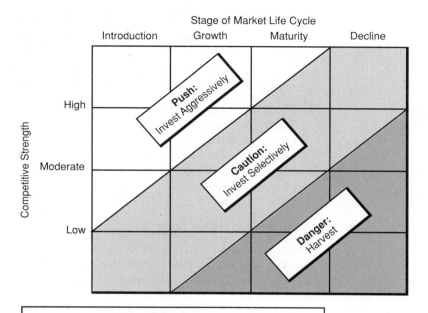

Description of Dimensions

Stage of Market Life Cycle: See page 184.

Competitive Strength: Overall subjective rating, based on a wide range of factors regarding the likelihood of gaining and maintaining a competitive advantage

Does Our Business Portfolio Achieve Appropriate Levels of Risk and Growth?

Diversification has traditionally been recommended as a way to manage, or diversify, risk. Said another way, "not having all your eggs in one basket" allows corporate managers to potentially reduce risk to company stockholders. Balancing cyclical revenue streams to reduce earnings volatility is one way diversification may reduce risk. So managers need to ask this question as a part of their strategic analysis and subsequent choice. Likewise, revenue growth can be enhanced by diversification. Many companies in the hazardous waste industry maintained the steady growth investors had come to expect by continuously making acquisitions of other businesses to gain immediate sales growth.

Both risk and growth are assumptions or priorities corporate managers should carefully examine as they undertake strategic analysis and choice. Is growth always desirable? Can risks truly be managed most effectively by corporate management? Many companies have pursued growth to gain market share without accompanying attention to profitability. Similarly, companies have built diverse business portfolios in part to manage overall risk. In both instances, the outcome is often a later time when subsequent management must "look in the bag" of businesses and aggressively divest and downsize the company until true value-adding activities and synergies linked to sustained competitive advantages are uncovered. Global Strategy-in-Action 9–1 describes just such a situation at Germany's largest company, Daimler Benz.

BEHAVORIAL CONSIDERATIONS AFFECTING STRATEGIC CHOICE

After alternative strategies have been analyzed, managers choose one of those strategies. If the analysis identified a clearly superior strategy or if the current strategy will clearly meet future company objectives, then the decision is relatively simple. Such clarity is the exception, however, and strategic decision makers often are confronted with several viable alternatives rather than the luxury of a clear-cut choice. Under these circumstances, several factors influence the strategic choice. Some of the more important are:

1. Role of the current strategy.
2. Degree of the firm's external dependence.
3. Attitudes toward risk.
4. Internal political considerations.
5. Timing.
6. Competitive reaction.

Role of the Current Strategy

Current strategists are often the architects of past strategies. If they have invested substantial time, resources, and interest in those strategies, they logically would be more comfortable with a choice that closely parallels or involves only incremental alterations to the current strategy.

Such familiarity with and commitment to past strategy permeates the entire firm. Thus, lower-level managers reinforce the top managers' inclination toward continuity with past strategy during the choice process. Research in several companies found lower-level managers suggested strategic choices that were consistent with current strategy and likely to be accepted while withholding suggestions with less probability of approval. Research by Henry Mintzberg suggests that past strategy strongly influences current strategic choice. The older and more successful a strategy has been, the harder it is to replace. Similarly, once a strategy has been initiated, it is very difficult to change because organizational momentum keeps it going. Even as a strategy begins to fail due to changing conditions, strategists often increase their commitment to it. Thus, firms may replace top executives when performance has been inadequate for an extended period because replacing these executives lessens the influence of unsuccessful past strategy on future strategic choice.

Degree of the Firm's External Dependence

If a firm is highly dependent on one or more environmental elements, its strategic alternatives and its ultimate strategic choice must accommodate that dependence. The greater a firm's external dependence, the lower its range and flexibility in strategic choice.

Bama Pies is a great family business success story. It makes excellent pies—apple turnovers. For many years, Bama Pies sold most of its pie output to one customer—McDonald's. With its massive retail coverage and its access to alternative suppliers. McDonald's was a major external dependence for Bama Pies. Bama Pies' strategic alternatives and ultimate choice of strategy were limited and strongly influenced by McDonald's demands. Bama Pies carefully narrowed its grand strategy and important related decisions in areas such as research and development, pricing, distribution, and product design with its critical dependence on McDonald's in mind.

Progressive firms accept external dependencies as a more positive reality—perhaps a source of competitive advantage. In the push for higher, more consistent quality, these firms seek to view key suppliers and customers as "partners" in strategic and operating decisions. More on this in Chapter 11.

Attitudes toward Risk

Attitudes toward risk exert considerable influence on strategic choice. Where attitudes favor risk, the range of the strategic choices expands and high-risk strategies are acceptable and desirable. Where management is risk averse, the range of strategic choices is limited and risky alternatives are eliminated before strategic choices are made. Past strategy exerts far more influence on the strategic choices of risk-averse managers.

Industry volatility influences the propensity of managers toward risk. Top managers in highly volatile industries absorb and operate with greater amounts of risk than do their counterparts in stable industries. Therefore, top managers in volatile industries consider a broader, more diverse range of strategies in the strategic choice process.

Industry evolution is another determinant of managerial propensity toward risk. A firm in the early stages of the product-market cycle must operate with considerably greater risk and uncertainty than a firm in the later stages of that cycle.

In making a strategic choice, risk-oriented managers lean toward opportunistic strategies with higher payoffs. They are drawn to offensive strategies based on innovation, company strengths, and operating potential. Risk-averse managers lean toward safe, conservative strategies with reasonable, highly probable returns. They are drawn to defensive strategies that minimize a firm's weaknesses, external threats, and the uncertainty associated with innovation-based strategies.

Internal Political Considerations

Power/political factors influence strategic choice. The use of power to further individual or group interest is common in organizational life. A major source of power in most firms is the chief executive officer (CEO). In smaller firms, the CEO is consistently the dominant force in strategic choice. Regardless of firm size, when the CEO begins to favor a particular choice, it is often selected unanimously.

Coalitions are power sources that influence strategic choice. In large firms, subunits and individuals (particularly key managers) have reason to support some alternatives and oppose others. Mutual interest draws certain groups together in coalitions to enhance their position on major strategic issues. These coalitions, particularly the more powerful ones (often called *dominant coalitions*), exert considerable influence on the strategic choice process. Numerous studies confirm the frequent use of power and coalitions in strategic decision making.

Figure 9–6 shows that the *content* of strategic decisions and the *processes* of arriving at such decisions are politically charged. Each phase in the process of strategic choice presents an opportunity for political action intended to influence the outcome. The challenge for strategists lies in recognizing and managing this political influence. For example, selecting the criteria used to compare alternative strategies or collecting and appraising information regarding those criteria may be particularly susceptible to political influence. This possibility must be recognized and, where necessary, "managed" to avoid dysfunctional political bias. Relying on different sources to collect and appraise information might serve this purpose.

Organizational politics must be viewed as an inevitable dimension of organizational decision making that strategic management must accommodate. Some authors argue that politics is a key ingredient in the "glue" that holds an organization together. Formal and

FIGURE 9–6
Political Activities in Phases of Strategic Decision Making

Phases of Strategic Decision Making	Focus of Political Action	Examples of Political Activity
Identification and diagnosis of strategic issues.	Control of: Issues to be discussed. Cause-and-effect relationships to be examined.	Control agenda. Interpretation of past events and future trends.
Narrowing the alternative strategies for serious consideration.	Control of alternatives.	Mobilization: Coalition formation. Resource commitment for information search.
Examining and choosing the strategy.	Control of choice.	Selective advocacy of criteria. Search and representation of information to justify choice.
Initiating implementation of the strategy.	Interaction between winners and losers.	Winners attempt to "sell" or co-opt losers. Losers attempt to thwart decisions and trigger fresh strategic issues.
Designing procedures for the evaluation of results.	Representing oneself as successful.	Selective advocacy of criteria.

Source: Adapted from Liam Fahey and V. K. Naroyanan, "The Politics of Strategic Decision Making," in *The Strategic Management Handbook*, ed. Kenneth J. Albert (New York: McGraw-Hill, 1983), pp. 21–20.

informal negotiating and bargaining between individuals, subunits, and coalitions are indispensable mechanisms for organizational coordination. Accommodating these mechanisms in the choice of strategy will result in greater commitment and more realistic strategy. The costs of doing so, however, are likely to be increased time spent on decision making and incremental (as opposed to drastic) change.

Timing

The time issue can have considerable influence on strategic choice. The most obvious way is when a time limit constrains strategic choice. A company has a six-month option to acquire another company or a key location is an example.

Another aspect of the time issue is the timing of a strategic decision. A good strategy may be disastrous if it is undertaken at the wrong time. The sudden outbreak of the Gulf War in 1991 proved disastrous for many small U.S. retailers who had expanded inventories for Spring 1991. And the sudden end of the war proved equally problematic for small military suppliers of products like Patriot missiles and body bags who had geared up for considerably increased demand.

Competitive Reaction

In weighing strategic choices, top management frequently incorporates perceptions of likely competitor reactions to those choices. For example, if it chooses an aggressive strategy directly challenging a key competitor, that competitor can be expected to mount an aggressive counterstrategy. In weighing strategic choices, top management must consider the probable impact of such reactions on the success of the chosen strategy.

The beer industry provides a good illustration. In the early 1970s, Anheuser-Busch dominated the industry, and Miller Brewing Company, recently acquired by Philip Morris, was a weak and declining competitor. Miller's management decided to adopt an expensive advertising-oriented strategy that challenged the big three (Anheuser-Busch, Pabst, and Schlitz) head-on because it assumed that their reaction would be delayed due to Miller's current declining status in the industry. This assumption proved correct, and Miller was able to reverse its trend in market share before Anheuser-Busch countered with an equally intense advertising strategy.

Miller's management took another approach in its next major strategic decision. In the mid-1970s, it introduced (and heavily advertised) a low-calorie beer—Miller Lite. Other industry members had introduced such products without much success. Miller chose a strategy that did not directly challenge its key competitors and was not expected to elicit immediate counterattacks from them. This choice proved highly successful, because Miller was able to establish a dominant share of the low-calorie beer market before those competitors decided to react. In this case, as in the preceding case, expectations regarding the reactions of competitors were a key determinant in the strategic choice made by Miller's management.

SUMMARY

This chapter examined how managers evaluate and choose their company's strategy in multibusiness settings. They look to rationalize their efforts to diversify and their current or anticipated collection of businesses. Doing this means identifying opportunities to share skills and core competencies across businesses or from corporate capabilities to business operational needs. Such opportunities usually arise in marketing, operations, management, or a combination of these activities when a capability in one area contributes to a competitive advantage in another.

Diversified, multibusiness companies face yet another, more complicated process of strategy analysis and choice. This chapter looked at the evolution of this challenge from portfolio approaches to value-based ways to decide which set of businesses maximizes opportunities to build shareholder value.

Critical, often overlooked in the process of strategic analysis and choice, are behavioral considerations that may well determine a company's choice of strategy as much or more so than solely rational analysis. Commitment to the current strategy, external dependence, political considerations, timing, and competitive considerations combine to exercise a major influence on how managers eventually evaluate and choose strategies.

QUESTIONS FOR DISCUSSION

1. How does strategic analysis at the corporate level differ from strategic analysis at the business unit level? How are they related?

2. When would multi-industry companies find the portfolio approach to strategic analysis and choice useful?

3. What are three types of opportunities for sharing that form a sound basis for diversification or vertical integration? Give an example of each from companies you have read about.

4. What role might power and politics play in strategic analysis within a multibusiness company? Strategic choice within that same company? Would you expect these issues to be more prominent in a diversified company or in a single–product line company? Why or why not?

5. Read Global Strategy in Action 9–1 about the German manufacturer Daimler Benz. Which behavioral considerations discussed in this chapter appear to have influenced strategic analysis and choice within that company over the last 10 years? Explain.

BIBLIOGRAPHY

Bart, K. Christopher. "Implementing 'Growth' and 'Harvest' Product Strategies." *California Management Review*, Summer 1987, p. 139.

Barwise, Patrick; Paul R. Marsh; and Robin Wensley. "Must Finance and Strategy Clash?" *Harvard Business Review*, September–October 1989, p. 85.

Bettis, Richard A., and William K. Hall. "Strategic Portfolio Management in the Multibusiness Firm." *California Management Review* 24 (Fall 1981), pp. 23–38.

———. "The Business Portfolio Approach—Where It Falls Down in Practice." *Long Range Planning* 16, no. 2 (April 1983), pp. 95–104.

Buzzell, R. D. "Is Vertical Integration Profitable?" *Harvard Business Review* 61 (January–February 1994), pp. 92–102.

Christensen, H. Kurt; Arnold C. Cooper; and Cornelius A. Dekluyuer. "The Dog Business: A Reexamination." *Business Horizons* 25, no. 6 (November–December 1982), pp. 12–18.

Davis, R., and L. G. Thomas "Direct Estimation of Synergy: A New Approach to the Diversity-Performance Debate." *Management Science* 39 (1993), pp. 1334–46.

Dess, Gregory G., and Nancy K. Orizer. "Environment, Structure, and Consensus in Strategy Formulation." *Academy of Management Review*, April 1987, p. 313.

Fry, J. N., and P. J. Killing. "Vision-Check." *Business Quarterly* [Canada] 54, no. 2 (1989), pp. 64–69.

Ginter, P. M.; W. J. Duncan; L. E. Swayne; and A. G. Shelfer. "When Merger Means Death: Organizational Euthanasia and Strategic Choice." *Organizational Dynamics* 20, no. 3 (1992), pp. 21–33.

Haspeslagh, Phillippe. "Portfolio Planning: Uses and Limits." *Harvard Business Review* 60, no. 1 (January–February 1982), pp. 58–73.

Haspeslagh, Phillippe C., and David B. Jamison. *Managing Acquisitions: Creating Value through Corporate Renewal*. New York: Free Press, 1991.

Hax, Arnoldo, and Nicolas S. Majluf. *Strategic Management: An Integrative Perspective*. Englewood Cliffs, NJ: Prentice Hall, 1984, chaps. 7–9.

———. *The Strategy Concept and Process*. Englewood Cliffs, NJ: Prentice Hall, 1991, chaps. 8–11 and 15.

Henderson, Bruce D. "The Application and Misapplication of the Experience Curve." *Journal of Business Strategy* 4, no. 3 (Winter 1984), pp. 3–9.

———. "The Origin of Strategy." *Harvard Business Review*, November–December 1989, p. 139.

Hill, Charles W. L., and Robert E. Hoskisson. "Strategy and Structure in the Multi-Product Firm." *Academy of Management Review*, April 1987, p. 331.

Hoskisson, Robert E. "Multidivisional Structure and Performance: The Contingency of Diversification Strategy." *Academy of Management Journal*, December 1987, p. 621.

Kelly, K. "Learning from Japan." *Business Week*, January 27, 1992, p. 53.

Lubatkin, M., and S. Chatterjee. "Extending Modern Portfolio Theory into the Domain of Corporate Diversification: Does It Apply?" *Academy of Management Journal* 37 (1994), pp. 109–136.

Mason, David H., and Robert G. Wilson. "Future-Mapping: A New Approach to Managing Strategic Uncertainty." *Planning Review*, May–June 1987, p. 20.

McConkey, Dale D. "Planning in a Changing Environment." *Business Horizons*, September–October 1988, p. 64.

Naugle, David G., and Garret A. Davies. "Strategic-Skill Pools and Competitive Advantage." *Business Horizons* 30, no. 6 (November–December 1987), pp. 35–42.

Porter, Michael E. *Competitive Advantage*. New York: Free Press, 1984, chaps. 9–11.

———. "From Competitive Advantage to Corporate Strategy." *Harvard Business Review* 65, no. 3 (May–June 1987), pp. 43–59.

Zweig, L. "Who Says the Conglomerate is Dead?" *Business Week*, January 23, 1995, p. 92.

CHAPTER 9 COHESION CASE ILLUSTRATION

BUILDING SHAREHOLDER VALUE AS A MULTIBUSINESS COMPANY AT COCA-COLA

A historical synopsis is useful to illustrate the "evolutionary perspective" on strategic choice at Coca-Cola. Coca-Cola focused its initial efforts on single-business concentration for an extended time. Through the 1960s, The Coca-Cola Company focused on market development and product development in its core business—soft drinks. This focus on a single-business concentration built Coke a domestic dominance and a growing dominance in the selected overseas markets it gradually entered. Facing some regulatory restrictions from vertically integrating into bottling—as well as hesitance to aggressively commit to such a capital-intensive arena when it "controlled" these businesses through franchising the rights to bottle Coke and other soft drinks—Coke found itself with a "cash cow" in the early 1970s.

Similar to other large U.S. companies, The Coca-Cola Company chose to pursue diversification as a way to spread its risks and opportunities. It principally chose the acquisition approach, entering over 15 diverse businesses already described in the cohesion case at the end of Chapter 1. By the early 1980s, Coke's management found itself facing increased losses to a rejuvenated PepsiCo, with weaknesses in its bottling franchise network relative to Pepsi's, and gradual maturation of the domestic market while facing rapidly expanding market opportunities abroad. While Coke remained financially strong, it found itself needing resources to respond to challenges and opportunities facing its core business at home and abroad. So Coke gradually divested itself of most of its nonbeverage businesses, culminating in the divestiture of Columbia Pictures, which alone generated $1.3 billion for investment in Coca-Cola's beverage-related businesses. Each of these shifts in strategy at Coke including its mid-1990s refocus on its core business, soft drinks (along with its citrus beverage business), and soft-drink bottling (vertical integration forward) is consistent with the evolutionary pattern discussed in Chapter 9.

As we described at the end of Chapter 1, Coca-Cola was a multibusiness company in the 1970s and early 1980s. Strategic analysis and choice during this period could be aided by a matrix approach similar to the industry attractive–business strength matrix. A selective assessment of some of Coke's businesses at the time would look something like this:

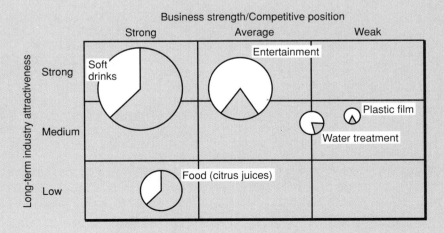

This assessment would suggest increased investment in soft drinks, harvesting water treatment and plastic films, selective investment and managing the juice business for cash generation, and investment to grow entertainment or harvesting the attractive opportunity if the company couldn't financially support the opportunity represented by both this business and soft drinks.

Strategic analysis and choice of Coca-Cola's generic strategy toward the 21st century is an important element we must consider to appreciate this perspective on strategic management and to understand fundamentals behind Coke's key strategic decisions. Coca-Cola's management under the new leadership of Roberto Goizueta set a new tone within The Coca-Cola Company of the 1980s. Some analysts have likened it to waking a sleeping giant. Regardless of the analogy you choose, it is abundantly clear that Coca-Cola reinvigorated the "Cola Wars" with aggressive behavior toward competitors and toward proving its uniqueness in every market it served throughout the world. If you refer back to Figures 9–2 to 9–4 in Chapter 9, you will see the commonly required skills, resources, and organizational requirements of the three basic generic business strategies. Coca-Cola has long possessed most of those required by a differentiation strategy—strong marketing abilities, product engineering, reputation for quality, a long tradition in the industry, and a strong coordination among R&D, product development, and marketing. The decisions made by Goizueta and his management team at that time and followed today seek to build Coke's success on differentiating it from every other source of refreshment in the world.

Finally, Coke's decision to focus on soft drinks, expand control of its primary distribution channel, and aggressively expand internationally is consistent with an industry that is in a transition to maturity in the United States, while the global market is rapidly emerging as a stable (for the sale of soft drinks) modern setting worldwide. And Coca-Cola's industry analysis shows that the main threats to industry profitability come from buyer power (bottlers), rivalry (Pepsi), and, perhaps, substitutes. Suppliers and potential entrants offer little concern. Coke is very strong relative to suppliers, and the capital requirement of serious entry is high. So Coca-Cola's differentiation strategy, combined with its swift, aggressive program of vertical integration acquiring bottlers or major interests in them, is a logical strategy to deal with rivalry and substitutes on the one hand and buyer power on the other. Coca-Cola's strategic decision to sell Columbia Pictures to Sony, whereby Coke netted $1.3 billion, was a clear decision to redirect substantial resources toward an aggressive vertical integration strategy suggested by the industry analysis as well as the other approaches outlined earlier.

Goizueta, speaking in late 1995, described Coca-Cola's "portfolio analysis" this way:

> We decided to evaluate our businesses based on economic value added [EVA], which we define as net operating profit after taxes less a charge for the average cost of debt and equity capital employed to produce that profit. The difference, if positive, is contributing value to shareholders. If negative, it is not. This shift in evaluation methodology prompted us to begin divesting ourselves of businesses with financial characteristics inferior to the remarkable fundamentals of our core soft drink business. Over ten years we divested our entertainment business, water treatment, plastic film, and other investments that did not produce an acceptable EVA. We have purposefully narrowed our businesses to focus almost entirely on a soft drink concentrate business that consistently generates returns 3Xs greater than our cost of capital. That business is augmented by selected bottling investments around the world and Coca Cola Foods.

So Coca-Cola management took an EVA-based look at the value-building capability of its portfolio of businesses and, based on that analysis, chose to divert resources from lesser performers toward the business that added the greatest value and held the best promise to continue to do so.

Focusing on Superior Lines of Business
By selling off businesses not sharing the same attractive financial fundamentals as the soft drink business, we now operate only in high-return businesses.

1994 Operating Income

97% Soft Drinks — 3% Other

77% Soft Drinks — 23% Other

1984 Operating Income

III STRATEGY IMPLEMENTATION

The last section of this book examines what is often called the *action phase* of the strategic management process: implementation of the chosen strategy. Up to this point, three phases of that process have been covered—strategy formulation, analysis of alternative strategies, and strategic choice. Although important, these phases alone cannot ensure success. To ensure success, the strategy must be translated into carefully implemented action. This means that:

1. The strategy must be translated into guidelines for the daily activities of the firm's members.
2. The strategy and the firm must become one—that is, the strategy must be reflected in the way the firm organizes its activities and in the firm's values, beliefs, and tone.
3. In implementing the strategy, the firm's managers must direct and control actions and outcomes and adjust to change.

Chapter 10 explains how organizational action is successfully initiated in three interrelated steps:

1. Creation of clear *action plans* and *short-term objectives*.
2. Development of specific *functional tactics* that create competitive advantage.
3. Empowerment of operating personnel through *policies* to guide decisions.

Action plans guide implementation by converting long-term objectives into short-term actions and targets. Functional tactics translate the business strategy into activities that build advantage. Policies empower operating personnel by defining guidelines for making decisions.

Today's competitive environment often necessitates restructuring and reengineering the organization to sustain competitive advantage. Chapter 11 examines how restructuring and reengineering are pursued in four organizational elements that provide fundamental, long-term means for institutionalizing the firm's strategy:

1. The firm's *structure*.
2. The *leadership* provided by the firm's CEO and key managers.
3. The fit between the strategy and the firm's *culture*.
4. The firm's *reward systems*.

Since the firm's strategy is implemented in a changing environment, successful implementation requires that execution be controlled and continuously improved. The control and improvement process must include at least these dimensions:

1. *Strategic controls* that "steer" execution of the strategy.
2. *Operations control systems* that monitor performance, evaluate deviations, and initiate corrective action.
3. *Continuous improvement* through total quality initiatives.

Chapter 12 examines the dimensions of the control and improvement process. It explains the essence of change as an ever-present force driving the need for strategic control. The chapter concludes with a look at the global "quality imperative," which is redefining the essence of control into the 21st century.

Implementation is "where the action is." It is the arena that most students enter at the start of their business careers. It is the strategic phase in which staying close to the customer, achieving competitive advantage, and pursuing excellence become realities. The chapters in this part will help you understand how this is done.

10

IMPLEMENTING STRATEGY THROUGH ACTION PLANS, FUNCTIONAL TACTICS AND EMPLOYEE EMPOWERMENT

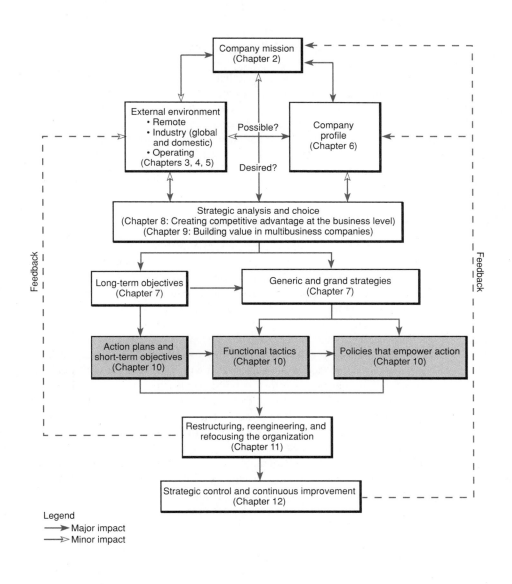

Legend
→ Major impact
⇾ Minor impact

Once corporate and business strategies have been agreed upon and long-term objectives set, the strategic management process moves into a critical new phase—translating strategic thought into organizational action. In the words of two well-worn phrases, they move from "planning their work" to "working their plan" as they shift their focus from strategy formulation to strategy implementation. This shift gives rise to four interrelated concerns:

1. Identifying action plans and short-term objectives.
2. Initiating specific functional tactics.
3. Communicating policies that empower people in the organization.
4. Committing to continuous improvement.

Action plans and short-term objectives translate long-range aspirations into this year's actions. If well developed, these objectives provide clarity, a powerful motivator and facilitator of effective strategy implementation.

Functional tactics translate business strategy into daily activities people need to execute. Functional managers participate in the development of these tactics, and their participation, in turn, helps clarify what their units are expected to do in implementing the business's strategy.

Policies are empowerment tools that simplify decision making by empowering operating managers and their subordinates. Policies can empower the "doers" in an organization by reducing the time required to decide and act.

Continuous improvement has become essential to the ability of any business to remain competitive. This quality orientation wherein functional managers seek best practices in each area's activities keeps businesses current, competitive, and value oriented.

ACTION PLANS AND SHORT-TERM OBJECTIVES

Chapter 7 described business strategies, grand strategies, and long-term objectives that are critically important in crafting a successful future. To make them become a reality, however, the people in an organization that actually "do the work" of the business need guidance in exactly what needs to be done today and tomorrow to make those long-term strategies become reality. Action plans and short-term objectives help do this. They provide much more specific guidance for what is to be done, a clear delineation of impending actions needed, which helps translate vision into action.

Action plans are effective when they incorporate four elements. First, they identify specific functional tactics and actions that will be done in the next week, month, or quarter as part of the business's effort to build competitive advantage. The next major section examines some of the functional tactics they usually deal with. The important point here is *specificity*—what exactly is to be done. The second element of an action plan is a clear *time frame for completion*—when the effort will begin and when its results will be accomplished. A third element action plans contain is identification of *who is responsible* for each action in the plan. This accountability is very important to ensure action plans are acted upon. Strategy in Action 10–1 provides excerpts from the action plan of a small oil distribution company in the northeastern United States that was part of its 1996–98 strategic plan.

The fourth element associated with action plans are short-term objectives. Usually, each action in an action plan has one or more specific objectives that are identified as outcomes

FIGURE 10–1
Creating Measurable Objectives

Examples of Deficient Objectives	Examples of Objectives with Measurable Criteria for Performance
To improve morale in the division (plant, department, etc.)	To reduce turnover (absenteeism, number of rejects, etc.) among sales managers by 10 percent by January 1, 1998.
	Assumption: Morale is related to measurable outcomes (i.e., high and low morale are associated with different results).
To improve support of the sales effort	To reduce the time lapse between order data and delivery by 8 percent (two days) by June 1, 1998.
	To reduce the cost of goods produced by 6 percent to support a product price decrease of 2 percent by December 1, 1998.
	To increase the rate of before- or on-schedule delivery by 5 percent by June 1, 1998.
To improve the firm's image	To conduct a public opinion poll using random samples in the five largest U.S. metropolitan markets to determine average scores on 10 dimensions of corporate responsibility by May 15, 1998. To increase our score on those dimensions by an average of 7.5 percent by May 1, 1999.

Source: Adapted from Laurence G. Hrebiniak and William F. Joyce, *Implementing Strategy* (New York: Macmillan, 1984), p. 116.

the action generates. There is also the need for other short-term objectives to be identified that "operationalize" long-term objectives. If we commit to a 20 percent gain in revenue over five years, what is our specific target or objective in revenue during the current year, month, or week to indicate we are making appropriate progress. Finally, short-term objectives are often useful topics to help raise issues that require coordination across functional activities within an organization. Meeting certain revenue objectives for the next month may cause difficulties for production managers or marketing managers also concerned with other objectives as well. Identifying and discussing short-term objectives help raise such issues. Because of the particular importance of short-term objectives in action plans, the following section addresses how to develop meaningful short-term objectives.

Qualities of Effective Short-Term Objectives

Measurable

Short-term objectives are more consistent when they clearly state *what* is to be accomplished, *when* it will be accomplished, and *how* its accomplishment will be *measured*. Such objectives can be used to monitor both the effectiveness of each activity and the collective progress across several interrelated activities. Figure 10–1 illustrates several effective and ineffective short-term objectives. Measurable objectives make misunderstanding less likely among interdependent managers who must implement action plans. It is far easier to quantify the objectives of *line* units (e.g., production) than of certain *staff* areas (e.g., personnel). Difficulties in quantifying objectives often can be overcome by initially focusing on *measurable activity* and then identifying *measurable outcomes*.

Priorities

Although all annual objectives are important, some deserve priority because of a timing consideration or their particular impact on a strategy's success. If such priorities are not established, conflicting assumptions about the relative importance of annual objectives

STRATEGY
IN ACTION
10–1

FROM OBSCURITY TO BEING A LEADER IN FUEL DISTRIBUTION ALONG VIRGINIA'S COAST

EnergyCo is an exciting, closely-held fuel distribution company located in coastal Virginia. Its management team has undertaken regular strategic analysis and planning to guide its growth aspirations. Its most recent planning efforts generated a comprehensive strategic plan to exploit several attractive opportunities. A key part of their ongoing strategic planning effort is the identification of action plans and annual objectives to make their wide-ranging planning discussions and efforts become concrete actions for which each member of the management team accepts some responsibility. They also insist on reducing the action plans into a few pages with minimal wording so that they can easily be reviewed, updated, and discussed at each weekly management meeting. Included below is an excerpt from their most recent action plan.

Objective	Assumption	1996	1998
Sales: Commercial fuels	12.5% annual growth	$16.9 mm	$21.0 mm
Sales: Oil Futures Hedging	Approximately 5% annual growth	$ 6.5 mm	$ 7.0 mm
Sales: Retail/C stores	Approximately 5% annual growth	$ 4.3 mm	$ 5.0 mm
Sales: Branding	4 sites per year 97–98	$ 4.0 mm	$12.0 mm
Sales: Home heat	1 or 2 acquisitions 97–98	$ 1.5 mm	$ 3.0 mm
Sales: Fleet pump	Aggressive growth 97–98	$ 750 k	$ 2.5 mm
Sales: Lubricants	12.5% + growth	$ 2.3 mm	$ 2.6 mm
Sales: Marine	Approximately 5% annual growth	$ 3.7 mm	$ 4.0 mm
Sales: Heating & cooling	Flat with 1998 acquisition?	$ 530 k	$ 800 k
Sales: Trucking	Approximately 5% annual growth	$ 2.7 mm	$ 3.0 mm
Total sales		$43.9 mm	$60.9 mm
Operating income		$ 1.2 mm	$ 1.7 mm
Return on equity		40%	37%
Debt to equity		3.5/1	3/1

may inhibit progress toward strategic effectiveness. Facing the most rapid, dramatic decline in profitability of any major computer manufacturer as it confronted relentless lower pricing by Dell Computer and AST, Compaq Computer formulated a retrenchment strategy with several important annual objectives in pricing, product design, distribution, and financial condition. But its highest priority was to dramatically lower overhead and production costs so as to satisfy the difficult challenge of dramatically lowering prices while also restoring profitability.

Priorities are established in various ways. A simple *ranking* may be based on discussion and negotiation during the planning process. However, this does not necessarily communicate the real difference in the importance of objectives, so such terms as *primary, top,* and

STRATEGY
IN ACTION   **continued**
10–1

Strategic Assignment	Who's Responsible	Due
Present outline of timing/format for sharing the results of EnergyCo planning retreat and the 1998 Vision with Eees (see 3/1/96 too).	Sam	Xmas Party
Get info on employee leasing from Laser Tech to Sarah	Richard	12/20/96
Sales—Operations Coordination and Integration—Report on initial ideas to increase the level of coordination and to pursue group meetings; after work meetings; coordination and interaction with admin personnel to. . . . Report on initial thoughts & get input	Leigh Jack Kate	Report initial ideas by 1/3/97
Real good assessment & recommendations on HVAC situation	Jack and Ginger	2/3/97
Create drawings and explanation of the adjacent property deal/use	Jack, Sarah, & Sam	3/3/97
Sales—Operations (Administration) Coordination Procedure Plan (the plan that results from the above ideas discussed, refined, etc.)	Leigh and Jack	4/30/97
Assess, do P&L, & implement hiring of Harbor Lube sales rep	Sam & Sarah	5/30/97
Computerization Task Force—assemble team, set agenda, and plan to proceed to examine, get a handle on, get input/involvement of EnergyCo employees doing the real work, and implement a comprehensive, integrated computer automation of the daily management of all of EnergyCo's sales, operations, administrative activities . . . & consideration of hiring someone to help early on	Sarah Kate Leigh Jack	6/30/97
Analysis, evaluation & develop a plan to deal with out of town product acquisition & $0.015 premium on low rack	Sarah & Jack	7/15/97
Retail Joint Venture: Evaluate EnergyCo direct ownership; franchise operations; owner equity lease financing to EnergyCo; and the potential for real estate syndication	Sam Sarah Kate	8/15/97
Partner buyout life insurance and evaluate risk of shared ownership	Leigh & Jack	9/15/97
EnergyCo Proformas on D/E ratios with capital proposed; set up EnergyCo's financial report to reflect investment by revenue stream/division and calculate ROI & SPI for each, etc.	Sarah	10/1/97
Implement series of meetings with employees to explain EnergyCo 1998 strategic plan and to answer questions; get their feedback, etc. One of the key issues to develop and discuss with EnergyCo employees is the new, greater emphasis and commitment to the retail and branding sides of the business.	Sam with management team	11/1/97
Finish Commission Program for Sales organization	Sarah and Leigh	12/30/97

secondary may be used to indicate priority. Some firms assign *weights* (e.g., 0 to 100 percent) to establish and communicate the relative priority of objectives. Whatever the method, recognizing priorities is an important dimension in the implementation value of short-term objectives.

Linked to Long-Term Objectives

Short-term objectives can add breadth and specificity in identifying *what* must be accomplished to achieve long-term objectives. For example, Wal-Mart's top management recently set out "to obtain 45 percent market share in five years" as a long-term objective. Achieving that objective can be greatly enhanced if a series of specific short-term objectives identify what must be accomplished each year in order to do so. If Wal-Mart's market share is now 25 percent, then one likely annual objective might be "to have each regional office achieve a minimum 4 percent increase in market share in the next year." "Open two regional distribution centers in the Southwest in 1998" might be an annual objective that Wal-Mart's marketing and distribution managers consider essential if the firm is to achieve a 45 percent market share in five years. "Conclude arrangements for a $1 billion line of credit at 0.25 percent above prime in 1994" might be an annual objective of Wal-Mart's financial managers to support the operation of new distribution centers and the purchase of increased inventory in reaching the firm's long-term objective.

The link between short-term and long-term objectives should resemble cascades through the firm from basic long-term objectives to specific short-term objectives in key operation areas. The cascading effect has the added advantage of providing a clear reference for communication and negotiation, which may be necessary to integrate and coordinate objectives and activities at the operating level.

The qualities of good objectives discussed in Chapter 7—acceptable, flexible, suitable, motivating, understandable, and achievable—also apply to short-term objectives. They will not be discussed again here, but the reader should review the discussion in Chapter 7 to appreciate these qualities, common to all good objectives.

The Value-Added Benefits of Action Plans and Short-Term Objectives

One benefit of action plans and short-term objectives is that they give operating personnel a better understanding of their role in the firm's mission. "Achieve $2.5 million in 1998 sales in the Chicago territory," "Develop an OSHA-approved safety program for handling acids at all Georgia Pacific plants in 1998," and "Reduce Ryder Truck's average age of accounts receivable to 31 days by the end of 1998" are examples of how short-term objectives clarify the role of particular personnel in their firm's broader mission. Such *clarity of purpose* can be a major force in helping use a firm's "people assets" more effectively, which may add tangible value.

A second benefit of action plans and short-term objectives comes from the process of developing them. If the managers responsible for this accomplishment have participated in their development, action plans and short-term objectives provide valid bases for addressing and accommodating conflicting concerns that might interfere with strategic effectiveness. Meetings to set action plans and short-term objectives become the forum for raising and resolving conflicts between strategic intentions and operating realities.

A third benefit of action plans and short-term objectives is that they provide *a basis for strategic control*. The control of strategy will be examined in detail in Chapter 12. However, it is important to recognize here that action plans and short-term objectives provide a clear, measurable basis for developing budgets, schedules, trigger points, and other mechanisms for controlling the implementation of strategy.

A fourth benefit is often a *motivational payoff*. Action plans and short-term objectives that clarify personal and group roles in a firm's strategies and are also measurable, realistic, and challenging can be powerful motivators of managerial performance—particularly when these objectives are linked to the firm's reward structure.

Strategy in Action 10–1 excerpts selected short-term objectives and action plans from the strategic plan of EnergyCo Fuel Company. Bought out of bankruptcy 10 years ago, founder Sam Rutledge has led an outstanding management team that has made EnergyCo a major player in eastern Virginia. One of the key aspects the firm emphasizes is action plans and annual objectives.

FIGURE 10–2
Role of Functional Tactics at General Cinema Corporation

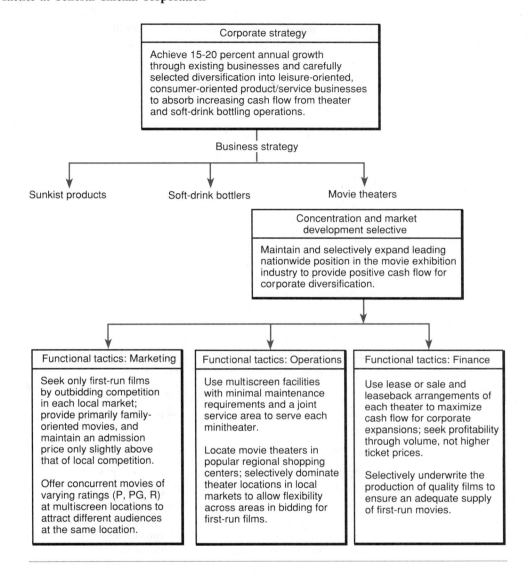

Corporate strategy

Achieve 15-20 percent annual growth through existing businesses and carefully selected diversification into leisure-oriented, consumer-oriented product/service businesses to absorb increasing cash flow from theater and soft-drink bottling operations.

Business strategy

Sunkist products   Soft-drink bottlers   Movie theaters

Concentration and market development selective

Maintain and selectively expand leading nationwide position in the movie exhibition industry to provide positive cash flow for corporate diversification.

Functional tactics: Marketing	Functional tactics: Operations	Functional tactics: Finance
Seek only first-run films by outbidding competition in each local market; provide primarily family-oriented movies, and maintain an admission price only slightly above that of local competition.	Use multiscreen facilities with minimal maintenance requirements and a joint service area to serve each minitheater.	Use lease or sale and leaseback arrangements of each theater to maximize cash flow for corporate expansions; seek profitability through volume, not higher ticket prices.
Offer concurrent movies of varying ratings (P, PG, R) at multiscreen locations to attract different audiences at the same location.	Locate movie theaters in popular regional shopping centers; selectively dominate theater locations in local markets to allow flexibility across areas in bidding for first-run films.	Selectively underwrite the production of quality films to ensure an adequate supply of first-run movies.

FUNCTIONAL TACTICS THAT IMPLEMENT BUSINESS STRATEGIES

Functional tactics are the key, routine activities that must be undertaken in each functional area—marketing, finance, production/operations, R&D, and human resource management—to provide the business's products and services. In a sense, functional tactics translate thought (grand strategy) into action designed to accomplish specific short-term objectives. Every value chain activity in a company executes functional tactics that support the business's strategy and help accomplish strategic objectives.

Figure 10–2 illustrates the difference between functional tactics and corporate and business strategy. It also shows that functional tactics are essential to implement business strategy. The corporate strategy defined General Cinema Corporation's general posture in the broad economy. The business strategy outlined the competitive posture of its operations in the movie theater industry. To increase the likelihood that these strategies would be successful, specific functional tactics were needed for the firm's operating components. These functional tactics clarified the business strategy, giving specific, short-term guidance to operating managers in the areas of marketing, operations, and finance.

Differences between Business Strategies and Functional Tactics

Functional tactics are different from business or corporate strategies in three fundamental ways:

1. Time horizon.
2. Specificity.
3. Participants who develop them.

Time Horizon

Functional tactics identify activities to be undertaken "now" or in the immediate future. Business strategies focus on the firm's posture three to five years out. Delta Air lines is committed to a concentration/market development business strategy that seeks competitive advantage via differentiation in its level of service and focus on the business traveler. Its pricing tactics are often to price above industry averages, but it often lowers fares on selected routes to thwart low-cost competition. Its business strategy is focused 10 years out; its pricing tactics change weekly.

The shorter time horizon of functional tactics is critical to the successful implementation of a business strategy for two reasons. First, it focuses the attention of functional managers on what needs to be done *now* to make the business strategy work. Second, it allows functional managers like those at Delta to adjust to changing current conditions.

Specificity

Functional tactics are more specific than business strategies. Business strategies provide general direction. Functional tactics identify the specific activities that are to be undertaken in each functional area and thus allow operating managers to work out *how* their unit is expected to pursue short-term objectives. General Cinema's business strategy gave its movie theater division broad direction on how to pursue a concentration and selective market development strategy. Two functional tactics in the marketing area gave managers specific direction on what types of movies (first-run, primarily family-oriented, P, PG, R) should be shown and what pricing strategy (competitive in the local area) should be followed.

Specificity in functional tactics contributes to successful implementation by:

· Helping ensure that functional managers know what needs to be done and can focus on accomplishing results.
· Clarifying for top management how functional managers intend to accomplish the business strategy, which increases top management's confidence in and sense of control over the business strategy.
· Facilitating coordination among operating units *within* the firm by clarifying areas of interdependence and potential conflict.

Participants

Different people participate in strategy development at the functional and business levels. Business strategy is the responsibility of the general manager of a business unit. That manager typically delegates the development of functional tactics to subordinates charged with running the operating areas of the business. The manager of a business unit must establish long-term objectives and a strategy that corporate management feels contributes to corporate-level goals. Similarly, key operating managers must establish short-term objectives and operating strategies that contribute to business-level goals. Just as business strategies and objectives are approved through negotiation between corporate managers and business managers, so, too, are short-term objectives and functional tactics approved through negotiation between business managers and operating managers.

Involving operating managers in the development of functional tactics improves their understanding of what must be done to achieve long-term objectives and, thus, contributes to successful implementation. It also helps ensure that functional tactics reflect the reality of the day-to-day operating situation. And perhaps most important, it can increase the commitment of operating managers to the strategies developed.

The next several sections will highlight key tactics around which managers can build competitive advantage and add value in each of the various functional areas.

Functional Tactics in Production/Operations

Basic Issues

Production/operations management (POM) is the core function of any organization. That function converts inputs (raw materials, supplies, machines, and people) into value-enhanced output. The POM function is most easily associated with manufacturing firms, but it also applies to all other types of businesses (service and retail firms, for example). POM tactics must guide decisions regarding (1) the basic nature of the firm's POM system, seeking an optimum balance between investment input and production/operations output and (2) location, facilities design, and process planning on a short-term basis. Figure 10–3 highlights key decision areas in which the POM tactics should provide guidance to functional personnel.

POM facility and equipment tactics involve decisions regarding plant location, size, equipment replacement, and facilities utilization that should be consistent with grand strategy and other operating strategies. In the mobile home industry, for example, the facilities and equipment tactic of Winnebago was to locate one large centralized, highly integrated production center (in Iowa) near its raw materials. On the other extreme, Fleetwood, Inc., a California-based competitor, located dispersed, decentralized production facilities near markets and emphasized maximum equipment life and less-integrated, labor-intensive production processes. Both firms are leaders in the mobile home industry, but have taken very different tactical approaches.

The interplay between computers and rapid technological advancement has made flexible manufacturing systems (FMS) a major consideration for today's POM tacticians. FMS allows managers to automatically and rapidly shift production systems to retool for different products or other steps in a manufacturing process. Changes that previously took hours or days can be done in minutes. The result is decreased labor cost, greater efficiency, and increased quality associated with computer-based precision. Global Strategy in Action 10–1 summarizes the "responsive factory" of tomorrow based on a global study by *Business Week*.

Purchasing has become an increasingly important component in the POM area. Many companies now accord purchasing a separate status like any other functional area. Purchasing tactics provide guidelines about questions like: Are the cost advantages of using only a

FIGURE 10–3
Key Functional Strategies in POM

Functional Strategy	Typical Questions That the Functional Strategy Should Answer
Facilities and equipment	How centralized should the facilities be? (One big facility or several small facilities?)
	How integrated should the separate processes be?
	To what extent should further mechanization or automation be pursued?
	Should size and capacity be oriented toward peak or normal operating levels?
Purchasing	How many sources are needed?
	How should suppliers be selected, and how should relationships with suppliers be managed over time?
	What level of forward buying (hedging) is appropriate?
Operations planning and control	Should work be scheduled to order or to stock?
	What level of inventory is appropriate?
	How should inventory be used (FIFO/LIFO), controlled, and replenished?
	What are the key foci for control efforts (quality, labor cost, downtime, product use, other)?
	Should maintenance efforts be oriented to prevention or to breakdown?
	What emphasis should be placed on job specialization? Plant safety? The use of standards?

few suppliers outweighed by the risk of overdependence? What criteria (e.g., payment requirements) should be used in selecting vendors? Which vendors can provide "just-in-time" inventory and how can the business provide it to our customers? How can operations be supported by the volume and delivery requirements of purchases?

POM planning and control tactics involve approaches to the management of ongoing production operations and are intended to match production/operations resources with longer range, overall demand. These tactical decisions usually determine whether production/operations will be demand oriented, inventory oriented, or outsourcing oriented to seek a balance between the two extremes. Tactics in this component also address how issues like maintenance, safety, and work organization are handled. Quality control procedures are yet another focus of tactical priorities in this area.

Just in time (JIT) delivery, outsourcing, and statistical process control (SPC) have become prominent aspects of the way today's POM managers create tactics that build greater value and quality in their POM system. JIT delivery was initially a way to coordinate with suppliers to reduce inventory carrying costs of items needed to make products. It also became a quality control tactic because smaller inventories made quality checking easier on smaller, frequent deliveries. It has become an important aspect of supplier-customer relationships in today's best businesses.

Outsourcing, or the use of a source other than internal capacity to accomplish some task or process, has become a major operational tactic in today's downsizing-oriented firms. Outsourcing is based on the notion that strategies should be built around core competencies that add the most value in the value chain, and functions or activities that add little value or that cannot be done cost effectively should be done outside the firm—outsourced. When done well, the firm gains a supplier that provides superior quality at lower cost than it could provide itself. JIT and outsourcing have increased the strategic importance of the purchasing function. Outsourcing must include intense quality control by the buyer. ValuJet's

WHAT DOES THE TRULY "RESPONSIVE" FACTORY OF THE 21ST CENTURY GLOBAL ECONOMY LOOK LIKE?

Manufacturers worldwide are scrambling to create the factories of the future today. Flexible manufacturing systems are an important component. But that's not all. Total quality control, concurrent engineering, process reengineering, computerization, and computer-aided logistical support are just some of today's insisted-upon characteristics. Convened by *Business Week* to probe the vision of the responsive factory more clearly, operations managers around the globe agreed on five key characteristics.

CHARACTERISTICS OF THE TRULY RESPONSIVE FACTORY

Concurrent everything	Enterprisewide computer integration, with electronic links to customers and suppliers, means that transactions occur mostly between computers, which will automatically route information to all the proper departments or operations.
Fast development cycles	A real-time database will unite the distributed-processing computers used by design, engineering, production, logistics, marketing, and customer service—whether the work is done in-house or outsourced. All parties will have instant access to the latest information, eliminating the rework now caused by delays in shuffling paper.
Flexible production	Flexibility will be built into all levels of manufacturing, from the controls on each machine to the computers that coordinate work cells and factorywide systems. Products can thus be turned out in greater variety and customized easily, with no cost penalty for small production runs.
Quick response	Dynamic factory-scheduling systems will put production "on call" and thus pare inventories to the bone. Production will begin only after a customer places an order.
Commitment to lifelong quality	Ongoing quality programs will lead to continuous improvement of both processes and products. A primary focus will be to make products easier to recycle or dispose of in environmentally sound ways.

Source: Reprinted from October 22, 1993, issue of *Business Week* by special permission. Copyright © 1993 by The McGraw-Hill Companies.

tragic 1996 crash in the Everglades was caused by poor quality control over its outsourced maintenance providers.

Statistical process control (SPC) refers to a series of quantitative-oriented management practices designed to improve quality at several phases in the production/operations process. Identifying measurable aspects of every function from inbound logistics through operations and then outbound parts of the value chain—and then subjecting them to systematic scrutiny to ensure that every phase is in control and compliance—is the heart of SPC. At the heart of the total quality management (TQM) movement, SPC has become very important tactically, particularly for businesses selling solely to other businesses that seek to meet international quality certifications.

Functional Tactics in Marketing

The role of the marketing function is to achieve the firm's objectives by bringing about the profitable sale of the business's products/services in target markets. Marketing tactics should guide sales and marketing managers in determining who will sell what, where, to

FIGURE 10–4
Key Functional Tactics in Marketing

Functional Tactic	Typical Questions That the Functional Tactic Should Answer
Product (or service)	Which products do we emphasize?
	Which products/services contribute most to profitability?
	What product/service image do we seek to project?
	What consumer needs does the product/service seek to meet?
	What changes should be influencing our customer orientation?
Price	Are we competing primarily on price?
	Can we offer discounts or other pricing modifications?
	Are our pricing policies standard nationally, or is there regional control?
	What price segments are we targeting (high, medium, low, and so on)?
	What is the gross profit margin?
	Do we emphasize cost/demand or competition-oriented pricing?
Place	What level of market coverage is necessary?
	Are there priority geographic areas?
	What are the key channels of distribution?
	What are the channel objectives, structure, and management?
	Should the marketing managers change their degree of reliance on distributors, sales reps, and direct selling?
	What sales organization do we want?
	Is the sales force organized around territory, market, or product?
Promotion	What are the key promotion priorities and approaches?
	Which advertising/communication priorities and approaches are linked to different products, markets, and territories?
	Which media would be most consistent with the total marketing strategy?

whom, in what quantity, and how. Marketing tactics at a minimum should address four fundamental areas: products, price, place, and promotion. Figure 10–4 highlights typical questions marketing tactics should address. Strategy in Action 10–2 shows how the San Luis Sourdough Company, a small California baker, developed pricing tactics to address different levels of service they rendered to different customers with the bread they sold.

In addition to the basic issues raised in Figure 10–4, marketing tactics today must guide managers addressing the impact of *the communication revolution* and the *increased diversity* among market niches worldwide. The Internet and the accelerating blend of computers and telecommunications has facilitated instantaneous access to several places around the world. A producer of plastic kayaks in Easley, South Carolina, receives orders from somewhere in the world about every 30 minutes over the Internet without any traditional distribution structure or global advertising. It fills the order within five days without any transportation capability. Speed linked to the ability to communicate instantaneously is causing marketing tacticians to radically rethink what they need to do to remain competitive and maximize value.

Diversity has accelerated because of communication technology, logistical capability worldwide, and advancements in flexible manufacturing systems. The diversity that has resulted is a virtual explosion of market niches, adaptations of products to serve hundreds of distinct and diverse customer segments that would previously have been served with more mass-market, generic products or services. Where firms used to rely on volume associated with mass markets to lower costs, they now encounter smaller niche players carving out subsegments they can serve more timely *and* more cost effectively. These new, smaller players lack the bureaucracy and committee approach that burdens the larger firms. They make decisions, outsource, incorporate product modifications, and make other agile adjustments to niche market needs before their larger competitors get through the first phase of committee-based decision making. Jack Welch, the CEO of General Electric, commented on this recently with the editors of *Business Week*:

> Size is no longer the trump card it once was in today's brutally competitive world marketplace—a marketplace that is unimpressed with logos and sales numbers but demands, instead, value and performance. At GE we're trying to get that small-company soul—and small-company speed—inside our big-company body. Faster products, faster product cycles to market. Better response time. New niches. Satisfying customers, getting faster communications, moving with more agility, all these are easier when one is small. All these are essential to succeed in the diverse, fast-moving global environment.

Functional Tactics in Accounting and Finance

While most functional tactics guide implementation in the immediate future, the time frame for functional tactics in the area of finance varies, because these tactics direct the use of financial resources in support of the business strategy, long-term goals, and annual objectives. Financial tactics with longer time perspectives guide financial managers in long-term capital investment, debt financing, dividend allocation, and leveraging. Financial tactics designed to manage working capital and short-term assets have a more immediate focus. Figure 10–5 highlights some key questions that financial tactics must answer.

Accounting managers have seen their need to contribute value increasingly scrutinized. Traditional expectations centered around financial accounting—reporting requirements from bank and SEC entities and tax law compliance—remain areas in which actions are dictated by outside governance. Managerial accounting, where managers are responsible for keeping records of costs and the use of funds within their company, has taken on increased strategic significance in the 1990s. This change has involved two tactical areas: (1) how to account for costs of creating and providing their business's products and services, and (2) valuing the business, particularly among publicly traded companies.

Managerial cost accounting has traditionally provided information for managers using cost categories like those shown on the left side below. However, value chain advocates have been increasingly successful getting managers to seek activity-based cost accounting information like that shown on the right side below. In so doing, accounting is becoming a more critical, relevant source of information that truly benefits strategic management.

Traditional Cost Accounting in a Purchasing Department		Activity-Based Cost Accounting in the Same Purchasing Department	
Wages and salaries	$350,000	Evaluate supplier capabilities	$135,750
Employee benefits	115,000	Process purchase orders	82,100
Supplies	6,500	Expedite supplier deliveries	23,500
Travel	2,400	Expedite internal processing	15,840
Depreciation	17,000	Check quality of items purchased	94,300
Other fixed charges	124,000	Check incoming deliveries against purchase orders	48,450
Miscellaneous operating expenses	25,250	Resolve problems	110,000
		Internal administration	130,210
	$640,150		$640,150

Source: Adapted from information in Terence P. Paré, "A New Tool for Managing Costs," *Fortune*, June 14, 1993, pp. 124–29. *Fortune*, © 1993, Time, Inc. All rights reserved.

REAL-WORLD PRICING DILEMMAS:
PRICING SERVICE

Most companies charge their customers the same price for a product—even if it costs more to satisfy some of them. Some customers require no after-sale service; others demand a tremendous amount of hand holding, support, and service. To David and Linda ("Charlie") West, owners of the San Luis Sourdough Company, it didn't make sense to charge *everyone* the same price. So the Wests designed a system that sets prices for their sourdough bread based on how much service their customers—local supermarkets and specialty food shops—require.

Here's how the pricing strategy works: If a customer chooses Level 1 service, having San Luis Sourdough deliver the bread to its back door, the wholesale price is 97 cents per loaf. If the store also wants to be able to return day-old bread for a full credit (Level 2 service) the cost of a loaf is $1.02. If the customer wants the convenience of returns plus the service of having San Luis Sourdough put the bread on the shelf and price it by sticking a bar code label on each bag and another on the shelf (Level 3 service), the price is $1.05 per loaf.

The Wests' prices are not arbitrary; they simply cover the cost of the extra service. The 5-cent premium per loaf for the privilege of returning day-old loaves covers the cost of the bread and handling the returns. Similarly, the 8-cent-per-loaf charge for stocking, pricing, and accepting returns pays for the Level 3 service. Studies show it takes a driver 30 minutes to stock and price a shelf, and drivers earn $8 per hour (salary and benefits). The average customer order is 100 loaves, producing a cost of 8 cents per loaf. "We don't care which pricing option you choose," says Dave. "They're all the same to us." About 60 percent of San Luis Sourdough's customers choose Level 2 service; the remainder are evenly divided between Levels 1 and 3.

In essence, San Luis Sourdough is passing the cost of service on to its customers. Rather than absorb the extra 5 cents or 8 cents per loaf to charge everyone the same price, the Wests let their customers pay for it. How can they get away with it? After all, Sourdough's customers typically require their other bread suppliers to charge one price, whatever the level of service.

Source: Adapted from Paul Brown, "You Get What You Pay For," *Inc.*, October 1990, pp. 155–56; and N. Scarborough and T. Zimmerer, *Effective Small Business Management* (Englewood Cliffs, NJ: Prentice Hall, 1995), p. 395.

Another area of concern is value—whether or not business strategies and management actions are creating real value for stockholders. Perhaps the most prominent technique that has guided tactical decisions for many companies during the last five years is *economic value added* (EVA). EVA is simply a way of measuring an operation's real profitability. It takes into account the "true" cost of capital—after-tax operating profit minus the total annual cost of capital. Incredibly, most corporate groups have looked at the cost of their borrowed capital, but the cost of equity capital that shareholders have contributed appears nowhere in their financial statements. Until managerial accounting takes this into account, so that managers know whether they are covering all their costs and adding value to the company, company managers won't achieve the benefits that have accrued to several companies described in Strategy in Action 10–3 on page 320.

Functional Tactics in Research and Development

With the increasing rate of technological change in most competitive industries, research and development (R&D) has assumed a key strategic role in many firms. In the technology-intensive computer and pharmaceutical industries, for example, firms typically spend

continued

The Wests cite three reasons. First, their big customers recognize that Sourdough is a small business, and they're willing to give the little guy a break. Second, the Wests bake a superior loaf of bread. Their customers recognize Sourdough's higher quality product and are willing to be more flexible in order to stock it. Third, the Wests are honest when dealing with their customers. "What we've told all our customers—and it's true—is that we just don't have the resources of a huge bread company," says Charlie. "We have to compete on the quality of our product, not our level of service."

Very few customers ever complain. Costco Wholesale, Inc., a national supermarket chain touting its reputation for the lowest prices, has no problem paying the 8-cent premium for Level 3 service. "I'm happy," explains the buyer. "We don't have the manpower here to stock the shelves, price, and handle returns. As long as I'm still able to offer the lowest price on their bread, it's a very workable arrangement."

Charlie and David West offer these rules for keeping customers happy while asking them to pay for extra service:

Don't gouge. Charge exactly what the service costs. Don't add a surcharge; it only alienates customers.

Don't play favorites. If customers choose to get extra service, they pay for it. "If we started providing Level 3 service to one company for the price of Level 2 or even Level 1, pretty soon we'd have to do it for everybody," says Dave. "By handling every customer the same way, we don't run the risk of alienating anyone."

Give them a reason to go along. Unless your product is unique, it's difficult to convince customers to pay a premium for service.

Let them establish the level of service they want. Don't force service on customers; let them tell you what service they want. You'll both be better off.

between 4 and 6 percent of their sales dollars on R&D. In other industries, such as the hotel/motel and construction industries, R&D spending is less than 1 percent of sales. Thus, functional R&D tactics may be more critical instruments of the business strategy in some industries than in others.

Figure 10–6, on page 322, illustrates the types of questions addressed by R&D tactics. First, R&D tactics should clarify whether basic research or product development research will be emphasized. Several major oil companies now have solar energy subsidiaries in which basic research is emphasized, while the smaller oil companies emphasize product development research.

The choice of emphasis between basic research and product development also involves the time horizon for R&D efforts. Should these efforts be focused on the near term or the long term? The solar energy subsidiaries of the major oil companies have long-term perspectives, while the smaller oil companies focus on creating products now in order to establish a competitive niche in the growing solar industry.

R&D tactics also involve organization of the R&D function. For example, should R&D work be conducted solely within the firm, or should portions of that work be contracted out? A closely related issue is whether R&D should be centralized or decentralized. What emphasis should be placed on process R&D versus product R&D?

Decisions on all of the above questions are influenced by the firm's R&D posture, which can be offensive or defensive, or both. If that posture is offensive, as is true for small

FIGURE 10–5
Key Functional Tactics in Finance

Functional Tactic	Typical Questions That the Functional Tactics Should Answer
Capital acquisition	What is an acceptable cost of capital?
	What is the desired proportion of short- and long-term debt? Preferred and common equity?
	What balance is desired between internal and external funding?
	What risk and ownership restrictions are appropriate?
	What level and forms of leasing should be used?
Capital allocation	What are the priorities for capital allocation projects?
	On what basis should the final selection of projects be made?
	What level of capital allocation can be made by operating managers without higher approval?
Dividend and working capital management	What portion of earnings should be paid out as dividends?
	How important is dividend stability?
	Are things other than cash appropriate as dividends?
	What are the cash flow requirements? The minimum and maximum cash balances?
	How liberal/conservative should the credit policies be?
	What limits, payment terms, and collection procedures are necessary?
	What payment timing and procedure should be followed?

high-technology firms, the firm will emphasize technological innovation and new product development as the basis for its future success. This orientation entails high risks (and high payoffs) and demands considerable technological skill, forecasting expertise, and the ability to quickly transform innovations into commercial products.

A defensive R&D posture emphasizes product modification and the ability to copy or acquire new technology. Converse Shoes is a good example of a firm with such an R&D posture. Faced with the massive R&D budgets of Nike and Reebok, Converse placed R&D emphasis on bolstering the product life cycle of its prime products (particularly canvas shoes).

Large companies with some degree of technological leadership often use a combination of offensive and defensive R&D strategy. GE in the electrical industry, IBM in the computer industry, and Du Pont in the chemical industry all have a defensive R&D posture for currently available products *and* an offensive R&D posture in basic, long-term research.

Functional Tactics in Human Resource Management (HRM)

The strategic importance of HRM tactics received widespread endorsement in the 1990s. HRM tactics aid long-term success in the development of managerial talent and competent employees; the creation of systems to manage compensation or regulatory concerns; and guiding the effective utilization of human resources to achieve both the firm's short-term objectives and employees' satisfaction and development. HRM tactics are helpful in the areas shown in Figure 10–7, on page 323. The recruitment, selection, and orientation should establish the basic parameters for bringing new people into a firm and adapting them to "the way things are done" in the firm. The career development and training component should guide the action that personnel takes to meet the future human resources needs of the overall business strategy. Merrill Lynch, a major broker-age firm whose long-term corporate strategy is to become a diversified financial service institution, has moved into such areas as investment banking, consumer credit, and venture capital. In support of its long-term objectives, it has incorporated extensive early-career training and ongoing career development programs to meet its expanding need for personnel with multiple competencies. Larger organizations need HRM tactics that guide decisions regarding labor relations; EEOC requirements; and employee compensation, discipline, and control.

Current trends in HRM parallel the reorientation of managerial accounting by looking at their cost structure anew. HRM's "paradigm shift" involves looking at people expense as an investment in human capital. This involves looking at the business's value chain and the "value" of human resource components along the various links in that chain. One of the results of this shift in perspective has been the downsizing phenomenon of the late 1980s and 1990s. While this has been traumatic for millions of employees in companies world-wide, its underlying basis involves an effort to examine the use of "human capital" to create value in ways that maximize the human contribution. This scrutiny continues to challenge the HRM area, as the recent *FORTUNE* article reprinted in Strategy in Action 10–4 details on page 324. The emerging implications for human resource management tactics may be a value-oriented perspective on the role of human resources in a business's value chain as suggested below.

Traditional HRM Ideas	Emerging HRM Ideas
Emphasis solely on physical skills	Emphasis on total contribution to the firm
Expectation of predictable, repetitive behavior	Expectation of innovative and creative behavior
Comfort with stability and conformity	Tolerance of ambiguity and change
Avoidance of responsibility and decision making	Accepting responsibility for making decisions
Training covering only specific tasks	Open-ended commitment; broad continuous development
Emphasis placed on outcomes and results	Emphasis placed on processes and means
High concern for quantity and throughput	High concern for total customer value
Concern for individual efficiency	Concern for overall effectiveness
Functional and subfunctional specialization	Cross-functional integration
Labor force seen as unnecessary expense	Labor force seen as critical investment
Work force is management's adversary	Management and work force are partners

Source: G. G. Dess and A. Miller, *Strategic Management*, p. 159. © 1993 by McGraw-Hill, Inc. Reproduced with the permission of The McGraw-Hill Companies.

To summarize, functional tactics reflect how each major activity of a firm contributes to the implementation of the business strategy. The specificity of functional tactics and the involvement of operating managers in their development help ensure understanding of and commitment to the chosen strategy. A related step in implementation is the development of policies that empower operating managers and their subordinates to make decisions and to act autonomously.

STRATEGY
IN ACTION
10–3

THE HIP MANAGERIAL ACCOUNTANT:
"WHAT'S YOUR EVA?"

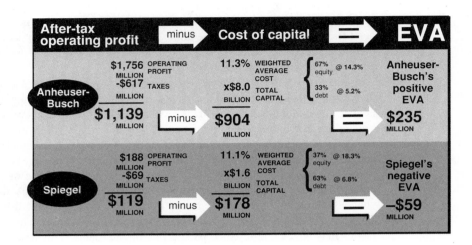

The power of the economic value added (EVA) concept comes from the insight that you can't know if an operation is really creating value until you apply the *true* cost of capital to *all* the capital employed. Most operations within companies—and some companies themselves—have no idea what either amount is. Finding out is fascinating and often startling.

▶Question No. 1: What's the true cost of your capital? You know the cost of your borrowed capital; at least in the short term it's the interest you pay, adjusted to reflect its tax deductibility. (In the longer term it's more complicated, and we'll leave that aside.) But what about equity capital, the money the shareholders provided? Since you aren't required to pay for it, you may think it's free. But it isn't—and its cost is much more than many managers would imagine.

Your true cost of equity is what your shareholders could be getting in price appreciation and dividends if they invested instead in a portfolio of companies about as risky as yours. It's what

EMPOWERING OPERATING PERSONNEL: THE ROLE OF POLICIES

Specific functional tactics provide guidance and initiate action implementing a business's strategy, but more is needed. Supervisors and personnel in the field have been charged in today's competitive environment with being responsible for customer value—for being the "front line" of the company's effort to truly meet customers' needs. Meeting customer needs, becoming obsessed with quality service, was the buzzword that started organizational revolutions in the 1980s. Efforts to do so often failed because employees that were the real contact point between the business and its customers were not *empowered* to make decisions or act to fulfill customer needs. One solution has been to empower operating personnel by pushing down decision making to their level. General Electric allows

STRATEGY
IN ACTION
10–3   **continued**

economists call the opportunity cost. Many managers resist this idea—how can it be a real cost if I don't have to write a check every month?

If that's your reaction, think of it from the point of view of the shareholder who has given his money to you instead of to Coca-Cola or Berkshire Hathaway or the Magellan Fund. If you're not employing his money as successfully as they are—and not showing any promise of doing so—he will take his money back by selling your stock, sending its price down. Other investors will be less inclined to supply any capital. So as long as you're not at least matching the investor's opportunity cost, you're on the road to oblivion. Says Talton Embry, an EVA enthusiast whose New York investment firm owns stakes in a host of big companies: "Capital looks free to a lot of managers. It doesn't look free to investors who hand them the money."

So what is equity's cost today? Over time, shareholders have received on average a return that is six percentage points higher on stocks than on long-term government bonds. With bond rates around 6.3%, that puts the average cost of equity at 12.3%, though it goes much higher for companies with volatile stocks and lower for those with more stable stocks. Assuming you use debt as well as equity capital, the cost is the weighted average of the two.

▶Question No. 2: How much capital is tied up in your operation? Even if you don't know the answer, you know what it consists of: what you paid for real estate, machines, vehicles, and the like, plus working capital. But proponents of EVA say there's more. What about the money your company spends on R&D? On employee training? Those are investments meant to pay off for years, but accounting rules say you can't treat them that way; you have to call them expenses, like the amount you spend on electricity. EVA proponents say forget the accounting rules. For internal purposes, call these things what they are: capital investments. No one can say what their useful life is, so make your best guess—say five years. It's truer than calling them expenses.

When you've answered these questions, you can multiply the capital from Question 2 by the rate from Question 1 and get the dollar cost of the capital in your operation. Now it's a simple matter to figure your EVA. Start with the commonest management yardstick, operating earnings. Subtract taxes. Then subtract the capital cost. What's left is your EVA.

If it's positive, congratulations—your operation is creating wealth. If it's negative, you've just learned your operation is destroying capital. You'd better fix it, fast.

Don't assume that because capital costs a lot, it's a bad thing. Look at the EVAs of Anheuser-Busch and Spiegel (above). It isn't how much capital you've got, but how you manage it.

appliance repair personnel to decide about warranty credits on the spot, a decision that used to take several days and multiple organizational levels. Delta Air Lines allows customer service personnel and their supervisors wide range in resolving customer ticket pricing decisions. Federal Express couriers make decisions and handle package routing information that involves five management levels in the U.S. Postal Service.

Empowerment is being created in many ways. Training, self-managed work groups, eliminating whole levels of management in organizations, and aggressive use of automation are some of the ways and ramifications of this fundamental change in the way business organizations function. At the heart of the effort is the need to ensure that decision making is consistent with the mission, strategy, and tactics of the business while at the same time allowing considerable latitude to operating personnel. One way operating managers do this is through the use of policies.

FIGURE 10–6
Key Functional Tactic in R&D

R&D Decision Area	Typical Questions That the Functional Tactic Should Answer
Basic research versus product and process development	To what extent should innovation and breakthrough research be emphasized? In relation to the emphasis on product development, refinement, and modification?
	What critical operating processes need R&D attention?
	What new projects are necessary to support growth?
Time horizon	Is the emphasis short term or long term?
	Which orientation best supports the business strategy? The marketing and production strategy
Organizational fit	Should R&D be done in-house or contracted out?
	Should R&D be centralized or decentralized?
	What should be the relationship between the R&D units and product managers? Marketing managers? Production managers?
Basic R&D posture	Should the firm maintain an offensive posture, seeking to lead innovation in its industry?
	Should the firm adopt a defensive posture, responding to the innovations of its competitors?

Policies are directives designed to guide the thinking, decisions, and actions of managers and their subordinates in implementing a firm's strategy. Previously referred to as *standard operating procedures*, policies increase managerial effectiveness by standardizing many routine decisions and clarifying the discretion managers and subordinates can exercise in implementing functional tactics. Logically, policies should be derived from functional tactics (and, in some instances, from corporate or business strategies) with the key purpose of aiding strategy execution.[2] Strategy in Action 10–5, on page 326, illustrates selected policies of several well-known firms.

Creating Policies That Empower

Policies communicate guidelines to decisions. They are designed to control decisions while defining allowable discretion within which operational personnel can execute business activities. They do this in several ways:

1. *Policies establish indirect control over independent action* by clearly stating how things are to be done *now*. By defining discretion, policies in effect control decisions yet empower employees to conduct activities without direct intervention by top management.

2. *Policies promote uniform handling of similar activities.* This facilitates the coordination of work tasks and helps reduce friction arising from favoritism, discrimination,

---

[2] The term *policy* has various definitions in management literature. Some authors and practitioners equate policy with strategy. Others do this inadvertently by using "policy" as a synonym for company mission, purpose, or culture. Still other authors and practitioners differentiate policy in terms of "levels" associated respectively with purpose, mission, and strategy. "Our policy is to make a positive contribution to the communities and societies we live in" and "our policy is not to diversify out of the hamburger business" are two examples of the breadth of what some call policies. This book defines *policy* much more narrowly as specific guides to managerial action and decisions in the implementation of strategy. This definition permits a sharper distinction between the formulation and implementation of functional strategies. And, of even greater importance, it focuses the tangible value of the policy concept where it can be most useful—as a key administrative tool to enhance effective implementation and execution of strategy.

FIGURE 10–7
Key Functional Tactics in HRM

Functional Tactic	Typical Questions That HRM Tactics Should Answer
Recruitment, selection, and orientation	What key human resources are needed to support the chosen strategy?
	How do we recruit these human resources?
	How sophisticated should our selection process be?
	How should we introduce new employees to the organization?
Career development and training	What are our future human resource needs?
	How can we prepare our people to meet these needs?
	How can we help our people develop?
Compensation	What levels of pay are appropriate for the tasks we require?
	How can we motivate and retain good people?
	How should we interpret our payment, incentive, benefit, and seniority policies?
Evaluation, discipline, and control	How often should we evaluate our people? Formally or informally?
	What disciplinary steps should we take to deal with poor performance or inappropriate behavior?
	In what ways should we "control" individual and group performance?
Labor relations and equal opportunity requirements	How can we maximize labor-management cooperation?
	How do our personnel practices affect women/minorities?
	Should we have hiring policies?

and the disparate handling of common functions—something that often hampers operating personnel.

3. *Policies ensure quicker decisions* by standardizing answers to previously answered questions that otherwise would recur and be pushed up the management hierarchy again and again—something that required unnecessary levels of management between senior decision makers and field personnel.

4. *Policies institutionalize basic aspects of organization behavior.* This minimizes conflicting practices and establishes consistent patterns of action in attempts to make the strategy work—again, freeing operating personnel to act.

5. *Policies reduce uncertainty in repetitive and day-to-day decision making*, thereby providing a necessary foundation for coordinated, efficient efforts and freeing operating personnel to act.

6. *Policies counteract resistance to or rejection of chosen strategies by organization members.* When major strategic change is undertaken, unambiguous operating policies clarify what is expected and facilitate acceptance, particularly when operating managers participate in policy development.

7. *Policies offer predetermined answers to routine problems.* This greatly expedites dealing with both ordinary and extraordinary problems—with the former, by referring to these answers; with the latter, by giving operating personnel more time to cope with them.

8. *Policies afford managers a mechanism for avoiding hasty and ill-conceived decisions in changing operations.* Prevailing policy can always be used as a reason for not yielding to emotion-based, expedient, or temporarily valid arguments for altering procedures and practices.

WHAT'S NEXT FOR HRM? AN EXPERT SAYS IT'S TIME FOR HRM DEPARTMENTS TO PUT UP OR SHUT UP!

Fortune magazine editor Tom Stewart (74774.3555@compuserve.com) made these observations recently:

> Nestling warm and sleepy in your company is a department whose employees spend 80 percent of their time on routine administrative tasks. Nearly every function of this department can be performed more expertly for less by others. It is your human resources department. Consider what HR does and whether it should do it.

Start with payroll. Outside providers now cut an estimated 25 percent of all paychecks issued in the United States. The reason, says payroll services leader ADP's CFO: "As companies move off mainframes, they are taking a look at what applications are strategic to them. When they decide that payroll and HR functions are not strategic, they outsource them."

The same is happening with benefits administration. A 1995 survey of 314 large U.S. companies found 87 percent outsource record keeping and 59 percent administration service. The Corporate Leadership Council conducts research for 500 member companies concluded that there is significant potential and value in outsourcing four HR functions: benefit design and administration; information systems and record keeping; employee services such as retirement counseling, outplacement, and relocation; and health and safety. None, the Council noted, have much potential to produce competitive advantage for a company that does them especially well in-house.

But why stop there? Take recruiting. The rule of thumb among managers is to involve HR as little as possible in the recruiting process. While HR professionals are themselves looking for work, two-thirds of the time they find it by networking or using (outside) search firms. Another candidate is

Policies may be written and formal or unwritten and informal. Informal, unwritten policies are usually associated with a strategic need for competitive secrecy. Some policies of this kind, such as promotion from within, are widely known (or expected) by employees and implicitly sanctioned by management. Managers and employees often like the latitude granted by unwritten and informal policies. However, such policies may detract from the long-term success of a strategy. Formal, written policies have at least seven advantages:

1. They require managers to think through the policy's meaning, content, and intended use.
2. They reduce misunderstanding.
3. They make equitable and consistent treatment of problems more likely.
4. They ensure unalterable transmission of policies.
5. They communicate the authorization or sanction of policies more clearly.
6. They supply a convenient and authoritative reference.
7. They systematically enhance indirect control and organizationwide coordination of the key purposes of policies.

The strategic significance of policies can vary. At one extreme are such policies as travel reimbursement procedures, which are really work rules and may not be linked to the implementation of a strategy. At the other extreme are organizationwide policies that are virtually functional strategies, such as Wendy's requirement that every location invest 1 percent of its gross revenue in local advertising.

continued

designing and running compensation and reward systems—ironically, especially when state-of-the-art reward mechanisms are of paramount importance to competing. Many managers have decided that it is much better to buy the state of the art from outside, customize it, and instill responsibility for running it as far down in the organization as possible. And as for training: Will every reader who has taken a training course sponsored by their HR department and found it very valuable raise his hand? There's lot of evidence that training is a good thing . . . if it's just-in-time, close-to-the-work training—training that should be lodged in the line function, not off the shelf.

Says Vikesh Mahendroo, Executive VP of HR consultants W.M. Mercer says "HR is often out of sync with the needs of the business." He thinks reengineering HR can fix that. But how far should they go? Steel giant Nucor, with 6,000 employees, runs HR with a headquarters staff of three people—a secretary and two HR professionals, one HR agent at each plant reporting to the plant manager, and a set of company HR principles. Says Corporate Leadership Council executive director Matt Olsen: "This is a make-or-break moment for the HR function."

HR people say that they are the trustee of the asset that matters above all others, proactive custodians of our core competence, holders of the keys to competitive advantage in the new economy. Just so much rhetoric say others. There may be a reason that more and more new HR executives come to the post with backgrounds in line management or consulting rather than from HR's own ranks. Says Mahendroo, "There are two messages here. One is that human capital management is important enough that it is an acceptable career path for an up-and-comer. The second is that many people doing the work now can't cut it in the HR of the future."

Policies can be externally imposed or internally derived. Policies regarding equal employment practices are often developed in compliance with external (government) requirements, and policies regarding leasing or depreciation may be strongly influenced by current tax regulations.

Regardless of the origin, formality, and nature of policies, the key point to bear in mind is the valuable role that they can play in strategy implementation. Existing policies should be reviewed periodically so as to ensure their guidance and control of operating activities in a manner consistent with current business and functional strategies. Lotus Development Corporation (Lotus 1–2–3) recently halted a policy forcing customers to destroy spreadsheet programs from competing software makers. Aimed at preventing unauthorized use of 1–2–3 software, Lotus found it was creating major problems for some customers. Communicating specific policies will help overcome resistance to strategic change and foster commitment to successful strategy implementation.

SUMMARY

The first concern in the implementation of business strategy is to translate that strategy into action throughout the organization. This chapter discussed three important tools for accomplishing this.

Action plans and short-term objectives are derived from long-term objectives, which are then translated into current actions and targets. They differ from long-term objectives in time frame, specificity, and measurement. To be effective in strategy implementation, they must be integrated and coordinated. They also must be consistent, measurable, and prioritized.

STRATEGY
IN ACTION
10–5

SELECTED POLICIES THAT
AID STRATEGY IMPLEMENTATION

3M Corporation has a *personnel policy*, called the *15 percent rule*, that allows virtually any employee to spend up to 15 percent of the workweek on anything that he or she wants to, as long as it's product related.

(This policy supports 3M's corporate strategy of being a highly innovative manufacturer, with each division required to have a quarter of its annual sales come from products introduced within the past five years.)

Wendy's has a *purchasing policy* that gives local store managers the authority to buy fresh meat and produce locally, rather than from regionally designated or company-owned sources.

(This policy supports Wendy's functional strategy of having fresh, unfrozen hamburgers daily.)

General Cinema has a *financial policy* that requires annual capital investment in movie theaters not to exceed annual depreciation.

(By seeing that capital investment is no greater than depreciation, this policy supports General Cinema's financial strategy of maximizing cash flow—in this case, all profit—to its growth areas. The policy also reinforces General Cinema's financial strategy of leasing as much as possible.)

IBM had a *marketing policy* of not giving free IBM personal computers (PCs) to any person or organization.

(This policy attempted to support IBM's image strategy by maintaining its image as professional, high-value, service business as it sought to dominate the PC market.)

Crown, Cork, and Seal Company has an *R&D policy* of not investing any financial or people resources in basic research.

(This policy supports Crown, Cork, and Seal's functional strategy, which emphasizes customer services, not technical leadership.)

NationsBank of South Carolina has an *operating policy* that requires annual renewal of the financial statement of all personal borrowers.

(This policy supports NationsBank's financial strategy, which seeks to maintain a loan-to-loss ratio below the industry norm.)

Functional tactics are derived from the business strategy. They identify the specific, immediate actions that must be taken in key functional areas to implement the business strategy.

Employee empowerment through policies provides another means for guiding behavior, decisions, and actions at the firm's operating levels in a manner consistent with its business and functional strategies. Effective policies channel actions, behavior, decisions, and practices to promote strategic accomplishment.

Action plans, functional tactics, and policies represent only the start of the strategy implementation. The strategy must be institutionalized—must permeate the firm. The next chapter examines this phase of strategy implementation.

QUESTIONS FOR DISCUSSION

1. How does the concept "translate thought into action" bear on the relationship between business strategy and operating strategy? Between long-term and short-term objectives?

2. How do functional tactics differ from corporate and business strategies?

3. What key concerns must functional tactics address in marketing? Finance? POM? Personnel?

4. How do policies aid strategy implementation? Illustrate your answer.

5. Illustrate a policy, an objective, and a functional tactic in your personal career strategy.

6. Why are short-term objectives needed when long-term objectives are already available.

BIBLIOGRAPHY

Allio, R. J. "Formulating Global Strategy." *Planning Review*, March–April 1989, pp. 22–29.

Boag, David A., and Ali Dastmalchian. "Market Vulnerability and the Design and Management of the Marketing Function in Small Firms." *Journal of Small Business Management*, October 1988, p. 37.

Charalambides, L. C. "Designing Communication Support Systems for Strategic Planning." *Long Range Planning*, December 1988, pp. 93–100.

Coates, N. "The Globalization of the Motor Vehicle Manufacturing Industry." *Planning Review*, January–February 1989, pp. 34–39.

Coy, P. "The New Realism in Office Systems." *Business Week*, June 15, 1992, p. 128.

David, F. R. "How Companies Define Their Mission." *Long Range Planning*, February 1989, pp. 90–97.

Freund, Y. P. "Critical Success Factors." *Planning Review*, March–April 1988, pp. 20–23.

Fulmer, William E. "Human Resource Management: The Right Hand of Strategy Implementation." *Human Resource Planning* 13, no. 1 (1990), pp.1–11.

Garavan, Thomas N. "Strategic Human Resource Development." *International Journal of Manpower* 12, no. 6 (1991), pp. 21–34.

Giles, William D. "Making Strategy Work." *Long Range Planning* 24, no. 5 (1991), pp. 75–91.

Lado, A. A., and M. C. Wilson. "Human Resource Systems and Sustained Competitive Advantage: A Competency Based Perspective." *Academy of Management Review* 19 (1994), pp. 699–727.

Marucheck, Ann; Ronald Pamnesi; and Carl Anderson. "An Exploratory Study of the Manufacturing Strategy Process in Practice." *Journal of Operations Management* 9, no. 1 pp. 101–23.

Miller, J. G., and W. Hayslip. "Implementing Manufacturing Strategic Planning." *Planning Review*, July–August 1989, pp. 22–29.

Nielson, Richard P. "Cooperative Strategy in Marketing." *Business Horizons*, July–August 1987, p. 61.

Ohmae, K. "Getting Back to Strategy." *Harvard Business Review*, September–October 1988, pp. 149–56.

Parnell, J. A. "Functional Background and Business Strategy: The Impact of Executive Strategy Fit on Performance." *Journal of Business Strategies* 11, no. 1 (1994), pp. 49–62.

Perkins, A. G. "Manufacturing: Maximizing Service, Minimizing Inventory." *Harvard Business Review* 72, no. 2, pp. 13–14.

Peterson, R. T. "An Analysis of New Product Ideas." *Journal of Small Business Management*, April 1988, pp. 25–31.

Prahalad, C. K., and Gary Hamel. "The Core Competence of the Corporation." *Harvard Business Review* 68 (May–June 1990), pp. 79–93.

Quinn, James Brian. *Intelligent Enterprise.* (New York: Free Press, 1992), chaps. 2 and 3.

Randolph, W. A., and B. Z. Posner. "What Every Manager Needs to Know about Project Management." *Sloan Management Review*, Summer 1988, pp. 64–74.

Roth, Kendall; David M. Schweiger; and Allen J. Morrison. "Global Strategy Implementation at the Business Unit Level: Operational Capabilities and Administrative Mechanisms." *Journal of International Business Studies* 22, no. 3 (1991), pp. 369–402.

Shank, J. K., and V. Govindarajan. "Making Strategy Explicit in Cost Analysis." *Sloan Management Review*, Spring 1988, pp. 19–30.

Stalk, George; Philip Evans; and Lawrence E. Shulman. "Competing on Capabilities: The New Rules of Corporate Strategy." *Harvard Business Review* 70, no. 2 (March–April 1992), pp. 57–69.

Stern, Joel. "Think Cash and Risk—Forget ESP." *Planning Review*, January–February 1988, p. 6.

Stonich, Paul. *Implementing Strategy: Making Strategy Happen.* (New York: Ballinger, 1982).

Wheelwright, S., and N. S. Langowitz. "Plus Development Corporation: Joint Venturing a Breakthrough Product." *Planning Review*, July–August 1989, pp. 6–21.

Wright, Norman B. "The Driving Force: An Action-Oriented Solution to Strategy Implementation." *Canadian Business Quarterly* 54, no. 1 (1989), pp. 51–54, 66.

Yip, George S. *Total Global Strategy: Managing for Worldwide Competitive Advantage.* (Englewood Cliffs, NJ: Prentice Hall, 1992), chap. 8.

CHAPTER 10 COHESION CASE ILLUSTRATION

IMPLEMENTING STRATEGY THROUGH THE BUSINESS FUNCTIONS AT COCA-COLA

The Coca Cola Company is exciting to examine when it comes to the detail with which they craft and execute value chain activities and functional tactics designated to accomplish their business strategy. In this case we show you some of the activities and tactics Coca-Cola has used to implement the four elements of its business strategy.

Before we do that, it is useful to see how Coca-Cola management views their company from a value chain perspective. Their value chain view of themselves is as a "global business system," as they describe below:

> A successful global company must have a global business system through which to reach consumers. In our case, the system comprises not only the Company itself, but a worldwide network of employees, bottling partners, vendors, and customers. This system is made up of dedicated people working long and hard to sell products they believe in. . . . Such a system must do much more than just deliver products. In order to appeal to cultures as diverse as those in Switzerland and Swaziland, it must also tailor products and messages to local markets. . . . Graphically, this system can best be represented as an inverted triangle or pyramid comprising many levels, of which the Company is only the base. The following figure depicts this incomparable global system, which builds from 650,000 employees through more than 8 million customers to satisfy the thirst of the world's more than 5 billion consumers. And most important, the system is growing and expanding every day. As impressive as the numbers in the figure are, by the time, you read them, they will have been surpassed.

Remember that Coca Cola's business strategy had four elements: (1) geographic expansion, (2) infrastructure fortification, (3) financial reformation, and (4) differentiation. Let's look at some specific ways they implement these four elements.

GEOGRAPHIC EXPANSION

Says Roberto Goizueta, "We refuse to neglect any territory anywhere in the world. We have long pursued geographic expansion as a fundamental means of growth. We have divided the world into six regions in which we have major organizations in place to pursue aggressive expansion." A summary of Coca Cola's geographic expansion efforts over the last three years is provided below and on pages 329–32.

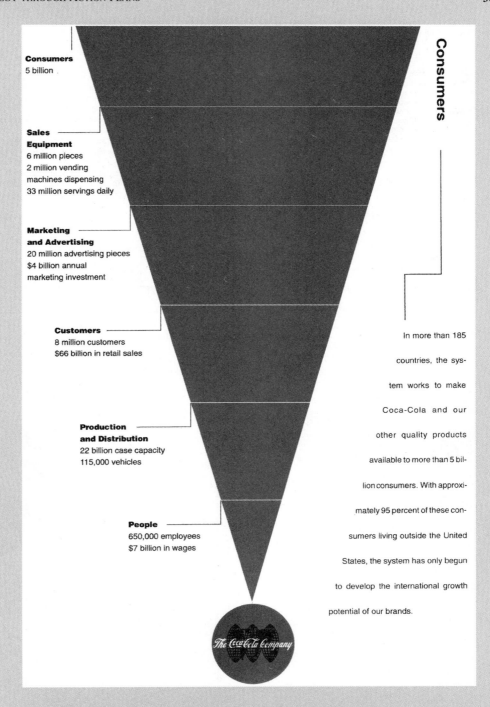

Consumers
5 billion

Sales Equipment
6 million pieces
2 million vending
machines dispensing
33 million servings daily

Marketing and Advertising
20 million advertising pieces
$4 billion annual
marketing investment

Customers
8 million customers
$66 billion in retail sales

Production and Distribution
22 billion case capacity
115,000 vehicles

People
650,000 employees
$7 billion in wages

Consumers

In more than 185 countries, the system works to make Coca-Cola and our other quality products available to more than 5 billion consumers. With approximately 95 percent of these consumers living outside the United States, the system has only begun to develop the international growth potential of our brands.

The Coca-Cola Company

COCA-COLA USA

Led by solid increases in the Company's core brands, the world's largest market for Coca-Cola achieved solid growth in 1994, again outperforming the industry. Unit case volume grew 7 percent, while gallon sales grew 8 percent. Complementing the strong growth of Coca-Cola and Sprite, supporting brands such as Fruitopia, Powerade and Minute Maid Juices To Go contributed meaningful volume gains. Continued focus on programs designed to help customers increase their profits through the sale of our products also contributed to the results.

Average Annual Growth
Unit Case Volume*

1 Year
Coca-Cola USA　　　7%
Rest of Industry　　2%

5 Years
Coca-Cola USA　　　4%
Rest of Industry　　2%

*Coca-Cola USA includes non-carbonated soft drinks.

Coca-Cola USA Per Capita Consumption**
Even in leading-edge markets such as the United States, enormous opportunities for growth still exist. If we were to elevate territories with below-average per capitas to our national average, our overall per capita would increase 27 drinks, generating 300 million incremental unit cases – roughly the equivalent of our total 1994 unit case volume in Spain, one of our top 10 markets worldwide.

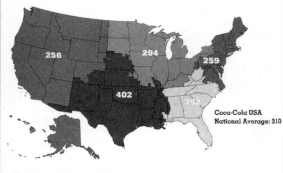

Coca-Cola USA
National Average: 310

**8-ounce servings of Company soft drinks per person per year.

AFRICA GROUP

Difficult economic and political conditions in key markets continued to affect industry performance in Africa. Declines in economically troubled Nigeria offset unit case increases throughout most of the Group. Gallon sales declined slightly, affected primarily by a decrease in Nigeria. Nonetheless, the Africa Group continues to improve and expand the foundations for strong long-term growth. Those foundations include restructured bottling operations, increasingly efficient business systems, aggressive marketing programs and improved customer service. While Company products account for 84 percent of industry sales, overall per capita consumption of Company products remains a relatively low 23 servings per year, representing significant potential for growth.

Growth Rate
(1994 vs. 1993)

Africa	Gallon Sales	Unit Case Sales
Central Africa Region	7%	11%
Nigeria	(19)%	(14)%
Southern Africa Division	(5)%	3%
Other	12%	9%
Total	**(4)%**	**1%**

Africa Group
1994 Unit Case Sales

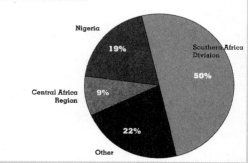

PACIFIC GROUP

Aggressive marketing and expanded production and distribution capacity fueled strong across-the-board volume increases in the Pacific Group in 1994. Unit case volume grew 12 percent and gallon sales increased 13 percent, as an unusually warm summer over most of Asia offset continued weakness in the Japanese economy. In 1995, the Group assumed responsibility for India and the Middle East, markets with opportunities that mirror those of many of our developed markets in Asia. Accordingly, the Group was renamed the Middle and Far East Group.

Growth Rate
(1994 vs. 1993)

Pacific	Gallon Sales	Unit Case Sales
Australia	13%	10%
China	50%	36%
Japan	9%	8%
Korea	19%	11%
Philippines	12%	14%
Thailand	14%	14%
Other	10%	10%
Total	**13%**	**12%**

Pacific Group
1994 Unit Case Sales

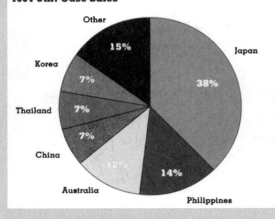

EUROPEAN COMMUNITY GROUP

Focused marketplace activity, complemented by favorable summer weather and a recovering economy, yielded strong results in 1994. Momentum accelerated in the second half of the year as unit case volume grew 13 percent. For the full year, unit case volume grew 7 percent and gallon sales rose 5 percent. These gains were fueled by a number of initiatives, including a new push behind contour packaging and strong World Cup and Olympic Winter Games marketing efforts. In early 1995, Eastern Europe, Scandinavia and the former Soviet Union were added to the Group's responsibilities, providing a single leadership point for greater Europe. The combined group was renamed the Greater Europe Group.

Growth Rate
(1994 vs. 1993)

European Community	Gallon Sales	Unit Case Sales
Benelux/Denmark	4%	9%
France	7%	9%
Germany	3%	4%
Great Britain	6%	7%
Italy	3%	5%
Spain	7%	9%
Other	11%	11%
Total	**5%**	**7%**

European Community Group
1994 Unit Case Sales

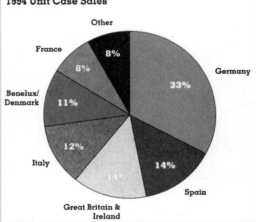

NORTHEAST EUROPE/MIDDLE EAST GROUP

The diverse markets of the Northeast Europe/Middle East (NEME) Group recorded another year of exceptionally strong growth. Unit case volume grew 35 percent and gallon shipments increased 32 percent, continuing the strong momentum of 1993. The NEME Group also picked up significant volume in India, where Coca-Cola returned in late 1993 after a 16-year absence.

Growth Rate
(1994 vs. 1993)

Northeast Europe/ Middle East (NEME)	Gallon Sales	Unit Case Sales
East Central European Division	17%	23%
Middle East Division	34%	33%
Nordic and N. Eurasia Division	13%	16%
India	*	*
Total	**32%**	**35%**

*Sales began in late 1993.

LATIN AMERICA GROUP

The Latin America Group continued to capitalize on the liberalization of economies throughout the region with aggressive infrastructure investments and new product and package introductions. These measures, coupled with focused brand-building initiatives, contributed to a solid performance in 1994. Driven by strong growth from Mexico and Argentina and a second-half surge in demand in Brazil, unit case volume grew 10 percent and gallon sales increased 9 percent, while profitability increased significantly.

Growth Rate
(1994 vs. 1993)

Latin America	Gallon Sales	Unit Case Sales
Argentina	11%	12%
Brazil	8%	10%
Chile	8%	8%
Colombia	4%	4%
Mexico	11%	11%
Other	7%	9%
Total	**9%**	**10%**

**Northeast Europe/Middle East Group
1994 Unit Case Sales**

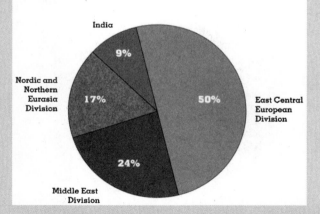

**Latin America Group
1994 Unit Case Sales**

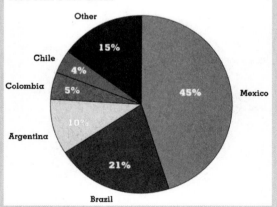

INFRASTRUCTURE FORTIFICATION

Coca-Cola has sought to improve and expand its inbound logistics, operating capabilities, and outbound logistics throughout its global bottling system. Management had this to say about infrastructure tactics:

> As our customers grow and expand, we continue to stimulate positive changes in our global bottling system, equipping it to meet their needs more effectively and efficiently. Depending on the situation, we have used three approaches: 1. Taking noncontrolling ownership positions, infusing capital and management. 2. Facilitating the creation of large, efficient anchor bottlers who share our commitment to growth. 3. Investing in consolidated operations, compensating for limited local resources. Bottling companies in which we hold an ownership position sold over 5 billion unit cases for 42 percent of our worldwide volume. Unit case volume grew at approximately the same rate in both those bottling companies in which we have ownership positions and those in which we have no holdings, reaffirming the effectiveness of the strategy of infrastructure fortification.

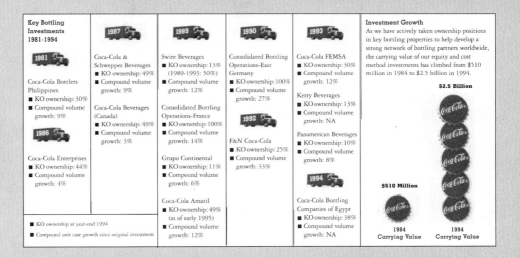

Another way to see this more graphically is to look at what Coca-Cola has invested in nonbottling infrastructure to consolidate production and distribution networks and to adapt the latest operating technology and information systems:

	Year Ended December 31		
	1994	**1993**	**1992**
Capital expenditures	**$878**	$800	$1,083
United States	**32%**	23%	22%
Africa	**3%**	1%	1%
European Community	**26%**	33%	41%
Latin America	**16%**	19%	20%
Northeast Europe/Middle East	**19%**	18%	13%
Pacific & Canada	**4%**	6%	3%

FINANCIAL REFORMATION

Coca-Cola management has used four financial/accounting tactics to implement its business strategy and to generate the capacity to support the other parts of its strategy to build competitive advantage. Those four tactics are:

1. Increase the use of debt.
2. Lower the dividend payout rate to increase reinvestment.
3. Repurchase Coca-Cola shares.
4. Adopt the economic value-added approach to evaluate results.

These tactics are described below and on the next page.

Using Debt Effectively

Capitalizing on our ability to generate returns well above our borrowing rates, we began taking on prudent amounts of debt in the early 1980s. With a return on capital roughly three times our cost of capital, this strategy makes even more sense now than before.

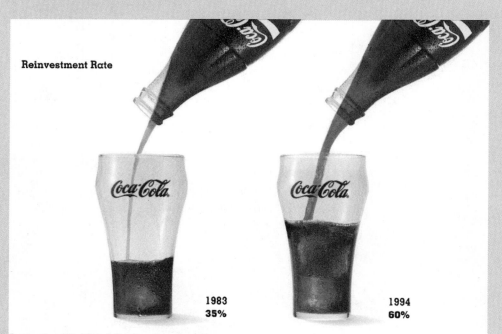

Reinvestment Rate

1983
35%

1994
60%

Lowering Dividend Payout Ratio

With our dividend payout ratio cresting as high as 65 percent in 1983, we began increasing our dividends at a slower rate than our earnings growth, eventually lowering that ratio to 40 percent. Reducing our payout ratio allowed us to reinvest over $660 million into our business in 1994 alone, bringing the total amount freed up for reinvestment since 1983 to $3.4 billion.

Repurchasing of Shares

Acting on the conviction that our shares represent one of the best uses of our excess cash, we repurchased 25 million of our own shares in 1994, bringing our total repurchases since 1984 to approximately 454 million, at an average cost of $15.45 per share.

$15.45

$51.50

Average Purchase Price

1994 Market Value

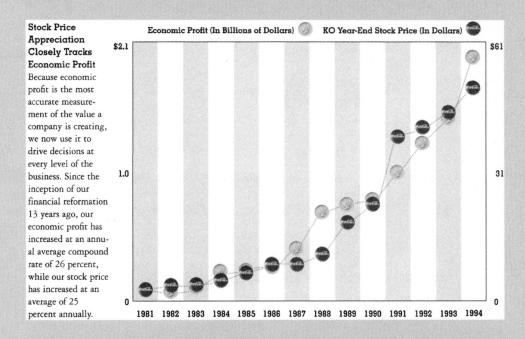

Stock Price Appreciation Closely Tracks Economic Profit

Because economic profit is the most accurate measurement of the value a company is creating, we now use it to drive decisions at every level of the business. Since the inception of our financial reformation 13 years ago, our economic profit has increased at an annual average compound rate of 26 percent, while our stock price has increased at an average of 25 percent annually.

Economic Profit (In Billions of Dollars)   KO Year-End Stock Price (In Dollars)

$2.1

1.0

0

$61

31

0

1981 1982 1983 1984 1985 1986 1987 1988 1989 1990 1991 1992 1993 1994

DIFFERENTIATION

Focusing on the Consumer

4 If our ongoing geographic expansion, financial reformation and infrastructure fortification initiatives are designed to gear up the machine, then our fourth initiative is designed to put that machine to work. Where we once might have been tempted to rely on the sheer strength of our global availability, our substantial financial resources and our powerful distribution network, we now are driving growth by aggressively expanding demand for our brands. **1994** To increase that demand to levels that will meet our own ambitious expectations, we have set out to become undeniably the world's premier consumer marketing company, taking decisive actions to differentiate our brands wherever we do business.

Differentiation With Customers

Further differentiating our brands with consumers also helps us further differentiate ourselves with our customers, the people who make our products available at the retail level. The logic is simple: the greater the consumer demand for our brands, the greater our ability to add value to our cus-tomers' businesses by attracting more consumers into their outlets.

This important point of differentiation is complemented by our ability to provide superior delivery, promotional services and sales support that clearly differentiate us as the beverage supplier most capable of driving sustained, profitable growth in their businesses.

Disappearing at stores daily.

Differentiation in Size and Scope Already the world's largest beverage company, we continued to increase in size and scope in 1994, further enhancing another key point of differentiation we bring to any marketplace.

● In 1994, the *increase* in our market value exceeded the *total* 1994 market value of all but 106 of the publicly traded companies based in the United States. ● In 1994, unit case sales for Fanta and Sprite, our third and fourth largest-selling brands, respectively, each crossed the **1,** mark for the first time. If the two brands existed as independent companies, Fanta would rank as the third largest soft drink marketer in the world, while Sprite would be the fourth. ● In 1994, our unit case sales in Latin America alone exceeded our nearest international competitor's total international unit case sales. ● In 1994, sales of Coca-Cola *increased* by 500 million unit cases – more than we sold in our first 34 years *combined*.

● In 1995, Coca-Cola made its third trip into space – aboard the *Discovery*.

Differentiation with Consumers

Through the decades, we have quite effectively built brand Coca-Cola on a horizontal basis, extending its appeal across national boundaries

Time magazine
May 15, 1950

until there is virtually no place on earth where the people do not both know and like Coca-Cola. That horizontal expansion continues to serve us well in driving growth. But now, as the number of nations where Coca-Cola is not sold dwindles to fewer than 20, we are intensifying our efforts to build our brands vertically.

Building a brand vertically means simply creating deeper consumer desire for that brand than existed the day before. It's simply making sure we continue to give people additional reasons to

Tokyo's Ginza
1994

buy our brands instead of somebody else's. That's the essence of *differentiation*, and we are determined to make sure every consumer understands that our brands are different, better and special.

In building brand Coca-Cola vertically, our challenge is daunting. Increasing the strength of a new brand is relatively easy; making the world's most powerful brand even more powerful is not. After all, most of the world's 5.6 billion people already have a well-established understanding of what Coca-Cola means to them.

But if our challenge is daunting, our tools are uniquely suited to the task. First, the Coca-Cola trademark itself is a remarkably resilient and multi-dimensional piece of cultural iconography. Second, we are continually building on our unique marketing expertise, consumer understanding, financial firepower and access to creative resources. And third, we are developing an increasingly strong penchant for action.

Differentiation in Action

Differentiation is not created by mere philosophy. Differentiation is created by action.

In other words, the world will judge us as its premier consumer marketing company based not on how much we know or how clever our ideas are, but on how well we translate those ideas into actions that produce results in the marketplace.

Consequently, if our marketing efforts are guided by our bias for differentiation, then they are propelled by our prejudice for action. This means that we must be willing to take risks. And, yes, it means we must be willing to

MIND BODY *Fruitopia™* PLANET

Fruitopia:
taking action to
meet changing
consumer
needs

fail occasionally.

In 1994, all of our major consumer marketing actions generated significant value for The Coca-Cola Company, either by directly driving volume increases or by helping us gain a deeper understanding of our consumers, on which we will build with future actions.

11

IMPLEMENTING STRATEGY THROUGH RESTRUCTURING AND REENGINEERING THE COMPANY'S STRUCTURE, LEADERSHIP, CULTURE, AND REWARDS

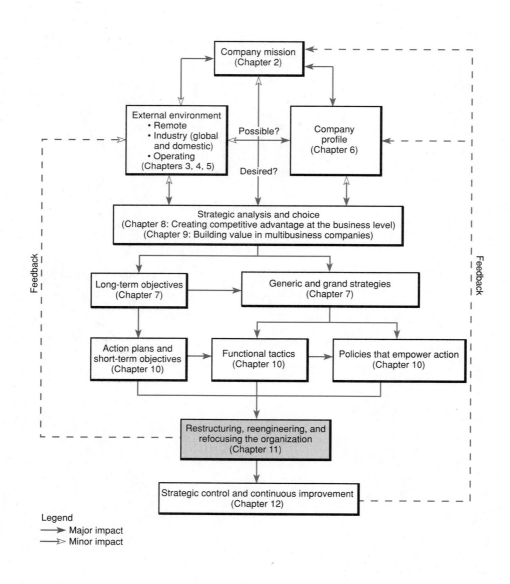

Company mission
(Chapter 2)

External environment
• Remote
• Industry (global and domestic)
• Operating
(Chapters 3, 4, 5)

Possible?

Desired?

Company profile
(Chapter 6)

Strategic analysis and choice
(Chapter 8: Creating competitive advantage at the business level)
(Chapter 9: Building value in multibusiness companies)

Long-term objectives
(Chapter 7)

Generic and grand strategies
(Chapter 7)

Action plans and short-term objectives
(Chapter 10)

Functional tactics
(Chapter 10)

Policies that empower action
(Chapter 10)

Restructuring, reengineering, and refocusing the organization
(Chapter 11)

Strategic control and continuous improvement
(Chapter 12)

Feedback

Feedback

Legend
⟶ Major impact
⟶ Minor impact

Until this point in the strategic management process, managers have maintained a decidedly market-oriented focus as they formulate strategies and begin implementation through action plans detailing the tactics and actions that will be taken in each functional activity. Now the process takes a decidedly operations focus—getting the work of the business done efficiently and effectively so as to make the strategy work. What is the best way to organize ourselves to accomplish the mission? Where should leadership come from? What values should guide our activities each day? What should this organization and its people be like? How can we shape rewards that encourage appropriate action? These are some of the fundamental issues managers face as they turn to the heart of strategy implementation.

While the focus is internal, the firm must still consider external factors as well. The intense competition in the global marketplace of the 1990s has led most companies to consider their structure, or how the activities within their business are conducted, with an unprecedented attentiveness to what that marketplace—customers, competitors, suppliers, distribution partners—suggests or needs from the "internal" structure, business processes, leadership, and culture of their company. *Downsizing, restructuring, reengineering, outsourcing*, and *empowerment* are all emblazoned in our minds as a result of the extraordinary speed with which companies worldwide have incorporated them as part of their adjustment to the rigors of competing as a part of the global economic village of the 21st century. You no doubt recognize and have been touched in several ways by the ramification of these concepts over the last five years. This contemporary vocabulary reflects managers' attempts to rationalize their organizational structure, leadership, culture, and reward systems to ensure a basic level of cost competitiveness, capacity for responsive quality, and the need to shape each one of them to accommodate the requirements of their strategies.

These topics received considerable attention from executives, authors, and researchers during the last decade as they sought to understand the reasons behind the superior performance of the world's "best companies." One of the early and widely accepted frameworks that identify the key factors that best explain superior performance was the McKinsey 7-S Framework, provided in Figure 11–1. This framework provides a useful visualization of the key components managers must consider in making sure a strategy permeates the day-to-day life of the firm.

Once the strategy has been designed, the McKinsey Framework suggests that managers focus on six components to ensure effective execution: structure, systems, shared values (culture), skills, style, and staff. This chapter organizes these six components into four basic elements through which managers can implement strategy. The first is structure—the basic way the firm's different activities are organized. Second is leadership, encompassing the need to establish an effective style as well as the necessary staff and skills to execute the strategy. The third element is culture—the shared values that create the norms of individual behavior and the tone of the organization. The final elements are the systems for rewarding performance as well as monitoring and controlling organizational action. Reward systems are examined in this chapter, while a discussion of systems for monitoring and controlling organizational action is reserved for Chapter 12.

STRUCTURING AN EFFECTIVE ORGANIZATION

Successful strategy implementation depends in large part on the firm's primary organizational structure. Structure helps identify the firm's key activities and the manner in which they will be coordinated to achieve the firm's strategic purpose. IBM changed from a highly centralized, functional structure in the early 1990s to a highly decentralized, strategic business unit structure that IBM's top managers viewed as more consistent with the firm's "network-centric" product development strategy for the 21st century.

FIGURE 11–1
McKinsey 7-S Framework

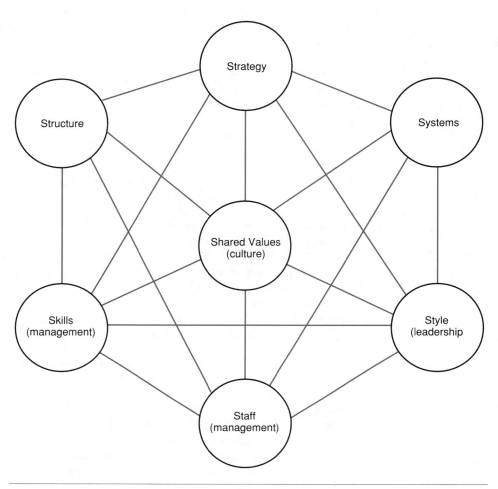

A primary organizational structure comprises the firm's major elements, components, or differentiated units. Such a structure portrays how key tasks and activities have been divided to achieve efficiency and effectiveness.

The primary structure is not the only means for getting "organized" to implement the strategy. Reward systems, coordination terms, planning procedures, alliances, information, and budgetary systems are among the other means that facilitate getting organized. However, it is through the primary structure that strategists attempt to position the firm so as to execute its strategy in a manner that balances internal efficiency and overall effectiveness.

Primary Organizational Structures and Their Strategy-Related Pros and Cons

Matching the structure to the strategy is a fundamental task of company strategists. To understand how that task is handled, we first must review the five basic primary structures. We will then turn to guidelines for matching structure to strategy.

FIGURE 11–2
Functional Organization Structures

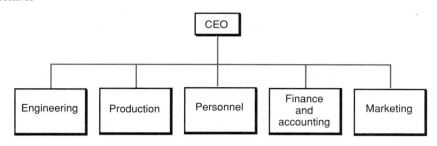

A process-oriented functional structure (an electronics distributor):

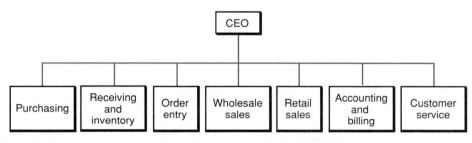

Strategic Advantages	Strategic Disadvantages
1. Achieves efficiency through specialization.	1. Promotes narrow specialization and functional rivalry or conflict.
2. Develops functional expertise.	2. Creates difficulties in functional coordination and interfunctional decision making.
3. Differentiates and delegates day-to-day operating decisions.	
4. Retains centralized control of strategic decisions.	3. Limits development of general managers.
5. Tightly links structure to strategy by designating key activities as separate units.	4. Has a strong potential for interfunctional conflict—priority placed on functional areas, not the entire business.

The five basic primary structures are: (1) functional organization, (2) geographic organization, (3) divisional organization, (4) strategic business units, and (5) matrix organization. Each structure has advantages and disadvantages that strategists must consider when choosing an organization form.

Functional Organizational Structure

Functional structures predominate in firms with a single or narrow product focus. Such firms require well-defined skills and areas of specialization to build competitive advantages in providing their products or services. Dividing tasks into functional specialties enables the personnel of these firms to concentrate on only one aspect of the necessary work. This allows use of the latest technical skills and develops a high level of efficiency.

Product, customer, or technology considerations determine the identity of the parts in a functional structure. A hotel business might be organized around housekeeping (maids), the front desk, maintenance, restaurant operations, reservations and sales, accounting, and personnel. An equipment manufacturer might be organized around production, engineering/quality control, purchasing, marketing, personnel, and finance/accounting. Two examples of functional organizations are illustrated in Figure 11–2.

The strategic challenge presented by the functional structure is effective coordination of the functional units. The narrow technical expertise achieved through specialization can lead to limited perspectives and to differences in the priorities of the functional units. Specialists may see the firm's strategic issues primarily as "marketing" problems or "production" problems. The potential conflict among functional units makes the coordinating role of the chief executive critical. Integrating devices (such as project teams or planning committees) are frequently used in functionally organized firms to enhance coordination and to facilitate understanding across functional areas.

Geographic Organizational Structure

Firms often grow by expanding the sale of their products or services to new geographic areas. In these areas, they frequently encounter differences that necessitate different approaches in producing, providing, or selling their products or services. Structuring by geographic areas is usually required to accommodate these differences. Thus, Holiday Inns is organized by regions of the world because of differences among nations in the laws, customs, and economies affecting the lodging industry. And even within its U.S. organization, Holiday Inns is organized geographically because of regional differences in traveling requirements, lodging regulations, and customer mix.

The key strategic advantage of geographic organizational structures is responsiveness to local market conditions. Figure 11–3 illustrates a typical geographic organizational structure and itemizes the strategic advantages and disadvantages of such structures.

Divisional Organizational Structure

When a firm diversifies its product/service lines, utilizes unrelated market channels, or begins to serve heterogeneous customer groups, a functional structure rapidly becomes inadequate. If a functional structure is retained under these circumstances, production managers may have to oversee the production of numerous and varied products or services, marketing managers may have to create sales programs for vastly different products or sell through vastly different distribution channels, and top management may be confronted with excessive coordination demands. A new organizational structure is often necessary to meet the increased coordination and decision-making requirements that result from increased diversity and size, and the divisional organizational structure is the form often chosen.

For many years, Ford and General Motors have used divisional structures organized by product groups. Manufacturers often organize sales into divisions based on differences in distribution channels.

A divisional structure allows corporate management to delegate authority for the strategic management of distinct business entities—the divisions. This expedites decision making in response to varied competitive environments and enables corporate management to concentrate on corporate-level strategic decisions. The divisions usually are given profit responsibility, which facilitates accurate assessment of profit and loss.

Figure 11–4 illustrates a divisional organizational structure and specifies the strategic advantages and disadvantages of such structures.

Strategic Business Units

Some firms encounter difficulty in evaluating and controlling the operations of their divisions as the diversity, size, and number of these units continue to increase. Under these conditions, a firm may add another layer of management to improve strategy implementation, to promote synergy, and to gain greater control over the firm's diverse business interests. This can be accomplished by creating groups that combine various divisions (or parts of some divisions)

FIGURE 11-3
A Geographic Organizational Structure

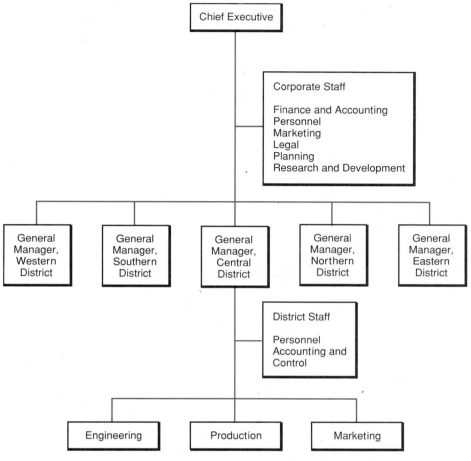

Strategic Advantages

1. Allows tailoring of strategy to needs of each geographic market.
2. Delegates profit/loss responsibility to lowest strategic level.
3. Improves functional coordination within the target market.
4. Takes advantage of economies of local operations.
5. Provides excellent training grounds for higher level general managers.

Strategic Disadvantages

1. Poses problem of deciding whether headquarters should impose geographic uniformity or geographic diversity should be allowed.
2. Makes it more difficult to maintain consistent company image/reputation from area to area.
3. Adds layer of management to run the geographic units.
4. Can result in duplication of staff services at headquarters and district levels.

in terms of common strategic elements. These groups, commonly called *strategic business units* (SBUs), usually are based on the independent product-market segments served by the firm. Figure 11–5 illustrates an SBU organizational structure.

As companies grow, they often adopt a new structure from among the alternatives we have described as a way to help them manage complexity brought on by growth. The SBU structure's main value appears to be that it provides a way for the largest companies to

FIGURE 11–4
Divisional Organization Structure

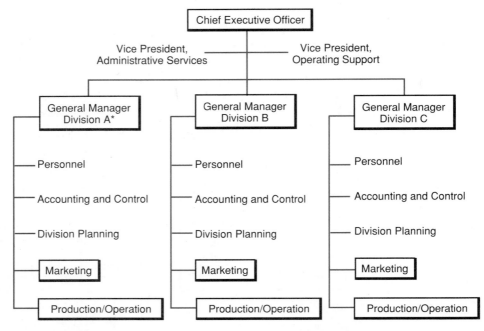

Strategic Advantages

1. Forces coordination and necessary authority down to the appropriate level for rapid response.
2. Places strategy development and implementation in closer proximity to the unique environments of the divisions.
3. Frees chief executive officer for broader strategic decision making.
4. Sharply focuses accountability for performance.
5. Retains functional specialization within each division.
6. Provides good training grounds for strategic managers.

Strategic Disadvantages

1. Fosters potentially dysfunctional competition for corporate-level resources.
2. Presents the problem of determining how much authority should be given to division managers.
3. Creates a potential for policy inconsistencies among divisions.
4. Presents the problem of distributing corporate overhead costs in a way that's acceptable to division managers with profit responsibility.

regain focus in different parts of their business that were central to earlier success yet which became "lost" or dysfunctional in the complexity and size brought on by the company's success. IBM adopted the SBU approach in 1995 by creating 11 distinct SBUs, or "Baby Blues," out of its highly centralized structure. These SBUs are distinct SBUs that provide marketing, services, and support for their customers in five global regions. These SBUs have worldwide responsibility for product development, manufacturing, and delivery of their own distinct product lines.

Matrix Organization

In large companies, increased diversity leads to numerous product and project efforts of major strategic significance. The result is a need for an organizational form that provides skills and resources where and when they are most vital. The matrix organization has been used increas-

FIGURE 11–5
Strategic Business Unit Organizational Structure

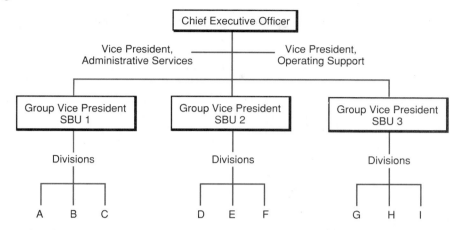

Strategic Advantages	Strategic Disadvantages
1. Improves coordination between divisions with similar strategic concerns and product-market environments.	1. Places another layer of management between the divisions and corporate management.
2. Tightens the strategic management and control of large, diverse business enterprises.	2. May increase dysfunctional competition for corporate resources.
3. Facilitates distinct and in-depth business planning at the corporate and business levels.	3. May present difficulties in defining the role of the group vice president.
4. Channels accountability to distinct business units.	4. May present difficulties in defining how much autonomy should be given to the group vice presidents and division managers.

ingly to meet this need. Among the firms that now use some form of matrix organization are Citicorp, Matsushita, Unilever, Shell Oil, Dow Chemical, and Texas Instruments.

The matrix organization provides dual channels of authority, performance responsibility, evaluation, and control, as shown in Figure 11–6. Essentially, subordinates are assigned both to a basic functional area and to a project or product manager. The matrix form is intended to make the best use of talented people within a firm by combining the advantages of functional specialization and product-project specialization.

The matrix structure also increases the number of middle managers who exercise general management responsibilities (through the project manager role) and, thus, broaden their exposure to organizationwide strategic concerns. In this way, the matrix structure overcomes a key deficiency of functional organizations while retaining the advantages of functional specialization.

Although the matrix structure is easy to design, it is difficult to implement. Dual chains of command challenge fundamental organizational orientations. Negotiating shared responsibilities, the use of resources, and priorities can create misunderstanding or confusion among subordinates. These problems are heightened in an international context with the complications introduced by distance, language, time, and culture.

To avoid the deficiencies that might arise from a permanent matrix structure, some firms are accomplishing particular strategic tasks, by means of a "temporary" or "flexible" *overlay structure*. This approach, used recently by such firms as NEC, Matsushita, Phillips, and Unilever, is meant to take *temporary* advantage of a matrix-type team while preserving an

FIGURE 11–6
Matrix Organizational Structure

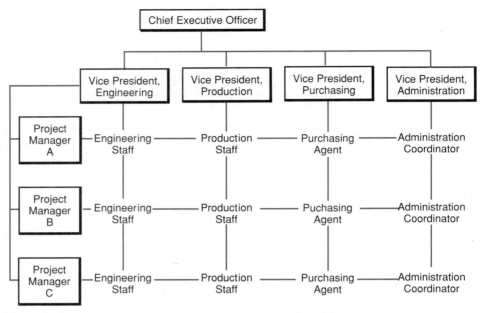

Strategic Advantages

1. Accommodates a wide variety of project-oriented business activity.
2. Provides good training grounds for strategic managers.
3. Maximizes efficient use of functional managers.
4. Fosters creativity and multiple sources of diversity.
5. Gives middle management broader exposure to strategic issues.

Strategic Disadvantages

1. May result in confusion and contradictory policies.
2. Necessitates tremendous horizontal and vertical coordination.
3. Can proliferate information logjams and excess reporting.
4. Can trigger turf battles and loss of accountability.

underlying divisional structure. Thus, the basic idea of the matrix structure—*to simplify and amplify the focus of resources on a narrow but strategically important product, project, or market*—appears to be an important structural alternative for large, diverse organizations.

Guidelines to Match Structure to Strategy

Which organizational structure is the best? Considerable research has addressed this issue, and the consensus is that *it depends on the strategy of the firm*. Since the structural design ties together key activities and resources of the firm, it must be closely aligned with the demands of the firm's strategy. What follows are some guidelines that emerge from this line of research and the restructuring revolution that has altered the corporate landscape at the dawn of the 21st century.

Restructure to Emphasize and Support Strategically Critical Activities

Restructuring has been the buzzword of global enterprise for the last 10 years. Its contemporary meaning is multifaceted. At the heart of the restructuring trend is the notion that some activities within a business's value chain are more critical to the success of the business's strategy than others. Wal-Mart's organizational structure is designed to ensure that its impressive logistics and purchasing competitive advantages operate flawlessly. Coordinating daily logistical and purchasing efficiencies among separate stores lets Wal-Mart lead the industry in profitability yet sell retail for less than many competitors buy the same merchandise at wholesale. Motorola's organizational structure is designed to protect and nurture its legendary R&D and new product development capabilities—spending over twice the industry average in R&D alone each year. Motorola's R&D emphasis continually spawns proprietary technologies that support its technology-based competitive advantage. Coca-Cola emphasizes the importance of distribution activities, advertising, and retail support to its bottlers in its organizational structure. All three of these companies emphasize very different parts of the value chain process, but they are extraordinarily successful in part because they have designed their organizational structures to emphasize and support strategically critical activities. Strategy in Action 11–1 provides some guidelines that should influence how an organization is structured depending on which among five different sources of competitive advantage are emphasized in its strategy.

Two critical considerations arise when restructuring the organization to emphasize and support strategically critical activities. First, managers need to make the strategically critical activities the central building blocks for designing organization structure. Those activities should be identified and separated as much as possible into self-contained parts of the organization. Then the remaining structure must be designed so as to ensure timely integration with other parts of the organization.

While this is easily proposed, managers need to recognize that strategically relevant activities may still reside in different parts of the organization, particularly in functionally organized structures. Support activities like finance, engineering, or information processing are usually self-contained units, often outside the unit around which core competencies are built. This often results in an emphasis on departments obsessed with performing their own tasks more than emphasizing the key results (customer satisfaction, differentiation, low costs, speed) the business as a whole seeks. So the second consideration is to design the organizational structure so that it helps coordinate and integrate these support activities to (1) maximize their support of strategy-critical primary activities in the firm's value chain and (2) does so in a way to minimize the costs for support activities and the time spent on internal coordination. Managerial efforts to do this in the 1990s have placed reengineering, downsizing, and outsourcing as prominent tools for strategists restructuring their organizations.

Reengineer Strategic Business Processes

Business process reengineering (BPR), popularized by consultants Michael Hammer and James Champy,[1] is one of the more popular methods by which organizations worldwide are undergoing restructuring efforts to remain competitive in the 21st century. BPR is intended to reorganize a company so that it can best create value for the customer by eliminating barriers that create distance between employees and customers. It involves fundamental rethinking and radical redesign of a business process. It is characterized as radical because it strives to structure organizational efforts and activities around results and value creation by focusing on the processes that are undertaken to meet customer needs, not specific tasks and functional areas such as marketing and sales.

Business reengineering reduces fragmentation by crossing traditional departmental lines and reducing overhead to compress formerly separate steps and tasks that are

---

[1] Michael Hammer and James Champy, *Reengineering the Corporation* (New York: HarperBusiness, 1993).

STRATEGY
IN ACTION
11–1

GUIDELINES FOR DESIGNING A STRUCTURE TO ACCOMMODATE FIVE DIFFERENT STRATEGIC PRIORITIES

One of the key things business managers should keep in mind when restructuring their organizations is to devise the new structure so that it emphasizes strategically critical activities within the business's value chain. This means that the structure should allow those activities to have considerable autonomy over issues that influence their operating excellence and timeliness; they should be in a position to easily coordinate with other parts of the business—to get decisions made fast.

Below are five different types of critical activities that may be at the heart of a business's effort to build and sustain competitive advantage. Beside each one are typical conditions that will affect and shape the nature of the organization's structure:

Potential Strategic Priority and Critical Activities	Concomitant Conditions That May Affect or Place Demands on the Organizational Structure and Operating Activities to Build Competitive Advantage
1. Compete as low-cost provider of goods or services.	Broadens market. Requires longer production runs and fewer product changes. Requires special-purpose equipment and facilities.
2. Compete as high-quality provider.	Often possible to obtain more profit per unit, and perhaps more total profit from a smaller volume of sales. Requires more quality-assurance effort and higher operating cost. Requires more precise equipment, which is more expensive. Requires highly skilled workers, necessitating higher wages and greater training efforts.
3. Stress customer service.	Requires broader development of servicepeople and service parts and equipment. Requires rapid response to customer needs or changes in customer tastes, rapid and accurate information system, careful coordination. Requires a higher inventory investment.
4. Provide rapid and frequent introduction of new products.	Requires versatile equipment and people. Has higher research and development costs. Has high retraining costs and high tooling and changeover costs. Provides lower volumes for each product and fewer opportunities for improvements due to the learning curve.
5. Seek vertical integration.	Enables firm to control more of the process. May not have economies of scale at some stages of process. May require high capital investment as well as technology and skills beyond those currently available within the firm.

strategically intertwined in the process of meeting customer needs. This "process orientation," rather than a traditional functional orientation, becomes the perspective around which various activities and tasks are then grouped to create the building blocks of the organization's structure. This is usually accomplished by assembling a multifunctional, multilevel team that begins by identifying customer needs and how the customer wants to deal with the firm. Customer focus must permeate all phases. Companies that have successfully reengineered their operations around strategically critical business processes have pursued the following steps:[2]

---

[2] Judy Wade, "How to Make Reengineering Really Work," *Harvard Business Review* 71, no. 6 (November–December 1993), pp. 119–31.

- Develop a flow chart of the total business process, including its interfaces with other value chain activities.
- Try to simplify the process first, eliminating tasks and steps where possible and analyzing how to streamline the performance of what remains.
- Determine which parts of the process can be automated (usually those that are repetitive, time-consuming, and require little thought or decision); consider introducing advanced technologies that can be upgraded to achieve next-generation capability and provide a basis for further productivity gains down the road.
- Evaluate each activity in the process to determine whether it is strategy-critical or not. Strategy-critical activities are candidates for benchmarking to achieve best-in-industry or best-in-world performance status.
- Weigh the pros and cons of outsourcing activities that are noncritical or that contribute little to organizational capabilities and core competencies.
- Design a structure for performing the activities that remain; reorganize the personnel and groups who perform these activities into the new structure.

When asked recently about his new networking-oriented direction for IBM, IBM CEO Gerstner responded: "It's called *reengineering*. It's called *getting competitive*. It's called *reducing cycle time and cost, flattening organizations, increasing customer responsiveness*. All of these require a collaboration with the customer and with suppliers and with vendors."

Downsize, Outsource, and Self-Manage

Reengineering and a value orientation have led managers to scrutinize even further the way their organizational structures are crucial to strategy implementation. That scrutiny has led to downsizing, outsourcing, and self-management as three important themes influencing the organizational structures into the 21st century. *Downsizing* is eliminating the number of employees, particularly middle management, in a company. The arrival of a global marketplace, information technology, and intense competition caused many companies to reevaluate middle management activities to determine just what value was really being added to the company's products and services. The result of this scrutiny, along with continuous improvements in information processing technology, has been widespread downsizing in the number of management personnel in thousands of companies worldwide. These companies often eliminate whole levels of management. General Electric went from 400,000 to 280,000 employees in this decade while its sales have almost tripled and its profit risen fivefold. AT&T has experienced similar numbers of job reductions. The results of a survey of companies worldwide that have been actively downsizing (which attempts to extract guidelines for downsizing) is shown in Global Strategy in Action 11–1.

One of the outcomes of downsizing was increased *self-management* at operating levels of the company. Cutbacks in the number of management people left those that remained with more work to do. The result was that they had to give up a good measure of control to workers, and they had to rely on those workers to help out. Spans-of-control, traditionally thought to maximize under 10 people, have become much larger due to information technology, running "lean and mean," and delegation to lower levels. Ameritech, one of the Baby Bells, has seen its spans-of-control rise to as much as 30 to 1 in some divisions because most of the people that did staff work—financial analysts, assistant managers, and so on—have disappeared. This delegation, also known as empowerment, is accomplished through concepts like self-managed work groups, reengineering, and automation. It is also seen through efforts to create distinct businesses within a business—conceiving a business

HOW LEAN IS YOUR COMPANY?

It's hard to find a major corporation that hasn't downsized in recent years. But simple reductions in staffing don't make for lean management. Here's a checklist, developed from interviews with executives and consultants, that may tell you if your company needs a diet.

Company Characteristic	Analysis
1. Layers of management between CEO and the shop floor.	Some companies, such as Ameritech, now have as few as four or five where as many as 12 had been common. More than six is most likely too many.
2. Number of employees managed by the typical executive.	At lean companies, spans of control range up to one manager to 30 staffers. A ratio of lower than 1:10 is a warning of arterial sclerosis.
3. Amount of work cut out by your downsizing.	Eliminating jobs without cutting out work can bring disaster. A downsizing should be accompanied by at least a 25% reduction in the number of tasks performed. Some lean companies have hit 50%.
4. Skill levels of the surviving management group.	Managers must learn to accept more responsibility and to eliminate unneeded work. Have you taught them how?
5. Size of your largest profit center by number of employees.	Break down large operating units into smaller profit centers—less than 500 employees is a popular cutoff—to gain the economies of entrepreneurship and offset the burdens of scale.
6. Post-downsizing size of staff at corporate headquarters.	The largest layoffs, on a percentage basis, should be at corporate headquarters. It is often the most overstaffed— and the most removed from customers.

as a confederation of many "small" businesses, rather than one large, interconnected business. Whatever the terminology, the idea is to push decision making down in the organization by allowing major management decisions to be made at operating levels. The result is often the elimination of up to half the levels of management previously existing in an organizational structure.

Another driving force behind downsizing has been outsourcing. *Outsourcing* is simply obtaining work previous done by employees inside the companies from sources outside the company. Managers have found that as they attempt to restructure their organizations, particularly if they do so from a business process orientation, numerous activities can often be found in their company that are not "strategically critical activities." This has particularly been the case of numerous staff activities and administrative control processes previously the domain of various middle management levels in an organization. But it can also refer to primary activities that are steps in their business's value chain—purchasing, shipping, making certain parts, and so on. Further scrutiny has led managers to conclude that these activities not only add little or no value to the product or services, but that they are either unnecessary or they can be done much more cost effectively (and competently) by other businesses specializing in these activities. If this is so, then the business can enhance its competitive advantage by outsourcing the activities it can't outright eliminate. Many organizations have outsourced information processing, various personnel activities, and production of parts that can be done better outside the company. Outsourcing, then, can be a source of competitive advantage and result in a leaner, flatter organizational structure.

Recognize That Strategy and Structure Often Evolve in a Predictable Pattern

Predating some of the recent guidelines reviewed above, still-relevant research suggests businesses frequently grow in a rather predictable pattern that has ramifications for which structure would be most effective. Alfred Chandler first observed a common sequence of evolution in strategy and structure among American firms.[3] The sequence reflected their increasing scope. Most firms began as simple functional units operating at a single site (e.g., a plant, a warehouse, or a sales office) and within a single industry. The initial growth strategy of such firms was *volume expansion*, which created a need for an administrative office to manage the increased volume. The next growth strategy was *geographic expansion*, which required multiple field units, still performing the same function but in different locations. Administrative problems with regard to standardization, specialization, and interunit coordination then gave rise to the need for geographic units and for a central administrative unit to oversee them. *Vertical integration* was usually the next growth strategy. Firms remained within the same industry but performed additional functions. Problems associated with the flow of information and materials among the various functions led to the functional organization, in which staff personnel developed forecasts and schedules that facilitated overall coordination.

The final growth strategy was *product diversification*. Firms entered other industries in which they could use their existing resources. Problems in managing diverse product divisions and evaluating their capital investment proposals led to the multidivisional structure in which similar activities were grouped. Separate divisions handled independent products and were responsible for short-run operating decisions. General managers (i.e., group managers) at a central office were responsible for long-term strategic decisions. These managers had to relate divisional decisions and performance to strategic direction and to balance divisional autonomy against central control.

Larry Wrigley and Richard Rumelt built on Chandler's work by examining how a firm's degree of diversification from its core business affected its choice of structure. They identified four growth strategies: (1) *single-product businesses*; (2) *single dominant businesses*, with one business accounting for 70–95 percent of sales; (3) *related diversified businesses* based on a common distribution channel or technology, with more than 30 percent of sales outside the primary business; and (4) *unrelated diversified businesses*, with more than 30 percent of sales outside the primary business.[4] They found that greater diversity led to greater divisionalization: single-product businesses used a functional structure; related and unrelated businesses used a divisionalized structure; and single dominant businesses used a functional structure in the dominant business and a divisional structure in the remaining businesses.

More-recent research has extended our understanding of the strategy-structure fit.[5] This research continues to suggest that, in smaller firms with a single product or product line, the

---

[3] Alfred D. Chandler, *Strategy and Structure* (Cambridge, MA: MIT Press, 1962).

[4] Larry Wrigley, *Divisional Autonomy and Diversification*, doctoral dissertation, Harvard Business School, 1970; Richard Rumelt, *Diversification Strategy and Performance, Strategic Management Journal* 3 (January–February 1982), pp. 359–69; Richard Rumelt, *Strategy, Structure and Economic Performance* (Boston: HBS Press, 1986). Rumelt used a similar, but more detailed classification scheme.

[5] D. A. Nathanson and J. S. Cassano, "Organization, Diversity, and Performance," *Wharton's Magazine* 6 (1982), pp. 19–26; and Christopher A. Bartlett and Sumantra Ghoshal, "Matrix Management: Not a Structure, a Frame of Mind," *Harvard Business Review* 68, no. 4 (1990), pp. 138–45.

functional structure significantly outperforms the multidivisional structure. In larger firms, however, the roles of corporate- and lower-level staffs significantly affect performance. The greater the diversity among a firm's businesses, the more desirable it is to have strong, decentralized staffs within the businesses (or divisions); with less diversity, firms with strong staffs at higher organizational levels are more effective. In other words, the greater the diversity among the businesses in multibusiness firms, the greater is the necessary degree of decentralization and self-containment. This need has only been heightened by the rapid globalization among many countries. On the other hand, where the diversity among a firm's businesses is low and the interdependence of these businesses is high, more integration at the corporate level is needed.

Four significant conclusions can be drawn from this research:[6]

1. *A single-product firm or single dominant business firm should employ a functional structure.* This structure allows for strong task focus through an emphasis on specialization and efficiency, while providing opportunity for adequate controls through centralized review and decision making.

2. *A firm in several lines of business that are somehow related should employ a multidivisional structure.* Closely related divisions should be combined into groups within this structure. When synergies (i.e., shared or linked activities) are possible within such a group, the appropriate location for staff influence and decision making is at the group level, with a lesser role for corporate-level staff. The greater the degree of diversity across the firm's businesses, the greater should be the extent to which the power of staff and decision-making authority is lodged within the divisions.

3. *A firm in several unrelated lines of business should be organized into strategic business units.* Although the strategic business unit structure resembles the multidivisional structure, there are significant differences between the two. With a strategic business unit structure, finance, accounting, planning, legal, and related activities should be centralized at the corporate office. Since there are no synergies across the firm's businesses, the corporate office serves largely as a capital allocation and control mechanism. Otherwise, its major decisions involve acquisitions and divestitures. All operational and business-level strategic plans are delegated to the strategic business units.

4. *Early achievement of a strategy-structure fit can be a competitive advantage.* A competitive advantage is obtained by the first firm among competitors to achieve appropriate strategy-structure fit. That advantage will disappear as the firm's competitors also attain such a fit. Moreover, if the firm alters its strategy, its structure must obviously change as well. Otherwise, a loss of fit will lead to a competitive disadvantage for the firm.

ORGANIZATIONAL LEADERSHIP

The introduction to this chapter showed the McKinsey 7-S framework as a way to understand the implementation challenge. Figure 11–1 shows that framework identifies management and leadership as two separate elements. Management is identified with skills and leadership with style. This distinction is important. John Kotter, a widely recognized leadership expert, helps explain this distinction:[7]

---

[6] V. R. Galbraith and R. K. Kazanjian, *Strategy Implementation: Structure, Systems & Processes* (St. Paul, MN: West Publishing, 1986).

[7] John P. Kotter, "What Leaders Really Do," *Harvard Business Review* 68, no. 3 (May–June 1990), p. 104.

Management is about coping with complexity. Its practices and procedures are largely a response to one of the most significant developments of the 20th century: the emergence of large organizations. Without good management, complex enterprises tend to become chaotic in ways that threaten their very existence. Good management brings a degree of order and consistency to key dimensions like the quality and profitability of products.

Leadership, by contrast, is about coping with change. Part of the reason it has become so important in recent years is that the business world has become more competitive and more volatile. . . . The net result is that doing what was done yesterday, or doing it 5 percent better, is no longer a formula for success. Major changes are more and more necessary to survive and compete effectively in this new environment. More change always demands more leadership.

Organizational leadership, then, involves two considerations. One is strategic leadership, usually coming from the CEO. The other is management skill to cope with complexity.

Strategic Leadership: Embracing Change

The blending of telecommunications, computers, the Internet, and one global marketplace have increased the pace of change exponentially during the last 10 years. All business organizations are affected. Change has become an integral part of what leaders and managers deal with daily.

The leadership challenge is to galvanize commitment among people within an organization as well as stakeholders outside the organization to embrace change and implement strategies intended to position the organization to do so. Leaders galvanize commitment to embrace change through three, interrelated activities: clarifying strategic intent, building an organization, and shaping organizational culture.

Clarifying Strategic Intent

Leaders help stakeholders embrace change by setting forth a clear vision of where the business's strategy needs to take the organization. Traditionally, the concept of vision has been a description or picture of what the company could be that accommodates the needs of all its stakeholders. The intensely competitive, rapidly changing global marketplace has refined this to be targeting a very narrowly defined strategic intent—*an articulation of a simple criterion or characterization of what the company must become to establish and sustain global leadership.* Lou Gerstner is a good example of a leader in the middle of trying to shape strategic intent. "One of the great things about this industry is that every decade or so, you get a chance to redefine the playing field," said Gerstner. "We're in that phase of redefinition right now, and winners or losers are going to emerge from it. We've got to become *the leader in 'network-centric computing.'* " It's an opportunity brought about by telecommunications-based change that will change IBM more than semiconductors did in the 1980s. Says Gerstner, "I sensed there were too many people inside IBM who wanted to fight the war we lost," referring to PCs and PC software, so now he is aggressively trying to shape network-centric computing as the strategic intent for IBM in the next century.

Clarifying strategic intent can come in many different forms. Coca-Cola's CEO and Chairman Roberto Goizueta says that the company he leads is "a global business system for which we raise capital to make concentrate and sell it at an operating profit. Then we pay the cost of that capital. Shareholders pocket the difference." Coke has average 27% annual return on stockholder equity for 18 years under his leadership. Travelers Insurance lost $200 million in 1992. Sanford Weill assumed leadership, focusing on a short term turnaround. Among other things, he says, "We sent letters to all suppliers saying: Dear Supplier, either we rebid your business or you lower your costs 15%." Within two years, nonpersonnel costs were cut 49% in addition to 15,000 jobs. Travelers' made $700 million in 1996. Mr. Weill was effective in setting forth strategic intent for Travelers' turnaround. While Coke and Travelers are very different situations, their leaders were both very effective in shaping and clarifying strategic intent in a way that helped stakeholders understand what needed to be done.

Building an Organization

The previous section examined alternative structures to use in designing the organization necessary to implement strategy. Leaders spend considerable time shaping and refining their organizational structure and making it function effectively to accomplish strategic intent. Since leaders are attempting to embrace change, they are often rebuilding or remaking their organization to align it with the ever changing environment and needs of the strategy. And since embracing change often involves overcoming resistance to change, leaders find themselves addressing problems like the following as they attempt to build or rebuild their organization:

- Ensuring a common understanding about organizational priorities
- Clarifying responsibilities among managers and organizational units
- Empowering newer managers and pushing authority lower in the organization
- Uncovering and remedying problems in coordination and communication across the organization
- Gaining the personal commitment to a shared vision from managers throughout the organization
- Keeping closely connected with "what's going on in the organization and with its customers"

Leaders do this through many ways. Larry Bossidy, the CEO who had quadrupled Allied Signal's stock price in the last four years, spends 50 percent of his time each year flying to Allied Signal's various operations around the world meeting with managers, discussing decisions, results and progress. Bill Gates at Microsoft spends two hours each day reading and sending E-mail to any of Microsoft's 16,000 employees that want to contact him. All managers adapt structures, create teams, implement systems, and otherwise generate ways to coordinate, integrate and share information about what their organization is doing and might do. Others create customer advisory groups, supplier partnerships, R&D joint ventures and other adjustments to build an adaptable, learning organization that embraces the leader's vision, strategic intent and the change driving the future opportunities facing the business. These, in addition to the fundamental structural guidelines described in the previous section for restructuring to support strategically critical activities, are the issues leaders constantly address as they attempt to build a supportive organization.

Shaping Organization Culture

Leaders know well that the values and beliefs shared throughout their organization will shape how the work of the organization is done. And when attempting to embrace accelerated change, reshaping their organization's culture is an activity that occupies considerable time for most leaders. Listen to these observations by and about MCI and CEO Bert Roberts about competing in the rapidly changing telecommunications industry:[8]

---

[8] Alison Sprout, "MCI: Can It Become the Communications Company of the Next Century?" *Fortune*, October 2, 1995, p. 110.

Says Roberts: "We run like mad and then we change directions." Indeed, the ever-changing wireless initiative (reselling wireless services rather than creating its own capacity) illustrates a trait that sets apart MCI from its competitors—a willingness to try new things, and if they don't work, to try something else. "Over at AT&T, people are afraid to make mistakes," says Jeff Kagan, president of Kagan Telecom in Atlanta, Ga. "At MCI, people are afraid not to make mistakes."

It appears that MCI CEO Bert Roberts wants an organizational culture that is risk taking and somewhat free wheeling in order to take advantage of change in the telecommunications industry. He is doing this by example, by expectations felt by his managers, and in the way decision making is approached within MCI.

Leaders use reward systems, symbols, and structure among other means to shape the organization's culture. Travelers' turnaround was accomplished in part by changing its "hidebound" culture through a change in its agent reward system. Employees previously on salary with occasional bonuses were given rewards that involved substantial cash bonuses and stock options. Observed a customer and risk management director at drugmaker Becton Dickinson, "They're hungrier now. They want to make deals. They're different than the old, hidebound Travelers' culture."

As leaders clarify strategic intent, build an organization, and shape their organization's culture, they look to one key element to help—their management team throughout their organization. As Allied Signal's visible CEO Lary Bossidy candidly observed when asked about how after 38 years at General Electric and now at Allied Signal with seemingly drab businesses he could expect exciting growth: "There's no such thing as a mature market. What we need is mature executives who can find ways to grow." Leaders look to managers they need to execute strategy as another source of leadership to accept risk and cope with the complexity that change brings about. So assignment of key managers becomes a leadership tool.

Assignment of Key Managers

A major concern of top management in implementing a strategy, particularly if it involves a major change, is that the right managers be in the right positions to facilitate execution of the new strategy. Of all the means for ensuring successful implementation, this is the one that CEOs mention first. Confidence in the individuals occupying pivotal managerial positions is directly correlated with top-management expectations that a strategy can be executed successfully.

This confidence is based on the answers to two fundamental questions:

1. Which persons hold the leadership positions that are especially critical to execution of the strategy?
2. Do these persons have the characteristics needed to ensure effective implementation of the strategy?

Although it is impossible to specify the characteristics that are most important in this context, they probably include (1) ability and education, (2) previous track record and experience, and (3) personality and temperament. An individual's suitability on these counts, combined with top managers' gut feelings about the individual, provides the basis for top management's confidence in the individual.

One practical consideration in making key managerial assignments when implementing strategy is whether to utilize current (or promotable) executives or bring in new personnel. This is obviously a difficult, sensitive, and strategic issue. Figure 11–7 highlights the key advantages and disadvantages of these alternatives.

FIGURE 11–7
Using Existing Executives versus Bringing in Outsiders in Managerial Assignments to Implement a New Strategy

	Advantages	Disadvantages
Using existing executives to implement a new strategy	Existing executives already know key people, practices, and conditions. Personal qualities of existing executives are better known and understood by associates. Existing executives have established relationships with peers, subordinates, suppliers, buyers, and the like. Use of existing executives symbolizes organizational commitment to individual careers.	Existing executives are less adaptable to major strategic changes because of their knowledge, attitudes, and values. Past commitments of existing executives hamper the hard decisions required in executing a new strategy. Existing executives have less ability to become inspired and credibly convey the need for change.
Bringing in outsiders to implement a new strategy	Outsiders may already believe in and have "lived" the new strategy. Outsiders are unencumbered by internal commitments to people. Outsiders come to the new assignment with heightened commitment and enthusiasm. Bringing in outsiders can send powerful signals throughout the organization that change is expected.	Bringing in outsiders often is costly in terms of both compensation and "learning-to-work-together" time. Candidates suitable in all respects (i.e., exact experience) may not be available, leading to compromise choices. Uncertainty exists in selecting the right outsiders to bring in. "Morale costs" are incurred when an outsider takes a job that several insiders want. The "what to do with poor ol' Fred" problem arises when outsiders are brought in.

The other consideration that has become prominent in an environment of restructuring, downsizing, and self-management is managers' ability to delegate and to handle larger spans of control. As companies adapt employee empowerment and self-managed work group practices, managers that remain face greater workloads and different management challenges. The result is the need for skills consistent with this new environment—delegation, coaching, electronic savvy, and a results orientation.

ORGANIZATIONAL CULTURE

Organizational culture is the set of important assumptions (often unstated) that members of an organization share in common. Every organization has its own culture. An organization's culture is similar to an individual's personality—an intangible yet ever-present theme that provides meaning, direction, and the basis for action. In much the same way as personality influences the behavior of an individual, the shared assumptions (beliefs and values) among a firm's members influence opinions and actions within that firm.

A member of an organization can simply be aware of the organization's beliefs and values without sharing them in a personally significant way. Those beliefs and values have more personal meaning if the member views them as a guide to appropriate behavior in the organization and, therefore, complies with them. The member becomes fundamentally committed to the beliefs and values when he or she internalizes them; that is, comes to hold them as personal beliefs and values. In this case, the corresponding behavior is *intrinsically rewarding* for the member—the member derives personal satisfaction from his or her actions in the organization because those actions are congruent with corresponding personal beliefs and values. *Assumptions become shared assumptions through internalization among an organization's individual members.* And those shared, internalized beliefs and values shape the content and account for the strength of an organization's culture.

Leaders typically attempt to manage and create distinct cultures through a variety of ways. Some of the most common ways are as follows:

Emphasize Key Themes or Dominant Values

Businesses build strategies around distinct competitive advantages they possess or seek. Quality, differentiation, cost advantages, or speed are three key sources of competitive advantage. So insightful leaders nurture key themes or dominant values within their organization that reinforce competitive advantages they seek to maintain or build. Key themes or dominant values may center around wording in an advertisement. They are often found in internal company communications. They are most often found as a new vocabulary used by company personnel to explain "who we are." At Xerox, the key themes include respect for the individual and services to the customer. At Procter & Gamble (P&G), the overarching value is product quality; McDonald's uncompromising emphasis on QSCV—quality, service, cleanliness, and value—through meticulous attention to detail is legendary; Delta Airlines is driven by the "family feeling" theme, which builds a team spirit and nurtures each employee's cooperative attitude toward others, cheerful outlook toward life, and pride in a job well done. Du Pont's safety orientation—a report of every accident must be on the chairman's desk within 24 hours—has resulted in a safety record that was 17 times better than the chemical industry average and 68 times better than the all-manufacturing average.

Encourage Dissemination of Stories and Legends about Core Values

Companies with strong cultures are enthusiastic collectors and tellers of stories, anecdotes, and legends in support of basic beliefs. Frito-Lay's zealous emphasis on customer service is reflected in frequent stories about potato chip route salespeople who have slogged through sleet, mud, hail, snow, and rain to uphold the 99.5 percent service level to customers in which the entire company takes great pride. Milliken (a textile leader) holds "sharing" rallies once every quarter at which teams from all over the company swap success stories and ideas. Typically, more than 100 teams make five-minute presentations over a two-day period. Every rally is designed around a major theme, such as quality, cost reduction, or customer service. No criticisms are allowed, and awards are given to reinforce this institutionalized approach to storytelling. L. L. Bean tells customer service stories; 3M tells innovation stories; P&G, Johnson & Johnson, IBM, and Maytag tell quality stories. These stories are very important in developing an organizational culture, because organization members identify strongly with them and come to share the beliefs and values they support.

Institutionalize Practices That Systematically Reinforce Desired Beliefs and Values

Companies with strong cultures are clear on what their beliefs and values need to be and take the process of shaping those beliefs and values very seriously. Most important, the values these companies espouse undergird the strategies they employ. For example, McDonald's has a yearly contest to determine the best hamburger cooker in its chain. First, there is a competition to determine the best hamburger cooker in each store; next, the store winners compete in regional championships; finally, the regional winners compete in the

"All-American" contest. The winners, who are widely publicized throughout the company, get trophies and All-American patches to wear on their McDonald's uniforms.

Adapt Some Very Common Themes in Their Own Unique Ways   The most typical beliefs that shape organizational culture include (1) a belief in being the best (or, as at GE, "better than the best"); (2) a belief in superior quality and service; (3) a belief in the importance of people as individuals and a faith in their ability to make a strong contribution; (4) a belief in the importance of the details of execution, the nuts and bolts of doing the job well; (5) a belief that customers should reign supreme; (6) a belief in inspiring people to do their best, whatever their ability; (7) a belief in the importance of informal communication; and (8) a belief that growth and profits are essential to a company's well-being. Every company implements these beliefs differently (to fit its particular situation), and every company's values are the handiwork of one or two legendary figures in leadership positions. Accordingly, every company has a distinct culture that it believes no other company can copy successfully. And in companies with strong cultures, managers and workers either accept the norms of the culture or opt out from the culture and leave the company.

The stronger a company's culture and the more that culture is directed toward customers and markets, the less the company uses policy manuals, organization charts, and detailed rules and procedures to enforce discipline and norms. The reason is that the guiding values inherent in the culture convey in crystal-clear fashion what everybody is supposed to do in most situations. Poorly performing companies often have strong cultures. However, their cultures are dysfunctional, being focused on internal politics or operating by the numbers as opposed to emphasizing customers and the people who make and sell the product.

Managing Organizational Culture in a Global Organization[9]

The reality of today's global organizations is that organizational culture must recognize cultural diversity. *Social norms* create differences across national boundaries that influence how people interact, read personal cues, and otherwise interrelate socially. *Values* and *attitudes* about similar circumstances also vary from country to country. Where individualism is central to a North American's value structure, the needs of the group dominate the value structure of their Japanese counterparts. *Religion* is yet another source of cultural differences. Holidays, practices, and belief structures differ in very fundamental ways that must be taken into account as one attempts to shape organizational culture in a global setting. Finally, *education*, or ways people are accustomed to learning, differ across national borders. Formal classroom learning in the United States may teach things that are only learned via apprenticeship in other cultures. Since the process of shaping an organizational culture often involves considerable "education," leaders should be sensitive to global differences in approaches to education to make sure their cultural education efforts

[9]Differing backgrounds, often referred to as *cultural diversity*, is something that most managers will certainly see more of, both because of the growing cultural diversity domestically and the obvious diversification of cultural backgrounds that result from global acquisitions and mergers. For example, Harold Epps, manager of DEC's computer keyboard plant in Boston, manages 350 employees representing 44 countries of origin and 19 languages. Useful reading on cultural diversity can be found in David Jamieson and Julie O'Mara, *Managing Workforce 2000: Gaining the Diversity Advantage* (San Francisco: Josey-Bass, 1991), and R. R. Thomas, *Beyond Race and Gender: Unleashing the Power of Your Total Workforce by Managing Diversity* (New York: AMACOM Books, 1991). To get an informative appreciation of the global scene, see Rosabeth Moss Kanter, "Transcending Business Boundaries: 12,000 World Managers View Change," *Harvard Business Review* 69, no. 3 (1991), pp. 151–64.

FIGURE 11–8
Managing the Strategy-Culture Relationship

	High	Low
Many	Link changes to basic mission and fundamental organizational norms. 1	Reformulate strategy or prepare carefully for long-term, difficult cultural change. 4
Few	2 Synergistic—focus on reinforcing culture.	3 Manage around the culture.

Changes in key organizational factors that are necessary to implement the new strategy

Potential compatibility of changes with existing culture

are effective. The Cohesion Case on Coca-Cola at the end of this chapter provides some relevant examples of how Coke has successfully managed organizational culture in a global organization.

Managing the Strategy-Culture Relationship

Managers find it difficult to think through the relationship between a firm's culture and the critical factors on which strategy depends. They quickly recognize, however, that key components of the firm—structure, staff, systems, people, style—influence the ways in which key managerial tasks are executed and how critical management relationships are formed. And implementation of a new strategy is largely concerned with adjustments in these components to accommodate the perceived needs of the strategy. Consequently, managing the strategy-culture relationship requires sensitivity to the interaction between the changes necessary to implement the new strategy and the compatibility or "fit" between those changes and the firm's culture. Figure 11–8 provides a simple framework for managing the strategy-culture relationship by identifying four basic situations a firm might face.

Link to Mission

A firm in cell 1 is faced with a situation in which implementing a new strategy requires several changes in structure, systems, managerial assignments, operating procedures, or other fundamental aspects of the firm. However, most of the changes are potentially compatible with the existing organizational culture. Firms in this situation usually have a tradition of effective performance and are either seeking to take advantage of a major opportunity or are attempting to redirect major product-market operations consistent with proven core capabilities. Such firms are in a very promising position: they can pursue a strategy requiring major changes but still benefit from the power of cultural reinforcement.

Four basic considerations should be emphasized by firms seeking to manage a strategy-culture relationship in this context. First, *key changes should be visibly linked to the basic company mission*. Since the company mission provides a broad official foundation for the organizational culture, top executives should use all available internal and external forums to reinforce the message that the changes are inextricably linked to it. Second, *emphasis should be placed on the use of existing personnel* where possible to fill positions created to implement the new strategy. Existing personnel embody the shared values and norms that help ensure cultural compatibility as major changes are implemented. Third, *care should be taken if adjustments in the reward system are needed*. These adjustments should be consistent with the current reward system. If, for example, a new product-market thrust requires significant changes in the way sales are made, and, therefore, in incentive compensation, common themes (e.g., incentive oriented) should be emphasized. In this way, current and future reward approaches are related and the changes in the reward system are justified (encourage development of less familiar markets). Fourth, *key attention should be paid to the changes that are least compatible with the current culture*, so current norms are not disrupted. For example, a firm may choose to subcontract an important step in a production process because that step would be incompatible with the current culture.

IBM's strategy in entering the Internet-based market is an illustration. Serving this radically different market required numerous organizational changes. To maintain maximum compatibility with its existing culture while doing so, IBM went to considerable public and internal effort to link its new Internet focus with its long-standing mission. Numerous messages relating the network-centric computing to IBM's tradition of top-quality service appeared on television and in magazines, and every IBM manager was encouraged to go online. Where feasible, IBM personnel were used to fill the new positions created to implement the strategy. But because the software requirements were not compatible with IBM's current operations, virtually all of its initial efforts were linked to newly acquired Lotus Notes.

Maximize Synergy

A firm in cell 2 needs only a few organizational changes to implement its new strategy, and those changes are potentially quite compatible with its current culture. A firm in this situation should emphasize two broad themes: (1) *take advantage of the situation to reinforce and solidify the current culture* and (2) *use this time of relative stability to remove organizational roadblocks to the desired culture*. Holiday Inns' move into casino gambling required a few major organizational changes. Holiday Inns saw casinos as resort locations requiring lodging, dining, and gambling/entertainment services. It only had to incorporate gambling/entertainment expertise into its management team, which was already capable of managing the lodging and dining requirements of casino (or any other) resort locations. It successfully inculcated this single major change by selling the change internally as completely compatible with its mission of providing high-quality accommodations for business and leisure travelers. The resignation of Roy Clymer, its CEO, removed an organizational roadblock, legitimizing a culture that placed its highest priority on quality service to the middle-to-upper-income business traveler, rather than a culture that placed its highest priority on family-oriented service. The latter priority was fast disappearing from Holiday Inns' culture, with the encouragement of most of the firm's top management, but its disappearance had not yet been fully sanctioned because of Clymer's personal beliefs. His voluntary departure helped solidify the new values that top management wanted.

Manage around the Culture

A firm in cell 3 must make a few major organizational changes to implement its new strategy, but these changes are potentially inconsistent with the firm's current organizational culture. The critical question for a firm in this situation is whether it can make the changes with a reasonable chance of success.

A firm can manage around the culture in various ways: create a separate firm or division; use task forces, teams, or program coordinators; subcontract; bring in an outsider; or sell out. These are a few of the available options, but the key idea is to create a method of achieving the change desired that avoids confronting the incompatible cultural norms. As cultural resistance diminishes, the change may be absorbed into the firm.

In the 1970s, Rich's was a highly successful, quality-oriented department store chain that served higher income customers in several southeastern locations. With Wal-Mart and Kmart experiencing rapid growth in the sale of mid- to low-priced merchandise, Rich's decided to serve this market as well. Finding such merchandise inconsistent with the successful values and norms of its traditional business, it created a separate business called *Richway* to tap this growth area in retailing. Through a new store network, it was able to *manage around its culture*. Both Rich's and Richway have since flourished, though their cultures are radically different in some respects.

Reformulate the Strategy or Culture

A firm in cell 4 faces the most difficult challenge in managing the strategy-culture relationship. To implement its new strategy, such a firm must make organizational changes that are incompatible with its current, usually entrenched, values and norms. A firm in this situation faces the complex, expensive, and often long-term challenge of changing its culture; it is a challenge that borders on impossible. Strategy in Action 11–2 describes the challenge faced by Robert Daniell, CEO of United Technologies, as he attempted to change the culture of his firm.

When a strategy requires massive organizational change and engenders cultural resistance, a firm should determine whether reformulation of the strategy is appropriate. Are all of the organizational changes really necessary? Is there any real expectation that the changes will be acceptable and successful? If these answers are yes, then massive changes in management personnel are often necessary. AT&T offered early retirement to over 20,000 managers as part of a massive recreation of its culture to go along with major strategic changes in 1996. If the answer to these questions is no, the firm might reformulate its strategic plan so as to make it more consistent with established organizational norms and practices.

Merrill Lynch faced the challenge of strategy-culture incompatibility in the last decade. Seeking to remain number one in the newly deregulated financial services industry, it chose to pursue a product development strategy in its brokerage business. Under this strategy, Merrill Lynch would sell a broader range of investment products to a more diverse customer base and would integrate other financial services, such as real estate sales, into the Merrill Lynch organization. The new strategy could succeed only if Merrill Lynch's traditionally service-oriented brokerage network became sales and marketing oriented. Initial efforts to implement the strategy generated substantial resistance from Merrill Lynch's highly successful brokerage network. The strategy was fundamentally inconsistent with long-standing cultural norms at Merrill Lynch that emphasized personalized service and very close broker-client relationships. Merrill Lynch ultimately divested its real estate operation, reintroduced specialists that supported broker/retailers, and refocused its brokers more narrowly on basic client investment needs.

REWARD SYSTEMS: MOTIVATING STRATEGY EXECUTION

The execution of strategy ultimately depends on individual organizational members, particularly key managers. So motivating and rewarding good performance by individuals and organizational units are key ingredients in effective strategy implementation. If strategy accomplishment is a top priority, then the reward system must be clearly and tightly linked to strategic performance. Motivating and controlling managerial personnel in the execution

STRATEGY
IN ACTION
11–2

TRANSFORMING ORGANIZATIONAL CULTURE AT UNITED TECHNOLOGIES

It was with some urgency that Robert F. Daniell, the newly appointed CEO of United Technologies Corporation, summoned his top executives. Just weeks after taking the reins from Harry J. Gray, Daniell called a management powwow at the Jupiter Beach Hilton in Florida. The subject? UTC's shaky future. Customers of its Pratt & Whitney jet engines, outraged by lousy service, were defecting in droves to archrival General Electric Company. Market shares at UTC's once dominant Otis elevator unit and Carrier air-conditioning company were evaporating. Profits had hit a 13-year low. "Things had to change," says Daniell.

Unlike the iron-fisted Gray, however, Daniell did not lecture at management meetings. Instead, a Boston consultant moderated a roiling discussion in which managers put forth their remedies: dump divisions wholesale, diversify, pump up research-and-development spending. "Just the fact that we went through all of that yelling and screaming was unusual," says one executive who attended. After two days, Daniell and his team decided to remake UTC—to level its autocratic structure and bring more of its 186,800 employees into the decision-making process. *The ultimate goal: To get UTC's haughty culture to take marching orders from its customers.*

Worker empowerment. Team building. Getting close to your customer. While a lot of companies are just starting to talk about such methods, Bob Daniell is already proving that they can work wonders on the bottom line. The changes are nowhere more apparent than at jet-engine maker Pratt & Whitney, which pulls in more than half of UTC's operating profit. Orders have increased eightfold, to nearly $8 billion, since 1987.

When Daniell finally became CEO, he inherited a divided, argumentative management. Executives were too frightened to admit mistakes, and they directed their staffs like armies. All the way down the line, staffers refused to take responsibility for errors.

At the same time, Daniell was working on a long-term goal: changing Pratt's by-the-book structure. Dictatorial management and a Byzantine approval process made employees feel powerless. Take the case of an airplane builder who wants to mount an engine a fraction of a millimeter closer to the wing than the blueprint specifies. Normally, a good engineer at Pratt could just eyeball the

Source: "Changes at United Technologies," *Forbes,* August 28, 1989, pp. 42–46.

of strategy are accomplished through a firm's reward mechanisms—compensation, raises, bonuses, stock options, incentives, benefits, promotions, demotions, recognition, praise, criticism, more (or less) responsibility, group norms, performance appraisal, tension, and fear. These mechanisms can be positive and negative, short run and long run.

Guidelines for Structuring Effective Reward Systems

Regardless of the short- or long-term strategic considerations, managers face additional challenges in structuring rewards in a manner that energizes every person in their organization. One success story in meeting this challenge has been Nucor Corporation. Described in Strategy in Action 11–3, Nucor's reward system is largely credited with driving the success of its strategy in a U.S. steel industry where experts have said the United States has "lost its comparative advantage, can no longer compete in world markets, and should exit the business altogether." Managers at every level within Nucor, and any other business, can improve the effectiveness of their reward system by following these nine guidelines:

1. **Link rewards tightly to the strategic plan.** As the earlier discussion pointed out, rewards linked to a firm's strategy logically enhance its chance of success. Linking rewards

blueprint and give the customer the nod for such a change. But until Pratt changed the system in February 1988, the request would wind through nine departments, including a committee that met only once a week.

Now, the design engineer makes the decision and only needs to get three signatures. Says Garvey: "It's all part of quality—taking responsibility." As a result, average response time has gone from 82 days to 10, and the request backlog has shrunk from 1,900 cases to fewer than 100.

Daniell went further with this campaign to improve service. He increased the number of service representatives in the field by nearly 70 percent—despite 30 percent staff cuts in the rest of the company.

Overall, Daniell's effort to change the culture is based on four approaches:

Flatten the hierarchy. Daniell leveled a Byzantine corporate structure by cutting many layers of decision making. At Pratt & Whitney, for instance, he cut eight levels of management to as few as four.

Empower your workers. Managers pushed decision making down. For instance, field representatives at Pratt & Whitney now make multimillion-dollar decisions about reimbursing customers on warranty claims. Before, they would have to wait for approvals from numerous layers above.

Get close to your customers. This is Daniell's battle cry. Worker empowerment helps, but the imperative goes even further than that. For instance, Pratt & Whitney lends some of its top engineers to customers for a year—and pays their salaries.

Train, train, train. Daniell uses training to revamp the corporate culture. More than 5,000 senior and middle managers are getting at least 40 hours of classroom work. In some classes, customers are brought in for gripe sessions, and a problem-solving team gathered from many different departments must come up with solutions.

to the accomplishment of key objectives, milestones, completion of key projects, or actions that sustain competitive advantage (like Nucor's high productivity) keeps people energized and focused on the right things and on doing them right.

2. **Use variable incentives and make them a major part of everyone's compensation.** If a significant portion of a person's compensation (usually 25 to 60 percent) varies with successful execution of his or her responsibilities, then a person should be very attentive to do them well. Nucor did this with low base pay and virtually open-ended bonus capability. AT&T has introduced "internal venturing," whereby employees with approved new product ideas can forgo a part of their compensation as a "co-investment" in their own internal venture and receive up to eight times that investment if the venture is successful within five years. This guideline obviously can backfire on any manager if the incentive is not fair, not understood, and not consistent with the next guideline.

3. **Rewards and incentives must be linked to an individual's job and the outcomes the individual can personally effect.** People are more accepting of incentive compensation when they control what needs to be done to accomplish the outcomes that earn them the incentive. While easier for salespeople to visualize than for production or administrative personnel, effective managers strive to introduce this guideline in all areas of the

NUCOR'S SECRET TO SUCCESS: A LOGICAL REWARD SYSTEM

The last 10 years have seen most analysts write off the U.S. steel industry as outdated, inefficient, and no match for Japan, Taiwan, and Europe. But they should come down to Charlotte, North Carolina. In an industry where the giants are hemorrhaging red ink, closing plants, and diversifying, midsized Nucor Corporation is an unprecedented success. Nucor is taking market share *away* from Japan and Taiwan!

Nucor is the low-cost producer, combining outfront technology with innovative incentive systems. The results are globally competitive steel products, highly productive steel mills, and a well-paid work force.

Nucor's reward system is based on four principles: (1) earnings according to productivity, (2) job security for proper performance, (3) fair and consistent treatment, and (4) easy and direct avenues of appeal. Nucor believes that "money is the best motivator." The compensation system is incentive oriented, with those incentives tied directly to productivity. Base salaries are low; but incentives can easily add 50 to 100 percent of base salary to total compensation, with no upper limit. All employees have a significant part of their compensation based around productivity. All incentive systems are designed around groups, not individuals. This applies to everyone, from production workers to clerks and secretaries to senior officers.

In the production incentive program, groups range from 25 to 35 people who are working as a team on some complete task. There are nine production bonus groups in Nucor's typical minimill—three each in melting and casting (M&C), rolling, and finishing and shipping. The M&C group begins with a base goal of 12 tons of good billets per hour; above this, every person in the group gets a 4 percent bonus for every ton per hour produced. If over a week they average 30 tons per hour—which is considered low—they earn a 72 percent bonus $[4 \times (30 - 12)]$ for that week. The multiplier affects all pay—overtime and regular. In the joist production line, bonuses are based on 90 percent of the historical time it takes to make a particular product. If during the week a group makes the product at 40 percent less than standard time, its members receive a 40 percent bonus—with the *next* paycheck.

Source: Nucor Corporation 1994 annual report.

company. Team bonuses are one way this is done. Employee participation in designing the rewards is another.

4. **Reward performance and link value to success, rather than to position in the hierarchy.** While seniority has its place, and positions of responsibility in a management hierarchy often correlate with contribution to results, progressive managers increasingly are recognizing the importance of structuring incentives and compensation to reward the key skills or expertise necessary for a strategy to be successful. In the rapidly growing environmental and bio-engineering industries, several companies have compensation and bonus programs under which technical personnel can earn significantly more than managers of their units or managers at higher levels in the organization. The reason is simple. The skills those people possess are essential to successful strategic outcomes.

5. **Reward everyone and be sensitive to discrepancies between the top and bottom of the organization.** A successful strategy requires energized, cooperative effort from every organization member. Incentive-based reward systems should reflect this by including programs wherein every member participates in some fashion. And while varying skills, levels of responsibility, and roles must be recognized with significantly different incentive amounts, inexplicably high rewards at high executive levels with little or none at the lowest level can erode confidence and commitment. A major controversy has arisen in

STRATEGY
IN ACTION
11–3   **continued**

Managerial bonuses are based on return on assets. Top managers have no employment contracts, nor do they receive guaranteed or discretionary bonuses, profit sharing, pension plans, or other executive perks (no company cars, planes, country club memberships, executive dining rooms, or reserved parking). Base salaries are set at 75 percent of what executives earn in comparable positions in other companies. If the company produces below par (9 percent return on equity), that's all they get. For every pretax dollar above this base, 5 percent goes into an officers' pool that is divided according to salary. For example, if return on equity goes to 24 percent, which it has, Nucor executives receive up to 270 percent of their base in cash and an additional 180 percent in stock.

All Nucor employees receive the same insurance, holidays, and vacations. Everyone, including the CEO, flies coach. There is a profit-sharing plan for all nonexecutive employees. Nucor provides a scholarship of $2,000 per year for four years of college or vocational training for every child of every employee. (When the children graduate, many come to work for Nucor.) The company has not laid off a single employee for more than 20 years. Ken Iverson, Nucor's president, confessed he was proud to be the lowest compensated Fortune 500 CEO in the recession of the early 1980s. Why? During that period, to avoid layoffs, Nucor had to cut back to four- or even three-and-a-half-day workweeks, which cut employee pay 20 to 25 percent below normal. But few complained: they knew that department heads were cut more (35 to 40 percent) and officers even more (60 to 70 percent). Iverson calls it our "Share the Pain" program. If a company isn't successful, the reasons are irrelevant. Management should take the biggest cut because they are the most responsible.

Can Nucor's incentive compensation be applied to other companies and industries? There are limitations. Two elements are necessary: (1) it must make sense to break out small groups of people who work as a team on a particular function and (2) that particular function must be both self-contained and measurable.

the United States over CEO compensation as a result of extraordinary bonuses accruing to selected executives in the auto industry and others while their companies were losing billions, massive layoffs were commonplace, and their highly successful Japanese and German counterparts were much more modestly compensated.[10] In smaller firms the discrepancy usually arises in perks or special founding-family compensation. But whether the reward involves cash, stock, options, perks, or other benefits, a reward system designed to incentivize everyone in the organization to share in strategic success (or a lack thereof) will be more effective long term.

6. **Be scrupulously fair, accurate, and informative.** Related to the previous guideline, reward systems that are perceived to be fair work better than those that are not. Where

---

[10] The issue of CEO compensation is a complex, highly charged issue. Some people question the high compensation and bonus package accruing to executives like Lee Iacocca (Chrysler), Steve Ross (Time-Warner), Mike Eisner (Disney), and Roberto Goizueta (Coke) to name a few. Others strongly defend their high compensation, pointing to the rise in market value of their respective firm's stock since they took control. For thoughtful analyses of this issue, see Andrew R. Brownstein and Morris J. Panner, "Who Should Set CEO Pay? The Press? Congress? Shareholders?" *Harvard Business Review* 70, no. 3 (1992), pp. 28–39; and "CEO Pay: How Much Is Enough?" *Harvard Business Review* 70, no. 4 (1992), pp. 130–39. For practical guidelines on handling executive pay in an atmosphere of increased public scrutiny, see John D. McMillan, "Executive Pay a New Way," *HRMagazine* 37, no. 6 (1992), pp. 46–48, 194.

incentives are linked to work teams, groups, or units, fairness among individuals' contribution and reward often will be an issue facing operating-level managers. Accurate measurement of the outcomes triggering rewards, timing considerations, and amounts paid play a key role in perceived fairness. Complete openness in sharing information about "how we're doing," so participants can see clearly the reasons behind compensation results, is another important way to reinforce fairness.

7. **Reward generously when successful; minimally when not.** Reward systems that reinforce success do just that. Systems that provide similar rewards (or a lack thereof) whether successful or not can send the message that extra effort doesn't matter. Food Lion has butchers and cashiers, while Wal-Mart has greeters and cashiers that have seen their small stock incentives valued at a few thousand dollars 20 years ago make them worth in excess of $2 million today. Nucor's management took 40 to 70 percent cuts and employees 20 to 25 percent cuts (via shorter work weeks) during the recession-induced reduction in demand for steel. Whether long term or short term, incentive compensation linked to results provides appropriate reinforcement of the need to formulate and implement good strategies effectively, regardless of organizational level.

8. **Don't underestimate the value of a rewarding and motivational environment.** While cash, stock, and perks get people's attention, a motivating environment is a very important part of a sound reward system. Increased responsibility, autonomy, participation in decision making, recognition, and opportunity for growth are long-advocated and proven "rewards" that motivate most people. Significant attention to creating ways to structure these elements into an individual and work team environment can provide any manager with a powerful tool for motivating strategy execution.

9. **Be open to changing the reward systems.** Strategies and tactics change. Situations change. Organization members come and go or encounter different needs. Certain aspects of a reward system prove inappropriate or counterproductive. These and other reasons should keep managers looking at reward systems as evolving, rather than permanent, indefinitely. Tempered with the need to avoid confusion and any sense of unfairness, a thoughtful change in reward systems can be an effective management option.

Following these guidelines in structuring reward systems will not guarantee successful strategy implementation. But a system so designed will make a big difference, particularly at operating levels of the company. For decisions on incentive compensations, salary increases, promotions, and key assignments, as well as perks, praise, and recognition are operational managers' foremost attention-getting and commitment-generating devices.

SUMMARY

This chapter examined the idea that a key aspect of implementing a strategy is the *institutionalization* of the strategy so it permeates daily decisions and actions in a manner consistent with long-term strategic success. Four fundamental elements must be managed to "fit" a strategy if the strategy is to be effectively institutionalized: *organizational structure, leadership, culture,* and *rewards.*

Five fundamental organizational structures were examined, and the advantages and disadvantages of each were identified. Institutionalizing a strategy requires a good strategy-structure fit. This chapter dealt with how this requirement often is overlooked until performance becomes inadequate and then indicated the conditions under which the various structures would be appropriate.

Organizational leadership is essential to effective strategy implementation. The CEO plays a critical role in this regard. Assignment of key managers, particularly within the top-management team, is an important aspect of organizational leadership. Deciding whether to promote insiders or hire outsiders is often a central leadership issue in strategy implementation. This chapter showed how this decision could be made in a manner that would best institutionalize the new strategy.

Organizational culture has been recognized as a pervasive influence on organizational life. Organizational culture, which is the shared beliefs and values of an organization's members, may be a major help or hindrance to strategy implementation. This chapter discussed an approach to managing the strategy-culture fit. It identified four fundamentally different strategy-culture situations and provided recommendations for managing the strategy-culture fit in each of these situations.

The reward system is a key ingredient in motivating managers to execute a firm's strategy. Firms should emphasize incentive systems that ensure adequate attention to strategic thrusts. This usually requires a concerted effort to emphasize long-term strategic performance as well as short-term measures of performance. In addition to timing, nine key guidelines must be accommodated to have an effective reward system.

QUESTIONS FOR DISCUSSION

1. What key structural considerations must be incorporated into strategy implementation? Why does structural change often lag a change in strategy?

2. Which organizational structure is most appropriate for successful strategy implementation? Explain how state of development affects your answer.

3. Why is leadership an important element in strategy implementation? Find an example in a major business periodical of the CEO's key role in strategy implementation.

4. Under what conditions would it be more appropriate to fill a key management position with someone from outside the firm when a qualified insider is available?

5. What is organizational culture? Why is it important? Explain two different situations a firm might face in managing the strategy-culture relationship.

6. How would you vary an incentive system for a growth-oriented versus a harvest-oriented business?

7. What do you anticipate your first management job may be? Outline a reward system for your employees based on the guidelines provided at the end of this chapter.

BIBLIOGRAPHY

Bailey, G., and J. Szerdy. "Is There Life after Downsizing?" *Journal of Business Strategy*, January 1988, pp. 8–11.

Barney, J. B. "Organizational Culture: Can It Be a Source of Sustained Competitive Advantage?" *Academy of Management Review*, July 1986, p. 656.

Bethel, J. E., and J. Liebeskind. "The Effects of Ownership Structure on Corporate Restructuring." *Strategic Management Journal* 14 (1993), pp. 15–31.

Bettinger, Cass. "Use Corporate Culture to Trigger High Performance." *Journal of Business Strategy* 10, no. 2 (March–April 1989), pp. 38–42.

Block, Barbara. "Creating a Culture All Employees Can Accept." *Management Review*, July 1989, p. 41.

Botterill, M. "Changing Corporate Culture." *Management Services* (UK) 34, no. 6 (1990), pp. 14–18.

Bower, Joseph Lyon, and Martha Wagner Weinberg. "Statecraft, Strategy, and Corporate Leadership." *California Management Review*, Winter 1988, p. 107.

Bowman, E. H., and H. Singh. "Corporate Restructuring: Reconfiguring the Firm." *Strategic Management Journal* 14 (1993), pp. 5–14.

Byles, C. M., and R. J. Keating. "Strength of Organizational Culture and Performance: Strategic Implications." *Journal of Business Strategy*, Spring 1989, pp. 45–55.

Chapman, P. "Changing the Corporate Culture of Rank Xerox." *Long Range Planning*, April 1988, pp. 23–28.

Chandler, A. D., *Strategy and Structure*. Cambridge: MIT Press, 1962.

Chingos, P. T., and V. J. Elliott. "Using Incentives to Foster Business Unit Results." *Bottomline* 8, no. 3 (1991), pp. 15–19.

Cowherd, D. M., and R. H. Luchs. "Linking Organization Structures and Processes to Business Strategy." *Long Range Planning*, October 1988, pp. 47–53.

"Cultural Transition at AT&T." *Sloan Management Review*, Fall 1983, pp. 15–26.

Daft, R. L.; J. Sormunen; and D. Parks. "Chief Executive Scanning." *Strategic Management Journal*, March 1988, pp. 123–40.

Donaldson, G. "Voluntary Restructuring: The Case of General Mills." *Journal of Financial Economics* 27 (1990), pp. 117–41.

Drake, Bruce H., and Eileen Drake. "Ethical and Legal Aspects of Managing Corporate Cultures." *California Management Review*, Winter 1988, p. 107.

Eccles, Robert G. "The Performance Measurement Manifesto." *Harvard Business Review* 69 (January–February 1991), pp. 131–37.

Fitzgerald, T. H. "Can Change in Organizational Culture Really Be Managed?" *Organizational Dynamics* 17, no. 2 (1988), pp. 5–15.

Floyd, Steven W., and Bill Wooldridge. "Managing Strategic Consensus: The Foundation of Effective Implementation." *Academy of Management Executive* 6, no. 4 (November 1992), pp. 27–39.

Forman, R. "Strategic Planning and the Chief Executive." *Long Range Planning*, August 1988, pp. 57–64.

Fredrickson, James W.; Donald C. Hambrick; and Sara Bawmrin. "A Model of CEO Dismissal." *Academy of Management Review*, April 1988, p. 255.

Freeman, R. Edward, and Daniel R. Gilbert, Jr. *Corporate Strategy and the Search for Ethics*. Englewood Cliffs, NJ: Prentice Hall, 1988.

Freund, York P. "Critical Success Factors." *Planning Review*, July–August 1988, p. 20.

Gabarro, J. J. "When a New Manager Takes Charge." *Harvard Business Review* 64, no. 3 (May–June 1985), pp. 110–23.

Ginsburg, Lee, and Neil Miller. "Value-Driven Management." *Business Horizons* (May–June 1992), pp. 25–27.

Gomez-Mejia, Luis R.; Henri Tose; and Timothy Hinkin. "Managerial Control, Performance, and Executive Compensation." *Academy of Management Journal*, March 1987, p. 51.

Gomez-Mejia, L. R., and T. Welbourne. "Compensation Strategies in a Global Context." *Human Resource Planning* 14, no. 1 (1991), pp. 29–41.

Green, Sebastian. "Strategy, Organizational Culture, and Symbolism." *Long Range Planning* 21, no. 4 (August 1988), pp. 121–29.

Gupta, Anil K. "SBU Strategies, Corporate-SBU Relations, and SBU Effectiveness in Strategy Implementation." *Academy of Management Journal*, September 1987, p. 477.

Hinterhuber, H. H., and W. Popp. "Are You a Strategist or Just a Manager?" *Harvard Business Review* 70, no. 1 (1992), pp. 105–14.

Hosking, D. M. "Organizing, Leadership and Skillful Process." *Journal of Management Studies*, March 1988, pp. 147–66.

Jensen, M. C., and K. J. Murphy. "Performance Pay and Top-Management Incentives." *Journal of Political Economy* 98 (1990), pp. 225–64.

Johnson, G. "Managing Strategic Change—Strategy, Culture, and Action." *Long Range Planning* 25, no. 1 (1992), pp. 28–36.

Kim, W. C., and R. A. Mauborgne. "Parables of Leadership." *Harvard Business Review* 70, no. 4 (1992), pp. 123–28.

Kirkpatrick, Shelley A., and Edwin A. Locke. "Leadership: Do Traits Matter?" *Academy of Management Executive* 5, no. 2 (May 1991), pp. 48–60.

Koch, D. L., and D. W. Steinhauser. "Changing the Corporate Culture." *Datamotion*, October 1983, pp. 247–52.

Kotter, John P. "What Leaders Really Do." *Harvard Business Review* 68 (May–June 1990), pp. 103–11.

Kotter, John P., and James L. Heskett. *Corporate Culture and Performance*. New York: Free Press, 1992.

Larson, Erik W., and David H. Gobeli. "Matrix Management: Contradictions and Insights." *California Management Review*, Summer 1987, p. 126.

Lei, D.; J. Slocum; and R. Slater. "Global Strategy and Reward Systems: The Key Roles of Management Development and Corporate Culture." *Organizational Dynamics* 19, no. 2 (1990), pp. 27–41.

Lewis, P. "Performance Related Pay: Pretexts and Pitfalls." *Employee Relations* (U.K.) 13, no. 1 (1991), pp. 12–16.

Liden, Robert C., and Terence R. Mitchell. "Ingratiatory Behavior in Organizational Settings." *Academy of Management Review*, October 1988, p. 572.

Main, John G., and John Thackray. "The Logic of Restructuring." *Planning Review*, May–June 1987, p. 5.

Meindl, James R., and Sanford B. Ehrlich. "The Romance of Leadership and Evaluation of Organizational Performance." *Academy of Management Journal*, March 1987, p. 91.

Miller, Danny. "Strategy Making and Structure: Analysis and Implications for Performance." *Academy of Management Journal*, March 1987, p. 7.

Nichols, Don. "Bottom-Up Strategies." *Management Review*, December 1989, p. 44.

O'Toole, James. "Employee Practices at the Best-Managed Companies." *California Management Review* 28, no. 1 (Fall 1985), pp. 35–66.

Paine, Lynn Sharp. "Managing for Organizational Integrity." *Harvard Business Review* 72, no. 2 (March–April 1994), pp. 106–117.

Putz, B. J. "Productivity Improvement: Changing Values, Beliefs, and Assumptions." *SAM Advanced Management Journal* 56, no. 4 (1991), pp. 9–12.

Reed, R., and M. Reed. "CEO Experience and Diversification Strategy Fit." *Journal of Management Studies*, March 1988, pp. 251–70.

Reimann, Bernard C., and Yoash Wiener. "Corporate Culture: Avoiding the Elitist Trap." *Business Horizons*, March–April 1988, p. 36.

Saffold, Guy S., III. "Culture Traits, Strength, and Settings." *Academy of Management Review*, October 1988, p. 546.

Schneier, C. E. "Capitalizing on Performance Management, Recognition, and Rewards Systems." *Compensation and Benefit Review* 21, no. 2 (1989), pp. 20–30.

Spector, Bert A. "From Bogged-Down to Fired-Up: Inspiring Organizational Change." *Sloan Management Review*, Summer 1989, p. 29.

Spohn, A. G. "The Relationship of Reward Systems and Employee Performance." *Compensation and Benefits Management* 6, no. 2 (1990), pp. 128–32.

Stone, N. "Building Corporate Character." *Harvard Business Review* 70, no. 2 (1992), pp. 94–104.

"Strategic Leaders and Leadership." *Strategic Management Journal*, special issue, Summer 1989.

Vancil, Richard F. "A Look at CEO Succession." *Harvard Business Review*, March–April 1987, p. 107.

Vincent, D. R. "Understanding Organization Power." *Journal of Business Strategy*, March 1988, pp. 40–44.

Wagner, John A., III, and Richard Z. Gooding. "Shared Influence and Organizational Behavior: A Meta-Analysis of Situational Variables Expected to Moderate Participation-Outcome Relationships." *Academy of Management Review*, September 1987, p. 524.

Webber, Alvin M. "The CEO Is the Company." *Harvard Business Review*, January–February 1987, p. 114.

———. "Consensus, Continuity, and Common Sense." *Harvard Business Review* 68, no. 4 (1990), pp. 115–23.

Zabriskie, N., and A. Huellmantel. "Implementing Strategies for Human Resources." *Long Range Planning*, April 1989, pp. 70–77.

Zajac, E. J., and M. S. Kraatz. "A Diametric Forces Model of Strategic Change: Assessing the Antecedents and Consequences of Restructuring in the Higher Education Industry." *Strategic Management Journal* 14 (1993), pp. 83–102.

Zaleznik, A. "Managers and Leaders: Are They Different?" *Harvard Business Review* 70, no. 2 (1992), pp. 126–35.

Zemke, R. "Rewards and Recognition: Yes, They Really Work." *Training* 25, no. 1 (1988), pp. 48–53.

CHAPTER 11 COHESION CASE ILLUSTRATION

IMPLEMENTING STRATEGY BY RESTRUCTURING AND REENGINEERING COCA-COLA'S ORGANIZATIONAL STRUCTURE, LEADERSHIP, CULTURE, AND REWARDS

STRUCTURE

The Coca-Cola Company had the following basic structure at the beginning of the 1980s:

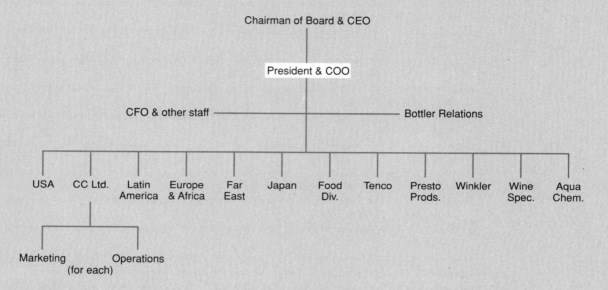

The figure suggests Coke was a rather decentralized company with relatively autonomous operating units based on both the product-service of the business and geographic location. This facilitated local decision making and aided Coke's rapid advance in international markets.

By the mid-1980s, Roberto Goizueta had completed significant restructuring and consolidation of Coca-Cola to allow for decentralized decision making while also retaining more centralized control. The following figure shows Coke's structure by 1984. According to Goizueta:

> To operate more effectively in today's business environment and more sharply focus management's attention on the expansion opportunities within the industries in which they operate, we have regrouped the Company's various units into four business sectors . . . Each of our four business sectors is operating according to a well-defined plan. Each is moving forward in line with a broad strategy to capitalize on its superior positioning and expertise, while drawing from complementary corporate resources that bind the sectors into a single, powerful enterprise.

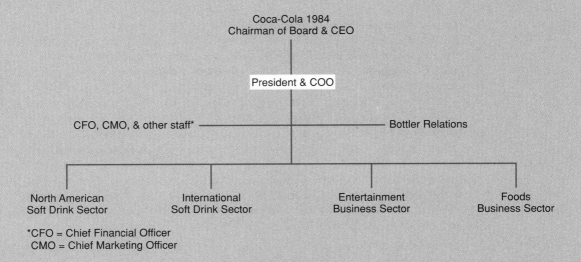

Coca-Cola 1984
Chairman of Board & CEO

President & COO

CFO, CMO, & other staff* ———————————— Bottler Relations

North American Soft Drink Sector | International Soft Drink Sector | Entertainment Business Sector | Foods Business Sector

*CFO = Chief Financial Officer
 CMO = Chief Marketing Officer

By 1993, the structure looked as follows:

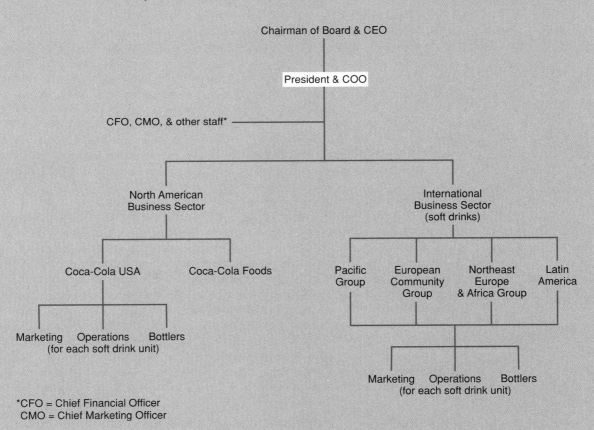

Chairman of Board & CEO

President & COO

CFO, CMO, & other staff* ————————————

North American Business Sector

International Business Sector (soft drinks)

Coca-Cola USA | Coca-Cola Foods

Pacific Group | European Community Group | Northeast Europe & Africa Group | Latin America

Marketing Operations Bottlers
(for each soft drink unit)

Marketing Operations Bottlers
(for each soft drink unit)

*CFO = Chief Financial Officer
 CMO = Chief Marketing Officer

The Coke structure of the mid-1990s reflected subtle but key adjustments designed to implement its key strategies more effectively. First, it had essentially two lines of business—soft drinks and foods (citrus juices). Second, it operated in two broad arenas—domestic (United States) and international. Goizueta's management team felt geographic focus was the most logical and fundamental organizing dimension to implement an international emphasized strategy. Then, in the case of the United States, the team's preference was to place the two main U.S. businesses (soft drinks and foods) within the U.S. geographic organization. Perhaps synergies involving deliveries to many retail outlets could be better supported or conflicts overcome by having these two under one roof.

A second dimension of this new organization kept bottling relations and overall marketing support as a corporate function, while giving each unit control of operations and day-to-day marketing and distribution. This allowed corporate control of broad themes, resources, and guidelines, while also allowing significant autonomy within each basic geographic sector. It also allowed for greater coordination of resources across international markets—an essential ingredient if Coke's aggressive international growth posture was to be maintained or indeed accelerated. Overall, the changes reflected in this structure point to Coca-Cola's major emphasis on international development and aggressive marketing adapted to local markets.

LEADERSHIP

Coca-Cola has many incidents of leadership selection that appear well coordinated with its strategies and changing strategic needs. Let's look at a few examples.

First, and perhaps most notable, was the selection of Roberto Goizueta as CEO and soon thereafter chairman in 1980. As we have briefly described earlier, Goizueta is Cuban by birth. His family owned a sugar refinery, which had made them wealthy. After finishing school in Cuba, Roberto chose to start to work for a major Coke bottler in Cuba, rather than join his family's business. Soon thereafter, Fidel Castro's rebellion took control of the island nation and, stripped of their sugar business, the Goizueta family left Cuba for the United States. Roberto Goizueta soon joined his family and went to work for a Florida bottler partially owned by the parent company. His background was in engineering and chemistry, which aided his rise within the organization, quickly turning into a position in Atlanta. From there he became a star in operations and rose quickly to the executive V.P. level.

When Paul Austin decided to step down in 1978, Coke had embarked on a serious effort to grow its international sales. While facing some lingering doubt as a rather conservative group, Coke's board was impressed with Roberto Goizueta's ability to articulate what Coke stood for and certainly was aware of the positive message it would convey to its budding international partners, employees, and investors. His appointment also reinforced Coke's long-standing policy of promotion from within, while sending a clear message to domestic personnel that it was serious about its long-term international commitment.

Goizueta has set a precedence of expecting managers to bring results-oriented commitment and dedication to their assignments at Coke. When results miss expectations, he is quick to move to support his managers and their ideas for improvement—or to change managers where their ideas engender a lack of confidence. In 1989, Coca-Cola USA—the big domestic arm selling Coke syrups and concentrates—was steadily losing modest market share to Pepsi in selected outlets. Goizueta's reaction was to suddenly bring in then 61-year-old Ira Herbert out of headquarters staff obscurity and put him in charge of this subsidiary. Herbert, marketing guru during Coca-Cola's very successful "Coke is it" and "It's the real thing" campaigns, insisted that he had not been called in "to pull the cart out of a ditch." Business writers thought otherwise. By 1992, Herbert had returned to staff duties and pending retirement, with Coca-Cola USA now leading Pepsi in every distribution outlet, including Pepsi's powerful grocery store channel. The lesson we see from this is the decisive decision to adjust leadership to the growth demands and aggressive marketing posture inherent in Coke's strategy for the 1990s. Rather than just talk about what it will take, Goizueta communicated his total commitment and expectation of the same from others by this action.

Goizueta, 65 in 1996, has been the subject of much speculation about the possibility of retirement. This speculation began in 1994. A story about Coke's handling this helps illustrate Coke's leadership orientation. Other illustrations of Coke's leadership priorities, which center around speeding up decision making and taking initiative, can be seen in the next section on culture. First the story:

> ATLANTA, 1994: Coca-Cola Co. was gripped with succession fever. Who would become the next in line to succeed Roberto C. Goizueta, the company's chairman and chief executive officer, who normally would be due to retire in 1996?
>
> Employees gossiped behind closed doors. They totted up the stock options of the company's young turks. They tried to divine the real reasons certain top executives were deciding such minutiae as where to place Olympic billboards or whether Diet Coke needed a new logo.
>
> "People constantly are speculating over who's going to succeed whom in top-level jobs," even on their car phones, one former employee said not long ago.
>
> The guessing game is over. Three weeks ago, the company announced that Mr. Goizueta, who turns 63 later this year, would remain at the helm for "an indefinite period" beyond the normal retirement age of 65. And the chairman seems in no rush to move on. Let's say "that I'm going to stay until 1999," he says cagily. "You mean to tell me you can pick in 1994 who is going to be the chief executive in 1999? Only God can do that. So many things happen in five years."
>
> The move to keep Mr. Goizueta was widely regarded by both insiders and outsiders as smart, coming at a time when Coke's stock has been weak and it faces new challenges both at home and abroad. The Cuban-born aristocrat, who joined Coke as a chemical engineer 40 years ago, has had a wildly successful run at Coke and has been a big hit on Wall Street.
>
> Many of the company's followers simply see no reason to turn him out. He is passionate about his job, regularly working 10-hour days, traveling to Coke's far-flung operations and perusing overseas strategy reports over weekends. He is in good health. And although he has been the CEO for 13 years, few believe that his management has ossified.
>
> Indeed, Coca-Cola may be representative of a new way of thinking enunciated by management experts and echoed by Coke's directors: There really is no reason—in fact, it may be foolish—to let go an experienced, successful chief executive just because he turns 65.
>
> "Talent is so scarce that when you have it, you don't let an arbitrary age retire it," says Warren Buffett, the respected Omaha, Neb., investor and Coke board member. "As long as the board thinks Roberto is the best person in the world to be head of the Coca-Cola company, there is no room for anyone else to head it."

BUILDING A SPEED-ORIENTED CULTURE AND REWARD SYSTEM

The culture Goizueta and other Coca-Cola managers think best reinforces their strategy is one that is synonymous with speed, rapid response, and aggressive decisions and actions. They seek to continually build an organization of people with initiative, commitment, understanding of how to make Coke forever remain the true pause that refreshes; people who take unabashed pleasure in (and are rewarded for) their efforts. Goizueta feels this must be the very foundation of Coke's worldwide business system. An interesting way to illustrate this culture is to look at Coke's reaction to the sudden fall of the Berlin Wall as the decade of the 1990s was about to begin.

The Berlin Wall was daily being destroyed in 1991 as millions watched on worldwide TV. Coke's chairman, Roberto Goizueta, and president, Don Keough, worried that a large, fast push into eastern Germany—with its ill-suited market structure—might become a colossal failure. But Horst Muller and Heinz Weizorek pressed their argument and quickly succeeded in changing the minds of Coke's top brass, especially Goizueta. The two Germans argued that monetary union would come faster than most people expected, which in turn would make doing business in eastern Germany much easier. They also saw economic advantages via tax breaks and investment assistance going to those companies and investors that moved quickly into a decrepit East Germany once it opened to the West. Also, they were aware of pent-up demand among East Germans, who consumed colas as frequently as their West German counterparts but were forced to drink poor-quality sodas provided by state-run factories.

Horst Muller, the new head of Coca-Cola's East German operations, first asked himself how to find sales reps in a country that has never had any. He needed people to handle store merchandising, order taking, and delivery. For Muller the dilemma, or one of many, was that East Germans lived in a culture where "selling" was a completely foreign idea.

Muller's choice was to scrutinize his 2,000+ employees in East Germany, most of whom worked at six old bottling plants Coca-Cola had bought from East Germany just weeks earlier. With the aid of his West German managers, Muller picked out the most friendly and engaging clerks, factory workers, and technicians from the old East German work force and sent them off to West Germany (and the United States) for a special version of Coke's sales personnel training programs. They returned in 30 days as obsessed market ambassadors and hustlers for Coca-Cola.

German personnel used "anything with wheels" to get their product and vending machines and other items into any outlet that would sell it. They jury-rigged the old East German bottling plants to keep up with demand and worked long hours, resulting in a dominant cola position in East Germany by the end of 1993—even before Pepsi had been seriously able to attempt to compete. And at the heart of this success was again a "can-do culture" found throughout the Coca-Cola worldwide business system.

Within one year, Coke had taken East Germany by storm and sold over 75 million cases in a territory where none were sold the previous year. Sales topped 100 million cases in 1992. Since Muller started, Coke has invested $500 million in eastern Germany, and Germany has become Coke's largest market in the European Community, which in turn generated more operating profits than the U.S. market since 1990. Indeed, it appears that Coke will usurp Pepsi's previous advantage in most of Eastern Europe and the old Soviet Union based on its aggressive move into East Germany from its strong position in West Germany. Today, unified Germany is one of Coke's strongest markets.

Another story from late 1995 describes how Coke's actions in Russia and other spots around the world seek to foster its culture and leadership to make *speed* synonymous with Coca-Cola:

Late one recent night, Neville Isdell, Coca-Cola Co.'s European chief, got a frantic call at home in Atlanta.

It was one of his managers in Russia asking for $340,000 to buy a stake in a bottling plant in the remote town of Nagutsky. The manager hadn't done any of the usual studies or liability checks. He wasn't even sure if local laws would permit Coke to own the property.

Mr. Isdell's response: Go for it. Two hours later, Coke was a part owner of the plant and later gained controlling interest. "The old Coca-Cola would have picked over every detail in the book, and maybe lost the chance to bid," he says. "Now, we know the value of intelligent risks."

In the race to quench the world's thirst, Coca-Cola has always had a reputation as the soft-drink industry's plodding old giant. Though a successful marketer, when it came to speed or innovation, the company faltered. It was swamped by the wave of teas, juices and flavored waters in the U.S. in the early 1990s. It was late entering India when that market began opening in the late

1980s. It shrugged off attacks by private-label soft-drink makers in the United Kingdom until they had siphoned off sizable sales.

But lately, Coca-Cola is charging around faster than a 10-year-old on a soda buzz—and with equal daring.

In the U.S., after nearly a decade without a new product, the company is pushing new drinks out the door at a record pace—everything from Mountain Blast Powerade sports drink to Strawberry Passion Awareness Fruitopia fruit drink. Its new marketing force has unleashed a flood of new packaging and promotions, including its signature curvy bottle, lucratively reborn in plastic. Coca-Cola says the efforts have helped it capture more than 80% of the growth in the U.S. soft-drink market this year—nearly twice last year's rate.

"Nothing energizes an organization like speed," says Roberto Goizueta, the company's chairman and chief executive.

Coca-Cola's hyperactivity has posed special challenges for PepsiCo Inc., which has always banked on its image as the industry's young rebel. It prided itself on coming out with the latest products and the hippest advertising campaigns (even if they flopped, as did Crystal Pepsi), and touted its flexibility overseas.

Now that Coca-Cola is assuming some of those same qualities, Pepsi acknowledges that it is scrambling to keep its edge. "Coke has definitely raised the bar," says Brian Swette, Pepsi's marketing chief.

The most important battles are in developing markets. With growth in soft-drink consumption maturing in markets such as the U.S., Western Europe, Mexico and Japan, most agree that the future of the beverage industry lies in emerging nations such as China and Russia.

Just this year, Coca-Cola has opened plants in Romania, Norway, Fiji and India. At least 10 more are slated, including plants in China, Hungary, Lithuania, Russia and Thailand. Big Red also is the first U.S. company to enter a joint venture in Vietnam since the embargo was lifted this summer. Coca-Cola now derives about 80% of its earnings from overseas, and makes more than half the soft drinks consumed outside the U.S.

In part, Coca-Cola is adapting to a changing industry, where teas, juices, sports drinks, bottled waters and other elixirs have transformed a largely two-cola world. Having recovered from the failure of New Coke, Coca-Cola is more willing to enter the fray and risk its name.

Credit new personalities. Coca-Cola's president, Douglas Ivester, is a fiercely competitive former financial chief who made his debut as president last year with a speech comparing company managers to a pack of "hungry wolves." What's more, as part of a recent marketing shake-up, Sergio Zyman, the creative whiz who left the company after New Coke bombed, has returned as chief marketing officer. He now is prodding his staff to make bolder, swifter moves.

For the most part, though, the changes are an extension of Mr. Goizueta's own career-long campaign to break institutional habits. During his 14-year tenure, he has overhauled the company's financial operations, trimmed the corporate structure, redefined its relationship with bottlers and reined in overseas operations that used to be run as distant fiefs. What is different about the latest moves, he says, is that many of them relate to marketing "and that's what people see."

Indeed, while Mr. Goizueta first started preaching "fast and flexible" in 1990, the effort has accelerated under Mr. Ivester. A champion of technology, Mr. Ivester has imposed a culture of voice and electronic mail and video conferencing, cutting the blizzard of memos by more than a third. He is known to send messages late at night and on weekends, leaving few excuses for delays.

"Neville's in Europe this morning, but I've already left him five voice mails," says Mr. Ivester, rushing through the halls of headquarters in Atlanta early one recent morning. "I've dealt with Spain, Italy, France and a personnel issue in Eastern Europe. And I didn't even need to talk to him once."

The company also has brought in new blood, especially in marketing. When Mr. Zyman took over, he went on a search for the "best marketing minds in the world" to bring in fresh ideas and keep pace with the company's growth. He has since hired between 40 and 50 new officers—some from sports teams and entertainment companies. Coca-Cola also has pushed its system of cross-training managers—shuttling them through different divisions—further down into the ranks, making it more difficult for the bureaucracy to solidify.

Coca-Cola's stuffy culture also is loosening up. Along with the company's collection of 19th-century oil paintings, basketball hoops now are popping up. And during a recent meeting between Coke's Asian manager and the company's Philippine bottler, Mr. Ivester and other top executives frequently dropped in to ask questions and give advice—a big change from the formal, closed-door sessions of old.

"The bottler told me, 'Doug, we used to just sit here and have a boring conversation. Now I'm talking to the president and working out all kinds of things,'" says Douglas Daft, the Asian manager. "He couldn't believe it."

Lower-level staff meetings also have taken on a more freewheeling air. "Now, in the Monday meetings, it's cool to talk about the movie you saw, or rock concert you went to and how it relates to Coke," says John Kao, a Harvard management professor who recently studied the rise in creativity at Coca-Cola.

Clearly, Coca-Cola is still a far cry from becoming the industry's wild child. The company continues to roll over competitors with its heaps of capital and tight control over bottlers, and it remains conservative among scrappier rivals.

What's more, continuing to engineer a faster, more daring Coca-Cola may be a tough task. Obsessed with shareholder value and steady growth, Coca-Cola has gained a reputation as a reliable earnings wonder. Largely on the strength of its international performance, the company's stock is up more than 50% in the past year—it closed yesterday at $63.125—boosting its market value by about $28 billion. A more-adventurous company, some say, might become a riskier investment.

"That's the hard balance," Prof. Kao says. "They have to simultaneously feed the machine that thrives on efficiency, format and market share and at the same time try to be a lab for risk-taking and invention."

Adds Mr. Isdell, the European chief: "Change driven by crisis is easy. Changing the way an organization thinks while it's successful, without being dysfunctional to what's good, that's the interesting challenge."

But it is a challenge the company will have to face as it enters new markets. Whereas the West may have been won with money and marketing muscle, emerging markets also will require quick response, a healthy thirst for risk and the ability to forge ties with a new breed of consumers. In these markets, politics and economies can change daily, demand is uncertain and customers can crave everything from pepper colas to rice punch.

In this new environment, Coke's new personality appears to be paying off.

Consider Japan, Coke's most-profitable market. Consumers there are notorious for constantly demanding fresh products. Companies typically launch between 700 and 800 drinks a year, and few stay in vending machines for more than a month.

While dominant in the market, Coca-Cola had trouble for years keeping pace. Two years ago, the company built a sophisticated product-development center to crank out new beverages faster. The result: Launch time for new drinks has been cut to 30 days from 90 days, and the company now releases as many as 50 new beverages a year. The development center has begun to serve the rest of Asia, and the lessons learned in Japan are being applied to the U.S. and Europe, too.

"We're getting it down to a fine art," says Mr. Daft, the Asian manager.

Japan also has taught the company the art of retreat. Traditionally, Coca-Cola stayed behind its products no matter how disastrous, fearing public defeat. Mr. Goizueta tells the story of a fortified tomato juice launched in the 1960s called ViProMin. The juice stayed on the shelves for several years, even though sales never materialized. "We tried to make it work for too long," he says.

Now, the company pushes products in and out of markets with greater ease, and shrugs off failures. In Japan, it launched a "lactic-based" drink called Ambasa Whitewater that initially sold millions of cases. But the market started to fade after 18 months and Ambasa was pulled.

"We see that as taking advantage of an opportunity," Mr. Daft says, "not failure."

Speed also has become more important in financial decisions. In a meeting with managers in Hanoi last month, Mr. Ivester made a quick decision to double the size of the company's new plant with a $10 million investment—even though the market was untested. To further speed things up, Mr. Ivester ordered a manufacturing line rerouted to Hanoi from a dock in Singapore.

"We had good information from our people on the ground, so we went for it," says Mr. Ivester. The plant will open next month.

In Eastern Europe, and especially in Russia, Coca-Cola's newfound agility has helped it blow past Pepsi. When the Soviet Union collapsed, for instance, the two companies followed opposite strategies. PepsiCo clung to its network of rickety, state-run bottlers, hoping to make use of their ties to old-line management. Coca-Cola quickly severed its links to the government system and built a new business from scratch. The company spent more than $1.5 billion in former East bloc countries to bring in manufacturing, distribution and marketing operations. Coca-Cola is now seen as the "milk of capitalism," especially among the young.

Of course, Coca-Cola's record overseas is far from perfect, and some spills have been costly. In Europe, the company's Tab Clear bombed. In Poland, Coca-Cola got stuck with a giant plant full of returnable bottles in its scramble to capture the expected market. And in Southeast Asia, the company's partnership with a politically well-connected bottler floundered and the company had to find an additional partner with more business acumen.

Still, Coca-Cola seems more willing than ever to swallow its failures in the name of risk and speed.

"You can't stumble if you're not moving," Mr. Goizueta says. "And if you stumble and make a decision that doesn't pan out, then you move quickly to change it. But it's better than standing still."

The Wall Street Journal, August 22, 1995, p. A1.

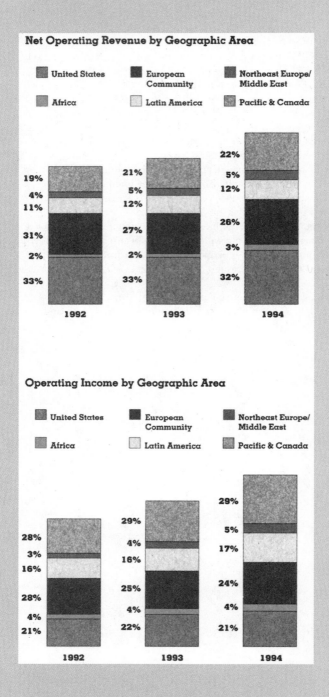

Net Operating Revenue by Geographic Area

United States | European Community | Northeast Europe/Middle East

Africa | Latin America | Pacific & Canada

1992

19%
4%
11%
31%
2%
33%

1993

21%
5%
12%
27%
2%
33%

1994

22%
5%
12%
26%
3%
32%

Operating Income by Geographic Area

United States | European Community | Northeast Europe/Middle East

Africa | Latin America | Pacific & Canada

1992

28%
3%
16%
28%
4%
21%

1993

29%
4%
16%
25%
4%
22%

1994

29%
5%
17%
24%
4%
21%

STRATEGIC CONTROL AND CONTINUOUS IMPROVEMENT

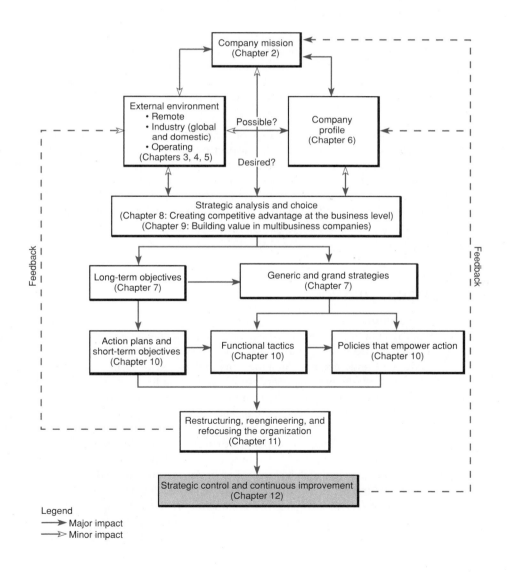

Legend

→ Major impact

⇾ Minor impact

Strategies are forward looking, designed to be accomplished several years into the future, and based on management assumptions about numerous events that have not yet occurred. How should managers control a strategy? The traditional approach to control compares actual results against a standard. After work is done, the manager evaluates it and then uses that evaluation as input to control further work. Although this approach has its place, it is inappropriate as a means for controlling a strategy. The full execution of a strategy often takes five or more years, during which time many changes occur that have major ramifications for the strategy's ultimate success. Consequently, the traditional approaches to control must be replaced by an approach that recognizes the unique control needs of long-term strategies.

Strategic control is concerned with tracking a strategy as it is being implemented, detecting problems or changes in its underlying premises, and making necessary adjustments. In contrast to postaction control, strategic control is concerned with guiding action in behalf of the strategy as that action is taking place and when the end result is still several years off. Managers responsible for the success of a strategy typically are concerned with two sets of questions:

1. Are we moving in the proper direction? Are key things falling into place? Are our assumptions about major trends and changes correct? Are we doing the critical things that need to be done? Should we adjust or abort the strategy?
2. How are we performing? Are objectives and schedules being met? Are costs, revenues, and cash flows matching projections? Do we need to make operational changes?

The rapid, accelerating change of the global marketplace of the last 10 years has made *continuous improvement* another aspect of strategic control in many business organizations. Synonymous with the total quality movement, continuous improvement provides a way for organizations to provide strategic control that allows an organization to respond more proactively and timely to rapid developments in hundreds of areas that influence a business's success. This chapter discusses traditional strategic controls and then explains ways that the *continuous improvement quality imperative* can be a vehicle for strategic control.

ESTABLISHING STRATEGIC CONTROLS

The control of strategy can be characterized as a form of "steering control." Ordinarily, a good deal of time elapses between the initial implementation of a strategy and achievement of its intended results. During that time, investments are made and numerous projects and actions are undertaken to implement the strategy. Also, during that time, changes are taking place in both the environmental situation and the firm's internal situation. Strategic controls are necessary to steer the firm through these events. They must provide the basis for adapting the firm's strategic actions and directions in response to these developments and changes.

Prudential Insurance Company provides a useful example of the proactive, steering nature of strategic control. Several years ago, Prudential adopted a long-term market development strategy in which it sought to attain the top position in the life insurance industry by differentiating its level of service from those of its competitors. It decided to achieve a differential service advantage by establishing regional home offices. Exercising strategic control, its managers used the experience of the first regional offices to reproject the overall expenses and income associated with this strategy. The predicted expenses were so high

FIGURE 12–1
Four Types of Strategic Control

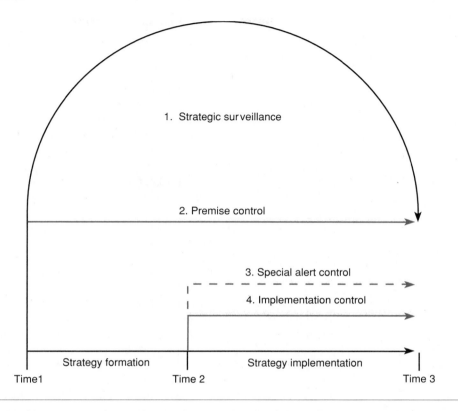

Source: Adapted from G. Schreyogg and H. Steinmann, "Strategic Control: A New Perspective," *Academy of Management Review* 12, no. 1 (1987), p. 96.

that the original schedule for establishing other regional offices had to be modified. And on the basis of other early feedback, the restructuring of the services performed at Prudential's corporate headquarters was sharply revised. Thus, the steering control (or strategic control) exercised by Prudential managers significantly altered the firm's strategy. In this case, the major objectives of the strategy remained in place; in other cases, strategic control has led to changes in the major strategic objectives.

The four basic types of strategic control are:

1. Premise control.
2. Implementation control.
3. Strategic surveillance.
4. Special alert control.

The nature of these four types is summarized in Figure 12–1.

Premise Control

Every strategy is based on certain planning premises—assumptions or predictions. *Premise control is designed to check systematically and continuously whether the premises on which the strategy is based are still valid.* If a vital premise is no longer valid, the strategy may have to be changed. The sooner an invalid premise can be recognized and rejected, the better are the chances that an acceptable shift in the strategy can be devised.

Which Premises Should Be Monitored?

Planning premises are primarily concerned with environmental and industry factors. These are described next.

Environmental Factors   Although a firm has little or no control over environmental factors, these factors exercise considerable influence over the success of its strategy, and strategies usually are based on key premises about them. Inflation, technology, interest rates, regulation, and demographic/social changes are examples of such factors.

EPA regulations and federal laws concerning the handling, use, and disposal of toxic chemicals have a major effect on the strategy of Velsicol Chemical Company, a market leader in pesticide chemicals sold to farmers and exterminators. So Velsicol's management makes and constantly updates premises about future regulatory actions.

Industry Factors   The performance of the firms in a given industry is affected by industry factors. These differ among industries, and a firm should be aware of the factors that influence success in its particular industry. Competitors, suppliers, product substitutes, and barriers to entry are a few of the industry factors about which strategic assumptions are made.

Rubbermaid has long been held up as a model of predictable growth, creative management, and rapid innovation in the plastic housewares and toy industry. Its premise going into the 21st century was that large retail chains would continue to prefer its products over competitors' because of this core competence. This premise included continued receptivity to regular price increases when necessitated by raw materials costs. Late 1995 found retailers, most notably Wal-Mart, balking at Rubbermaid's attempt to raise prices to offset the doubling of resin costs. Furthermore, traditionally overlooked competitors have begun to make inroads with computerized stocking services. Rubbermaid is moving aggressively to adjust its strategy because of the response of Wal-Mart and other key retailers.

Strategies are often based on numerous premises, some major and some minor, about environmental and industry variables. Tracking all of these premises is unnecessarily expensive and time consuming. Managers must select premises whose change (1) is likely and (2) would have a major impact on the firm and its strategy.

How Are Premise Controls Enacted?

A strategy's key premises should be identified and recorded during the planning process. Responsibility for monitoring those premises should be assigned to the persons or departments that are qualified sources of information. To illustrate, members of the sales force might be assigned to monitor the expected price policy of major competitors and the finance department might be assigned to monitor interest rate trends. The required amount of monitoring effort varies for different premises; to avoid information overload, emphasis should be placed on the monitoring of key premises. These premises should be updated (and new predictions should be made) on the basis of updated information. Finally, key areas within the firm, or key aspects of the strategy that would be significantly affected by changes in certain premises, should be preidentified so adjustments necessitated by revisions in those premises can be determined and initiated. For example, senior marketing executives should be alerted to changes in competitors' pricing policies so these executives can determine whether revised pricing, product repositioning, or other strategy adjustments are necessary. Global Strategy in Action 12–1 reports an interview with IBM CEO Lou Gerstner that discusses the premise control changes in IBM's strategy that IBM has made in response to the Internet.

Implementation Control

Strategy implementation takes place as series of steps, programs, investments, and moves that occur over an extended time. Special programs are undertaken. Functional areas initiate strategy-related activities. Key people are added or reassigned. Resources are mobilized. In other words, managers implement strategy by converting broad plans into the concrete, incremental actions and results of specific units and individuals.

Implementation control is the type of strategic control that must be exercised as those events unfold. *Implementation control is designed to assess whether the overall strategy should be changed in light of the results associated with the incremental actions that implement the overall strategy.* Prudential's updating of cost and revenue projections based on early experiences with regional home offices is an example of implementation control. The two basic types of implementation control are (1) monitoring strategic thrusts and (2) milestone reviews.

Monitoring Strategic Thrusts

As a means of implementing broad strategies, narrow strategic projects often are undertaken—projects that represent part of what needs to be done if the overall strategy is to be accomplished. These strategic thrusts provide managers with information that helps them determine whether the overall strategy is progressing as planned or needs to be adjusted.

Although the utility of strategic thrusts seems readily apparent, it is not always easy to use them for control purposes. It may be difficult to interpret early experience or to evaluate the overall strategy in light of such experience. One approach is to agree early in the planning process on which thrusts or which phases of thrusts are critical factors in the success of the strategy. Managers responsible for these implementation controls will single them out from other activities and observe them frequently. Another approach is to use stop/go assessments that are linked to a series of meaningful thresholds (time, costs, research and development, success, and so forth) associated with particular thrusts. A program of regional development via company-owned inns in the Rocky Mountain area was a monitoring thrust that Days Inn used to test its strategy of becoming a nationwide motel chain. Problems in meeting time targets and unexpectedly large capital needs led Days Inn's executives to abandon the overall strategy and eventually sell the firm.

Milestone Reviews

Managers often attempt to identify significant milestones that will be reached during strategy implementation. These milestones may be critical events, major resource allocations, or simply the passage of a certain amount of time. The milestone reviews that then take place usually involve a full-scale reassessment of the strategy and of the advisability of continuing or refocusing the firm's direction.

A useful example of implementation control based on milestone review is offered by Boeing's product development strategy of entering the supersonic transport (SST) airplane market. Boeing had invested millions of dollars and years of scarce engineering talent during the first phase of its SST venture, and competition from the British/French

WHOOSH . . . THE INTERNET, WORLDWIDE WEB, AND IBM: PREMISE CONTROL AT IBM

IBM was supposed to be dying. And it may still die. But it is endeavoring to apply premise control to build its future in "network-centric" directions. Let's see what this involves by looking at IBM's old premise and the effects of the Internet.

1. *Old premise.* Software programs are written for specific types of hardware (IBM or Apple). Programs don't go from one hardware configuration to the other. And even if written for the same operating system, programs don't adapt from one to the other. Even same-supplier programs don't always work together. Solution: bloatware, "suites," with a bunch of applications thrown together to interface better. But this requires greater speed and capacity on your computer so a new chip and new computer is needed. And so begins an "unholy" alliance between software and hardware makers. Not always best for the computer consumer but few alternatives exist.

2. *Enter the Internet.* Since the Web and Mosaic and Netscape programs for viewing pages emerged, the Web has turned into a huge virtual disk drive. Suddenly, barriers that kept information from flowing between brands of computers and software are gone. Next, using the Web not only to make the same information available to all wired machines but to let them share the same programs. If it works, the software industry is destroyed and reconstructed overnite. That's exactly what's beginning to happen—at a pace nobody in the computer industry anticipated.

IBM's CEO Lou Gerstner, speaking with *Business Week* editor Ira Sager in a conference room where Gerstner keeps a couple of computers to check on everything from kids' software to Web browsers, shared IBM's premise control reactions, as reported in the following *Business Week* article:

> *Louis V. Gerstner Jr. caused a stir two summers ago when he declared that the last thing IBM needed was to proclaim a grand vision. Gerstner proceeded to focus on cost-cutting and other management issues and proved the vision-hungry pundits wrong. But having studied IBM, the computer industry, and technology trends, the former McKinsey & Co. consultant has come up with, if not a vision, at least a plan for IBM. Relaxing in a conference room where he keeps a couple of computers to check out everything from kids' software to Web browsers, Gerstner shared his ideas with Information Processing Editor Ira Sager.*
>
> **Q:** *You speak of "network-centric" computing. What is it?*
> **A:** The first wave of computing, 30 years ago, was driven by the technologies of host-based processors [mainframes] and storage devices. Twenty years later, we moved into a second wave, which was driven by microprocessors and simplified operating systems. The third wave of computing is being driven by very powerful networked technologies that provide very inexpensive and very wide [communications] bandwidth.
>
> **Q:** *What will happen to existing computers?*
> **A:** People have argued that the host-based [mainframe] model is dead. Well, it isn't dead. People are buying more of those units than they ever have. And no one should say that the stand-

Source: "Lou Gerstner on Catching the Third Wave," *Business Week,* October 30, 1995, p. 152.

Concorde effort was intense. Since the next phase represented a billion-dollar decision, Boeing's management established the initiation of the phase as a milestone. The milestone reviews greatly increased the estimates of production costs; predicted relatively few passengers and rising fuel costs, thus raising the estimated operating costs; and noted that the Concorde, unlike Boeing, had the benefit of massive government subsidies. These factors led Boeing's management to scrap its SST strategy in spite of high

alone personal computer is going to go away. But there is no question that the PC-based model is now not the future. The future is a network-centric model. The focus moves to a network that draws out the best of both worlds. That model drives the strategy of this company. When people talk about IBM, it's interesting to hear them say: "Well, I wonder if they'll get their new businesses to grow fast enough while their old businesses die." What they don't understand is, we are reconceptualizing our old businesses. We're bringing them into this new model.

Q: *Will IBM put applications on a network and charge per-transaction or volume-based fees?*

A: Absolutely. We call this business process outsourcing. For example, this Internet or networked world will put extreme pressure on traditional providers of financial services. We have no interest in going into the banking business. But we do have an interest in working with a series of banks in which we will provide networking capability through the IBM Global Network and networking applications that we will build. We'll take part of the transaction revenue. It could very well be on a per-click, per-communication unit. It is a strategy that brings our customers into this world of network services. Yes, we will be compensated in nontraditional ways.

Q: *That provides a recurring source of revenue—as opposed to one-time product sales. Is this where you see network computing leading IBM?*

A: That's the model IBM created with its mainframe software—monthly license revenue. We understand the concept of software paid for on a usage basis as opposed to a shrink-wrap, buy-it-once basis. Now, all of this is going to take time. It's going to evolve differently in different industries, in different companies, depending on their strategies. Large customers are going to take a very long time before they're going to rent mission-critical applications. People will not convert their own legacy systems to this. What will go on a rental model is the new stuff, like electronic commerce.

Q: *In a wired world, must IBM remain a big maker of hardware and software?*

A: People are going to need a lot of very powerful servers. They're going to need a lot of transaction software. They're going to need a lot of database software. They're going to need a lot of communications software. You don't necessarily have to provide all of these things, but we do. And as long as we're successful in each of them, we're going to continue to provide them. [If] we're not successful, we'll get out of the business.

Q: *How does Prodigy fit into IBM's network-computing plans?*

A: We are taking a hard look at our Prodigy strategy right now, along with [Prodigy partner] Sears. Short term, we're making a lot of changes. We brought in new management. They've done some new things with their system. Certainly their merchandising and marketing has gotten better. But the long-term strategy for IBM and Prodigy is not clear. We will sort that out in a relatively short time. The fundamental issue is: In the world of the Internet, is there a place for a packager of services? Does the customer want to go surf the Net and go to every one of 50,000 Web sites? Or will people pay a reasonable amount for somebody to go out and preselect and package what they want? My guess is they will both coexist.

sunk costs, pride, and patriotism. Only an objective, full-scale strategy reassessment could have led to such a decision.

In this example, a milestone review occurred at a major resource allocation decision point. Milestone reviews may also occur concurrently when a major step in a strategy's implementation is being taken or when a key uncertainty is resolved. Managers even may set an arbitrary period, say two years, as a milestone review point. Whatever the basis for

STRATEGY
IN ACTION
12–1

EXAMPLES OF STRATEGIC CONTROL

IMPLEMENTATION CONTROL AT DAYS INN

When Days Inn pioneered the budget segment of the lodging industry, its strategy placed primary emphasis on company-owned facilities and it insisted on maintaining a roughly 3-to-1 company-owned/franchise ratio. This ratio ensured the parent company's total control over standards, rates, and so forth.

As other firms moved into the budget segment, Days Inn saw the need to expand rapidly throughout the United States and, therefore, reversed its conservative franchise posture. This reversal would rapidly accelerate its ability to open new locations. Longtime executives, concerned about potential loss of control over local standards, instituted *implementation controls* requiring both franchise evaluation and annual milestone reviews. Two years into the program, Days Inn executives were convinced that a high franchise-to-company ratio was manageable, and so they accelerated the growth of franchising by doubling the franchise sales department.

STRATEGIC SURVEILLANCE AT CITICORP

Citicorp has been pursuing an aggressive product development strategy intended to achieve an annual earnings growth of 15 percent while it becomes an institution capable of supplying clients with any kind of financial service anywhere in the world. A major obstacle to the achievement of this earnings growth is Citicorp's exposure to default because of its extensive earlier loans to troubled Third World countries. Citicorp is sensitive to the wide variety of predictions about impending Third World defaults.

Source: Adapted from conversations with selected Days Inn executives; "Is the Worst over for Citi?" *Forbes,* May 11, 1992; and "How Companies Prepare for the Worst," *Business Week,* December 23 1985, p. 74.

selecting that point, the critical purpose of a milestone review is to thoroughly scrutinize the firm's strategy so as to control the strategy's future.

Strategic Surveillance

By their nature, premise control and implementation control are focused controls; strategic surveillance, however, is unfocused. *Strategic surveillance is designed to monitor a broad range of events inside and outside the firm that are likely to affect the course of its strategy.*[1] The basic idea behind strategic surveillance is that important yet unanticipated information may be uncovered by a general monitoring of multiple information sources.

Strategic surveillance must be kept as unfocused as possible. It should be a loose "environmental scanning" activity. Trade magazines, *The Wall Street Journal,* trade conferences, conversations, and intended and unintended observations are all subjects of strategic surveillance. Despite its looseness, strategic surveillance provides an ongoing, broad-based vigilance in all daily operations that may uncover information relevant to the firm's strategy. Citicorp benefited significantly from a Peruvian manager's strategic surveillance of political speeches by Peru's former president, as discussed in Strategy in Action 12–1.

[1] G. Schreyogg and H. Steinmann, "Strategic Control: A New Perspective," *Academy of Management Review* 12, no. 1 (1987), p. 101.

continued

Citicorp's long-range plan assumes an annual 10 percent default on its Third World loans over any five-year period. Yet it maintains active *strategic surveillance control* by having each of its international branches monitor daily announcements from key governments and from inside contacts for signs of changes in a host country's financial environment. When that surveillance detects a potential problem, management attempts to adjust Citicorp's posture. For example, when Peru's former president, Alan Garcia, stated that his country would not pay interest on its debt as scheduled, Citicorp raised its annual default charge to 20 percent of its $100 million Peruvian exposure.

SPECIAL ALERT CONTROL AT UNITED AIRLINES

The sudden impact of an airline crash can be devastating to a major airline. United Airlines has made elaborate preparations to deal with this contingency. Its executive vice president, James M. Guyette, heads a crisis team that is permanently prepared to respond. Members of the team carry beepers and are always on call. If United's Chicago headquarters receives word that a plane has crashed, for example, they can be in a "war room" within an hour to direct the response. Beds are set up nearby so team members can catch a few winks; while they sleep, alternates take their places.

Members of the team have been carefully screened through simulated crisis drills. "The point is to weed out those who don't hold up well under stress," says Guyette. Although the team was established to handle flight disasters, it has since assumed an expanded role. The crisis team was activated when American Airlines launched a fare war. And according to Guyette, "We're brainstorming about how we would be affected by everything from a competitor who had a serious problem to a crisis involving a hijacking or taking a United employee hostage."

Special Alert Control

Another type of strategic control, really a subset of the other three, is special alert control. *A special alert control is the thorough, and often rapid, reconsideration of the firm's strategy because of a sudden, unexpected event.* A political coup in the Middle East, an outside firm's sudden acquisition of a leading competitor, an unexpected product difficulty, such as the poisoned Tylenol capsules—events of these kinds can drastically alter the firm's strategy.

Such an event should trigger an immediate and intense reassessment of the firm's strategy and its current strategic situation. In many firms, crisis teams handle the firm's initial response to unforeseen events that may have an immediate effect on its strategy. Increasingly, firms have developed contingency plans along with crisis teams to respond to circumstances such as those illustrated in Strategy in Action 12–1.

Figure 12–2 summarizes the major characteristics of the four types of strategic control. Unlike operational controls, which are concerned with the control of action, strategic controls are designed to continuously and proactively question the basic direction and appropriateness of a strategy. Each type of strategic control shares a common purpose: to assess whether the strategic direction should be altered in light of unfolding events. Many of us have heard the axiom, "The only thing that is constant is change itself." Organizations face the constancy of change from endless sources within and without the organization, all occurring at an ever accelerating pace. There is very little that organizations can do to directly control the many sources of change. Yet, with performance and long-term

FIGURE 12–2

Characteristics of the Four Types of Strategic Control

Basic Characteristics	Types of Strategic Control			
	Premise Control	Implementation Control	Strategic Surveillance	Special Alert Control
Objects of control	Planning premises and projections	Key strategic thrusts and milestones	Potential threats and opportunities related to the strategy	Occurrence of recognizable but unlikely events
Degree of focusing	High	High	Low	High
Data acquisition:				
Formalization	Medium	High	Low	High
Centralization	Low	Medium	Low	High
Use with:				
Environmental factors	Yes	Seldom	Yes	Yes
Industry factors	Yes	Seldom	Yes	Yes
Strategy-specific factors	No	Yes	Seldom	Yes
Company-specific factors	No	Yes	Seldom	Seldom

Source: Adapted from G. Schreyogg and H. Steinmann, "Strategic Control: A New Perspective," *Academy of Management Review* 12, no. 1 (1987), pp. 91–103.

survival at stake, better organizations adopt and regularly refine strategic controls as a way to deal with pervasive change.

IBM's CEO Lou Gerstner's explanation of the rationale behind some of the fundamental changes at IBM toward the end of the 20th century illustrates the pervasive, dramatic character of change and the essence of strategic control as a means to deal with it:

> One of the great things about this [computer] industry is that every decade or so, you get a chance to redefine the playing field. We're in that phase of redefinition right now, and winners or losers are going to emerge from it . . . Network centric computing . . . Providing time on computers rather than selling the hardware . . . The Internet . . . There's no question that the speed with which the Internet has emerged has caught all industries related to this technology by surprise . . . But there is no question that the PC-based model is now not the future.

Both operational and strategic controls are needed to guide the strategic management process. The next section examines the key types of operational control systems that are used to aid the strategic management process.

OPERATIONAL CONTROL SYSTEMS

Operational control systems guide, monitor, and evaluate progress in meeting short-term objectives. While strategic controls attempt to steer the company over an extended period (usually five years of more), operational controls provide postaction evaluation and control over short periods—usually from one month to one year. To be effective, operational control systems must take four steps common to all postaction controls:

1. Set standards of performance.
2. Measure actual performance.
3. Identify deviations from standards set.
4. Initiate corrective action.

Three types of operational control system are *budgets, schedules,* and *key success factors.* The nature and use of these three types of systems are described in the next sections.

Budgets

The budgetary process was the forerunner of strategic planning. A budget is a resource allocation plan that helps managers coordinate operations and facilitates managerial control of performance. Budgets themselves do not control anything. They simply set standards against which action can be measured. They also provide a basis for negotiating short-term resource requirements to implement strategy at the operating level. Most firms employ at least three budgets as a part of their planning and control activities. These types of budgets are the following:

1. *Profit and loss (P&L) budgets* are perhaps the most common. These budgets serve as the basis to monitor sales on a monthly or more frequent basis, as well as to monitor expense categories on a comparable time frame against what has actually occurred. Sales and expense numbers often are subdivided by department, location, product lines, and other relevant subunits to more closely project and monitor organizational activities.

2. *Capital budgets* usually are developed to show the timing of specific expenditures for plant, equipment, machinery, inventories, and other capital items needed during the budget period.

3. *Cash flow budgets* forecast receipt and disbursement of cash during the budget period. They tie together P&L expectations, capital expenditures, collection of receivables, expense payments, and borrowing needs to show just where the life blood of any business—cash—will come from and go to each month.

The budgeting system serves as an important and early indicator about the effectiveness of a firm's strategy by serving as a frame of reference against which to examine month-to-month results in the execution of that strategy.

Scheduling

Timing is often a key factor in the success of a strategy. Scheduling considerations in allocating time-constrained resources and sequencing interdependent activities often determine the success of strategy implementation. Scheduling offers a mechanism with which to plan for, monitor, and control these dependencies.[2] For example, a firm committed to a vertical integration strategy must carefully absorb expended operations into its existing core. Such absorption, given either forward or backward integration, will require numerous changes in the operational practices of the firm's organizational units. A good illustration is Coors Brewery's decision to integrate backward by producing its own beer cans. A comprehensive two-year schedule of actions and targets for incorporating the manufacture of beer cans and bottles into the product chain contributed to the success of this strategy. Purchasing, production scheduling, machinery, and production systems were but a few of the critical operating areas that Coors's scheduling efforts were meant to accommodate and coordinate.

---

[2] A useful primer on scheduling considerations in strategic project planning is provided by Steven Wheelwright and Kim Clark in "Creating Project Plans to Focus Project Development," *Harvard Business Review* 70, no. 2 (1992), pp. 70–82; and Steven Wheelwright and Kim Clark, *Revolutionizing Product Development: Quantum Leaps in Speed, Efficiency, and Quality* (New York: The Free Press, 1992).

FIGURE 12–3
Key Success Factors at Lotus Corporation

Key Success Factor	Measurable Performance Indicator
1. Product quality	a. Performance data versus specification. b. Percentage of product returns. c. Number of customer complaints.
2. Customer service	a. Delivery cycle in days. b. Percentage of orders shipped complete. c. Field service delays.
3. Employee morale	a. Trends in employee attitude survey. b. Absenteeism versus plan. c. Employee turnover trends.
4. Competition	a. Number of firms competing directly. b. Number of new products introduced. c. Percentage of bids awarded versus the standard.

Key Success Factors

Another useful way to effect operational control is to focus on "key success factors." These factors identify the performance areas that are of greatest importance in implementing the company's strategies and, therefore, must receive continuous management attention. Each key success factor must have measurable performance indicators. Lotus Corporation management, for example, having identified product quality, customer service, employee morale, and competition as the key determinants of success in the firm's strategy of rapidly expanding its software offerings, then specified three indicators to monitor and control each of these key success factors, as shown in Figure 12–3.

Key success factors succinctly communicate the critical elements for which operational managers are responsible. These factors require the successful performance of several key individuals and, thus, can be a foundation for teamwork among managers in meeting the firm's strategic objectives.

Budgeting, scheduling, and monitoring key success factors are important means of controlling strategy implementation at the operational level. Common to all of these operational control systems is the need to establish measurable standards and to monitor performance against those standards. The next section examines how to accomplish this.

USING OPERATIONAL CONTROL SYSTEMS: MONITORING PERFORMANCE AND EVALUATING DEVIATIONS

Operational control systems require performance standards. *Control* is the process of obtaining timely information on deviations from these standards, determining the causes of the deviations, and taking corrective action.

Figure 12–4 illustrates a simplified report that links the current status of key performance indicators to a firm's strategy. These indicators represent progress after two years of a five-year strategy intended to differentiate the firm as a customer-service-oriented provider of high-quality products. Management's concern is to compare *progress to date* with *expected progress*. The *current deviation* is of particular interest, because it provides a basis for examining *suggested actions* (usually suggested by subordinate managers) and for finalizing decisions on changes or adjustments in the firm's operations.

FIGURE 12–4
Monitoring and Evaluating Performance Deviations

Key Success Factors	Objective, Assumption, or Budget	Forecast Performance at This Time	Current Performance	Current Deviation	Analysis
Cost control: Ratio of indirect overhead costs to direct field and labor costs	10%	15%	12%	+3 (ahead)	Are we moving too fast, or is there more unnecessary overhead than was originally thought?
Gross profit	39%	40%	40%	0%	
Customer service: Installation cycle in days	2.5 days	3.2 days	2.7 days	+0.5 (ahead)	Can this progress be maintained?
Ratio of service to sales personnel	3.2	2.7	2.1	−0.6 (behind)	Why are we behind here? How can we maintain the installation-cycle progress?
Product quality: Percentage of products returned	1.0%	2.0%	2.1%	−0.1% (behind)	Why are we behind here? What are the ramifications for other operations?
Product performance versus specification	100%	92%	80%	−12% (behind)	
Marketing: Monthly sales per employee	$12,500	$11,500	$12,100	+$600 (ahead)	Good progress. Is it creating any problems to support?
Expansion of product line	6	3	5	+2 products (ahead)	Are the products ready? Are the perfect standards met?
Employee morale in service area: Absenteeism rate	2.5%	3.0%	3.0%	(on target)	
Turnover rate	5%	10%	15%	−8% (behind)	Looks like a problem! Why are we so far behind?
Competition: New product introductions (average number)	6	3	6	−3 (behind)	Did we underestimate timing? What are the implications for our basic assumptions?

From Figure 12–4, it appears that the firm is maintaining control of its cost structure. Indeed, it is ahead of schedule on reducing overhead. The firm is well ahead of its delivery cycle target, while slightly below its target service-to-sales personnel ratio. Its product returns look OK, although product performance versus specification is below standard. Sales per employee and expansion of the product line are ahead of schedule. The absenteeism rate in the service area is on target, but the turnover rate is higher than that targeted. Competitors appear to be introducing products more rapidly than expected.

After deviations and their causes have been identified, the implications of the deviations for the ultimate success of the strategy must be considered. For example, the rapid product-line expansion indicated in Figure 12–4 may have been a response to the increased rate of competitors' product expansion. At the same time, product performance is still low; and, while the installation cycle is slightly above standard (improving customer service), the ratio of service to sales personnel is below the targeted ratio. Contributing to this substandard ratio (and perhaps reflecting a lack of organizational commitment to customer service) is the exceptionally high turnover in customer service personnel. The rapid reduction in indirect overhead costs might mean that administration integration of customer service and product development requirements has been cut back too quickly.

This information presents operations managers with several options. They may attribute the deviations primarily to internal discrepancies. In that case, they can scale priorities up or down. For example, they might place more emphasis on retaining customer service personnel and less emphasis on overhead reduction and new product development. On the other hand, they might decide to continue as planned in the face of increasing competition and to accept or gradually improve the customer service situation. Another possibility is reformulating the strategy or a component of the strategy in the face of rapidly increasing competition. For example, the firm might decide to emphasize more standardized or lower-priced products to overcome customer service problems and take advantage of an apparently ambitious sales force.

This is but one of many possible interpretations of Figure 12–4. The important point here is the critical need to monitor progress against standards and to give serious in-depth attention to both the causes of observed deviations and the most appropriate responses to them. After the deviations have been evaluated, slight adjustments may be made to keep progress, expenditure, or other factors in line with the strategy's programmed needs. In the unusual event of extreme deviations—generally because of unforeseen changes—management is alerted to the possible need for revising the budget, reconsidering certain functional plans related to budgeted expenditures, or examining the units concerned and the effectiveness of their managers.

An acceptable level of deviation should be allowed; otherwise, the control process will become an administrative overload. Standards should not be regarded as absolute, because the estimates used to formulate them typically are based on historical data, which, by definition, are after the fact. Absolute standards (keep equipment busy 100 percent of the time or meet 100 percent of quota) make no provision for variability. Standards are also often derived from averages, which, by definition, ignore variability. These difficulties suggest the need to define acceptable *ranges* of deviation in budgetary figures or key indicators of strategic success. This approach helps in avoiding administrative difficulties, in recognizing measurement variability, in delegating more realistic authority for short-term decisions to operating managers, and in improving motivation.

Some firms use trigger points for the clarification of standards, particularly in monitoring key success factors. A *trigger point* is a level of deviation of a key indicator or figure (such as a competitor's actions or a critical cost category) that management identifies in the planning process as representing either a major threat or an unusual opportunity. When that point is reached, management immediately is altered (triggered) to consider necessary adjustments in the firm's strategy. Some firms take this idea a step forward and develop one or more *contingency plans* that are to be implemented when predetermined trigger points are reached. These contingency plans redirect priorities and actions so rapidly that valuable reaction time is not wasted on administrative assessment of the extreme deviation.

Correcting deviations in performance brings the entire management task into focus. Managers can correct such deviations by changing measures or plans. They also can eliminate poor performance by changing how things are done, by hiring or retraining workers, by changing job assignments, and so on. Correcting deviations, therefore, can involve all of the functions, tasks, and responsibilities of operations managers. Managers in other cultures, most notably Japan, have for some time achieved operational control by seeking their unit's continuous improvement. Companies worldwide have adapted this point of view that operational control is best achieved through a pervasive commitment to quality, often called *total quality management* (TQM), which is seen as essential to strategic success into the 21st century.

THE QUALITY IMPERATIVE: CONTINUOUS IMPROVEMENT TO BUILD CUSTOMER VALUE

The initials TQM have become the most popular abbreviation in business management literature since MBO (management by objectives).[3] TQM Stands for *total quality management,* an umbrella term for the quality programs that have been implemented in many businesses worldwide in the last two decades. TQM was first implemented in several large U.S. manufacturers in the face of the overwhelming success of Japanese and German competitors. Japanese manufacturers embraced the quality messages of Americans W. Edward Deming and J. M. Juran following World War II, and by the 1970s Japanese products had acquired unquestioned reputations for superior high quality.

Growing numbers of U.S. manufacturers have attempted to change this imbalance with their own quality programs, and the practice has spread to large retail and service companies as well. Increasingly, smaller companies that supply big TQM companies have adopted quality programs, often because big companies have required small suppliers to adopt quality programs of their own. Strategy in Action 12–2 describes the quality program in one such company, Dallas-based Marlow Industries, a recent winner of the Malcolm Baldrige National Quality Award.

TQM is viewed as virtually a new organizational culture and way of thinking. It is built around an intense focus on customer satisfaction; on accurate measurement of every critical variable in a business's operation; on continuous improvement of products, services, and processes; and on work relationships based on trust and teamwork. One useful explanation of the quality imperative suggests 10 essential elements of implementing total quality management, as follows:[4]

1. **Define *quality* and *customer value*.** Rather than be left to individual interpretation, company personnel should have a clear definition of what *quality* means in the job, department, and throughout the company. It should be developed from your customer's perspective and communicated as a written policy.

Thinking in terms of customer value broadens the definition of *quality* to include efficiency and responsiveness. Said another way, quality to your customer often means that the product performs well; that it is priced competitively (efficiency); and that you provide it quickly and adapt it when needed (responsiveness). Customer value is found in the combination of all three—quality, price, and speed.

2. **Develop a customer orientation.** Customer value is what the customer says it is. Don't rely on secondary information—talk to your customers directly. Also recognize your "internal" customers. Usually less than 20 percent of company employees come into contact with external customers, while the other 80 percent serve internal customers—other units with real performance expectations.

The value chain provides an important way to think about customer orientation, particularly to recognize *internal* as well as external (ultimate) customers. Operating personnel

---

[3] This section draws on total quality management ideas found in the following: G. Stalk, P. Evans, and L. E. Shulman, "Competing on Capabilities: The New Rules of Corporate Strategy," *Harvard Business Review,* March–April 1992, pp. 57–69; M. Barrier, "Small Firms Put Quality First," *Nation's Business,* May 1992, pp. 22–31; Ernst & Young, *Total Quality,* SCORE Retrieval File no. A49003, 1991; and Mary Walton, *The Deming Management Method* (New York: Perigee Books, 1986).

[4] Ideas about these 10 elements are based in part on excellent work by the firm Ernst and Young, in *Total Quality,* SCORE Retrieval File no. A49003, 1991.

STRATEGY
IN ACTION
12–2

DO OR DIE: MARLOW INDUSTRIES ADOPTS
TOTAL QUALITY MANAGEMENT

Congress created the Baldrige Award in 1987 to recognize U.S. firms with outstanding records of quality improvement and quality management. Marlow Industries, the Dallas-based firm that was the 1992 small-business winner of the Malcolm Baldrige National Quality Award, is one of those companies that adopted TQM under pressure from its customers.

There's a simple reason for such customer pressure: When an appliance maker is trying to produce defect-free products, it cannot tolerate defects in the parts provided by its small suppliers.

Marlow, with 160 employees, is the smallest business yet to win the award. Only three small firms have ever won, out of 125 that have applied. Marlow makes thermoelectric coolers—small solid-state devices used to spot cooling in critical applications for telecommunications, aerospace, and the military. Most of Marlow's products are custom made for customers who impose their own quality requirements on their suppliers. Marlow had to come up with comprehensive quality systems that would meet all of those requirements.

That might sound like an intimidating task for so small a company, but Marlow successfully introduced profound changes in the way it operates. For example, about two years ago Marlow broke up its quality-assurance department, assigning product inspectors to "minifactories"—self-contained units, made up of approximately 15 people each. Today, according to Chris Witzke, Marlow's COO, the inspectors "look after the quality systems, set training standards, do audits—but they're not in the product-inspection business."

In other words, Marlow switched from product inspection to process control—from catching and correcting defects at the end of the process to monitoring the process itself, so defects do not occur. It was not easy to adopt TQM at Marlow. Raymond Marlow, founder and president of Marlow, said "You've got to have patience, because it takes a couple of years" before employees can work together smoothly in problem-solving teams. While the transition is taking place, Marlow says, top management must display "consistency of purpose. You have to keep the quality thing moving."

Measurement was critical at Marlow. "If you measure something," said Chris Witzke, "it improves." Simply posting measurements—putting up a chart showing how well departments

Source: Excerpted from "Small Firms Put Quality First," *Nation's Business*, May 1992, pp. 22–31.

are *internal* customers of the accounting department for useful information and also the purchasing department for quality, timely supplies. When they are "served" with quality, efficiency, and responsiveness, value is added to their efforts, and is passed on to their internal customers and, eventually, external (ultimate) customers.

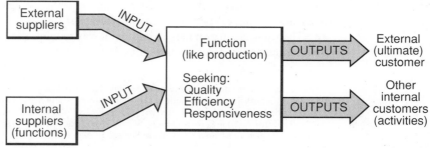

Source: G. G. Dess and A. Miller, *Strategic Management*, p. 143. © 1993 by McGraw-Hill, Inc. Reprinted with the permission of The McGraw-Hill Companies.

continued

are doing at turning in their time cards on schedule, for instance—can sometimes solve a problem. But deciding what to measure is not always easy. Marlow devoted a full year to developing statistical process controls. "We really dedicated ourselves to understanding our processes and finding the key variables," Witzke said. "All this stuff used to be black art. Now it's science." Marlow at one time measured 52 variables in a plating process—but had constant problems anyway. Now it measures only 14 variables (including seven new ones), and the problems have disappeared. Measurements sometimes can reveal things about a business that no one would have suspected if the measurements hadn't been made. When Marlow began subjecting employee turnover to Pareto analysis, it discovered that a 90-day probationary period was contributing to turnover by encouraging supervisors to make marginal hires. Once the supervisors understood the cost of that turnover, they tightened their hiring practices. At Marlow, decisions on what should be measured usually have followed surveys of "internal customers" so what was important could be measured.

As any TQM company would be expected to do, Marlow measures its suppliers' performances— and it also tells them how they're doing. "It's amazing how quick a reaction you can get just from sending out a letter saying, 'Hey, your supplier index has dropped to 1.1,' " said Marlow's Witzke. One of Marlow's minifactories, responding to just such a review, came up with a "service guarantee" for its internal customers. Posted prominently in a hall at the plant, the guarantee promises replacement of any unsatisfactory part within 24 hours. After that guarantee went up, Witzke said, "it wasn't long before they started popping up in other places. That's the ideal situation—where management doesn't have to spend all of its time making things happen."

Marlow does a lot of in-house training, in both work skills and quality techniques—the average employee spent almost 50 hours in training last year—and the training helps managers as well as employees. Said Witzke: "By the time you've taught a course three or four times, you begin to believe it."

When a quality program is working, Witzke says—when customers are happy, products are defect-free, deliveries are on time—"all of a sudden you've got 30 percent more staff than you thought you had," because employees are spending less time correcting problems.

3. **Focus on the company's business processes.** Break down every minute step in the process of providing the company's product or service and look at ways to improve it, rather than focusing simply on the finished product or service. Each process contributes value in some way, which can be improved or adapted to help other processes (internal customers) improve. Examples of ways customer value is enhanced across business processes in several functions are:

	Quality	**Efficiency**	**Responsiveness**
Marketing	Provides accurate assessment of customer's product preferences to R&D	Targets advertising campaign at customers, using cost-effective medium	Quickly uncovers and reacts to changing market trends
Operations	Consistently produces goods matching engineering design	Minimizes scrap and rework through high-production yield	Quickly adapts to latest demands with production flexibility
Research and development	Designs products that combine customer demand and production capabilities	Uses computers to test feasibility of idea before going to more expensive full-scale prototype	Carries out parallel product/process designs to speed up overall innovation

(*continued*)

	Quality	Efficiency	Responsiveness
Accounting	Provides the information that managers in other functions need to make decisions	Simplifies and computerizes to decrease the cost of gathering information	Provides information in "real time" (as the events described are still happening)
Purchasing	Selects vendors for their ability to join in an effective "partnership"	Given the required vendor quality, negotiates prices to provide good value	Schedules inbound deliveries efficiently, avoiding both extensive inventories and stock-outs
Personnel	Trains work force to perform required tasks	Minimizes employee turnover reducing hiring and training expenses	In response to strong growth in sales, finds large numbers of employees and quickly teaches needed skills

Source: G. G. Dess and A. Miller, Strategic Management, p. 143 ©1993 by McGraw-Hill, Inc. Reproduced with the permission of The McGraw-Hill Companies.

4. **Develop customer and supplier partnerships.** Organizations have a destructive tendency to view suppliers and even customers adversarially. It is better to understand the horizontal flow of a business—outside suppliers to internal suppliers/customers (a company's various departments) to external customers. This view suggests suppliers are partners in meeting customer needs, and customers are partners by providing input so the company and suppliers can meet and exceed those expectations.

Ford Motor Company's Dearborn, Michigan, plant is linked electronically with supplier Allied Signal's Kansas City, Missouri, plant. A Ford computer recently sent the design for a car's connecting rod to an Allied Signal factory computer, which transformed the design into instructions that it fed to a machine tool on the shop floor. The result: quality, efficiency, and responsiveness.

5. **Take a preventive approach.** Many organizations reward "fire fighters," not "fire preventers," and identify errors after the work is done. Management, instead, should be rewarded for being prevention oriented and seeking to eliminate nonvalue-added work.

Strategy in Action 12–2 describes how Marlow Industries discovered that a traditional 90-day probationary period for new hires was increasing employee turnover, encouraging marginal hires, and lowering all three sources of customer value.

6. **Adopt an error-free attitude.** Instill an attitude that "good enough" is not good enough anymore. "Error free" should become each individual's performance standard, with managers taking every opportunity to demonstrate and communicate the importance of this imperative.

Strategy in Action 12–2 describes how Marlow Industries reoriented its complete organization from a "get the job done no matter what" attitude to a "no job is done until it's done right" way of thinking.

7. **Get the facts first.** Continuous improvement–oriented companies make decisions based on facts, not on opinions. Accurate measurement, often using readily available statistical techniques, of every critical variable in a business's operation—and using those measurements to trace problems to their roots and eliminate their causes—is a better way.

8. **Encourage every manager and employee to participate.** Employee participation, empowerment, participative decision making, and extensive training in quality techniques, in statistical techniques, and in measurement tools are the ingredients continuous improvement companies employ to support and instill a commitment to customer value.

9. **Create an atmosphere of total involvement.** Quality management cannot be the job of a few managers or of one department. Maximum customer value cannot be achieved unless all areas of the organization apply quality concepts simultaneously.

10. **Strive for continuous improvement.** Stephen Yearout, director of Ernst & Young's Quality Management Center, recently observed that, "In the '80s, meeting your customers' expectations would distinguish you from your competitors. The '90s will require you to anticipate customer expectations and deliver quality service faster than the competition." Quality, efficiency, and responsiveness are not one-time programs of competitive response, for they create a new standard to measure up to. Organizations quickly find that continually improving quality, efficiency, and responsiveness in their processes, products, and services is not just good business; it's a necessity for long-term survival.

Continuous improvement and strategic control are two sides of the same "coin"— attention to factors that, in themselves, or because of change impacting them, influence the long-term success and survival of an organization. So it is not surprising, in the face of increasing global competition, that continuous improvement has evolved as a prominent factor that strategic-thinking managers are instilling in the way their organizations do business in the 21st century.

SUMMARY

Three fundamental perspectives—strategic control, operational control, and total quality/continuous improvement—provide the basis for designing strategy control systems. Strategic controls are intended to steer the company toward its long-term strategic goals. Premise controls, implementation controls, strategic surveillance, and special alert controls are types of strategic control. All four types are designed to meet top management's needs to track the strategy as it is being implemented, to detect underlying problems, and to make necessary adjustments. These strategic controls are linked to the environmental assumptions and the key operating requirements necessary for successful strategy implementation. Ever-present forces of change fuel the need for and focus of strategic control.

Operational control systems identify the performance standards associated with allocation and use of the firm's financial, physical, and human resources in pursuit of its strategy. Budgets, schedules, and key success factors are the primary means of operational control.

Operational control systems require systematic evaluation of performance against predetermined standards or targets. A critical concern here is identification and evaluation of performance deviations, with careful attention paid to determining the underlying reasons for and strategic implications of observed deviations before management reacts. Some firms use trigger points and contingency plans in this process.

The "quality imperative" of the last 20 years has redefined global competitiveness to include reshaping the way many businesses approach strategic and operational control. What has emerged is a commitment to continuous improvement in which personnel across all levels in an organization define customer value, identify ways every process within the business influences customer value, and seek continuously to enhance the quality, efficiency, and responsiveness with which the processes, products, and services are created and supplied. This includes attending to internal as well as external customers.

QUESTIONS FOR DISCUSSION

1. Distinguish strategic control from operating control. Give an example of each.
2. Select a business whose strategy is familiar to you. Identify what you think are the key premises of the strategy. Then select the key indicators that you would use to monitor each of these premises.

3. Explain the differences between implementation controls, strategic surveillance, and special alert controls. Give an example of each.
4. Why are budgets, schedules, and key success factors essential to operations control and evaluation?
5. What are key considerations in monitoring deviations from performance standards?
6. What are five key elements of quality management? How are quality imperative and continuous improvement related to strategic and operational control?
7. How might customer value be linked to quality, efficiency, and responsiveness?
8. Is it realistic that a commitment to continuous improvement could actually replace operational controls? Strategic controls?

BIBLIOGRAPHY

Asch, D. "Strategic Control: A Problem Looking for a Solution." *Long Range Planning* 25, no. 2 (1992), pp. 97–104.

Baysinger, B., and R. E Hoskisson. "The Composition of Boards of Directors and Strategic Control: Effects on Corporate Strategy." *Academy of Management Review* 15, no. 1 (1990), pp. 72–87.

Boeker, Warren. "Strategic Change: The Effects of Founding and History." *Academy of Management Journal*, September 1989, p. 489.

Bungay, S., and M. Goold. "Creating a Strategic Control System." *Long Range Planning* 24, no. 3 (1991), pp. 32–39.

Cowen, S. S., and J. K. Middaugh. "Designing an Effective Financial Planning and Control System," *Long Range Planning,* December 1988, pp. 83–92.

Duchessi, P., and J. Hobbs. "Implementing a Manufacturing Planning and Control System." *California Management Review,* Spring 1989, pp. 75–90.

Finkin, E. F. "Expense Control in Sales and Marketing." *Journal of Business Strategy,* May 1988, pp. 52–55.

Goold, M. "Strategic Control in the Decentralized Firm." *Sloan Management Review* 32, no. 2 (1991), pp. 69–81.

Goold, M., and J. J. Quinn. "The Paradox of Strategic Control." *Strategic Management Journal* 11, no. 1 (1990), pp. 43–57.

Grant, Robert M.; Rami Shani; and R. Krishnan. "TQM's Challenge to Management Theory and Practice." *Sloan Management Review,* Winter 1994, pp. 25–35.

Gundy, T., and D. King. "Using Strategic Planning to Drive Strategic Change." *Long Range Planning* 25, no. 1 (1992), pp. 100–09.

Gupta, A. K., and V. Govindarajan. "Knowledge Flows and the Structure of Control within Multinational Corporations." *Academy of Management Review* 16, no. 4 (1991), pp. 768–92.

Harrison, E. F. "Strategic Control at the CEO Level." *Long Range Planning* 24, no. 6 (1991), pp. 78–87.

Herzberg, Frederick. "One More Time: How Do You Motivate Employees?" *Harvard Business Review* 65, no. 4 (September–October 1987), pp. 109–20.

Hill, C. W. L. "Corporate Control Type, Strategy, Size and Financial Performance," *Journal of Management Studies,* September 1988, pp. 403–18.

Johnson, G. N. "Managing Strategic Change: Strategy, Culture and Action," *Long Range Planning* 25, no. 1 (1992), pp. 28–36.

Johnson, H. Thomas. *Relevance Regained.* New York: Free Press, 1992.

Kellinghusen, G., and K. Wiebbenhorst. "Strategic Control for Improved Performance." *Long Range Planning* 25, no. 3 (1992), pp. 30–37.

Kelly, D., and T. L. Amburgey. "Organizational Inertia and Momentum: A Dynamic Model of Strategic Change." *Academy of Management Journal* 34, no. 3 (1991), pp. 591–612.

Kiernan, Matthew J. "The New Strategic Architecture: Learning to Compete in the Twenty-First Century." *Academy of Management Executive* 7, no. 1 (February 1993), pp. 7–21.

King, E. M.; W. Norvell; and D. Deines. "Budgeting: A Strategic Managerial Tool." *Journal of Business Strategy,* Fall 1988, pp. 69–75.

Klein, Howard J. "An Integrated Control Theory Model of Work Motivation." *Academy of Management Review,* April 1989, p. 50.

Kohn, Alfie. "Why Incentive Plans Cannot Work." *Harvard Business Review* 71, no. 5 (September–October 1993), pp. 54–63.

Murphy, T. "Pay for Performance—An Instrument of Strategy." *Long Range Planning,* August 1989, pp. 40–45.

Norburn, D., and S. Birley. "The Top Management Team and Corporate Performance." *Strategic Management Journal,* May 1988, pp. 225–38.

Odiorne, George S. "Measuring the Unmeasurable: Setting Standards for Management Performance." *Business Horizons,* July–August 1987, p. 69.

Olian, Judy D., and Sara L. Rynes, "Making Total Quality Work: Aligning Organizational Processes, Performance Measures, and Stakeholders." *Human Resource Management* 30, no. 3 (Fall 1991), pp. 303–333.

Quinn, James Brian. *Intelligent Enterprise.* New York: Free Press, 1992, chap. 4.

Reichheld, F. F., and W. E. Sasser. "Zero Defects: Quality Comes to Services." *Harvard Business Review* 68, no. 3 (1990), pp. 94–111.

Rogers, T. J. "No Excuses Management." *Harvard Business Review* 68, no. 4 (1990), pp. 105–13.

Ross, Joel, and David Georgoff. "A Survey of Productivity and Quality Issues in Manufacturing: The State of the Industry." *Industrial Management* 33, no. 1 (1991), pp. 3–5, 22–25.

Shetty, Y. K. "Aiming High: Competitive Benchmarking for Superior Performance," *Long Range Planning* 26, no. 1 (February 1993), pp. 39–44.

Taguchi, G., and D. Clausing. "Robust Quality." *Harvard Business Review* 68, no. 1 (1990), pp. 65–75.

Wiley, Carolyn. "Incentive Plan Pushes Production." *Personnel Journal* (August 1993), pp. 86–91.

Zahra, S. "Increasing the Board's Involvement in Strategy." *Long Range Planning* 23, no. 6 (1990), pp. 10–16.

Zent, Charles H. "Using Shareholder Value to Design Business Unit Manager Incentive Plans." *Planning Review,* March–April 1988, p. 40.

CHAPTER 12 COHESION CASE ILLUSTRATION

STRATEGIC CONTROL AND CONTINUOUS IMPROVEMENT AT COCA-COLA

Fundamental to Coca-Cola's strategic control in its soft-drink business is daily monitoring of unit case sales in each of the thousands of markets Coke serves around the world. The following table of selected country results illustrates Coke's unit case volume in selected countries on an annual basis. The same scrutiny is applied to all markets, sales territories, routes, and customers (stores selling or disbursing soft drinks) on a weekly basis throughout the Coca-Cola system.

A second critical strategic variable monitored by Coke management is the sales volume or market share attained by independently owned as well as company-owned (full or partially) bottling franchises worldwide. You will recall that a major element of Coke's strategy for the 1990s has been its decision to vertically integrate forward into bottling as necessary to ensure accelerated access to consumers. And where Coke already has long-time franchisees in place, it is aggressively monitoring and evaluating their sales results, choosing quickly when necessary to buy out underperforming franchises. This has been true even in international markets, where some international business experts consider such a move, usually accompanied with inserting an American manager in charge, as being too aggressive. Yet Coke has pushed forward and done so successfully, most notably in Great Britain and France. Recent comments by Coke management on this activity include:

> Our accelerated growth rate of the past five years would seem to indicate that we are doing business differently than before, and we are. Without question, the biggest difference is our willingness to do whatever is advisable to grow our concentrate and syrup business around the world. In large measure, around the world we are able to maximize profitable growth with the traditional bottler system. Sometimes, however, the practical action is taking significant equity positions in important components of our global bottling network. Taking ownership positions in approximately 60 different bottling, canning, and distribution operations around the world and, often, assuming management responsibility has been a way to ensure ourselves of working with the bottling partners who share our commitment to reinvestment in, and profitable growth of, the business.
>
> The results speak for themselves. The accompanying table illustrates the success we have had in a number of individual markets (and also serves to show the focus of a key aspect of Coke's strategic control system).

Another element of Coca-Cola's strategic control centers around the basic goal the company seeks to accomplish. Speaking to business analysts, Roberto Goizueta put it simply: "Management doesn't get paid to make the shareholders comfortable. We get paid to make the shareholders rich." So fundamental strategic control at Coca-Cola monitors the market valuation of Coke and continuously tries to evaluate strategies, assumptions, and actions in light of their effect on this situation. Coca-Cola's chief financial officer recently explained this approach to strategic control:

> Economic Profit and Economic Value Added provide a direct framework for measuring the impact of value-oriented actions. Economic Profit is defined as net operating profit after taxes in excess of a computed capital charge for average operating capital employed. Economic Value Added represents the growth in Economic Profit from year to year.
>
> Beginning in 1994, the Company expanded the use of Economic Value Added as a performance measurement tool. Measured over a three year time frame, long-term incentive bonuses for

Bottling Investments

Region	Year of Investment	Company Ownership (%)	Share (%) Before	Share (%) 1995	Annual Unit Case Sales Growth (%)
Philippines	1981	30%	31%	78%	14%
Taiwan	1985	35	10	52	48
Great Britain	1986	49	21	36	22
Indonesia	1987	29	58	79	18
Netherlands	1988	30	24	34	16
France	1989	100	32	41	24
Australia	1989	51	52	57	9

certain employees of the Company are now determined, in part, by comparison against Economic Profit target levels. This change in performance measures was made to more closely align management's focus on the key drivers of the business. Management believes that a clear focus on the components of Economic Profit, and the resultant growth in Economic Value Added over time, leads to the creating of share-owner wealth.

Over the last 13 years, the Company has increased its Economic Profit at an average annual compound rate of 26 percent, resulting in Economic Value Added to the Company of $1.9 billion. Over the same period, the Company's stock price has increased at an average annual compound rate of 25 percent. During the past decade, share owners of the Company have received an excellent return on their investment. A $100 investment in the Company's common stock at December 31, 1984, together with reinvested dividends, would be worth approximately $1,237 at December 31, 1994, an average annual compound return of 29 percent.

1994 OPERATIONS REVIEW

SELECTED COUNTRY RESULTS

Estimated Unit Case[1] Volume

	Average Annual Growth				1994 Results			
	10 Years		5 Years		Unit Case Growth		Company	
	Company[3]	Industry[4]	Company[3]	Industry[4]	Company[3]	Industry[4]	Share[4]	Per Capita[4] Consumption
Worldwide[6]	7%	5%	6%	3%	10%	6%	46%	49
North America Business Sector[2]	4	3	4	3	7	4	41	296
United States	4	3	4	3	7	4	41	310
International Business Sector[6]	8	5	7	3	11	7	49	35
European Community	9	5	6	3	7	5	49	130
Benelux/Denmark	8	4	8	4	9	4	46	152
France	13	7	11	5	9	(1)	47	65
Germany	7	5	8	1	4	3	55	191
Great Britain	12	6	2	3	7	10	31	101
Italy	8	6	4	3	5	2	55	94
Spain	8	4	5	2	9	8	54	166
Pacific[5]	8	8	7	6	12	12	39	20
Australia	9	7	8	3	10	9	65	274
Japan[5]	6	1	6	2	8	8	30	133
Korea	5	5	4	1	11	5	52	59
Philippines	6	3	3	3	14	14	75	96
Thailand	12	14	9	9	14	11	48	54
Northeast Europe/Middle East (NEME)[6]	14	4	17	1	35	17	32	11
Egypt	5	2	4	0	47	4	55	26
Hungary	20	2	37	6	4	12	42	111
Norway	11	7	8	5	9	15	59	256
Poland	33	2	69	8	44	47	24	29
Africa	5	2	5	(1)	1	(7)	84	23
Nigeria	2	0	6	0	(14)	(25)	82	22
South Africa	5	3	5	1	4	0	88	146
Zimbabwe	8	6	5	(1)	9	4	87	62
Latin America	8	6	6	4	10	4	55	148
Argentina	7	6	14	11	12	12	57	189
Brazil	8	7	0	1	10	14	56	92
Chile	15	14	12	8	8	6	64	217
Mexico	8	6	6	4	11	7	57	333

[1]Unit case equals 24 8-ounce drinks.
[2]Consists of United States and Canada.
[3]Includes non-carbonated soft drinks.
[4]Includes only flavored, carbonated soft drinks.
[5]Company share and per capita include Japanese non-carbonated soft drinks; revised to conform with Japanese industry standards (equivalent Company share for Japan in 1993 was 31).
[6]The calculation of per capita consumption includes India and several former Soviet republics.

Perhaps the best-known example of its willingness to react quickly is Coke's reaction to consumers' reception of New Coke in the mid-1980s. After extensive market tests showed Pepsi's slightly sweeter cola was preferred in blind taste tests to traditional Coke, and after still further ruminations, Goizueta's relatively new management team introduced New Coke in an extraordinarily expensive promotional and distribution blitz while also having it take the place of Coke's traditional beverage. Coke was surprised by the consumer rebellion of loyal Coke drinkers who adamantly refused to let the old Coke die. While Coke management had invested millions in this new move—literally changing distribution practices, promotional material, and the like nationwide in 1985—it quickly readjusted its strategy, apologized for its decision, brought back a new "Coke Classic," and ended up with more shelf space in grocery stores (Pepsi's stronghold) as retailers allowed Coke to keep both New Coke & Coke Classic (as well as other brands) for sale. Even with the huge mistake, Coke management's rapid response (strategic control) resulted in yet another record year, in terms of sales and profitability, as well as a valuable lesson in and reinforcement of consumer loyalty to the Coke brand.

Two key trends in global markets will occupy the attention of Coke executives' strategic control:

· Private-label colas sold by large retailers.
· Rise in demand for noncola, "new age" beverages.

For example, Cott Corporation, still a very small player in the beverage industry, has made some inroads in key markets like Japan, Canada, Great Britain, and the United States with an improved quality beverage that it sells to retailers who relabel it using their own labels and sell it to consumers at prices 50 percent below Coke's retail price. They also receive greater profit margins, even at this drastically lower price, than they receive from handling Coke products. Developments in Japan help illustrate this dilemma.[5]

TOKYO—Coke is no longer "It" in Japan, as big retailers come out with discount colas and force the giant U.S. beverage maker Coca-Cola Co. to trim its prices.

"Coca-Cola's biggest fear right now is price deflation for soft drinks spreading to vending machines," which account for about 55% of Coca-Cola's overall soft-drink sales in Japan, said Nikko's Ms. Sudo. That is already happening: Coca-Cola has recently slashed the price of its soft drinks to 100 yen ($1.19) from 110 yen at some of its vending machines.

The root of Coca-Cola's problem in Japan is the brand's slipping ability to defend its suggested retail prices. The problem stems from tougher competition from other beverage companies and the onslaught of inexpensive, generic soft drinks, which last year began flooding Japanese supermarkets at prices as low as 40 yen a can, hurting the sales and influence of brand-name sodas.

Together, Japan's 17 Coca-Cola bottlers, which produce soft drinks with syrups provided by Coca-Cola (Japan) Co., still sell almost one out of every three soft drinks in the country. But at the retail level, excluding vending-machine sales, their dominance is waning. At some major chain stores, analysts said, Coca-Cola's share now is as little as 10%.

As a result of Coca-Cola's diminishing presence in retail stores, the balance of power has tipped in favor of large retailers, so much so that Coca-Cola is under growing pressure to do something it hasn't done much in the past: hand out discounts for retailers.

---

[5] Norihiko Shirouzu, "World Markets: Stocks of Coca-Cola Bottlers in Japan Pressured by Price-driven Inroads by Retailers, Rivals," *The Wall Street Journal,* May 2, 1995, p. C12.

The clearest indication of Coca-Cola's compromised position, Ms. Sudo said, is recent talk among the Coca-Cola bottlers about unifying their distribution, now segmented into 17 regional blocks—a system that has achieved stable retail prices. While a new operation could boost efficiency, it is being considered only at the strong urging of large retail chains such as Seven-Eleven Japan Co. and Daiei Inc. "It's not something Coca-Cola is volunteering to do," Ms. Sudo said.

Because Coca-Cola products, which include coffees and Chinese and Japanese teas, are distributed exclusively by one Coca-Cola bottler per region, large retailers are prevented from using volume buying as leverage for discounts or other incentives. So for the bottlers, altering this system may be necessary but suicidal, analysts said, because a superstore chain could demand lower Coke prices in return for shelf space.

Coke's strategic control has focused on creating alternate responses as it monitors the developments in this critical Pacific region market. Reactions include selling colas, at least Coke Classic, directly from the U.S. West Coast, bypassing Coca-Cola's 17 Japanese bottlers. But long term, the issue speaks to the need for Coke to reconsider its cost structure to address this price-based competition and the high relative strength of large retailers.

Coke's response to the development of new age beverages has been much more direct. Coke has introduced several new beverages to compete directly with these beverages. It has rapidly and aggressively introduced new beverages to leverage the strength of its existing infrastructure and relationship with retailers to immediately take market share away from new entrants once they prove a viable niche exists. The next page highlights some of Coke's recent successes with this approach, which it calls *capitalizing on supporting brands*.

Action: Capitalize On Supporting Brands

Objective: Strengthen consumer loyalty; tap into shifting consumer preferences; source volume from competitors.

Tactics: Positioned supporting brands to address specific market opportunities.

Point of Differentiation: A portfolio of unparalleled strength and depth.

Results: Strong growth from virtually all major supporting brands.

The Complete Beverage Source

Our Company owns some 100 supporting brands around the world. Some have an appeal that transcends geographic and cultural boundaries. Others fill uniquely local needs, often with modest investment. We're eyeing each one with the same scrutiny we used to refocus our lines of business, energizing those that complement our core brands and justify their costs of capital and shedding the rest.

Brand	Detail	Market note		Growth
Powerade Introduced in 1990. Expanding to 20 countries in 1995.	Advertising campaign featuring new look and attitude launched in 1995.			Compounded unit case volume growth*: **346%**
Aquarius Introduced in 1983. Available in 20 countries.		Two new flavors launched in Japan; new advertising under way in Europe.		Compounded unit case volume growth*: **19%**
Hi-C Acquired in 1960. Available in 21 countries.	New packaging graphics and advertising introduced in 1995.			Compounded unit case volume growth**: **6%**
Georgia Introduced in 1975. Available in Japan.	Japan's canned coffee segment leader.			Compounded unit case volume growth*: **30%**
Thums Up & Limca Acquired in late 1993. Available primarily in India.	Leaders in respective flavor segments in India.			No prior year comparison.
Sparletta Brands Once a bottler brand. Available primarily in South Africa.	Our second largest brand in South Africa behind Coca-Cola.			Compounded unit case volume growth***: **22%**

Teas

Ready-to-drink teas represent a small but growing fraction of the soft drink industry. In 1995, we will enhance our product line with new iced teas under the Fruitopia and Nestea trademarks, complemented by local teas in select markets.

Brand	Detail	Market note		Growth
Fruitopia Teas New in 1995.	Initial line to include four all-natural flavors.			No prior year comparison.
Nestea Distributed by the Company since 1992. Now in 41 countries.		Customized flavors and styles with pure iced tea taste launched in 1995.		Compounded unit case volume growth*: **104%**
Seiryusabo Introduced in 1994. Available in Japan.	Nearly 19 million unit cases sold in 1994; one of the fastest growing brands in its category.			No prior year comparison.

*Since first full year after introduction/acquisition.
**Since 1975. ***Since 1970.

SEEKING CONTINUOUS IMPROVEMENT

Coca-Cola has placed much greater emphasis on empowering operating personnel to seek continuous improvement and quality, believing that it is critical to control the strategic priority to keep their global business system better than any other in the world. This often translates into continuously improving local operations, syrup plants, and other parts of Coca-Cola. Below are two internal documents that characterize what Coke seeks to do in empowering plant personnel to act and react quickly—with the speed long utilized by executives.

Managing in the New System vs.
Managing in the Old System

Old System (Traditional)	New System (Contemporary)
Individual	Team
Fickleness	Commitment
Generalities	Details
Finance focus	Production focus
Dollars	Things and ideas
Sales focus	Marketing focus
Printed or spoken word	Diagram oriented
Single function	System
Opinion	Data
Why?	How?
Fragmented (single focus)	Holistic (integrated)
Deductive	Inductive
Short range	Long range
Product	Process
Debate/conversation	Planning/action
Correction	Prevention
Blame	Help
Just-in-case	Just-in-time
Management control	Leadership
Technology/machines	Human resources
Bureaucratic	Entrepreneurial
Information is power	Communicative
Compartmentalized	Cooperation
Quality-problem	Quality-solution
Control	Breakthrough
Fire fighting to preserve the status quo	Continuous improvement

Source: Coca-Cola USA

Values Sustain Continuous Improvement

· Belief in the employees' ability to solve problems
· Belief that the people doing the work know the most about it and, therefore, are the best able to improve it
· Belief that innovation requires tapping into the resources, contributions, and growth of all employees
· Belief that CIP, team building, and problem solving can create a culture where everyone is responsible for quality
· Willingness to respond fairly and promptly to team recommendations
· Willingness to allow time for team meetings
· Willingness to develop incentives which reward team performance for quality improvement
· Willingness to change structure, policies, and the system as teams develop skills
· Willingness to place decisions for quality with the individuals who do the work
· Willingness to create the opportunity for personal growth, development, and contributions of all employees.

Subject Index

A

ABC/Capital Cities, 173
Acceptable objectives, 214
Acceptable quality level, 43
Accountability, 16
Accounting, 315–316
Accounts receivable turnover, 195
Achievable objectives, 215
Acquisition strategy, 232–233
Action plans, 16
  elements of, 304–305
  EnergyCo, 305–306
  value-added benefits, 308
Activity-based cost accounting,
    179, 315
Activity ratios, 195–196
Adaptive mode, 9
Age distribution, 65
AIDS, 53
Airborne Express, 5
Aircraft industry, 84
Air pollution, 67
  laws, 72
Air Quality Act, 72
Albert, Kenneth J., 294
Alcoa, 7
Allied Signal, 354, 355, 396
American Express, 64, 88
  customer segmentation, 91
America OnLine, 172
Ameritech, 349
Amoco, 228
Andreessen, Marc, 261
Andrews, K. R., 45 n
Anfuso, Dawn, 118
Apple Computer, 152, 175, 222
Apple Macintosh, 85
ARCO, 39
Arthur D. Little Company,
    148–149, 285 n
Ashley, Laura, 169
Asset reduction, 231
Asset turnover, 195
AT&T, 64, 124, 225, 277
  downsizing, 361
Austin, Paul, 372
Auto emissions, 68
Avery Denison, benchmarking at,
    185

B

Backward vertical integration, 228
Baeder, Robert W., 109
Bama Pies, 292
Bare bones posture, 263
Barnard, Chester, 173
Barrier, M., 393 n
Barriers to entry, 76–77
  experience curve, 78
  industry concentration, 84
  and industry structure, 85–86
Bartlett, Christopher A., 212,
    351 n
BCG growth-share matrix,
    283–285
Becker, Dan, 68
Begley, S., 68
Benchmarking, 43, 162
  at Avery Denison, 185
  for cost leadership opportunities,
    249
  for differentiation, 252–253
  in internal analysis, 185–188
  at Kmart, 188
  at SAS, 186–187
Bethlehem Steel, 237
Bice restaurant, 6–7
Bleackley, Mark, 230 n
BMW, 85, 253
Boards of directors
  and company mission, 42–45
  empowerment, 11
  and stakeholders, 46
Boeing Corporation, 85, 383–384
Bonoma, Thomas V., 93
Booz Allen and Hamilton, 226
Bossidy, Larry, 354, 355
Boston Consulting Group, 283
Boulton, W., 45 n
Bracker, J. S., 48 n, 162
Brainstorming, 145, 151
Brand loyalty, and new entrants,
    253
Broad-line global competition, 264
Brown, Paul, 316
Brownstein, Andrew R., 365 n
Buckley, J. T., 238
Budgets, 389
Buffet, Warren, 373
Burrows, Peter, 174

Bush administration, 68
Business-level decisions, 6, 8
Business processes, 395
  reengineering, 347–349
Business Week, 313
Buyer behavior, 92
Buyer group, 79–80

C

CACI, Inc., 215
Cadillac Motor Company, 44
Calloway, Wayne, 269
Camillus, J. C., 12 n, 13, 19, 95
Campbell, A., 9 n
Campbell Soup Company, 11
Capabilities sharing, 278–280
Capital budget, 389
Capitalizing on supporting brands,
    404, 405
Capital requirements, 76
Carter, Jimmy, 100
Cash cows, 284
Cash flow budget, 389
Cassano, J. S., 351 n
Caterpillar Tractor, 39, 212, 213
CBS, Inc., 235
Central America, 154
CEOs; *see* Chief executive officers
Chaebol, 240
Champy, James, 347
Chancellor, Andrea, 109
Chandler, Alfred D., 351
Chapter 11 bankruptcy, 235
  Wang Laboratories, 236
Chase Econometric, 145
Chemlawn, 218–219
Chesebrough-Ponds, 224
Chief executive officers
  compensation issues, 365 n
  in strategic management, 10
Chrysler Corporation, 237
Citicorp, 172, 386–387
Clark, Kim, 389 n
Clean Air Act, 68, 72
Clean Air Act Amendments, 72
Clean Water Act, 73
Clearly Canadian, 102
Cleary, M. J., 158
Cleland, David I., 12 n, 13, 19,
    29 n, 47, 95

Clymer, Roy, 360
Coalitions, 293
*Coca-Cola, a Business System
    toward 2000*, 57–60, 244
Coca-Cola Company, 281, 347,
    353
  acquisitions, 23
  company mission, 57–60
  competitive advantage, 273–275
  continuous improvement,
    404–405
  corporate culture and reward
    system, 373–378
  differentiation at, 336–337
  external environment, 99–102
  financial reformation, 334–335
  forecasting, 164–167
  geographical expansion,
    328–332
  global corporation, 373–378
  in global environment, 131–135
  grand strategies, 245–246
  history, 22–25
  in Hungary, 135
  infrastructure fortification, 333
  internal analysis, 203–209
  in Japan, 134
  leadership at, 372–373
  long-term objectives, 24–245
  shareholder value, 297–299
  strategic controls, 400–404
  strategy implementation,
    328–337
  structure, 370–372
Cohen, Jonathan, 261
Cohen, Richard, 254
Colgate-Palmolive Company,
    118–119
Commerce Department Export
    Now Program, 123
Communications revolution, 314
Community and economic
    development, 52
Companies; *see* Firms
Company creed, 34–35
Company goals, 32–34, 121
Company mission, 13–14
  at Coca-Cola, 57–60
  and company responsibility,
    45–51
  core competencies, 120–121
  customer orientation, 39–40
  definition, 29

409